URBAN
MASS
TRANSPORTATION
PLANNING

McGraw-Hill Series in Transportation

CONSULTING EDITOR

Edward K. Morlok, *University of Pennsylvania*

URBAN MASS TRANSPORTATION PLANNING

Alan Black
University of Kansas

McGRAW-HILL, INC.

New York   St. Louis   San Francisco   Auckland   Bogotá   Caracas   Lisbon
London   Madrid   Mexico City   Milan   Montreal   New Delhi
San Juan   Singapore   Sydney   Tokyo   Toronto

This book was set in Times Roman by Ruttle, Shaw & Wetherill, Inc.
The editors were B. J. Clark and James W. Bradley;
the production supervisor was Leroy A. Young.
The cover was designed by Carla Bauer.
R. R. Donnelley & Sons Company was printer and binder.

URBAN MASS TRANSPORTATION PLANNING

1 2 3 4 5 6 7 8 9 0 DOC DOC 9 0 9 8 7 6 5

ISBN 0-07-005557-2

Library of Congress Cataloging-in-Publication Data

Black, Alan, (date).
   Urban mass transportation planning / Alan Black.
      p.   cm.— (McGraw-Hill series in transportation)
   Includes index.
   ISBN 0-07-005557-2
      1. Urban transportation policy—United States.   2. Transportation—
   United States—Planning.   3. Urban transportation policy—United
   States—History.   I. Title.   II. Series.
   HE308.B53   1995
   388.4'068—dc20
                                                              94-33904

ABOUT
THE AUTHOR

ALAN BLACK has been involved in urban transportation planning for the past 35 years. He served on the staffs of the Chicago Area Transportation Study and the Tri-State Transportation Commission in New York City in the 1960s. Later he worked for the consulting firm of Creighton, Hamburg, Inc., in Delmar, New York. He began a full-time teaching career in 1975 at the University of Texas at Austin. Since 1981 he has been at the University of Kansas, where he is professor and former chair of the Graduate Program in Urban Planning.

Professor Black earned a Master of City Planning degree from the University of California, Berkeley, and a Ph.D. in City and Regional Planning from Cornell University. He has published numerous articles on transportation and city planning and has been active in several professional organizations.

CONTENTS

PREFACE

No doubt it seems odd for someone living in a small city in Kansas to write a book about urban mass transportation. I should explain my background. I grew up in a suburb of Boston and regularly used subways, streetcars, and buses, since teenagers did not have cars in those days. Later I lived in Chicago and New York City, where I often rode public transit (for 3 years I commuted on the Lexington Avenue subway).

I began my professional planning career with the Chicago Area Transportation Study in the early 1960s. At first I was mainly a highway planner, but I performed an analysis of a rail transit proposal. I gave a paper summarizing this study at the Highway Research Board's meeting in 1962.

At this time the staff of the Chicago study were doing pioneering work on the optimal spacing of highway routes. I was impressed by this work and felt that a similar approach could be applied to mass transit. I did some exploratory calculations, but then put them aside. Several years later, as a graduate student at Cornell, I resurrected my notes for a term project. My instructor, Charles ReVelle, was enthusiastic, and I decided to expand on the project for my dissertation. This led me to specializing in urban transit.

Upon completing my dissertation in 1975, I took my first full-time teaching position at the University of Texas at Austin. I offered a course in urban mass transportation, which I have now taught about 15 times. I never found a satisfactory textbook for the course. I tried a few, but for various reasons found them unsuitable. Mostly I relied on collections of journal articles for reading assignments. When I talked to professors at other schools who taught similar courses, I found they had the same problem.

Finally I decided there was a need I could fill. I began by writing out my lecture notes and having them photocopied for students to read. Over the last 5 years, I have revised, expanded, and updated this material; the result is this book.

Some people believe mass transit to be a panacea for many urban problems. It has been propounded as an answer for such concerns as degradation of the environment, urban sprawl, the energy crisis, and even racial strife. Transit usually receives favorable press; politicians endorse it in their campaigns; and public opinion polls show that a majority of people in the United States favor it (although a far smaller number actually use it).

It must be recognized that transit has become an ideological issue. Promoting transit is part of the liberal agenda. Consequently, debates about transit are often emotional, and it appears that no arguments could change the minds of true believers or skeptics. This has interfered with rational planning and decision making in urban transportation. I am not a diehard transit advocate, and I hope that this book presents an objective view.

This may disappoint transit boosters who are looking for ammunition to use in their battles. There are plenty of books available to bolster their case, but I believe that many contain exaggerations and half-truths. I have tried to write a book that presents unbiased factual information. I give a lot of attention to controversies, because they are interesting and important, but I try to let the reader make the final judgments. Obviously my personal opinions have crept into the book at many points, but I think that overall it will not seem a polemic.

In my mind, I have addressed the book to urban planning students, since this is the group with whom I work on a daily basis. I have also taught many students from architecture, civil engineering, environmental studies, geography, and public administration. In addition, there are many persons who are interested in mass transit and would like to know more about it. I think that my audience will be heterogeneous, and I expect that most will be master's-degree candidates or upper-level undergraduates.

This book should be ideal for a course fashioned after mine that focuses on urban mass transportation. It should be useful in courses that deal generally with transportation planning or the urban transportation problem. It emphasizes policy issues and has only a modicum of technical material, thus requiring little mathematical knowledge. Professors of civil engineering may find the book lacking in this area, but it still could be useful as a supplemental text.

The geographic scope of the book is largely confined to the United States. I do not discuss bicycles, pedestrians, or rural transportation, because I have little expertise in these topics. I give cursory coverage to travel-demand forecasting and none to evaluation methods such as benefit/cost analysis. These subjects are well presented in other works.

This is my first book, and it is the culmination of 35 years of experience and learning. I owe debts to many people but name only the most significant. These include teachers—T. J. Kent, Jr., Barclay G. Jones, and Pierre Clavel—and transportation planners—the late J. Douglas Carroll, Jr., Roger L. Creighton, John R. Hamburg, Morton Schneider, and George Haikalis. Among later colleagues who helped me greatly were Sandra Rosenbloom, C. Michael Walton, and Samuel L. Zimmerman.

I am grateful to the University of Kansas for granting me a sabbatical leave during which I did the major work of fleshing out my lecture notes. The Department of Urban Studies and Planning at the Massachusetts Institute of Technology helped by appointing me a visiting scholar and providing resources to facilitate my research. I want to thank my sister Margaret and her husband, James H. Flanagan, for their generous hospitality during an extended retreat at their home.

Finally, McGraw-Hill and I would like to thank the following reviewers for their many helpful comments and suggestions: David J. Brower, University of North Carolina; Erik Ferguson, Georgia Institute of Technology; and Kumares Sinha, Purdue University.

Alan Black

URBAN
MASS
TRANSPORTATION
PLANNING

1

THE ROLE OF TRANSIT

Transportation has a pervasive influence on modern society. It is very important economically: Transportation activity (including the manufacture of vehicles) amounts to about one-fifth of the U.S. gross national product (GNP) [Morlok 1978, p. 64]. On the average, U.S. households spend about $1 of every $8 on personal transportation. In the past, transportation routes played a major role in the siting of cities, and today the transportation system affects where and how urban areas grow. Transportation has social and cultural impacts; it shapes our lifestyles. Issues involving transportation sometimes have a prominent place on political agendas.

The technologies used in transportation have evolved through history. In the 19th century, railroads were the principal means of travel for long distances. Today railroads have been largely replaced by automobiles and aviation. Within cities, various forms of public transportation (ranging from horse-drawn carriages to electric subway trains) were dominant in the hundred years from 1820 to 1920. Since then the automobile has become the most popular means of urban travel, but mass transit has continued to play a role.

None of this happened easily or painlessly. Overcoming the barrier of distance in a speedy fashion has always required money and effort; it has often had negative side effects. Experts on travel behavior believe that most people regard travel as a necessary evil to be minimized or traded off against other desires. Complaints abound. Although the United States probably has the best transportation system in world history, few people think it is satisfactory.

THE URBAN TRANSPORTATION PROBLEM

For decades there has been talk about the "urban transportation problem" (or sometimes the "urban transportation crisis"). Popular magazines run cover stories about it from

1

time to time. Politicians discuss it in their campaigns. In public opinion surveys, people often rank it as one of the most serious local problems. It was also the title of a very influential book [Meyer et al. 1965].

The urban transportation problem is actually a complex bundle of interrelated problems. They can be grouped in three major categories: congestion, mobility, and ancillary impacts.

Congestion

Congestion causes increased costs for travelers and freight movement, loss of time, accidents, and psychological strain. This is not simply congestion on streets and highways, although this is the most common example. There is also congestion of transit vehicles during peak periods, not just in large cities like New York and Chicago, but also in small cities. Congestion of pedestrians on sidewalks frequently occurs in the downtown areas of large cities at lunchtime. In Holland there is congestion of bicycles.

Congestion is nothing new; it has existed in cities for centuries. It is not something introduced by the automobile (see Figure 1-1). In the following passage, Lewis Mumford [1961, p. 218] described the situation in ancient Rome:

> As soon as the increase of population created a demand for wheeled traffic in Rome, the congestion became intolerable. One of Julius Caesar's first acts on seizing power was to ban wheeled traffic from the center of Rome during the day. . . . Just as motor car congestion now affects small towns as well as big ones, so the increase of animal-drawn vehicles impeded circulation everywhere. Hence Claudius extended Caesar's prohibition to the municipalities of Italy; and Marcus Aurelius, still later, applied it without regard to their municipal status to every town in the Empire.

Caesar's innovation was the forerunner of what is now called an *auto-free zone,* which is common in Europe and often proposed for U.S. cities.

Congestion is what most people find objectionable about traveling in cities. It is the most common complaint. If there were no congestion, most people would be happy with their cars, and transportation would not be a widely discussed problem.

Congestion has several generic causes. The first is urbanization—the concentration of people and economic activities in urban areas. If everyone lived and worked on farms or in small towns scattered over the landscape, congestion would be rare. But most people want to live in cities or suburbs, and it is efficient for most productive activities to cluster in cities. Ironically, the main reason to locate in cities is to reduce travel. Indeed, travel distances are reduced, but the trade-off is that travel becomes slower.

The second cause is specialization within cities. People want to travel between different activities (or land uses), which are dispersed around the city. Workplaces are concentrated in some areas, living places in other areas, and recreation activities in still others. But these activities are interdependent, and people must travel between them.

The most important part of this is the separation of workplaces and homes, creating the journey to work. This became widespread with industrialization; it was uncommon earlier. In the Middle Ages, the usual pattern in European cities was for a building to

FIGURE 1-1
Traffic congestion before automobiles. This photograph of the intersection of 42d Street and Fifth Avenue in New York City was taken between 1900 and 1910. (*Source:* Library of Congress.)

have a shop and workroom on the first floor, kitchen and dining room on the second floor, and sleeping quarters on the upper floors. Going to work simply meant going downstairs.

The third cause is the problem of matching supply and demand temporally. The supply of transportation facilities in U.S. cities is very large, but relatively fixed. Demand, however, varies greatly over the day; this is the peaking problem. It stems largely from the journey to work and the practice of having most people start and end their workdays at about the same time.

A fourth cause of congestion is that supply often stimulates demand. Increases in transportation capacity can be self-defeating. A new highway that seems spacious when it opens may fill up with traffic in a few years. People seize opportunities to travel more; this comes with a rising standard of living. Furthermore, development is attracted to sites with superior accessibility because of better movement facilities. In time, this advantage may decline because of congestion.

Consequently, increasing transportation supply is not sufficient to end congestion. It is also not economic: The cost of building enough capacity to eliminate congestion (particularly during rush hour) would be overwhelming. It is more economic to allow some congestion. Hence it is likely that as long as we live in cities, we shall have to put up with some amount of congestion. People complain about it, but most tolerate it rather than move elsewhere.

One form of transportation supply with potentially great capacity is transit service. This people-moving capacity continues to be important in large cities. This probably applies to all metropolitan areas of at least 1 million population, but it is most true of the older, dense cities of the northeast and midwest. There the agglomeration of human activities in a small area is so intense that circulation by private vehicles causes recurrent congestion, which no feasible expansion of the street system could eliminate.

This is particularly true of highly centralized cities where the worst congestion is found on approaches to the central business district (CBD). Such cities as New York, Chicago, Philadelphia, and Boston could not continue to function without extensive transit service. It would be impossible to move hundreds of thousands of workers to the CBD during the peak period entirely by automobiles. While these cities have experienced suburban dispersal, they also have seen downtown growth that indicates the CBD will remain a strong focal point.

The greatest transit use occurs in large cities. This is shown by Census data; the Census Bureau asks several questions about the journey to work, and one concerns the means of transportation used. Table 1-1 lists the 25 metropolitan areas that had the largest number of transit work trips in 1990. The top seven areas on the list accounted for almost 70 percent of all the transit work trips in the nation.

Many of these cities developed in the 19th century, when transit was the dominant mode of urban transportation. They became dense because of transit, they had good transit systems then, and they still have relatively superior transit service. Other cities did not become large until the 20th century, when the automobile was replacing transit as the most popular means of conveyance. These cities developed in a dispersed pattern, and their CBDs were not so dominant. Some of them are now huge—such as Los Angeles, Dallas–Fort Worth, and Houston—and they have severe congestion problems despite their low densities and generally excellent freeway systems. Apparently when a city reaches a certain size, regardless of its density, an automobile-only system of transportation does not work.

Because of their growth, many suburbs now have the kind of traffic congestion historically associated with the inner city. These areas often have antiquated street systems inherited from their rural origins, while transit service is poor or nonexistent. The result has been termed *suburban gridlock* [Cervero 1986]. Some transportation experts see it as the issue of the 1990s.

The problem stems partly from the emergence of suburban "megacenters" such as City Post Oak in Houston, Texas, Tyson's Corner in Virginia, and the Denver Technological Center in Colorado. These clusters have amounts of floor space and employment that rival (and sometimes exceed) the CBD of their areas. Offices play a major role, but these developments often include shopping malls, hotels, entertainment facilities, and housing. These projects were planned for automobiles and have ample free parking. Their design does not favor transit use, and the distances between buildings discourage walking.

TABLE 1-1
LEADING METROPOLITAN AREAS IN TRANSIT WORK TRIPS, 1990

Rank	Metropolitan area	Total workers	Transit trips	Percentage of transit
1	New York	8,550,473	2,271,949	26.57
2	Chicago	3,841,337	524,756	13.66
3	Los Angeles	6,809,043	310,563	4.56
4	Washington	2,214,350	302,351	13.65
5	San Francisco	3,200,833	297,363	9.29
6	Philadelphia	2,794,917	284,579	10.18
7	Boston	2,141,717	227,948	10.64
8	Baltimore	1,191,813	91,176	7.65
9	Seattle	1,308,338	82,619	6.31
10	Pittsburgh	956,154	75,995	7.95
11	Atlanta	1,481,781	69,822	4.71
12	Minneapolis	1,307,624	69,125	5.29
13	Houston	1,759,796	66,540	3.78
14	Miami	1,476,085	64,240	4.35
15	Cleveland	1,242,099	56,675	4.56
16	Detroit	2,079,880	50,568	2.43
17	Dallas	1,976,606	46,504	2.35
18	Denver	964,912	40,961	4.25
19	Honolulu	437,518	40,643	9.29
20	San Diego	1,230,446	40,378	3.28
21	Portland, OR	724,532	39,259	5.42
22	Milwaukee	772,752	37,737	4.88
23	New Orleans	514,726	37,337	7.25
24	St. Louis	1,144,336	33,994	2.97
25	Cincinnati	812,766	29,758	3.66

Note: Transit modes include taxicab.
Source: 1990 Census of Population.

It is unclear whether transit can help much in ameliorating suburban gridlock. While some measures would increase transit use, the main approach being taken involves traffic mitigation programs that try to increase ride sharing and reduce peak-hour travel. Some companies have formed *transportation management associations*, and some suburban municipalities have enacted *traffic reduction ordinances*, to accomplish these objectives.

Mobility

The second aspect of the transportation problem is usually labeled *mobility*, or *accessibility*. Our society requires a great deal of travel, but people do not have equal abilities to travel or equal access to the transportation system. In the United States, we have emphasized the automotive highway system of transportation. Most people find this more or less satisfactory, but some people are unable to use this system. They have been called the *transportation-disadvantaged.*

The exact size of this group depends on definition and estimation techniques, but it is at least a sizable minority. According to the 1990 Census, 10.6 million U.S. households (or 11.5 percent of the total) did not have any motor vehicle available. The share rose to 12.3 percent for residents of metropolitan areas and 20.6 percent for central-city residents. Not all these people live in large cities, of course; some live in suburbs, small towns, and rural areas.

In some studies, this group is defined to include persons who do not have a car available at the time they want to make a trip. Many families have only one car, which the father takes to work; the mother has to get along without, not to mention the children. With this broader definition, some have estimated the transportation-disadvantaged at more than half the population.

One proposal to remedy this is to guarantee everyone a personal vehicle [Myers 1970]. It might even be cheaper for the government to pay for this rather than preserving mass transit, which requires large subsidies. However, it is not just economics that makes some people "carless." There will always be some in the population who cannot use a car or who do not want to. Some people are physically or mentally unable to drive. Many children are too young to get a driver's license. And some people prefer not to drive, even if they could (especially the elderly).

Hence some form of public transportation will always be necessary. It may not be one of the forms common today (buses and subways). Perhaps in the future some form of *paratransit* (discussed in Chapter 6) will be the means used by most people who do not have a personal car.

Transportation for the disabled has been a political issue for two decades. Several million people in the United States have physical or mental problems that interfere with their travel, and how to provide transit service for such people has been a vexing question. One approach is to offer door-to-door service with taxis or vans. Another is to make all transit vehicles accessible to the disabled, including those with wheelchairs. Many of the disabled prefer the latter course, which is called *mainstreaming*.

The federal government vacillated between the two approaches for years. The matter now seems to be settled by taking both approaches at once. The Americans with Disabilties Act of 1990 requires all future transit vehicles to be accessible to wheelchairs. In addition, transit agencies must provide demand-responsive service to those unable to use regular transit vehicles.

Obviously congestion is more serious in large cities than in small ones. In smaller places, it would be physically feasible, and perhaps economically efficient, to handle all travel by automobiles (including rental vehicles and taxis). There would be some congestion, but it would be tolerable by any objective standards. No city has an ideal street system, but incremental improvements are continually made. A street system could be developed in a city of a few hundred thousand people that would handle all travel adequately.

In small cities, the primary role of transit is to provide mobility to the transportation-disadvantaged. This is a matter of equity more than efficiency. It reflects the view that travel is essential to human beings and that all citizens are entitled to some form of transportation service, regardless of their circumstances.

Ancillary Impacts

The ancillary impacts of the transportation system (what economists call *externalities*) make up the third aspect of the transportation problem. A brief listing of major impacts follows:

Accidents   While U.S. highway accident rates are lower than those in other countries, the annual death toll of more than 40,000 is still a matter of concern. On the average, each motorist is involved in an accident every 5 years. Although politicians have been preoccupied with rural driving (Congress agreed in 1987 to let states raise the speed limit to 65 miles per hour on rural expressways), transit is clearly a safer mode than automobiles for moving people in urban areas.

Energy Consumption   The transportation sector relies almost wholly on petroleum for energy and accounts for 65 percent of the U.S. demand for oil. Gasoline prices fell during the 1980s, and the energy problem faded for a while, but the war over Kuwait brought it back to the limelight. It is bound to be a continuing concern since petroleum is a nonrenewable resource. This is partly a strategic problem because more than half of the world's crude oil reserves are in the Middle East.

Transit has the potential to reduce oil consumption (European cities, which are more transit-oriented, use much less energy per capita than their U.S. counterparts). Whether it will ever make a sizable impact on energy use in this country is debatable. The current approach is to make automobiles more fuel-efficient, and this is producing results. One good argument for expanding transit systems is the uncertainty about the future energy situation.

Environmental Impacts   These include air and water pollution and noise. While air quality nationwide has improved somewhat, smog remains a problem in more than 100 cities. Motor vehicles are major sources of carbon monoxide and ozone, the two most common pollutants. In 1990 Congress enacted a new Clean Air Act that makes a renewed attack on smog. Transit vehicles have the capacity to cause less air pollution per passenger, and a large shift of motorists to transit would improve the air quality. By the same token, a modest shift in modal split would have modest impacts.

Land Consumption   The transportation system occupies over 30 percent of the developed land in most U.S. cities. The automobile is a voracious user of urban space. In the CBDs of some cities, streets and parking take up 60 to 70 percent of the surface area. Freeway interchanges and parking lots consume vast expanses in the suburbs.

Aesthetics   This space consumption has contributed to the visual blight of urban areas. Neither a parking lot nor a freeway nor a strip commercial street is very pleasant to look at. Motor vehicles, moving or stationary, tend to dominate the cityscape. Billboards spoil rural vistas. Even transit facilities can have deleterious effects: Old-time elevated tracks cast deep shadows and lower property values nearby.

Disruption of the Urban Fabric   Major transportation routes can form physical barriers that divide neighborhoods, separate pupils from their schools, and cut off stores from their trade areas. The construction of new facilities requires taking property and forces relocation of families and businesses. This kind of damage stimulated the "highway revolt" that began in the 1960s and led some cities to cancel proposed expressways. Transit facilities are less obtrusive, although occasionally they create barriers.

Land Use   Since World War II, the country has adapted its economy and lifestyle to the automotive highway system, and this has altered urban development patterns. Multicentered, low-density metropolises create many problems: They consume a lot of land, increase costs and energy use, and reduce walking to a minimum. While many planners and pundits have criticized urban sprawl, it is obvious that a majority of people in the United States prefer living in single-family homes in the suburbs, despite the costs and disadvantages.

The suburban explosion and the depopulation of central cities have created difficult conditions for transit and caused ridership to fall. It is uneconomic for transit to serve low-density residential areas and scattered activity centers. Transit is efficient and attractive in older, dense cities, but mostly these are not the growth centers of the country. The sprawling, multinodal cities of the south and west are growing the fastest.

Consequently, relatively weak consumer demand for transit has been a constant problem since the 1950s. The benefits of transit occur only if transit vehicles carry large numbers of passengers, which they can do. Too often, though, transit vehicles carry light loads, and the benefits do not materialize. A bus carrying one passenger is more expensive, consumes more energy, and causes more air pollution than if that one person drove a car.

The weak demand for transit is understandable because usually transit is second-class transport. It is difficult to make transit service competitive with the automobile for those who can afford the latter. There are exceptions for people who live and work close to transit routes, but the dispersal of U.S. cities means that fewer and fewer people find themselves in this situation.

Transit, when combined with appropriate land-use controls, has the potential to produce a more compact, higher-density urban form that would alleviate some of the problems. But it appears that a major shift to transit will require unpopular restrictive measures such as very high fuel taxes, strict land-use controls, and constraints that make the automobile less convenient.

These impacts have existed for a long time but were largely ignored until the 1960s. Up to then, transportation problems were regarded as mainly technical engineering problems and outside the arena of political discussion. Technocrats (planners and engineers) dominated the decision-making process.

One result was lack of citizen input, especially from underrepresented groups such as the poor, elderly, disabled, and minorities. Since transportation problems were considered to be technical, there was no reason to consult the public. However, the automotive highway interests had great influence in decision making. Many companies with a stake in transportation, including carmakers, oil companies, and firms involved in highway construction lobbied effectively in Washington, D.C., and state capitals.

This has changed in recent years. The transportation decision-making process is now quite political. There are legal requirements for public hearings and environmental impact statements. Citizen and environmental groups are active and even militant in expressing their views. Ancillary impacts have attracted much attention and sometimes become the overriding issues in planning transportation facilities.

Transit also has a role as a standby or backup service, an alternative to the automobile that is available when needed. This was evident in the gasoline shortages that occurred during the Arab Oil Embargo in 1973 to 1974 and the Iranian crisis in 1979. However, transit seems to have limited promise in such emergencies; most transit systems cannot greatly expand their service on short notice because of limitations of equipment and personnel. More prosiac, but perhaps more useful, is the availability of the transit option for such temporary incidents as when the weather is bad or the car is at the garage.

What the U.S. public wants should be considered also. In the last 30 years, there have been many public elections on transit issues. The results have been mixed, but in many cases, voters have approved transit proposals. There have also been many legislators who favored transit; the existence of federal transit programs is proof of this. This suggests that a sizable number of people in the United States think transit is beneficial.

MAJOR ISSUES INVOLVING TRANSIT

Several basic policy issues involving transit have persisted for many years and will certainly continue to attract attention. Although they will be discussed in detail in later chapters, a brief introduction here will provide a preview of the material to come.

Highways versus Transit

The oldest debate is whether public transportation or the automotive highway system should be favored in U.S. cities. This has been the dominant issue in urban transportation since the 1950s. It is an emotional and ideological dispute that has produced extremists on both sides. There have been countless books and articles that attacked the automobile and promoted transit. There is also a pro-automobile literature; a striking example is a book titled *The War Against the Automobile* [Bruce-Briggs 1977].

Highway advocates had the upper hand in the 1950s. There was little opposition to the concept of the interstate highway system; it was a popular program. The first substantial dissent began around 1960, when some eastern mayors got upset over curtailment of commuter rail services, and San Francisco declared a moratorium on building freeways within the city. Wholesale clearance for the interstates aroused protest all over the country. This grassroots movement soon impressed politicians. By 1970 it had produced wide public opposition to urban freeways and support of transit as an alternative.

Transit proponents did very well in the 1970s, when Congress passed many pro-transit measures. This included "busting" the Highway Trust Fund and initiating federal operating subsidies for transit. Urban highway building virtually came to a halt. In the 1980s, highway backers made a comeback as the Reagan and Bush administrations curtailed transit programs. The Clinton administration appears to be more supportive of transit; the first budget it submitted to Congress contained a substantial increase in funding for transit.

Choice of Transit Technology

Another debate has come to the fore in recent years: Should transit improvements take the form of rail or bus? There is strong pressure to make the bus the principal mode of mass transit, often from people who formerly supported highways over transit. Others, including many politicians, favor rail transit. This controversy can also be emotional; some people seem to be psychologically attached to a particular type of hardware.

The bus side has some strong arguments, such as the fact that buses carry the majority of U.S. transit passengers. Conventional bus service has a bad image, but it has the advantage that it uses existing streets and has low capital costs. There are innovative ways to improve the quality of bus transit, ranging from subscription services to exclusive bus lanes.

The debate often centers on whether to build new rail systems. This is the question of *new starts*. Since 1972, new heavy rail systems (which get power from a third rail) have opened in six U.S. cities. From 1981 through 1993, new light rail systems (which get power from an overhead wire) have opened in eight cities. Whether these projects have been successes or failures is controversial. Some people favor light rail as a compromise, claiming it has some advantages of both buses and heavy rail systems.

The Reagan and Bush administrations were reluctant to approve new starts. Washington officials preferred to allocate money to buses and rehabilitation of older rail systems. The only new heavy rail system approved in the past decade was a subway in Los Angeles, 4.4 miles long, which opened in January 1993.

However, rail transit has remained popular with others. Congress has often inserted appropriations for rail projects in the budget; some of these survived the political process and were approved. In 1991 Congress passed the *Intermodal Surface Transportation Efficiency Act* (ISTEA), which gives great flexibility to state and local governments in how they spend federal aid. Probably some of them will choose to build new rail systems.

Responsibility for Transit

There has been continuing controversy over what institutions should own and/or operate transit systems; and over who would take responsibility for them. Transit operations began in this country as private enterprises and largely continued that way through World War II. Then gradually most of the companies went bankrupt; smaller ones ceased operation while larger ones were taken over by local governments. This was a considerable burden for many of them, and the local governments looked to state capitals and Washington, D.C., for help. In the 1960s and 1970s, the federal government largely assumed responsibility for ensuring that local transit services were maintained throughout the country.

The Reagan administration tried to reverse this trend and reduce the federal role in transit. It tried to give responsibility back to state and local governments (and partly succeeded). It also encouraged the private sector to return to the transit field. This was in line with the Reaganites' policy of favoring private enterprise in general and transferring public activities to the private sector where possible.

Privatization became a major issue in the 1980s. Proponents argue that public officials are not entrepreneurial, that lack of competition removes the incentives for better management. They claim that private firms can operate transit more efficiently than public agencies can. There is some evidence that private firms have lower operating costs, but in part they achieve this result by using nonunion labor and paying lower wages. Both local transit officials and labor unions have strongly opposed the privatization movement.

Actually, private firms never completely left the transit business. Some profitable transit services patronized by the well-to-do, such as express buses from suburbs to downtown, have survived in the private sector. But the best opportunities for private firms lie in contracting for specific services, such as transporting the elderly and disabled or vehicle maintenance. It appears that the private sector can play a limited role in transit, but not a major one. Private firms need to make a profit; most transit riders are poor, and it is difficult to make money serving the poor. That is why most transit firms were taken over by government in the past.

State and local governments have taken more responsibility for transit, and it appears that this trend will continue. The ISTEA legislation gives them more power in decision making, but also imposes stricter planning requirements. The most important question, though, is, Who will provide the money needed to support transit services?

Financing

Among those responsible for running transit systems, the most pressing issue is finance. Where will the money come from? The costs of building, equipping, and operating transit systems have soared, while revenues have grown modestly, and deficits sometimes seem to be out of control. There are several reasons for this; perhaps most important is the power held by transit labor unions, as occasionally manifested in strikes. Costs of construction and transit vehicles have also risen faster than the cost of living.

Since transit started in the private sector, the original attitude was that transit should pay for itself. In the 1960s, it became acceptable to subsidize capital costs (for vehicles and rail lines), but it was felt that fare revenues should cover operating costs. Soon, however, most transit systems were running deficits on their operations. In 1974, Congress enacted a program of federal subsidies for local transit operating costs.

The Reagan administration tried to phase out operating subsidies, but Congress never concurred. Every year the Reagan administration proposed sharp cuts in transit funding, but it was always forced to compromise. Federal transit funding decreased in the 1980s, but all the transit aid programs continued.

No one now expects transit to break even or hopes for revenues to cover operating costs. There are few exceptions to the rule that all U.S. transit systems are subsidized. Much attention has been given to federal operating subsidies, but this source is relatively minor compared to state and local subsidies. These levels of government have often had financial problems in recent years and have sometimes faced taxpayer revolts.

The situation reached the crisis stage in a few cities where transit service was temporarily suspended for lack of funds. Often cost-cutting measures have been adopted, such as reducing hours of service and dropping lightly patronized routes. Many transit systems have raised fares, which inevitably causes a loss in ridership. Some metropolitan areas have enacted new taxes to support transit. A sales tax dedicated to transit seems to be acceptable to voters in many areas. This has the drawback that, according to economists, the sales tax is one of the most regressive forms of taxation.

Other problems confronting transit will be discussed later in the book. The intent here was to sketch the four major issues that have preoccupied the transit field for many years. The nature of the urban transportation problem changes over time—in response to changes in technology, economic structure, legislation, and lifestyle—but the problem has persisted for centuries. It appears that it will always be with us.

QUESTIONS

1 What are the most serious problems in the United States caused by people's reliance on private motor vehicles for personal travel? To what extent can expansion of mass transit services solve these problems?
2 Will it ever be possible to eliminate traffic congestion from U.S. cities?
3 Should the government undertake measures to get people to live closer to their jobs, thus reducing journey-to-work traffic? Should these measures be voluntary or mandatory?
4 Is there any justification for providing public transportation service in small cities and towns?
5 What can be done to increase the demand for transit? Would you favor making transit use more attractive, making automobile use less attractive, or doing some of both?

REFERENCES

Bruce-Briggs, B.: *The War Against the Automobile* (New York: E. P. Dutton, 1977).
Cervero, Robert: *Suburban Gridlock* (New Brunswick, NJ: Center for Urban Policy Research, Rutgers University, 1986).
Meyer, John R., John F. Kain, and Martin Wohl: *The Urban Transportation Problem* (Cambridge, MA: Harvard University Press, 1965).
Morlok, Edward K.: *Introduction to Transportation Engineering and Planning* (New York: McGraw-Hill, 1978).
Mumford, Lewis: *The City in History* (New York: Harcourt, Brace & World, 1961).
Myers, Sumner: "Personal Transportation for the Poor," *Traffic Quarterly*, vol. 24, no. 2 (April 1970), pp. 191–206.

2

THE HISTORY OF URBAN TRANSIT

THE BEGINNINGS

The first public transportation known to history was introduced by the Romans, who established a system of vehicles for hire during the reigns of Emperors Augustus and Tiberius [Thrupp 1877]. These two- or four-wheel wagons were stationed at inns every 5 or 6 miles along the fine highways for which the Romans were famous.

Coaches that ran on regular schedules between major towns appeared in Europe during the 16th century. Stagecoaches (similar in appearance to those seen in western movies) were introduced in the 17th century. However, most roads were poor, fares were high, and the service was slow and uncomfortable. For example, in 1706 a stage-coach left from London for York every Monday, Wednesday, and Friday. The journey of approximately 175 miles took 4 days.

The first form of public transportation to operate solely within cities was the hackney carriage, the forerunner of the taxi, which appeared in Paris and London shortly after 1600. The name came from the French word *haquenée*, meaning a horse of middling size and quality used for riding, but not for war or hunting. It soon came to mean a horse for hire and then a vehicle as well [Gilbert and Samuels 1982]. By 1700 there were about 600 hackneys operating in London [McKay 1976]. The name has survived: Some U.S. cities have a Hackney Bureau that issues "hack licenses" for taxicabs.

In 1662 the French philosopher-mathematician Blaise Pascal obtained a patent from the King and began a low-fare coach service on five fixed routes in Paris. Although successful at first, the service lasted less than 2 years. This was partly because Pascal died, at the age of 39, but also because hackneys offered competition and people in certain classes (e.g., soldiers and servants) were not allowed to ride the coaches [Thrupp 1877].

As the 19th century opened, the average person walked to work. Cities were dense and compact; the geographical area of a city was largely limited to the radius of walking distance from the center. Some wealthy families lived on the outskirts and traveled by horseback or carriage, but horses were too expensive for common people to keep.

The modern era of urban mass transit began in 1819 with a coach line in Paris [Miller 1941]. It used an existing type of stagecoach called a *diligence*. The first transit service in the United States was started by Abraham Brower on Broadway in New York City in 1827. For this he designed a modified stagecoach seating 12 passengers, and he had it built by the coach-making firm of Wade & Leverich. It was named the *Accommodation*. Business was good, and 2 years later he ordered a second vehicle with different design: All the seats ran lengthwise, and there was a door at the rear with an iron stairway to the ground. This vehicle he named the *Sociable*.

MAJOR MOVERS OF THE 19TH CENTURY

Omnibus

In 1825 a coach builder named George Shillibeer was commissioned to build specially designed coaches with large seating capacity for use in Paris. The vehicle was called an *omnibus*, a name coined by a Frenchman named Baudry for a coach he ran in the town of Nantes. Shillibeer moved to London and started an omnibus line there in 1829. The vehicle was drawn by three horses and could seat 18 passengers. In 1832 Parliament passed the Stage Carriage Act, which made it legal to pick up and let off passengers anywhere along a route—a right previously reserved for hackneys.

The omnibus was introduced in New York City in 1831 by John Stephenson, who became the largest manufacturer of transit vehicles in the 19th century. It was successful and competitors appeared; by 1835 more than a hundred omnibuses were running in New York. Philadelphia got them in 1831, Boston in 1835, and Baltimore in 1844. Typically each vehicle was individually owned and operated. The first large transit firm was the London General Omnibus Company, formed in 1856, which tried to buy out all the small operators. In the first year, it acquired 580 omnibuses and 6400 horses, but it never secured a complete monopoly in London.

Although the omnibus was designed to operate in cities, it was slow and uncomfortable. There were few paved streets, and those were usually paved with cobblestones. Nevertheless, omnibuses continued to operate throughout the 19th century on routes with light patronage. They ran on Fifth Avenue in New York City until they were replaced by motor buses between 1905 and 1908.

Horse-Drawn Street Railway

A major advance came in the form of the horse-drawn street railway. The first one in the world was the New York & Harlem Railroad, which began service on November 26, 1832. It was the brainchild of John Mason, president of Chemical Bank, who formed a company and raised $350,000 in capital. The cars were built by Stephenson. The use of horses was first considered temporary, to last only until the steam railroad could be extended from Albany to New York, but the horses performed well and were never replaced by steam engines.

This mode, popularly called the *horsecar*, eventually replaced omnibuses on the busiest routes. New Orleans started a horsecar line in 1834, Boston in 1855, Philadelphia in 1857, and Pittsburgh in 1859. Baltimore, Chicago, and Cincinnati also had horsecars before the Civil War. The first horsecars in Europe began operation in Paris in 1853, and a U.S. entrepreneur introduced them to England in 1859. Horsecars appeared in other European cities in the 1860s and 1870s, but they were never as common as in the United States.

Horsecars came in many sizes and shapes; there was no standard model (see Figure 2-1). There were short "bobtail" cars drawn by a single horse and large cars capable of seating 50 persons and pulled by three or four horses. The most common vehicle was 23 feet long, had 22 seats, and was pulled by two horses. Mules were sometimes used instead of horses; they were slower but more durable.

The horsecar was a great improvement. It ran on iron rails laid in the middle of the street, which greatly reduced friction and roughly doubled the load that horses could pull. The average speed was also about double that of the omnibus. The wheels could be smaller, which permitted design of lower and wider vehicles. And according to McKay [1976, p. 15],

> There were other advantages. The horsecar was faster, smoother, and less noisy. There was also more room inside, easier entry and exit, and somewhat greater safety due to the brake,

FIGURE 2-1
A horsecar. This photograph was taken in Red Cloud, Nebraska, in 1910. Horsecars were used in hundreds of cities and towns throughout the country. Notice that the street is not paved. (*Source:* Kansas Collection, University of Kansas Libraries.)

which increased control. Finally, since the investment in rails paid for itself handsomely, the operators could reduce fares and tap a new clientele.

However, the horsecar had its disadvantages. Horses were expensive—they accounted for 40 percent of the capital investment. Teams had to be changed several times a day, so the majority of the stock was always idle. The horses caused an early form of pollution, described by Hilton [1971, p. 15]:

> A horse dropped over ten pounds of fecal material a day on the street and periodically drenched the pavement with urine. Not only was this offensive per se, but the feces contained the virus of tetanus, such that any skin abrasion on the streets entailed the risk of an absolutely fatal disease. Urination was so frequent that smooth pavements such as asphalt were not practical; either dirt or cobblestones had to be provided to assure traction between a horse's hooves and the street.

Another problem was that the horses survived this kind of use for only a few years and then had to be retired. Further, they were liable to disease and injury. This came to a head in 1872, when the Great Epizootic (an equine-influenza epidemic) killed 2250 horses in Philadelphia in 3 weeks and killed or disabled 18,000 horses in New York. This was a disaster for the operators, who began seeking other means of propulsion.

Cable Car

The answer first appeared to be the cable car. In this system, a cable is laid in a small trough between the rails and is kept in continuous motion by a steam engine located at the end of the line. A car is propelled by gripping onto the cable with a metal arm that reaches down; the grip is released when the car brakes to a stop. The car itself has no motor. Besides a driver-conductor, each car carries a gripman, who must develop skill at the trade.

This invention is usually attributed to Andrew S. Hallidie, but it is more accurate to say that he built the first commercially successful cable car line [Hilton 1971]. Cable-drawn wagons had been used in British mines since the 1830s, and Hallidie had run a company that manufactured wire cables for the California gold fields. He got the idea of applying the system to urban transport and secured financing to build a line 6/10 mile long on the Clay Street hill (which had a 12 percent grade) in San Francisco.

Hallidie successfully demonstrated his system on August 1, 1873, and began revenue service a month later. The financial results were impressive: At times the company reported a return of 35 percent on its investment. Rival companies were formed; San Francisco got its second cable car line in 1877, the third in 1878, and two more in 1880.

San Francisco was an attractive site for cable cars because horses could not pull cars up the steep hills, the city had a gridiron street system (no curves), and the climate was mild (no snow or ice). However, cable cars ran perfectly well on flat ground, and the problem of going around corners was eventually solved. After visiting San Francisco in 1880, the president of the Chicago City Railway built a line on State Street that opened on January 28, 1882, in the depth of winter. It proved that climate was no obstacle. To the contrary: "The fact that the cars did not depend on adhesion was a positive advantage in winters; cable cars were marvelously superior to horsecars in the snow." [Hilton 1971, p. 31]

Cable cars spread across the United States in the 1880s and were installed in about 30 cities. There was cable car service on the Brooklyn Bridge when it opened in 1883. Boston and Detroit were the only large cities that never had them, and they were never built in the south. San Francisco had the largest system (52.8 miles), while Chicago was second with 41.2 miles and Kansas City was third with 37.8 miles. They were also built in Europe, Australia, and New Zealand.

The cable cars represented a major advance: They attained speeds of 7 to 9 miles per hour in business districts and 12 to 13 miles per hour elsewhere. They were cheaper to operate than horsecars. However, capital investment was very high—about four times that of horsecars—and the cables occasionally snapped or frayed, which interrupted service for several hours.

Cable cars started to be replaced by electric streetcars in the 1890s. The peak year was 1893, when there were 305.1 miles in service throughout the country. After Kansas City closed its last line in 1913, only three cities (all hilly) retained them. Tacoma abandoned its line in 1938, and Seattle ended service in 1940, making San Francisco the only city with cable cars.

There are three cable car lines operating in San Francisco (see Figure 2-2). The system was rebuilt in 1983 to 1984 at a cost of $60 million, and it is now in excellent condition. While it is a tourist attraction, it also carries a substantial number of commuters. During midday, the cable car operators sometimes stop to let passengers take pictures, but during rush hour the cars keep to schedule.

Electric Streetcar

The streetcar—also called the *electric railway, trolley*, or *tram*—was the next and most important innovation. The first successful demonstration was staged by Werner von Siemens, of the famous German family of inventors, at an industrial exposition in Berlin in 1879. His company, Siemens and Halske, built a 1.5-mile line in Lichterfelde, a suburb of Berlin, that began revenue passenger service in 1881.

Meanwhile, Thomas A. Edison was also experimenting with an electric railway. He built a test track at his laboratory in Menlo Park, New Jersey, and in May 1880 he staged the first demonstration of an electrically propelled locomotive in the United States [Passer 1953]. It worked very well, but street railway officials were skeptical. Edison was more interested in lighting and never followed through on his promising early results. Thus he failed to become a major figure in electric transportation.

The major problem the inventors faced was how to supply electricity to the vehicles. Both Siemens and Edison used the two rails to carry the current, but experience in Lichterfelde showed that this was hazardous. "Although the rails were placed to the side of the road and raised six inches above the surface, shocks to horses and inattentive pedestrians touching both rails simultaneously did occur" [McKay 1976, p. 38].

Edward M. Bentley and Walter H. Knight built a 1-mile line in East Cleveland that "commenced regular operation in July 1884 and had the distinction of being the first commercial electric street railway in the United States" [Passer 1953, p. 225]. An un-

FIGURE 2-2
A San Francisco cable car. San Francisco was the first city with cable cars and now is the only one in the world. There are three lines operating. This is the California Street line at its terminal at Market Street. (Photo by author.)

derground wooden conduit between the rails contained two copper conductors that carried the current; each car had a plow that fitted into a slot in the conduit. This line was abandoned after a year when the street was torn up to install sewers. Bentley and Knight built several other installations, but their business did not thrive. Later, streetcars in New York City and Washington, D.C., used underground conduits because overhead wiring was banned, but this design was inferior.

Leo Daft had demonstrated an electric locomotive capable of hauling a railroad coach at Saratoga, New York, in 1883. In 1885 he electrified a line of the Baltimore Union Passenger Railway, "which proved to be the first American electric line to operate commercially for any extended period" [Hilton 1971, p. 15]. Power came from a third rail on the ground, which posed a hazard. That year he also built a line in Orange, New Jersey, in which a four-wheeled "trolley" ran along two overhead wires that carried the current. But the trolley kept falling off; this design proved inadequate.

Charles J. Van Depoele, an immigrant from Belgium, operated electric railways at expositions in Chicago in 1883 and Toronto in 1884. In 1885, he extended the Toronto line and introduced a design with a single overhead wire. Each car had a spring-loaded pole on the roof with a single trolley wheel that kept in continuous contact with the wire; current was returned through the track, completing the electric circuit. In 1886,

Van Depoele built a 2-mile line in Montgomery, Alabama, which functioned very well. By the end of 1887, his company had built a dozen electric railways and was far ahead of its competitors. However, this dominance did not last long.

It was Frank J. Sprague who became the leader in electric traction. Sprague graduated from the U.S. Naval Academy and worked briefly for Edison, but Edison had lost interest in electric motors. In 1884 Sprague resigned and formed his own company. He designed motors for industrial use that sold well and gave him a sound financial base; meanwhile he concentrated on electric railway design. He completed his first streetcar installation in 1887 in St. Joseph, Missouri, but it got little attention.

Sprague's second project was in Richmond, Virginia, and this proved to be the breakthrough system. The contract called for 40 cars, 12 miles of track, and a power plant of 375 horsepower. Richmond had steep hills, and the cars had to ascend a grade of 8 percent. The system began revenue service on February 2, 1888, and by the end of that year it was operating efficiently and reliably. It was the largest streetcar system in the world, and it established Sprague as the premier designer in the field. His achievement was explained by Passer [1953, pp. 245–246]:

> The real significance of the Richmond installation was that it contained the technical features which permitted successful operation on a large scale and set the pattern for electric street-railway development. An overhead conductor was used, and the current was picked up by a universal swiveling, underrunning trolley. The motors—two in each car—were mounted beneath the car and suspended by what was called the wheelbarrow suspension. Each motor was mounted by three points, two on the car axle and one on the car. This arrangement permitted the car to move relative to the axle and motor without misaligning the gearing. . . . One controller was mounted on each end of the car, permitting operation from either end. The tracks were part of the return circuit, and only one overhead conductor was used.

One of the most influential transit magnates was Henry M. Whitney, president of the West End Street Railway in Boston. It was the largest street railway system in the United States, with 212 miles of track, 1700 cars, and 8000 horses. He was planning to install a cable system when he heard about the excellent performance of the Richmond railway. He visited Richmond three times in 1888. Whitney was skeptical that electricity could handle rush-hour demand, so Sprague held a demonstration in which 22 cars started in succession and kept running at the same time. Whitney was convinced and forgot about cable cars (which is why Boston never had them). Instead, he converted the Boston system to electricity; the first electric cars ran in January 1889.

Whitney's decision impressed many transit operators throughout the country, who rapidly switched to electric power during the 1890s. This was not an easy change, as it required much additional investment. Besides stringing overhead wires, the track had to be replaced because electric cars were much heavier than horsecars [McKay 1976]. Still, by 1902 more than 90 percent of the street railway mileage in the country was electrified. Horsecars lingered on lightly used lines that did not justify the investment. A few horsecars continued to run on Bleecker Street in New York City until 1917.

The streetcar dominated urban transportation in the United States for four decades. Lines were built in every city and even in small towns (see Figure 2-3). Many specialized vehicles were designed: open-sided cars for the summer, roofless cars for carrying

FIGURE 2-3
An early streetcar. This photo was taken on Massachusetts Street in Lawrence, Kansas, circa 1907 to 1909. Cyclists abound, although the street is not paved. (*Source:* Kansas Collection, University of Kansas Libraries.)

tourists, sprinkler cars for cleaning the streets, hearses, and rolling post offices. Philadelphia had a car that delivered milk in the morning, and Duluth had a car outfitted as a fire engine. Company presidents had private cars with luxurious fittings such as easy chairs and bathrooms.

The streetcar network was so extensive that in 1912 a party of officials rode from Boston to New York entirely by streetcar. They used a dozen lines and went through Worcester, Springfield, Hartford, New Haven, and Bridgeport. If they had been required to pay fares, the total cost would have been $2.40.

At the turn of the century, the streetcar business was very good, and huge profits were made, even though the standard fare was 5¢. The services were privately owned, and competition was bitter. This had several results:

First, there was overextension of routes and duplication of service. Two companies would run parallel lines on streets a block apart. Many companies extended lines into the countryside, hoping that suburbs would grow up around them. Sometimes they did, but not always.

Second, in many cities, there was a battle to secure a monopoly over all streetcar service. Strong companies were continually buying out weaker rivals. Often one company was able to obtain a complete monopoly (such as the West End Street Railway in Boston).

Third, corruption and graft permeated the transit business. Companies bribed public officials to get exclusive franchises and stifle competition. One of the most infamous "traction kings" was Charles T. Yerkes of Chicago, who was a master at financial manipulation and bribery [Roberts 1961]. He gained control of all streetcar lines on the North and West Sides of Chicago. Many of the scandals exposed by Lincoln Steffens, the muckraking journalist, involved streetcar companies. The transit industry acquired a poor public image, and few people cared to defend it in times of trouble.

Just after World War I, the streetcar industry suffered a major crisis. Many transit companies began to collapse, largely because management had sought to milk as much quick profit as possible. Some companies had "watered stock," which means the book value of their stock was far greater than the actual value of their assets. Costs rose rapidly at this time because of inflation caused by World War I and the spread of unions among transit workers. However, many companies had franchises that permanently fixed the fare at 5¢ (they had favored this to prevent price wars).

Between 1916 and 1923, more than one-third of U.S. transit companies went bankrupt. In 1919 Woodrow Wilson appointed a Federal Electrical Railway Commission to investigate the problem. It made some good recommendations, but few of them were carried out. After the shakeout, the streetcar industry entered a period of stability, which lasted until the onset of the depression.

The Steam Railroads

The 19th century also witnessed the development of steam railroads. The first intercity railroad service began in 1830 between Liverpool and Manchester in England. This inaugurated a century in which steel wheels on steel rails became the dominant form of intercity transportation. The railroad industry formed a major part of the economy, much as the automotive industry does now.

Some people started riding the trains to work every day from small towns near the large cities. There was enough demand so that railroads began running special trains for the commuters. London opened the first strictly suburban line in 1838. A large network of suburban tracks was built around London between 1840 and 1875 and is still in use. Other European cities that built suburban routes included Paris, Berlin, Hamburg, Liverpool, and Glasgow.

This also occurred in the United States. Commuter trains began running from Worcester to Boston in 1843 [Kennedy 1962]. New York, Philadelphia, and Chicago also built large networks of suburban lines. Other cities such as Washington, Pittsburgh, and San Francisco had a few routes. Although the steam locomotive is long gone, many of these services continue to operate with trains powered by diesel engines or electricity.

SUBWAY AND ELEVATED SYSTEMS

Several attempts were made to introduce steam trains into the heart of cities. The first subway in the world, 3.7 miles long, opened in London on January 10, 1863 [Bobrick 1981]. The trains were pulled by steam locomotives, and while special efforts were made to expel the smoke, ventilation remained a major problem. The line was popularly called the *sewer railway*. However, it continued to operate for many years and eventually was electrified.

A better idea seemed to be to put steam trains on elevated tracks over the street. Charles T. Harvey built an elevated line with cable traction on Greenwich Street in New York City in 1868, but the venture was not successful economically, and in 1871 new management switched to small steam locomotives called *dummies*. Elevated steam trains ran in Manhattan, Brooklyn, and Queens until the end of the century. When Chicago opened its first elevated line in 1892, the trains were pulled by steam engines. Other elevated steam railways operated briefly in Kansas City and Sioux City, Iowa [Cudahy 1990].

This arrangement was never satisfactory, though, and soon disappeared: "Steam power on the elevated lines . . . was a pronounced civic liability. The engines were sooty, messy and noisy. They started fires in awnings, startled teams of horses, and in general wreaked havoc with efforts to lead a quiet and tranquil life" [Cudahy 1979, p. 19].

Other power sources were tried. The first U.S. subway was built by Alfred Ely Beach, publisher of *Scientific American*, and opened in New York City in 1870 [Bobrick 1981]. It ran for 312 feet under Broadway and was powered by pneumatic pressure. Beach could not obtain a franchise for the line, so he built it secretly. This enraged the powerful Boss Tweed, who killed plans to extend the line. Beach operated the service until 1874.

The first subway in the world using electricity (from a third rail) opened in London in 1890. In May 1896, Budapest began operating an underground tram line. In December 1896, Glasgow initiated service on a 6.6-mile underground loop powered by cables (but later converted to electricity).

The first electric elevated line in the world was the Metropolitan West Side Elevated Railroad in Chicago, which began service on May 6, 1895 [Cudahy 1982]. It used a locomotive equipped with motors and able to pull one or two unpowered trailer cars. This was not an efficient design.

In 1897, the South Side Elevated Railway in Chicago decided to switch to electricity and awarded a contract to Sprague. He made another important contribution by inventing the *multiple-unit system*, in which every car has motors, all controlled by the train operator in the first car. Sprague worked on this at General Electric's test track in Schenectady, New York. In July 1897, "he demonstrated a six-car train there before South Side officials and engineers. To indicate the ease with which the six cars could be operated, he permitted his ten-year-old son to handle the controls" [Passer 1953, p. 273]. All steam locomotives were removed from the South Side by August 1898.

The multiple-unit system was important for several reasons. It meant you could add cars to trains without any diminution of power, since each car had the correct amount of propulsive power for itself. Tractive power is a function of the weight on the driving wheels, and in the multiple-unit system, the weight of the entire train (instead of just the locomotive) is applied to the driving wheels. Individually powered cars also have faster acceleration, which increases average speed and reduces operating cost. All subway elevated systems in the world use this system today.

Boston was the first U.S. city with an electrically powered subway; a streetcar line under Tremont Street began operating on September 1, 1897. The line was later equipped with a third rail and extended on elevated tracks to Dudley Street in Roxbury and Sullivan Square in Charlestown. This service began in June 1901 and continued for 7 years. Then a second tunnel was built under Washington Street, connecting with the elevated, and streetcars returned to the Tremont Street tunnel. Elevated tracks on Washington Street were used until 1987, when the new Orange Line inaugurated service; they have now been torn down. The historic Tremont Street tunnel is still in use (for those familiar with Boston, it is the upper level at the Park Street station).

Boston expanded its system over the years: A tunnel to East Boston opened in 1904 (this is now the Blue Line). A route to Cambridge, which crosses Charles River on a bridge, began operating in 1912 (this is now the Red Line). This line was brought into the Park Street station by burrowing under the original tunnel; this is known as *Park Street Under* [Cudahy 1972]. The system was owned by the Boston Elevated Railway Company until 1947, when it was taken over by a public authority. Boston is unique in having few buses running through its downtown area; the concentration of subway stations makes them superfluous.

New York City leaders debated building subways for many years; finally ground was broken in 1900 [Cudahy 1979]. The contractor had trouble with financing and enlisted the aid of August Belmont, who is regarded as the father of the New York City subway. The Interborough Rapid Transit (IRT) Company was formed in 1902 to operate the line, with Belmont as president. Service began on October 27, 1904. By the end of the first year, 400,000 passengers a day were paying the 5¢ fare to ride the line.

The route began at City Hall and ran north under Fourth Avenue to 42d Street, where it turned west to Times Square. There it turned north and ran under Broadway to 145th Street. The portion from City Hall to Grand Central Station is now part of the Lexington Avenue line. The crosstown leg became the shuttle between Grand Central and Times Square. This subway was the first in the world with four tracks, allowing both local and express trains. In a curious error, Times Square was first made a local stop, although today it is one of the busiest stations in the city.

The success of this line aroused interest in building more subways. A competitor to Belmont's group emerged in the Brooklyn Rapid Transit (BRT) Company, which operated elevated and streetcar service in Brooklyn and Queens. Finally in 1913, the IRT, BRT, and New York City signed the Dual Contracts, which laid out an extensive network of subways and elevateds and divided them between the two rivals. Most of the planned routes were eventually built, even though the BRT entered receivership in 1918 and was reorganized as the Brooklyn-Manhattan Transit (BMT) Corporation.

Although the two companies received long-term leases on the facilities, there was continuing agitation for public transit service. This bore fruit in 1925, when New York City broke ground for an independent route under Eighth Avenue. Construction proceeded slowly, but it was finally completed in 1932. This began the Independent (IND) system, the third element of the triad, which was operated by the city. The IRT and BMT fared poorly in the depression, and in 1940 the city bought them out. Later the city tried to expunge memory of the separate systems, but many New Yorkers still refer to the IRT, BMT, and IND.

Rapid transit came to Philadelphia in 1907, with a combination subway and elevated line along Market Street. This subway has four tracks; streetcars provide local service on one pair, while heavy rail cars using a third rail operate express service on the other pair of tracks. The Frankford Elevated was added to the eastern end in 1922. A second subway under Broad Street, perpendicular to the first, went into service in 1928.

Chicago relied on its extensive elevated network and for years opted not to build subways. Samuel Insull, who started his career as personal secretary to Thomas Edison, came to control all the elevated companies and merged them into the Chicago Rapid Transit Company in 1924 [Cudahy 1982]. He was the best-known transit tycoon of his time, but his empire collapsed in the depression. He was indicted for embezzlement and fraud in 1932; it took 18 months to have him extradited from Europe. Then he was acquitted on all counts.

Subways were proposed in a few other U.S. cities, including Los Angeles, in the period between the two world wars. Several of these plans were aborted when bond issues failed at elections. Cincinnati did begin construction of a 16-mile rapid transit loop in 1920 after voters approved a $6 million bond issue [Condit 1977]. Work was halted in 1923, after 11 miles of right-of-way had been prepared, when Cincinnati ran out of money because of inflation. There was a political change in the city government, and construction was never resumed. Most of the route was later buried under the Mill Creek Expressway, although part of the subway tunnel is still there.

When World War II began, Boston, New York, and Philadelphia were the only U.S. cities with subways. But ground had been broken for Chicago's first subway, under State Street, in 1938. It began revenue service on October 17, 1943. Construction of a second subway, under Dearborn Street, was halted because of the war; it was finally completed in 1951.

Several European cities had subways before World War II, but elevated lines were not so common as in the United States. The first Metro line in Paris was completed in 1900 [Bobrick 1981]. Berlin's subway, called the *U-Bahn*, began service in 1902. Hamburg opened one in 1912, Madrid in 1919, Barcelona in 1924, and Stockholm in 1933. Because of the midday siesta, the Spanish systems have four peak periods per day. Today London has the largest system in the world with 252 route miles; New York is second with 231 [Cudahy 1979].

The first subway in Latin America was opened in Buenos Aires in 1913. Australia became the fourth continent with a subway when streetcars started using a 3-mile tunnel in Sydney in 1926. The first subway in Asia was the Ginza line in Tokyo, completed in 1927. Finally Africa got a subway when Cairo began service through a tunnel connecting two railroad stations in 1987.

One of the most famous subways is in Moscow, where the first line was opened in 1935. The older stations are elaborately decorated with statues, chandeliers, and marble walls, but newer ones are more austere [Grava 1976]. The tunnels are unusually deep, and the subways got heavy use as air raid shelters in World War II. The system has grown continually and now carries more passengers than any other in the world, although Tokyo is a close second.

INTERURBAN ELECTRIC RAILWAYS

A slightly different form of public transportation was important for several decades. The *interurban electric railway* was midway between a street railway and an intercity train. The vehicles were heavier than streetcars and sometimes capable of travel at 60 miles per hour. Routes began at the city center and ran into the country, often continuing to another city. Typically the tracks ran in the middle of city streets, but in the country the tracks were laid alongside highways or on a separate right-of-way. Power came from an overhead wire, as with streetcars. Most of the business involved carrying passengers, but the trains also carried mail and freight. Farmers used them to ship produce into the city; stores used the trains to deliver packages. For an example of a vehicle, see Figure 2-4.

One of the Siemens brothers designed the first interurban electric railway in the world, which began service at Giant's Causeway, Northern Ireland, in 1883. However, the concept attained its greatest popularity in the United States. The first U.S. interurban electric railway was built between Newark and Granville in Ohio and began operation in 1889. The first important line was opened in Oregon in 1893 between Portland and Oregon City; it continued in service until 1958.

Hilton and Due [1960] compiled an exhaustive history of the interurban electric railways that catalogues every line built in the United States (and there were hundreds). The period of greatest expansion was from 1900 to 1910. Eventually the lines formed a dense network covering the northeast and midwest. Ohio and Indiana had the most mileage, but there was some in almost every state. The peak year for total mileage was

FIGURE 2-4
An interurban electric car. This vehicle, built in 1925, was once used by the Philadelphia and West Chester Traction Company. It has been preserved at the Seashore Trolley Museum in Kennebunkport, Maine. (Photo by author.)

1916, when there were 15,580 miles in the United States. The longest continuous trip one could take (with transfers, of course) was from Elkhart Lake, Wisconsin, to Oneonta, New York—a distance of 1087 miles. There is no evidence that anyone ever took this trip.

At first there was great optimism about the future of the industry and much speculative investment. The major competition consisted of the steam railroads, which were more interested in long-distance traffic. "Interurbans had greatest success in attracting traffic from towns ten to forty miles from a major city; they offered service at two-thirds the speed of the railroads, but with at least four to six times the frequency, and at half to two-thirds the fare. Some interurbans with high-speed rights-of-way or exceptionally high frequency were able to attract as much as 95 per cent of the local traffic." [Hilton and Due 1960, p. 15]

But few of the companies ever made any substantial profits, according to Hilton and Due. Some logical routes were built, but too often entrepreneurial ambition and civic boosterism supplanted rational calculation of prospects for success. Many lines were built between small towns, which were eager to get the service and sometimes offered subsidies. Usually patronage was not enough to justify these ill-advised projects.

The most exotic venture was the Chicago–New York Electric Air Line Railroad, which was to be a double-track line straight from Chicago to New York City, with no grade crossings, curves, or grades over 0.5 percent. This was apparently a sincere but misguided enterprise, and 15 miles of track were built in Indiana before the company went bankrupt in 1915. One wonders what would have happened had the tracks reached the mountains of Pennsylvania.

The industry went into decline in the 1920s, largely because of competition from motor vehicles. Automobile ownership was rising rapidly, and intercity bus services were spreading. The depression was the death blow for the industry and caused wholesale abandonment of routes. The last new track was laid in 1939; the last new-car order was placed in 1946. As passenger traffic declined, many lines turned to freight and hung on for a few more years. Hilton and Due wrote in 1960 that only four lines still carried passengers—two in Chicago, one in Los Angeles, and one in Philadelphia.

The Insull empire included three interurban services into downtown Chicago. The Chicago, Aurora, and Elgin brought trains over the Garfield elevated line; it ended passenger service in 1957. Trains of the Chicago, North Shore, and Milwaukee used the northwestern elevated line and circled the Loop. The trip from the Loop to Milwaukee, 90 miles away, took 95 minutes. This service was carrying 1500 passengers a day when it was terminated in January 1963. The third route survives: The Chicago, South Shore, and South Bend still carries a large number of commuters from northern Indiana. It enters the city on Illinois Central tracks but has its own terminal downtown. Cudahy [1982, p. 99] called it "the country's last true interurban line."

The largest interurban electric railway system was the Pacific Electric in southern California. That is why you may read that Los Angeles once had the best rail transit system in the country. Between 1901 and 1910, Henry Huntington built a vast network of electric railways that blanketed the Los Angeles area [Crump 1970]. In 1910 he sold out to the Southern Pacific Railroad, and in 1911 the Pacific Electric Railway Company was formed by a merger of eight companies. At its height, it served over 50 communities with 1164 miles of track and 2700 trains a day. The "big red cars" became a familiar part of Los Angeles life. President Richard Nixon's father was a Pacific Electric motorman.

Pacific Electric began cutting back in the 1930s, and much of the track was abandoned between 1938 and 1941. The San Fernando Valley line, which was instrumental in developing that area, was vacated in 1950, and the roadbed was covered with a freeway. A Metropolitan Transit Authority was formed in 1958; it acquired all the electric railways and began replacing them with buses. The big red cars made their last official trip on the Long Beach line on April 9, 1961. Several of them have been preserved in trolley museums, and a few appeared in the motion picture "Who Framed Roger Rabbit?"

ARRIVAL OF THE MOTOR VEHICLE

The forerunner of the private motor vehicle was the road locomotive (or steam carriage). This was a steam engine on wheels—something like a railroad locomotive, but with flat-surfaced wheels to run on highways. The first one was built by Richard Trevithick in England in 1801, but it was too heavy for the roads of the time. Steam omnibuses operated in England for some years; they were considered a threat by both stagecoach operators and the railways. "The railway companies were the primary influence behind the Locomotives on Highways Act of 1867, which required self-propelled vehicles on a public highway to be limited to four miles an hour and to be preceded by a man on foot carrying a red flag" [Rae 1984, p. 3]. Hence the road locomotive never became a major mode of transport. Some surviving specimens have been restored by collectors; they are fascinating objects for the mechanically minded.

Steam was one of several power sources tried. One early automobile was the Stanley Steamer, which the Stanley twins started making in Newton, Massachusetts, in 1897. One brother was killed in an automobile accident in 1918, the other lost interest, and the company went out of business. Several U.S. companies made electric automobiles around the turn of the century, but the major one, Electric Vehicle Company, failed in the panic of 1907. Electric vehicles continued to be made for specialized applications (e.g., golf carts), but the weight of the batteries made them impractical for general use.

It was the internal-combustion engine, fueled by gasoline, that won the technological competition. The engine was perfected in 1878 by the German Nicholas Otto, who introduced the four-stroke cycle still used. Credit for inventing the automobile is shared by two other Germans, Karl Benz and Gottlieb Daimler, who both demonstrated practical vehicles in 1885. They argued about who was first the rest of their lives; after both died, their companies merged to form Mercedes-Benz. It was not until 1893 that the first U.S. automobile was built by the Duryea brothers in Springfield, Massachusetts. The pioneering developments took place in Europe, but the United States became the leading country in the manufacture of automobiles, largely because of Henry Ford.

Ford built his first automobile in 1896 and earned a reputation as a race driver. At the time, there were many small automobile manufacturers, that mostly sought to build either a luxury item for the wealthy or a mechanical toy for sporting types. Ford got the idea of building a high-quality, low-price vehicle that could be sold in large numbers to

FIGURE 2-5
Early automobiles. Henry Ford stands between the first automobile made by the Ford Motor Company and the ten-millionth, which was a Model T. The photograph was taken in 1924. (*Source:* Library of Congress.)

average people for everyday use. He wasn't the only one with this idea, but he was the one who succeeded (see Figure 2-5).

The Model T Ford, affectionately called the *Tin Lizzie*, went on sale in 1908 for a price of $850 [Rae 1965]. Ford knew this price was too high to achieve his goal, and he worked incessantly to lower the price. He kept improving the manufacturing process until he attained full assembly-line production in 1914. Visitors to the Ford plant marveled to see a complete Model T come off the line every 3 minutes. The time for chassis assembly had been reduced from 12 hours 28 minutes to 1 hour 30 minutes.

Table 2-1 shows the price and annual sales of the Model T from its introduction through 1916. This was the period in which automobile production virtually exploded. In 1908, the total U.S. production of motor vehicles was only 65,000. In 1916, Ford alone sold 577,000. By 1920, half of all the automobiles in the world were Model T Fords. Altogether 15,007,003 Model T's were manufactured. The last one in 1927 looked outwardly just about the same as the original version in 1908. During this period, Ford did not make any other model of car. The price reached its lowest point in 1926—just $290.

Ford had a natural genius for public relations. In 1914, he announced that the basic

TABLE 2-1
PRICE AND SALES OF THE MODEL T FORD

Year	Price, $	Cars sold
1908	850	5,986
1909	950	12,292
1910	780	19,293
1911	690	40,402
1912	600	78,611
1913	550	182,809
1914	490	260,720
1915	440	355,276
1916	360	577,036

Source: John B. Rae, *The American Automobile: A Brief History*
(Chicago: University of Chicago Press, 1965), p. 61.

wage rate at Ford Motor Company would be $5 per day. This was approximately twice the going rate in Detroit. Job applicants mobbed the Ford plant and had to be dispersed with fire hoses. The publicity certainly did not hurt Ford's sales. Ford had the foresight to realize that the workers were also consumers who might buy his cars.

Ford had been unable to borrow enough money from banks to start his company back in 1903, so he sold stock to colleagues. He became increasingly disenchanted with the other stockholders, and in 1919 he decided to buy them out so they could not question his judgment. James S. Couzens, who had been his business manager, held out after all the others accepted Ford's offers. Finally Couzens agreed on a price of $29 million for stock that had cost him $2500 in 1903 [Rae 1965].

For all his success, Ford made a serious mistake by staying with the Model T too long, as its popularity waned considerably in the 1920s. Finally production was halted in 1927, and the assembly line closed down for a year while a new model was prepared. This turned out to be the Model A, which was considered a good car but never attained the market share of the Model T.

Meanwhile, General Motors (GM) became the leading automobile manufacturer. GM had been founded in 1908 by W. C. "Billy" Durant, a colorful figure who was forced to resign as president in 1910 and went off to start making the Chevrolet. He accumulated GM stock and returned as president in 1915. He was forced out a second time in 1920 when his stock speculation threatened to bankrupt the company. Durant pioneered a major innovation—extending credit to car buyers—when he created General Motors Acceptance Corporation (GMAC) in 1919.

Alfred P. Sloan, another major figure in the history of the U.S. automobile industry, became president of General Motors in 1923. Sloan was not an expert in production, as Ford was, but he was a strong administrator and a marketing genius. He introduced two practices which many people now criticize, but which boosted GM's success: the annual model change and offering a wide variety of models and enticing buyers to "trade up" to a more expensive model.

FIGURE 2-6
A double-decker bus. This photo was taken in front of the New York City Public Library on Fifth Avenue. The Fifth Avenue line was the last one in the United States to use double-deckers in scheduled service. They were withdrawn in the 1950s. (*Source:* American Public Transit Association.)

The automobile was soon accompanied by the truck, the tractor, and the bus. The first motor bus service in the world began in London in 1899, and by 1911 the London General Omnibus Company had completely replaced horse-drawn omnibuses with motor buses [Miller 1941]. Because of the narrow streets, double-decker buses were designed to increase seating capacity. In 1905, the Fifth Avenue Coach Company began operating imported double-deckers in New York City. Double-deckers have remained the most popular type of bus vehicle in Great Britain, but aside from Fifth Avenue (where they ran until the 1950s), they were seldom used in the United States (see Figure 2-6).

The first U.S.-made buses were improvisations based on touring cars, trucks, or even streetcars (see Figure 2-7). They were unsatisfactory; the motors and springs were inadequate. About 1920 two brothers, Frank and William Fageol, designed a bus from the ground up that was a vast improvement and became very popular. In 1927 they introduced the Feagol Twin Coach, which had two engines placed under the floor, instead of in front as automobiles do. This design became almost universal. In 1938 the Fageols designed an articulated bus which could seat 58 persons. Many U.S. cities now use articulated buses on high-volume routes.

FIGURE 2-7
An early bus. This vehicle provided free service for customers of a department store in downtown Detroit. The photo was taken between 1905 and 1910. (*Source:* Library of Congress.)

Early buses ran on gasoline, but its high price in Europe led to experimentation with the engine invented by the German Rudolf Diesel back in the 1890s. Public Service of New Jersey imported two Mercedes-Benz diesel buses in 1929; the buses performed well, but importing parts was a problem. Finally Yellow Coach Company of Pontiac, Michigan, designed a diesel bus. A fleet of 27 diesel buses began service in Newark in 1937. Today almost all buses worldwide use diesel engines.

DECLINE OF THE STREETCAR

The Facts

The peak year for U.S. streetcars was 1923, when they carried 13.6 billion passengers. The totals declined thereafter, as buses became common. The transit industry trade association first reported a national total of bus passengers for 1922: The figure was 404 million passengers. The totals rose rapidly and reached 2.6 billion in 1929. Operators kept streetcars on the busiest lines, but switched to buses on routes with low patronage.

In addition to its declining ridership, more than half of the national streetcar fleet was over 20 years old. Transit operators had long resisted standardized vehicle design, but in 1929 a group of executives formed the Presidents' Conference Committee (PCC) to design a model streetcar that could be mass-produced and would hopefully revive the industry. After 5 years of exhaustive research, the committee released specifications for what came to be called the *PCC car* in 1935.

Fiorello La Guardia, New York City's famous mayor, cut a ribbon on October 1, 1936, to inaugurate revenue service by the first PCC streetcar. Over the next 16 years, 30 cities purchased almost 5000 of the vehicles. Most were manufactured by either St. Louis Car Company or Pullman-Standard Manufacturing Company. The other major car builder, J.G. Brill Company, refused to cooperate and marketed a rival car called the Brilliner, which did not sell well. Brill made an abortive effort to produce buses, but would not adopt the diesel engine. The company went out of business in 1954.

There is often misunderstanding about the PCC car. It was not actually a single, standardized streetcar; rather it was a set of standard components that could be combined in various ways to meet the requirements of different transit systems. The cars varied in length, width, weight, and many design features. Chicago and Boston purchased rapid transit cars based on the PCC design. According to Carlson and Schneider [1980, p. 59], "The PCC car was not just another modular vehicle but the result of the first and only systems engineering approach to mass producing a rail car."

The Presidents' Conference Committee was replaced by an organization called Transit Research Corporation, whose primary function was to administer the 144 patents obtained in the design effort. The corporation considered any vehicle licensed to use one of its patents to be a PCC car.

The PCC car was an excellent vehicle: It had high acceleration and braking capabilities and was quieter and more comfortable than previous streetcars. The major breakthrough was the development of a resilient wheel that included rubber parts and reduced transmission of vibrations to the car body. This made it possible to use lightweight materials, which reduced power requirements and made the car more economic. PCC cars proved to be very durable and sometimes remained in service for 40 years (see Figure 2-8). However, the new streetcar came too late to halt the shift to buses.

In 1937, Paris became the first large city in the world to abandon streetcars entirely. This was followed by Manchester (1949), London (1952), Birmingham (1953), Liverpool (1957), Edinburgh (1958), Sydney (1961), Glasgow (1962), and Bombay (1964). Every British city scrapped its trams except the seaside resort of Blackpool.

Abandonment was also the rule in U.S. cities. San Antonio was the first, in 1933, but most cities kept some streetcars until after World War II. In fact, during the war, conversion to buses was prohibited. In 1956, New York City, Detroit, and Dallas all closed down their last streetcar lines. Kansas City took this step in 1957, Chicago in 1958, Washington, D.C., in 1962, Baltimore and Los Angeles in 1963, and St. Louis in 1966. Only seven cities retained any streetcars, the major examples being Boston, Philadelphia, Pittsburgh, and San Francisco. Cleveland still has the Shaker Heights line,

FIGURE 2-8
A PCC streetcar. This vehicle was still in use on the Mattapan shuttle in Boston in 1990. No PCC
cars have been manufactured in the United States since 1952. (Photo by author.)

Newark has its City Subway, and New Orleans has preserved the picturesque St.
Charles line, which is a tourist attraction and a National Historic Landmark.

The last U.S. order for PCC cars was delivered to San Francisco in 1952; after that
no streetcar was made in the United States for more than 20 years. Foreign companies
continued to make PCC cars, since streetcars remained popular in some foreign countries. Nearly 25,000 vehicles of the PCC design have been built by 20 manufacturers on
four continents [Schneider and Carlson 1983]. The most prolific version is the Tatra T3
made in the former Czechoslovakia, which is used throughout Eastern Europe.

Recently the streetcar has made a comeback in the guise of *light rail transit*, which
is discussed in Chapter 5. The U.S. government played a part; in 1973 it induced Boston
and San Francisco to order a new Standard Light Rail Vehicle, which was intended as a
replacement for the PCC car. However, the cars had many mechanical problems, and
they are no longer made. Now U.S. orders for light railcars go to foreign companies
(see Chapter 4).

The Controversy

In the early years of streetcars, many transit firms built their own electric generating
plants and sometimes sold electricity to other customers. What started as a sideline

often grew into the dominant business as the demand for electricity multiplied. Thus, electric utilities were deeply involved in the streetcar business. By 1931 utility holding companies controlled about 50 percent of the U.S. transit companies, which carried more than 80 percent of the passengers [Saltzman and Solomon 1972]. The transit firms were losing money, but it was covered by profits made in other lines of business.

The utility holding companies were called *trusts* and were unpopular because they had monopoly power and were sometimes involved in scandals. Hence Congress enacted the Public Utility Holding Company Act of 1935, which required each holding company to limit its operations to "a single integrated public utility system." The act took effect in 1938. Most electric trusts used this opportunity to dispose of their money-losing transit operations. There were a few exceptions, as in New Orleans, where the transit system was owned by a utility company until a few years ago.

Meanwhile, General Motors had become the dominant U.S. manufacturer of buses through its Yellow Truck and Coach subsidiary. In 1936, a company called National City Lines (NCL) was formed for the purpose of buying up streetcar companies and replacing the trolleys with buses. This was financed by selling stock to General Motors, Firestone Tire and Rubber, Phillips Petroleum, Standard Oil of California, and similar companies. By 1947 NCL had acquired 46 transit systems. This included the Key System, which ran trains over the San Francisco–Oakland Bay Bridge. Train service was terminated in 1959, and the tracks were removed to build more lanes for motor vehicles on the bridge.

General Motors secured a virtual monopoly in bus manufacturing. Besides the transit companies it controlled, other companies were persuaded to switch to buses because GM offered credit on attractive terms. Little money was available to modernize streetcar operations: Who would invest in a dying business?

In 1947 the Justice Department sued NCL and its suppliers for violation of antitrust laws. The case dragged on for years, but in 1954 the defendants were convicted. General Motors was fined $5000, and its treasurer was fined $1. After the decision, National City Lines disposed of most of its transit operations. Unfortunately, this deprived the transit industry of an ample source of capital.

The Justice Department filed a new complaint in 1956, accusing GM of "illegally monopolizing the manufacture and sale of buses." This case never went to trial. It was concluded in 1965 when GM signed a consent decree that restricted its activities with regard to buses [Saltzman and Solomon 1972]. This had little practical effect, as no other U.S. firm emerged as a major supplier of buses. However, GM's share of the bus market fell over the years because of foreign competition.

The thrust of the report was that GM and its pro-auto allies had engaged in a conspiracy to replace electric streetcars with buses throughout the country. Allegedly the conspirators realized that buses were inferior and expected that many passengers would eventually purchase automobiles. The implication was that GM had deliberately tried to put mass transit out of business [Fischler 1979].

> The essence of the study alleged that General Motors, along with oil, tire, and highway interests, more than fifty years ago deliberately began to wreck the mass transport systems of this country in order to increase sales of their products. The suggestion, right or wrong, was that GM tried to wreck the mass transit system.

Snell's charges were backed up by testimony from the mayors of San Francisco and Los Angeles. This did cause a brouhaha, and GM issued a rebuttal, which critics dismissed as a public relations cover-up. It appears that the issue will not die, as it is regularly revived in the national media. It is surprising that so much passion is vented about something that happened long ago and cannot be changed.

Did General Motors really instigate a conspiracy to kill off streetcars? The evidence suggests that it did, but it is unlikely that the plot made much difference. Electric streetcars were already being replaced by buses on a large scale, not only in the United States but also in other countries, where GM did not have such power. Perhaps GM pushed the streetcar over the edge, but it was already teetering.

A new bus cost two-thirds as much as a PCC streetcar and by the late 1930s had almost as many seats. Comparison of operating costs was clouded by the common practice of using both a motorman and a conductor on streetcars, while buses had only a driver. But even with one-person operation, a streetcar cost more to operate, according to Dewees [1970]. Streetcar companies had to maintain the street around the tracks, while buses got their right-of-way free of charge. This amounted to a public subsidy for buses, which apparently occurred without thought of the consequences. A factor often overlooked is that the growing mass of motorists found streetcars and their tracks to be a huge nuisance. Paving over the tracks was usually a popular solution.

RIDERSHIP TRENDS

The American Public Transit Association (APTA) and its predecessors have collected statistics on transit use throughout this century (Figure 2-9 shows the trend of total transit passengers in the United States). Transit riding rose to a peak of 17.2 billion passengers in 1926 and remained high throughout the 1920s, a period of prosperity. After the depression began in 1929, the total dropped to 11.3 billion in 1933 and remained low during the 1930s. For several years the national unemployment rate hovered around 25 percent. Work trips form a large part of the transit market, and when people don't go to work, they don't ride transit.

During World War II, production of automobiles and tires for civilian use was stopped, gasoline was rationed, and transit riding rose sharply to levels exceeding those of the 1920s. This continued for several years after the war ended; the best years for transit were in the 1940s. In 1946, the industry carried 23.4 billion passengers, the highest total in history. During this period, there was an explosion of consumer spending because people had saved a great deal of money during the war, when there wasn't much to buy. One result was a surge in the demand for travel. However, new cars were hard to obtain since Detroit had to retool for peacetime production. Not until 1949 did the industry match its prewar production level.

After 1950, transit riding fell sharply. New cars were now plentiful, and the movement to the suburbs began, aided by government-insured mortgages. Millions of veterans qualified for Veterans Administration home mortgages, which required no money down. Shopping centers appeared, cutting into downtown business. Soon factories and offices started moving to the suburbs. The 5-day workweek became common, reducing transit use on Saturdays. Television was also a factor: Many families stayed home in-

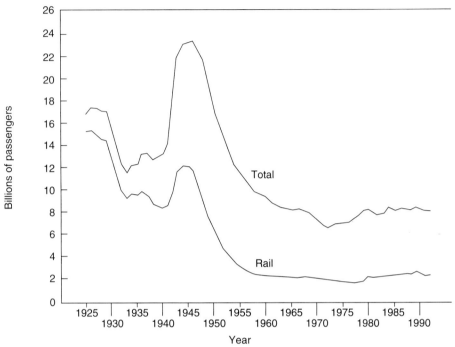

FIGURE 2-9
Total transit passengers in the United States, 1925 to 1992. The total peaked during and immediately after World War II and then declined sharply until 1972. The trend since then has been
mostly upward, but gradual. Rail includes light rail (streetcars), while the total includes bus and
trolley coach. (*Source:* American Public Transit Association, *Transit Fact Book,* 1993 and earlier
years.)

stead of going out for entertainment. Attendance at movie theaters fell drastically, and
thousands of them closed.

Transit companies were in poor shape. The systems were old, equipment was worn
out, and maintenance costs were high. Labor costs rose, especially after New York City
suffered a transit strike in January 1966. The strike paralyzed the city for 12 days; absenteeism was high and retail sales suffered terribly. The generous settlement provided
an impetus for a national trend toward higher transit wages.

The companies replied by raising fares and cutting service, both of which caused
further losses in patronage. The downward spiral couldn't be stopped. Hundreds of
transit systems in small cities went out of business in the 1950s and 1960s. Eventually
all urban rail systems and most of the bus systems were taken over by local governments, and now they remain in operation only because they are subsidized by the general public.

Transit riding fell continuously from 1947 to its lowest level in 1972, when there
were just 6.6 billion passengers in the United States. This was slightly over one-quarter

of the 1946 total. There was an upturn in 1973 because of the fuel shortage caused by the Arab Oil Embargo (it would have been bigger, but service could not be expanded rapidly enough to handle the sudden demand).

Ridership totals then increased each year through 1980. Besides the high price of gasoline, the federal transit programs (discussed in Chapter 3) were starting to have some effect. There were slight decreases in 1981 and 1982, probably because of a recession. Since 1984, the trend has been approximately flat: Small gains have alternated with small drops. In 1992, the last year reported, the national total was 8.05 billion passengers. Note that while total transit trips have climbed in the past 15 years, they have not increased as fast as automobile travel.

There is another source of time-series data: Since 1960 the decennial Census has contained questions on the journey to work. One of these asks the principal mode of transport used; from the results one can determine how many persons take transit to work. Table 2-2 shows the national totals reported by the Census Bureau. There was a large decline in transit trips from 1960 to 1970, and there were smaller ones in the 1970s and 1980s. The Census figures do not mesh well with APTA data, which suggest an increase in ridership of about 10 percent from 1970 to 1990. The reason for the discrepancy is uncertain, but the Census data cover only work trips, while the APTA data include all trips.

It is interesting to analyze the trends in individual cities. In the 1960s, the number of transit work trips declined in every metropolitan area with five exceptions. But the 1970s were different: In 107 metropolitan areas, the number of transit work trips went up. Most of these areas were in rapidly growing states in the south and west. Some increases were large: In 32 cases, the number of transit trips more than doubled. This included such large western cities as Denver, Phoenix, Portland, Sacramento, Salt Lake City, and San Jose [Black 1986].

Nonetheless, it is clear that recent population shifts have had a negative impact upon transit use [Fulton 1983]. People and jobs are moving to places where public transportation is either unavailable or inconvenient. There are two major trends involved, both bad for transit:

TABLE 2-2
TOTAL JOURNEY-TO-WORK TRIPS IN THE UNITED STATES
(As Reported in the Decennial Census)

Year	Total trips	Transit trips	Percentage by transit
1960	61,873,929	7,806,932	12.62
1970	76,852,389	6,514,012	8.48
1980	96,617,296	6,007,728	6.22
1990	115,070,274	5,890,155	5.12

Notes:
   1 The 1960 numbers exclude "Mode Not Reported." In later years Census computers were programmed to allocate blank responses.
   2 Taxicab not counted as a transit mode.

First, people are migrating to regions of the country where historically transit service has been poorer (largely because cities in these regions developed at a later time when automobile ownership was becoming common). This is the well-known movement from the frostbelt to the sunbelt.

Second, within metropolitan areas, suburbs have grown much faster than central cities, in both population and employment. The traditional functions of mass transit have been to move people around within central cities and to carry suburban residents downtown and back. The number of people whose travel habits fit this pattern is declining. The dominant commuter movement now is from suburb to suburb [Pisarski 1987].

During the 1970s, there was another trend: The population outside *standard metropolitan statistical areas* (SMSAs) grew faster than that inside them. Of course, public transportation is almost nonexistent in rural areas. But this trend was reversed in the 1980s, when metropolitan-area populations grew by 11.6 percent and the population outside by only 3.9 percent.

GENERAL OBSERVATIONS

The pace of transit-related inventions during the 19th century was very rapid. In 75 years the country went from the horse-drawn omnibus to the motor bus and electric subway trains. All the major technologies were developed by 1900. In the last 95 years, there have been incremental improvements but no breakthroughs comparable in impact to those of the 19th century.

The dissemination of innovations and the construction of facilities also happened very rapidly. When a new technology such as the cable car or electric streetcar was proved viable in one city, it spread like the proverbial wildfire to other cities. Almost all the street railways in the country switched from animals to electricity within a dozen years.

It is significant that major improvements in the technology of building construction occurred while mass transit was the primary mode of urban travel. Elisha Otis perfected the elevator in 1852; without this, tall buildings would have been impractical. The first steel-frame skyscraper was erected in Chicago in 1885. A wave of skyscraper construction followed, and heights rose higher and higher. As early as 1913, the Woolworth Building in New York City reached 792 feet. It was the tallest building in the world until 1929, when the Chrysler Building was completed (it was the first to top 1000 feet).

Tall buildings and high densities were compatible with mass transit. Transit made it possible to bring many thousands of workers into the city center in a short time each day, which could not have happened if people were still walking to work. On the other hand, the dense city centers created a market for transit that was attractive to entrepreneurs.

One can speculate on what would have happened if the automobile had been invented earlier. If it had preceded the electric streetcar, instead of coming later, perhaps U.S. cities would never have developed the centralized, high-density form characteristic of the late 19th and early 20th centuries. We'll never know.

QUESTIONS

1 Two of the most important forms of urban transportation in the 19th century were horsecars and cable cars. What disadvantages finally caused the disappearance of these two modes (except for the cable cars in San Francisco)?

2 Why did streetcars of the PCC design become more popular in other countries than in the United States?

3 What were the principal factors that led to the decline of the transit industry in the United States, resulting in abandonment of many transit systems and the conversion to public ownership of most of the rest?

4 Some people claim that the decline of transit resulted from a conspiracy by automobile companies and their corporate allies. Others argue that private automobiles and suburban living have natural advantages, and that U.S. consumers simply indicated their preferences in the marketplace. Which view do you think is correct?

5 If the automobile had been invented several decades earlier, would U.S. cities look much different? Would skyscrapers ever have been built?

REFERENCES

Black, Alan: *Analysis of 1970 and 1980 Census Data on Transit Work Trips* (Lawrence: Transportation Center, University of Kansas, 1986).

Bobrick, Benson: *Labyrinths of Iron: A History of the World's Subways* (New York: Newsweek Books, 1981).

Carlson, Stephen P., and Fred W. Schneider III: *PCC—The Car That Fought Back* (Glendale, CA: Interurban Press, 1980).

Condit, Carl W. *The Railroad and the City: A Technological and Urbanistic History of Cincinnati* (Columbus: Ohio State University Press, 1977).

Crump, Spencer: *Ride the Big Red Cars: How Trolleys Helped Build Southern California*, 3d ed. (Corona del Mar, CA: Trans-Anglo Books, 1970).

Cudahy, Brian J.: *Change at Park Street Under: The Story of Boston's Subways* (Brattleboro, VT: Stephen Greene Press, 1972).

————: *Under the Sidewalks of New York: The Story of the Greatest Subway System in the World* (Brattleboro, VT: Stephen Greene Press, 1979).

————: *Destination Loop: The Story of Rapid Transit Railroading in and Around Chicago* (Brattleboro, VT: Stephen Greene Press, 1982).

————: *Cash, Tokens, and Transfers: A History of Urban Mass Transit in North America* (New York: Fordham University Press, 1990).

Dewees, Donald N.: "The Decline of the American Street Railway," *Traffic Quarterly*, vol. 24, no. 4 (October 1970), pp. 563–581.

Fischler, Stanley I.: *Moving Millions: An Inside Look at Mass Transit* (New York: Harper & Row, 1979).

Fulton, Philip N.: "Public Transportation: Solving the Commuting Problem?" *Transportation Research Record*, no. 928 (1983), pp. 1–10.

Gilbert, Gorman, and Robert E. Samuels: *The Taxicab: An Urban Transportation Survivor* (Chapel Hill: University of North Carolina Press, 1982).

Grava, Sigurd: "The Metro in Moscow," *Traffic Quarterly*, vol. 30, no. 2 (April 1976), pp. 241–267.

Hilton, George W.: *The Cable Car in America: A New Treatise upon Cable or Rope Traction as Applied to the Working of Street and Other Railways* (Berkeley, CA: Howell-North Books, 1971).

————— and John F. Due: *The Electric Interurban Railways in America* (Stanford, CA: Stanford University Press, 1960).

Kennedy, Charles J.: "Commuter Services in the Boston Area, 1835–1860," *Business History Review*, vol. 36, no. 2 (Summer 1962), pp. 153–170.

McKay, John P. *Tramways and Trolleys: The Rise of Urban Mass Transport in Europe* (Princeton, NJ: Princeton University Press, 1976).

Miller, John Anderson: *Fares, Please! A Popular History of Trolleys, Streetcars, Buses, Elevateds, and Subways* (New York: D. Appleton-Century Company, 1941).

Passer, Harold C.: *The Electrical Manufacturers, 1875–1900* (Cambridge, MA: Harvard University Press, 1953).

Pisarksi, Alan E.: *Commuting in America: A National Report on Commuting Patterns and Trends* (Westport, CT: Eno Foundation for Transportation, 1987).

Rae, John B.: *The American Automobile: A Brief History* (Chicago: University of Chicago Press, 1965).

—————: *The American Automobile Industry* (Boston: Twayne Publishers, 1984).

Roberts, Sidney I.: "Portrait of a Robber Baron: Charles T. Yerkes," *Business History Review*, vol. 35, no. 3 (Autumn 1961), pp. 344–371.

Saltzman, Arthur, and Richard J. Solomon: "Historical Overview of the Decline of the Transit Industry," *Highway Research Record*, no. 417 (1972), pp. 1–11.

Schneider, Fred W., and Stephen P. Carlson: *PCC—From Coast to Coast* (Glendale, CA: Interurban Press, 1983).

Thrupp, G. A.: *The History of Coaches* (London: Kerby & Endean, 1877).

3

THE FEDERAL ROLE IN
URBAN TRANSIT

BACKGROUND OF HIGHWAY PROGRAMS

The first national highway was the Cumberland Road, between Cumberland, Maryland, and Vandalia, Illinois, completed in 1841. But as a rule, the U.S. government took little part in building roads until the 20th century. Before 1900, pressure for paving roads came from cyclists, let by the League of American Wheelmen [Flink 1970]. The first Federal Highway Act was passed in 1916 and authorized $5 million in grants to states for road construction. It was a rural program administered by the Department of Agriculture, and no money could be spent in a community with 2500 or more people. This law established the policies that federal aid could not be spent on maintenance and that no tolls could be charged on a federally aided highway.

Rural interests dominated the federal highway program for many years. The slogan was, "Get the farmer out of the mud." In 1928, federal law was broadened slightly to allow expenditures in towns with more than 2500 people, but only to build highways on which houses were at least 200 feet apart.

State and local governments carried out the bulk of road construction. The states began levying taxes on gasoline in 1919, and by 1929 every state had a gas tax [Rose 1990]. Most states put these tax receipts in the general fund, and part was spent for nonhighway purposes. Highway interests naturally opposed this, and the Hayden-Cartwright Act passed by Congress in 1934 stipulated that any state that increased the diversion of its own gas taxes to nonhighway purposes would be penalized by reduction in federal aid [Burch 1962]. Subsequently a majority of the states adopted constitutional amendments prohibiting diversion of highway funds.

Meanwhile, Congress adopted the first federal gasoline tax, 1¢ per gallon, in 1932. It was considered a luxury tax with which wealthy car owners would help pull the country out of the depression. The receipts were not earmarked for highways; for years much of the money went for other purposes.

The U.S. government first participated in urban highway building after the 1944 Highway Act established an urban primary system in places with a population of 5000 or more and allotted 25 percent of federal aid to this system. Federal grants could finance one-half of the construction cost and one-third of land acquisition.

The flagship of the federal highway program is the National System of Interstate and Defense Highways. It did not appear overnight but was preceded by years of preparation and planning [Robertson 1985]. Its origin can be traced to a 1939 report by the Bureau of Public Roads recommending development of a 26,700-mile network of interregional highways. The 1944 Highway Act established the system as a separate network, but appropriated no money for construction. The states were asked to propose routes, and in 1947 the Federal Works Administrator approved a map with 37,700 miles of intercity routes. Congress appropriated small sums of money in 1952 and 1954, but little was accomplished.

There was widespread agreement on the need to build new roads, as automobile ownership and traffic were increasing rapidly. However, dissension on how to finance the interstate system and how to distribute the funds blocked action for several years [Rose 1990]. The farmers wanted one thing, the truckers something else, and car owners (represented by the American Automobile Association) had still other goals. Some people thought the highways should be used to clear slums and revitalize city centers.

President Eisenhower was strongly interested in the program and finally effected a compromise. In 1956 Congress approved the system and adopted a financing mechanism that guaranteed implementation. The federal gas tax was raised by 2¢ per gallon, the Highway Trust Fund was created, and expenditures from the fund were restricted to highway construction. The federal government would pay 90 percent of the costs; the states, 10 percent. About 45 percent of the money was scheduled for urban areas, but only 13 percent of the mileage. The system contained 41,000 miles and was estimated to cost $41 billion. Completion was scheduled for 1972.

Proceeding with the Interstate System was warmly welcomed at the time. Secretary of Commerce Sinclair Weeks called it "the greatest public-works program in the history of the world" [New York Times, 1956, p. 1]. In the key votes, the House approved the bill by 388 to 19; the Senate, by 89 to 1. The program was widely hailed in the press. The only prominent critic was Lewis Mumford, who called it an "ill-conceived and preposterously unbalanced program" [Mumford 1964, p. 244].

THE REVIVAL OF INTEREST IN TRANSIT

At this time there was little public support for mass transit. Most transit systems were owned by private firms, and it was felt that transit should meet the test of the marketplace: If passengers didn't pay enough to finance a service, it should be dropped, as with any failing business. The same standard was applied to those systems operated by public agencies: They should break even and not get subsidies. For example, the Chicago Transit Authority was required to balance its budget every year. If a deficit loomed, the fare was raised.

Public opinion began to change around 1960. Both local and national politicians responded to this, and pro-transit measures gained increasing support. There were six major causes:

1 The first interstate links built were rural, but by 1960 highway construction was having a severe impact on cities. In the early 1960s, the federal-aid highway program displaced an annual average of 32,395 families and individuals plus 3199 businesses [U.S. Congress, House Committee on Public Works 1965]. About 80 percent of the displacements were in urban areas. The only federal program causing more disruption was urban renewal.

Grassroots opposition to the superhighways grew into the "Highway Revolt." This first appeared in San Francisco in 1959 when the Board of Supervisors declared that it would not permit the state to build any more freeways through residential areas in the city (under California law, cities can veto proposals to build state highways within their city limits). Aesthetics was a factor: People were outraged by the elevated Embarcadero Freeway, which spoiled the view of the historic Ferry Building at the foot of Market Street (see Figure 3-1). The city proposed several times to tear down the Embarcadero Freeway [Hall 1990]. It finally happened when the structure was damaged in the 1989 earthquake and could no longer carry traffic.

Similar confrontations occurred elsewhere as the antihighway movement spread.

FIGURE 3-1
Aesthetic intrusion by highways. This view on Market Street in San Francisco shows how the double-decked Embarcadero Freeway blocked the view of the historic Ferry Building. The freeway was closed after being damaged by the 1989 earthquake and was subsequently demolished. (Photo by author.)

The governor of Massachusetts ordered a moratorium on highway construction in the Boston area, and the proposed Inner Belt was abandoned [Lupo et al. 1971]. New Orleans stopped the Riverfront Expressway that would have passed through the French Quarter [O'Leary 1969]. In New York City, the Lower Manhattan Expressway urged by Robert Moses was never built. The Crosstown Expressway in Chicago met the same fate [Pikarsky 1967].

2 The new expressways did not end traffic congestion; they seemed to fill up as soon as they opened [Downs 1962]. People felt disillusioned; the promises of the highway builders did not materialize. Actually there were improvements in traffic flow, but they were incremental. Some commuters expected to be able to drive downtown at rush hour at 60 miles per hour, and that never happened.

3 Another factor was the rise of the environmental movement. Air pollution was first recognized as a problem in Los Angeles in the 1950s. For years the highway lobby claimed this was due to the unique topography and climate of that city. But by 1970 air pollution was evident in all the large cities. (See Chapter 11 for further discussion of air pollution.)

4 Automobile safety was another issue. Ralph Nader's book *Unsafe at Any Speed* [1965] contained harsh criticism of General Motors and singled out the Corvair as a dangerous car. The book had modest sales until a committee of Congress held hearings on the matter. Nader testified that he had been followed, his mail had been opened, his phone had been tapped, and he had been solicited by prostitutes. The committee subpoenaed the president of General Motors (GM), who flew to Washington the next day. He confessed that GM had hired private detectives to "get the goods" on Nader and issued a public apology.

The incident made Nader a national hero and the design of motor vehicles a national issue. In 1966 Congress enacted the National Traffic and Motor Vehicle Safety Act, which authorized the government both to regulate the design and manufacture of motor vehicles and to force manufacturers to recall vehicles with safety defects. GM pulled the Corvair off the market in 1969 because sales had plummeted by 93 percent.

5 Poverty became a major concern. Rioting in the Watts section of Los Angeles in 1965 was the first of a string of civil disturbances that erupted in many cities with large minority populations. These were serious affairs: In Watts, 35 people died, and property damage totaled $200 million. The McCone Commission that studied the Watts case concluded that poor public transportation in Los Angeles was one cause of discontent.

The federal government responded with a series of demonstration projects targeting transit services on poor areas. Most of these were disappointing and were eventually dropped [Hilton 1974]. A less tangible but more lasting result was the consciousness raising: People realized that while the highway-oriented transportation system satisfied the white middle-class majority, there was a minority of people who received little benefit from it. Serving the poor became a major goal in transportation planning.

6 These issues generated some support for transit, but the thing that affected the most people was the energy crisis caused by the Arab Oil Embargo in 1973. The gasoline shortage in the winter of 1973 to 1974 was severe. Motorists grumbled because prices doubled within a short time, but what really upset them was to drive by station after station with "no gas" signs posted or the waiting in line an hour for gas. The

Iranian crisis in 1979 brought another gas shortage that reminded people of the problem, although it was milder.

These factors produced a strong antiauto sentiment and support for transit as an alternative. The prevailing attitude toward transit changed from indifference to a belief that transit has a permanent role, at least in large cities. The idea of subsidizing public transportation became acceptable.

FEDERAL TRANSIT LEGISLATION

The federal government ignored urban mass transit until the 1960s. One reason was that historically most transit systems were privately owned, and the government was reluctant to intervene in the private sector. Another reason was that urban transportation was considered a responsibility of local governments and not an appropriate area for federal activity. Concern about mass transit was strong in large cities, but it was a service with a limited clientele.

However, since 1887 the federal Interstate Commerce Commission (ICC) had regulated the railroads. After World War II, the railroads suffered declining revenues as passengers switched to automobiles and airplanes and freight switched to trucks. Passenger service had been declining for years, and the railroads saw retrenchment as a way to bolster their financial situation.

Congress passed the Transportation Act of 1958 to give the railroads some relief [Hilton 1969]. Among other things, the law made it easier for railroads to drop passenger trains: Petitions to abandon service could be decided by the ICC instead of state regulatory boards, which tended to disallow cutbacks. Protesters often appeared before the state boards; they were less likely to go to ICC meetings in Washington, D.C.

Soon many commuter trains were dropped in Boston, New York, and Philadelphia, causing consternation in those cities. Richardson Dilworth, mayor of Philadelphia, organized municipal leaders and lobbied for Washington to take a positive role in promoting transit. He found an ally in Congress in Harrison Williams, a first-time Senator from New Jersey. Williams was looking for an issue that was important to his state and might also propel him to national prominence [Smerk 1974]. Urban transit fit the description. Williams introduced a transit aid bill that was passed by the Senate in 1960 but never got out of committee in the House of Representatives.

John F. Kennedy made urban problems a major part of his presidential campaign, and his administration was more urban-oriented than any previous one. Congress was not ready to establish a separate transit program, but the 1961 Housing Act included the first federal funds for transit: $25 million in grants for demonstration projects and $50 million in loans for facilities and equipment. The loans had to be repaid, which was so unappealing to transit operators that there were few applications [Hilton 1974].

Kennedy declared support for mass transit in his Transportation Message of 1962. However, transit bills filed in 1962 and 1963 were stopped in the House of Representatives, where rural interests were strong. The pro-transit bloc, led by Senator Williams, gradually gathered strength and did more effective lobbying. In 1964, Congress enacted the Urban Mass Transportation Act, which passed the Senate by a vote of 52 to 41 and the House by 221 to 189. The law continued the demonstration grant and loan programs, but more importantly it authorized $375 million in capital grants for any transit project "essential to the comprehensively planned development of the urban area." Federal funds would pay two-thirds of project cost. This law firmly established a federal role in urban transit; most subsequent federal laws have technically been amendments to the Urban Mass Transportation Act of 1964.

In 1966 Congress passed a bill amending the act and extending funding for capital grants for 3 more years. The law also established three new grant programs for (1) planning, engineering, and design of transit projects; (2) management training; and (3) university research and training.

There was a debate within the administration over what agency would manage the urban transit program. In 1961 responsibility was given to the Housing and Home Finance Administration, which was merged into the Department of Housing and Urban Development (HUD) in 1966. Some thought it should have the transit program because it was the leading agency for urban problems. In 1967, the Department of Transportation (DOT) was created; some thought it should have the transit program because it was the leading agency for transportation. President Johnson settled the argument in 1968 by deciding to switch the program to the DOT. The Urban Mass Transportation Administration (UMTA) was then created, on a par with the other modal administrations. This move was beneficial for transit, as the program had been neglected in an agency whose main interests were housing and urban renewal [Smerk 1974].

The transit program received less than $150 million a year in the late 1960s, which transit supporters felt was far short of the needs. Richard Nixon became President, and to the surprise of many, his administration proved to be a strong advocate for transit. In 1969 Nixon proposed to commit the federal government to spending $10 billion on transit over a 12-year period. Secretary of Transportation John A. Volpe, formerly a highway builder, gave his endorsement, and for the first time the transit people put together a powerful lobby. Even the highway interests gave lukewarm support, once they were assured that the Highway Trust Fund would not be touched.

Congress passed the Urban Mass Transportation Assistance Act of 1970 by overwhelming votes: 83 to 4 in the Senate and 327 to 16 in the House. There had been a reversal in political sentiment in 10 years, as disappointment with the highway program grew and transit's image improved. The law implemented Nixon's plan and authorized spending $3.1 billion over the next 5 years.

However, the transit bloc still wanted to "bust the Trust." Transit appropriations came from general funds, but highway appropriations came from the Highway Trust Fund, which could be spent only on highways. There is a great advantage to having such an earmarked fund: It means that a flow of money is guaranteed and does not depend on annual appropriations by Congress. Senator Williams had introduced bills to create a transit trust fund since 1969, but they had gotten nowhere.

The highway lobby looked on the Highway Trust Fund as its personal domain and jealously resisted efforts to invade it. However, this monopoly had been gradually eroded. The 1968 Highway Act permitted Highway Trust Fund money to be spent for relocation assistance and fringe parking facilities for the central business district

(CBD). This was the first time the Highway Trust Fund could be spent on something other than a highway. The 1970 Highway Act allowed Highway Trust Fund money to be spent on building exclusive or preferential bus lanes and related facilities, such as traffic control devices, passenger loading areas, and parking. Such a project had to replace a highway project and provide an equivalent capacity for moving persons.

The transit lobby finally got its wish when the 1973 Highway Act truly "busted" the Highway Trust Fund by permitting up to $1 billion to be spent on transit facilities, including up to $800 million for rail projects. Actually the law gave the states the choice of spending the money on highways or transit; not all of it was used for transit. The Nixon administration backed the bill; the key vote came in the Senate, where it passed by 49 to 44.

The 1973 act also contained a unique provision permitting an unwanted link of the interstate highway system to be deleted and an equivalent amount of money from general funds to be appropriated for transit. This must be requested by the local government and the governor of the state, and it must be approved by the Secretary of Transportation. This is the "interstate transfer" provision, which has been used many times. The law also increased the federal share of the cost of transit projects from two-thirds to 80 percent, provided $40 million for bicycle and pedestrian pathways, and authorized $55 million for rural public transportation.

Transit interests had another major objective: to get federal aid for operating expenses. At this time, federal grants were limited to capital investment (new facilities and vehicles) or for special uses like planning, research, and training (which took relatively little money). Most large transit systems could no longer cover operating expenses with fare revenues, and the systems ran larger deficits every year. Either the losses were paid by state and local governments, or the transit operators raised fares and reduced service.

The Nixon administration opposed operating subsidies, and Congress had also been reluctant. It was feared this would be a bottomless pit that would require escalating amounts of federal money. However, it was clear that the existing system biased local decisions in favor of capital-intensive projects. Rather than maintain old buses, transit agencies bought new ones every few years. It was also one reason why many cities wanted to build rail systems.

The transit lobby scored again with the National Mass Transportation Assistance Act of 1974, which provided operating subsidies for transit. The bill had a stormy passage through Congress, with jurisdictional squabbling among the House, Senate, and the Nixon administration. Included were a capital grants program of $7.8 billion and a new formula grants program of $3.975 billion. Under the latter, each metropolitan area is eligible for a maximum grant determined by formula which can be used for either capital investment or operating expenses. The federal government pays 80 percent of the cost of capital projects and 50 percent of operating losses.

Federal operating subsidies have not solved the financial problems of local transit agencies, but for several years the subsidies allowed fares to be stabilized. It is claimed that subsidies encourage labor unions to demand higher wages, and management to give in fairly easily. The formula grants program has been criticized on the grounds that it allocates more money than is needed to small cities, but not enough to large cities. At times a sizable balance of money has accumulated that no one can use because of restrictions in the law.

The transit people were optimistic when Jimmy Carter became President, as Democrats have generally supported their wishes. However, the transit people were disappointed: Carter was preoccupied with the growing federal deficit and opposed expansion of the UMTA budget. When Carter issued a national energy policy, he made no mention of mass transit, which seemed like a glaring omission. Many people finally concluded that Carter had an antitransit bias [Smerk 1991]. He tried to make amends when he addressed the annual convention of the American Public Transit Association in 1979; he was the first President to do so.

The major transit legislation of the Carter era was included in the Surface Transportation Assistance Act of 1978 and authorized $13.5 billion in transit aid over a 4-year period. Responding to the interests of large, old cities, the law required that at least $350 million per year be spent on modernization of older rail systems, and it increased funding of operating subsidies for cities of more than 750,000. The law created a new program of capital grants and operating assistance for nonurbanized and rural areas. It also authorized $200 million per year for intermodal terminals and transit-related urban development projects. The idea was to integrate land-use development with transit stations so that transit systems could get continuing income from leasing property rights. The Reagan administration later ended this program.

There were early signs that Ronald Reagan would be unfriendly to the interests of the transit lobby, and this turned out to be true. The Reagan administration sought to downsize the federal government, and transit was seen as an expendable program. Administration officials placed a moratorium on new starts (initiation of new rail systems); they also proposed to reduce operating subsidies and phase them out entirely by 1985. The moratorium was later rescinded; operating aid was lowered but never eliminated, as the program was popular in Congress.

Nevertheless, the transit bloc achieved another landmark with the Surface Transportation Assistance Act of 1982, which raised the federal fuel tax by 5¢ per gallon and earmarked 1¢ for a new fund restricted to transit capital improvements. Now there is a mass transit account in the Highway Trust Fund. Credit belongs to Transportation Secretary Drew Lewis, who persuaded Reagan that the 5¢ really represented a user charge instead of a tax increase [Smerk 1991]. The administration tried to limit all transit aid to this source, but Congress never accepted this idea.

The act extended the transit and highway programs for 4 years and authorized expenditures of $17.7 billion for transit. Under the discretionary capital grant program, the federal share was reduced from 80 to 75 percent. A new block grant formula program was created that apportioned funds to urbanized areas for both capital improvements and operating costs. Urban areas had some flexibility in spending the money, but a cap was put on operating aid. There was a major shift in fund allocation: The formula grant program received twice as much money as the discretionary grant program. Previously the proportions had been reversed.

Transportation issues did not receive high priority during the second Reagan term, when attention focused on the federal deficit and the Iran-Contra scandal. Both transit and highway programs expired in 1986, but the Senate and House could not agree on a bill to reauthorize them. Finally the formula grant program for transit was continued for another year.

Early in 1987 Congress took up a combined highway-transit bill, which passed by lopsided votes. However, President Reagan vetoed the bill, calling it a "budget-buster." The House overrode the veto by a huge margin, while the Senate barely overrode by a 67-to-33 vote. The law reauthorized the highway and transit programs for 5 years. Transit expenditures over this period were set at $17.8 billion. There were numerous minor changes in the transit program, but they "really amounted to fine-tuning" [Smerk 1991, p. 258].

With the deficit ever growing, Congress raised the federal gas tax by another 5¢ in 1990, bringing the total to 14¢ per gallon. Half of the increase went to the general fund to help reduce the deficit; the other half went to the Highway Trust Fund. Of this, 20 percent (½¢ per gallon) was earmarked for the mass transit account. This brought transit's share to 1.5¢ per gallon, which currently generates annual receipts of about $2 billion.

Because of the deficit, the administration does not spend all the money in the trust funds. Annual receipts exceed expenditures, and the surplus accumulates in the funds. As of 1991, the mass transit account had a balance of $7 billion, while the highway account had a balance of $11 billion. There is also a trust fund for aviation, which had a balance of $13 billion. It is charged that this is one reason why there is supposedly an infrastructure problem in the country.

Federal highway and transit programs both expired in 1991, and Congress worked for 2 years fashioning legislation to revamp them. The outcome was the Intermodal Surface Transportation Efficiency Act of 1991, popularly called ISTEA (pronounced like *iced tea*). It was passed in November 1991 by votes of 79 to 8 in the Senate and 372 to 47 in the House of Representatives. The law authorized expenditures of $151 billion for highways and transit over 6 years. It is considered the most important transportation legislation in many years, and its consequences are still unfolding. Among the major programs were the following:

1 Expenditures of $31.5 billion were authorized to continue existing mass transit programs. Over the 6 years, this is an average of $5.3 billion per year, almost twice the funding for transit in recent years.

2 ISTEA created a new National Highway System, consisting of Interstate Highways and other primary roads, expected to total 150,000 miles. It authorized $21 billion for this network. Among other things, this is to provide, finally, for completion of the Interstate Highway System. States submitted proposed routes in 1993, and Congress was required to adopt the system by December 18, 1995.

3 A new Surface Transportation Program was established and funded at $23.9 billion. This will fund a variety of transportation modes, including highway, bridge, transit, ride sharing, bicycle, and pedestrian projects.

4 A new Congestion Mitigation and Air Quality Program was funded at $6 billion. This is intended to help urbanized areas meet the air quality standards of the 1990 Clean Air Act Amendments as well as to reduce urban congestion. The 200 or so *nonattainment areas* that do not meet federal standards for ozone and/or carbon monoxide have first priority for this money. Both highway and transit projects are eligible.

5 Another $3 billion was set aside for "transportation enhancement." The ten eligible activities include rehabilitation and operation of historic transportation buildings and facilities, provision of facilities for pedestrians and bicycles, landscaping, acquisition of scenic easements, preservation of abandoned railway corridors, and removal of billboards.

6 Major research projects include $725 million for development of a prototype magnetic levitation (maglev) train and $660 million for intelligent vehicle/highway systems (these topics are discussed in Chapter 7).

The law grants unprecedented flexibility to state and local officials to decide whether to spend federal aid on highways or transit. States may transfer up to 50 percent of the money from the National Highway System Program to transit projects (and up to 100 percent with the approval of the Secretary of Transportation). To do so, it must be shown that the transit project would be more cost-effective than highway investment in improving the level of service in a corridor.

However, transfers can also go in the other direction. States may use section 9 transit capital funds for highway projects, but only under fairly strict conditions.

Most transit programs will be eligible for the same matching ratio as highway programs: 80 percent federal. In the past, many transit programs received a smaller federal share than highway projects did.

The law strengthens state and local planning requirements. All urbanized areas must prepare long-range transportation plans, and for the first time, all states must prepare statewide transportation plans. A total of $1.5 billion was authorized for metropolitan transportation planning, which doubles the previous funding level for this purpose. There is new funding for transit research, including the creation of the National Transit Institute.

The law also changed the name of UMTA to the Federal Transit Administration (FTA) and changed the name of the Urban Mass Transportation Act to the Federal Transit Act.

ISTEA was warmly welcomed by the transit community, as it embodied numerous features that the transit lobby had sought. The discretion accorded to the states probably means that urban states will increase spending on transit and some major projects may be undertaken. Rural states, of course, are not likely to divert money from highways to transit.

U.S. DEPARTMENT OF TRANSPORTATION

There had been many unsuccessful attempts to consolidate transportation agencies within the federal government when President Johnson made another bid in 1966. Congress squabbled over the proposal for eight months and finally passed a bill that Johnson signed, although the provisions were weaker than he wanted [Burby 1971]. The Department of Transportation officially came into being on April 1, 1967. Through 1993, twelve persons had occupied the position of Secretary of Transportation, as listed in Table 3-1. Five of them had substantial previous experience in transportation, to wit:

TABLE 3-1
U.S. SECRETARIES OF TRANSPORTATION

Number	Tenure	Name and background
1.	1967–1969	Alan S. Boyd. Chairman of the Civil Aeronautics Board and Undersecretary of Commerce for Transportation. Headed task force that recommended formation of DOT.
2.	1969–1973	John A. Volpe. Owner of a highway construction firm. Three times elected Governor of Massachusetts.
3.	1973–1975	Claude S. Brinegar. Vice President for Mobil Oil Company. Has Ph.D. in economics.
4.	1975–1977	William T. Coleman, Jr. Distinguished labor lawyer. Graduate of Harvard Law School.
5.	1977–1979	Brock Adams. Congressman from the state of Washington who specialized in transportation policy. Later elected United States Senator.
6.	1979–1981	Neil E. Goldschmidt. Mayor of Portland, Oregon. Later became Governor of Oregon.
7.	1981–1983	Andrew L. "Drew" Lewis, Jr. Corporate executive and business consultant. Ran unsuccessfully for Governor of Pennsylvania. Graduate of Harvard Business School. Later became president of Union Pacific Railroad.
8.	1983–1987	Elizabeth H. Dole. Member of Reagan's White House staff. Resigned to assist her husband, Senator Robert Dole, in his Presidential election campaign. Graduate of Harvard Law School. Later Secretary of Labor under Bush.
9.	1987–1989	James H. Burnley IV. Deputy Secretary of DOT since 1983. Graduate of Harvard Law School.
10.	1989–1991	Samuel K. Skinner. Lawyer. Chairman of Regional Transportation Authority of Northeastern Illinois. Resigned to become Bush's chief of staff.
11.	1992–1993	Andrew H. Card, Jr. Member of Bush's White House staff. Previously served 10 years in the Massachusetts state legislature.
12.	1993–	Federico F. Pena. Mayor of Denver from 1983 to 1991. Led Clinton's transition team on transportation.

Alan S. Boyd, the first one, had been chair of the Civil Aeronautics Board and Undersecretary of Commerce for Transportation.

John A. Volpe, Nixon's first appointee, had been the first Federal Highway Administrator. He owned a large highway construction firm in Massachusetts and had also been governor of that state. He surprised many people by giving strong support to transit.

Brock Adams, appointed by Jimmy Carter in 1977, was a congressman considered to be an expert in transportation matters. He and Carter had a falling out in 1979, and he resigned.

James H. Burnley, the last Secretary under Reagan, had been Deputy Secretary for 4 years when he was appointed in 1987.

Samuel K. Skinner, appointed by George Bush, had been chair of the Chicago Transit Authority.

Neil Goldschmidt had no personal experience in the transportation field, but he supported mass transit as mayor of Portland, Oregon. During his tenure, the city decided to build a light rail line. Likewise, Federico Pena, appointed by President Clinton, was mayor of Denver when that city initiated a light rail project.

One transportation expert who evaluated the performance of the first eight secretaries gave the best ratings to Volpe and Lewis [Hazard 1988]. They were quite dissimilar persons. Volpe was the son of Italian immigrants and attended a technical school. He worked his way up from a laborer's job to ownership of a major construction company. Lewis graduated from Haverford College and Harvard Business School. He was an executive for National Gypsum Co. and American Olean Title Co. and then started a consulting firm that specialized in helping businesses in trouble. Unlike Volpe, he had no background in transportation. The one thing the two had in common was experience in managing large organizations.

There has been much turnover in the position; the average secretary has served a little more than 2 years. The one with the longest tenure was Elizabeth Dole, who served 57 months from 1983 until she resigned in 1987 to help her husband's unsuccessful Presidential campaign. She had no background in transportation; her preceding job was as a member of Reagan's White House staff. She was the first woman named to the Cabinet by Reagan, who was claimed to suffer a "gender gap" in the polls [Hazard 1988]. She later became Bush's first Secretary of Labor and then head of the American Red Cross.

The Department of Transportation has about 100,000 employees and an annual budget approaching $30 billion. There are nine line agencies (or operating administrations) within the department, as follows:

The *Federal Transit Administration* (FTA) administers the mass transit programs that will be described below. The name was changed by the 1991 law; previously it was called the Urban Mass Transportation Administration (UMTA). The designation as UMTA is frequently used in this book, since people in the transit field have been accustomed to it for 25 years.

The *Federal Highway Administration* (FHWA) controls about half of DOT's budget, most of which is passed to the states in grants for highway building. It was called the Bureau of Public Roads when it was in the Department of Commerce.

The *Federal Aviation Administration* (FAA) is responsible for aviation safety and airport operations. It has the largest staff of the agencies, about half of them being air traffic controllers. It was formerly an independent agency, and it is still known for independence.

The *Federal Railroad Administration* is mostly concerned with intercity railroads and oversees Amtrak and Conrail. It has jurisdiction over suburban rail service, which exists in about ten cities.

The *National Highway Traffic Safety Administration* is the agency that investigates safety defects in motor vehicles and orders manufacturers to recall automobiles. It also sets the fuel economy standards for new cars.

The *Coast Guard* was formerly in the Department of Defense, and it is still considered a branch of the armed forces. Its principal concern is safety, but it also enforces laws against smuggling (including drugs).

The *St. Lawrence Seaway Development Corporation* manages (in cooperation with Canada) the system of dams and locks that has made the Great Lakes accessible to ocean-going vessels since 1959.

The *Research and Special Programs Administration,* created in 1977, handles an assortment of topics such as pipeline safety, transportation of hazardous materials, antiterrorism, and transportation emergency preparedness. It conducts ongoing research through the Transportation Systems Center in Cambridge, Massachusetts, and grants to universities.

The *Maritime Administration* is responsible for the nation's merchant marine, which is the most heavily subsidized of all transportation modes. It was originally left out of DOT because of lobbying from both unions and industry, but in 1981 it was transferred from the Department of Commerce.

The *National Transportation Safety Board* is also part of the Department of Transportation, but it is independent of the secretary and other DOT officials. The board has five members who are appointed by the President for 5-year terms. This agency is often in the news because it investigates major accidents involving all transportation modes.

The argument for forming DOT was to rationalize organization by grouping together all the agencies that were involved in transportation. Presumably this would produce better coordination and more effective allocation of money. But when the time came to write the law, some agencies did not want to join, and they had strong supporters in Congress. The law passed was a compromise .

Congress decided to leave out agencies whose primary function was economic regulation of transportation modes. One of these was the Maritime Administration. A second was the Civil Aeronautics Board, which assigned routes to the airlines and set fares. Perhaps most important was the Interstate Commerce Commission (ICC), which regulated railroads, trucks, intercity buses, pipelines, and internal water transportation.

Much of the transportation industry was deregulated, starting in the 1970s. ICC control over railroads, trucking, and bus lines was reduced. The Airline Deregulation Act of 1978 freed the aviation industry, and the Civil Aeronautics Board was phased out in 1985. Pipelines are now regulated by the Federal Energy Regulatory Commission, part of the Department of Energy.

Also independent of DOT is the Army Corps of Engineers, which dredges harbors, builds canals and locks, and manages the inland waterways. It has always had a special relationship with Congress; the annual "rivers and harbors" bill is the most cited example of pork-barrel politics.

DOT is organized along modal lines. All the old agencies were retained; no multimodal agencies were created. This was the intent of Congress; each agency and its allies were afraid that they might suffer in any merger and lose their money and influence. The operating administrations were given unusual stature for a Cabinet department, and the office of the secretary was made weak [Hazard 1988]. The assistant secretaries primarily function as staff for the secretary; they have no direct control over line agencies.

The modal agencies are suspicious of any effort to make intermodal comparisons. The legislation creating DOT effectively prevents this by prohibiting the Secretary of Transportation from applying economic evaluation to investment proposals made under federal grant programs [Burby 1971]. The secretary is also forbidden to implement any investment standards or criteria without appropriate action by Congress. In other words, DOT cannot perform analysis to decide whether air, water, rail, or highways would be the best mode to accomplish a particular transportation objective.

In 1979 Brock Adams announced that he would combine UMTA and FHWA into a single surface transportation administration. He argued that this would reduce competition between highway people and transit people and lead to more rational decisions. The proposal was vehemently opposed by the transit lobby, which feared that highway people would dominate the combined agency. At the time, FHWA had about 4900 employees and UMTA had only about 600 [Smerk 1991]. Adams resigned shortly afterward, and Goldschmidt reversed his decision.

The administrator of UMTA/FTA is nominated by the President and confirmed by the Senate. Hence the selection may be based on politics, rather than expertise. For example, the second administrator (appointed by Nixon) was Carlos C. Villarreal, an executive with an aerospace company. One reason for his selection was that he was Hispanic, and Nixon was being criticized because there were no high-ranking minorities in his administration.

There have been eleven administrators of UMTA/FTA, listed in Table 3-2. Only two had any full-time experience in urban transit at the time of appointment: Theodore Lutz, a Carter appointee, had been general manager of the Washington Metropolitan Area Transit Authority. Alfred A. DelliBovi, the last administrator under Reagan, had been on the UMTA staff since 1981 and served as deputy administrator from 1984 to 1987.

Two other administrators took jobs in transit after leaving office. Frank C. Herringer, appointed by Nixon, became head of the Bay Area Rapid Transit (BART) system in San Francisco. Richard S. Page, Carter's first appointee, took Lutz's old job with the Washington, D.C., system.

President Clinton's choice for administrator was Gordon J. Linton, a Pennsylvania state legislator known as an advocate for transit. In 1991, Linton pushed a bill through the state legislature establishing dedicated funding for transit authorities in Pennsylvania. He was also a board member of the Southeastern Pennsylvania Transportation Authority (SEPTA), which runs the transit system in Philadelphia. Before entering politics, Linton had been an administrator for the auditor general of Pennsylvania.

FTA is not large, as federal agencies go, but neither is it trivial. Through the 1992 fiscal year, more than $61.5 billion in federal transit aid was given out (see Table 3-3). This included $47.3 billion in capital grants and $14.2 billion for operating assistance. UMTA's budget for the 1993–1994 fiscal year was $4.6 billion.

FTA is not the only unit in DOT involved in transit. FHWA has a highway public transportation branch, which deals with the operation of buses on federally aided highways. The Transportation Systems Center sometimes does research on transit. DOT built a National Ground Transportation Test Facility in Pueblo, Colorado, to test rail equipment, both urban and intercity. Under Reagan, the facility was turned over to a private firm under the privatization policy.

TABLE 3-2
ADMINISTRATORS OF UMTA/FTA

Number	Tenure	Name and background
1.	September 1968–April 1969	Paul L. Sitton. Bureau of the Budget analyst, deputy undersecretary of DOT since 1967. Later on staff of National Academy of Sciences. Died in 1987.
2.	April 1969–February 1973	Carlos C. Villarreal. Executive for an aerospace firm in California. Later a member of U.S. Postal Rate Commission.
3.	February 1973–June 1975	Frank C. Herringer. Member of President Nixon's White House staff. Left to become general manager of BART.
4.	August 1975–February 1977	Robert E. Patricelli. Executive director of Greater Hartford Processes, a civic group, since 1971. Later a vice president of Connecticut General Life Insurance Co.
5.	July 1977–May 1979	Richard S. Page. Executive director of Municipalities of Metropolitan Seattle since 1974. Left to become general manager of Washington Metropolitan Area Transit Authority.
6.	December 1979–January 1981	Theodore C. Lutz. General manager of Washington Metropolitan Area Transit Authority since 1976. Later vice president of *The Washington Post*.
7.	March 1981–August 1983	Arthur E. Teele, Jr. Head of President Reagan's transition team for DOT. Labor lawyer from Florida. Later ran unsuccessfully for mayor of Miami.
8.	November 1983–May 1987	Ralph L. Stanley. Worked on Reagan's Presidential campaign in 1980, then served on DOT staff. Later head of Toll Road Corporation of Virginia.
9.	June 1987–June 1989	Alfred A. DelliBovi. Deputy administrator of UMTA since 1984. UMTA's mid-Atlantic regional administrator from 1981 to 1984. Earlier elected to four terms in New York State Assembly. Later deputy secretary of HUD.
10.	November 1989–January 1993	Bryan W. Clymer. Partner in accounting firm. Board member of SEPTA (Philadelphia transit authority) since 1981.
11.	August 1993–	Gordon J. Linton. Pennsylvania state legislator known as an advocate for transit. Also a board member of SEPTA.

TABLE 3-3
FEDERAL FINANCIAL AID TO TRANSIT
(Millions of Dollars in Approved Grants)

Year	Capital investment	Operating expenses	Total
1965	50.7	0	50.7
1966	106.1	0	106.1
1967	120.9	0	120.9
1968	121.8	0	121.8
1969	148.3	0	148.3
1970	132.8	0	132.8
1971	284.0	0	284.0
1972	508.6	0	508.6
1973	863.7	0	863.7
1974	955.9	0	955.9
1975	1,287.1	142.5	1,429.6
1976	1,954.8	411.8	2,366.6
1977	1,723.7	571.8	2,295.5
1978	2,036.9	685.3	2,722.2
1979	2,101.6	868.5	2,970.1
1980	2,787.1	1,120.7	3,907.8
1981	2,945.7	1,129.5	4,075.2
1982	2,554.1	1,055.5	3,609.6
1983	3,161.6	887.9	4,049.5
1984	2,876.0	922.4	3,798.4
1985	2,510.3	881.1	3,391.4
1986	3,138.2	872.5	4,010.7
1987	2,474.7	820.4	3,295.1
1988	2,520.8	780.0	3,300.8
1989	2,589.5	779.1	3,368.6
1990	2,380.0	765.4	3,145.4
1991	2,396.4	779.4	3,175.8
1992	2,612.9	768.4	3,381.3
Totals	47,344.2	14,242.2	61,586.4

Source: American Public Transit Association, *Transit Fact Book* (Washington: APTA, 1993 and earlier years).

FEDERAL TRANSIT AID PROGRAMS

Following is a summary of the federal transit aid programs administered by FTA. These are known by the relevant sections of the Federal Transit Act, which was called the Urban Mass Transportation Act until the ISTEA legislation of 1991. Table 3-4 shows recent appropriations for the major programs.

Section 3 offers discretionary grants for capital improvements, which include equip-

TABLE 3-4
RECENT APPROPRIATIONS FOR UMTA/FTA
(Millions of Dollars)

	Federal fiscal year							
	1987	1988	1989	1990	1991	1992	1993	1994
Section 3	915	980	985	982	1115	1342	1725	1785
Section 9 Operating	861	805	805	802	802	802	802	802
Section 9 Capital	1064	928	799	822	932	1021	758	1424
Section 18	75	69	71	71	71	106	91	130
Elderly and disabled	35	35	35	35	35	55	49	59
Interstate transfer	200	124	200	160	160	160	75	45
Washington Metro	201	180	168	85	64	124	170	200
Planning and research	45	45	45	45	45	109	85	92
Other	56	49	47	46	46	44	45	46
Total	3452	3215	3155	3048	3270	3763	3800	4583

Source: American Public Transit Association, *1992 Transit Fact Book* (Washington: American Public Transit Association, 1992), and *Passenger Transport,* vol. 51, no. 43 (November 1, 1993).

ment and buyout of private transit firms. The fact that grants are discretionary means that localities must submit applications and have them judged on merit; no one is guaranteed any funds. This is a matching program: The federal government pays 80 percent of the cost; the rest must come from state or local governments (state transit aid programs vary widely; some states may pay the entire 20 percent, while others pay nothing). Currently 40 percent of the available money is allocated for new rail starts or extensions, 40 percent for modernization of old rail systems, and 20 percent for bus capital improvements. This program started in 1964 and for many years took the largest portion of UMTA's budget. Money for this now comes from the mass transit account of the Highway Trust Fund.

Section 6 authorizes grants for research, development, and demonstration projects. In the early years of UMTA, much emphasis was put on such projects [Hilton 1974]. There were experiments aimed at finding whether ridership could be increased by improving service or lowering fares (such as the Skokie Swift rail extension in Chicago and projects involving commuter rail service in Boston and Philadelphia). Other projects were intended to serve poverty areas and test new equipment. There was a demonstration of dial-a-ride in Haddonfield, New Jersey, and of Personal Rapid Transit in Morgantown, West Virginia (these are described in later chapters). In recent years this program has received little attention.

Section 8 funds technical studies for planning, engineering, and evaluation. This is an important program for planners and engineers because it supplies money to pay their salaries. This is a discretionary program and a matching program (the federal share is 80 percent). This money may be used to pay staff to prepare applications for other types of grants.

Section 9 provides formula grants that may be used for either capital expenditures or operating assistance, as decided at the local level. The fact that it is a formula program means that each urbanized area in the country is entitled to a quota of money each year, as calculated by formulas specified in the law. This is a matching program; the federal share is 80 percent for capital grants, but only 50 percent for operating assistance. This program was started in 1974, and originally money for it came entirely from general funds. In 1987 the law was amended so that section 9 also gets one-half of mass transit account receipts exceeding $1 billion a year (this amount must be used for capital projects).

The formulas used to distribute section 9 money have been revised several times and are now very complicated. Different formulas apply to fixed guideway operations and bus operations, and the formulas vary according to the population of the urbanized area. Among the variables used are the total population, population density, revenue vehicle miles operated, route miles, passenger miles traveled, and passenger miles traveled per dollar of operating cost. For the details, see American Public Transit Association [1993].

Section 10 provides fellowships for persons employed in managerial, technical, or professional positions in the public transportation field. A maximum of 1 year of training is permitted, so the fellowships do not normally allow study in degree programs. In practice, they have mostly been used for short courses of 2 to 6 weeks.

Section 11 was intended to promote university research and training in mass transit. At first open-ended grants were made to about 35 universities to finance both faculty research and fellowships for students [Hilton 1974]. One object was to train young people who would make their careers in the transit field. Later the program was changed: Grants were given only for research on topics specified by UMTA, and the training aspect was deemphasized. In 1978 Congress revamped the program so that all money is funneled through ten designated University Research Centers. However, this scheme was not implemented for about 10 years. In recent years, annual funding has been at a level of $5 or $6 million.

Section 16 is intended to assist in transporting elderly and disabled persons. Funds may be used to purchase equipment or contract for service by private providers. Section 16(b)(1) provides grants for public agencies, while section 16(b)(2) provides them to private nonprofit organizations. The federal government pays 80 percent of costs. Transportation for the elderly and disabled is discussed further in Chapter 13.

Section 18 is the rural public transportation program. Other types of grants go only to urbanized areas (which have a population of at least 50,000), but this program provides grants for transit service in rural areas and small towns. The grants can be used for either capital expenditures (80 percent federal share) or operating assistance (50 percent federal). Funds are distributed to governors according to a formula based on the nonurbanized area population of each state.

Other sections of the act do not include financing programs. Section 13 deals with labor standards and is discussed in Chapter 4. Section 15 requires recipients of FTA grants to follow a uniform accounting system and report an exhaustive set of data to FTA every year. Before the system took effect (in the 1978–1979 fiscal year), different transit agencies used different accounting systems, and it was difficult to compile comparable data for research and policy analysis.

Besides these FTA programs, the Federal Highway Administration gives grants from the Highway Trust Fund that can be spent on "highway public mass transportation." This includes exclusive bus lanes, traffic control devices, bus passenger loading areas and facilities, and park-and-ride lots. If such a project is built as part of an interstate highway, it is eligible for the interstate matching formula (90 percent federal). Otherwise the federal government pays 75 percent of the cost. There is also a small amount of highway money available for bicycle and pedestrian facilities.

More important is the interstate transfer program that was inserted in the 1973 Highway Act after it became obvious that certain links of the interstate system would never be built because of local opposition. If requested by a local government agency and the governor of the state, a transit project may be substituted for a segment of the interstate system deemed to be "nonessential." This program is funded separately, and Congress approves specific projects. The federal government pays 85 percent of the costs. This provision has been used many times (e.g., in building the light rail lines in Portland, Oregon, and Sacramento, California).

PLANNING REQUIREMENTS

Transportation planning has a a fairly long history, as described by Weiner [1987]. In 1934 the Hayden-Cartwright Act authorized states to use 1.5 percent of federal highway aid for surveys, planning, and engineering (research was added in 1944). These are the Highway Planning and Research (HPR) funds. This was optional at first, but in 1962 it was made mandatory to use the money for these purposes, and another 0.5 percent was permitted at the option of the states. Since 1973, 0.5 percent of federal-aid highway funds have been set aside for transportation planning in urbanized areas.

Near the end of World War II, the Bureau of Public Roads turned its attention to urban traffic problems. The bureau developed the home-interview origin-destination (O-D) survey as a methodology for measuring travel behavior and laying the basis for planning future roads. The first O-D survey was made in Little Rock, Arkansas, in 1944; many others were conducted in succeeding years.

In 1953, the first comprehensive metropolitan transportation study was started in Detroit. It was financed with HPR funds plus token contributions from state and local governments. A dozen more metropolitan transportation studies were launched in the following 10 years. The most important in terms of pioneering methodology were the Chicago Area Transportation Study (begun in 1956) and the Penn-Jersey Study of Philadelphia (begun in 1959). These studies were encouraged by the Bureau of Public Roads, but they involved some local financial participation. Although they tended to emphasize highways, they included studies and plans for mass transit.

Meanwhile, there was mounting concern from urban interests about the impacts of the highway program and the decline of public transportation. Hence in 1960, the Housing and Home Finance Administration signed an agreement with the Bureau of Public Roads to share in financing the transportation studies. The 1961 Housing Act authorized the use of section 701 comprehensive planning funds for transportation planning.

This arrangement was solidified by the 1962 Highway Act, which required that after July 1, 1965, all federal-aid highway projects in an urban area with 50,000 or more people be "based on a continuing, comprehensive transportation planning process carried on cooperatively by the states and local communities." This is called the "3-c" require-ment. It means that every metropolitan area must perform comprehensive transporta-tion planning that includes mass transit as well as highways. Since 1973, the agency that does this has been called the *metropolitan planning organization* (or MPO); it is se-lected by the governor of the state.

Under the National Environmental Policy Act of 1969, an Environmental Impact Statement must be submitted for any federally aided transportation project that might significantly affect the environment. More than half of all such statements involve transportation projects, mostly highways. This device has been used to stop some high-way projects, but it has also been used a few times to stop transit projects. Overall it has helped transit because transit alternatives to highway proposals are often considered.

In 1975, UMTA and FHWA jointly issued regulations requiring each MPO to adopt annually a Transportation Improvement Program (TIP), a 5-year program of capital improvements for highways and transit. This includes an annual element, listing the projects to be implemented in the next year. Each MPO is also required to prepare a transportation system management (TSM) program. The idea of TSM is to maximize productivity of the existing transportation system by making short-term improvements that require little or no capital investment. The improvements may involve measures to increase the capacity and safety of streets or to assist transit, bicycles, or pedestrians.

As the years went by, requests for transit capital grants increased, far exceeding the funds available. More and more cities made proposals to build new rail lines. Hence UMTA grew more discriminating and demanded better proof of the worth of proposals. In 1976, UMTA issued a policy on major mass transportation investments requiring that an analysis of transportation alternatives accompany an application for a capital grant and that cost-effectiveness be demonstrated (however, this was defined only in general terms). This planning study is known as *alternatives analysis*. The policy also required major fixed guideway projects to be implemented in stages, rather than in one fell swoop as San Francisco's BART system was done.

In 1978, UMTA issued a policy on rail transit that specified criteria for approving new rail transit lines or extensions and reaffirmed the need to examine alternatives. UMTA also sought to put some limits on federal financial commitments and generate more local backing for rail proposals.

The Reagan administration conducted an extensive review of planning requirements and decided that they were too burdensome. New regulations issued in 1983 gave state and local officials more discretion in carrying out the planning process. It was still re-quired that areas with more than 200,000 people have an MPO that adopts a TIP. It was left to the discretion of the states whether to designate an MPO in smaller areas.

President Reagan also abolished the *A-95 review* process that emphasized compre-hensive planning for metropolitan areas (of course, transportation planning is an impor-tant part of comprehensive planning). This began with section 204 of the Demonstra-tion Cities and Metropolitan Development Act of 1966, which required that an "areawide agency" review federally assisted construction projects in 36 programs (in-cluding highways, transit, and airports) to ensure that each project conform with a long-range comprehensive plan for the area. This was strengthened by the Intergovernmental

Cooperation Act of 1968, which required coordination among federal, state, and local agencies in comprehensive areawide planning.

This was called the A-95 review because Circular no. A-95, issued by the Office of Management and Budget (OMB) in 1969, spelled out the rules. The idea was that transportation projects should conform to a metropolitan comprehensive plan (presumably including land use) as well as a metropolitan transportation plan. The review agencies, also called *clearinghouses*, were designated by OMB. They were often the same as the MPO agencies, but not always. One popular form of clearinghouse was the council of governments, which has representation from all local governments in a metropolitan area.

The A-95 system received much criticism for causing delays, generating paperwork, and increasing the bureaucracy. It was alleged that many clearinghouses rubber-stamped proposals, and indeed few projects were disapproved. One of Reagan's policies was to reduce federal interference in state and local government. Consequently he signed an Executive Order in 1982 rescinding the A-95 process. States were given the option of substituting their own review processes, but it was not required.

In 1984 UMTA promulgated quantitative cost-effectiveness criteria for evaluating fixed-guideway projects (these are usually rail, but could be bus lanes). The most important criterion is the federal cost of generating each new transit user. Passing the test makes a project eligible for funding, but does not guarantee it. Of the first eleven projects rated, five were declared eligible for federal aid, including the Los Angeles subway and a light rail line in Detroit [Zimmerman 1989]. Many transit proponents criticized the criteria as too strict. Sometimes Congress has ignored them by earmarking funds for specific rail projects that were not recommended by UMTA.

The ISTEA passed in 1991 has greatly revamped the transportation planning process, and the details are still being worked out. Every MPO is required to prepare a 20-year transportation plan that meets a new set of criteria including energy conservation, impacts on land use, intermodal access, and social, economic, and environmental effects. A Transportation Improvement Program is still required, but the time frame was changed to 3 years. For the first time, every state must also prepare a long-range transportation plan that has its own set of criteria. In all cases, the funding sources for proposed projects must be identified.

The law calls for more public participation in plan making. Groups that advocate on behalf of mass transit, bicycles, the environment, and historic preservation must be allowed to participate in the planning process from the beginning. An MPO must include representatives of agencies that operate major modes of transportation, including transit.

In addition, every urbanized area with a population over 200,000 is designated as a *transportation management area* (TMA). Additional areas may be designated by the Secretary of Transportation at the request of the governor and local MPO. In each TMA, the MPO must adopt a congestion management system intended to make existing transportation systems as efficient as possible.

In TMAs, projects under the ISTEA multimodal programs are to be selected by the MPO in consultation with the state government. In other urbanized areas, project selection is to be made by the state in cooperation with the MPO. This gives more power to local officials vis-à-vis state agencies. The intent is to ensure that a state does not commit flexible funds to highways when this is not the wish of an MPO.

FEDERAL POLICIES

The United States has never had a consistent set of long-term policies for transportation. From time to time DOT has issued policy documents. However, these statements primarily represent the views of the current administration, and sometimes Congress has had different ideas. In theory, the Secretary of Transportation may not establish policies without the consent of Congress.

Nevertheless, it is possible to infer policies from explicit actions that have been taken, such as legislation passed by Congress or decisions made by the administration. Following is a summary of what appear to be the major federal policies with regard to mass transit over the last few decades.

Up to 1980

Prior to 1961, the federal government had a hands-off policy toward urban transit. Transit was considered to be either in the domain of private enterprise or a problem for cities to handle. Thus, the federal government should not interfere. This was reflected in the 1958 Transportation Act, which made it easier for railroads to drop unprofitable commuter trains.

The first federal transit aid was enacted in 1961. From then through 1968, it was gradually accepted that transit might become a public service, but it was still felt that fare revenues should cover operating costs. In 1964, the federal government assumed responsibility for assisting with capital investment, but localities were to contribute a share of these capital costs. It was believed that improving the capital stock would increase efficiency and reduce operating costs, which would solve the problem of operating deficits.

Between 1968 and 1974, the federal government accepted urban transit as a problem of national concern by creating UMTA and passing the Urban Mass Transportation Assistance Act of 1970, which committed $10 billion in federal aid. There was still resistance to federal operating assistance. There was emphasis on hardware development (the Morgantown PRT, the Haddonfield dial-a-ride) and on capital-intensive projects (BART and the Washington Metro). Transit came to be seen as an aid to solving other problems not traditionally part of transportation (poverty, air pollution, and later the energy shortage). In 1973, the Highway Trust Fund was opened to transit.

Between 1974 and 1980, there was a shift away from capital-intensive projects toward service improvements, fare reductions, and transportation system management (including restraints on the automobile). Federal operating assistance was enacted, as Washington finally accepted the idea that transit would be a money-losing public service. With the profit motive irrelevant, increased ridership became the criterion of success. There was a shift from rail to bus solutions, plus a strong interest in paratransit. Investment in new technology was curtailed, except for the Downtown People-Mover program (described in Chapter 7).

Reagan Administration

The Reagan administration brought a marked change in federal policies in transportation, as in other areas. An article by a DOT official [Weiner 1984] articulated the new policy principles as follows:

1 Federal transportation expenditures should be financed by user charges when possible. To quote Weiner, "In regard to equity, those receiving the benefits from transportation services should pay for them." Previously income redistribution had been a major objective of transit programs.

The administration tried to end operating subsidies for transit. In 1981, it announced that subsidies would be phased out after fiscal year 1985. This never happened, and the subsidies continue. The administration regularly proposed reductions, but Congress resisted them, and the administration finally compromised by accepting continuation of the grants. However, the amount spent on operating aid gradually declined, from $1.3 billion in fiscal year 1980 to $805 million in fiscal year 1988.

2 The federal role in transportation should be reduced, while state and local governments should take responsibility for activities not considered national in scope. In 1986, Secretary Dole stated, "There's a real need to rethink the proper role of the federal government in transportation. Areas such as mass transit would be better funded at the local or state level."

3 The private sector should have a larger role in providing transport facilities and services, and opportunities for private enterprise should be created. This policy was applied to urban transit as well as other areas.

4 Federal interference in private and state and local decisions should be reduced. This meant continuing the deregulation policy begun under Carter, plus relaxing requirements imposed on state and local governments.

5 Federal transportation investments should be subjected to rigorous analysis to ensure that their benefits exceed the costs. It has always been hard to justify transit projects by benefit/cost analysis because many of the benefits are hard to measure in monetary terms.

An additional policy was to emphasize the rehabilitation of the existing transportation system rather than construction of new routes. This implied no new starts (such as new rail lines). The administration put a moratorium on new starts in 1981, but later removed it, and there were new starts in several cities, such as the Los Angeles subway.

The transit bloc fought a holding action during the Reagan era and tried to prevent earlier gains from being wiped out. It was fairly successful. Although federal operating aid decreased, state and local governments made up the difference in most cases, and few services were terminated. The push for privatization (discussed in Chapter 4) brought many private firms into the transit business, but the threat to public agencies now seems to have been exaggerated. The transit people scored one major victory in the establishment of a federal trust fund earmarked for transit capital investment.

Bush Administration

The Bush administration took a more proactive stance regarding urban transportation. Secretary Skinner arranged a series of public hearings on transportation policy that were held around the country in 1989. In March 1990 he released a report enunciating a proposed national transportation policy [U.S. Department of Transportation 1990]. There were six major themes:

1 Maintain and expand the nation's transportation system. Emphasis was on preserving the infrastructure and making the best use of existing capacity by maximizing efficiency. Capacity increases were advocated to relieve congestion in the aviation and highway systems. Transit did not receive such favorable mention: With regard to new rapid rail systems built in several cities, the report stated, "The results were often disappointing" [p. 62]. It proposed to move away from narrow categorical grants to more flexible federal funding and to renew emphasis on integrated transportation planning.

2 Foster a sound financial base for transportation. It was proposed to emphasize reliance on user charges, encourage state and local governments to use innovative financing options, stimulate private investment, and encourage joint public-private initiatives. Relaxing of restrictions on state and local governments and the private sector was advocated.

3 Keep the transportation industry strong and competitive. The report implied that federal subsidies have lowered productivity and competitiveness. Thus, it proposed to reduce operating assistance for urban transit and to end operating subsidies for Amtrak by the year 2000. More welcome was a suggestion to remove unnecessary federal regulations and requirements.

4 Ensure that the transportation system supports public safety and national security. The report stated, "The Department will not deregulate safety" [p. 81]. Among specific concerns were air traffic control, shipping of hazardous materials, drug interdiction, and terrorism.

5 Protect the environment and the quality of life. This would include responding to the threat of oil spills, conserving energy resources, and extending access and mobility improvements to all people in the United States, including the disabled and other transportation-disadvantaged citizens.

6 Advance U.S. transportation technology and expertise. High-speed rail and magnetically levitated trains were cited as potential means to serve high-density intercity travel. Improvement in the design of motor vehicles and intelligent vehicle/highway systems were proposed. The report also stressed the need for improved transportation education, data, and planning.

Transit interests gave mixed reviews to the policy document. The American Public Transit Association stated, "We are very disappointed with its view that the federal government should reduce its promotion and funding of mass transit service and turn over to cities and states the main responsibility for dealing with this critical issue" [*Passenger Transport* 1990, p. 8]. Another criticism was that the report did not mention transit as a way to cope with environmental and energy problems.

Generally the report maintained policies of the Reagan administration. It claimed, "Transportation deregulation has been a notable success" [p. 6], an opinion that is strongly opposed by some experts [Dempsey 1989]. It proposed to reduce the federal share of funding for transportation projects, to increase reliance on user fees, and to encourage further privatization. The goal of reducing operating subsidies for urban transit remained.

Clinton Administration

Transportation issues were little discussed during the 1992 Presidential campaign, except that Clinton indicated support for high-speed intercity trains. As of this writing, the administration has not issued any explicit policies like those of Secretary Skinner, nor has it taken any major initiatives. Nonetheless, this administration is viewed as more pro-transit than its immediate predecessors. Selection of Federico Pena as Secretary of Transportation and Gordon Linton as FTA administrator was well received by transit people.

The major sign of a change of attitude in Washington, D.C., came when the administration submitted its proposed budget for fiscal year 1994. This included a substantial increase in funding for FTA. The House and Senate made some changes but finally agreed on a funding level very close to that recommended by the administration. The Appropriations Act signed by President Clinton in October 1993 allocates $4.58 billion for FTA for fiscal year 1994. This is an increase of 20.6 percent over the appropriation for fiscal year 1993 (see Table 3-4). It is the largest FTA budget in 10 years.

Transit advocates were heartened by this action, although some complained that the funding is still less than the $5.325 billion authorized by ISTEA. However, it is not unusual for Congress to appropriate less money than authorized. With ISTEA permitting some highway money to be transferred to transit projects, it is likely that expenditures on transit will be greater than the FTA budget. All in all, it appears that the Clinton era will be good for transit.

QUESTIONS

1 Describe the negative impacts of the interstate highway system.
2 Over the years, automobile and highway interests have been more effective in lobbying for government programs than mass transit interests have. Why do you think this is true?
3 Should the federal government take a larger or smaller role in promoting and financing urban mass transit? Should the responsibility for transit be left to state and local governments?
4 Should the users of transportation facilities and services pay their full costs through user charges? Would you apply this rule to all transportation modes and all users?

5 Now that there is a mass transit account in the Highway Trust Fund, motorists are paying for some of the costs of transit through the fuel tax. Is this fair?

6 Suggest some ideas that you think belong in a national transportation policy.

REFERENCES

American Public Transit Association: *1993 Transit Fact Book* (Washington: American Public Transit Association, 1993).

Burby, John: *The Great American Motion Sickness, or Why You Can't Get There from Here* (Boston: Little, Brown, 1971).

Burch, Philip H., Jr.: *Highway Revenue and Expenditure Policy in the United States* (New Brunswick, NJ: Rutgers University Press, 1962).

Dempsey, Paul Stephen: *The Social and Economic Consequences of Deregulation* (New York: Quorum Books, 1989).

Downs, Anthony: "The Law of Peak-Hour Expressway Congestion," *Traffic Quarterly*, vol. 16, no. 3 (July 1962), pp. 393–409.

Flink, James J.: *America Adopts the Automobile, 1895–1910* (Cambridge, MA: MIT Press, 1970).

Hall, Peter: *Shall We Tear Down the Embarcadero?* Working Paper 512 (Berkeley: Institute of Urban and Regional Development, University of California, March 1990).

Hazard, John L.: *Managing National Transportation Policy* (Westport, CT: Eno Foundation for Transportation, 1988).

Hilton, George W.: *The Transportation Act of 1958: A Decade of Experience* (Bloomington: Indiana University Press, 1969).

———: *Federal Transit Subsidies: The Urban Mass Transportation Assistance Program* (Washington: American Enterprise Institute for Public Policy Research, 1974).

Lupo, Alan, Frank Colcord, and Edmund P. Fowler: *Rites of Way: The Politics of Transportation in Boston and the U.S. City* (Boston: Little, Brown, 1971).

Mumford, Lewis: *The Highway and the City* (New York: New American Library, 1964).

Nader, Ralph: *Unsafe at Any Speed* (New York: Grossman, 1965).

New York Times, June 30, 1956, "Eisenhower Signs Road Bill; Weeks Allocates 1.1 Billion," by John D. Morris, p.1.

O'Leary, Jeremiah D.: "Evaluating the Environmental Impact of an Urban Expressway," *Traffic (Quarterly*, vol. 23, no. 3, July 1969), pp. 341–351.

Passenger Transport, vol. 48, no. 11, p. 8 (March 12, 1990), "APTA Statement on the Administration's National Transportation Policy."

Pikarsky, Milton: "Comprehensive Planning for the Chicago Crosstown Expressway," *Highway Research Record*, no. 180 (1967), pp. 35–51.

Robertson, Richard B.: "The Evolution of Transportation Planning: A Federal Perspective," *Transportation Research Record,* no. 1014 (1985), pp. 1–10.

Rose, Mark H.: *Interstate: Express Highway Politics, 1939–1989*, rev. ed. (Knoxville: University of Tennessee Press, 1990).

Smerk, George M.: *Urban Mass Transportation: A Dozen Years of Federal Policy* (Bloomington: Indiana University Press, 1974).

———: *The Federal Role in Urban Mass Transportation* (Bloomington: Indiana University Press, 1991).

U.S. Congress, House Committee on Public Works: *Study of Compensation and Assistance for*

Persons Affected by Real Property Acquisition in Federal Assisted Programs (Washington: Government Printing Office, 1965).

U.S. Department of Transportation: *Moving America: New Directions, New Opportunities* (Washington: Department of Transportation, February 1990).

Weiner, Edward: "Redefinition of Roles and Responsibilities in U.S. Transportation," *Transportation*, vol. 12, no. 3 (May 1984), pp. 211–224.

————: *Urban Transportation Planning in the United States: An Historical Overview* (New York: Praeger, 1987).

Zimmerman, Samuel L.: "UMTA and Major Investments: Evaluation Process and Results," *Transportation Research Record*, no. 1209 (1989), pp. 32–36.

4

INSTITUTIONS AND ISSUES

THE ROLE OF THE STATES

Some state governments have played an important part in preserving and expanding local transit systems. The extent of state involvement and support varies greatly. It is high in most states with large metropolitan areas, such as those in the northeast, Illinois, and California. Most rural states, such as those in the great plains and mountain regions, pay little attention to urban transit.

Several types of state assistance are described below, ranging from minimal to heavy commitment.

Administration and Planning

Most of the states have enlarged their highway departments into multimodal departments of transportation. Three states did this even before the U.S. Department of Transportation (DOT) was created in 1967. By 1974, 39 states had formed departments of transportation. While highways tend to dominate in staff and budget, these agencies are responsible for passenger and freight movement by all modes. Railroads and aviation are major concerns in some states.

Some states do general planning for urban transit, especially if they also offer financial assistance. In Iowa, e.g., each urban area submits a local transit plan; the state incorporates these in a statewide transit plan, which is updated regularly. The Maryland department of transportation has identified 24 corridors throughout the state where it does multimodal planning for surface passenger transportation. A number of state departments of transportation have transit branches that provide technical assistance to local transit systems.

Under ISTEA, every state must initiate a statewide transportation planning process that covers all modes of travel. Each must prepare a long-range plan that considers a list of 20 factors and must adopt a statewide transportation improvement program specifying projects to be implemented in the next 3 years. Several states have adopted multimodal state transportation plans in the past, but many have not.

Legislative Authorization

Many states have provided indirect assistance by passing legislation authorizing the creation of metropolitan transit districts or authorities. Sometimes this is broad enabling legislation that provides a framework for local areas to follow. In other cases, state legislatures pass special acts creating a transit authority in one metropolitan area. Sometimes local voters must approve the formation of an authority, sometimes not.

Such laws normally provide a revenue source for the transit authority besides passenger fares. Typically the laws permit the authority to levy a sales or property tax, but occasionally other taxes are used. Often the authority is given power to sell bonds, subject to voter approval. In this way, state governments can aid urban areas without assuming any financial burden.

Financial Assistance

According to a survey conducted by the Council of State Governments in 1987, 37 states provided some direct financial assistance (or subsidy) to urban transit systems [Krause et al. 1987]. This is the aspect that varies most from state to state. Highly urban states regularly give more than $100 million a year for transit. Some of the rural states have never given a penny.

State aid became increasingly important with the cutback in federal aid in the 1980s. The states' contribution increased steadily and came to about $3.5 billion in 1987. Seven states accounted for three-quarters of this total: California, Illinois, Maryland, Massachusetts, New Jersey, New York, and Pennsylvania.

State aid may be given for capital investment, operating expenses, or demonstration projects. Some states provide a specified share of the local match required with federal grants. The share varies; a few states pay 100 percent of the match for capital improvement grants. Many states distribute operating assistance annually on a formula basis. Michigan and California have earmarked a portion of state fuel tax receipts for local transit.

Maryland has perhaps the most comprehensive program of financial aid. The state has a single transportation trust fund that finances not only highways and transit, but also the Port of Baltimore and the Baltimore-Washington International Airport. The state operates the Baltimore transit system and commuter trains; it also provides financing for portions of the Washington Metro that reach into Maryland.

Several states have allocated state bond funds for transit capital outlays. In 1967, New York voters approved a transportation bond issue that included $1 billion for transit improvements. The following year New Jersey voters approved a bond issue that included $200 million for transit. Pennsylvania also issues bonds to finance local transit projects.

Several states provide money to reduce fares for students. For example, Illinois inaugurated a program in 1965 under which pupils pay reduced fares (up to half) and the state makes up the difference. Several states reimburse local agencies for reduced fares for the elderly or disabled.

Most states exempt local transit agencies from paying certain taxes and fees. These may include fuel taxes, vehicle registration fees, sales taxes, and local property taxes. This contribution is small, but it is helpful.

Operating Transit Systems

A few state governments own, manage, and even operate urban transit systems. For reasons of local history, they have assumed this function from local governments. Sometimes state agencies run the operation from top to bottom; in other cases the state provides overall management but contracts out for day-to-day operations.

The Baltimore case has been mentioned. There are other examples: New York State bought the Long Island Railroad when it went bankrupt in 1949. Nebraska took over Omaha's transit system in 1972. Following a long strike in 1976, Connecticut purchased the company that operates transit in Hartford, New Haven, and Stamford. The Rhode Island Public Transit Authority, a state agency, provides most bus service within the state.

ELECTIONS ON TRANSIT ISSUES

One indication of public support for transit is how people vote on transit issues. There have been numerous state and local elections on transit questions, usually involving the creation of a transit authority, bond issues, or tax increases. Appendix B lists some of the important elections (this was compiled by the author over the years from press accounts). Transit's records at the polls is mixed: some wins, some losses.

Some transit proposals succeeded right away. A landmark was the 1962 election in which San Francisco Bay Area voters approved a $792 million bond issue to build the BART system. This occurred before there was federal aid for capital improvements; financing was to come from state and local sources. Because of cost overruns, some federal aid was needed to complete the project.

Congress made the decision to build the Washington Metro, but voters in Maryland and Virginia approved bonds to finance suburban segments in 1968. A bond issue for Miami's rail transit system passed in 1972 and survived an attempt to repeal the decision in 1978. Denver voters approved $425 million in bonds in 1973 to build 98 miles of guideways for automated 12-person vehicles. But UMTA did not approve the plan, and the money was never used.

On the other hand, proposals for rail transit have never succeeded in some cities. Seattle voters defeated rail proposals in 1968 and 1970; since then the area has invested heavily in bus improvements. A proposed heavy rail system for Detroit was rejected in 1974. The most costly transit proposal ever put to voters was the $8.5 billion ValTrans system planned for Phoenix. It included 103 miles of automated rapid transit lines, improved bus service, commuter trains, paratransit, and priority lanes for freeways. Only 39 percent of voters favored the plan in 1989 [Bingham 1989].

In many places there has been a mixed record of victories and defeats. Some proposals failed at first but on subsequent tries gained voter approval. The proposal to build the MARTA system in Atlanta failed in 1968 but was resubmitted in 1971 and passed. The Los Angeles subway had a stormy passage: Voters rejected it in 1968 and 1974, but approved it on a third try in 1980. In 1990 Los Angeles County voters passed a sales tax increase that partly finances transit.

Texas voters have been ambivalent. The state is very highway-oriented, but traffic congestion has become a major issue. In Dallas, a measure to create a transit authority lost in 1980 and then passed in 1983, when it was accompanied by a plan for a light rail network. But in 1988, voters soundly rejected a financial plan to build the system. In Houston, voters vetoed a proposed transit authority in 1973, but approved it in 1978. In 1983, voters rejected a bond issue to build a rail line, but in a nonbinding referendum in 1988, they approved a rail proposal. El Paso voters denied a sales tax increase for transit twice, but finally said yes in 1987.

Not all rail proposals require an election. The Buffalo light rail line is one case: Because New York State paid the entire nonfederal share of the cost, no local funds were involved. Baltimore built its subway without an election. The Tijuana Trolley in San Diego was never submitted to voters; it was entirely financed with state funds.

Overall, transit has done better at the ballot box than at the fare box. People seem willing to pay higher taxes to preserve or improve their transit systems, but many of these people seldom ride transit. For example, 61 percent of voters approved the BART proposal, but the system carries only about 5 percent of trips in the San Francisco Bay Area. Why the large difference? Harvard Prof. John Meyer claimed the principal reason that transit is attractive to people is "because they hope that it will attract *other* auto drivers off the roads" [1968, p. 50].

THE TRANSIT MANUFACTURING INDUSTRY

Once most transit vehicles used in this country were made here. Three firms became major producers of railcars: Budd Company, Pullman-Standard, and St. Louis Car Company. When transit riding declined after World War II, business was slack for a long time. Production lines were shut down and workers laid off. The companies did not invest in improving technology.

After federal grants for transit started, orders picked up in the late 1960s and in the 1970s. Two aerospace firms entered the market and won contracts: Rohr, which built the cars for BART and the Washington Metro, and Boeing, which built the Standard Light Rail Vehicle. These companies had no experience in making transit vehicles; they encountered many difficulties and lost a great deal of money. General Electric, which had long made components for electric railcars, made a brief venture as prime contractor. Finally all three companies withdrew from the business.

In the 1970s, foreign manufacturers moved into the vacuum and sought U.S. orders [Wiese 1980]. They often underbid U.S. firms. For example, Société Franco Belge of

Paris got the order to build cars for the MARTA system in Atlanta, and Cleveland ordered new light railcars from Breda, of Italy. Companies from Canada, Germany, and Japan also became active in the market.

This virtually spelled finis for the U.S. transit car manufacturing industry. St. Louis Car Company quit the business, and in 1979, Pullman—a famous name in history associated with sleeping cars, a planned community, and a bloody strike—announced that it would no longer make rail passenger cars [Young 1979]. That left Budd as the only U.S. railcar manufacturer, and it soon became a subsidiary of Thyssen A.G. of West Germany.

In an attempt to alter the situation, Congress added the "Buy America" clause to the 1978 Surface Transportation Assistance Act. On any contract of $500,000 or more for which UMTA funds are used, preferential treatment goes to any manufacturer who meets two conditions: (1) Final assembly of equipment occurs in the United States, and (2) "substantially all" the components are manufactured in the United States. UMTA interpreted this to mean at least 50 percent. A bidder who complies receives a 10 percent preference over bidders who do not comply. A waiver is possible if no U.S. firm can supply the equipment.

The clause was favored by both labor unions and U.S. manufacturers. It was, of course, opposed by foreign companies, and eventually some transit authorities objected on the grounds that it increased their costs: Sometimes they could not give a contract to the low bidder.

The chief argument for the rule is that federal grants should not be used to give jobs to foreign workers when there are unemployed workers in the United States. It is also claimed that some foreign governments give subsidies or favorable financing to their own manufacturers, which enables them to charge lower prices. For example, in 1982 the New York City Transit Authority ordered 825 railcars from Bombardier of Canada and 325 from Kawasaki of Japan. Budd was the only U.S. bidder and actually submitted the low bid. However, the foreign companies offered financing at below-market interest rates, while the U.S. Export-Import Bank would not provide similar financing for Budd. The Buy America clause did not apply because no federal funds were involved.

An article by Frost [1984] explained some causes of this situation. One factor is competitive bidding: Many state laws mandate awarding a contract to the low bidder. Sometimes this meant the order went to a company that used inferior materials. In other cases, the bid was really too low for the company's good, and it lost money. There has been some movement to repeal low-bid laws and permit transit agencies to negotiate their contracts, as is common in private enterprise. Some agencies are using *life-cycle costing,* in which awards are based on long-term costs rather than just the initial price. However, the method is difficult to apply and has led to disputes.

New technology in transit has often been unreliable. There has been a high rate of equipment failure, leading to a pattern of recalls, retrofitting, and disputes over who would pay the unexpected costs. For example, in 1981 New York City withdrew 637 new Flxible buses from service because some of them developed cracks in their frames. Several times the frames split, and the bodies partially collapsed. Chicago and Los Angeles had the same problem with this model. Ironically, at the time Flxible was a subsidiary of Grumman Corporation, which built the spacecraft that successfully landed on the moon.

Part of the problem is that the U.S. market for transit vehicles is small and irregular. Including both railcars and buses, it averages about $1 billion a year. In contrast, the market for automobiles is over $100 billion a year. Obviously making buses was a sideline for General Motors. Foreign companies seem able to produce efficiently on a smaller scale. Also, they have more consistent demand from year to year because their markets are worldwide. The U.S. companies have never sold much abroad.

The Buy America clause has not helped U.S. manufacturers much. Foreign companies responded by opening plants in this country or temporarily leasing sites where they could assemble equipment. They have subcontracted with U.S. suppliers so that a majority of components would be U.S.-made. And in some cases, they have no difficulty in underbidding domestic firms by 10 percent. Some observers believe that the Buy America clause is irrelevant.

The U.S. railcar market has been growing and now represents half of the world market open to competition [Carrington 1988]. Three international firms have become the leaders: (1) Bombardier of Canada, which opened an assembly plant in Barre, Vermont; (2) Kawasaki of Japan, which leased a former Otis Elevator plant in Yonkers, New York; and (3) Westinghouse-Amrail, a joint venture between the U.S. company (15 percent) and the French transit equipment industry (85 percent), which leased facilities in New York and California. One of the major manufacturers of light railcars is Siemens Duewag of Germany. In 1992 the company opened an assembly plant in Sacramento, where it expects to produce light rail vehicles for Denver, Sacramento, St. Louis, and San Diego.

However, a U.S. company has entered the market. Morrison Knudsen, based in Boise, Idaho, has long been in the business of rehabilitating locomotives and transit cars. In 1989 it received a contract for 232 new railcars from the Chicago Transit Authority.

The issue received national publicity early in 1992 when the Los Angeles County Transportation Commission rescinded a $122 million contract for railcars that it had awarded to Sumitomo Corporation, a Japanese firm. This appeared to be a reaction to criticism about taking jobs from U.S. workers. Morrison Knudsen actually submitted the low bid, but originally the commission decided that Sumitomo was better qualified. After changing its mind, the commission asked for new bids, but did not receive any that were acceptable.

The same situation has occurred in transit bus manufacturing. As noted in Chapter 2, General Motors once had a monopoly in this field. At one time it sold 85 percent of the transit buses in the United States, while a second firm, Flxible, supplied most of the rest. The government, in what now seems an unnecessary attempt to increase competition, induced American Motors to enter the market in the 1970s. It withdrew after a few years.

European companies gained a large share of the bus market in the 1980s [Young 1985]. Neoplan, from Germany, opened a bus manufacturing plant in Colorado, and M.A.N., also German, opened one in North Carolina. The largest bus order in recent years occurred in 1982 when the Pennsylvania Department of Transportation pooled orders from 16 cities and took bids for 1000 buses. Neoplan was the low bidder at $157,800 per bus. The U.S. bidders were General Motors ($164,000) and Flxible ($170,200).

General Motors sold its bus manufacturing subsidiary in 1987. It was renamed the Transportation Manufacturing Corporation and built new buses at a plant in Roswell, New Mexico. In November 1993, its parent company, Motor Coach Industries International, announced that it would close the Roswell plant and leave the U.S. market because it was losing money. However, it will continue to supply buses for the international market through a Canadian subsidiary.

LABOR UNIONS

Another major component of urban mass transit consists of the workers who operate the services. Employment in the transit industry peaked at 266,000 workers in 1947 and then declined continuously for the next 25 years [Barnum 1977]. By 1972 there were only 138,000 workers; the total gradually increased to 178,000 in 1979. Since then, the numbers have been calculated differently. In 1991, there were 282,000 full-time equivalent employees, but the number of individuals may be less because so many work overtime.

Transit workers have been organized in unions since the turn of the century. The Amalgamated Transit Union (ATU) has the largest membership and a majority of the contracts. The second largest union is the Transport Workers Union (TWU), which is concentrated in New York City and Philadelphia but also has locals in Houston, Miami, San Francisco, and some other cities. Both belong to the AFL-CIO. Other national unions (including the Teamsters) have locals in a few transit systems, and there are some independent unions. More than 95 percent of public transit systems in the country have unions [Barnum 1977].

The first national convention of transit workers was held in 1892 and resulted in the creation of the ATU. It affiliated with the American Federation of Labor (AFL) the next year. It was a craft-oriented union, and its concerns have always been primarily job-oriented. Power is highly centralized; one person, William D. Mahon, was president from 1893 to 1946.

Although there have been many transit strikes over the years, the ATU has been unique in the U.S. labor movement in favoring arbitration as the major means for resolving contract disputes. "Mahon was strongly in favor of voluntary arbitration from the very beginning of the ATU, arguing that the public nature of transit virtually compelled impasses to be resolved by arbitration" [Barnum 1977, p. 50].

The TWU was formed by IRT subway workers in New York City in 1934. According to an exhaustive history of the union written by Freeman, "The drive to organize New York City transit workers sprang from two sources: an incipient, diffuse process of self-organization and activity initiated by the Communist Party of the United States" [1989, p. 39]. Michael J. Quill, a flamboyant Irish immigrant, was elected president of the union at the end of 1935 and kept this position until his death in 1966. The TWU adhered to the philosophy of industrial unionism and joined the Congress of Industrial Organizations (CIO) in 1937. It was at first a left-wing union with broad concerns for the welfare of workers; several of its early leaders were Communists. Quill always denied (even under oath) that he was a Communist Party member, but others testified that he was. He certainly had close ties to the party.

The TWU brought a militant attitude to labor relations. Many of the workers were

Irish immigrants, and some had belonged to the Irish Republican Army. In 1937 the TWU achieved recognition on all the major New York City transit services except the Independent subway system owned by the city. The situation changed in 1940 when all three subway systems were brought under city control; at the time, public employees were not supposed to have unions. Mayor Fiorello La Guardia persistently resisted the union's demands, and a rocky period followed. Meanwhile, Quill became a powerful and famous figure. He was elected to the New York City Council three times, giving him another platform for expounding his views.

In 1947 William O'Dwyer was mayor and indicated that he favored raising the transit fare, which was still 5¢. This issue split the union and brought a watershed. The Communists and other left-wing groups opposed a fare hike; they saw it as a class issue. While most transit workers sympathized with this position, they also realized they could not get higher pay unless the fare went up. In private meetings, "O'Dwyer told Quill that without a fare hike there could be no wage increase. If, however, Quill agreed to support a higher fare, O'Dwyer would give the union a substantial wage increase and some form of union security" [Freeman 1989, p. 299].

In 1948 Quill came out for a fare increase and openly broke with the Communists. Although a bitter factional fight ensued, he maintained control of the TWU and soon purged all Communists from union offices. The fare was raised to 10¢; transit workers got a wage increase of 24¢ per hour.

While Robert F. Wagner, Jr., was mayor (1953 to 1965), the TWU had great political influence and achieved many gains (see Figure 4-1). Wagner issued an executive order formalizing collective bargaining for city employees. Contract negotiations took on a stereotyped pattern described by Freeman [1989, p. 327]:

> Every two years, as the January 1 expiration date of the TWU contract approached, the union would make extravagant demands that would be vehemently rejected by the transit agency. Usually mediators or a fact-finding board would be appointed as a crisis atmosphere developed. But out of public sight, Quill and Wagner would quietly work out an agreement that would be announced just before the union's strike deadline.

Quill never actually called a citywide strike until John V. Lindsay was elected mayor in 1965. Lindsay, a patrician who had represented Manhattan's "Silk Stocking District" in Congress, had no experience in labor negotiations and "spoke of lofty principles of collective bargaining and lectured Quill on his civic and moral responsibility. The strike became inevitable" [Cudahy 1979, p. 133]. At midnight on January 1, 1966, Lindsay became mayor; a few hours later, all New York City transit workers walked off their jobs.

The strike lasted 12 days and severely crippled the city (for a detailed account, see Marmo [1990]). It was an outright violation of New York State's Conlin-Wadlin Law, which prohibited strikes by public employees. The city secured an injunction against the union, but Quill ignored it. The court jailed him and eight other union leaders, but the strike continued. Two hours after entering jail, Quill suffered a heart attack. A week later, settlement was reached and the strike ended. Lindsay agreed to a 15 percent wage increase, spread over 2 years, and the fare was raised again in July. Some skeptics thought Quill had feigned his illness, but he died on January 28.

New York City had another strike in 1980, and Philadelphia (the TWU's other major

FIGURE 4-1
Mike Quill. The famous labor leader tears up a proposal offered by the New York City Transit Authority on a television program sponsored by the Transport Workers Union during contract negotiations in 1963. (Copyright, Devin-Adair Publishers, Inc., Old Greenwich, CT 06830, "Mike Quill, Himself," 1985.)

locale) has had several strikes in recent decades; but on the whole the transit industry has had fewer strikes than other industries that are as highly unionized. This is largely because of the ATU's preference for arbitration. However, the use of arbitration has declined in recent years because management has resisted it. The ATU has a unit, the Labor Bureau of the Middle West, which specializes in contract negotiations and sends experts to assist locals in bargaining. According to Jennings et al. [1978, p. 109], ". . . the Amalgamated (ATU) has outsmarted, outbargained, and in general used more effective strategy than has management. The main reason was that the ATU had centralized control and a highly professional team of advocates, while management had little coordination and less experience."

Until the 1960s, most transit systems were privately owned and fell under the jurisdiction of the National Labor Relations Act of 1935, which guaranteed employees the right to collective bargaining. When transit systems became public, they were no longer covered by the act, but often were covered by state laws that denied public workers the right to organize. As a result, transit locals in Dallas and Dade County, Florida, were eliminated.

This led union leaders to seek federal protection. Hence the Urban Mass Transportation Act has a "labor protection clause" stating that no federally aided transit project shall deprive any person of employment or worsen conditions of employment (thus preserving job rights, including the right to collective bargaining). This was in the original act and was renumbered as section 13(c) in 1966. The Department of Labor enforces this, not the Department of Transportation. Each application for federal transit aid must include a section 13(c) declaration regarding the impact on workers. The Department of Labor decided that transit unions must approve these declarations.

Section 13(c) gives transit workers at least as much protection as that afforded to railroad workers by the Interstate Commerce Act of 1887. This means that any worker who is dismissed or demoted receives compensation for 4 years or the length of employment, whichever is less. When Amtrak was created by the Rail Passenger Service Act of 1970, the Secretary of Labor arbitrated a union-management dispute and ruled that such compensation shall continue for 6 years. The 6-year rule is now customarily written into section 13(c) agreements [Barnum 1977]. However, few compensatory payments have been made under the rule, as the transit industry has an aversion to layoffs and has handled declining labor needs through attrition.

In 1975 a National Employee Protective Agreement was negotiated between the ATU, TWU, and American Public Transit Association (APTA), the national organization of transit operators. It is now widely used as a model section 13(c) agreement and has reduced controversy over labor rights in transit.

Sometimes the protection of section 13(c) is in direct conflict with state laws. Means of skirting this conflict have been developed. One is called the *Memphis formula,* under which the public agency contracts with a private management firm to run the transit system. The private firm employs the workers, who technically are not public employees [Barnum 1977]. Four firms specialize in this management business [Jennings et al. 1978]. One advantage of using them is that they have expertise in bargaining with unions.

One point often overlooked is that section 13(c) gives protection to all employees affected by a federal grant, whether or not they are employed by a transit system and whether or not they belong to unions. The issue has come up occasionally when a federally funded paratransit operation has competed with taxi services. The taxi drivers are entitled to job protection. But in practice, the federal government has interpreted the statute to apply only to transit employees [Jennings et al. 1978].

APTA has long opposed section 13(c), claiming that labor unions use it to obtain new benefits and higher wages, not just to protect existing benefits and wages. Allegedly when unions bargain with management, they threaten to withhold approval of grant applications and force management into arbitration, which has generally favored the unions. Section 13(c) makes it hard to try innovations such as paratransit that might decrease ridership on existing routes and cause layoffs. It has been used to fight attempts by transit agencies to hire part-time operators and to privatize services.

APTA proposed a change under which an applicant would only have to file a *negative declaration,* stating that the proposal would not adversely affect labor, and unions would not have to approve [Crosby 1982]. The Reagan administration, which also opposed section 13(c), tried to get the power to approve declarations shifted from the Secretary of Labor to the Secretary of Transportation. Neither of these changes was acceptable to Congress.

However, the evidence suggests that section 13(c) has not been a serious obstacle. According to Barnum [1977, pp. 34–35], ". . . of the more than 800 individual cases that the Department has ruled on between 1964 and 1975, only three grant applications have been denied because managements would or could not agree to the required minimum standards. Likewise, in only several cases has the Department certified an application over the union's opposition."

Most transit workers are semiskilled blue-collar workers, although some are clerical employees. Generally there are no educational requirements, and training is brief. The fact that the skills are easily learned is probably a deterrent to strikes, as replacements could readily be found. The majority of workers are vehicle operators; about one-fifth are involved in maintenance, and some of these positions require more skill. "In short, today's typical transit employee is a bus driver, who, although semi-skilled, has considerable responsibility because of his human cargo" [Barnum 1977, p. 137].

The dominance of vehicle operators means that disputes over craft jurisdiction are relatively rare. In most transit systems, there is a single union; bargaining involves the wages of operators, and those of other workers are adjusted accordingly. Exceptions exist in the largest systems. "In Boston's MBTA there are 28 different unions, ranging in size from the 4,295 member Carmen's Union (ATU) . . . to Local 4 of the Hoisting and Portable Engineers, which has one member" [Barnum 1977, pp. 40–41].

The wage rates of transit workers have risen substantially in recent decades. This is attributed to the ATU's success in arbitration cases. *Pattern bargaining* is the rule, which means that wages in one city are compared with what transit workers receive in other cities. Thus, increases tend to spread fairly uniformly across the country. For example, the contract at the San Francisco Municipal Railway specifies that "the Muni operators' wage rate should be the average of the two highest operator wage rates in the United States" [Meyer and Gomez-Ibanez 1977, p. 92].

Most transit workers receive generous fringe benefits such as health insurance, pensions, sick leave, holidays, and vacations. The cost of fringe benefits can amount to 50 percent of the direct wage bill. Absenteeism is a chronic problem in the industry, and sick pay is a major expense. Vacations start at a modest level, but workers with 20 years' experience may be entitled to 5 or 6 weeks off a year.

Most contracts contain elaborate work rules, and workers often receive premium payments and payment for nonoperating time. Premiums are paid for night work and overtime. Many transit workers routinely receive overtime pay, and some regard it as a perquisite of seniority. The difficulty of scheduling transit service creates this situation. Often there are short pieces of work late in the day, and it is more economical to pay overtime than to put on another worker. This is one reason why unions are against part-time workers.

In addition, most workers receive premiums for split shifts. These are based on the spread from first reporting to leaving for the day. The Massachusetts Bay Transportation Authority (MBTA) in Boston has a typical arrangement: If the spread exceeds 10 hours, time-and-a-half is paid for the eleventh and twelfth hours and double time for the thirteenth hour. A spread beyond 13 hours is prohibited. This feature is unique to the transit industry.

Most payments for nonoperating time derive from guaranteed minimums. Some workers are guaranteed a minimum of 8 hours' pay for any day. This provision was intended to discourage transit agencies from hiring part-time workers; it is disappearing as management insists on the right to use part-timers. There is also the *extra board*: Some extra workers must report each day to cover vacancies caused by illness, vacation, etc., or to handle emergencies. These workers are guaranteed some pay even if they don't have to work on a particular day.

Some transit systems have high absenteeism even though most contracts impose a waiting period before workers receive any sick pay, and then the workers must submit a doctor's confirmation. Absenteeism stems at least in part from occupational health hazards. In a review of numerous studies, Long and Perry found that "transit operators appear to be more susceptible to health disorders such as hypertension, gastrointestinal disorders, nervous disorders, and back problems than a variety of occupational groups" [1985, p. 257]. Major factors contributing to stress are exposure to violence, dealing with difficult passengers, and pressure to keep to schedule in congested traffic.

Work rules and premium pay are often attacked as sources of inefficiency and rising operating costs. It is a matter of opinion whether transit workers deserve the benefits they get. There has been some public reaction against them. In 1980, the Massachusetts Legislature passed the Management Rights Act, which overrode key provisions of contracts between the MBTA and its unions [Warner 1988]. Among other things, the law prohibited cost-of-living adjustments in wages and authorized hiring part-time employees and contracting with private firms.

Transit critics sometimes make claims of featherbedding, but in the opinion of those who have studied transit labor, it is not a major problem. According to Barnum [1977, pp. 160–161], "There have been few reports of extensive 'featherbedding' in the transit industry, as is alleged to occur on the railroads. There is little opportunity for such practices in bus systems. And, with the exception of Boston's MBTA, little featherbedding has been alleged on the rapid rail lines either." Meyer and Gomez-Ibanez [1977, pp. 76–77] commented, "Transit is not as troubled by archaic work rules or labor practices as are other transportation industries."

PRIVATIZATION

Background

Mass transportation originated wholly in the private sector. All the early means of transit described in Chapter 2 were built, owned, and operated by private companies. Entrepreneurs took the risks; some failed, but many made large profits. At first there was intense competition, but over time stronger companies bought out weaker ones, and monopolies emerged in many cities.

Public involvement in urban transit began with construction of subways, which required huge capital investments. The first subways in Boston and New York City were built with public funds, and long-term leases were given to private companies to operate them. The first municipal government to offer transit service was San Francisco, which in 1912 formed the San Francisco Municipal Railway to build two tunnels and operate streetcar routes in the western part of the city [Smerk 1986]. Soon after, the street railways in Seattle and Detroit became publicly operated. New York City's Independent subway was publicly owned and operated from the start.

Private transit companies became unpopular because they were involved in scandals exposed by crusading journalists. The usual reaction of government was to regulate the private firms more strictly, rather than to take them over. By 1940, only 20 transit systems in the country (2 percent of the total) were publicly owned [American Public Transit Association 1985]. New York City bought out two private companies that year and made the whole subway system public. A few other large cities did likewise: Cleveland created a public transit system in 1942, Chicago in 1946, and Boston in 1947.

When transit ridership fell precipitously in the 1950s, most private companies began to lose money. Eventually many went out of business, and hundreds of smaller cities lost all transit service. In some larger cities, where transit was deemed essential, the systems were taken over by government or given subsidies to keep them going, although often at a reduced scale.

The Urban Mass Transportation Act of 1964 introduced federal capital grants that could be used to buy out private companies. All remaining large transit companies, plus many smaller ones, went into public ownership during the 1960s and 1970s. By 1983, there were 599 publicly-owned systems, or 58 percent of all systems in the country. They owned 93 percent of the vehicles, operated 95 percent of the vehicle-miles, and carried 95 percent of the passenger trips [American Public Transit Association 1985].

The 1964 act included two protections for private enterprise. Section 3(e) restricted use of federal funds "for the operation of mass transportation facilities or equipment in competition with, or supplementary to, the service provided by an existing mass transportation company." Section 8(e) required that federally aided transportation plans and programs "shall encourage to the maximum extent feasible the participation of private enterprise." There were some efforts to avoid negative impacts on taxi companies; otherwise little was made of these provisions.

In most areas, all transit services were put under one public transit authority. This was considered desirable, as it fostered comprehensive planning and coordination of services. Federal law encouraged it: Federal aid went to public bodies (except for the services for the elderly and the disabled), and proposed changes had to fit into a metropolitan transportation plan.

However, the transit agencies were monopolies that could be indifferent to changing demand and hostile to competition. For example, the Washington Metropolitan Area Transit Authority refused to provide service to the new town of Reston, Virginia, claiming the route would not be cost-effective. In 1968 some Reston residents formed a "commuter club" and hired a private company to run express buses to downtown Washington [Kirby et al. 1974].

The Reagan administration sought to privatize transit services in order to reduce federal expenditures and create opportunities for private firms to make a profit. In 1984 UMTA issued a policy that "charged localities with the responsibility of demonstrating that they were *actively* encouraging private firms to participate in the provision of new and restructured local services. Unless UMTA was satisfied on this score, localities would not be able to obtain or retain matching funds for these services" [Sclar et al. 1989, p. 9]. In 1986 UMTA published guidelines requiring applicants for transit aid to submit documentation of their privatization efforts, including analysis of whether existing public services could be provided by private operators.

This policy was opposed by many transit officials, some members of Congress, and especially labor unions. Hence privatization has "produced the most intense controversy of any federal transit policy initiative of the past twenty years" [Teal 1987, p. 10]. Under the Clinton administration, there has apparently been a reversal of policy. In April 1994, the Federal Transit Administration announced that it was rescinding the 1984 policy statement.

Opportunities for Private Enterprise

There are numerous opportunities for private firms in urban transit. Actually they never totally left transit; many companies continued to function in the field in various capacities, but they remained in the background. In some places, private firms supply all transit service under contract to public bodies. There are four private management firms that run 20 to 25 percent of the publicly owned systems. Private companies provide all bus service in Honolulu, Phoenix, and Westchester County, New York.

More commonly transit authorities contract with private companies for only part of their service or for certain specific functions. Smerk [1986] described the following opportunities for the private sector:

1 Private companies can perform support activities, such as building and vehicle maintenance and cleaning, printing of schedules, advertising, and accounting.

2 They can provide demand-responsive transit, such as dial-a-ride or shared taxi. According to a national survey conducted in 1985, one-third of all demand-responsive services are contracted to private firms [Teal 1988]. A majority of special services for the elderly and disabled are run by private firms. Some transit agencies have replaced fixed routes that had low ridership with demand-responsive service provided by private carriers. Examples are routes in low-density areas and evening and weekend service.

3 Private companies can cover long commuter runs from residential areas to downtown. Some private railroads still operate commuter trains under contract to public agencies, but the most common examples are express buses that run only in the peak period and peak direction. Private firms offer such services in Boston, New York, Chicago, Houston, Los Angeles, and several other cities (see Figure 4–2). Often the routes tap high- or upper-middle-income areas and have high fares. Some of these services are subsidized, but others are not; this is one form of transit that can be profitable [Morlok and Viton 1984].

FIGURE 4-2
Privately owned buses parked all day next to South Station in Boston. These buses make one round trip a day between the suburbs and downtown. They are owned by the Plymouth & Brockton Street Railway Company, which has been in business since 1888. (Photo by author.)

4 Private companies can undertake joint development at transit stations. This idea is not new—it was done in some early subways—but it has received attention recently as a way of increasing income for transit agencies. An example from Atlanta is ReSurgens Plaza, a 27-story office building erected over the Lenox rail station. Passengers leaving trains walk a few feet to elevators that go to any floor of the building. The developer leased air rights from 40 feet aboveground upward, plus toeholds for the columns that support the building.

5 Private companies can contract out ordinary fixed routes to private operators. The idea is to solicit bids for individual routes. Supposedly competing private firms will become more efficient in order to make low bids, and the public will benefit. This approach has been tried in many places. For example, in 1988 the Colorado Legislature ordered the Denver Regional Transportation District to privatize at least 20 percent of its bus service. For an analysis of first-year results under this arrangement, see Peskin et al. [1992].

Another scenario occurs occasionally: A private company provides a specialized transit service as an adjunct of real estate development. In Fort Worth, the Tandy Corporation runs free streetcars between a parking lot and Tandy Center, a downtown shopping mall. The developer of Harbour Island in Tampa Bay spent $7 million to build an automated people mover that connects with downtown. A privately financed people mover was also built at the Las Colinas new town near Dallas.

Arguments for Privatization

Proponents of privatization do not claim that private enterprise is always superior to public operation. In the past, they note, many private transit companies suffered from bad or corrupt management, and many were monopolies. The real issue is monopoly versus competition. As Teal noted, "Monopoly organization, particularly when combined with dedicated transit subsidies, insulates transit managers from economic or political pressures to stress cost-effectiveness when making service delivery decisions" [1985, p. 34].

Specific claims for privatization of transit are as follows:

1 It lowers the costs of providing transit service. Although a private firm under contract makes a profit, its costs are so much lower that the transit authority spends less money and the public pays less in taxes. This is the most important argument because the operating costs of public transit systems have soared in recent years.

2. Private firms are more efficient. They have better management since compensation is related to performance and is not limited by rigid pay scales.

3 Private firms have higher productivity than public agencies. There are several measures of transit productivity such as vehicle-miles supplied per worker or passengers carried per worker. The recent record of transit has been poor. By most measures, productivity has been stagnant or has declined.

4 Private firms are more flexible. They are less hampered by bureaucracy and more immune to political influence. A private boss can fire a worker who is performing badly, but this may be difficult in a civil service system. A private manager tries to cut out parts of the business that lose money; public officials resist cutting services because of the political risk.

5 Private firms are more innovative, more responsive to changes in demand, more willing to take risks. For example, in New York City, numerous private services have emerged spontaneously to fill gaps left by the Transit Authority [Grava et al. 1987]. Entrepreneurs are motivated by the lure of large profits; public employees do not have this incentive and are more concerned with security. They can suffer harsh penalties for being wrong.

These arguments are based on the virtues of competition. Some people have questioned the extent to which privatization produces competition. Since the public sector has long dominated urban transit, there are few private firms ready to supply bus service to the general public. Sometimes there have been no responses to a call for bids or only one response. Hence competitive bidding may not occur; many contracts are negotiated. While the majority of contracts are for 1 year, often they are renewed without seeking new bids.

However, it is argued that free entry to the market poses the threat of potential competition, which forces a monopoly to act in a competitive manner. Morlok claimed that "there need not be overt competition between prospective service producers to provide the pressure necessary to keep costs low. All that is necessary is the possibility that another firm could enter the market if the present producer became inefficient" [1984, p. 56].

Comparison of Public and Private Costs

There have been many studies comparing the costs of transit services operated by public agencies and private companies. It is difficult to make fair comparisons because so many factors vary. Although the costs of private firms are known from contracts, it is harder to determine public agency costs for individual routes within a large system. Often these are estimated from cost allocation models that can only approximate. There are systematic biases that can mask the comparison. Costs tend to be lower in small cities than in large metropolitan areas; generally costs are lower for small systems than for large ones. The private operations are small to medium-sized; all the large systems in the country are public.

Teal has collected the most data on comparative costs. In one paper, he concluded that "private sector contracting can produce cost savings of 15 to 60 percent" [1985, p. 28]. For all-day, fixed-route bus systems, he found that private contractors achieved savings ranging from 22 to 54 percent. For commuter bus services, private contractors had cost advantages ranging from 25 to 58 percent. For demand-responsive service for the general public, the cost savings were around 50 percent, with one exception.

Later Teal [1988] conducted a national survey of government bodies that sponsor transit and received more than 800 responses. About 35 percent of the agencies contracted at least part of their service. The survey revealed small differences between average public and private costs: For small systems (up to 50 vehicles), private costs were less than 10 percent lower. For medium-sized systems, the cost advantages of private firms ranged from 9 to 23 percent.

Morlok [1988] obtained detailed cost data from 17 transit systems that had engaged in competitive contracting of service operation. The mean saving was 28.7 percent, but there was substantial variation: The range extended from essentially zero to just over 50 percent.

In New York City, six private companies operate local bus service, primarily in Queens. Researchers at Columbia University compared these firms with the New York City Transit Authority (NYCTA). They found, "The private companies as a group are consistently more efficient and more cost-effective than the NYCTA. In 1984, operating cost per vehicle mile for the privates was 76 percent of the TA level, while the privates obtained 74 percent more vehicle miles per employee hour" [Downs 1988, p. 562].

Why Private Costs Are Lower

Thus there is considerable evidence that private firms can supply transit services at lower cost than public agencies can. Whether this is desirable depends on why private costs are lower. Critics of privatization have suggested that the cost comparisons are specious. Sclar et al. [1989] argued that there is a bias because the fully allocated costs of a public system are compared with the incremental costs of a private firm for operating one or a few routes. The public costs include overhead, administration, planning, etc., while the private costs do not.

Another argument is that private firms lower the quality of service. Teal noted that "the fact that negative experiences do occur gives credence to the belief of many transit managers that service quality can be a problem in contracting" [1985, p. 35]. The public agency should carefully specify quality standards in contracts and should monitor the performance of private firms.

These points are valid, but they cannot explain all the large cost differences reported. Clearly some private companies do manage better than public agencies. Here are some examples: (1) Private firms use smaller vehicles (minibuses and vans) that are sufficient for low demand, while a transit authority may have only full-sized buses. (2) The private firms spend less on spare parts (federal aid makes it attractive for public agencies to stock parts). (3) The private companies schedule their workforce more efficiently, paying less overtime and keeping fewer operators on standby. (4) Private firms use part-time workers more than public agencies do.

It appears that many private firms have lower overhead. In part this is because they tend to be small enterprises, and evidence suggests there are diseconomies of scale in bus systems. It is often alleged that public agencies are swollen bureaucracies with redundant staff, and it may be true. Whatever the reason, private companies seem to have fewer employees who are not engaged in the actual delivery of transportation services.

Political interference raises costs in some public transit systems. Proposals to reduce service often generate neighborhood protests which reach the ears of elected officials. Transit authority boards of directors are frequently political appointees who are sensitive to such reactions. In addition, there are patronage jobs at some transit agencies.

But the major reason why private costs are lower is that the workers receive less income. Transit service is labor-intensive; nationally labor costs (including fringe benefits) made up 73 percent of operating costs in 1992 [American Public Transit Association 1993]. The main way to reduce total costs is to cut labor costs. As Rosenbloom noted, "Some of the current cost advantages enjoyed by private providers are simply a result of lower labor costs and not more efficient management or production" [1988, p. 44].

The private companies achieve lower labor costs mainly because they use nonunion labor, pay lower wages, and offer fewer benefits. For example, bus drivers for the Kansas City Area Transportation Authority, who have a union, received a top scale of $13.07 per hour in 1990. In nearby Johnson County, Kansas, where a private firm supplied the service and there was no union, the maximum wage was $7.00 per hour. A Florida union official stated that private firms "can hire people easily for half the price that they pay our people" [Ryan 1987, p. 68].

The presence or absence of unions may be the significant factor, rather than whether the enterprise is public or private. What is needed to clarify the issue is a 2 × 2 table comparing union versus nonunion as well as public versus private. Since almost all public transit agencies have unions, the cell for public nonunion systems would be virtually empty.

Workers at some private companies do have unions, usually in older firms that escaped the transition to public ownership. Transit unions spread during the era when the industry was mostly in private hands. But today private company locals are small and weak compared to those at large public transit authorities. A union that can paralyze the daily travel of a major metropolis is to be feared; one that controls a minor bus service has little clout.

One study did make a national comparison of transit labor costs. Peterson et al. [1986] collected data on transit worker compensation in eight metropolitan areas ranging in size from New York City to Seattle. This was not a systematic sample, but the areas contained 35 percent of public bus operators in the country and 95 percent of rail operators. The study showed that on average, the compensation level (wages plus fringe benefits) for unionized bus drivers at private firms was 21 percent less than that for public agency bus drivers. Compensation for nonunionized bus drivers at private companies was 45 percent lower than that for drivers at public systems.

Lower labor costs stem from differences in benefits and work rules as well as hourly wages. Herzenberg [1982] did a detailed cost analysis of 12 MBTA bus routes that were considered candidates for privatization. She concluded that the MBTA could save about $12,000 a day by contracting with private firms for drivers and maintenance (this is equivalent to at least $3 million a year). The total was broken down as follows: $2000 to $4000 due to the difference in basic wage rates, $3700 due to fringe benefits, $1400 due to work rules, and $3000 to $4000 due to maintenance labor costs.

The New York City case mentioned earlier is interesting because all the private companies were unionized and their wage rates were close to what the Transit Authority paid. Even so, the private firms had much lower labor costs, largely because of work rules: They did not pay penalties for split shifts, resulting in a 30 percent savings in operator costs [Downs 1988].

The Impact on Transit Workers

Most writers on privatization realize that cost reductions come from lower wages and using nonunion workers, but many see no objection to this. Some argue that the private company workers are satisfied because they might not have jobs otherwise and because there are compensating advantages. Morlok [1984] suggested some reasons why employees of small private firms might be content:

1 Workers seem willing to trade off the increased recognition of their work and importance of their position in a smaller firm for somewhat lower wages.

2 There is probably less chance of a labor-management agreement in small firms specifying regulations that lead to some workers being paid for time during which no work is performed. In a small firm there tends to be a lack of anonymity among workers, and workers in jobs that require a full effort would be aware and resentful of other workers with an easy job or nothing to do.

3 Firms that are successful in keeping wages low seem to choose their workers carefully. Often they try to hire persons who want to work part time only and who are not the main breadwinners for their families.

As for the last point, a study of part-time operators at public transit agencies found that the majority would prefer full-time work [Chomitz et al. 1985]. It was expected that most part-timers would be college students, retirees, or mothers of young children who wanted permanent part-time work. Instead, most were people unable to find full-time jobs.

Others believe that unionized transit workers are overpaid and get extravagant benefits. Transit operators are semiskilled workers, but they bear a sizable responsibility for public safety and their work is not easy. It is difficult to determine fair wages by comparing with other occupations. Peterson et al. [1986] found that in the areas they studied, on the average public bus drivers received compensation 5 percent greater than public elementary school teachers did, but 20 percent less than police officers.

Some believe the situation is temporary: Eventually employees of private transit firms will form unions, and their wages will go up. This is uncertain. Teal commented, "the prospects for organizing the employees of the private contractor are not particularly bright, as a policy of competitive procurement of services will favor private companies with low to moderate wages" [1987, p. 11]. That is, companies that pay higher wages won't get much business.

The transit unions have indeed secured substantial wage increases and other benefits for their members in the past 25 years. It is debatable whether these benefits should be curtailed. It may seem appealing to achieve "efficiency" by eliminating work rules that invoke penalties for split shifts. But split shifts are unpleasant; there may be a span of 13 hours between first reporting to work and finally leaving for the day. It is reasonable that some financial compensation be given for working under undesirable conditions.

Conclusion

There are advantages to encouraging private firms to enter the transit business. In some cases they operate services more efficiently, probably because they are less affected by bureaucratic and political constraints. The existence of private competitors should stimulate public transit authorities to improve their marketing and management. Some of the cost-saving measures used by private companies could be adopted by public agencies.

In many areas the transit authority has a monopoly position and has blocked private firms and other public agencies from introducing independent services. These barriers to entry should be removed; private firms should be permitted to compete. The same holds for suburban governments; transit authorities are based in the central city and often neglect the suburbs.

The reason for the cost savings reported for private firms needs more investigation. The savings may have been achieved largely at the expense of transit workers. Herzenberg framed the issue well: "Policy makers deciding whether or not to subcontract private operators to provide drivers and maintenance services should understand that, in doing so, they are implying that the wages and working conditions for MBTA drivers are less reasonable than those for private company drivers" [1982, p. 130].

SUBURBAN GRIDLOCK

The growth of U.S. suburbs is a phenomenon well known to everyone. The suburban movement is not a recent event; it started after the Civil War and was abetted during the late 19th century by commuter trains, interurban electric railways, and extension of city streetcar lines. The prosperity of the 1920s spurred a wave of suburban building; another came after World War II.

Most of these buildings were single-family homes; their occupants usually continued to work, shop, and recreate in the central city. In the 1950s, nonresidential uses began choosing suburban locations. First came stores, led by large shopping centers such as Shoppers' World near Boston, Northland in suburban Detroit, and Southdale outside Minneapolis. Soon factories followed; manufacturers found it efficient to build low structures either on isolated sites or in industrial parks. Next came offices, especially those intended for paperwork rather than sales and managerial functions. The bulk of office space constructed in the 1980s was in office parks or freestanding buildings on suburban highways. In addition, numerous hotels, restaurants, and movie theaters were built in the suburbs, so that entertainment is now largely a suburban activity. The suburbs now contain most of the functions once associated with the central city. This trend is thoroughly described in the book *Edge City* by Joel Garreau [1991].

At first, most of the nonresidential uses were scattered. The major activity nodes were shopping malls, which were surrounded by vast parking lots. But in the past 15 years, some immense clusters of buildings have emerged across the country. They are called sometimes *suburban activity centers* and sometimes *megacenters*. They contain huge numbers of jobs: As of 1986, Tysons Corner near Washington, D.C., had 70,000 workers, and City Post Oak in Houston had a daytime population of 85,000. These centers usually have high-rise buildings, which serve as landmarks and architectural showpieces. City Post Oak includes the 65-story Transco Tower, reportedly the tallest building in the world outside a central business district (CBD) [Cervero 1986].

These are multiple-use developments, although offices predominate. Most have shopping facilities, while hotels and multiplex cinemas are common. In some cases, residential buildings are included (typically apartment buildings or town houses). Sometimes a single developer designs and manages a center (as is the case with the Las Colinas new town near Dallas), while elsewhere several developers are involved.

Many people spend most of their daily lives in the suburbs and rarely visit the central city. They not only live in the suburbs but also work, relax, and do their personal business there. According to the 1980 Census, 40 percent of all work trips in the United States were from suburb to suburb [Pisarski 1987]. This is the fastest-growing component of commuting; work trips between the suburbs and the central city are declining. Hence peak-hour travel flows are multidirectional; many have a circumferential orientation. No longer are the largest volumes on roads between the suburbs and the CBD.

This travel pattern has put a severe strain on suburban highways. Many were built as two-lane rural roads and were lined with buildings before they could be widened. Cutting new freeways and arterials through the suburbs would often entail condemning properties as well as forcing many people to relocate. Many states and localities do not have the money to implement large-scale suburban highway building. The result has been growing traffic congestion in the suburbs, now frequently the site of the worst traffic buildups in a metropolitan area. The outcome is often called *suburban gridlock,* a term popularized by Cervero [1986].

Transit service in most suburbs is weak or nonexistent. Most transit routes are radials focusing on the CBD. Because of the dispersion of suburban trip ends, most circumferential bus routes carry few passengers at a high cost per passenger. Transit authorities may experiment with such routes, but often the routes are abandoned because they are inefficient in comparison with central-city routes. There has been some recent expansion of suburban transit service, but on the whole, the suburbs are poorly served by transit.

Developers normally assume that all occupants of their buildings will drive to work (and, in fact, will make all their trips by automobile). They provide ample parking, which is usually free. Under U.S. tax law, the fringe benefit of free parking is taxable only if the value exceeds $155 per month. Once, developers grudgingly added more parking when forced by local planning boards. Now developers willingly add more parking because it is vital to marketing their properties. Zoning ordinances with minimum parking requirements have become obsolete; most projects have more parking than required.

Site planning reenforces dependence on the automobile. Many office parks have a campuslike setting with medium- or high-rise buildings widely spaced in landscaped or wooded grounds (see Figure 4-3). The buildings are so far apart that people who must travel between them take their cars. Many projects have no sidewalks, bus stops, or facilities for bicycles. Often the internal street system consists of winding lanes that are attractive but inconvenient for buses or pedestrians. In addition, many office and industrial parks contain no restaurants or shops; occupants are forced to drive out on their lunch hour.

According to Cervero [1989], the problem is greater because there is an imbalance of jobs and housing in many suburban communities. Many suburban workers are un-

FIGURE 4-3
Typical suburban development. These high-rise buildings are located in Johnson County, Kansas, a booming suburban area of Kansas City. As is common, they have parklike surroundings plus huge parking lots. (Photo by author.)

able to find suitable homes near their workplaces and must commute long distances. Several factors contribute to this. One is that traditional zoning practice isolates nonresidential uses, supposedly to protect residential areas from the nuisances caused by factories and stores. Some suburban governments compete for nonresidential uses to enrich the tax base; they discourage residential building because homes require expensive services (especially schools) and pay less in taxes. There is also much economic segregation: Blue-collar workers may have to look far and wide to find homes within their financial means. Finally, an increasing number of families have two wage-earners, who usually work in different places. A family may locate near one parent's job, but far from the other parent's job.

An opposing view was given by Gordon et al. [1991], who claimed that people are moving closer to their jobs. They compared average automobile commuting times from the 1980 Census with the 1985 American Housing Survey for the 20 largest U.S. metropolitan areas. They found that commuting times fell in 18 of the 20 areas; in most cases the differences were statistically significant. The reason, they say, is that "spontaneous relocation decisions by firms and households do a very nice job of achieving balance, and of keeping commuting times within tolerable limits without costly planning interventions" [p. 419]. They concede that congestion may have increased on some routes, but claim that in most urban areas, "congestion is unlikely to get much worse" [p. 419].

Which view is correct remains uncertain. Gordon et al. compared data from two different sources and did not report any data on commuting distances. To prove their hypothesis that suburbanites react to congestion by moving to homes closer to work, it would be necessary to show that average commuting distances have declined. Unfortunately, the Census question does not concern travel distance, only travel time. However, many public and private officials believe that suburban gridlock is a real problem, and they have taken steps to solve it.

The conventional response to congestion is to increase the supply of transportation service. This means building new highways and improving old ones, which are being done in some places. But it is costly and difficult. Transit service can be increased, but it is unlikely that fixed-route bus service will play a major role in suburban travel. Paratransit and ride sharing (discussed in Chapter 6) seem more promising. Some companies have hired buses to transport their employees, such as blue-collar workers who live in the central city. In cities with rail systems, some firms have arranged shuttle services from rail stations to permit reverse commuting.

The approach now often used is called *transportation demand management* [Ferguson 1990]. The emphasis is on increasing ride sharing to reduce the number of single-occupant vehicles on the road. Many companies offer matching services to help employees locate others who live nearby and have the same working hours. Some firms designate coordinators to manage and publicize this service. Frequently the parking spaces nearest the building are reserved for car pools. In addition, many companies have established vanpooling programs.

Time shifting is another way to limit travel during peak hours. Many suburban companies have adopted staggered work hours, a practice that some central-city employers (such as the U.S. government in Washington) have followed for a long time. Flextime, in which workers select their own starting and finishing times (within limits), is also seeing increased use. It reduces the peak because some workers like to start early and finish early, while others prefer to sleep late. A more radical change is the 4-day workweek, which in theory could lower average weekday commuting trips by 20 percent. Most workers would prefer a 3-day weekend, so the effect would largely be felt on Fridays and Mondays. Some firms have initiated a 4-day workweek, but the practice is not yet widespread.

The jobs-housing imbalance might be ameliorated by encouraging mixed land uses. Zoning ordinances could offer incentives to developers to provide residences and services in the same projects with offices and factories (provided that any potential nuisances are controlled). While it may not appeal to everyone, some workers would like to live near their jobs and walk or bike to work. Cervero [1988] believes that mixed-use development does encourage more foot and bicycle travel.

There has been experimentation with institutional means for implementing such measures. One is the *transportation management association (TMA)* representing major employers in a suburban area. Many of these organizations are purely private, and membership is voluntary. Companies join and donate money because their workers are bothered by the hassle of commuting. In other cases, local governments participate in TMAs. The groups implement programs like carpooling, vanpooling, time shifting, and arranging bus service. Some have actively lobbied state legislatures for highway improvements. According to one survey, there were 53 TMAs in the United States in 1989, 40 percent of them in California [Ferguson 1990].

A more coercive approach is the *traffic reduction ordinance (TRO)*, with which a local government tries to force employers to reduce the number of single-occupant vehicles traveling in the peak period. As of 1990, 46 political jurisdictions (two-thirds of them in California) had enacted TROs of some type [Ferguson 1990]. Typically the ordinances require companies to prepare a multiyear plan with quantitative targets. Compliance with the plan is monitored, and penalties may be imposed on those who miss the targets.

Pleasanton, California, adopted a TRO in 1984 and is a well-known example, although it was not the first [Curry and Fraser-Middleton 1985]. The TRO applied to employers of 50 or more persons in a single shift and to all employers located in complexes. Each was required to prepare and implement a program to reduce the number of vehicle commute trips during the peak period by 45 percent with in 4 years. The program could involve any combination of measures; that was left flexible. Each company had to name a workplace coordinator, disseminate information to employees, conduct an annual survey of employee travel, and report results to a city coordinator. Fines up to $250 a day were authorized. The ordinance appears to be effective: By the second year all employers had implemented programs, and 12 companies had already exceeded the goal of 45 percent of employees commuting by some means other than driving alone during the peak period [Flynn and Glazer 1989].

A more ambitious effort is going on in the Los Angeles area, where the South Coast Air Quality Management District enacted Regulation XV in 1988. It set targets for the average number of persons per vehicle and required employers of 100 or more workers to submit plans for achieving them. The primary goal in this case is to combat air pollution (see Chapter 11 for further discussion).

Besides these corrective measures, some communities try to head off problems by negotiating with developers during the planning stage. Developers often need rezoning, variances, or site plan approval, and they may be willing to grant concessions. These might include reducing the amount of parking, charging for parking, committing to trip reduction programs, and providing facilities for pedestrians, bicycles, and buses. Some suburban towns impose development impact fees, which may be used to improve streets. A few communities require the developer of a large office project to build a certain number of homes with an affordable price (this is called *linkage*).

Ride sharing appears to have the greatest impact in reducing suburban gridlock. However, there are promising opportunities for expanding suburban transit service. Wherever 25,000 people work within a small area, there should be enough patrons to justify scheduled bus service. The timed-transfer system (discussed in Chapter 8) can make suburb-to-suburb bus trips faster and more convenient. Transit planners need to devote more attention to designing new suburban routes, as suburban service has often been neglected.

QUESTIONS

1 Harvard Prof. John Meyer claims that many citizens vote for mass transit proposals not because they want to ride transit, but simply to "get other drivers off the road." Do you agree?
2 Is foreign competition in the manufacture of transit vehicles a matter for serious concern? Do you agree with the law that gives U.S. companies an advantage, even if they are more expensive?
3 Should public transit workers have the right to strike? Would you give the same answer for large, transit-oriented cities and for small cities where relatively few people ride transit?
4 Do you think unionized public transit workers are overpaid? Does it seem right that, on the average, bus drivers receive more than elementary school teachers?
5 Is privatization of urban transit a desirable policy? Do you believe that, in general, private firms are better managed and more efficient than government agencies?
6 Traffic congestion has grown to disturbing levels in many suburban areas. Why is conventional mass transit poorly suited to serve this kind of travel? What measures could reduce traffic congestion by attracting people out of their cars? Or is the best approach to expand highway capacity?

REFERENCES

American Public Transit Association: *Transit Fact Book* (Washington: American Public Transit Association, 1985 and 1993).

Barnum, Darold T.: *From Private to Public: Labor Relations in Urban Mass Transit* (Lubbock: College of Business Administration, Texas Tech University, 1977).

Bingham, Maren S.: "Phoenix Kisses Transit Goodbye," *Planning,* vol. 55, no. 6 (June 1989), pp. 6–10.

Carrington, Burr: "The New Big Three: Transit Car Builders in the U.S.," *Mass Transit,* vol. 15, no. 10 (October 1988), pp. 20–22, 56.

Cervero, Robert: *Suburban Gridlock* (New Brunswick, NJ: Center for Urban Policy Research, Rutgers University, 1986).

————: "Land-Use Mixing and Suburban Mobility," *Transportation Quarterly,* vol. 42, no. 3 (July 1988), pp. 429–446.

————: "Jobs-Housing Balancing and Regional Mobility," *Journal of the American Planning Association,* vol. 55, no. 2 (Spring 1989), pp. 136–150.

Chomitz, Kenneth M., Genevieve Giuliano, and Charles A. Lave: *Fiscal and Organizational Impacts of Part-Time Labor in Public Transit* (Washington: Urban Mass Transportation Administration, 1985).

Crosby, Thomas: "13(c): To Be or Not to Be," *Mass Transit,* vol. 9, no. 6 (June 1982), pp. 16–19.

Cudahy, Brian J.: *Under the Sidewalks of New York: The Story of the Greatest Subway System in the World* (Brattleboro, VT: Stephen Greene Press, 1979).

Curry, David, and Karen Fraser-Middleton: "Pleasanton TSM Ordinance: A New Approach to Traffic Mitigation," *Transportation Research Record,* no. 1018 (1985), pp. 41–46.

Downs, Charles: "Private and Public Local Bus Services Compared: The Case of New York City," *Transportation Quarterly,* vol. 42, no. 4 (October 1988), pp. 553–570.

Ferguson, Erik: "Transportation Demand Management: Planning, Development, and Implementation," *Journal of the American Planning Association,* vol. 56, no. 4 (Autumn 1990), pp. 442–456.

Flynn, Carolyn P., and Lawrence Jesse Glazer: "Ten Cities' Strategies for Transportation Demand Management," *Transportation Research Record,* no. 1212 (1989), pp. 11–23.

Freeman, Joshua B.: *In Transit: The Transport Workers Union in New York City, 1933–1966* (New York: Oxford University Press, 1989).

Frost, William H.: "Changes in the U.S. Rail Transit Car Manufacturing Industry," *Transportation Research Record,* no. 992 (1984), pp. 14–23.

Garreau, Joel: *Edge City: Life on the New Frontier* (New York: Doubleday, 1991).

Gordon, Peter, Harry W. Richardson, and Myung-Jin Jun: "The Commuting Paradox: Evidence from the Top Twenty," *Journal of the American Planning Association,* vol. 57, no. 4 (Autumn 1991), pp. 416–420.

Grava, Sigurd, Elliott Sclar, and Charles Downs: *The Potentials and Problems of Private Sector Transportation Services: Activities in the New York Region* (Washington: Urban Mass Transportation Administration, 1987).

Herzenberg, Anne Yvette: "Who Should Run Boston's Buses?" M.S. thesis (Cambridge: Massachusetts Institute of Technology, 1982).

Jennings, Kenneth M., Jay A. Smith, Jr., and Earle C. Traynham, Jr.: *Labor Relations in a Public Service Industry: Unions, Management, and the Public Interest in Mass Transit* (New York: Praeger Publishers, 1978).

Kirby, Ronald F., Kiran V. Bhatt, Michael A. Kemp, Robert G. McGillivray, and Martin Wohl: *Para-Transit: Neglected Options for Urban Mobility* (Washington: The Urban Institute, 1974).

Krause, Robert A., Dinker I. Patel, and Brian D. Gathy: *Financing for the Future: Changing Roles in Mass Transit* (Washington: U.S. Department of Transportation, 1987).

Long, Lyn, and James L. Perry: "Economic and Occupational Causes of Transit Operator Absenteeism: A Review of Research," *Transport Reviews,* vol. 5, no. 3 (1985), pp. 247–267.

Marmo, Michael: *More Profile than Courage: The New York City Transit Strike of 1966* (Albany: State University of New York Press, 1990).

Meyer, John R.: "Urban Transportation," in James Q. Wilson, ed., *The Metropolitan Enigma: Inquiries into the Nature and Dimensions of America's "Urban Crisis"* (Cambridge, MA: Harvard University Press, 1968), pp. 41–69.

———— and Jose A. Gomez-Ibanez: *Improving Urban Mass Transportation Productivity* (Cambridge, MA: Department of City and Regional Planning, Harvard University, February 1977).

Morlok, Edward K.: "Economics of Private Operator Service," *Transportation Research Record,* no. 980 (1984), pp. 55–59.

————: "Privatizing Bus Transit: Cost Savings from Competitive Contracting," *Journal of the Transportation Research Forum,* vol. 28, no. 1 (1988), pp. 72–81.

———— and Philip A. Viton: "Feasibility of Profitable Transit Service in Radial Urban Corridors," *Transportation Research Record,* no. 980 (1984), pp. 46–54.

Peskin, Robert L., Subhash R. Mundle, and Scott D. Buhrer: "Transit Privatization in Denver: Experience in First Year," *Transportation Research Record,* no. 1349 (1992), pp. 75–84.

Peterson, George E., Walter G. Davis, Jr., and Christopher Walker: *Total Compensation of Mass Transit Employees in Large Metropolitan Areas* (Washington: The Urban Institute, 1986).

Pisarski, Alan E.: *Commuting in America: A National Report on Commuting Patterns and Trends* (Westport, CT: Eno Foundation for Transportation, 1987).

Rosenbloom, Sandra: "Role of the Private Sector in the Delivery of Transportation Services to the Elderly and Handicapped in the United States," *Transportation Research Record,* no. 1170 (1988), pp. 39–45.

Ryan, Andy: "Public vs. Private: Testing Buses in Miami," *Mass Transit,* vol. 14, no. 1/2 (January-February 1987), pp. 12, 68.

Sclar, Elliott D., K. H. Schaeffer, and Robert Brandwein: *The Emperor's New Clothes: Transit Privatization and Public Policy* (Washington: Economic Policy Institute, 1989).

Smerk, George M.: "Urban Mass Transportation: From Private to Public to Privatization," *Transportation Journal,* vol. 26, no. 1 (Fall 1986), pp. 83–91.

Teal, Roger F.: "Transit Service Contracting: Experiences and Issues," *Transportation Research Record,* no. 1036 (1985), pp. 28–36.

————: "Transportation Privatization: Experience and Issues," *Urban Resources,* vol. 4, no. 1 (1987), pp. 7–12.

————: "Public Transit Service Contracting: A Status Report," *Transportation Quarterly,* vol. 42, no. 2 (April 1988), pp. 207–222.

Warner, Marc G.: "Transit Management Rights: A Critical Appraisal and Assessment of Prospects," *Transportation Quarterly,* vol. 42, no. 1 (January 1988), pp. 43–62.

Wiese, Arthur E.: "The Battle of 'Buy America,' " *Mass Transit,* vol. 7, no. 10 (October 1980), pp. 6ff.

Young, David: "Pullman and Transit: End of an Era," *Mass Transit,* vol. 6, no. 7 (July 1979), pp. 8–11.

————: "U.S. Bus Industry: Fallen on Hard Times," *Mass Transit,* vol. 12, no. 3 (March 1985), pp. 8ff.

5

CONVENTIONAL TRANSIT MODES

A major part of the work of planning transit improvements is to select the particular transit mode to implement. Transit modes can be distinguished on at least three dimensions: technology, right-of-way, and type of service. Combining these aspects can lead to an elaborate classification, such as given by Vuchic [1981]. Here modes will be presented as they are commonly known by planners and decision makers, without regard to technical distinctions.

There are three general families of transit modes: rail, bus, and paratransit. Rail and bus modes operate on fixed routes and fixed schedules. Paratransit has a variable route and/or schedule; it is also called *demand-responsive transit*. This chapter begins with a description of rail and bus modes and then gives a comparison of conventional rail and bus technology. Paratransit is discussed in Chapter 6. Chapter 7 deals with innovative technology, including personal rapid transit, people movers, and monorail.

Selection of a transit mode is often a controversial issue and may be highly politicized. Claims and counterclaims provide material for public debate and media accounts. Planning studies frequently involve the comparison of modes; this is part of the alternatives analysis that the Federal Transit Administration (FTA) requires with grant applications for major investment in fixed-guideway facilities.

SUBURBAN RAILROAD

Suburban railroad service for commuters, also called *commuter rail* or *regional rail*, was started by the intercity railroads as a sideline before the Civil War. It became important in several large cities. After a long period of decline, it has recently experienced a revival and currently exists in about ten U.S. cities. There are suburban railroads in many foreign cities; London and Paris have large networks. Suburban railroads also operate in Canada, Asia, Australia, and other parts of Europe.

This system is characterized by heavy equipment, high maximum speeds, and slow acceleration and deceleration. Usually locomotives pull trains of passenger coaches, but some self-propelled cars were made (e.g., the Budd car). The locomotives have either diesel or electric motors (the latter requires overhead wires). The routes are typically 25 to 50 miles long and lead to a stub-end terminal in the central business district (CBD). Most other stations are in the suburbs and are several miles apart. Usually ridership is highly concentrated in the peak periods.

One distinctive aspect of this mode is that the service is often of high quality. Trains run at speeds up to 80 miles per hour, and there are enough seats so that normally every passenger gets one. Some lines use double-decker coaches to increase seating capacity (see Figure 5-1). This is the only transit mode with average speeds that compete with driving on freeways; not surprisingly, many of the passengers own automobiles and choose to leave them at home (or at the station). The fares are high, but regular riders save by purchasing monthly passes. The average income of passengers is higher than that of other transit users or even of automobile drivers.

After World War II, the private railroads began losing money on suburban service, and much of it was abandoned. It survived in five U.S. cities: New York City, Chicago, Philadelphia, Boston, and San Francisco. New York City has the largest system, carrying over 500,000 passenger trips each weekday. The Long Island Railroad (owned by

FIGURE 5-1
A commuter railroad passenger car. This double-decked car, parked in a rail yard next to Michigan Avenue in Chicago, is used by the Regional Transportation Authority in suburban service. (Photo by author.)

New York State) has the largest single commuter operation in the country. Chicago has the second largest system, while Philadelphia and Boston have fairly extensive networks. A line running between San Francisco and San Jose was taken over by the state of California when the Southern Pacific Railroad sought to abandon it in 1980. All the systems are now under government control, although a few private railroads operate them under contract to public bodies. Amtrak operates the Boston system for the Massachusetts Bay Transportation Authority.

Suburban rail has made a comeback in recent years. Tri-Rail in Florida, which opened in 1989, is a 67-mile line from West Palm Beach through Fort Lauderdale to the Miami International Airport, where passengers can transfer free to Miami's urban rail line. The state of Florida bought the track for $264 million from CSX, Inc., and leases it to an operating agency. Passenger volumes have been growing; the line averaged 6600 passengers per day in 1991 and carried 10,677 passengers on one day in February 1992.

The state of Maryland contracts for service on three lines serving Baltimore and Washington, D.C.; they carried a total of 15,900 trips per day in 1991. Ridership has grown steadily, and additional service is planned. The Virginia Railway Express began operating from Fredericksburg and Manassas to Washington, D.C., in the summer of 1992. It averaged 6500 passenger trips per day in March 1993.

In October 1992, the Southern California Regional Rail Authority began service on three lines leading to Union Station in Los Angeles from Moorpark, Santa Clarita, and Pomona. A fourth line from Riverside opened in June 1993, and a fifth line from Oceanside, in March 1994. The system is called Metrolink and is operated by Amtrak under contract to the Authority. Metrolink seemed to be a godsend when a major earthquake rocked Southern California on January 17, 1994. With several freeways blocked, thousands of commuters turned to trains. Metrolink carried a single-day record of 31,276 passengers on January 25, 1994 [Middleton 1994].

The new services run on existing tracks that were formerly used exclusively by freight trains. Hence the capital investment needed to start such a service is relatively small; the major item is the acquisition of locomotives and passenger cars. Since most large cities have an ample supply of freight tracks, there are probably more opportunities to bring back commuter trains. Because of their high speed and long routes, the operating cost per passenger-mile is very low. For a summary of operating statistics of several systems, see Gray [1992].

HEAVY RAIL

This mode used to be referred to as *subway-elevated* because most tracks were located either underground or on structures elevated over streets and alleys. Now it is common to lay tracks at ground level, especially in the median strip of an expressway (a practice initiated on the Congress Expressway in Chicago in 1958). The term *heavy rail* came into use to distinguish it from *light rail*, but the equipment is actually lighter than that of suburban railroads. The term *rail rapid transit* is sometimes used, and in foreign countries the popular appellation is *metro*.

Heavy rail is intended primarily to serve travel within the central city, although the newer systems often have lines extending into the suburbs. Stations are fairly close together; the average spacing is about a mile. New York City has some stops that are only one-quarter mile apart, but this is considered inefficient by modern standards. All systems are electrically powered, and each car has its own motor. Electricity usually comes from a third rail, which typically carries 600 volts. This can kill anyone who touches the rail, so the roadbed must be protected. Hence stations have high platforms, and tracks put at ground level are fenced.

Five U.S. cities have older heavy rail systems. As noted in Chapter 2, Boston, New York City, and Philadelphia were the U.S. pioneers in building subways. These cities also erected some elevated lines. Chicago developed an extensive elevated network before World War II and completed two subways in the 1940s. Cleveland opened one line in 1955; it was the first urban rail line in the United States begun after World War II.

These cities have added to their rail networks in recent decades. Boston extended its Red Line and replaced the Washington Street elevated with the new Orange Line. Chicago built rail lines in the median strips of three expressways and also added the Skokie Swift. Cleveland extended its line to Hopkins Airport in 1968, becoming the first U.S. city with rail service to its airport. The Lindenwold Line, connecting downtown Philadelphia with southern New Jersey, began service in 1969. The New York system has added some short links but no major extension.

Six new systems have opened in the last 25 years. The BART system in the San Francisco Bay Area began service in 1972; it is discussed further later in this chapter. The Washington Metro opened in 1976; there are now five lines, and it is approaching its ultimate size of 103 miles (see Figure 5-2). The total construction cost has passed $7

FIGURE 5-2
A heavy rail car. This Washington, D.C., Metro car waits at the elevated station at National Airport. It draws electricity from a third rail, which is visible at the lower left. (Photo by author.)

billion. Atlanta's MARTA system opened in 1979; there are north-south and east-west routes that cross in the downtown area. Baltimore's single line began operation in 1983; Miami opened a line in 1984.

The latest new system is in Los Angeles, and it has also been one of the most controversial. There were several decades of debate before construction of the subway began in 1987. The first leg of the Red Line, 4.4 miles long, began operation in January 1993. It cost $1.4 billion. Ground has been broken for a second segment, 6.7 miles long. Further extensions are under study; local officials hope that the line will eventually reach 18 miles.

Table 5-1 gives some statistics for the heavy rail systems, listed in rank order by the number of average weekday passenger trips. The New York City Transit Authority system dwarfs all the others, accounting for 60 percent of the vehicles and 62 percent of the passenger trips. New York City has a second heavy rail operation—the PATH system that links Manhattan with northern New Jersey. Philadelphia also has two systems; the Lindenwold Line is operated by PATCO and is separate from the SEPTA network.

Most heavy rail systems use the standard gauge of intercity railroads, with tracks 4 feet 8 ½ inches apart. BART is an exception; it was designed with a gauge of 5 feet ¾ inch. BART cars are noticeably lower and wider. Most foreign countries use standard gauge (but not Russia, where the gauge is exactly 5 feet).

Most systems use steel wheels on steel rails. The French pioneered a design in which vehicles have rubber tires and run on a concrete guideway. It is now used throughout the Paris system as well as in Montreal and Mexico City, where the French did the en-

TABLE 5-1
HEAVY RAIL SYSTEMS IN THE UNITED STATES
(Data for Fiscal Years Ending in 1992)

City	Vehicles operated in max. service	Route miles	Annual passenger trips	Average weekday trips
New York (NYCTA)	4923	492.9	1,373,625,314	4,637,993
Washington	534	162.1	186,781,930	649,266
Boston	368	76.7	180,672,743	551,040
Chicago	924	191.0	137,372,830	473,297
Philadelphia (SEPTA)	300	75.8	79,807,489	271,614
San Francisco	415	142.0	77,247,042	259,953
New York (PATH)	282	28.6	60,142,914	211,567
Atlanta	136	67.0	64,078,000	210,518
Miami	82	42.2	13,701,605	46,230
Baltimore	48	26.6	11,996,972	41,421
Philadelphia (PATCO)	102	31.5	11,150,707	40,411
Cleveland	30	38.2	5,556,481	19,075

Source: Transit Profiles; Agencies in Urbanized Areas Exceeding 200,000 Population; for the 1992 Section 15 Report Year (Washington: Federal Transit Administration, December 1993).

gineering. This design has the advantages that it is quieter, the ride is more comfortable, and vibrations from trains are not transmitted to the ground. However, energy consumption is higher, and there are climatic limitations: The tires can generate excessive heat in the summer. Snow and ice cause traction problems, so an underground alignment is required in cities with cold winters.

LIGHT RAIL

Light rail transit (or *LRT*) is currently the most popular form of rail transit being proposed for U.S. cities [Black 1993]. It is really a modern version of the electric streetcar; most of the vehicles are not intrinsically different from the PCC car. Often the track is laid in the street in places, but much of it is located underground, on elevated guideway, or within a freeway right-of-way (see Figure 5-3).

Some of the advantages claimed for light rail are as follows:

1 It is safer than heavy rail because the electricity comes from an overhead wire instead of a third rail. There is no need to fence the track, and it can operate in the street.

2 It offers more flexibility of location than heavy rail. Where land is expensive (as

FIGURE 5-3
A light railcar. This is the downtown portion of the San Diego system, where trains run in the middle of the street. Power is drawn from an overhead wire through a pantagraph on top of the car. (Photo by author.)

in a downtown area), it can be put in a street and passengers can board and alight from the sidewalk. Right-of-way acquisition and construction can be much cheaper than for heavy rail.

3 Hence it is viable in situations with a lower level of demand than that needed to justify costly heavy rail projects. This might include medium-sized cities where the only alternative is bus service.

4 If most of a route is on separate right-of-way, average speeds are higher than for buses in mixed traffic. Hence light rail should attract more passengers than buses.

5 The technology is well known and has been proved by experience. There is little risk of encountering mechanical problems or big cost overruns.

LRT proponents claim that LRT is cheaper to build and operate than heavy rail. However, some construction costs have been comparable to those of heavy rail. Prices for new cars are higher than originally expected and approximate those for heavy rail-cars (currently more than $1 million apiece). Evidence on operating costs is mixed; it depends on what measures are used.

Background

The decline of the streetcar was described in Chapter 2. Most large U.S. cities abandoned streetcars in the 1950s and 1960s. Only seven cities retained any part of their streetcar operations: Boston, Cleveland, Newark, New Orleans, Philadelphia, Pittsburgh, and San Francisco.

During this period of retrenchment, Leonard's Department Store in Fort Worth spent $1 million to construct a streetcar line just over 1 mile long between a large parking lot and the basement of the store. It opened in 1963; in 1967, the Tandy Corporation bought both the store and the trolley line. Both the trolley ride and parking are free [Scott 1978].

Streetcars were also abandoned in many foreign cities, but they were retained in other places, including some European countries, and some new lines were built. A tally in 1975 showed that 310 cities in the world had streetcar/LRT systems operating [Diamant et al. 1976, p. 25]. The streetcar is the prime mode of urban transportation in Eastern European countries, where automobile ownership is low. Because of the demand for new equipment, foreign companies continued to manufacture streetcars and to improve the design.

In the early 1970s, UMTA financed the design of a new Standard Light Rail Vehicle. Boston and San Francisco ordered 275 of the new cars from Boeing-Vertol in 1973. The first cars Boston received suffered many technical problems and allegedly did not meet specifications. After a long dispute, Boeing agreed in 1979 to pay $40 million for modifications to the cars. Boeing lost a lot of money on the orders and later withdrew from the business.

Recent Projects

Light rail was the preferred technology for new rail systems built in the 1980s. Following is a summary of recent projects (Table 5-2 gives some data about the systems):

TABLE 5-2
NEW LIGHT RAIL TRANSIT SYSTEMS IN NORTH AMERICA

City	Year opened	Length, miles	Cost,* $	Average weekday riders†
Edmonton	1978	6.5	185	25,000
Calgary	1981	17.1	500	111,000
San Diego	1981	33.2	292	50,000
Buffalo	1985	6.4	536	29,900
Vancouver	1986	15.2	1033	110,000
Portland	1986	15.1	240	22,500
Sacramento	1987	18.3	176	23,400
San Jose	1987	20.3	500	19,700
Los Angeles	1990	21.5	877	34,200
Baltimore	1992	22.7	364	18,600
St. Louis	1993	18.0	351	23,000

*Investment cost in millions of current dollars, including vehicles. In Canadian dollars where appropriate.
†In 1992 or 1993 for U.S. systems; in 1990 or 1991 for Canadian systems.

Canada actually led the revival of light rail transit in North America. *Edmonton* opened the first line in North America in 1978. It was 4.5 miles long, with a 1-mile subway downtown, and has since been extended. *Calgary* opened the South Line of its C-Train system in May 1981. The Northeast Line was opened in 1985, and the Northwest Line in the fall of 1987, in time for the 1988 Winter Olympics.

San Diego opened the first LRT line in the United States in July 1981. Called the *Tijuana Trolley*, it runs 16 miles from downtown San Diego to San Ysidro at the Mexican border. It cost only $86 million, partly because the transit agency was able to purchase 109 miles of little-used freight lines from a subsidiary of Southern Pacific for $18 million. No federal aid was used; most of the money came from state gasoline taxes. A second line to the eastern suburb of El Cajon, 11 miles long, was completed in 1989, and a downtown loop opened in 1990 (federal aid was used for these projects). Construction of a third line is under way.

Buffalo built a line after UMTA rejected plans for heavy rail. Part was opened in 1985; the project was completed in November 1986. Trains run in a 1.2-mile transit mall downtown; the rest of the route is subway (the original plan to make this elevated aroused heavy opposition). The final cost of $536 million makes this the most expensive project on a per-mile basis.

Vancouver opened its Skytrain in 1986 in time for the exposition held that year. It is unique in that it is powered by linear induction and the operation is totally automatic (there are no personnel on the trains or in the stations). The Skytrain carried as many as 160,000 passengers per day during Expo. The original section, 13 miles long, has since been extended over the Fraser River on a lovely cable-stayed bridge (see Figure 5-4). The total cost for the system has passed $1 billion Canadian.

FIGURE 5-4
The Vancouver Skytrain. Here a train crosses the cable-stayed bridge over the Fraser River.
These trains are fully automatic and carry no personnel, a practice not used in the United States.
(*Source:* American Public Transit Association.)

Some experts do not classify this technology as light rail. It is like heavy rail in that the guideway must be protected (a plate between the tracks carries 600 volts), and the stations are substantial structures. Others call it *advanced light rail transit.* The speed and capacity are similar to those for light rail: Trains cruise at 50 miles per hour; each car has 40 seats and can hold 35 standees.

Portland opened the MAX line in September 1986. It makes a loop through downtown on city streets. Elsewhere parts run on streets and parts alongside the Banfield Freeway. Interstate Transfer funds helped pay the cost after plans for the Mount Hood Freeway were abandoned. In November 1990, voters passed a $125 million bond issue to build a second line.

Sacramento completed its RT Metro system in September 1987. Two radial lines meet at a downtown transit mall. The system originally had 11 miles of single-track sections, which required headways of at least 15 minutes. This project also used Interstate Transfer funds; in this case, the canceled freeway was already under construction. Part of one line was built on this right-of-way, and some of the freeway pavement is used for parking. Other parts use former railroad right-of-way.

San Jose built the Guadalupe Line through the heart of Silicon Valley in Santa Clara County, California. It consists of two radial lines which meet at a downtown transit mall. A 6-mile section opened in December 1987, and the project was completed in April 1991.

Los Angeles began service in July 1990 on the Blue Line between central Los Angeles and Long Beach. It uses 16 miles of former right-of-way of the Pacific Electric interurban system; there was much publicity about the return of rail transit to Los Angeles after 30 years. The project was completed when a six-block tunnel in downtown Los Angeles opened in February 1991. The Green Line, 20 miles long, is being constructed in the Century Freeway right-of-way with a spur to Los Angeles International Airport.

Baltimore opened the first section of its Central Light Rail Line in May 1992. When completed, it will reach 22.5 miles from the northern suburbs through a downtown transit mall to the southern suburbs. The project was briefly halted in 1989 when the cost estimate escalated from $290 million to $468 million, but it was decided to proceed.

St. Louis built an 18-mile line called *Metro Link* that began service in July 1993. It extends from the Illinois side of the Mississippi River, across the historic Eads Bridge, through downtown in an old railroad tunnel, and then to Lambert Airport. The entire line is on exclusive right-of-way.

Dallas is also building a light rail system. An 18.5-mile "starter" line that will cost $828 million is scheduled to open in 1996. The ultimate goal is a 66-mile network.

Denver held a "start of construction" ceremony in September 1992 for yet another new LRT system.

Several of the cities with old streetcar systems have undertaken major renovations. Pittsburgh spent $542 million to convert 10.5 miles of streetcar lines to an LRT system entirely on separate right-of-way, including a new downtown subway. The project was completed in 1987. The streetcars on Market Street in San Francisco were moved underground when BART was built. Boston, Cleveland, and Newark have also made large investments in their systems.

Schumann [1992] compiled detailed information on all the streetcar/light rail systems operating in the United States and Canada. Demoro and Harder [1989] wrote a popular account of the systems on the west coast.

Proposals to build LRT are under study in many other cities, including Austin, Charlotte, Columbus, Detroit, Kansas City, Memphis, Minneapolis, Norfolk, Orlando, Salt Lake City, Seattle, and Tampa. Note that none of these cities has a heavy rail system. LRT offers an entree to the elite circle of cities with rail transit if you cannot afford heavy rail.

Another idea with growing popularity is the *vintage trolley* [Phraner 1992]. This involves using antique streetcars that have been restored or else replicas of old cars. These are not buses made to look like trolleys; these vehicles run on electricity. In some places they use part of an LRT line (as in San Jose); in others, they have the tracks all to themselves (as in Dallas, Detroit, and Seattle). This concept is mostly seen as a tourist attraction.

BUS

Bus transit is well known since it is the most common form of urban public transportation in the United States. There are about 60,000 urban transit buses in use in the country, compared with about 10,000 heavy rail vehicles and about 1000 light railcars.

TABLE 5-3
LARGEST MOTOR BUS SYSTEMS IN THE UNITED STATES
(Data for Fiscal Years Ending in 1992)

City	Vehicles operated in maximum service	Annual passenger trips	Average weekday trips
New York (NYCTA)	3050	650,522,389	2,170,062
Los Angeles	1897	402,885,250	1,270,096
Chicago	1791	370,335,119	1,198,253
Newark	2536	175,016,649	597,705
Washington	1436	167,165,685	564,524
Philadelphia	1120	168,645,196	555,769
San Francisco	386	102,740,036	339,042
Boston	838	94,040,291	308,841
Baltimore	751	89,072,647	302,524
Houston	961	84,357,831	284,702
Detroit	474	75,762,094	259,463
Atlanta	579	76,934,710	252,423
Pittsburgh	757	65,632,509	239,991
Honolulu	415	72,985,610	230,241
Oakland	614	69,682,121	224,234
Minneapolis	869	66,303,403	223,204
Dallas	751	56,635,906	202,667
Denver	652	58,865,608	196,687
New Orleans	373	60,949,631	195,772
Seattle	939	57,991,507	195,024

Source: Transit Profiles; Agencies in Urbanized Areas Exceeding 200,000 Population; for the 1992 Section 15 Report Year (Washington: Federal Transit Administration, December 1993).

About two-thirds of all transit passenger trips are made by bus. Table 5-3 lists the 20 largest bus systems in the country, ranked by average weekday passenger trips.

The Vehicles

Most transit agencies use a type of bus designed specifically for urban use (see Figure 5-5). It is approximately 40 feet long; some manufacturers offer shorter models. Seating configurations vary, but most buses have 47 to 53 seats. Large cities like New York City often use longitudinal seating, which reduces the number of seats but provides more room for standing passengers.

Many smaller models of buses are available; sometimes they are called *minibuses*.

FIGURE 5-5
A standard urban transit bus. This vehicle, operated by the Kansas City Area Transportation Authority, was manufactured by the Transportation Manufacturing Group in New Mexico. (Photo by author.)

Usually they have 20 to 30 seats. They are most often used in paratransit services, and they will be discussed further in Chapter 6.

There are also larger buses, which have long been common in Europe. Double-decker buses are still predominant in Great Britain (see Figure 5-6) as well as other places that were once part of the British Empire (such as Hong Kong). They are not antiques; double-decker buses are still being manufactured. There are few of them in the United States.

More popular worldwide are *articulated buses*, which have a hinge in the middle and bend to go around corners (see Figure 5-7). They have 66 to 72 seats and three or four doors, instead of the usual two. Some U.S. cities acquired articulated buses in the 1980s to raise the productivity of drivers. Often the buses are used only during peak periods, when demand is high and the extra seats are needed.

Most buses have diesel engines, although some operate on propane gas, and there is currently experimentation with other alternative fuels. Electric buses (also called *trolley buses* or *trackless trolleys*) are still used in five U.S. cities: Boston, Dayton, Philadelphia, San Francisco, and Seattle. They are common in some foreign countries (such as China). Trolley buses have two trolley poles and use two overhead wires, one bringing

FIGURE 5-6
A double-decker bus. This is still the most common type of bus used in Great Britain, as well as several countries that were formerly part of the British Empire. This photograph was taken in Oxford, England. (Photo by author.)

the current and one returning it (see Figure 5-8). They ride on rubber tires and can maneuver in the street, as long as the trolleys do not become disengaged. Of course, they cannot pass one another.

In the 1980s, many U.S. cities and towns began using fake trolleys, which are actually buses with bodies that resemble old-fashioned streetcars. Sometimes they are called *trolley replicas.* Generally they are used for specialized services, such as downtown circulation or tourist-oriented routes. For example, Kansas City has a popular route that connects the downtown area with two shopping centers, an entertainment district, and numerous hotels (see Figure 5-9). However, some transit purists are offended at the idea of buses masquerading as electric streetcars.

The following sections deal with the physical facilities on which buses run and different ways of operating bus service.

Separate Roadways or Freeway Lanes

Traditionally buses ran on the same streets as other vehicles and thus suffered from traffic congestion. In the past 20 years, many cities have built special roadways or desig-

FIGURE 5-7
An articulated bus. This type of bus, which can bend in the middle, is used by several large U.S. cities, especially during the peak period on high-volume routes. This one is operated by the Metropolitan Atlanta Rapid Transit Authority. (Photo by author.)

nated special lanes for buses to raise their speed. Sometimes these are called *busways*, sometimes *transitways*. Because buses use little capacity, it is common to let vanpools and car pools also use the lanes, which are then called *high-occupancy vehicle (HOV) lanes*. As of 1989, there were 40 such facilities, totaling about 300 miles, in almost 20 metropolitan areas in the United States and Canada [Turnbull and Hanks 1990].

The most ambitious scheme is to build a roadway on an independent alignment that is for buses only. There are two in Pittsburgh: The South Busway opened in 1977, and the East Busway, in 1983. Ottawa, Canada, has an 11-mile busway on separate right-of-way. Seattle built a 1.3-mile bus tunnel costing $450 million under the downtown area; it opened in September 1990. Years ago networks of separate busways were proposed in Milwaukee and St. Louis, but the plans were never implemented.

It is more common to construct a separate roadway that is located on freeway right-of-way but separated from other traffic by a railing or concrete barrier. These facilities involve different designs and modes of operation. Some have one lane; others have two lanes operating in the same direction; still others have two lanes and bidirectional flow. In the first two cases, the direction is reversed in the middle of the day. Sometimes the lanes are restricted only in peak periods; others operate 24 hours a day. Some HOV lanes require car pools to have at least two persons, others at least three.

FIGURE 5-8
A trolley bus. This vehicle has rubber tires but runs on electricity. It requires two overhead wires and two poles to complete the electric circuit. Trolley buses are still used in five U.S. cities including San Francisco, where this picture was taken. (Photo by author.)

The first demonstration of exclusive bus lanes was the Shirley Busway, which opened in 1969 [Fisher 1972]. It is 11 miles long and runs through the Virginia suburbs of Washington, D.C., ending near the Pentagon (see Figure 5-10). The second was an 11-mile busway on the San Bernardino Freeway in Los Angeles, which opened in 1973. Both were originally restricted to buses but now operate as HOV lanes.

Houston now has the largest system, totaling 46.5 miles as of 1990. HOV lanes were opened on the Katy Freeway in 1984, the North Freeway in 1985, and the Northwest and Gulf Freeways in 1988. Similar facilities will be built on the Southwest and Eastex Freeways. Other cities with HOV lanes on freeway right-of-way include Hartford, Minneapolis, Pittsburgh, and San Diego.

A special case is a 10-mile segment of Interstate 66 in Virginia between the Potomac River and the Beltway, which opened in 1982. It was originally planned as an eight-lane freeway but became controversial and was redesigned twice [Page 1983]. The final design has two lanes in each direction (plus a Metro line in the median strip). During peak periods, the peak-direction lanes are restricted to buses and other vehicles with three or more persons. At other times the highway is open to all traffic except heavy trucks.

A different design that requires minimal investment is a *concurrent flow lane*. Here a freeway lane is designated as an HOV lane but is not physically separated. It is usually

FIGURE 5-9
A trolley replica. This is actually a small bus, but it is designed to resemble an old-fashioned electric streetcar. Many cities use such vehicles on selected routes, particularly those patronized by tourists. This one boards passengers at the Crown Center shopping complex in Kansas City, Missouri. (Photo by author.)

marked with a wide paint stripe; there may be overhead signs or signals as well. In some cases, large diamonds are painted on the pavement, in which case it is popularly called a *diamond lane*.

One of the first examples of a diamond lane operated on the Santa Monica Freeway in Los Angeles for 5 months in 1976. It encountered many problems and was abandoned after protests [Billheimer 1978]. Since then, the approach has been refined and has become more acceptable to the driving public. Among the cities now using concurrent flow lanes on freeways are Denver, Honolulu, Los Angeles, Miami, Orlando, Phoenix, San Francisco, San Jose, and Seattle.

HOV lane restrictions are prone to violation because the lanes move at a higher speed than adjacent lanes open to all traffic. In some places, there is a considerable effort at enforcement, which keeps violation rates low. In Virginia, police record the license plates of violators and send tickets by mail. In other places, there is no special enforcement, and a few cities have reported violation rates exceeding 30 percent [Turnbull and Hanks 1990].

Another arrangement is a *contraflow lane*, in which buses run in the opposite direc-

FIGURE 5-10
The Shirley Busway. The first exclusive busway in the world opened in northern Virginia in 1969. The special lanes are now open to car pools and vanpools as well as buses. This picture was taken during a Friday afternoon rush hour; the advantage of the special lanes is obvious. (Photo by author.)

tion from other vehicles on the same side of the median strip. The lane is separated by plastic posts rather than permanent barriers. Normally it is used only during peak hours; the posts are removed, and the lane is opened to all traffic at other times. This system is suitable where traffic flow in the peak period is very unbalanced; the lane is taken away from the lighter direction of movement.

The first contraflow lane opened in New Jersey in 1970 on the approach to the Lincoln Tunnel [Goodman and Selinger 1972]. It is still operating, as are contraflow lanes on two other expressways in New York City. Boston, San Francisco, and Houston used them in the 1970s, but in these cities contraflow lanes have since been replaced by other types of operations. Contraflow lanes are adaptations of existing freeways; they are never considered in designing a new freeway.

Some cities give buses priority at freeway ramps. Chicago, Pittsburgh, and Seattle have freeways with separate entry ramps for buses. There are metered entry ramps with bus bypass lanes in Los Angeles, Minneapolis, and San Diego. This can be helpful because there are often long backups at ramps.

The San Francisco–Oakland Bay Bridge has a special lane on which buses and car pools may bypass the toll booths. This point is a major bottleneck; waits of 15 minutes are common.

City Street Treatments

Another way to improve bus service is to turn an entire city street over to buses, excluding cars and trucks. This may be called a *transit mall* or *transitway*; it is done only in the downtown area. The sidewalks are widened, leaving one or two lanes for the buses. Sometimes benches and plantings are installed to make the area more attractive. Since the volume of buses is low, people walk back and forth across the street; the effect is similar to having a pedestrian mall. Some cities let taxis use these streets; emergency vehicles are also permitted.

One example is the Sixteenth Street Mall in Denver, where buses shuttle between two terminals about 2 miles apart (see Figure 5-11). Headways are short, and there is no fare. The whole bus network was redesigned to center on this mall; all radial routes stop at one of the terminals, where passengers can transfer to the shuttle. Other examples include State Street in Chicago, Nicollet Mall in Minneapolis, Chestnut Street in

FIGURE 5-11
A downtown transit-pedestrian mall. This is Sixteenth Street in Denver, where buses are the only motor vehicles regularly allowed to use a 2-mile stretch. Several other U.S. cities have implemented this concept. (Photo by author.)

Philadelphia, Fifth and Sixth Streets in Portland, Oregon, and Granville Street in Vancouver, British Columbia.

An interesting experiment is seen in the British new town of Runcorn, which was designed with a 13-mile busway roughly forming a figure eight [Dupree 1987, pp. 162–165]. The buses travel at 20 miles per hour; this is not a high-speed service.

Another arrangement is to reserve one or two lanes of a wide street for buses. One example is Canal Street in New Orleans, which has a median strip, guarded by curbs, that was once used by streetcars. When the streetcar tracks were removed, the strip was paved to make two lanes that are for buses only.

Reserved bus lanes are used in many cities but are not usually separated by physical barriers. They are usually curb lanes and suffer from interference by illegally parked vehicles and vehicles making right turns. Madison Avenue in New York City has two adjacent lanes reserved for buses so that those stopped to unload and load passengers do not delay others. Several cities have contraflow bus lanes on downtown streets.

Another innovation is to give buses priority at traffic signals. Some buses are equipped with radio transmitters that send pulses that make traffic signals turn green as the bus approaches an intersection.

Service Alternatives

Besides these special facilities, there are different ways of operating bus routes. These apply when buses run in mixed traffic as well as on separate lanes.

Conventional bus service involves frequent stops along the entire route (8 to 10 designated stops per mile is typical). Buses stop only on demand, when a passenger signals to get off or someone is waiting at a bus stop to get on. With low demand, buses skip many of the stops, but during rush hour they must stop at most of the designated points, which reduces speed.

One alternative is *limited-stop service* with stops spaced much farther apart (usually 2 to 4 stops per mile). Chicago has operated such service for many years. New York City experimented with this approach on five routes in Manhattan [Ercolano 1984]. The limited-stop buses were 50 to 100 percent faster than other buses in light traffic, but there was little difference in heavy traffic. Because of the faster operation, fewer buses were needed to meet the schedule, which reduced costs.

Express service implies a long nonstop run, which may occur on an arterial street, expressway, or HOV lane. Typically such routes connect a residential area (which may be in the suburbs) with the central business district (CBD). At the outer end, there may be a series of stops for collection and distribution or one stop at a park-and-ride lot. There may be a single stop in the CBD or an area where buses make several stops. These services are used almost wholly by commuters, and often they operate only in peak periods.

Express routes offer superior transit service: The average speed is fairly high (depending on the nonstop portion), and usually passengers are guaranteed seats. The clientele is typically middle-income, and the fares are relatively high. This is one type of transit service that can be profitable, and there are numerous private companies operating such routes in New York City, Chicago, Boston, Washington, and other large cities.

THE RAIL VERSUS BUS DEBATE

There has been a prolonged debate in transportation planning between those who want to build new rail systems and those who favor all-bus transit. Some people feel strongly about the issue, and there is much rhetoric. It is surprising how professionals can become emotionally attached to a particular kind of technology.

There are institutional factors that influence the positions people take on the issue. The automobile, oil, and highway lobby prefers the bus because it is a road vehicle. For a long time General Motors was the largest U.S. manufacturer of buses. Oil companies supply the fuel for buses. Most highway engineers now concede the need for transit improvements, at least in large cities, but they tend to be strong advocates of bus proposals.

Construction of a busway usually implies construction of a freeway, although, as noted, Pittsburgh and Ottawa built busways on separate right-of-way. Some rail lines have been built on freeway right-of-way, but usually they are located elsewhere. Most analyses of busway schemes assume that a freeway is built in the same alignment. Hence the busway is charged only the marginal cost of the bus lanes; i.e., the busway is treated as an add-on to the freeway. There may be no additional land cost for bus lanes because building a freeway typically requires acquiring a block-wide strip of land. This makes a busway seem cheaper than if it were built separately.

Federal funding formulas favor the bus in some situations. For bus lanes built as part of an interstate highway, the federal government pays 90 percent of the cost. For a rail facility, the federal share is 80 percent. Thus you get more leverage from local money if you build a busway instead of a rail line. For a busway, $1 in local money generates $9 in federal money. For a rail line, $1 in local money generates $4 in federal money.

There are also reasons why some people favor rail. During the early years of federal transit aid, UMTA encouraged proposals for rail systems. Until 1974, federal money was available only for capital investment, which usually meant rail projects. After requests for money grew beyond the amounts available, UMTA became more discriminating and rejected some rail proposals.

Another factor is that rail is more capital-intensive. It is argued that operating costs can be reduced through automation, which is more feasible with rail than with bus. There is now federal aid for operating costs, but there is a limit, based on a formula, to how much operating aid a city can receive. Capital grants are awarded on a discretionary basis, and there is no statutory limit to the amount that an individual city can receive.

Light rail has become a popular option in part because it seems to be a compromise between heavy rail and bus improvements. Cervero wrote, "LRT seems particularly well-suited to a host of medium-sized North American cities where rapid rail systems cannot be economically justified" [1984, p. 146]. He gave reasons for its popularity: "it is relatively quiet, thus environmentally unobtrusive, is electrically propelled, thus less dependent than buses on the availability of petrochemical fuels; and can operate effectively along available railroad rights-of-way and street medians, thus is far cheaper, less disruptive, and easier to build than heavy rail. LRT's lack of exhaust fumes and comparatively slow speeds make it particularly compatible with pedestrian settings such as downtown malls" [p. 134].

Several writers have alleged that the planning studies for recent rail projects were manipulated in order to justify the proposals. Hamer [1976] devoted a book to the subject, *The Selling of Rail Rapid Transit,* in which he presented several case studies. The implication is that if objective analyses had been made, the rail proposals would have been rejected and bus alternatives would have been selected instead.

Rail proponents often cite the work of Pushkarev et al. [1982], who developed criteria for building heavy and light rail lines. Their approach was to estimate the minimum weekday passenger volume for which savings in land, energy, labor, and passenger travel time would justify the capital investment required. The results depended greatly on how much underground construction was involved, as this is very expensive. The threshold for heavy rail above ground was 15,000 passengers; if built fully in a tunnel, the minimum rose to 29,000 passengers. A very low-capital light rail line would be justified by 4000 passengers; one with one-fifth of the route in a tunnel required a volume of 13,500 passengers.

The authors applied their findings to existing U.S. cities. They found only four cities that were serious candidates for new heavy rail lines: Los Angeles, Seattle, Honolulu, and Houston. They identified 10 cities as good candidates for light rail, plus several that were marginal.

Pickrell "corrected" this study by substituting revised estimates of some benefits and costs that he felt were more realistic. He came up with threshold levels two to four times greater. He also criticized Pushkarev for focusing exclusively on the line-haul portion of the trip and omitting feeder modes, which gave rail an artificial advantage. Pickrell concluded that "no new heavy rail lines appear to be economically justified in U.S. cities" and that "the number of urban travel corridors . . . where constructing light rail lines can be justified by realistic estimates of their likely costs and attendant benefits also appears to be extremely limited" [1984, p. 52].

Gomez-Ibanez analyzed early ridership and financial data from the new light rail lines in San Diego, Calgary, and Edmonton and concluded that "LRT proponents indeed have overstated their case" [1985, p. 339]. Transit ridership rose in all three cities, but only modestly. In all three cases, the total cost per passenger went up considerably because of the capital investment involved. Gomez-Ibanez warned that "other cities considering LRT should be skeptical of claims that light rail will reduce transit costs, improve service quality, or increase ridership significantly" [p. 349].

Gomez-Ibanez noted the conflict between two supposed merits of light rail: "LRT proponents are sometimes inconsistent . . . in claiming both that the LRT offers better service than buses because it often operates on an exclusive right of way and that the LRT is much cheaper than heavy rail because it can run in existing surface streets" [p. 339]. You cannot have it both ways.

Wachs wrote that forecasts are often manipulated to give preconceived outcomes: "I am convinced that most of the forecasts used in the planning of America's rail transit systems are statements of advocacy rather than unbiased estimates produced by politically neutral applied social scientists. . . . the pressures to produce self-serving forecasts which are cloaked in the guise of technical objectivity is overwhelming" [1986, p. 28].

Since forecasting models are complex and involve hidden assumptions, few can tell whether the results are valid. Forecasts usually support the wishes of the agencies that pay to have them made. Wachs blamed this practice on the federal funding system: Since capital investment is funded by discretionary grants, each agency has an incentive to make its proposal look better than those of competitors. In contrast, highways are funded by formula grants, which do not vary with the attractiveness of individual projects.

Wachs has discussed the ethical dilemma facing forecasters, who are responsible to both the public interest and employers or clients. Those who give priority to the public interest may suffer. "I am aware of at least five individuals who have been fired and blacklisted from employment in the field . . . because they have objected to instructions to 'revise' their forecasts to suit the needs of their clients or supervisors, or because they have given newspapers information showing that forecasts made in support of a proposed public program have been distorted for political reasons" [1990, p. 154].

Johnston et al. [1987] did a case study of Sacramento's decision to build light rail. In alternatives analysis, LRT was compared with building HOV lanes and a Transportation Systems Management option that included more than doubling the bus fleet. LRT came out best on only one of eleven technical criteria, and even that advantage resulted from forecasting errors. The review by Johnston et al. of the analysis "reveals a project that apparently has little to recommend it into the foreseeable future. It is a fixed guideway project located in a low-density metropolitan area superimposed upon an automobile-dominated transportation system" [1987, p. 466].

Politicians, local organizations, and the public (as shown in two polls conducted by the *Sacramento Bee*) still preferred light rail. Johnston et al. believe it was "preselected," and the alternatives analysis did not sway anyone. They suggested local political support should be given some weight; in view of the inevitable uncertainty in forecasting, decisions should not be based solely on technical grounds. They concluded that "the choice of LRT, to the extent that it reflected legitimate local concerns, was valid" [p. 450].

Kain criticized building light rail lines in low-density sunbelt cities such as Los Angeles and Dallas. By his analysis, heavy rail is superior in handling high peak-hour volumes, and buses are superior for low volumes. He remarked, "I continue to be puzzled by the persistent popularity of Light Rail Transit. LRT seems to me to be nothing more than a slow and expensive bus that cannot pass and is unable to operate on the city streets" [1988, p. 202].

In another article, Kain analyzed the forecasting used to justify the 92-mile LRT system proposed for Dallas. A referendum to let the transit district issue bonds was badly defeated by voters in 1988. Kain charged, "the Dallas Area Rapid Transit District . . . overstated the benefits and understated the costs of the proposed system and attempted, first, to conceal and then to misrepresent the results of unfavorable travel forecasts" [1990, p. 184].

In a retrospective study, Pickrell [1989] reviewed the performance of 10 recent rail projects: 4 heavy rail systems, 4 light rail lines, and 2 downtown people movers. He compared forecasts of ridership, construction costs, and operating costs with the values that actually occurred after system completion. In 8 of 9 cases, the number of weekday rail passengers was less than half of that predicted; the Washington Metro did best, with a shortfall of only 28 percent. With costs measured in constant 1988 dollars, capital outlays were above forecasts in 9 cases (Pittsburgh completed its LRT upgrading at 11 percent below estimate). Annual operating expenses were higher than predicted in 7 of 8 cases (in Sacramento they were 10 percent below estimate).

Forecasting remains something of an art, and errors are to be expected. But if the inherent uncertainty of the methodology were responsible for the errors, they should be randomly distributed above and below. This was not the case. Pickrell later wrote, "the transit planning process has been reduced to a forum in which local officials use exaggerated forecasts to compete against their counterparts from other cities to obtain federal financing of projects they have already committed themselves to support, but realize cannot prevail in an unbiased comparison to plausible alternatives" [1992, p. 169].

The federal government financed most of the costs of these projects, including the cost overruns. Pickrell suggested there is little incentive for accurate forecasting. "The most effective way to induce planners and decision-makers to choose projects on the basis of more accurate ridership and cost projections would be to transfer the financial risk of forecasting errors from the federal treasury to local government" [1992, p. 170]. One way would be for the federal government to put a dollar ceiling on its contribution; another would be to distribute funds on a formula basis.

A major factor in the popularity of rail transit is that it has a better public image than buses do. People rarely boast about their city's having a good bus system; they are more likely to complain that the buses are slow, crowded, and unsafe. A rail system, on the other hand, makes a city "big-league," like a major league sports team or a domed stadium. It is argued that a rail system helps to attract business, tourists, and conventions to the city.

Turnbull [1991] confirmed the existence of this opinion by interviewing officials in four cities that had recently built rail systems. She found a consensus that rail transit has intangible benefits and gives a city a positive image. The fact of having rail transit was prominently featured in marketing and promotional efforts. However, business leaders said transit was only a secondary consideration when they made location decisions.

Richmond made a case study of the decision-making process that led to building the Blue Line in Los Angeles. He interviewed many of the officials involved and concluded that "symbols, images and metaphors combine to form a compelling myth of the power of rail to solve the transportation problems of Los Angeles. Objects are polarized into good and bad—and trains are clearly good" [1989, p. 14]. Trains were seen as speedy, exciting, powerful, and representing advanced technology. He quoted a county transportation commissioner as saying, "Trains are sexy, buses are not." Several people were upset that San Diego had rail before Los Angeles did.

Richmond urged planners to forget about alternatives analysis and become psychiatrists. He summed up as follows:

> UMTA administrators, academics or other planners immune to the myth of rail who simply throw reams of statistical evidence at rail-hungry cities will be ignored because rail is not

something emerging from a process of analytic reason but from drives such as penis envy and the lust for power; from fantastic imagery; from impressions formed during expense-paid junkets to cities with rail; from hopes and dreams fueled by memories of the past; from metaphors which make a complex set of choices look alluringly simple [1989, p. 15].

COMPARISON OF MODES

There have been many studies that purported to make objective comparisons of rail and bus modes. The first formed a major part of a book by Meyer et al. [1965] called *The Urban Transportation Problem.* This study, ordered by President Kennedy, influenced the government's decision to construct a busway on the Shirley Highway.

The study posited a hypothetical corridor leading to a central business district and considered only the peak period. The trip was divided into three parts: residential collection, line-haul service (with three alternatives: rail, buses on exclusive lanes, and automobiles on a freeway), and downtown distribution. Ranges of values were used for key variables: the length of the corridor, population density, size of the CBD, and one-way hourly passenger volumes from 5000 to 50,000. The study attempted to make service levels for the alternatives comparable in terms of speed, frequency, and seating capacity. Evaluation was based on the sum of operating, vehicle, and construction costs. Travel time was not included.

The findings were complex but can be summarized as follows: (1) Driving an automobile all the way is cheapest with volumes up to 5000 passengers per hour. (2) Taking a bus all the way (and using a busway) is generally cheapest when volumes are 10,000 per hour or higher. (3) Rail with feeder buses for residential collection and with a downtown subway for distribution is cheapest with high population density and volumes of at least 40,000 persons per hour. Rail has a very small advantage over bus in this range.

The authors concluded that rail transit can be justified in only a few large cities of the northeast and midwest. New York City and Chicago were the only cities with a peak-hour corridor volume of 40,000 passengers, while Boston, Philadelphia, and Washington, D.C., had corridors with 20,000 to 30,000 passengers per hour [Meyer et al. 1965, p. 86]. No other U.S. city had a corridor carrying over 20,000 persons per hour.

This book made a large impression, and other comparisons of rail and bus followed. Some included travel by automobile; others were confined to transit modes. Most studies posited hypothetical situations, compared typical characteristics of the modes, and sought to determine the range of conditions under which each mode was superior. Often the object was to find the threshold level of demand that would justify building a rail facility. The usual approach was to assume equivalent service levels and declare the least-cost mode to be the winner.

Two of the early studies were very favorable to rail. Deen and James [1969] compared busway and rail alternatives in Atlanta for hourly corridor volumes of 4000 and 12,000 passengers. They found that rail was slightly less costly at the higher volume and concluded that rail is superior for any volume higher than 12,000 passengers.

Miller et al. [1973] compared busway and rail alternatives as part of a transit study for Los Angeles. They found the cost almost equal for volumes from 2000 to 5000 passengers per hour. Rail was clearly superior for any volume above 5000. This, of course, would justify rail in dozens of cities.

Several analysts claimed to prove that the bus is best in all conditions. Stover and Glennon [1969] advocated a *freeway flyer* system in which buses operate in mixed traffic on freeways, with separate ramps and electronic surveillance of all traffic. Using English data, Smith [1973] compared this scheme with a subway and found the bus option to be better in all respects. He suggested that some rail lines should be torn up and replaced with motorways. Keeler and Small [1975] compared alternatives for the San Francisco Bay area and concluded there was no economic rationale for building the BART system. Bhatt [1976] did both a hypothetical analysis and a case study of Washington, D.C., and calculated that a busway surpassed a rail line in respect to both cost and travel time.

Boyd et al. [1973] did a thorough updating of the Meyer et al. study and included passengers' travel time in the tally of total costs. They concluded that buses operating on city streets are cheapest at low levels of demand, while buses operating on exclusive lanes are cheapest at higher levels. They found no conditions under which rail is the best alternative. They also claimed that rail transit causes more air pollution than buses because many riders use their automobiles to reach the stations.

Vuchic and Stanger [1973] did a different kind of analysis that supported rail. It was not framed in a hypothetical context, but compared two facilities that opened in 1969: the Lindenwold rail line and the Shirley Busway. The comparison covered three viewpoints—those of the passengers, the transit operator, and the community. The analysis included many qualitative factors and did not reduce the evaluation to finding the least-cost solution. Out of 17 characteristics examined, the Lindenwold line was rated superior on 13.

Vuchic and Olanipekun [1990] used the same approach to compare rail and bus in the same area, southern New Jersey. Again the Lindenwold line was used; it was compared with a 562-mile network of 26 bus routes operated by New Jersey Transit. Out of 19 attributes, the rail line was rated higher on 16. The authors noted that the services are really not comparable: The rail line mostly attracts commuters to Philadelphia and Camden (80 percent of the riders reach their station by automobile), while the bus network provides for local travel over a much larger area. Vuchic and Olanipekun concluded that "rail transit can in many cases represent the most effective and, in the long run, most economical transit mode for both high-density cities and low-density suburbs" [1990, p. 138].

It is difficult to draw firm conclusions from this conflicting evidence. Perhaps none of the studies was really objective; it appears that some of the researchers did have biases. Rail proponents have made several convincing points. Hypothetical analyses do not provide adequate guidance because any real decision depends on factors unique to the situation. The assumption of equivalent service levels is unrealistic because modes are inherently different. Transit ridership in a corridor is not fixed; a rail line will probably attract more passengers than bus service. Public choice involves many values, some of them unmeasurable, and economic analysis does not provide the ultimate answer.

In an attempt to shed light on a murky topic, there follows a discussion of the main points of comparison between rail and bus:

Passenger Capacity

Many believe that a rail line can carry more passengers than a busway; thus it provides a reserve to handle future increases in demand. The effective capacity of a line can be increased by running more trains and longer trains, although eventually limits are reached. The counterargument is that the few U.S. cities where demand requires such large capacity already have rail systems. Other cities will never need rail because they are growing in a dispersed pattern and will never have a sufficiently large volume of travel in any single corridor.

Capacity is usually measured by the maximum number of persons that can be moved on a single track or single lane in 1 hour. This is important in determining whether a line can handle peak-hour demand. Heavy rail lines do indeed have high capacity. The highest passenger volume measured in recent years was on the Queens–53d Street tunnel in New York City: 65,340 passengers in 1 hour. No other U.S. city comes close, but lines in Moscow, Tokyo, and Sao Paulo carry more than 50,000 persons in one track in the peak hour.

The capacity of a bus lane is much greater than generally assumed. Based on experiments conducted at the General Motors Proving Ground, a single lane can carry 1450 buses per hour [Rothery et al. 1964]. If each bus had 50 passengers, that would come to 72,500 passengers per hour. However, the figure was extrapolated from a measurement for 20 minutes made under ideal conditions, with no stops or delays. No bus lane has approached this number in the real world. The highest volume ever observed was 735 buses and 32,560 passengers in 1 hour in the Lincoln Tunnel between New Jersey and New York City.

Table 5-4 shows theoretical estimates of the capacity of three modes (automobiles, bus, and rail) as well as the highest values ever observed in the field, as reported in the *Highway Capacity Manual* [Transportation Research Board 1985].

Speed

Since a rail line has a separate right-of-way, trains are not bothered by traffic congestion and supposedly compete better with the automobile in speed. Buses running in mixed traffic are slow, and they get slower as the highway becomes more crowded. However, buses running on exclusive lanes are not affected by congestion; they are constrained only by the speed limit.

There are three different measures of speed in a transit system. The one that gets the most publicity is the *maximum speed* that vehicles are able to attain. However, the glamour of high speed is specious; this is not the most important measure.

Technology does not limit the maximum speed of either trains or buses. It is a matter of design objectives: Any vehicle is designed for a certain top speed. Modern railcars are designed for 70 to 80 miles per hour, but they seldom run at top speed because this is an inefficient use of electricity. Buses must comply with the speed limit, which is no

TABLE 5-4
CAPACITY OF URBAN TRANSPORTATION MODES
(Single Lane or Track)

Mode	Vehicles per hour	Passengers per vehicle	Passengers per hour
Theoretical			
Automobiles on freeway	2,000	1.5	3,000
Bus	1,400	50	70,000
Subway	400	200	80,000
Observed			
Automobiles on freeway	2,628	1.4*	3,680
Bus	600	46	27,600
Subway	320	204.2	65,340

*Estimated.
Locations for observed values:

    Automobiles on freeway: I-70 in Kansas City, MO. This was the highest average volume per lane ever observed on an urban freeway.
    Bus: Contraflow lane on I-495 in New Jersey, approaching Lincoln Tunnel.
    Subway: Queens–53d Street IND tunnel in New York City.

Source: Highway Capacity Manual, Special Report 209 (Washington: Transportation Research Board, 1985).

more than 55 miles per hour in urban areas. If you have ever been passed by a Greyhound bus on the highway, you know some buses can go much faster. Buses intended for use on city streets are usually geared for low speeds and may have a top speed of only 45 miles per hour. Buses intended for use on freeways or suburban highways are geared for higher speeds.

The *average vehicle speed* is based on the total time it takes a vehicle to cover a route from end to end. The critical factor is not the technology but the spacing of stops. Close spacing of stops means slow speed for both rail and bus. Rail systems potentially have higher average speeds, but an express bus on an exclusive lane can also maintain a high speed.

Actual average speeds are surprisingly low. Based on 1992 data for revenue vehicle-miles and revenue vehicle-hours [U.S. Federal Transit Administration 1993], heavy rail systems had speeds ranging from 19.8 miles per hour for Boston to 32.1 for San Francisco, with an average of 21.9. The national average for old streetcar systems was 11.2 miles per hour, while new light rail systems had an average of 17.7 miles per hour. For the 20 largest bus systems (listed in Table 5-3), the average speed was 11.9 miles per hour. This mostly reflects operation on city streets; speeds on HOV lanes would be much higher.

The *door-to-door speed* is the average speed for a traveler from origin to destination, including time spent walking and waiting for a transit vehicle. This is the most important measure because it is believed that most travelers base their modal choice on door-to-door time. This speed depends on several factors besides average vehicle speed. One is route coverage, which affects walking distance. Another is frequency of service, which determines waiting time. Whether one must transfer between routes also has an effect.

Rail has less advantage over bus by this measure because the access distance tends to be greater. On the average, rail passengers travel farther to reach a station, and a high portion of them use another mode (bus or automobile). Rail lines are widely spaced because they are expensive to build; the route coverage is sparse. A dense network of bus routes can be provided at relatively low cost, so most passengers walk a short distance to a bus stop.

Table 5-5 shows the results of travel surveys made in three large cities around 1960. Suburban railroad consistently had the highest speed of any mode. People traveling by subway-elevated had a faster door-to-door speed than those using bus or streetcar (all bus service was in mixed traffic; only Philadelphia had streetcars). The subway-elevated mode was a bit slower than travel by automobile, but close enough to be competitive in some circumstances.

These are averages for a sample of all persons in the metropolitan areas. People who are favorably located with respect to rail stations can enjoy high door-to-door speed. In the ideal case, you live next to a station, and your job is next to another station on the same line (hence no transfer). Then taking the train may be faster than driving a car. People in this situation will probably choose transit even if they own cars. However, urban areas have become so dispersed that there are not many people in this situation.

Costs

There is thorough coverage of transit costs in Chapter 14; only a few points relevant to the present discussion will be made here. There are three major categories of cost re-

TABLE 5-5
AVERAGE AIRLINE SPEED OF TRAVEL BY MODE IN SELECTED
TRANSPORTATION STUDIES, MILES PER HOUR

Mode	New York	Chicago	Philadelphia
Bus or streetcar	5.5	6.2	5.4
Subway-elevated	9.8	8.9	7.4
Suburban railroad	22.4	14.4	13.4
All transit	9.0	8.0	6.8
Automobile driver	11.7	11.1	11.4
Automobile passenger	11.0	10.4	11.3

Sources:
New York: Tri-State Transportation Commission. Unpublished tabulations of data collected in 1963–1964 home interview survey.
Chicago: *Chicago Area Transportation Study: Final Report,* vol. 2, *Data Projections,* July 1960, p. 123.
Philadelphia: *Penn Jersey Transportation Study: PJ Reports,* vol. 1, *The State of the Region,* April 1964, p. 82.

quired to install and operate a rail or bus line. The first is the *construction cost* involved in acquiring land and providing guideway, stations, and ancillary facilities.

A heavy rail system requires a huge capital investment. For example, BART (completed in 1974) cost $1.6 billion. The bill for the Washington Metro has reached $7 billion, and it is not finished. A light rail line is inexpensive if located in a city street (but then the service is slow). If it is on a separate right-of-way, the cost can be similar to that of heavy rail. In comparison, all types of bus improvements are relatively cheap.

The fair comparison is between the cost of building a rail line or a busway in the same location. Vertical alignment is a key factor. It is more expensive to build a rail line than a busway on the surface or on an elevated structure. This is partly because a rail line requires some things that a busway does not, such as power supply, signals, and a safety control system. However, in a tunnel it is cheaper to build a rail line for two reasons: (1) Buses have a larger cross section, and the tunnel must be larger. (2) Strong ventilation is needed to remove the diesel exhaust. The latter problem was avoided in Seattle by having the buses switch to electric power in the tunnel, but this was a very expensive solution.

The cost of building a heavy rail line usually exceeds $100 million per mile, although it depends on how much is underground (which costs much more). The most expensive project has been the Los Angeles subway; the first link came in at more than $300 million per mile. Costs of building light rail lines were given in Table 5-2. The incremental cost of adding HOV lanes to a freeway typically runs $3 million to $4 million per mile.

There is almost no capital cost in starting a bus route on an existing city street—only the installation of signs and passenger shelters. More significant bus improvements can be installed with modest capital investment, such as a concurrent flow lane, a contraflow lane, and express service.

Vehicle cost is another component of capital investment. Examples of recent prices for new vehicles are given in Chapter 14. Railcars cost much more than buses, but they have more seats and last longer. Current prices for both heavy and light rail vehicles exceed $1 million each. Standard-sized buses cost from $150,000 to $200,000, depending on accessories (such as air conditioning, automatic transmission, and a wheelchair lift).

Because of the differences between vehicles, comparison should be made on an annualized per-seat basis. Make the following assumptions: (1) A bus has 50 seats, an expected life of 10 years, and costs $180,000. (2) A railcar has 80 seats, an expected life of 30 years, and costs $1,100,000. (3) The interest rate is 8 percent. The calculations show that a bus has an annual cost per seat of $536, while for a railcar it is $1221.

Operating cost is the third category of cost. It is often claimed that rail has a lower operating cost, but this depends on the measures used. Some experts consider cost per vehicle-hour to be the critical measure because labor costs are so important. Cost per vehicle-mile is another common indicator. But some analysts point to cost per passenger or passenger-mile because railcars are larger and people tend to make longer trips on rail.

A simple comparison of national averages is biased toward the bus. The reason is that wage rates are usually higher in larger cities (because the cost of living is higher and large cities have stronger unions). All cities with rail are large cities with high wages, while a large share of bus operations occur in small cities with low wages.

TABLE 5-6
OPERATING EXPENSE RATIOS FOR THREE TRANSIT MODES
(Data for Fiscal Years Ending in 1992)

	Heavy rail	Light rail	Bus*
Per revenue vehicle-hour	$152.29	$150.29	$76.50
Per revenue vehicle-mile	6.96	11.02	6.42
Per passenger trip	1.61	1.63	1.61
Per passenger mile	0.33	0.44	0.47

*For the 20 largest systems in average weekday passengers.

Source: Transit Profiles; Agencies in Urbanized Areas Exceeding 200,000 Population; for the 1992 Section 15 Report Year (Washington: Federal Transit Administration, December 1993).

Table 5-6 shows four operating-expense ratios for 1992, based on all heavy and light rail systems and the 20 largest bus systems. Bus has a clear advantage in cost per vehicle-hour and per vehicle-mile. The three modes have virtually the same cost per passenger trip. Heavy rail is lowest in cost per passenger-mile, while light rail and bus are very close. Thus the data mostly favor bus.

Labor Requirements

It is argued that rail uses less labor input and that therefore rail costs are less vulnerable to inflation. This is an advantage of a capital-intensive mode: Once you have paid to construct a facility, that cost is fixed and does not increase. A labor-intensive mode faces rising operating costs in the future. This point has been raised because historically transit labor costs have risen rapidly, at a greater rate than the cost of living.

However, the evidence shows that rail has a minor advantage over bus in this respect. It is true that one person operating a subway train can carry a 1000 passengers, while a bus driver can carry perhaps 100 persons (in an articulated bus). But a rail system requires many more workers who are not vehicle operators, for the maintenance of vehicles and right-of-way, management, and policing. Rail systems are more complicated and liable to failure; even the computers have required a great deal of attention.

Based on data reported for 1990 [U.S. Federal Transit Administration 1991], labor expenses (including fringe benefits) made up the following percentages of total operating expenses:

Old heavy rail systems	81.9 percent
New heavy rail systems	70.2 percent
Old light rail systems	82.7 percent
New light rail systems	62.3 percent
Twenty largest bus systems	80.2 percent

Thus, old rail systems have no advantage over bus, but new rail systems are somewhat less labor-intensive. This is mostly because new rail systems use either automatic or self-service fare collection.

Energy and Air Pollution

Most people assume that rail is more energy-efficient because a train carries large loads of people. However, many studies claim the opposite. The result depends on assumptions about the average passenger load (the comparison is usually based on energy per passenger), and one can manipulate assumptions to alter the result. Still, a majority of analysts have concluded that a full accounting of energy consumption indicates that the bus mode is more efficient.

The key is the huge amount of energy consumed in building a rail system; modern construction is very energy-intensive. Further, rail has some inherent inefficiencies. There is a sizable loss in transmitting electricity from the power plant to the train motor.

From a strategic standpoint, rail may be preferable because buses run on diesel fuel, a petroleum product. The electricity that powers rail lines comes from several sources, occasionally including petroleum. But it is possible to generate all the electricity needed without petroleum. On the other hand, there is currently much research on alternative fuels for buses.

Many people think that buses create more air pollution than trains; this is often cited as an advantage of rail. The dirty exhaust produced by the bus diesel engines is obvious, while you cannot see anything coming from trains. Still, one study found that rail systems cause more air pollution [Boyd et al. 1973]. Note that most ways to generate electricity pollute the air. Of course, the pollution occurs at the power plants, which may be located miles outside the city. The type of fuel makes a difference: Natural gas is cleaner than coal; hydroelectric and nuclear power cause no air pollution, but they create other environmental problems.

Energy and air pollution issues are discussed further in Chapter 11.

Other Advantages of Rail

Planners believe that a major advantage of a rail line is its impact on land-use development. It is argued that a rail line is a permanent facility in which a lot of money has been invested, so it is unlikely to disappear. In contrast, a bus route can be changed overnight at little cost. Real estate developers are eager to build next to rail stations, but they pay no attention to bus stops. The evidence for this argument is discussed in Chapter 10.

Most studies have dealt with heavy rail lines. There has been little research on busways, which *are* permanent facilities. Cervero concluded that the potential for light rail to affect land use is "moderately high, where there are pro-development policy environments and other complementary forces" [1984, p. 133]. However, often policy-makers put more emphasis on costs. Low-cost alignments can be poor locations for development (e.g., much of the Tijuana Trolley passes through industrial areas and scrubland).

Rail systems have some operational advantages. Everyone agrees that trains give a more comfortable ride than buses. Steel rails are smoother than pavement, and trains are less likely to get into stop-and-go traffic.

The length of trains can be varied, which enables better adjustment to changes in demand. Many systems run longer trains during the peak period than during the rest of the day. Adding cars to a train increases capacity with little increase in operating cost, since no additional personnel are needed.

Boarding is faster in heavy rail systems because the stations have high platforms and each car has three or four doors. This is valuable in high-demand situations, where delays from boarding can cripple the average speed. Thus rail systems can handle large passenger volumes in small stations. Buses would need huge stations to accommodate similar volumes. The Port Authority Bus Terminal in New York has handled 730 buses and 32,600 persons in 1 hour, but it covers a whole city block and has 184 loading docks on three levels.

As one would expect, rail lines on separate guideway have a lower rate of collisions per vehicle-mile than do buses. Injuries on rail systems occur mostly at stations and mostly to transit workers. Buses have a fairly high accident rate per vehicle-mile, but a low rate per passenger-mile. Both modes have much lower rates than automobiles; shifting travelers from cars to transit greatly reduces the accident toll.

Other Advantages of Bus

Bus transit's other advantages stem from its flexibility. First, buses can pass each other; a stalled vehicle causes inconvenience for only one load of passengers. A train that breaks down blocks the track and may interrupt service on the entire line. Thousands of riders may be delayed.

Second, the routing of buses is more flexible, except where there are permanent physical facilities like a busway. A transit authority can drop, modify, or start routes at any time. The importance of this point has probably been exaggerated; transit operators change bus routes infrequently because they tend to lose passengers when they do.

Even a busway has some flexibility. If use is low, the lanes can be given to automobiles and trucks. There is little expense in making such a conversion. This is not true for rail; if a rail line attracts so few travelers as to be useless, it is a white elephant. However, no urban rail lines in the United States have been abandoned since the 1950s.

To summarize, both rail and bus systems have particular advantages, and neither dominates in all respects. The choice should depend on the conditions of the individual situation and should be made after thorough planning studies and public debate. The major factor working against rail is its construction cost; the major factor in favor is its prestige value. Probably the romantic appeal of rail has swayed too many people; there are good bus alternatives that have not been selected as often as they should be.

EVALUATION OF BART

The most publicized transit project in recent decades is San Francisco's BART system, which opened in 1972. It also may be the most controversial. Rail proponents hail it as a great success. Others have been very critical; Peter Hall [1982] made it a case in his book *Great Planning Disasters*.

The first critique to receive national attention was written by Melvin Webber [1976], professor of planning at the University of California, Berkeley. Webber was in charge of a research project on the impact of BART; his overall conclusion was that BART was a mistake. He had been an early advocate of BART and was personally involved in planning it in the 1950s.

Three objectives guided the design of BART's network: (1) to promote growth of the Bay Area's central business district (defined as a tripartite center containing the CBDs of San Francisco, Oakland, and Berkeley) and to concentrate other development in subcenters at the stations; (2) to reduce highway traffic, especially on the San Francisco–Oakland Bay Bridge, by pulling drivers out of their cars; and (3) to be financially viable.

The resulting plan resembled a suburban railroad system more than a central-city heavy rail system. The average spacing between stations is 2.5 miles, which means most travelers take a bus or use their cars to reach the station. The suburban stations are surrounded by huge parking lots. Emphasis on high speed dominated the design of the system (Webber said this was the biggest mistake). While the trains are fast, most people spend so much time in access and waiting that door-to-door travel times do not compete with those for driving.

Here are Webber's findings on how well the objectives were attained:

1 The effect on metropolitan development was mixed. An office building boom occurred along Market Street in San Francisco, under which BART runs. This was aided by two large redevelopment projects that created much vacant land adjacent to Market Street. In the centers of Oakland and Berkeley, there was little new construction. There was almost no nonresidential development around suburban stations. Webber thought that the overall impact of BART was to encourage suburban sprawl, rather than to concentrate development.

2 There was little effect on highway traffic. Only 35 percent of BART riders formerly made the trip by car (compared with a forecast of 61 percent). Half of the transbay riders switched from buses. There was a large increase in the total amount of transbay travel by both automobile and transit. The impact on Bay Bridge traffic was "so slight as to be undetectable" [Webber 1976, p. 87].

3 The plan called for property taxes to retire the bonds which financed construction, while fare revenues were projected to cover operating costs and produce a surplus. Because of cost overruns, the original $792 million bond issue was inadequate; in 1969 the state legislature authorized another $150 million in bonds, which are being retired by a sales tax. BART also received $305 million in federal grants to purchase rolling stock, which was not in the original plan. Fare revenues have never exceeded operating expenses; BART has always operated at a deficit.

Webber found that BART passengers were heavily subsidized: On the average, each rider paid a fare of $0.72 and received a subsidy of $3.76. It would be cheaper to transport all BART riders by automobile. It would be cheapest, though, to carry them on buses. Webber also raised the equity issue. BART riders tended to have higher-than-average incomes, while the subsidies came from regressive sales and property taxes. Webber concluded that "the poor are paying and the rich are riding" [1976, p. 93].

The main problem was that not enough people used BART; patronage was way below the prediction. It was forecast that BART would carry 258,500 trips per day in 1975. In 1976, it actually carried 131,370 trips per day (51 percent). This is important because the justification for BART was based on the forecast; this is what voters believed when they approved the plan in 1962.

There were also equipment problems. There was much embarrassment on the day BART opened when a train plowed through a barrier at the end of the track (fortunately no one was hurt). The system was designed "from the ground up," rather than by using existing hardware, and it was supposed to bring a quantum leap in transit technology. It proved impossible to accomplish so many innovations at once. The average speed of trains has never reached the goal of 50 miles per hour. Many Bay Area residents considered BART unreliable and unsafe.

In 1979 a fire started in a train midway through the tunnel under the bay [Demoro 1979]. It turned out that materials used in the car interiors were flammable and generated poisonous gases when they burned. To evacuate the passengers, power had to be turned off. Firefighters hiked more than 2 miles through the tunnel to reach the train. One firefighter died and 46 persons were injured. The tube was closed for 11 weeks. After that, a fire safety aide was assigned to ride every train through the tunnel. In 1989 the State Public Utilities Commission completed 10 years of investigating the fire and ordered some additional safety measures.

In defense of BART, note that the plan was prepared and adopted at a time when building more highways was the popular approach to the urban transportation problem. The decision ran counter to the national trend. Further, it came before any federal transit aid was available; all financing was expected to come from state and local sources.

It is now many years since Webber's critique, and in that time, ridership has grown considerably. From 131,370 trips per day in 1976, it increased as follows:

1981	162,000
1982	180,000
1984	210,000
1986	215,000
1989	219,000
1990	254,800
1992	260,000

There have been several fare increases, causing temporary declines, but patronage has always rebounded. However, the 1992 figure barely exceeds the forecast of 258,000 made for 1975. By comparison, the Washington Metro averaged 660,000 riders per day in 1992.

The operational bugs were worked out long ago, and BART is now regarded as reliable by most people. Speeds have increased, and peak-hour headways have been reduced. The financial picture has improved: Fare revenues now cover about 50 percent of operating expenses, which is a good performance by national standards.

BART turned out to be a tremendous boon to the Bay Area in the 1989 earthquake, when the Bay Bridge was damaged and closed to traffic. Ridership doubled for a time, and even after the bridge reopened, ridership remained higher than previously. Tourists and other visitors have always had a good impression of BART; now Bay Area residents regard it more favorably.

BART has begun a $491 million expansion program that will nearly double the system's capacity. This includes installation of a new central computer to permit lower headways, purchase of 150 new cars, and construction of a storage yard and maintenance facility. There are plans for several extensions that will add 52 route-miles by the year 2000. In 1988 BART reached agreement with San Mateo County for an extension to the San Francisco Airport. Originally the county had chosen to stay out of the BART district.

No one questions that BART has enhanced the image of San Francisco and made it more attractive to business, tourists, and conventions. Perhaps BART was a luxury and buses could have provided increased transit service more economically. But U.S. consumers regularly pay more to acquire goods of higher quality than is necessary to satisfy their basic needs, and San Francisco was more able than most cities to afford a luxury.

QUESTIONS

1 Should any more rail transit systems be built in the United States? If you think so, what cities would be good candidates?

2 Why is the electric streetcar making a comeback as light rail transit? What advantages does it enjoy compared to heavy rail systems? To buses? Do you think light rail is a good option for medium-sized cities?

3 Suppose a city decides not to build a rail system but wants to provide better transit service. What measures could be taken to improve and expand bus service? Evaluate each as to cost, ease of implementation, and which riders would benefit.

4 It is claimed that transit officials, city planners, and politicians tend to favor rail transit, while academic researchers usually criticize rail projects and favor bus transit. What is the explanation for this?

5 Why is the high speed potentially attainable by trains a deceptive indicator of the quality of service they provide?

6 Do you agree with Melvin Webber that building the BART system in the San Francisco Bay Area was a mistake? If so, why is it being extended? Discuss the good and bad points about the experience with BART.

REFERENCES

Bhatt, Kiran: "Comparative Analysis of Urban Transportation Costs," *Transportation Research Record*, no. 559 (1976), pp. 101–125.

Billheimer, John W.: "The Santa Monica Freeway Diamond Lanes: Evaluation Overview," *Transportation Research Record*, no. 663 (1978), pp. 8–16.

Black, Alan: "The Recent Popularity of Light Rail Transit in North America," *Journal of Planning Education and Research*, vol. 12, no. 2 (Winter 1993), pp. 150–159.

Boyd, J. Hayden, Norman J. Asher, and Elliot S. Wetzler: *Evaluation of Rail Rapid Transit and Express Bus Service in the Urban Commuter Market* (Washington: Government Printing Office, 1973).

Cervero, Robert: "Light Rail Transit and Urban Development," *Journal of American Planning Association*, vol. 50, no. 2 (Spring 1984), pp. 133–147.

Deen, Thomas B., and Donald H. James: "Relative Costs of Bus and Rail Transit Systems," *Highway Research Record*, no. 293 (1969), pp. 33–53.

Demoro, Harre: "Fire Blackens BART Image," *Mass Transit*, vol. 6, no. 7 (July 1979), pp. 12–15, 53–62.

———— and John N. Harder: *Light Rail Transit on the West Coast* (New York: Quadrant Press, 1989).

Diamant, E. S., et al.: *Light Rail Transit: A State of the Art Review* (Washington: Government Printing Office, Spring 1976).

Dupree, Harry: *Urban Transportation: The New Town Solution* (Aldershot, U.K.: Gower Publishing Company, 1987).

Ercolano, James M.: "Limited-Stop Bus Operations: An Evaluation," *Transportation Research Record*, no. 994 (1984), pp. 24–29.

Fisher, Ronald J.: "Shirley Highway Express Bus on Freeway Demonstration Project," *Highway Research Record*, no. 415 (1972), pp. 25–37.

Gomez-Ibanez, Jose A.: "A Dark Side to Light Rail? The Experience of Three New Transit Systems," *Journal of American Planning Association*, vol. 51, no. 3 (Summer 1985), pp. 337–351.

Goodman, Leon, and Carl S. Selinger: "The Exclusive Bus Lane on the New Jersey Approach to the Lincoln Tunnel," *Highway Research Record*, no. 415 (1972), pp. 38–48.

Gray, George E.: "Statistical Summary of Operating North American Commuter Rail Services," *Transportation Research Record*, no. 1349 (1992), pp. 62–65.

Hall, Peter: *Great Planning Disasters* (Berkeley: University of California Press, 1982), chap. 5.

Hamer, Andrew Marshall: *The Selling of Rail Rapid Transit* (Lexington, MA: D.C. Heath, 1976).

Johnston, Robert A., Daniel Sperling, Mark A. DeLuchi, and Steve Tracy: "Politics and Technical Uncertainty in Transportation Investment Analysis," *Transportation Research*, vol. 21A, no. 6 (November 1987), pp. 459–475.

Kain, John F.: "Choosing the Wrong Technology: Or How to Spend Billions and Reduce Transit Use," *Journal of Advanced Transportation*, vol. 21, no. 3 (Winter 1988), pp. 197–213.

————: "Deception in Dallas: Strategic Misrepresentation in Rail Transit Promotion and Evaluation," *Journal of the American Planning Association*, vol. 56, no. 2 (Spring 1990), pp. 184–196.

Keeler, Theodore E., and Kenneth A. Small: *The Full Costs of Urban Transport, Part III: Automobile Costs and Final Intermodal Cost Comparisons* (Berkeley: Institute of Urban and Regional Development, University of California, 1975).

Meyer, John R., John F. Kain, and Martin Wohl: *The Urban Transportation Problem* (Cambridge, MA: Harvard University Press, 1965), chaps. 8 to 11.

Middleton, William D.: "Commuting in the Southland," *North American Commuter Rail 1994* (Pasadena, CA: Pentrex, 1994), pp. 20–26.

Miller, D. R., B. C. Goodwin, G. A. Hoffman, and W. H. T. Holden: "Cost Comparison of Busway and Railway Rapid Transit," *Highway Research Record*, no. 459 (1973), pp. 1–12.

Page, John H.: "I-66 Case Study: Evolution Process of Tomorrow's Urban Highways," *Transportation Quarterly*, vol. 37, no. 4 (October 1983), pp. 493–510.

Phraner, S. David: "Vintage Trolleys: A National Overview," *Transportation Research Record*, no. 1361 (1992), pp. 323–329.

Pickrell, Don H.: "How Many More Rail Systems Does the U.S. Need?" Paper presented at annual conference of the Association of Collegiate Schools of Planning, New York City, October 1984.

————: *Urban Rail Transit Projects: Forecast versus Actual Ridership and Costs* (Cambridge, MA: Transportation Systems Center, U.S. Department of Transportation, October 1989).

————: "A Desire Named Streetcar: Fantasy and Fact in Rail Transit Planning," *Journal of the American Planning Association*, vol. 58, no. 2 (Spring 1992), pp. 158–176.

Pushkarev, Boris S., with Jeffrey M. Zupan and Robert S. Cumella: *Urban Rail in America: An Exploration of Criteria for Fixed-Guideway Transit* (Bloomington: Indiana University Press, 1982).

Richmond, Jonathan E. D.: "Theories of Symbolism, Metaphor and Myth, and the Development of Western Rail Passenger Systems, or, Penis Envy in Los Angeles." Paper presented at 31st annual meeting of the Association of Collegiate Schools of Planning, Portland, OR, October 1989.

Rothery, R., R. Silver, R. Herman, and C. Torner: "Analysis of Experiments on Single-Lane Bus Flow," *Operations Research*, vol. 12, no. 6 (November-December 1964), pp. 913–933.

Schumann, John W.: "Status of North American LRT systems: 1992 Update," *Transportation Research Record*, no. 1361 (1992), pp. 3–13.

Scott, P. D.: "Fort Worth's Privately Owned Subway System," *Light Rail Transit: Planning and Technology*, Special Report 182 (Washington: Transportation Research Board, 1978), pp. 88–91.

Smith, Edward: "An Economic Comparison of Urban Railways and Express Bus Service," *Journal of Transport Economics and Policy*, vol. 7, no. 1 (January 1973), pp. 20–31.

Stover, Vergil G., and John G. Glennon: "A System for Bus Rapid Transit on Urban Freeways," *Traffic Quarterly*, vol. 23, no. 4 (October 1969), pp. 465–484.

Transportation Research Board: *Highway Capacity Manual*, Special Report 209 (Washington: Transportation Research Board, 1985).

Turnbull, Katherine F.: "Image of Rail Transit," *Transportation Research Record*, no. 1308 (1991), pp. 3–7.

——— and James W. Hanks: *A Description of High-Occupancy Vehicle Facilities in North America* (Washington: U.S. Department of Transportation, July 1990).

U.S. Federal Transit Administration: *Data Tables for the 1990 Section 15 Report Year* (Washington: Federal Transit Administration, December 1991).

———: *Transit Profiles; Agencies in Urbanized Areas Exceeding 200,000 Population; for the 1992 Section 15 Report Year* (Washington: Federal Transit Administration, December 1993).

Vuchic, Vukan R.: *Urban Public Transportation: Systems and Technology* (Englewood Cliffs, NJ: Prentice-Hall, 1981).

——— and Olayinka A. Olanipekun: "Lindenwold Rail Line and New Jersey Transit Buses: A Comparison," *Transportation Research Record*, no. 1266 (1990), pp. 123–138.

——— and R. M. Stanger: "Lindenwold Rail Line and Shirley Busway: A Comparison," *Highway Research Record*, no. 459 (1973), pp. 13–28.

Wachs, Martin: "Technique versus Advocacy in Forecasting: A Study of Rail Rapid Transit," *Urban Resources*, vol. 4, no. 1 (Fall 1986), pp. 23–30.

———: "Ethics and Advocacy in Forecasting for Public Policy," *Business and Professional Ethics Journal*, vol. 9, nos. 1, 2 (Spring, Summer 1990), pp. 141–157.

Webber, Melvin M.: "The BART Experience—What Have We Learned?" *The Public Interest*, no. 45 (Fall 1976), pp. 79–108.

6

PARATRANSIT

The term *paratransit* was coined in the 1970s to cover certain types of operations which are midway between conventional transit and the private automobile [Kirby et al. 1974]. They are similar to transit in that they are services available to the public. They are similar to the private automobile in that they operate on demand—not following a fixed route or fixed time schedule.

One type of paratransit is familiar: the taxi, which can be traced back to the hackney coach of the 17th century. Other forms did not become well known until the 1970s, when the federal government promoted paratransit as an innovative approach. Some experts think it will eventually replace conventional transit except in a few older cities that retain high densities and a strong central business district (CBD). Paratransit appears to be more economical and efficient in low-density and suburban settings.

Some paratransit services are limited to elderly and disabled persons. This application of the concept will be discussed in more detail in Chapter 13. This chapter explains the various types of paratransit without regard to the characteristics of users.

DIAL-A-RIDE

Definition and Service Patterns

Several terms are basically synonymous with *dial-a-ride: dial-a-bus, demand-responsive transit,* and *demand-actuated transit.* All describe a type of service that is more flexible than conventional transit service. Service can be demand-responsive in two ways: (1) routing—the vehicle goes exactly where the passenger wants (door-to-door service)—and (2) scheduling—the vehicle arrives when desired by the passenger. Of course, taxis provide exactly this kind of service. Most people reserve the term *dial-a-ride* for systems in which passengers going to different destinations may share the vehicle.

A dial-a-ride system has a defined service area rather than specific routes. It picks up and delivers riders within the service area, but does not go outside it. There are three service patterns:

1 *Many-to-one:* Passengers are picked up anywhere but are delivered to only one place, such as a major employment site. This is usually paired with one-to-many service.

2 *Many-to-few:* Passengers are taken to only a few places, such as downtown, a shopping center, and a hospital. This would be paired with few-to-many service.

3 *Many-to-many:* Origins and destinations may be anywhere in the service area.

Some operations vary the service patterns depending on the time of day. For example, in the morning peak period, passengers are only taken to a railroad station, and in the evening peak, they are only picked up at the station. During the rest of the day, many-to-many service is offered.

Some systems attempt to fill requests that are telephoned to a dispatcher as soon as possible, but some wait time is inevitable. Many systems require that reservations be made in advance, often the previous day. Most will provide service on a regular, subscription basis. For example, a person might be picked up every morning at the same time to go to work or every Thursday to go to a supermarket.

Dial-a-ride is intended for situations where the demand is too low for conventional transit service. These may be low-density areas such as suburbs, small cities and towns that have no scheduled bus service, or rural areas. Sometimes automobile ownership levels are high in these areas, but there are still some people without cars. Another approach is to offer dial-a-ride service during evening and weekend hours as a substitute for scheduled bus service that operates in the daytime Monday through Friday. This scheme has been successful at the Tidewater Transportation District in Virginia [Echols 1985].

The Vehicles

Most dial-a-ride services do not use the standard transit bus, which has at least 45 seats and costs from $175,000 upward. Instead they use smaller vehicles of four types [Pennsylvania Department of Transportation 1988]:

1 A standard van, which has 5 to 15 seats and costs $12,000 to $18,000 (prices are given as of 1988). This vehicle has the advantage that it can be purchased off the shelf, but it has a short service life (3 to 5 years) and its low roof makes getting in and out awkward.

2 A modified van, which usually has a higher roof and sometimes a lower floor and wider body. It has 9 to 16 seats and costs $22,000 to $25,000. It can be equipped with a wheelchair lift. The disadvantages are that it gets poor fuel mileage and that a raised roof makes it unstable in high winds. See Figure 6-1.

FIGURE 6-1
A typical paratransit vehicle. This modified van carries ten passengers and is equipped with a wheelchair lift at the rear. It provides demand-responsive service to senior citizens in Lawrence, Kansas.

3 A body-on-chassis vehicle, of which the best-known example is the standard school bus. This is made by putting a bus body on top of a chassis designed for a van, light-duty truck, or motor home. It has 12 to 30 seats and costs $35,000 to $45,000. It is more durable than vans, with a service life of 5 to 7 years, and has no significant disadvantages.

4 A small bus. This is designed like a standard bus, with the same chassis and diesel engine, but with smaller dimensions. Typically there are 18 to 35 seats. This is a very durable vehicle, with a service life of 10 to 15 years, and it has more interior space than the other types. The principal disadvantage is its price, which ranges from $100,000 to $120,000.

These vehicles have many other applications than dial-a-ride. One can normally observe a variety of all four types circulating at any major airport to carry travelers to hotels, car-rental agencies, parking lots, etc.

Background

There are several dial-a-ride services of long standing operated by private carriers. Davenport, Iowa, has had dial-a-ride since 1934, and Hicksville, New York, has had it since 1961 [Davis et al. 1976]. But these were isolated cases that received little publicity.

Interest in dial-a-ride increased when UMTA funded some demonstrations in the

1960s. The first was the Peoria Premium Special, a many-to-one subscription service to the Caterpillar Tractor plant in Peoria, Illinois, which started in December 1964 [Roos et al. 1971]. It was successful, and Peoria City Lines continued it after the demonstration period ended in February 1966. Unfortunately, the company went out of business in 1970, which terminated the service. A similar demonstration called the *Maxicab* operated in Flint, Michigan, from 1968 to 1971, but it was less successful. In 1970, UMTA funded an experiment on one bus route in Mansfield, Ohio, in which customers could telephone the driver and arrange to be picked up anywhere within four blocks of the route.

In 1969, UMTA gave a research grant to the Massachusetts Institute of Technology (MIT) for Project CARS (computer-aided routing system). The primary objective was to develop a computer program to automatically dispatch and route vehicles. It was believed that a good routing program was the key to making dial-a-ride a success. This was not an easy task: The program should operate in real time and respond to a telephone request by deciding what bus should deviate from its previous route to pick up the person (which delays passengers already on board). The MIT researchers could not find an algorithm that would optimize routing, but they developed a heuristic procedure that they believed would perform well [Roos et al. 1971].

The MIT people recommended a major field demonstration and evaluated possible sites. UMTA selected Haddonfield, New Jersey, a suburb of Philadelphia [Gwynn et al. 1973]. The area was served by the Lindenwold line, and it was thought that dial-a-ride would be an attractive feeder service to the high-speed rail line. UMTA sponsored the demonstration from 1972 to 1975. When federal funding stopped, the state of New Jersey had the opportunity to take over, but decided not to. The system was then abandoned.

MIT was not involved in the Haddonfield project, which was supervised by the MITRE Corporation. Most of the dispatching was manual. Near the end of the demonstration, a computer was used to automate processing of customer requests and dispatching of vehicles, but it received only limited testing. Later computer-based control systems were used in dial-a-ride systems in Santa Clara County, California, and Ann Arbor, Michigan [Wilson and Colvin 1977].

Meanwhile, officials of the Rochester-Genesee Regional Transportation District in New York had become interested in dial-a-ride through contacts with MIT. A small system was successfully implemented in Batavia, a town of 17,000 population 35 miles south of Rochester. In 1973, a larger test was begun in an area of about 10 square miles in northwest Rochester and the suburb of Greece, where fixed bus routes were replaced by dial-a-bus. UMTA began funding this project in 1975, with MIT providing overall management.

Rochester developed into another major demonstration of dial-a-ride. Service was extended to the suburbs of Irondequoit, Brighton, and Henrietta. Among several experiments attempted were subscription service to work sites, special services to schools and shopping centers, services for the elderly and disabled, and feeders to fixed bus routes. As might be expected when so many innovations are being tested, various problems occurred which caused the quality of service to deteriorate. While at first ridership increased, eventually it fell off sharply.

At first the Rochester system dispatched vehicles manually. Later a computer program based on the work at MIT was introduced, but it went through a shakedown period of several months, during which service quality was affected. Finally the program was debugged and operated successfully, but by then the dial-a-ride system had lost many of its customers. A comparison of computer dispatching and manual dispatching showed that the former had some advantages, but overall productivity was about the same for both. The level of demand was too low to give computerized dispatching a true test.

The Orange County Transit District in California began a demonstration of dial-a-ride service with computer dispatching in 1980 [Reinke et al. 1987]. It purchased computer software from Rochester and attempted to adapt it to a much larger operation. The transit district used 100 vehicles to cover an area of 350 square miles. The experiment was not considered successful, because the automated system was more expensive to operate than manual dispatching and a human scheduler had to override the computer in 20 to 25 percent of cases.

Present Situation

Despite these early setbacks, the dial-a-ride concept has become popular, and today there are hundreds of systems all over the country. Most are small, using less than 20 vehicles, and dispatching is done manually. They are operated by transit agencies, private nonprofit organizations, and sometimes for-profit firms under contract. Subsidization is the rule; rarely do passenger fares cover costs, and some services are free. However, they are popular and ridership has increased in most places. Hence there has been political support for them, and subsidies continue.

The majority of systems are limited to special clients like the elderly and disabled. Only a minority are available to the general public. Usually these are replacements for fixed bus routes that were abandoned because of low patronage. Often the new services lose less money than the older ones did. But ridership is lower, and the passengers tend to be different from those who rode previously.

The American Public Transit Association (APTA) began compiling statistics on demand-responsive transit in 1984. The national annual total of passengers rose from 62 million in 1984 to 79 million in 1992 [American Public Transit Association 1993]. This is less than 1 percent of all transit passengers in the United States. However, the total is probably incomplete, as many operations are small and may not report data to APTA.

Many of the systems now use microcomputers to aid in some of their functions, such as reservations, scheduling, dispatching, and record keeping. An article by Stone et al. [1993] lists 15 software packages that are available. Optimization of routing remains a challenge, but it may become common in the future. Stone et al. note that "real-time, shared-ride scheduling and dispatching are not . . . a widespread operational reality for paratransit" [p. 3].

Operating Results

There are several measures of the performance of a dial-a-ride system. One is *vehicle productivity*—the average number of passengers picked up per vehicle-hour. Usually this index is well below 10, whereas a value of 15 to 20 is needed to break even financially. Only subscription services attain the desired range; they are more efficient because they take the same route every day. Abkowitz and Ott [1980] made a study of six dial-a-ride systems and found that vehicle productivity ranged from 3.0 to 4.9.

Fares have generally been kept low to attract passengers, and substantial subsidies are required. In the Haddonfield experiment, the average fare was $0.50, while the average cost per passenger was more than $2.00. In the Abkowitz and Ott study, revenue per passenger ranged from $0.65 to $1.15, but the operating cost per passenger ranged from $2.45 to $11.88.

The situation has not changed much in recent years. Table 6-1 shows some operating statistics for 20 of the larger demand-responsive systems in the country for fiscal years ending in 1992. Vehicle productivity ranged from 1.44 to 5.31, with an average of 2.92.

TABLE 6-1
SELECTED DEMAND-RESPONSIVE TRANSIT SYSTEMS
(Data for Fiscal Years Ending in 1992)

Area	Annual passenger trips	Operating cost per passenger	Passengers per veh. hour	Average passenger load*
Allentown	269,464	$ 8.84	3.25	1.83
Ann Arbor	327,290	7.94	2.73	0.51
Chicago	1,566,410	9.01	4.08	1.36
Dallas	803,923	14.61	1.44	1.36
Detroit	1,019,773	9.65	4.49	2.22
Hartford	456,590	9.45	3.49	2.14
Honolulu	535,976	8.02	2.52	2.74
Houston	663,046	12.53	2.20	1.11
Los Angeles	2,365,895	8.74	4.85	1.29
Miami	1,110,617	11.98	2.16	1.14
Milwaukee	713,338	9.63	1.86	0.78
Norfolk	231,482	9.32	3.28	1.82
Orange County	1,742,633	6.23	5.31	2.14
Pittsburgh	2,018,730	9.86	2.30	0.93
Portland	410,746	12.93	2.92	2.11
Rochester	136,759	11.18	3.25	1.59
St. Louis	288,263	18.34	2.78	1.28
San Antonio	677,842	12.37	2.06	1.39
San Diego	566,148	9.70	3.37	1.78
Worcester	320,412	9.23	3.48	1.26
Means	811,267	9.88	2.92	1.39

*This is the ratio of passenger miles to vehicle revenue miles. It represents the average number of passengers on a vehicle during the time it is in service.
Source: Transit Profiles; Agencies in Urbanized Areas Exceeding 200,000 Population; for the 1992 Section 15 Report Year (Washington: Federal Transit Administration, December 1993).

The operating cost per passenger ranged from $6.23 to $18.34, with an average of $9.88. Fares are not shown, but they continue to be low, often no more than $1.

Another performance indicator is the *level-of-service index*, which is the ratio of request-to-arrival time by dial-a-ride to door-to-door travel time by automobile. The lower the ratio, the better the service. Experience shows that this index is usually in a range of 2.0 to 3.0, which means that dial-a-ride competes poorly with the private automobile.

The rightmost column of Table 6-1 shows the average number of passengers on a vehicle while it is in service. These numbers are very low, pointing up the basic inefficiency of such systems. A few of the figures are less than 1, meaning that a large portion of the time the vehicles are empty.

Legal and Institutional Problems

Dial-a-ride services must be operated or sponsored by a public agency to qualify for Federal Transportation Administration (FTA) grants, with one exception: Under section 16(b)(2) of the Mass Transportation Act, FTA makes grants to nonprofit private organizations that serve the elderly and disabled. Many services are operated by private firms (often taxi companies) under contract to public or nonprofit agencies.

Under section 13(c), transit workers are protected against losing their jobs or job rights because of introducing a federally funded dial-a-ride service. This has been a problem in some places. Dial-a-ride may compete with both taxis and conventional bus service and take passengers away from them. Cutbacks in regular bus service could make some workers superfluous.

The effect of section 13(c) on taxi drivers is problematical. The statute refers to "workers affected," but in practice the Department of Labor (DOL) has applied it only to transit workers. After a 1977 dispute in Pittsburgh, the DOL ruled that a taxi company falls within the definition of transit if at least 15 percent of its revenues come from shared-ride service [Gilbert and Samuels 1982]. If that criterion is met, the taxi drivers are protected.

Frequently dial-a-ride uses nonunion drivers, who receive lower wages than unionized bus drivers. At first, leaders of the transit workers' unions expressed support for the dial-a-ride concept, thinking it would expand job opportunities for members. They changed their position after many of the jobs went to nonunion workers. It is certainly a policy issue whether to encourage growth of a group of transit workers who receive less pay and benefits than those obtained by the unions.

Conclusions

Early expectations for dial-a-ride were high because of the idea of computer-controlled many-to-many service. It now appears that the potential of this approach was exaggerated. Vehicle productivity never reached the levels that were predicted. The publicity given to computer dispatching in the 1970s can be seen as part of the faith of UMTA officials in technological breakthroughs.

Nonetheless, dial-a-ride has found a permanent niche in public transportation, and the services are very useful to many people. While the services are not particularly efficient, they often serve travelers who have no other options. There are hundreds of dial-a-ride systems serving the elderly and disabled. Most have small service areas and use manual dispatching. However, computer software is being used increasingly and is being gradually improved.

There are some many-to-one systems serving the general public; often they act as feeders to rail lines or fixed bus routes. Many-to-one service achieves higher productivity than many-to-many service does. Subscription service gets high marks for efficiency and can even be profitable. Services that try to respond immediately to phone calls are quite costly; taxis handle this market better. A majority of dial-a-ride systems require advance reservations.

The market for dial-a-ride is bound to increase substantially. For one thing, the number of elderly persons in the United States is growing, and many services are targeted on them. The Americans with Disabilities Act of 1990 (discussed further in Chapter 13) requires transit agencies to offer complementary paratransit service in the same area as fixed routes, which means many new services will be started. Further, dial-a-ride may be the best way to provide transit service in suburban areas; it is one approach to the problem of suburban gridlock described in Chapter 4.

TAXI

Taxis play an important role in urban transportation in the United States. In numerous places, the taxi is the only form of public transportation available. More than 3000 communities have taxi service, compared to about 1000 that have transit service. See Figure 6-2.

Although statistics are not very complete, the general dimensions of the taxi industry are as follows:

1 It carries about one-third as many passengers as conventional transit.

2 Its total revenue is about twice that of conventional transit. This highlights one of its major characteristics: It is expensive.

3 It operates about twice as many vehicle-miles as conventional transit. This is another characteristic: It is inefficient.

4 It employs almost as many workers as conventional transit. A third characteristic: It is labor-intensive.

The taxi industry is 100 percent private enterprise and receives no direct government assistance. However, many taxi firms provide service under contract to local governments that is indirectly subsidized.

Ridership Characteristics

In New York City and Washington, D.C., the two cities that stand out for having superior service, taxis are widely used by all kinds of people, of all income levels. In other cities, they are used disproportionately by:

FIGURE 6-2
An early taxi. This was used in Kansas City, Missouri; the sign indicates that the picture was taken in 1910. Notice that it has no headlights and that it has a crank in front for starting. (*Source: Kansas City Public Library, Kansas City, Missouri.*)

1 *The poor.* The 1990–1991 Nationwide Personal Transportation Study showed that 29 percent of taxi users came from households with incomes below $15,000, although this group contained only 21 percent of all households [Pucher and Williams 1992]. This tendency is more pronounced in small cities than in large ones: Gilbert et al. [1976] surveyed taxi riders in eight North Carolina cities and found that 54 percent had household incomes below $5000.

2 *The elderly.* The national study showed that people over 65 years old made 16.2 percent of taxi trips, as compared with 6.2 percent of all trips.

3 *Out-of-town visitors*, particularly business people and tourists. For this reason, the greatest concentration of taxi trip ends usually occurs in the CBD and at the airport.

Taxis are seldom used for commuting to work. According to the 1990 Census, the proportion of persons in the United States who used taxi to go to work was 1 out of 640. The highest demand for taxis does not occur during normal rush hours, but in the evening. In the jargon of transportation planners, the most common purposes of taxi trips are *personal business* and *social-recreation*. Some people use them for weekly trips to the supermarket.

Service Characteristics

There are three arrangements for getting a cab:

1 The most common way is to summon one by telephone. The cabs are equipped with radios and routed by a dispatcher who answers the phone. This is the method used in most small cities and towns, but it is not so pervasive in larger places.

2 In big cities, it is customary to hail a passing cab from the sidewalk. This is the standard method in New York City, where the yellow *medallion cabs* have the exclusive right to operate in this way. Hence taxis cruise the streets looking for fares, which wastes gas and increases traffic. In Manhattan, which has the largest concentration of taxis in the country, taxis account for 25 percent of all vehicle-miles.

3 Many cities try to make taxis wait at designated stands to reduce cruising. Stands are usually located at hotels, theaters, and transportation terminals (including airports). The system can be inconvenient for customers, especially those from out of town, who do not know where to find the stands. Taxi drivers may not like where the stands are located and may ignore them.

All three systems are inefficient. About half of all taxi vehicle-miles occur with the driver alone. In the system of calling a cab by phone, the cab usually returns to base empty. Computer dispatching can raise efficiency. It is used in Los Angeles and has cut unproductive vehicle-miles to 45 percent.

There are three ways of determining the fare. The first and most common is to calculate it by a meter (the word *taxi* originated in the French word *taxi-metre*). There is a base fare when the flag is dropped; then the fare goes up with distance traveled. In large cities with heavy congestion, the fare also increases with waiting time when the vehicle is stopped. There may be an extra charge for carrying more than one passenger.

The second method is the zone system, in which the fare goes up when you cross a boundary into a new zone. A map showing the zones is posted in the cab so that you can tell your fare when you get in. One advantage is that the driver cannot cheat you by taking a roundabout route to your destination.

The third way is the flat fare, which does not change with distance traveled. This is mostly used in small communities where all trips are fairly short. It is often used for trips between the airport and the city center.

In the past, most taxi drivers were employees of moderately large firms such as Yellow and Checker [Gilbert and Samuels 1982]. The drivers were paid on a commission basis, receiving a percentage of fares ranging from 43 to 50 percent, plus tips. It is increasingly common for drivers to own their vehicles or lease them from a company that also provides dispatching service. One reason is that this arrangement avoids payment of Social Security and other earnings taxes.

Since 1984, applicants for a hack license in New York City have been required to attend the New York Taxi Drivers Institute, consisting of 20 hours of classroom instruction. This is one of the first such programs in the United States. An article by Morris [1986] reported on a survey of 4400 students who attended the institute in 1984–1985. She found that 74 percent were foreign-born (the most common country of origin was Haiti). The drivers were older and better educated than expected: The median age was 33, and 47 percent had completed at least 2 years of college.

New York City ended the commission system in 1979. Drivers now lease their vehicles, pay for gas, and keep everything they collect from passengers. Supposedly this has increased competition and improved service. The average driver clears $20,000 to $25,000 a year. Most work 12-hour shifts 6 days a week. This is typical: Most taxi drivers in the country work 70 to 80 hours per week.

Legal and Institutional Problems

The taxi business is mostly regulated by local governments; only a few states intervene. There are rules with regard to safety and insurance, and there is also economic regulation governing fares and entry. Until recently, entry into the business was restricted in every major city except Washington, Atlanta, and Honolulu. Generally a legal taxi must carry a *medallion*, a metal plate that is bolted onto the body where it can be easily seen (sometimes on the hood, sometimes on the trunk). In some cities the number of medallions is fixed; in others, the city grants franchises to one or two companies, which decide on the number of cabs.

One result is that the number of taxis may not increase in step with demand for them. Hence it is difficult to get a cab in some cities. Another result is high fares. It is a seller's market, which means high prices.

New York City has had 11,787 medallions in use for many years. The limit was set at 13,595 by the Haas Act in 1937. About 2000 were surrendered during the late years of the depression, when business was poor, and were never reissued. Boston maintained a limit of 1525 medallions from 1935 until 1990, when the city's Hackney Division was authorized to issue an additional 300 medallions. The intent was to increase service in outlying neighborhoods, which had come to rely on suburban taxi companies.

According to Rosenbloom [1985], in 1976 Washington, D.C., with free entry, had 8079 taxis—two-thirds of the legal number in New York City. Chicago, which is larger than Washington, D.C., had just 4600 cabs, and the number had not changed for many years. The three cities with free entry had the highest ratios of taxis per capita.

Another result of restrictions is that *gypsy cabs* (a popular term for illegal cabs) are common in some cities. This partly comes from economic motives, but there may be another reason: Many drivers of legal cabs refuse to take passengers into ghetto areas, which they consider to be dangerous. It is illegal for a driver to refuse a request for service, but they do it anyway. This deprives the ghetto areas of taxi service; in response, residents of these areas may start their own taxi operations without authorization. In many cities police do not enforce the laws and ignore gypsy cabs.

Grava et al. [1987] estimated that there are 35,500 nonmedallion taxis operating in New York City. They have varying degrees of legal status, but generally all are tolerated by the police. Most are radio-dispatched, which is legal, but some also pick up passengers by hail, which only medallion cabs are permitted to do. Some services are quite specialized, such as the "black cars," which are aimed at an upscale market. They are large black sedans and charge double or triple the rates of medallion taxis. They are popular for weddings and funerals.

Another legal problem is that most cities prohibit group riding (or sharing a taxi). A party (which can be more than one person) that gets into a cab has exclusive use of the cab until leaving it. This makes taxis less efficient and more expensive.

Taxis operate differently in Washington, D.C., than in most cities, and visitors to that city are often favorably impressed with the service. Group riding is allowed; a driver may pick up a second party if the first party agrees. Fares are based on a zone system; there are no meters. There are many independent owner-operators, instead of one or two large firms controlling the business. There are many part-time drivers (some are college students). They usually go out in the evening, which is exactly when more cabs are needed.

Taxi companies sometimes present an obstacle to planners. They may oppose plans for public paratransit services, which they regard as unfair competition. There is evidence that dial-a-ride services do take passengers away from taxis. In 1974, Santa Clara County, California, converted most of its bus system to dial-a-ride, and taxi companies sued. The court ruled that the county would have to buy out eight taxi companies at a cost estimated at $1.5 million. The county decided to discontinue dial-a-ride [Carlson 1976].

Attempts at Reform

It seems logical to remove restrictions and allow free entry to the taxi business, but two factors work against it. First, taxi operators have a monopoly they don't want to give up. Second, medallions are valuable assets; if a city suddenly declared medallions were no longer needed, these assets would be wiped out. The value of a medallion is not trivial: In 1987, the going price in New York City was $105,000 [Grava et al. 1987]. In 1990 it was reported that a Boston medallion was worth $70,000. The association of taxi operators sued the city to prevent it from issuing new medallions.

There have been experiments with deregulation in recent years, notably in Indianapolis, Portland, San Diego, and Seattle. According to Rosenbloom [1985], the results have been disappointing. There have not been large increases in the number of cabs. In some cases, the number went down because demand decreased at the same time. When fares were deregulated, the companies that were supposed to compete ended up charging the same fare.

Another approach has been more successful. In some cities the transit agency contracts with taxi firms to provide specific services. This includes many services for the elderly and disabled, but in other cases taxis serve the general public on weekends and nights or in low-density areas where demand for transit is low. Taxi service is offered as an alternative to running buses on fixed routes, which is inefficient because of low patronage. A transit authority might cancel all service in such a situation, but there may be pressure to preserve some kind of service for the few people who need it.

This kind of service is heavily subsidized. Passengers pay an arbitrarily low fare (from $0.50 to $1), but the cost is closer to $10. The transit agency covers the cost plus a profit for the taxi company. But the transit agency saves money because it would be more expensive to provide regular bus service—so everybody comes out ahead. One reason it is cheaper is that taxi drivers earn less than unionized bus drivers.

JITNEY

The *jitney* is a cross between taxi service and a regular bus route. The vehicle may be an automobile, van, or minibus. Unlike taxis, jitneys operate along a fixed route, usually a major street, and they may have fixed stops. There is no regular schedule, and passengers share the vehicle. There is a fixed fare, which is low. (Originally the standard fare was 5¢, and the nickel was popularly called a *jitney*.) In some places, jitneys will deviate from the route a few blocks to let people off at their doors; an extra fare is charged for this.

Jitneys have an interesting history, as described by Eckert and Hilton [1972]. Jitneys first appeared in Los Angeles in 1914 during a period of high unemployment when people with automobiles tried to turn them to some profit. Jitneys quickly spread to hundreds of cities across the country. By the summer of 1915, it was estimated that 62,000 jitneys were operating in the United States. They cut into the revenues of streetcar companies because they followed streetcar lines and picked up people waiting at stops. At first the streetcar operators thought jitneys would spontaneously disappear because they were uneconomical, but this did not happen.

The streetcar companies then took a political approach and managed to have laws passed that soon drove the jitneys out of business. The streetcar operators were quite ingenious in thinking up devices to make the jitney business unattractive. For example, jitney owners were required to obtain franchises, pay license fees, and post liability bonds (these were expensive because jitneys had bad accident records). Sometimes jitneys were forbidden to use streets with streetcar lines. Another trick was to limit their speed to a maximum of 10 miles per hour. These measures accomplished the goal, and jitneys had virtually disappeared by the early 1920s.

Two cities, Atlantic City and San Francisco, did not drive out jitneys, and they have continued to operate there [Saltzman and Solomon 1973]. In Atlantic City they run on Pacific Avenue; in San Francisco, on Mission Street. St. Louis had an extensive system, known as *service cars*, which began in 1916 or 1917 and lasted for 50 years. In 1965, the transit authority bought out the two companies operating them, and service was terminated.

Jitneys operate illegally in several cities, such as Chicago and Pittsburgh. In Chicago the jitneys use Martin Luther King, Jr., Boulevard, which is the main street of the historically black community. Davis and Johnson [1984] did a study of illegal jitneys in Pittsburgh; they estimated there were 495 of them compared to 225 legal taxis. Here also the jitneys were used mainly by the African-American population.

San Diego deregulated taxis in 1979 and at the same time made jitneys legal. According to Reinke [1986], in 1984 there were 21 jitney companies operating 58 vehicles (mostly vans with 12 to 20 seats). The jitneys must run on predetermined routes; most of these serve the airport, downtown, a hotel area, and military bases. About 40 percent of passengers are military personnel. San Diego has a major naval base, and when a ship enters the bay, spotters on the hills telephone ahead, and jitneys converge on the docks.

This service appears to be successful, although there have been some complaints of unfair competition from the transit system and taxi companies. On the other hand, the transit authority had to reduce night and weekend service, and jitneys have proved to be an acceptable substitute.

Some jitneys have operated in Miami for many years. In 1989 the Florida legislature passed a law prohibiting local governments from regulating intercity transportation. Starting in spring 1990, a large number of unlicensed jitneys began operating across city lines. The law was hastily amended, but it was too late. Efforts to control the jitneys have failed.

A study found almost 400 jitneys were operating and carrying 43,000 to 49,000 riders each weekday [Urban Mobility Corporation 1992]. This was 23 to 27 percent of ridership on the Metro-Dade Transit Agency bus system. At a fare of $1, a jitney driver could earn a profit of $40 to $55 a day, roughly equivalent to the minimum wage. The study found that some riders had shifted from buses, but the majority appeared to be a new market. The jitneys served many areas without bus service. Passengers were predominantly low-income, and 53 percent did not speak English.

There were mixed opinions on the desirability of the jitneys. Some officials believed they should be legally acknowledged and integrated with Metrobus service. However, the county periodically attempted to suppress unlicensed vehicles. The jitneys proved to be of value after Hurricane Andrew devastated Dade County in August 1992. Many were recruited and quickly legalized to provide emergency service on a dozen van routes.

Jitneys are important in many foreign cities, where they have local names. They are called *carros por puesto* in Caracas [Kudlick 1969]. In Manila, they are called *jeepneys* because they were originally made from jeeps left from World War II [Grava 1972]. Other cities with numerous jitneys include Beirut, Buenos Aires, Hong Kong, Istanbul, San Juan, and Teheran.

Roschlau [1981] made a study of jitneys in Mexico City, where they are called *peseros*. He found that 17,000 vehicles carry almost 2 million passengers a day, about 10 percent of all trips in the metropolitan area. They are more expensive than buses, but their average speed is twice as high, partly because the drivers are quite aggressive. These vehicles operate on fixed routes, and each route has an association with a director. The government classifies some routes as "authorized" and some as "tolerated."

There has been much talk of reviving jitneys in the United States. Many cities still have ordinances prohibiting group riding in taxis, which effectively precludes jitneys. A few cities have changed their laws, but there has been little response from providers. The jitney is a good approach in a particular kind of situation—high linear demand along a well-defined corridor—but it is unlikely to become a major carrier.

RIDE SHARING

The most common paratransit option is *ride sharing,* in which travelers form groups to share vehicles that operate when and where they want. There has been great effort in recent years to promote ride sharing, especially in response to the suburban transportation problems discussed in Chapter 4. Transportation management associations and traffic reduction ordinances generally emphasize measures to boost ride sharing and reduce solo commuting. Part of the appeal of ride sharing is that, unlike transit service, it usually involves little or no public expenditure.

Many metropolitan areas suffer from air pollution, and ride sharing is seen as a major way to take cars off the road and meet air quality standards. For example, in 1988 the South Coast Air Quality Management District adopted Regulation XV, which regulates firms with 100 or more employees in the Los Angeles area. The ordinance imposed standards for average vehicle ridership ranging from 1.75 in downtown Los Angeles to 1.3 in remote areas.

There are differences among the forms of ride sharing that relate to the vehicle used. Therefore, it is appropriate to discuss carpooling, vanpooling, and subscription bus service separately.

Carpooling

Carpooling is an obvious way to take vehicles off the road. The average number of persons per car for all kinds of urban trips is about 1.5. It is lower for trips to work (apparently about 1.1), despite the popular belief that car pools are common. Furthermore, car pools are becoming less common. According to the Census, of those persons who used private vehicles to go to work, 23.5 percent carpooled in 1980, but only 15.4 percent in 1990. The number of persons who carpooled decreased by 4 million in the decade [Pisarski 1992].

There are many empty seats in cars, which adds up to a lot of unused capacity. This is wasteful, but it also represents a reserve that is available for emergencies. For example, if another energy crisis and gasoline shortage occurred, carpooling would be the major response, unless the crisis went on for some time. Carpooling increases quickly and spontaneously in brief emergencies such as a transit strike or severe weather.

The author was working as a transportation planner in New York City at the time of the transit strike in 1966. One morning he was stationed on the Queensborough Bridge to count the number of persons in every automobile entering Manhattan. Over a 4-hour period, the average was 3.23 persons per automobile. The driver was alone in only 16 percent of the cars, while 44 percent of cars carried 4 or more persons.

However, as a habitual practice in normal times, carpooling is unpopular with most commuters [Margolin et al. 1978]. There are several reasons:

1 Scheduling and routing are usually rigid. You can't work late or make a side trip on the way home if you are in a car pool.

2 The dispersion of homes and workplaces, especially in low-density areas, reduces the probability of finding good matches. Car pools work best with large employers where many people work in the same location.

3 People who ride with someone else don't have a car available to run errands during the day or to go to lunch. Again, the dispersed character of suburban development often makes a car essential for such purposes. Many office and industrial parks have no eating places within walking distance.

4 Personality conflicts make car pools unattractive to some. The majority of car pools do not have long tenure. People who have had bad experiences may not want to try again.

Teal [1987] made an analysis of carpooling with data from the 1977–1978 Nationwide Personal Transportation Survey. He found that carpoolers do not form a homogeneous group; they have a wide range of characteristics. About 40 percent of car pools contain members of the same household. Most of these are two-person car pools with a wife and husband. About 20 percent of carpoolers do not have any vehicle available and are always passengers.

Teal concluded that "economics plays a major role in carpooling. The commuters most prone to carpool are those making long trips, those with relatively high commuting cost burdens if they drive alone, and those from households with fewer vehicles than workers" [1987, p. 210]. But in his study, economic variables were not very successful in predicting car pool use.

Owens [1981] analyzed interview data in an attempt to find out why some people remained in car pools while others dropped out. Attitudinal factors were very important. Durable car pools had members who liked each other and felt that the arrangement was fair. Of course, such factors are not ascertained by computer matching programs.

Car pools depend on individual initiative; there is dispersed decision making in this situation. However, the government or other authorities can do things to increase carpooling, such as:

1 Provide a matching service to pair people with the same general origin, destination, and time schedules. Matching can be done manually or by computer. It can be done for major employers or for the general public (some radio stations help promote it). This is basically an information service that can be offered, but people cannot be forced to use it. Evidence shows that only a small percentage of people given matches actually form car pools.

2 Give car pools the most convenient spaces in parking lots. This is a common practice, but if the car pool spaces go unused, there may be a backlash.

3 Arrange a *guaranteed ride home* program. People who occasionally must leave work at odd times, missing their car pools, can take a subsidized taxi ride home. In a demonstration in the Seattle area, 260 persons signed up, some of whom stopped driving alone [Kadesh and Elder 1989]. Each person was allowed a certain number of taxi miles per month, but had to pay $1 for each trip. The program, which cost the local government $8000 over 6 months, was deemed successful and was expanded.

4 Install high-occupancy vehicle (HOV) lanes. As discussed in Chapter 5, this is done in many places around the country. What started as exclusive bus lanes have generally become HOV lanes. There is a problem with cheating unless police make a concerted enforcement effort. There have been cases in which drivers carried dummies in their cars. The driver of a hearse in Los Angeles was ticketed for using an HOV lane; the police did not accept his argument that the body in the coffin counted as a passenger.

HOV lanes have given rise to a new phenomenon called *casual carpooling* or *instant carpooling,* in which drivers pick up hitchhikers in order to use the lanes. Commuters find a place where they can park their cars free all day, and then they wait for a ride at standard pickup points. According to Beroldo [1990], every weekday morning about 8000 commuters form casual car pools in the East Bay to cross the Bay Bridge to San Francisco. Automobiles with 3 or more persons may use a bypass lane at the toll plaza; this saves 10 to 20 minutes in travel time and lowers the toll by $1.

There are some remarkable things about this behavior. Some commuters from Contra Costa County actually start on BART and then get off to form a car pool to cross the bridge. There is a no bypass in the evening because tolls are collected only in the westbound direction. Hence the carpoolers find another way to get home. Indeed, BART carries about 5000 more passengers eastbound in the evening than westbound in the morning.

This custom seems like a logical way to remove cars from highways. However, Beroldo made a survey which showed that only 6 percent of the car pool passengers formerly drove alone, while 33 percent of the car pool drivers formerly used transit. Apparently the number of automobiles using the Bay Bridge has increased.

The other place this happens on a large scale is in Springfield, Virginia, where about 2500 persons a day form ad hoc car pools to use the HOV lanes on the Shirley Highway leading to Washington, D.C. [Reno et al. 1989]. The transit authority first objected to the practice on the grounds that it was unfair competition. Later the authority adjusted its service and was able to reduce operating costs. Reno et al. urged that this system be replicated elsewhere.

Planners often promote carpooling with the idea that it will reduce drive-alone commuting. However, Teal [1987] said that data indicate that it is transit use and carpooling that are close substitutes. In other words, greater carpooling will take passengers off the transit system, rather than drivers off the road. Teal found that carpooling is high in areas where the transit service is poor and low where transit service is good. He was pessimistic about efforts to increase carpooling significantly, but the record shows that it does happen when driving becomes difficult or expensive.

Vanpooling

The 3M Company in St. Paul began the first large vanpooling program in 1973. Since then, this means of commuting has become increasingly popular, and there are now hundreds of vanpool programs around the country. However, no national statistics exist because few of the programs are managed by public agencies. Houston has been called the "vanpool capital of the world." Several oil companies based there operate over 100 vans each. The Municipality of Metropolitan Seattle runs perhaps the largest public vanpool program in the United States, operating more than 500 vans and carrying an average of 5000 daily riders.

It may appear that vanpooling is just carpooling with a larger vehicle, but there are differences. For one, there are legal and institutional barriers peculiar to vanpooling:

1 Some states require vanpool drivers to get a chauffeur's or other higher class license. This license is more difficult and expensive than a driver's license and may involve a police investigation of the driver's background.

2 Some states regard commuter vans as common carriers, which require a permit from a public utilities commission. This may involve considerable paperwork, legal assistance, and a public hearing.

3 Insurance companies have been unsure how to handle vanpools. If vanpools are classified as common carriers, it means high insurance rates.

4 The Internal Revenue Service has ruled that if vanpool drivers are paid, they must pay income tax.

5 There are some practical questions: Who owns the van? Who pays the operating costs? Who uses the van on weekends? Where is it stored?

Consequently, most successful vanpool services have been organized by employers. Individual initiative does not work well in this case; a central authority is needed. In a typical system, the company buys and owns the van and pays administrative and operating costs. One person is selected as the permanent driver and is compensated with a small stipend and use of the van on weekends. Either riders pay a monthly fee, or the firm subsidizes the service.

Another difference from carpooling is that since a van is larger than an automobile, the van picks up more passengers, whose homes are more dispersed. If a van picks up everyone at home, it must make many detours. Often there is a pickup point where everyone gathers, but this may be several miles from home for some people. Either way this slows the trip. To offset this disadvantage, the van must travel a long way at high speed. Hence the system works best for people who live a long way from their jobs. Successful vanpools usually have a round trip of at least 50 miles. They are mostly found in a large cities where long commutes are common.

Table 6-2 gives some operating statistics for several large vanpool systems operated

TABLE 6-2
SELECTED VANPOOL SYSTEMS
(Data for Fiscal Years Ending in 1992)

Area	Annual passenger trips	Average trip length, miles	Average speed, miles per hour	Average passenger load*
Austin	190,638	16.0	40.0	6.26
Bremerton, WA	117,716	24.0	24.3	7.39
Charlotte	114,408	23.2	27.1	10.77
Chicago	133,137	36.2	35.0	8.19
Nashville	63,904	55.6	38.7	8.51
Norfolk	109,872	32.3	35.7	11.78
Phoenix	126,036	39.7	35.1	12.23
Spokane	62,127	19.4	31.0	7.43
Tacoma	158,176	30.1	40.5	9.07
Means	119,557	29.2	34.2	8.93

*This is the ratio of passenger miles to vehicle revenue miles. It represents the average number of passengers on a vehicle.
Source: Transit Profiles; Agencies in Urbanized Areas Exceeding 200,000 Population; for the 1992 Section 15 Report Year (Washington: Federal Transit Administration, December 1993).

by public agencies, which must report section 15 data. This is not a representative sample, as most vanpool operations are private and do not report data to the FTA. However, the numbers are probably fairly typical. Note that the average trip length is long and the average speed is high. Further, the average passenger load is quite high when compared to dial-a-ride, which indicates that vanpooling is an efficient mode.

Based on a survey of vanpool riders in Los Angeles by Kumar and Moilov [1991], it also appears that this is a mode preferred by people who have a choice. The mean income of riders was $55,000; 75 percent had graduated from college; and 67 percent had executive or professional occupations. Perhaps most surprising, more than 80 percent of the riders came from households that had two or more vehicles. This should be welcome news to planners who want to reduce the number of single-occupant cars during peak periods.

Vanpooling is an excellent option in the right situation. It is quite economical in terms of cost per passenger. It turns out to be the most energy-efficient of all urban transportation modes, as explained in Chapter 11. The problem is to make it more appealing to employers, since they must take the initiative. Sometimes they have an incentive. The 3M Company started its program when it faced a parking crisis because it ran out of land; the alternative was to build expensive multilevel parking garages. Probably vanpooling is popular in Houston because the freeways are congested and most bus service is slow. It is easier to attract and retain employees if commuting can be made less onerous.

Subscription Bus

Subscription bus services for commuters have operated for at least 30 years. Typically passengers pay by the month (usually in advance). They are guaranteed seats, and sometimes there are amenities not found in normal buses (such as coffee and newspapers). Usually each bus makes one round trip a day and is parked all day in the city center. Because the operation is repetitive, there is ample time to determine the best routing.

Such services have been organized by employers, private bus companies, transit authorities, and community groups [Kirby and Bhatt 1975]. For example, the National Geographic Society (NGS) decided to move its bindery operation from Washington, D.C., to suburban Gaithersburg, Maryland, in 1968. When workers objected, NGS contracted with D.C. Transit to operate 10 bus routes which carried 600 employees a day to the new plant. The same year, a group of residents of Reston, Virginia, formed a *commuter club* and contracted for buses running to downtown Washington, D.C., and the Pentagon.

In some cases, private bus companies have initiated these services, and they make a profit. Often they collect passengers in middle- and high-income suburban areas and charge fares higher than those of the local transit system. However, Specialty Transit in St. Louis ran a successful operation, serving a low-income area and using school buses instead of standard transit buses.

As with a van, the line-haul portion of the route is usually very long and follows expressways as much as possible. The bus does not pick up passengers at their doorstep;

instead they board at a few pickup points such as a shopping center parking lot. Some commuters park their cars all day; others get a ride to the stop.

This type of service presents no legal or institutional problems because it is usually operated by a private bus company or local transit authority, and there is a paid professional driver. Load factors are high (otherwise a route is canceled), and it is a very cost-effective form of transit. It is attractive in large metropolitan areas where commuting distances are long and parking charges are high, but it is unlikely to be feasible in smaller areas.

To sum up, there is a variety of paratransit options that planners should consider in situations where conventional transit service is uneconomical or otherwise unsuitable. Each alternative has particular characteristics; they are not interchangeable, and they need to be compared carefully [Black et al. 1980]. Paratransit services are increasing throughout the country and will undoubtedly continue to be important.

QUESTIONS

1 Describe the major forms of paratransit. For each one, discuss (*a*) the situation in which it generally occurs or seems most promising, (*b*) what advantages it has over conventional bus and rail service, and (*c*) any disadvantages or problems it has.

2 Compare dial-a-ride and taxis as means for providing transportation for people without cars in suburbs and small cities. Should local governments ensure that there is an alternative to the private automobile for travel in these areas, or should it be left to the marketplace?

3 Although taxi fares are high, surveys consistently show that low-income people use taxis more often than the average citizen. Why is this?

4 Local governments have regulated taxis for many years and in many cities have limited the number of legal cabs in use. Why is there opposition to deregulating the taxi business? If there were free entry, who would be hurt?

5 Efforts to increase carpooling have not been very successful on a national basis, although there are exceptions in some areas. Why is carpooling unpopular? Can anything be done to change this attitude?

6 Describe the differences between carpooling and vanpooling. Why do large employers usually take the initiative in arranging vanpools? What is their motivation?

REFERENCES

Abkowitz, Mark D., and Marian T. Ott: "Review of Recent Demonstration Experiences with Paratransit Services," *Transportation Research Record,* no. 778 (1980), pp. 13–19.

American Public Transit Association: *Transit Fact Book* (Washington: American Public Transit Association, 1993).

Beroldo, Stephen: "Casual Carpooling in the San Francisco Bay Area," *Transportation Quarterly,* vol. 44, no. 1 (January 1990), pp. 133–150.

Black, Alan, C. Michael Walton, Rita Ellison, and Gordon Derr: *Evaluation of Various Approaches to Providing Public Transportation Service in Areas Less Than 200,000 Population* (Austin: Center for Transportation Research, University of Texas, 1980).

Carlson, Robert C.: "Anatomy of a Systems Failure: Dial-a-Ride in Santa Clara County, California," *Transportation,* vol. 5, no. 1 (March 1976), pp. 3–16.

Davis, Frank W., Kenneth W. Heathington, Roger Alford, Richard Symons, and David Middendorf: "Comparison of Privately and Publicly Owned Demand-Responsive Systems," *Transportation Research Record,* no. 559 (1976), pp. 11–20.

Davis, Otto A., and Norman J. Johnson: "The Jitneys: A Study of Grassroots Capitalism," *Journal of Contemporary Studies,* vol. 7, no. 1 (Winter 1984), pp. 81–102.

Echols, James C.: "Use of Private Companies to Provide Public Transportation Services in Tidewater, Virginia," in Charles A. Lave, ed., *Urban Transit: The Private Challenge to Public Transportation* (San Francisco: Pacific Institute for Public Policy Research, 1985), pp. 79–100.

Eckert, Ross D., and George W. Hilton: "The Jitneys," *Journal of Law and Economics,* vol. 15, no. 2 (October 1972), pp. 293–325.

Gilbert, Gorman, Robert O. Bach, Frank C. Dilorio, and Frederick D. Fravel: *Taxicab User Characteristics in Small and Medium-Sized Cities* (Chapel Hill: Center for Urban and Regional Studies, University of North Carolina, January 1976).

——— and Robert E. Samuels: *The Taxicab: An Urban Transportation Survivor* (Chapel Hill: University of North Carolina Press, 1982).

Grava, Sigurd: "The Jeepneys of Manila," *Traffic Quarterly,* vol. 26 (1972), pp. 465–484.

——— Elliott Sclar, and Charles Downs: *The Potential and Problems of Private Sector Transportation Services: Activities in the New York Region* (Washington: Urban Mass Transportation Administration, January 1987).

Gwynn, David W., Anthony Y. Simpson, and Marcel J. Zobrak: "The Haddonfield, N.J., Dial-a-Ride Demonstration," *Traffic Quarterly,* vol. 27, no. 2 (April 1973), pp. 541–562.

Kadesh, Eileen, and Laurie Elder: "Guaranteed Ride Home: An Insurance Program for HOV Users," *Transportation Research Record,* no. 1212 (1989), pp. 72–75.

Kirby, Ronald F., and Kiran U. Bhatt: "An Analysis of Subscription Bus Service," *Traffic Quarterly,* vol. 29, no. 3 (July 1975), pp. 403–425.

———, Kiran U. Bhatt, Michael A. Kemp, Robert G. McGillivray, and Martin Wohl: *Para-Transit: Neglected Options for Urban Mobility* (Washington: The Urban Institute, 1974).

Kudlick, Walter: "Carros Por Puesto—The 'Jitney' Taxi System in Caracas, Venezuela," *Highway Research Record,* no. 283 (1969), pp. 1–10.

Kumar, Ajay, and Margaret Moilov: "Vanpools in Los Angeles," *Transportation Research Record,* no. 1321 (1991), pp. 103–108.

Margolin, Joseph B., Marion Ruth Misch, and Mark Stahr: "Incentives and Disincentives of Ride Sharing," *Transportation Research Record,* no. 673 (1978), pp. 7–15.

Morris, Anne G.: "Taxi School: A First Step in Professionalizing Taxi Driving," *Transportation Research Record,* no. 1103 (1986), pp. 40–48.

Owens, Dallas D., Jr.: "Ridesharing Programs: Governmental Response to Urban Transportation Problems," *Environment and Behavior,* vol. 13, no. 3 (May 1981), pp. 311–330.

Pennsylvania Department of Transportation: *Handbook for Purchasing a Small Transit Vehicle* (Harrisburg: Pennsylvania Department of Transportation, October 1988).

Pisarski, Alan E. *New Perspectives in Commuting* (Washington: U.S. Department of Transportation, 1992).

Pucher, John, and Fred Williams: "Socioeconomic Characteristics of Urban Travelers: Evidence from the 1990–91 NPTS," *Transportation Quarterly,* vol. 46, no. 4 (October 1992), pp. 561–581.

Reinke, David: "Update on Taxicab and Jitney Deregulation in San Diego," *Transportation Research Record,* no. 1103 (1986), pp. 9–11.

———, J. Moscovich, G. Rhyner, and S. Pultz: *Automated Dial-a-Ride Dispatching in Orange County, California* (Los Altos, CA: Crain & Associates, July 1987).

Reno, Arlee T., William A. Gellert, and Alex Verzosa: "Evaluation of Springfield Instant Carpooling," *Transportation Research Record,* no. 1212 (1989), pp. 53–62.

Roos, Daniel, Thomas Melone, Forbes Little, Edwin Porter, and Nigel Wilson: *The Dial-a-Ride
Transportation System* (Cambridge: Urban Systems Laboratory, Massachusetts Institute of
Technology, March 1971).

Roschlau, Michael Walter: *Urban Transport in Developing Countries: The Peseros of Mexico
City* (Vancouver: Centre for Transportation Studies, University of British Columbia, 1981).

Rosenbloom, Sandra: "The Taxi in the Urban Transport System," in Charles A. Lave, ed., *Urban
Transit: The Private Challenge to Public Transportation* (San Francisco: Pacific Institute for
Public Policy Research, 1985), pp. 181–213.

Saltzman, Arthur, and Richard J. Solomon: "Jitney Operations in the United States," *Highway
Research Record,* no. 449 (1973), pp. 63–70.

Stone, John R., Anna Nalevanko, and Jeffrey Tsai: "Assessment of Software for Computerized
Paratransit Operations," *Transportation Research Record,* no. 1378 (1993), pp. 1–9.

Teal, Roger F.: "Carpooling: Who, How, and Why," *Transportation Research,* vol. 21A, no. 3
(May 1987), pp. 203–214.

Urban Mobility Corporation: "The Miami Jitneys: An Update," *Private Sector Briefs,* vol. 4, no.
7 (September 1992).

Wilson, Nigel H. M., and Neil J. Colvin: *Computer Control of the Rochester Dial-a-Ride System*
(Cambridge: Center for Transportation Studies, Massachusetts Institute of Technology, July
1977).

7

INNOVATIVE TECHNOLOGY

There has always been great interest in finding technological solutions to transportation problems. Many people believe the United States remains the leading economic power in the world largely because of its skill in inventing new technology. Successes in space exploration, computers, and weaponry make people wonder why there cannot be comparable breakthroughs in urban transportation. However, government support for technological development as a policy approach to transportation has waxed and waned over the years.

Interest was high when the Department of Transportation (DOT) was formed. In 1966 Congress passed legislation mandating a study of "new systems of urban transportation." Seventeen contractors were hired in 1967 and submitted reports the following year. They were optimistic about the potential of breakthroughs in hardware, but the follow-up was spotty. Nonetheless, this study foreshadowed much of the work done in the ensuing years.

This chapter discusses new concepts and innovative technology that might apply to urban transportation. Many of these approaches are currently under development. Some of the technology has been available for years and has been selectively implemented.

PERSONAL RAPID TRANSIT

The Concept

The idea of *personal rapid transit* (often called *PRT*) is to make transit service competitive with the private automobile by approximating its advantages: (1) It goes anywhere in the city. (2) It leaves at any time; there is no fixed schedule. (3) There are no intermediate stops or transfers. (4) The average door-to-door speed is high. (5) You have exclusive use of the vehicle; it does not pick up other people.

To achieve this, PRT proponents try to design a system with an extensive route network (such as a grid with lines ¼ to ½ mile apart), small vehicles, and automatic control so there are no human operators. They claim that automation will keep labor costs to a minimum so that operating costs will be low. This is counterbalanced by the certainty that the initial investment to build a system will be high.

Early Prototypes

Federal involvement in developing automated rail systems began in 1963 when Westinghouse Electric Corporation received a grant to build a test track in South Park in Pittsburgh [Ruiter and Neumann 1984]. For $5 million, it constructed a one-way loop 9400 feet long carrying 30-foot vehicles controlled by computer. Called the *Transit Expressway* and also *Skybus,* the system was marketed by Westinghouse for several years, but there were no takers. Eventually the company won some contracts for similar systems.

Interest in PRT increased after UMTA, created in 1968, put strong emphasis on new technology (Carlos Villarreal, administrator from 1969 to 1973, had been an executive for an aerospace company). UMTA gave $1.5 million contracts to each of four companies to design and demonstrate prototypes of experimental systems at the Transpo 72 transportation exposition that DOT staged at Dulles Airport near Washington, D.C., in 1972. These were the companies:

1 Bendix Corporation built a system called *Dashaveyor.* One system was built at the Toronto zoo, but then Bendix abandoned this venture.

2 Ford Motor Company called its system *A.C.T.* (automatically controlled transportation). Ford installed systems at Bradley Airport near Hartford, Connecticut, and Dearborn, Michigan, but then left the business.

3 Rohr Industries built a system called *Monocab* with cars suspended from an overhead guideway (see Figure 7-1). No operating system was ever built. Rohr was an aerospace manufacturer which also built the original vehicles used in BART and the Washington Metro.

4 Transportation Technology Incorporated, an affiliate of Otis Elevator Company, built a system in a medical complex at Duke University in North Carolina and remains interested in the concept.

In 1974, UMTA gave additional grants to Boeing, Otis, and Rohr to develop more sophisticated systems. Rohr dropped out in 1978, but Boeing and Otis continued to receive federal support through the 1980s.

There was little direct impact from this program, except for the few systems built. The companies' interest was largely dependent on federal support. Boeing and Otis continue to do some research [Ruiter and Neumann 1984]. Otis built the Harbor Island shuttle in Tampa, which opened in 1985.

FIGURE 7-1
The Rohr Monocab. This is the prototype erected at the Transpo exposition at Dulles Airport in 1972. No commercial version of this system was ever built, but Rohr went on to manufacture heavy rail cars. (Photo by author.)

Morgantown

The one system that was actually built with federal support, and is currently operating, is at Morgantown, the site of the University of West Virginia (see Figure 7-2). This is not a good example of the true PRT concept, since there are only five stations and one line.

Samy Elias, an engineering professor at the University of West Virginia, was the motivating force behind the project. He obtained an UMTA research grant in 1969; then UMTA decided to implement his proposal as a demonstration. Construction started in 1971, and the first section began operating in 1975. It had three stations: one in downtown Morgantown, one on the old campus close to downtown, and one on the new campus about 2 miles away. The final cost was $62 million, compared to the initial estimate of $17 million.

The original prime contractor was Jet Propulsion Laboratory, but it was replaced early in the work by Boeing. Major subcontracts went to Bendix Corporation and William Alden (an inventor who held key patents on the control system). At first there was a great deal of technical trouble with the system, and construction took much

FIGURE 7-2
The Morgantown PRT system. This shows one of the cars on guideway on the University of West Virginia campus in Morgantown. The system is fully automatic; passengers push buttons to indicate their destinations. (Photo by author.)

longer than scheduled. The site is a difficult one with a steep grade, as the downtown and old campus are in a river valley and the new campus is on top of a bluff.

A 2-mile extension within the new campus was built in 1978 and 1979 while the system was closed down for over a year. The second section cost $64 million. The line is now slightly over 4 miles long and has five stations. Most of it is on an elevated structure, but parts are at ground level.

An article by Fisher [1981] described the system after it was fully operational for a couple of years. There were 73 cars, each having 8 seats and room for 12 standees. The system was completely automatic, with 14 different computers. While there were no drivers or ticket takers, altogether 72 persons were employed in the operation.

Vehicles had a maximum speed of 30 miles per hour and operated with a minimum headway of 15 seconds. The theoretical capacity was 1760 passengers in 20 minutes, or 5280 per hour. The system had actually carried a maximum of 1100 passengers in 20 minutes.

At this time the system carried 28,000 passengers per day, most of them students or staff at the university. This number is approximately the population of Morgantown (which was 27,605 in 1980). The impact study conducted by Elias et al. [1982] indicated there had been a substantial diversion of trips in the corridor from automobiles to the PRT system. However, most PRT users were diverted from the buses that formerly ran between the two campuses.

Students paid a fee of $25 per semester to use the PRT, plus a fare of $0.25 per ride. The state of West Virginia covered 60 percent of the annual $2 million operating costs.

Other Proposals

There have been proposals to build PRT elsewhere. In 1973, voters in the Denver area approved a $425 million bond issue to build a 98-mile network proposed by the consulting firm of Ian McHarg, the famous regional planner. This resembled a suburban railroad more than the basic PRT concept; it would have connected downtown Denver with major suburbs. However, UMTA was unwilling to provide federal aid to match the local money (partly because of the unhappy experience in Morgantown). UMTA insisted on a restudy of other alternatives, and finally the PRT idea was dropped.

In Minneapolis, PRT was aggressively promoted by J. Edward Anderson, formerly an engineering professor at the University of Minnesota. He and his colleagues have published extensively and held several national conferences on the subject. His ideas were taken seriously by some local politicians, but there was never a consensus to go ahead [Cassidy 1974]. Anderson, who moved to Boston University in 1986, formed the TAXI 2000 Corporation, which continues work on the concept. He contemplates a true PRT system, with a network covering an entire city and routes spaced 0.5 to 1 mile apart.

Chicago's Regional Transportation Authority began a study of PRT in 1990; the program was described by Ahlheim [1992]. In phase 1, contracts of $1.5 million each were given to two firms for preliminary engineering studies. In June 1993, the authority decided to proceed with phase 2 and approved spending up to $18 million. A contract was given to Raytheon Corporation, which said it would invest $20 million of its own money in the project. The company will build a prototype vehicle and a test track. If the results are satisfactory, phase 3 will involve construction of an operating system. The Chicago suburb of Rosemont has been chosen as the site for this experiment.

There has also been research on PRT abroad. In Germany, a prototype of the Cabin-taxi system was built, while Japan supported development of a computer-controlled vehicle system for several years. Great Britain and France also engaged in PRT research. However, none of these countries has yet built an operating system that fits the true PRT concept.

PEOPLE MOVERS

The Concept

There is much overlap in technology between PRT and people movers. The differences are in purpose and application. While PRT is supposed to provide citywide transportation, people movers are meant to substitute for pedestrian travel, to fill the gap between walking and conventional modes. It is thought that effective speeds of 6 to 10 miles per hour (including waiting) would be sufficient to attract many pedestrians. People movers are suitable for high-density activity centers, such as a central business district (CBD), airport, or theme park.

Mechanically, there are two types: (1) a moving belt on which pedestrians stand and (2) small vehicles operating on guideways with automatic control. These are analogous to the escalator and the elevator. The latter type is sometimes called *automated guideway transit* (or *AGT*). It is essentially the same as the Morgantown PRT.

The route system is usually very simple. Often there is only a single line with two terminals, and the vehicles shuttle back and forth. Some systems are larger and have as many as a dozen stops. There may be one or two tracks; a one-way loop is a common design.

Existing Systems

The largest system in the world is Airtrans at the Dallas–Fort Worth Airport, which opened in 1974 (see Figure 7-3). It has 13 miles of guideway and 14 stations. There are many junctions, and trains can bypass stations. The stations are divided into three sets (A, B, and C), and normally each train stops at only one set. The system was built by LTV Aerospace and largely financed with local money, although UMTA provided about $1 million in support.

Many other people movers have been installed in the United States since the 1970s [Fabian 1981, 1983]. Following are some currently in operation, classified by type of application:

1 *Airports:* Atlanta, Chicago (O'Hare Field), Houston, Las Vegas, Miami, Orlando, Seattle-Tacoma, and Tampa.

2 *Amusement or theme parks:* Busch Gardens (Virginia), Carowinds (South Carolina), Disneyland, Disney World, Dutch Wonderland (Pennsylvania), Hershey Park (Pennsylvania), King's Dominion (Virginia), and Magic Mountain (California).

3 *Downtown:* Detroit, Jacksonville, and Miami.

4 *Hospital complex:* Duke University in Durham, North Carolina.

5 *Shopping center:* Fairlane Town Center in Dearborn, Michigan.

6 *Zoos:* Bronx Zoo, Miami Metro Zoo, Minnesota Zoo, and San Diego Zoo.

In 1989 the Port Authority of New York and New Jersey awarded $126 million in contracts to construct and operate a people mover system at John F. Kennedy Airport. The plan for this airport was unique: Each major airline has its own terminal, and distances between them are great. Passengers take buses to transfer between airlines. Westinghouse is the major contractor for the new system, which is to be completed in 1995. In 1992 the Port Authority awarded contracts totaling $40.6 million to begin construction of a people mover at Newark Airport, and one is also planned for La Guardia Airport.

A people mover was built in the center of the Las Colinas new town north of Dallas and began operating in 1989. However, usage was disappointing, and in 1993 the developer closed down the system to save on operating expenses.

Las Vegas awarded a contract in 1985 for construction of a 1.3-mile line that would

FIGURE 7-3
The Airtrans system at the Dallas–Fort Worth Airport. This is the largest
people mover system operating at a U.S. airport. This view shows a
junction; trains that take the right guideway will bypass the station
ahead. (Photo by author.)

serve the convention center, a sports complex, and a new downtown transportation center. Some facilities were built, but at last report the project was on hold.

Three firms dominate the market for constructing such systems at airports and recreation centers: Walt Disney Enterprises, Universal Mobility, and VSL. Besides the facilities at its own amusement parks, Disney built the people mover at Houston Airport.
Universal Mobility has done most of the ones at non-Disney parks. VSL built an aerial
tramway that connects Roosevelt Island with Manhattan in New York City.

There are many people mover systems operating in foreign countries, including Australia, Canada, England, France, Japan, Singapore, and Germany ["AGT-Peoplemover

Guide" 1989]. Some foreign firms have reached technological levels equal or superior to those of U.S. companies [Ruiter and Neumann 1984]. The French company Matra is well known for its VAL system, which has been installed in Lille, Paris, and Toulouse. Matra built the people mover at O'Hare Airport in Chicago, which began service in May 1993.

The Downtown People Mover Program

In 1976 UMTA launched a nationwide demonstration program for downtown people movers. A solicitation attracted proposals from 38 cities. In December 1976, UMTA announced grants totaling $220 million to four cities: Cleveland ($41 million), Houston ($33 million), St. Paul ($45 million), and Los Angeles ($100 million plus $25 million in transferred highway funds). (Numbers are rounded off.) It also agreed to let Detroit and Miami implement their proposals with money reassigned from previous transit commitments.

There was much fanfare about downtown people movers at the time, but the final results were disappointing. Here is what happened in the six cities:

1 Dennis Kucinich was elected mayor of Cleveland in 1977 and declared he didn't want a people mover (which had been promoted by his predecessor). Kucinich (characterized as a populist) said it would only help downtown business interests and suburbanites who worked downtown. He would rather spend the money to improve bus service in low-income neighborhoods. UMTA would not transfer the money, but Cleveland dropped out anyway.

2 The Houston proposal was originally backed by Mayor Ron Hofheinz, Jr. But Houston also had a change of mayors, and the new one (Jim McConn) voiced skepticism. In 1978 there was an election campaign to form a metropolitan transit authority (MTA), during which the idea was hardly mentioned. The MTA was approved and took over planning for the proposal. In 1979, the MTA board voted to discontinue further study of the people mover and redirect attention to a system of reserved bus lanes.

3 In St. Paul, the state legislature refused to provide the local share of funding for the project, and the city dropped out.

4 Los Angeles canceled its plans after UMTA announced in 1981 that it was terminating the people mover program and would provide no money beyond that already committed.

5 Miami went ahead, and UMTA allowed the city to cut back on its heavy rail plan and reallocate $24 million of federal aid for construction of the *MetroMover.* There were technical problems during construction, which fell way behind schedule, and the cost escalated to $145 million. The 1.9 mile loop finally went into service in 1986. It was built by Westinghouse and has rubber-tire vehicles running on an elevated concrete guideway. It carried 9100 passengers per day in 1992 for an operating cost of $7 million. Two extensions were scheduled for completion in 1994. Westinghouse also got the $54 million contract for the second phase.

6 Detroit also proceeded, and the system was opened in 1987 (see Figure 7-4). It is a 2.9-mile loop through the downtown area with 13 stations. It takes 14 minutes to

FIGURE 7-4
Detroit's downtown people mover system. This elegant guideway winds through downtown Detroit and carries automated trains that stop at 13 stations. Trains are powered by linear induction motors. (Photo by author.)

complete the circuit, and the fare is $0.50. The project was in construction for 4 years and encountered many problems—mechanical, legal, and political [Bas 1986]. The final construction cost was expected to exceed $210 million. The builder was Urban Transportation Development Corporation, a company founded by the province of Ontario that went private in 1988. This system uses linear induction technology and has steel wheels on steel rails. It carried 6900 passengers per day in 1992.

Jacksonville also installed a downtown people mover with federal aid. It was designed by Matra and began operating in 1989. The first segment, 7/10 mile long, connects the downtown area with large parking lots. Another 1.8 miles is planned. It carried just 1000 passengers per day in 1992.

A people mover was built with private financing in Tampa, connecting the Harbour Island residential and commercial development with the downtown area. It is 3000 feet long and cost $7 million. City officials would like to add onto it and create a system that serves the whole downtown.

There is great interest in people movers, which seem to provide a valuable service in airports and other activity centers where distances are too long for walking. Surely more will be built in the future. Downtown people movers appear questionable because of the high cost (about $70 million per mile in Miami and Detroit). It seems proper for the FTA to regard people movers as a form of mass transit eligible for capital grants.

RAIL TRANSPORTATION

Monorail

Monorail is often included with futuristic technologies, but actually it has a considerable history. The first monorail in the world was built in Wuppertal, Germany, in 1901 and is still operating. It is 8.3 miles long and has 19 stations. Short monorail systems have been erected at numerous world fairs and amusement parks; hence millions of people have ridden monorail.

As indicated by its name, the distinguishing characteristic of monorail is that it uses one rail instead of two. There are two types: In one, the cars are suspended by sturdy hangers from an overhead rail; in the other, the cars ride on top of a concrete beam and wrap around it. Wuppertal has the suspended type, but most new systems are supported from below. Best known is the Alweg system, which was developed in the 1950s under the sponsorship of the Swedish industrialist Axel Wenner-Gren.

Monorails have received much publicity over the years, and interest has revived lately. However, many engineers have concluded that conventional two-rail systems are better. The major drawback is switching: The rails are heavy concrete beams that cannot be easily moved. In most existing systems, trains either reverse direction on the same track or operate in a loop.

An Alweg monorail was built over city streets in Seattle for the World's Fair held there in 1962. It links the downtown area with the fairgrounds and is still operating. There are two tracks; each carries a single train that shuttles between the terminals. With a fare of $0.90 for a 1.2-mile journey, the line is mostly used by tourists.

A monorail connecting downtown Tokyo with the Haneda Airport began service in 1964. It was built by Hitachi following an Alweg design. The line is 8.2 miles long and has 5 stations. This is the only modern monorail currently providing major urban transportation service, but there may be others in the near future.

Perhaps the largest monorail system in the world operates at Walt Disney World near Orlando, Florida (see Figure 7-5). It runs trains up to 6 cars long. In 1991, the MTA of Harris County voted to build a monorail system in Houston and selected a proposal for a design similar to the system at Walt Disney World. However, there was a political reaction, and after a change in mayors, the rail plan was shelved [Baron 1994]. Honolulu also considered the possibility of constructing a monorail line, but late in 1991 picked a consortium that uses more conventional technology to build a rail transit system.

Bullet Trains

High-speed trains, often called *bullet trains,* receive a great deal of publicity, and there have been several recent proposals to build lines in the United States. They may not seem to belong in a book on urban transportation, but the high speeds enable them to be

FIGURE 7-5
The monorail at Disney World in Orlando, Florida. This is the supported type of monorail in which cars straddle a concrete beam. This train is approaching a hotel where it will stop inside an atrium lobby. There are many monorails operating at amusement or theme parks, but only a few that provide true urban transit service. (Photo by author.)

used for commuting over considerable distances. There may be spin-offs from improvements in intercity trains that can be applied to urban rail transit.

Following are the best-known examples of high-speed trains currently in operation:

1 The pioneer was Japan's Shinkansen line, which began operating in 1964 between Tokyo and Osaka, 320 miles apart. The line was very profitable, and over the years the Japanese National Railways built more; there are now almost 1300 miles of high-speed lines. Each day Japan operates about 260 bullet trains carrying 400,000 passengers at speeds up to 170 miles per hour. The system runs 99 percent on time and has never had a fatal accident [Vranich 1991].

2 The world's fastest regularly scheduled train is the French TGV (this stands for *train à grande vitesse*). The first line covered the 210 miles between Paris and Lyon; partial service began in 1981, and the line was completed in 1983. It has a top speed of 168 miles per hour and carries 300,000 passengers per week. A second line, the TGV Atlantique, began operating between Paris and Le Mans in 1989. It has a top speed of 186 miles per hour. The TGV keeps rewriting the world speed record; at a test run on May 18, 1990, it raised the mark to 320.2 miles per hour [Vranich 1991].

3 The Metroliner, running between New York City and Washington, D.C., offers the fastest passenger service in the United States. Trains reach 125 miles per hour on straight stretches, but the average speed is less than 90 miles per hour. The entire line is electrified. This service began in 1969 as a demonstration project authorized by the High-Speed Ground Transportation Act of 1965. It is the most heavily used Amtrak route.

4 There was another demonstration project between New York City and Boston where for several years Turbotrains powered by gas-turbine engines operated. Although a Turbotrain reached 170 miles per hour in a test, the many curves on this route kept operating speeds below those of the Metroliner. Currently conventional locomotives are used, and the top speed is 90 miles per hour. Amtrak plans to upgrade the line at a cost of $800 million and to purchase Swedish X-2000 tilt trains, which can round curves at high speeds. While this will cut 1 hour off the travel time between the terminals, the average speed will be only 78 miles per hour [Levinson 1992].

The French TGVs go beyond the high-speed sections and continue at slower speeds on older tracks. They enter some adjacent countries such as Belgium, the Netherlands, and Switzerland. A version of the TGV will run through the English Channel tunnel, which was formally opened in a ceremony in May 1994 (passenger service was expected to begin in October 1994). The British government has invited proposals to build a high-speed link between the tunnel and London.

High-speed trains also operate in Great Britain, Germany, Spain, and Italy. Other countries are planning routes, and improved rail equipment is being designed. One problem is that a few countries (notably Spain and Russia) do not use standard gauge. There is also concern about environmental impacts. If these problems are overcome, there will probably be high-speed rail service all over Europe.

High-speed trains have been seriously considered in the United States in recent years. They are being promoted by an organization called the High Speed Rail Association, which issued a map indicating that eighteen proposals are under consideration. Following is a recap of the best-known ones:

Entrepreneurs formed the American High Speed Rail Corporation with the intent of building a 130-mile line between Los Angeles and San Diego. The state legislature established a Passenger Rail Financing Commission, which was authorized to issue $1.25 billion in tax-exempt bonds. However, the proposal met intense opposition from environmental groups and local governments; ridership forecasts were criticized as wildly optimistic. The corporation abandoned its efforts in 1984 [Smith and Shirley 1987].

In 1988 a California-Nevada Super Speed Train Commission was formed to promote a plan for 300 mile per hour magnetic levitation trains between Anaheim and Las Vegas, both meccas for tourists. A franchise was awarded to the Bechtel Group in 1990, but the scheme was abandoned the following year [Levinson 1992].

Florida created a High Speed Rail Commission that solicited proposals from private bidders for a 320-mile line linking Miami, Orlando, and Tampa [Klein 1988]. A consortium of European firms was selected but was unable to come up with a financing package and backed out in 1991 [Levinson 1992].

In 1989 Texas formed a High Speed Rail Authority, which proposed to build a triangle of high-speed lines linking Houston, Dallas, and San Antonio. In 1991 it selected a consortium headed by Morrison Knudsen and including French interests. Originally the $5.7 billion project was to be financed entirely with private capital, but later the group sought approval of $3 billion in taxfree bonds. The future of the project is in doubt.

In 1982 Ohio voters rejected a 1¢ sales tax increase that would pay for an $8.5 billion high-speed rail network. Then a more modest plan was developed for a single route costing $3.2 billion and linking Cleveland, Columbus, and Cincinnati. This project is also awaiting a financing package.

The Pennsylvania High Speed Rail Passenger Commission studied a route between Philadelphia and Pittsburgh. However, Governor Robert P. Casey abolished the commission and killed the proposal in 1987 [Vranich 1991].

High-speed trains seem to be an attractive travel option for distances between 150 and 500 miles. Most trips shorter than this are made by private vehicle, while aviation dominates the market for longer trips. Trains may have an advantage for intermediate-length trips because of the difficulty in getting to and from airports and the congestion at some of them. In fact, the airlines see fast trains as a threat and have opposed some recent proposals.

Financing is the principal obstacle to implementing the proposals. Some were promoted with the idea that the private sector would build and operate the lines without public assistance. This now seems unlikely. A committee of the Transportation Research Board (TRB) concluded that the "systems are costly and unlikely to pay for themselves under reasonable projections of ridership and farebox revenues" [Transportation Research Board 1991b, p. 121]. However, the systems would produce some external benefits—such as relieving highway and airport congestion, energy savings, and improved air quality—that might warrant public subsidy.

So far, state governments have taken the initiative, but they do not have the resources to make multibillion-dollar investments. The U.S. government has shown little interest in bullet trains. In part the problem is institutional: There is no federal agency charged with taking an overview of high-speed transportation, but there are agencies committed to advancing the interests of the air and highway systems. According to the TRB committee, incremental improvements in existing rail services "may offer the most cost-effective and practical means of providing better intercity transportation in some corridors" [Transportation Research Board 1991b, p. 14].

Advanced Technology

Most of these trains would involve slight advances in conventional technology. There has also been experimentation with more exotic improvements. Following are major examples:

The *linear induction motor* has now been proved by experience and can be considered state of the art. In this system, the force created by passing an electric current through a magnetic field is used to produce linear motion instead of rotary motion. Part of the motor is installed in the roadbed between the tracks; the other part is a plate on the underside of the vehicle. To save electricity, the part in the roadbed is automatically activated just before a train arrives and is turned off after the train passes. No power is carried to the wheels; they simply support and guide the train. The Urban Transportation Development Corporation of Canada used this technology in building the Vancouver Skytrain and the people mover in Detroit.

Magnetic levitation (often called *maglev*) is currently receiving a great deal of attention. In this system, powerful electromagnets raise a train above a metal guideway while a linear induction motor propels it forward. By eliminating friction between the wheels and the rail, speeds exceeding 300 miles per hour can be achieved. The concept was developed by U.S. scientists in the 1960s, but federal funding for the research was terminated in 1975 when it was decided that existing technology was adequate [Strandberg 1991].

Since then, Germany and Japan have each invested $1 billion in research and development of maglev trains. The German system uses attractive forces, which lift a train about ⅜ inch. The Transrapid International group built a 20-mile test track in Emsland, Germany, where trains have operated since 1983 at speeds over 250 miles per hour. Transrapid built a magnetic levitation people mover in Birmingham, England, that has been in use since 1984. It plans to build a 13-mile line between the Orlando airport and Walt Disney World [Vranich 1991].

The Japanese system uses repulsive forces, which create a 4-inch gap between the train and the roadbed. An unstaffed prototype designed by the Japanese National Railways reached 321.3 miles per hour on a 4.4-mile test track in 1979. Several Japanese magnetic levitation trains have operated at world fairs. The Japanese now plan to build a 27-mile test track and may use magnetic levitation to replace the bullet trains. A consortium of Japanese firms has received permission to build a line in Las Vegas connecting the airport with downtown.

U.S. interest in magnetic levitation trains has revived. Some defense contractors, looking for new lines of work, lobbied for renewed federal aid for research and were supported by some members of Congress, including Senator Daniel Moynihan [1989]. This bore fruit, and the Intermodal Surface Transportation Efficiency Act of 1991 authorized expenditure of $725 million to develop a prototype magnetic levitation train.

An alternative means to levitate a vehicle is to create an air cushion underneath it. This is done by directing powerful jets of air downward that lift the vehicle just enough to eliminate friction. There was considerable interest in air-cushion trains in the 1960s and 1970s. A Frenchman, Jean Bertin, built a protoype called the *Aerotrain* that reached a speed of 264 miles per hour on a test track in 1969 [Sjokvist 1988]. Great Britain and the United States sponsored research in which air-cushion vehicles were built and tested. However, the results of these experiments were not considered satisfactory. At present, magnetic levitation seems to be a more promising approach.

GUIDED BUSWAYS

One relatively modest innovation that could see wide application is a system in which buses are attached to a guideway and automatically controlled. The buses can collect passengers in a residential area, then travel on the guideway at high speed, leave the guideway, and fan out over a destination area such as a central business district.

This has been implemented in the O-Bahn, a guided bus system developed by Daimler-Benz in Germany [Vuchic 1985]. The first system in public service began operating in Adelaide, Australia, in 1986 [Wayte 1988] (see Figure 7-6). It uses standard buses to which guide rollers have been attached. The buses operate in the usual manner on city streets, but after they enter the concrete guideway, no control by the driver is required. The line is 7.5 miles long and cost $70 million. It is completely grade-separated, as the route was originally intended for a freeway. Compared with conventional bus lanes, the main advantages are high speed (the buses move at a constant 62 miles per hour), a narrower right-of-way, and a smoother ride.

This is reminiscent of the concept of *dual-mode transportation* that received considerable attention in the 1970s [Transportation Research Board 1976]. The idea was to have the same vehicle perform collection-distribution and line-haul functions, so that no transfer is required. This was another attempt to ape the automobile by combining the advantages of door-to-door service and high speed on trunk lines.

One approach was to design buses that could be connected into "bus trains" and travel at high speed on freeways. This would presumably reduce labor costs because only one driver would be needed for each train. However, nothing ever came of this proposal.

Another idea was to have small vehicles that operate on the streets as automobiles do and are attached to some kind of conveyor system on the main line. The vehicles might be individually owned, or they might be available on a rental basis. William Alden invented a system called the *StaRRcar* in which small electric vehicles can either be driven on the streets, running on batteries, or automatically steered on a guideway with power from a rail. He built one car and a short section of track as a demonstration. Because he obtained some important patents, he was hired to help design the Morgantown PRT.

There were several studies of the dual-mode concept, and a number of inventors besides Alden proposed hardware for it. By 1980, the idea was largely forgotten in the United States, but Adelaide's guided busway has revived interest. While this is the only operating example of such a system, probably it will be considered as an alternative in future planning. The concept is a good one. It is approximated by express buses that run on exclusive lanes. Adding a guidance system to a busway might not involve much incremental cost.

FIGURE 7-6
Adelaide's automated busway. This facility is for exclusive use of buses, which are automatically steered and attain high speeds. The buses are fitted with rollers that keep them in the guideway. (*Source:* Wayte 1988, p. 112.)

HIGHWAY TRANSPORTATION

Rent-by-the-Trip Cars

A different technology aimed at solving a different problem involves small electric vehicles that are rented for single trips. This has also been called *public automobile service.* The application usually contemplated is in the central business district, where there would be several stations scattered about. You could rent a car at any station, drive it to another station, and leave it there. You wouldn't have to return it.

One demonstration of the concept was the *witkar* system begun in Amsterdam in

1974. It was proposed by Luud Schimmelpennink, an industrial designer and city councilman, in 1969. The council refused to support the scheme, but he formed a cooperative, borrowed $250,000 from several sponsors, and started the system himself. He designed the vehicle, which was similar to an electric golf cart. It was small and boxy, with three wheels and seats for two persons. The top speed was 20 miles per hour. It was powered by an electric motor with a nickel-cadmium battery and could run for 40 to 65 minutes before requiring recharging, which took 7.5 minutes.

The system operated as follows: A person joined the cooperative by paying a $10 entry fee and $10 for a plastic key card. Members had to have an account at the Amsterdam Savings Bank (one of the sponsors). At a station, a traveler inserted the card in a panel, and a computer made a credit check. Then the vehicle was unlocked and could be driven away. At the destination station, the card was inserted in another panel, and the charge was deducted from the person's bank account.

The witkar system was described in an article by Bendixson and Richards [1976]. At that time, there were 5 stations and 35 vehicles. There were ambitious plans for expanding the system, but this never happened. At first, costs were low because all labor was donated by volunteers and sites for the stations were donated by the city. But eventually financing problems led to the end of the experiment.

The idea was recently revived with proposals for "station cars" that would take commuters back and forth from rail stations. These would be small electric cars whose batteries would be recharged while they were parked at the stations. Commuters might use them to go between home and the station at the residential end; there might be others in the downtown area to go between stations and job sites. Public agencies and electric companies in Boston, Chicago, and San Francisco are investigating this concept [Knack 1992].

Motor Vehicles

While Detroit has a vested interest in preserving existing automotive technology, several companies have explored new approaches. Much attention has been given to alternative power sources for automobiles, which could be critical in a petroleum shortage. William Lear, whose company makes the Learjet, tried to develop a steam-engine car, but finally abandoned the effort. There is also much interest in alternative fuels, which are discussed in Chapter 11.

Electric vehicles seem to be the most popular alternative. Some are being manufactured; but without a breakthrough in batteries, it appears that they are handicapped by heavy weight, short range, and low speed. General Motors unveiled an experimental electric car called the *Impact* in January 1990. It has high acceleration and can travel 120 miles at 55 miles per hour before needing recharging. It uses conventional batteries that weigh 870 pounds, one-third of the car's total weight. GM later announced that 50 families would be chosen to test drive the Impact for several months during 1994.

Intelligent Vehicle-Highway Systems

Driverless vehicles operating on elegant guideways were depicted in the General Motors Futurama exhibit at the 1939–1940 World's Fair, and since then there has been sporadic interest in automated highways [Shladover 1990]. In the 1950s, GM demonstrated an "electronic highway" on which vehicles were controlled through a wire buried in the pavement. U.S. interest in the concept had virtually disappeared by 1980, but work continued in other countries, particularly Germany and Japan.

In recent years there has been a rebirth of U.S. interest in what are now called *intelligent vehicle-highway systems* (or *IVHSs*). Sometimes they are popularly referred to as *smart streets*. The national transportation policy issued in 1990 indicated a federal commitment to pursue research on IVHSs. The Intermodal Surface Transportation Efficiency Act of 1991 authorized $660 million for such research. Work is currently progressing in three areas that involve personal travel [Transportation Research Board 1991a]:

1 *Advanced traveler information systems* would provide communication with cars on the road. Instead of road signs, radio messages would be automatically transmitted to drivers, informing them of the speed limit, hazards ahead, etc. Temporary messages could be sent to warn motorists of unusual events, such as detours, accidents, or weather problems. The system could also be used to distribute traffic, informing drivers which routes are congested and which are not (much as radio stations now do). A street map could be displayed on a screen on the dashboard, with streets color-coded to represent average speeds. It would even be possible for an onboard computer to determine the optimal route under current traffic conditions.

Several European governments, automakers, and universities are cooperating in the $700 million PROMETHEUS project to develop such communications ability. A prototype system called *Autoguide* developed by the Siemens AG conglomerate is in use in Berlin [Beck et al. 1988]. A central computer monitors about 400 miles of streets for traffic and dispatches information to small computers installed in 700 cars. One Siemens engineer claimed that it reduced his journey to work from 40 to 20 minutes.

2 *Advanced traffic management systems* are intended to optimize traffic flow on street networks. Freeway surveillance and control systems have been in use for 30 years, but they are not widespread. Many cities use a computer to optimize traffic signal timing over a large area. Washington, D.C., has a system that controls 1200 intersections; one in Tokyo controls 6000 intersections.

Another approach is to equip cars with *automatic vehicle identification* (AVI) devices to determine whether they are entitled to use HOV lanes, tollbooth bypasses, or even parking lots. Restrictions could also be enforced; cameras could automatically record the license plates of violators. Automatic toll collection, in which cars need not slow down, is another application that is being used in several cities.

3 The most ambitious research area involves *automatic vehicle control systems,* representing truly automatic highways. To eliminate the need for drivers, computers would have to perform several functions, including control of steering, speed, and spacing between vehicles. There would be sensors to avoid collisions with both vehicles and objects in the roadway. Controlling the merging of vehicles, changing of lanes, and exiting from the highway would be especially difficult. If all this could be accomplished, it is estimated that the capacity of a freeway would be increased 5 times.

Another attraction of automated highways is to eliminate the monotony of long-distance driving on superhighways. One idea is to attach cars to a conveyor belt system that would run between major cities. Something similar is already in operation: In several places, automobiles are carried on railroad flatcars while their occupants ride in coaches. Amtrak offers a service called the Auto Train between Lorton, Virginia, and Sanford, Florida. There is another in a tunnel through the Alps, and this will be done in the tunnel under the English Channel.

While automobile-related interests provide most of the support for this research, numerous applications to transit and paratransit could occur [Davies et al. 1991]. Some buses have *automatic vehicle location* devices that inform dispatchers where the buses are at all times. Some buses have transmitters that can alter the timing of traffic signals. AVI systems could be used to identify car pools and give them priority over single-occupant cars. Computers could form car pools on demand, with travelers meeting at designated places. Transit passengers could pay fares by passing a card over a scanner, which would identify persons eligible for reduced fares. This system could also record data for use in scheduling and revising routes.

The technology for many of these things already exists, but the question of economic feasibility remains. Mass production would lower costs, but it is unknown how many car owners would voluntarily pay to add the equipment to perform these sophisticated functions. It would require an enormous amount of capital investment to install the roadway components. Incremental improvements may not be feasible; it is uncertain whether "smart cars" and "dumb cars" can mix in the same traffic stream. It may be necessary to build some expensive large-scale systems to demonstrate convincing results.

Cost is not the only objection. Some people believe that the attention and expenditure directed to IVHS only reinforce the dominance of the automobile in U.S. transportation. If IVHS technology is successful, more and more people will drive cars and there will be less use of transit, bicycles, and walking. One engineer wrote, "This search for a technical fix to traffic congestion problems is really a Band-Aid approach that does nothing to address the cause of the disease—transportation and land use policies that encourage automobile dependency" [Thor 1992, p. 11].

WATER TRANSPORTATION

Ferry service was once common in U.S. cities; it is still important in several of them, as well as elsewhere in the world. The FTA considers ferries that carry pedestrians to be mass transit and has made grants for them.

According to Caba [1988], ferries have made a comeback in New York City because bridges and tunnels are choked to capacity during rush hour. Besides the historic Staten Island Ferry, three new services operate between New Jersey and Manhattan. The Port Authority has a $150 million plan to run four large boats (holding up to 630 passengers each) between Hoboken and Battery Park City. In part, this is to transfer passengers from five suburban railroad lines, who are currently overloading the PATH subways under the Hudson River.

Seattle has the largest ferry network in the country. There are 23 boats, which carry 7 million vehicles and 17 million passengers per year across Puget Sound. The nine routes are mostly used by commuters from suburban towns; the trips take between 10 minutes and 1 hour. The state of Washington took over this system in 1951; it subsidizes the operation, but fares pay 70 percent of operating costs.

The Vancouver transit system operates the Sea-Bus over Burrard Inlet between downtown and North Vancouver. This service, which began in 1977, connects with numerous bus routes at both ends as well as with the Skytrain. Boston and San Francisco operate passenger boats for commuters, while New Orleans has a ferry that crosses the Mississippi River.

These services all use conventional boats. However, two new types of water craft using advanced technology are suitable for ferries. One is the *hydrofoil,* which has "wings" submerged in the water. At a high speed (about 30 miles per hour), the hull rises out of the water, reducing drag, and the ship accelerates to a speed of 50 to 60 miles per hour. Hydrofoils have been widely used in Europe for years, particularly in Russia (which has over a thousand in operation), Norway, and Italy (see Figure 7-7). Although Boeing manufactures them, very few have been used in the United States.

The pioneering work on the hydrofoil was done by Alexander Graham Bell, inventor of the telephone. Late in his life he settled in Nova Scotia and did research on the airplane. Little came of this, but he applied some of the ideas to boats. He built a hydrofoil

FIGURE 7-7
A hydrofoil passenger ferry. This one is operating on the Moscow River in front of the Kremlin. Notice that the hull has risen out of the water, greatly reducing friction. Hydrofoils are widely used in Russia and several other European countries, but they are rare in the United States. (Photo by author.)

that reached a speed of 71 miles per hour on Lake Baddeck in 1918. This was the world speed record for boats for many years. The U.S. Navy supported his research during World War I, but later lost interest, and the momentum moved to other countries.

The second type of watercraft suitable for ferries is the *hovercraft*. It contains powerful fans that blow downward and lift the boat a few inches off the water; there are rubber skirts to confine the air. Another set of motors operates propellers that move the vehicle forward. In principle, hovercraft can run over land, but normally it is used only on water. It has some disadvantages: It is very noisy, cannot operate in high waves, and can be damaged by floating debris.

The best example is the ferry service across the English Channel. These ships are surprisingly large (each can carry 254 passengers plus 30 automobiles) and fast (cruising speed is 60 miles per hour). In the 1960s, UMTA funded a demonstration of hovercraft operating between downtown San Francisco and the San Francisco and Oakland airports. It was not considered successful and was discontinued. There are currently no hovercraft in commercial service in the United States.

AIR TRANSPORTATION

Air transportation is important to modern cities because it is the favored mode of long-distance travel. Atlanta, Dallas, and Denver have been boomtowns partly because they are major airline hubs. There is relatively little intraurban travel by air; most of that is by helicopter. A few U.S. cities have scheduled helicopter service, including New York, Chicago, Los Angeles, and San Francisco. This is mostly to link airports, but often there is a heliport in or near the downtown area.

Helicopter use has increased rapidly. Besides airport service, the helicopter is widely used in business and industry, by the police, and by hospitals to bring patients needing emergency treatment. Finding acceptable heliport sites is a common problem, as the craft are noisy and unpopular with people living or working nearby. At one time, helicopters landed on top of the Pan Am Building in New York City and took passengers to and from airports. This service was terminated after an accident in 1977 caused five deaths, but the real opposition was to the noise.

Ground access to airports is a major problem. Travelers often spend more time on the ground getting to and from airports than they do in the air. The increasing size and speed of planes require longer runways, which means larger landing fields located farther from the city. The Dallas–Fort Worth International Airport occupies 13 square miles, and the new Denver airport is even larger. Kansas City offers a typical example: All major airlines moved from the highly accessible Downtown Airport to Kansas City International Airport 15 miles away.

The majority of air travelers reach the airport by automobile. Bus and limousine services are mostly patronized by out-of-town visitors and do not serve residential areas. The transit network seldom offers a convenient, fast way of getting to the airport. No U.S. cities had rail service to their airports until 1968, when Cleveland extended its heavy rail line to Hopkins International Airport. Washington, D.C., opened a Metro line to National Airport in 1977, and Chicago extended a rail line to O'Hare International Airport in 1984. A light rail line is being built to the Los Angeles International Airport, and it is planned to extend a BART line to the San Francisco International Airport.

A possible solution is V/STOL aircraft (this stands for *vertical or short takeoff and landing*). Some, like the tilt-rotor plane, can rise vertically, while others require a short runway. It has been proposed to build several small fields dispersed throughout a metropolitan area. No such aircraft are currently in regular service, but demonstrations have shown they are feasible (in one, planes used a pier in the Hudson River in Manhattan as a landing field). These planes also have military applications, as demonstrated by the British Harrier "jump jets" in the Falkland Islands War.

CONCLUSION

As part of the New Systems Study in 1967–1968, Stanford Research Institute published a much-heralded report outlining an array of concepts for new urban transportation technology [Henderson et al. 1968]. It included a proposal for major activity center travel, which has been implemented in people movers. Suggestions for local area travel included dial-a-bus. The concept for extended area travel was essentially PRT, as demonstrated at Morgantown, West Virginia. The approach to fast transit link systems was based on bullet trains. While the report did not directly influence later developments, in retrospect it appears to have been remarkably prescient.

Everyone agrees that research and development is necessary, but it is debatable how much money it is worth. Some critics argue that the glamour of high technology engenders extravagant spending and often produces white elephants. They would rather allocate resources to expand conventional transit service and keep fares down. Automation offers the promise of cutting labor costs, which represent about two-thirds of transit operating costs, but the trade-off is that new systems will require enormous capital investment. Because of this, implementation of advanced transit technology is likely to be gradual.

Probably the worst approach is the on-again, off-again support of the U.S. government. Potentially useful ideas have been abandoned because funding was terminated. The private sector is willing to make some investment in research and development, but will not commit large sums for a product that will inevitably have to be subsidized. The federal government must give sustained support if progress is to be realized. Several other countries seem more willing to take the risk of uncertain payoffs than the United States.

QUESTIONS

1 People in the United States have long been fascinated by new technology. Achievements in areas such as space exploration, computers, and weaponry have encouraged the belief that scientists and engineers can solve any problem. If we can send men to the moon, why can't we get commuters to work on time?

2 Give some examples of new technology in mass transit that has been developed in recent decades. Which advances hold the most promise for greatly improving urban transportation in the future?

3 The U.S. government aborted its downtown people mover program, but several cities went ahead and constructed such facilities. Do you think people movers should be built in more cities, or would this be a waste of money? Would it bring about the revitalization of downtown areas?

4 Proponents of intelligent vehicle-highway systems offer visions of automated streets with huge volumes of driverless vehicles moving at high speed. Do you think this will ever happen? What are the obstacles?
5 Several foreign cities operate automated trains that are totally controlled by computers. Why has this technology never been fully applied in the United States? Would you object to riding in a train that did not have a human operator?
6 If you were a transportation policymaker, would you give high priority to the development of new technology? Or would you spend the money available to expand conventional transit service and keep fares down?

REFERENCES

"AGT-Peoplemover Guide," *Mass Transit,* vol. 16, no. 3 (March 1989), pp. 15–30.

Ahlheim, Mark C.: "Personal Rapid Transit: Developing a New Mode of Public Transportation," *Transportation Research Record,* no. 1349 (1992), pp. 133–141.

Baron, Steven M.: "Still Waiting for the Train in Houston," *The New Electric Railway Journal,* vol. 6, no. 4 (Summer 1994), pp. 12–19.

Bas, Ed: "Detroit's Troubled People Mover," *Mass Transit,* vol. 13, no. 10 (October 1986), pp. 8ff.

Beck, Melinda, Michael Meyer, Shawn D. Lewis, and Mary Hager: "Smart Cars, Smart Streets," *Newsweek,* December 5, 1988, pp. 86–87.

Bendixson, Terence, and Martin G. Richards: "Witkar: Amsterdam's Self-Drive Hire City Car," *Transportation,* vol. 5, no. 1 (March 1976), pp. 63–72.

Caba, Susan: "Reviving the Waterways: The Return of the Commuter Ferry," *Mass Transit,* vol. 15, no. 1/2 (January-February 1988), pp. 16–18.

Cassidy, Robert: "Gloria Mundi Is Sick of Transit," *Planning,* vol. 40, no. 6 (July 1974), pp. 20–22.

Davies, Peter, Chris Hill, Neil Emmott, and Jeremy Siviter: *Assessment of Advanced Technologies for Transit and Rideshare Applications* (Leesburg, VA: Castle Rock Consultants, 1991).

Elias, Samy E. G., Edward S. Neumann, and Wafik H. Iskander: "Impact of People Movers on Travel: Morgantown—A Case Study," *Transportation Research Record,* no. 882 (1982), pp. 7–12.

Fabian, Lawrence J.: "People Movers: The Emergence of Semi-Public Transit," *Traffic Quarterly,* vol. 35, no. 4 (October 1981), pp. 557–568.

———: "People-Movers: From Semi-Public to Public Transit," *Transportation Quarterly,* vol. 37, no. 1 (January 1983), pp. 85–98.

Fisher, Ken: "Morgantown: The One and Only?" *Mass Transit,* vol. 8, no. 6 (June 1981), pp. 10ff.

Henderson, Clark, et al.: *Future Urban Transportation Systems: Descriptions, Evaluations, and Programs* (Menlo Park, CA: Stanford Research Institute, 1968).

Klein, Gilbert F.: "High-Speed Rail Is Creeping toward Reality," *Governing,* November 1988, pp. 66–67.

Knack, Ruth: "Plug in and Commute," *Planning,* vol. 58, no. 10 (October 1992), p. 26.

Levinson, Marc: "The Little Engines That Can't," *Newsweek,* January 17, 1992, p. 46.

Moynihan, Daniel Patrick: "How to Lose: The Story of Maglev," *Scientific American,* vol. 261, no. 5 (November 1989), p. 130.

Ruiter, Earl R., and Lance A. Neumann: "Status and Prospects of the Automated Guideway Transit Industry in the United States," *Transportation Research Record,* no. 991 (1984), pp. 38–48.

Shladover, Steven E.: "Roadway Automation Technology—Research Needs," *Transportation Research Record,* no. 1283 (1990), pp. 158–167.

Sjokvist, Eric H.: "Worldwide Development of Propulsion Systems for High-Speed Trains," *Transportation Research Record,* no. 1177 (1988), pp. 54–83.

Smith, George C., and Earl Shirley: "High-Speed Rail in California: Avoidable Controversy," *TR News,* no. 130 (May-June 1987), pp. 2–7.

Strandberg, Keith W.: "Mass Transit's Orphan Technology: Maglev Prepares to Come Home," *Mass Transit,* vol. 18, no. 1/2 (January/February 1991), pp. 18–21.

Thor, Carl: "Intelligent Vehicle-Highway Systems: Boon or Boondoggle?" *TR News,* no. 160 (May-June 1992), pp. 11–14.

Transportation Research Board: *Dual-Mode Transportation,* Special Report 170 (Washington: Transportation Research Board, 1976).

————: *Advanced Vehicle and Highway Technologies,* Special Report 232 (Washington: Transportation Research Board, 1991a).

————: *In Pursuit of Speed: New Options for Intercity Passenger Transport,* Special Report 233 (Washington: Transportation Research Board, 1991b).

Vranich, Joseph: *Super-Trains: Solutions to America's Transportation Gridlock* (New York: St. Martin's Press, 1991).

Vuchic, Vukan R.: "O-Bahn: Description and Evaluation of a New Concept," *Transportation Research Record,* no. 1011 (1985), pp. 8–15.

Wayte, Alan: "Adelaide's Automated Busways," in Wayne Attoe, ed., *Transit, Land Use and Urban Form* (Austin: Center for the Study of American Architecture, University of Texas, 1988), pp. 107–118.

8

PLANNING TRANSIT NETWORKS

Besides selection of the transit technology to use, another important part of transit planning is the design of the route network and choice of specific locations for routes and stops. That is the subject of this chapter.

Transit planning tends to be more complex than highway planning. There are more variables involved, more decisions for planners to make. Here are some of the major differences between highway planning and transit planning:

1 Highway planning is strictly concerned with construction of physical facilities—the channels for movement. Operation of vehicles is decentralized to individual, autonomous drivers. Transit planning also involves scheduling service on the routes, since a central agency manages all vehicles.

2 Highway engineers are not involved in the design of vehicles. This is done by the manufacturers, although it is partially regulated by the U.S. government. Transit engineers usually pay considerable attention to the design of vehicles, as they write specifications for manufacturers to fulfill. Transit vehicles (even buses) are essentially custom-made for each order.

3 Highway planners are concerned with the capacity of facilities, while this is not a constraint in transit. Except in New York City, no transit lines in the United States operate at anywhere near capacity. Crowding occurs in transit vehicles, but it could be remedied by scheduling more service. Cost may prevent this from being done.

4 Highways and transit respond to peak-period demand in opposite ways. Congestion causes highway speeds to decline. But door-to-door transit speeds often improve because more frequent service reduces waiting time. This is one reason why transit attracts more passengers during the peak than the off-peak hours.

THE PLANNING PROCESS

A transit system is only one of many types of facilities and services that governments provide for their citizens. Its importance varies greatly from city to city, depending on the size, density, and settlement pattern of the city. Therefore, transit planning should be integrated with comprehensive planning for the future of a city so that the transit system complements other public goals. The relationship of transit routes to land use is particularly important (this is discussed further in Chapter 10). Transit planning should also be done in the context of multimodal planning, since transit vehicles frequently share space with private vehicles. Rail lines and high-occupancy vehicle (HOV) lanes are often built in freeway alignments.

Transportation planning has several levels and time frames. Long-range planning typically has a horizon of 20 years and involves major projects with a long lead time. Short-range planning focuses on the next 3 to 5 years and involves more modest changes that can be implemented fairly quickly. Service or operational planning deals with day-to-day operations of a transit system, such as scheduling of service and adjustments to bus routes.

The transportation planning process in the United States is largely dictated by the federal requirements described in Chapter 3. Since 1975, every urbanized area has had a metropolitan planning organization (MPO) that is responsible for multimodal planning. The ISTEA legislation of 1991 strengthened the role of MPOs and increased their responsibilities. Each MPO must prepare a long-range transportation plan that considers fifteen specified factors and must adopt a transportation improvement program (TIP), which is a 3-year program of improvements. This must be updated annually.

When seeking federal aid for major investments, a transit planning agency must go through a process involving four phases:

1 *System planning.* This is long-range planning for the entire urban area. It involves examining alternative systems at a general level, evaluating their potential cost-effectiveness, and identifying a priority corridor for the next major improvement. The output is a system planning report that is submitted to the FTA.

2 *Alternatives analysis.* This study is a detailed comparison of several alternatives for the priority corridor, including a base case or *null alternative.* It results in selection of a preferred alternative. This report must be accompanied by a draft Environmental Impact Statement.

3 *Preliminary engineering.* This work on the preferred alternative determines technical feasibility; establishes specific alignments, grades, and station locations; and makes detailed cost estimates. The output is submitted along with a final Environmental Impact Statement.

4 *Final design.* In this phase, engineers prepare the final plans and specifications that will be used by contractors. By this point, there should be only minor decisions to make, and cost estimates should not change much.

This whole process takes several years. Normally the FTA must approve the completion of each phase before the next phase starts, although sometimes the FTA permits overlap. The FTA makes the federal funding commitment at the end of the third phase. Until then, any proposal may be aborted.

A few transit agencies have also conducted *strategic planning* [Farkas et al. 1989]. The approach originated in the private sector but has been adapted to public organizations in recent years. It involves rethinking of the basic mission of an agency and identifying internal strengths and weaknesses and external opportunities and threats. The outcome is the development of strategic objectives and restatement of the agency's mission. Progress toward the objectives should be monitored over the ensuing years. The Transportation Research Board (TRB) has published a set of guidelines for strategic planning and management in transportation agencies [Tyndall et al. 1990].

Most planning agencies follow a rational planning paradigm that has been widely accepted in the planning profession. Black [1990] enumerated ten steps in this process in a case study of the Chicago Area Transportation Study. These important steps are emphasized here:

1 Establishing goals and objectives
2 Formulating alternatives
3 Estimating the performance of the alternatives
4 Evaluating the alternatives

Setting goals and objectives involves policy decisions at the highest level. While planners often make proposals, there should be concurrence by the relevant governing body, whether it be a transit authority board of directors or a city council. For examples of transportation goals and objectives, see Dickey [1983, chapter 4]. There is a tendency to adopt vague, noncontroversial statements such as "to provide for safe, efficient travel" or "to improve the quality of life." But some significant questions should be answered before the planning analysis proceeds.

First, is the transit system intended to attract drivers away from their automobiles, or is it mainly to aid people who do not have access to an automobile? The answer will depend on local conditions. In large metropolitan areas where freeway congestion seems intolerable, removing private vehicles from the roads may be the dominant goal. In smaller cities where traffic moves relatively well, priority should go to serving the transportation-disadvantaged.

Second, should transit service emphasize delivery of commuters to the CBD or dispersed travel throughout the central city and perhaps the suburbs? The two targets call for different kinds of service. They are not mutually exclusive; some large cities serve both markets well. The answer does not depend solely on the population's economic well-being. For example, San Francisco's large bus system makes it possible to travel anywhere in the city by transit, even though car ownership is high.

Third, who will pay for transit service, and how? Most transit systems operate at a deficit. While federal and state governments give some subsidies, usually local taxpayers must pay part of the bill. Policy makers must decide how much service is needed and how much tax support is acceptable. Often they adopt objectives or standards to guide such decisions. Problems of financing transit are discussed in Chapter 15.

Many environmentalists favor transit; goals of improving air quality, conserving energy, and reducing dependence on petroleum imports are often stated. Heavily used transit systems in large cities certainly do further these goals. But in small and medium-sized cities, transit is unlikely to remove enough vehicles from the road to have much impact. Direct approaches such as the regulation of motor vehicles seem to be more effective. Energy and environmental implications of transit are covered in Chapter 11.

The second step in the process—formulation of alternatives—remains something of an art. It is still largely an intuitive design exercise. Hence it will receive most of the attention in the following sections.

Estimating the performance of alternatives is the most highly developed part of the process. Although the methodology is summarized here, no attempt will be made to describe it fully, since there exist several good textbooks on the subject.

Evaluation often involves standard methodologies such as benefit/cost analysis or cost-effectiveness analysis. Because these topics are also well covered in other books, they will not be discussed here. While they have flaws, they are systematic procedures that bring some rationality to decision making. However, achievement of some goals cannot be quantified; intangible factors play a part in decisions, often rightfully so. In any case, evaluation should be based on the goals and objectives established in the first step.

PLANNING METHODOLOGY

Major advances in the methodology of transportation planning occurred in the 1960s, concurrently with the spread of electronic computers. Most of the techniques were first used in highway planning, which was stimulated by construction of the interstate highway system. Gradually the techniques were applied to transit planning, with suitable modifications. The Chicago Area Transportation Study, in the early 1960s, was the first planning agency to code transit networks for a computer, program models to forecast passenger flows, and evaluate the results with benefit/cost analysis [Black 1990].

The first computer models were developed as ad hoc efforts by a few large metropolitan transportation studies, such as those at Chicago, Philadelphia, and New York City. Then the 1962 Highway Act essentially mandated that every urbanized area in the country conduct a transportation study, so there was a need for standardized methodology. Soon the U.S. Department of Transportation prepared computer programs and disseminated them to planning agencies throughout the country. An integrated software package called the *Urban Transportation Planning System,* or *UTPS,* was widely used for many years [Dial 1976]. This synthesized highway and transit planning. UTPS required a large mainframe computer, but a simplified version using manual calculations was also available [Sosslau et al. 1978].

UTPS was applied to large networks, containing many thousands of links and representing the road or transit system of a whole metropolitan area. With the advent of microcomputers and a shift in emphasis to planning studies of individual corridors and smaller areas, UTPS is seldom used today. Instead, software has been developed to perform the models on personal computers; Ferguson et al. [1992] reviewed nine urban transportation planning packages on the market. QRS II, based on the methodology of Sosslau et al. [1978], is perhaps the most popular, but has limited capacity. EMME/2, developed at the University of Montreal, is considered the most advanced.

The main object of these computer programs is to estimate use; the process is called *travel demand forecasting.* This book does not cover it in detail, but it will be described briefly. Anyone expecting to become a transportation planner should take a course in this methodology. It makes use of networks, explained in the next section.

Transportation Networks

A network is a kind of *graph,* which is a geometric figure made up of points and lines. The branch of mathematics dealing with this is called *graph theory,* or *topology.* It can be theoretical and esoteric, but many linear systems can be represented as graphs. In practical applications, the points and lines are always interconnected. Each line has a point at each end, and several lines may meet at a single point. Other terms are often used. Transportation planners usually refer to a point as a *node* and to a line as a *link.* A *network* is defined as a graph in which there is some sort of flow.

A transit network resembles the route map that a transit operator publishes. The links represent segments of transit routes. For a rail line, a link is a section of track; for a bus route, it is a street on which buses run. All transit modes are included in the same network.

Each transit link has two dimensions: *flow* (the number of units that use the link) and *friction* (the cost or penalty incurred by each unit of flow on the link). The flow is the output of the estimating process; in transit planning, it is the number of passengers. The friction includes the time and cost to traverse the link. The friction must be estimated and assigned in describing the network.

In conventional coding of a transit network, each route is represented separately, even if two or more routes use the same street or track. This is another difference from highway planning; it makes a transit network more complicated. It is common for several bus routes to use the same downtown street; each must get its own link.

An alternative way of coding a transit network was developed by Dial [1967]. The network is coded in two files, one containing links and one containing lines (the transit routes). All lines using an individual link are designated, but you do not need multiple links for multiple routes. Dial devised a special minimum-path algorithm for this approach; it is slightly less efficient than the standard ones. The advantages are that coding the network is easier and there are fewer links.

Transit nodes represent (1) rail stations, (2) bus stops or groups of adjacent stops, or occasionally (3) major changes in a route, such as the point where buses enter an expressway and speed increases markedly.

There is a special kind of node called a *loading node,* which is artificial. This is a place where trips enter or leave the network. The region under study is divided into small geographic areas traditionally called *traffic zones.* Zones vary in size depending on the scale of the study; they may be as small as a city block or as large as 1 square mile. In a typical metropolitan area study, zones are approximately the size of census tracts. Each zone gets one loading node (also called the *zone centroid*), and it is assumed that all origins and destinations in the zone occur at this node.

A special kind of link called an *artificial link* connects a loading node with a node representing a transit stop. It gets a friction consisting of (1) the average time to walk to the transit stop plus (2) the average waiting time (usually assumed to be one-half of headway) plus (3) the fare. Since the friction is measured in minutes, the fare is converted to a time equivalent, by using an assumed value of travel time. Several artificial links may emanate from one loading node, since several transit routes may pass through a zone.

Artificial links are also used for transfers between two routes. Such a link gets a friction representing waiting time for the second route. If a person must walk between the routes (often necessary in a subway station), that time is added. If an additional fare is required, that is also included.

Travel Demand Forecasting

This process predicts what will happen in the future under hypothetical conditions (build a freeway here, or build a rail line there). It may be applied to present conditions in order to check the validity of the models or to *calibrate* them (to estimate the numerical values of key parameters). The process is based on division of the region under study into *traffic zones*; typically there are several hundred zones in a metropolitan area. Prior to travel forecasting, the land use, population, and economic activity in each zone are estimated for the forecast year.

Several books describe the travel demand forecasting process in detail, such as those by Dickey [1983] and Meyer and Miller [1984]. The process is composed of four major steps:

1 *Trip generation.* The number of person-trip ends in each zone is estimated based on the land use, population, and economic activity. A person-trip is undifferentiated by mode; it is one person making one trip, which has an origin and a destination (both are *trip ends*). Key variables in estimating trip ends at residential land use are income, automobile ownership, and household size. Trip ends at nonresidential land use are usually based on employment, floor space, and land area. This step is important because it establishes the total number of trips in the region as well as where the trips start and end.

2 *Trip distribution.* Where the trips will go is estimated. The number of trips starting in each zone and ending in every other zone is calculated (in other words, origins and destinations are paired). The result is a table of zone-to-zone trips called *zonal interchanges.* This step requires the largest volume of computations. Two categories of mathematical models are used: *Growth-factor models* start with a table of zonal interchanges for a base year and factor it up to match forecast totals. *Synthetic models* do not require an existing table; they estimate the interchanges on the basis of travel time and cost. The gravity model is the most popular of the synthetic models, but some planners prefer the opportunity model.

3 *Modal split.* The number of person-trips is divided into two modal groups: automobile trips or transit trips. This step will be covered in more detail in Chapter 12 as part of a discussion on travel behavior.

4 *Traffic* (or *network*) *assignment.* The routes that the trips will take are estimated. Each zonal interchange is sent over a network that has been coded and stored in the computer. Highways and transit have separate networks: Automobile trips go over a network containing expressways and arterial streets; transit trips go over a network of rail lines and bus routes. Early asssignment programs used a minimum-path algorithm to send each interchange over the path with the least travel friction. Recent programs calculate an equilibrium in which no interchange could benefit from switching to another route.

Assignments are made for a 24-hour period (the average weekday) but also for shorter times, such as the peak period. The number of trips assigned must correspond with the time period. The network may have to be adjusted; certain services operate only in the peaks, and schedules vary during the day.

The end product of this process is a listing or display of estimates of the numbers of vehicles using every link of the highway network and the numbers of passengers using every link of the transit network. The computer also produces summaries of total travel time, how many persons get on and off at each transit stop, and other statistics. These numbers are key ingredients of evaluation methods. For example, the volumes are compared with capacities of links to see whether congestion will occur (this is common with highways and can occur in transit when too few vehicles are scheduled). The numbers may become inputs for benefit/cost analysis or models that estimate air pollution or energy consumption.

Planning for the future involves trying to improve the network. Usually this means adding or deleting links; sometimes it means changing the frictions of certain links (perhaps to represent higher speed or less waiting time). The year for testing must be chosen. To use the existing numbers of trips implies that the revised network is implemented immediately. This may be appropriate for bus routes, which can be changed quickly. But normally the test is for a future year, in which case the number of trip ends in each zone must be forecast for that year.

A key part of the process is the generation of ideas for changes in the network (in other words, drafting a plan). This is one step that requires the human mind; computers have no imagination. Some planners have developed systematic procedures to add and subtract links, but typically the work of devising proposed changes is intuitive. Two guidelines are available: (1) Experience with existing transit networks suggests some design principles. (2) A number of analysts have done studies that optimize various dimensions of transit systems. These two subjects are discussed in the rest of this chapter.

CONFIGURATION OF THE NETWORK

Rail

Most rail transit routes are radials that end at or pass through the city center. This is true whether the technology is suburban railroad, heavy rail, or light rail. If a city has only one line, the line is inevitably a radial (as in Miami). If there are two lines, they usually cross at the center (this is true in Atlanta). Even when there are more lines, they normally meet at the center, forming what Lewis Mumford called the *asterisk plan* (Boston provides an example). The reason is that the largest market for transit is travel to or from the CBD.

Circumferential and crosstown rail routes rarely generate enough traffic to justify the investment. The main examples are found in foreign countries. When a circumferential

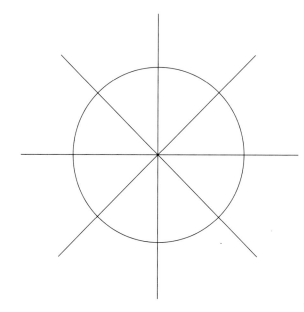

FIGURE 8-1
The radial-circumferential pattern. The circumferential or circle route is largely used to transfer between radial routes. In practice, not all the radial routes could meet at a single station in the center; they would have to be offset. The subway systems in London, Paris, and Moscow approximate this pattern. There is no example in the United States.

route is combined with radials, this creates the radial-circumferential or "cobweb" pattern (see Figure 8-1). The best example can be seen in Moscow, where there is heavy travel on the circle route. London and Paris also have circumferential subways. There is no example in the United States.

A crosstown route connects outlying areas but does not go through the center. It can be considered part of a circumferential. New York City has such a route—the G line between Brooklyn and Queens. All other rail routes in New York City go to Manhattan. Chicago once had a crosstown elevated running north-south near Ashland Avenue. Much of it was abandoned after World War II, but a portion remains as part of the Douglas line.

Many rail networks have branching routes, i.e., radial routes that divide into two or more lines outside the CBD (see Figure 8-2). The resulting pattern resembles the letter Y, with the base of the Y at the CBD. There are examples in New York City, Chicago, and Washington, D.C. The BART system divides into three branches in the East Bay. Boston's Green Line (which carries light rail) splits into four branches.

Branches have the advantage of covering a larger area so that more travelers are within walking distance of a station. Because service is less frequent, branches are often used in lower-density areas where passenger loads do not justify short headways. Branches have the disadvantage of requiring more construction cost than a single line. There are also operational problems: The branches should have roughly equal demand so trains may alternate among them. Incoming trains must stay on schedule so that they will merge properly at the junction of the branches.

Perhaps the oddest configuration occurs in Glasgow (this was the third underground in the world, opening in 1896). The entire subway consists of an oval 6.5 miles in cir-

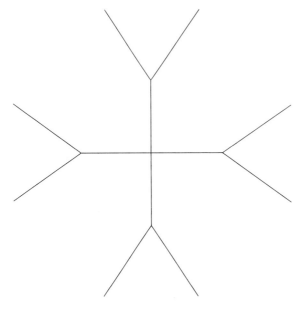

FIGURE 8-2
Radial routes with branches. This design provides greater coverage in outlying areas, but with less frequent service. Normally every other train will take each branch. This pattern is common in large U.S. cities such as New York, Chicago, and Washington. In some cases a main line divides into three branches (San Francisco) or even four (Boston).

cumference. One set of trains travels clockwise; another set, counterclockwise. One end of the oval passes under the CBD, so this amounts to having two radial routes that meet at their outer ends.

Downtown distribution is a weak point in some systems. Ideally stations are located near the major activity concentrations so that passengers can walk to and from them. Sometimes this does not occur (usually for historical reasons), and many passengers must take short bus trips within the CBD. When there are multiple routes, there should be convenient transfer points that require little walking. There is a good pattern in St. Petersburg, Russia: Three radial routes are offset and form a triangle in the city center. A passenger on any line can easily transfer to either of the other two lines.

Bus

In most small cities, bus routes are radials converging on the CBD. In medium-size and large cities, the bus networks are larger and more complex and may not resemble any simple pattern. Most routes follow major streets, so the network apes the street pattern. In cities where radial streets are prominent (such as Pittsburgh and Washington), the busiest routes are radials.

The gridiron street pattern is common in U.S. cities, so many bus networks approximate a grid. Chicago, Detroit, and Milwaukee offer examples. This design has the advantages of covering the entire city well and making it possible to travel between outer areas without passing through the CBD. The principal disadvantage is that a high percentage of passengers must transfer, since many desire lines that are diagonally oriented. The system works well if headways are short, which can be justified only in large cities. Of course, when two routes cross, they should have stops at the same intersection.

The likelihood of making passengers transfer is an important factor in designing a bus network. Although transfers are normally free, many travelers find the time and nuisance annoying. The need to transfer is a deterrent to transit use. Travel behavior studies show that out-of-vehicle time (including waiting time) is psychologically weighted more heavily than in-vehicle time is.

In a city with rail transit, many bus routes terminate at rail stations. In Boston, e.g., ten bus routes converge on the Harvard station on the Red Line. This pattern also forces many riders to transfer, but they benefit from higher speed on the rail portion of their trips.

Of course, other patterns than a grid or radials are possible. There have been analytical comparisons of different geometries for bus networks by Thompson [1977], Thelen et al. [1980], and Vaughan [1985].

Real bus networks differ from any ideal pattern. There may be irregular streets, topographical constraints, or barriers such as freeways and railroad tracks. Further, routes are adjusted according to demand. In low-density areas where most households have automobiles, routes are spaced farther apart than in high-density areas that generate more transit riders. Socioeconomic characteristics of the residents also play a part. Low-income communities may be served by numerous routes, while wealthy areas have little service.

Many automobile-oriented metropolitan areas have difficulty making bus service competitive with driving on freeways. Thompson [1977] argued that traditional transit networks have become dysfunctional, as these areas have dispersed activity centers and the CBD generally attracts less than 10 percent of all trips. One approach to this situation is to redesign the bus network to focus on *transit centers* or transfer points [Schneider and Smith 1981]. The region is divided into subregions, each with its own transit center (a shopping center is a recommended location) (see Figure 8-3). Three kinds of service are provided:

1 Local buses circulate within each subregion and bring people to or from the transit center. The buses do not cross into adjacent subregions. Buses may operate on fixed routes with fixed schedules, or if demand is low, there may be demand-responsive service instead.

2 Express buses, with limited stops, run between each transit center and the CBD. Ideally they operate on expressways at fairly high speeds. They may be given priority over other traffic, as with HOV lanes.

3 Express buses run on a circumferential route between transit centers. Again it is best if they use an expressway; many cities have a beltway.

This plan provides wide coverage of a metropolitan area, allowing a person without a car to go almost anywhere. However, most travelers will have to transfer. There is no direct service between residential areas and the CBD; passengers must transfer at a transit center unless they live within walking distance (unlikely if it is a suburban mall). Traveling between suburbs may require two transfers (from local to express and back to local).

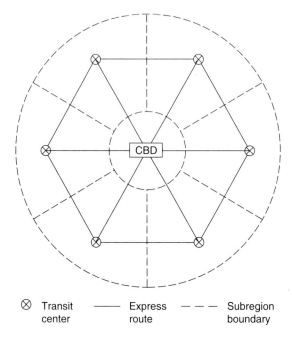

⊗ Transit   ——— Express   — — — Subregion
   center   route   boundary

FIGURE 8-3
The transit center system for buses. The region is divided into subregions, as indicated by the broken lines. The central one contains the central business district (CBD) and has conventional service. Each of the others has a transit center where buses circulating within the subregion (not shown) terminate. Express buses run between each transit center and the CBD. There is also circumferential express service connecting the transit centers.

The *timed-transfer* system can mitigate this problem. All buses are scheduled to arrive at a transit center almost simultaneously, and they wait there for 3 to 5 minutes. This keeps the transfer time to a minimum. However, the system can break down if a bus is more than a few minutes late at the transit center; then other buses must wait for it. Adhering to schedule is a persistent problem for buses. It may be difficult to schedule all the buses for simultaneous arrival, since travel times on the routes may vary greatly.

Park-and-ride travel fits well with the transit center scheme. If the center is located at a shopping mall, commuters can drive there, park all day for free, and take an express bus downtown.

The transit center plan has been adopted in several cities, including Denver, Portland, and Edmonton. There are case studies of implementation in Tacoma/Pierce County, Washington [Schneider et al. 1984], and Austin, Texas [Bakker et al. 1988]. The system appears to be successful at improving service, but in some cases this has involved considerable expenditure for expanding the bus fleet and constructing off-street transfer centers. Much planning work is required to coordinate the routes and schedules; the steps are described by Schneider and Smith [1981].

In some cities, the pattern of bus routes has changed little for years. In New York City, a route serving a ferry terminal was continued for 10 years after the ferry ceased operation. Bus routes may not fit well with recent development; new activity centers such as shopping malls may not be served. It is often possible to improve the system greatly by redesigning the route network. The Transportation Research Board [1980] has published a fine guide to the planning of bus routes and schedules. The book by Giannopoulos [1989] can also serve as a practical manual.

However, it is wise not to change routes too often. This always causes some confusion for passengers and may arouse public opposition. Further, people adapt to the routes, and the routes attract regular riders for whom they provide the best travel option, given the riders' circumstances. When a route is changed, some of these riders may find it is no longer the best option. Changing a route usually causes some loss of riders. Hence it should be done only if the loss is likely to be offset by the number of new riders gained.

DESIGNING A SINGLE ROUTE

Rail

The location of rail lines is often governed by the availability of right-of-way. However, there are choices to be made and logical rules to follow. There is a good discussion of design principles in a book by Tass [1971]. The basic problem is this: An individual rider wants only the stations where he or she joins and leaves the service. But there are many individuals wanting to get on and off at many points. A balance must be found between the contrasting mass and individual demands.

Routes should be as straight as possible, since detours and curves cause delays for most passengers. If detours are unavoidable, they should delay the least number of passengers. The alignment should not bend at a point where most passengers want to go straight on.

Compromise solutions sometimes arise whereby one (usually circuitous) route is constructed in place of two. This forces riders to make unavoidable detours and impairs the efficiency of the system. A branched route may be the best alternative in this situation.

Insofar as possible, passengers should not be forced to transfer. A trunk line that bypasses the CBD will cause heavy transfer movements (as occurred in Toronto with the Bloor-Danforth line).

Operation on extremely long routes is undesirable. Delays tend to accumulate so that trains fall behind schedule. Further, the outer sections of the route are often underutilized, resulting in uneconomical operation. It is better to design a set of feeder bus routes that bring passengers from lower-density areas to a rail terminal.

Stations should be sited near dense concentrations of activity so that many potential transit users will be within walking distance. Often these are commercial centers, but other examples include a university, a hospital complex, a sports stadium, and an airport. Normally stations should not be placed in primarily residential areas unless the areas are high-density.

Chicago pioneered in locating rail transit lines in the median strips of expressways, and this has become a popular choice (see Figure 8-4). The advantage is the low cost of land. Typically the highway project is charged for most of the cost, and the transit line pays only a fraction. An expressway requires a strip about 300 feet wide; a rail line needs only 30 or 40 feet.

However, this is a poor location in several ways. Transit routes should run through dense centers of activity and connect them. Expressways usually go through the less

FIGURE 8-4
Rapid transit line in the median strip of the Eisenhower Expressway, Chicago. This was the first instance in the United States in which a rail line was built in the middle of a freeway (it opened in 1958). This has become common practice since, although it has disadvantages (see text). (Photo by author.)

built-up spaces between the centers. Highway planners try to avoid the centers because of the high cost of acquiring property. If the activity pattern is visualized as a three-dimensional surface, then rail lines should follow the ridges and expressways should follow the valleys. This is a basic difference between locating rail lines and expressways.

There are also problems at the microscale. A transit station in the middle of an expressway is far from any buildings; people using the station must walk a long way. Stations are often located at interchanges, which tend to be surrounded by automobile-oriented businesses such as gas stations, rather than tall buildings which might supply a lot of transit users.

Another common mistake is to route rail lines along major streets, which may bend or miss some of the activity centers in the corridor. Again the temptation to deviate from good design practice derives of lower costs. A street is public property and available free of charge. A route that does not follow streets may require property acquisition (unless it is a deep subway).

Both shallow and deep tunnels have advantages. Shallow tunnels usually follow streets and are built by the *cut-and-cover* method. This is cheaper, although it involves extra work preserving utilities under the street and disrupts traffic during construction.

Deep tunnels need not follow streets and go below the utilities anyway. Besides cost, deep tunnels have the disadvantage of increasing vertical travel between street level and the train platform. This may seem a trivial item, but it mounts up when several hundred thousand persons a year use a station.

Because rail networks are sparse, many passengers reach them by another mode than walking. This should be considered in locating a route. Many people transfer from buses; hence rail stations should be sited at points where bus routes cross or merge (see Figure 8-5). Many persons drive to suburban stations, so the stations should have kiss-and-ride and park-and-ride facilities (this is always desirable for outer terminals). Availability of land for parking may influence site location. If stations are heavily used, parking garages may be indicated. Boston's Red Line has multilevel parking facilities at the Alewife terminal on the north end and the Quincy station near the south end.

Bus

Bus routes should follow arterial streets as much as possible and avoid minor streets. Arterial streets are wider (buses are difficult to maneuver) and have higher average speeds because of traffic engineering measures designed to increase flow. Side streets

FIGURE 8-5
The Silver Spring station on the Washington Metro. Adjacent are an area for buses to load and un-load and a parking lot (plus a multilevel parking garage, not shown). Many rail passengers transfer to and from other modes, and such a design facilitates transfers. (Photo by author.)

are more likely to be blocked by parked vehicles or children playing. Arterials are more likely to be lined with buildings that have high trip generation.

Ideally a bus route should be straight and direct. This is easier for people to understand, and usually it provides a faster trip from end to end. On the other hand, buses should stop in front of major trip generators. These goals may conflict, so a compromise is necessary. It is common to put deviations in routes so as to pass by major buildings such as a high school, hospital, or shopping center. But if a route becomes circuitous, service will be slowed to the point where it repels some travelers. Hence potential deviations deserve careful study to determine whether they are justified. If there are deviations, it is best to have them near the outer end of the route, where they will delay the fewest passengers.

Transit agencies regularly receive requests to add new routes or change existing ones. The best-managed agencies have adopted criteria and use a formal evaluation process. A booklet issued by the Toronto Transit Commission states that a proposal is acceptable if it is operationally feasible, it meets specified design guidelines, and it "confers a *net* benefit on existing and potential customers (e.g., measured as the number of new riders served vs. the number of existing riders inconvenienced)" [1984, p. 10].

Many bus routes terminate in the CBD. Instead of having each bus turn back on the same route, *through routing* offers some advantage. Routes on opposite sides of the CBD are paired, and each bus alternates between the routes. For example, a bus comes in from the west side, stops in the CBD, and then leaves for the east side. This will eliminate transfers for some riders going from the west side to the east side. However, very long routes should be avoided because they increase the probability of falling behind schedule.

Cycle routing may be used in low-density areas (see Figure 8-6). Instead of having each bus travel back and forth on the same line, all buses go in the same direction around a loop. Essentially a bus is outbound on half the route and inbound on the other half. This increases travel time for some riders who want to go in the direction opposite

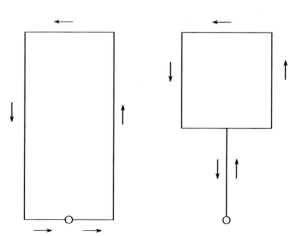

FIGURE 8-6
Cycle and balloon routing. These types of bus routes are often used in low-density areas where passenger volumes are light. In a cycle route (on the left), buses travel in one direction around the entire loop. In a balloon route (on the right), buses follow a one-way loop on the outer portion of the route, while two-way service is provided on the rest of the route.

to the bus and have to travel around the loop. This option is mostly used to provide some minimal service in areas of low demand.

A compromise is *balloon routing*. Here buses travel back and forth along most of the route, but there is a small one-way loop at the outer end. On a map the pattern resembles a balloon on a string, hence the name.

One question that has received much attention is whether to locate a bus stop on the near side or far side of an intersection, especially one with traffic signals. There is no consensus; practice varies from city to city. Giannopoulos itemized the pros and cons of each choice [1989, pp. 116–121]. A theoretical study by Ghoneim and Wirasinghe [1980] indicated that the key factor is whether demand for boarding and alighting is greater on the near side or far side.

SPACING OF ROUTES

Designing a transit network involves determination of the spacing between routes. For a grid pattern (typical of bus systems), this means the spacing between parallel lines. For a radial pattern (typical of rail systems and busways), it means the angular distance between radial lines.

There have been several analytical studies that used a grid pattern, in part because it simplified the mathematics. Holroyd [1967] assumed a grid of bus routes and derived a solution for optimal spacing of routes and frequency of service. The optimum produced an exact balancing of three cost components: walking time, waiting time, and cost of bus service. Matzzie [1968] posed and solved several problems involving grid systems of transit routes. Woodhull [1970] extended Holroyd's approach to two grids, one for rail and one for bus. These studies assumed uniform spacing of the grid, although Matzzie suggested that variable spacing might be better in realistic applications.

Similar are studies of the optimal spacing of parallel transit routes. Byrne and Vuchic [1972] assumed a rectangular corridor containing parallel routes leading to the CBD. They proved that routes should be located so that an equal number of passengers from either side use each one. Then they devised an iterative approach to find a simultaneous optimum for route spacing and headway. Hurdle [1973] assumed a set of parallel bus routes leading to a rapid transit main line. The feeder routes joined the main line at stations, so that the spacing of routes was also the spacing of stops on the main line.

Byrne [1975] took the other geometric approach by assuming a circular city and radial transit routes. He derived a solution for the optimal number of radial routes when population density varies with distance from the center.

These studies indicated several relationships. When the total amount of service is held constant, wide spacing between routes leads to (1) lower construction cost, because fewer routes are built; (2) more frequent service on each route and hence less waiting time; and (3) greater access distance to the routes (important if most people walk). The opposite results hold: Close spacing between routes means greater construction cost, less frequent service on each route, and shorter access distance.

The optimum depends on how large construction cost is compared to travelers' time costs. For rail systems, the cost of constructing routes is very large, so it is best to have few routes (wide spacing) and more frequent service on each route. Not everyone will reach the routes on foot; some people will take feeder buses, and others will drive. For conventional bus systems, routes follow existing streets and the construction cost is zero. Hence it is best to have many routes (close spacing) and less frequent service on each route. Walking will be less, but waiting time will be greater.

SPACING OF STOPS

The spacing of stops largely determines the average operating speed on a line, which affects the quality of service perceived by travelers. The maximum speed of the vehicles is only secondary. In deciding on the number of stops on a line, it is important to realize that each stop causes time losses for (1) braking to a stop, (2) unloading and loading passengers, and (3) accelerating back to running speed.

It is wasteful to have stops so close together that the vehicles cannot reach their cruising speed. High-speed vehicles (such as suburban trains) should be used only on lines with wide spacing between stops. Routes with frequent stops should use vehicles with low speeds (such as buses). Acceleration rates also play a part: Vehicles that accelerate slowly should have routes with long distances between stops (again, true of suburban trains.)

There is a certain spacing of stops that will minimize travel time for passengers. As stops come closer together, each person walks less distance to a stop. At the same time, average speed of the transit vehicles declines, and the ride takes longer. Feder [1973] found that the optimal spacing between bus stops should be 0.5 mile. Typical bus routes have 6 to 10 scheduled stops per mile (but they stop only on demand).

Including monetary costs yields a different optimum. A transit operator is likely to favor few stops on a line because this will raise the average speed and lower operating costs (labor cost is a function of time). Further, turnaround time will be faster, and fewer vehicles will be needed. But passengers will have longer access distances to the stops.

Sometimes there is community pressure to add stops. This is understandable: A transit line running through your neighborhood is of no value (and may be a nuisance) if you cannot get on or off. But if decision makers always yield to this pressure, the inevitable result is close spacing and slow speeds. Most optimization studies indicate that the spacing between stops should be greater than is customary in practice.

The mode (and speed) of access to stops makes a difference. Higher access speed increases the optimal spacing between stops. This applies when most people drive their cars to the stops. The BART system was designed largely for such travelers. There are large parking lots at most suburban stations, stops are about 2.5 miles apart on average, and train speeds are high.

Uniform spacing of stops is not necessarily desirable. The cumulative effect of the time delays caused by stops is interesting. Consider a train that starts in the suburbs and heads for the CBD during the morning peak. Most travelers are destined for the CBD. A person wanting to get on benefits when the train stops, but a person on board suffers a delay. If there are few people on the train and many who want to get on, there should be more stops. If there are many people on board and few who want to get on, there should be fewer stops. As the train approaches the CBD, there will be more and more people on board, and there should be fewer stops. This is contrary to usual practice, in which the spacings become closer as one nears the CBD.

Schneider [1961] analyzed this problem for a hypothetical corridor with a transit line. He assumed that every trip is destined for the CBD terminal at one end and origins are uniformly distributed throughout the corridor. The objective was to minimize the total travel time. He devised a recursive procedure to find the optimal number of stations and the set of optimal spacings. The outcome was that interstation spacings should increase as one approaches the CBD.

Vuchic [1966] also studied this problem and developed a general model in which the density of trip origins need not be regular. He found that the optimal location for the next stop depends on the ratio of the number of passengers already on a train to the number who want to get on. As the number of passengers on a train increases, there is a decreasing "propensity of the train to stop," and the spacings should be monotonically increasing.

Vuchic adopted a dynamic programming approach to calculate numerical solutions, wrote a computer program, and presented results for several density patterns. He analyzed the case in which the density of origins is uniform throughout the corridor. He found that the spacings between stations should increase arithmetically in the direction of cumulation of passengers—the same result obtained by Schneider.

FREQUENCY OF SERVICE

Although not strictly a network dimension, the *frequency of service* is an important feature of a transit system. This is the inverse of *headway,* which is the time interval between successive buses or trains. Scheduling has a major effect on the service level obtained by the riding public and the operating expenses of the transit agency. Furthermore, frequency of service and route spacing are interrelated. For the same cost, an operator can offer either many routes, each with long headways, or few routes, each with short headways.

Most transit operators follow different practices in setting headways during peak and off-peak periods. Peak-period scheduling is typically based on a loading standard. For example, at the Toronto Transit Commission, the standard for a 40-foot bus is 55 to 65 passengers in the maximum hour [Toronto Transit Commission 1984]. Since such a bus has no more than 53 seats, some passengers must stand. Other agencies may have different standards. Usually suburban railroad and express bus services try to guarantee everyone a seat, since fares are high.

During off-peak periods, most transit vehicles are underused, and no one has to stand. To apply the same loading standard as in the peak period would greatly reduce service. The setting of the off-peak headway is a policy decision that involves balancing travelers' needs with costs. For example, the policy may call for a headway of 15 or 30 minutes. This may vary on different routes (e.g., central city versus suburban). Thus, it is said that peak-period scheduling is demand-based, while off-peak scheduling is policy-based.

One can optimize off-peak scheduling by analyzing the trade-off between the two major cost components affected by headway: waiting time of passengers and operating expenses of the transit authority. Following is a simplified version of optimizing service on a bus route. It does not incorporate all factors and should be regarded as an illustration of the approach. Equipment costs are disregarded because they are determined by peak-period requirements.

Other assumptions are made: (1) The number of passengers is constant and unaffected by headway. (2) Passengers arrive at stops randomly (according to a uniform distribution). (3) The headway is uniform throughout the period. (4) The operating cost is constant regardless of the number of riders.

The variables in the formulation are

$$f \ = \ \text{frequency of service, buses per hour}$$
$$p \ = \ \text{passengers per hour}$$
$$q \ = \ \text{operating cost per bus-hour, \$}$$
$$t \ = \ \text{value of time, \$/hour}$$

Headway is the inverse of frequency, or $1/f$. Under the assumptions, the average waiting time is one-half of headway, or $1/2f$. Hence the total passenger waiting time is $p/(2f)$, and the dollar value of this time is

$$\frac{pt}{2f}$$

The operating cost for 1 hour is simply fq. Total costs C are given by

$$C = \frac{pt}{2f} + fq$$

From calculus, the derivative of C with respect to f is set equal to zero. The resulting expression for the optimal value of f is

$$f_{\text{opt}} \ = \ \sqrt{\frac{pt}{2q}} \qquad\qquad (8\text{-}1)$$

This turns out to be the point at which the waiting-time cost is equal to the operating cost. The result means that as the number of passengers increases, the optimal number of buses increases by the square root. It takes 4 times as many passengers to justify twice as many buses. The formula also indicates (as seems logical) that frequency should increase when the value of time is greater and should decrease when operating cost is greater.

Table 8-1 shows how costs vary with different frequencies of service for a passenger volume of 100 per hour (assuming an operating cost of $40 per bus-hour and a time value of $7.20 per hour). The optimum is 3 buses per hour, at which value the waiting-time cost equals the operating cost. Table 8-2 gives the optimal frequencies for varying passenger volumes. Note that the optimum for 100 passengers is twice that for 25 passengers; the optimum for 400 passengers is twice that for 100 passengers. However, at

TABLE 8-1
COST FOR SELECTED FREQUENCIES OF SERVICE WHEN PASSENGER VOLUME IS
100 PER HOUR

Buses per hour	Headway, minutes	Riders per bus	Time cost, $	Operating cost, $	Total cost, $
1	60	100	360	40	400
1.5	40	66.7	240	60	300
2	30	50	180	80	260
2.5	24	40	144	100	244
3	20	33.3	120	120	240
4	15	25	90	160	250
5	12	20	72	200	272
6	10	16.7	60	240	300
7.5	8	13.3	48	300	348
10	6	10	36	400	436
12	5	8.3	30	480	510

Assumed values: operating cost = $40 per bus-hour; time value = $7.20 per hour.

400 passengers, the number of riders per bus becomes unrealistically high. With high volumes of passengers, scheduling should be based on demand (as is customary for peak periods).

Bus service has a feature that complicates the problem. A bus route has designated stops, but each bus stops only when someone wants to get on or off. Thus, the probabil-

TABLE 8-2
OPTIMAL FREQUENCIES OF SERVICE FOR SELECTED VOLUMES OF PASSENGERS

Riders per hour	Buses per hour	Headway, minutes	Riders per bus	Time cost, $	Operating cost, $	Total cost, $
25	1.5	40	16.7	60.00	60.00	120.00
50	2.12	28.28	23.6	84.85	84.85	169.71
75	2.6	23.09	28.9	103.92	103.92	207.85
100	3	20	33.3	120.00	120.00	240.00
150	3.67	16.33	40.8	146.97	146.97	293.94
200	4.24	14.14	47.1	169.71	169.71	339.41
250	4.74	12.65	52.7	189.74	189.74	379.47
300	5.2	11.55	57.7	207.85	207.85	415.69
400	6	10	66.7	240.00	240.00	480.00
500	6.71	8.94	74.5	268.33	268.33	536.66

Assumed values: operating cost = $40 per bus-hour; time value = $7.20 per hour.

ity is less than 1 that a bus actually stops at a designated location. (This practice occurs only in bus operation; with rail transit, the usual rule is that every train stops at every station.)

Mohring [1972] developed a stochastic model to estimate the probability that a bus will actually stop at a designated location. When buses run more frequently, each one will carry fewer passengers and make fewer stops. Hence buses will achieve higher speeds; passengers will benefit from reduced waiting time and reduced in-vehicle time. However, more buses will be needed to serve the route, and operating costs will increase.

There is another complicating factor—the possibility that a bus is full so that waiting travelers cannot get on and have to wait for the next bus. This is also a probabilistic phenomenon. It is less likely to happen when buses run more frequently, which is another argument for shorter headways.

BUS SIZE

Vehicle size (in particular, seating capacity) is another variable that transit planners can manipulate. It is irrelevant to rail systems; there it is the size of trains (discussed below) that matters. But it is an important variable in bus systems. Large buses cost more to buy, and operating costs increase slightly. But labor cost is the major factor, and this does not increase, since a bus has only one driver regardless of its size.

Buses range from minibuses with 20 seats to articulated buses with as many as 75 seats. Conventional buses have 47 to 53 seats, and in the past most fleets had only these standard-size buses. In recent years, there has been experimentation with smaller and larger buses; now many systems have a variety of vehicles. Different-size buses may be used on different routes or at different times of day.

Bus size has been the subject of several optimization studies. Hauer [1971] held operating and equipment costs constant and sought to determine the bus size that would give the best quality of service. He found that small buses result in more frequent service and less waiting time. Since there are fewer passengers per bus, there is a lower probability of stopping on demand and buses attain a higher speed. However, small buses have a greater chance of being full and passing up waiting passengers, which increases waiting time.

Jansson [1980] developed a model of a single bus line and simultaneously optimized frequency of service and bus size. He concluded that social cost minimization would produce a service pattern different from most existing services in that buses would be smaller and would run more often. This is not done because it would increase operating costs of bus companies appreciably.

A later optimization study by Oldfield and Bly [1988] found that the optimal bus size varies with the square root of passenger demand. For typical urban operating conditions in the United Kingdom, they found that the optimal size is between 55 and 65 seats; even with improvements in the efficiency of small buses, the optimum is unlikely to be less than 40 seats. (Note that most British operations use double-decker buses with 70 seats.)

Rufolo [1986] investigated the cost-effectiveness of using articulated buses, which had just been introduced in Portland, Oregon. Typically two articulated buses substituted for three standard buses. He concluded that passengers pay a fairly large time cost for the larger buses on high-density, short-haul routes. Larger buses are at less of a disadvantage on long-haul routes, where passengers make long trips and there are fewer boardings per mile.

The most important trade-off is between operating cost and passengers' time. Transit operators would rather run large buses less often to reduce operating cost, even if many seats are empty most of the day. It is the users who pay the penalty, and their time does not appear on the transit agency's books. If fuel costs rise substantially, it *is* an incentive to transit operators to use smaller buses.

TRAIN LENGTH

The operator of a rail system must decide how many cars to put on each train. This decision is not taken lightly; usually it is given considerable study. Determining the optimal length of trains is analogous to determining optimal bus size. As with buses, there are economies of scale. The marginal operating cost of increasing the train length is fairly small because the number of personnel on a train does not change.

The maximum train length must be compatible with the length of station platforms or loading areas, and this must be analyzed in planning a new line. If platforms will only handle four-car trains, it is impossible to later use six-car trains. It is peak-hour demand that governs the maximum train length, so this must be estimated. In the case of light rail running in a city street, short blocks may limit the length of loading areas. In this case, the physical constraint will determine the maximum length of trains.

If the total number of cars scheduled over a time period is held constant, then shorter trains will result in lower headways and less waiting time. Platforms can be shorter, which will reduce construction cost. Running longer trains will reduce the operating cost. There will also be less probability of a train's being full so people must wait for the next train (a common event in New York City). The important trade-off is between waiting time and operating cost—another conflict between the interests of riders and those of the operator.

Many transit agencies change the train length during the day, using the maximum length only in the peak periods. There may be a third track in some places where cars are stored in midday. There is some cost to making these changes, but it is not large. The principal saving is seen in energy costs.

The efficiencies of longer trains make rail an attractive option in cases of high demand. Adding cars to trains raises capacity, but adds little to the operating cost. Cities that use long trains (e.g., New York City) have a lower operating cost per rider than cities that use short trains (e.g., Cleveland).

A COMPREHENSIVE STUDY

In one of the more ambitious studies, Black sought to simultaneously optimize the spacing of routes, the spacing of stops, and headway. A full account is given in his dissertation [1975]; a summary is available [Black 1978]. He assumed a hypothetical city that is a circle, uniform throughout 360 degrees and extending to infinity. The center of the circle represents the CBD. The transit network consists of radials emanating from the center and extending an unknown distance. Each line has discrete stops, and access is possible only at these points, which are to be determined. Because of the assumed symmetry of the city, the radial lines will be equally spaced. Each will have the same number of stops, spaced in the same way, and of the same length.

The transit system serves a fixed amount and distribution of travel demand (there was no modal-split analysis). The only alternative to using transit is to walk. Demand is highest at the center and declines with increasing distance from the center. After some empirical analysis, Black decided to represent this by the negative exponential function. The equation was

$$Y = Ae^{-bX} \qquad (8\text{-}2)$$

where Y = density of trip ends, X = distance from the center, e = base of natural logarithms, and A and b are parameters.

To make the problem mathematically manageable, only trips to or from the center of the city were considered. CBD trips form the largest market for transit, and this dominates the design of transit networks.

It was assumed that travel may occur anywhere on the city's surface, but only in radial and circumferential directions. There are no circumferential transit routes; all circumferential travel is on foot. Each inbound traveler starts from her or his origin and walks in a circumferential arc to the nearest radial transit route. There the traveler has a choice between walking inward or outward to reach a stop. The traveler chooses that stop which minimizes the total time from origin to destination. Near the center, some travelers find it faster to walk all the way and not use the transit service.

The objective was to minimize total costs, consisting of capital investment for guideway and vehicles, operating costs, and door-to-door travel time (which included walking, waiting, and delays when vehicles stopped for other passengers). Time was converted to dollars by assuming a monetary value. Operating costs were based on vehicle-miles; equipment costs, on the number of vehicles; and guideway costs, on miles and number of stations.

The decision variables were (1) the number of radial routes, (2) the number of stops on each route, (3) the spacings between the stops (each interstation spacing was an independent variable), and (4) the average headway. The last was included because frequency of service is related to the spacing of routes and stops. The length of routes is an implicit variable represented by the distance from the center to the outermost stop.

An equation encompassing all the costs was derived by integral calculus. With differential calculus, a set of equations was derived that must be solved simultaneously to find optimal values of all variables. Since the equations were nonlinear, an analytical solution was not possible. Black developed a recursive procedure and wrote a computer program to find the solution that satisfies all equations and optimizes all variables simultaneously.

He then calculated results for six hypothetical cities with varying parameters of the demand function. The values chosen were representative of those measured in cities ranging in size from Detroit down to Syracuse. In each case, he compared three types of transit service: ordinary bus service in mixed traffic, exclusive bus lanes, and rail transit. These differ in cost and performance values. In particular, the guideway cost was assumed to be zero for local bus, while the value for rail was twice that for busways.

No numerical results will be given, but the findings can be summarized as follows:

1 As one would expect, the more total transit trips in a city, the larger the transit network—more radial routes, longer routes, and more stops on each route. This was true of all three transit modes. The major impact of greater demand was on the length of radial routes and the number of stops. The average spacing between stops did not vary much.

2 A greater number of passengers led to lower headway, but less than proportionally. This suggests that when vehicle trips are added to handle increased demand, they should be divided between existing routes and newly created routes (which will reduce both waiting time and walking).

3 The construction cost greatly reduced the dimensions of the optimal networks. Optimal busway systems were much smaller than local bus systems for the corresponding cities, and rail systems were smaller than busway systems.

4 Results indicated some economies of scale, but they were not very large. An increase in the total number of trips reduced the cost per trip somewhat. Economies seemed to be largest when there were construction costs.

5 The same optimal pattern of spacing between stops was found in each case: The first stop from the center had a large spacing because of travelers who walked to and from the center. From there, the spacings decreased gradually to a point about four-fifths of the length of the route; then they increased slightly. Except for the first stop, the spacings were approximately equal. This differed from the findings of Schneider and of Vuchic. The reason is that they assumed a uniform density of trip ends, while Black assumed that the density of trip ends is highest at the city center and declines away from it.

6 The average spacing between stops was greater for busway systems than for local bus systems. This occurred because (1) people walk farther to reach a higher-speed service, (2) higher cruising speed increases the time penalty for stops, and (3) busway stops involved a construction cost, while there was none for local buses. Most of the average spacings for rail systems were slightly greater than those for busway systems.

7 Optimal headways for busways were much lower than those for local bus. The busway involved high costs for stations and route-miles, but the operating cost per vehicle-mile was lower. The outcome was a smaller route structure with more frequent service. The optimal headways for rail systems were greater than those for busway systems, but less than those for local bus systems.

8 In comparing the three modes, the busway had the least total cost for the largest hypothetical city, while the local bus system was optimal for the other five cities. The rail system had the highest cost in all cases.

Ordinary bus service came out surprisingly well in the comparisons. This was primarily because a dense network and close spacing of stops reduced walking distances greatly compared to the alternatives. The absence of construction cost permitted a large number of routes. The low cruising speed, although the bane of this type of service, imposed small penalties for stops. The routes were also longer than those for the fixed-guideway systems and thus served travelers from the outer areas better.

Perhaps the major generalization from the study is that when there is a construction cost, the optimum system has a small route structure with frequent service. When there is no construction cost, the route structure is larger and service on each route less frequent.

The study had its limitations, and some of the numerical results were unrealistic. The most important improvements would be to add circumferential transit routes and to make the level of demand sensitive to the quality of service (i.e., to include a modal-split model). To the author's knowledge, no one has attempted such a comprehensive analysis.

CONCLUSION

Optimization studies like Black's are not directly transferable to real cities, with their unique topographies, land-use patterns, and constraints of various kinds. Numerical results are not reliable guides, but sometimes they suggest that standard practices (e.g., regarding the spacing of stops) should be reexamined. They are most useful for giving insights into relationships among variables and various cost components.

In practice, planners use several methodologies for designing transit networks. Some of these are manual, relying on experience and intuition, while others involve mathematical models. Chua [1984] described several approaches to planning bus systems used in recent years. Some he classified as "systems analysis" because they use computer models to predict flows on hypothetical networks. This can be tedious work, making it feasible to examine only a few alternatives. Hence some agencies use interactive graphics systems such as the one developed at the University of Washington [Schneider et al. 1974]. These make it possible to enter network changes on a screen and get rapid feedback.

The mathematical approach involves programming models that start with an origin-destination matrix of person-trips and try to find the best transit network, according to specified criteria and constraints. The models are not guaranteed to find an optimal solution; they use heuristic procedures that improve on earlier solutions. One approach is to start with a basic network (perhaps the existing system) and search for the best links to add. Another is to start with a maximum network (perhaps consisting of the entire coded highway network) and search for links to delete. For recent examples of such models, see Ceder and Wilson [1986] and van Nes at al. [1988].

These methods are quite sophisticated and generally are used by only the largest transportation planning organizations. Most transit planners must rely on common sense, combined with personal knowledge of local conditions. In a survey of British bus operators who had reorganized their networks, Chua [1984] found that 71 percent had used the manual approach. Understanding principles of good design and the implications of analytical studies can help. It is clear that decisions on routes, stops, and frequency of service are among the most important that a transit planner ever makes.

QUESTIONS

1 If you were preparing a long-range transportation plan for an urban area, what goals would you establish? Can you suggest quantitative criteria by which to determine whether the goals are being achieved?

2 Compare the radial-circumferential and gridiron patterns for transit routes. What are the advantages and disadvantages of each? Would you use different patterns for rail lines and for bus routes?

3 Obtain a map of the transit routes in an actual city (perhaps the one where you live). Does it seem to follow any ideal pattern? Can you think of ways to improve the network by adding or changing routes?

4 Today the major commuting movement is from suburb to suburb, rather than from suburb to central city. How can some of these trips be attracted to transit?

5 Why is the spacing of stops important in planning a rail transit line? There is often community pressure to add more stops. Why is this not necessarily a good idea?

6 Optimization studies involve idealized problems and many simplifying assumptions. Do the findings of such analyses have any practical value? Do they suggest any principles that should be followed in planning real transit systems?

REFERENCES

Bakker, J. J., J. Calkin, and S. Sylvester: "Multi-Centered Time Transfer System for Capital Metro, Austin, Texas," *Transportation Research Record,* no. 1202 (1988), pp. 22–28.

Black, Alan: *Optimizing the Design of Urban Mass Transit Systems: A General Model* (Ithaca, NY: City and Regional Planning, Cornell University, 1975).

———: "Optimizing Urban Mass Transit Systems: A General Model," *Transportation Research Record,* no. 677 (1978), pp. 41–47.

———: "The Chicago Area Transportation Study: A Case Study of Rational Planning," *Journal of Planning Education and Research,* vol. 10, no. 1 (Fall 1990), pp. 27–37.

Byrne, Bernard F.: "Public Transportation Line Positions and Headways for Minimum User and System Cost in a Radial Case," *Transportation Research,* vol. 9 nos. 2/3 (July 1975), pp. 97–102.

——— and Vukan R. Vuchic: "Public Transportation Line Positions and Headways for Minimum Cost," in Gordon F. Newell, ed., *Traffic Flow and Transportation* (New York: American Elsevier, 1972), pp. 347–360.

Ceder, Avishai, and Nigel H. M. Wilson: "Bus Network Design," *Transportation Research,* vol. 20B, no. 4 (August 1986), pp. 331–344.

Chua, Tiong An: "The Planning of Urban Bus Routes and Frequencies: A Survey," *Transportation,* vol. 12, no. 2 (January 1984), pp. 147–172.

Dial, Robert B.: "Transit Pathfinder Algorithm," *Highway Research Record,* no. 205 (1967), pp. 67–85.

———: "Urban Transportation Planning System: Philosophy and Function," *Transportation Research Record,* no. 599 (1976), pp. 60–64.

Dickey, John W.: *Metropolitan Transportation Planning,* 2d ed. (New York: McGraw-Hill, 1983).

Farkas, Z. Andrew, Moges Ayele, Seifu Kerse, and Legesse Negash: "Strategic Planning Process for Transit Properties," *Transportation Research Record,* no. 1229 (1989), pp. 35–42.

Feder, Richard C.: *The Effect of Bus Stop Spacing and Location on Travel Time* (Pittsburgh: Transportation Research Institute, Carnegie-Mellon University, 1973).

Ferguson, Erik, Catherine Ross, and Michael Meyer: "PC Software for Urban Transportation Planning," *Journal of American Planning Association,* vol. 58, no. 2 (Spring 1992), pp. 238–243.

Ghoneim, Nadia S., and S. C. Wirasinghe: "Near-Side or Far-Side Bus Stops: A Transit Point of View," *Transportation Research Record,* no. 761 (1980), pp. 69–75.

Giannopoulos, G. A.: *Bus Planning and Operation in Urban Areas: A Practical Guide* (Aldershot, UK: Avebury, 1989).

Hauer, Ezra: "Fleet Selection for Public Transportation Routes," *Transportation Science,* vol. 5, no. 1 (February 1971), pp. 1–21.

Holroyd, E. M.: "The Optimum Bus Service: A Theoretical Model for a Large Uniform Urban Area," in Leslie C. Edie, Robert Herman, and Richard Rothery, eds., *Vehicular Traffic Science* (New York: American Elsevier, 1967), pp. 308–328.

Hurdle, V. F.: "Minimum Cost Locations for Parallel Public Transit Lines," *Transportation Science,* vol. 7, no. 4 (November 1973), pp. 340–350.

Jansson, J. O.: "A Simple Bus Line Model for Optimisation of Service Frequency and Bus Size," *Journal of Transport Economics and Policy,* vol. 14 (January 1980), pp. 53–80.

Matzzie, Donald E.: "Ubiquitous Rapid Transit Service in an Urban Area," Ph.D. dissertation, Carnegie-Mellon University, Pittsburgh, May 1968.

Meyer, Michael D., and Eric J. Miller: *Urban Transportation Planning: A Decision-Oriented Approach* (New York: McGraw-Hill, 1984).

Mohring, Herbert: "Optimization and Scale Economies in Urban Bus Transportation," *American Economic Review,* vol. 62, no. 4 (September 1972), pp. 591–604.

Oldfield, R. H., and P. H. Bly: "An Analytic Investigation of Optimal Bus Size," *Transportation Research,* vol. 22B, no. 5 (October 1988), pp. 319–337.

Rufolo, Anthony M.: "Cost Effectiveness of Articulated Buses When Passenger Time Is Treated as a Cost," *Transportation Research,* vol. 20A, no. 5 (1986), pp. 337–343.

Schneider, Jerry B., Claus D. Gehner, Dennis Porter, and James Clark: "Computer-Aided Design of Urban Transit Systems," *Transportation Engineering Journal of ASCE,* vol. 100, no. TE4 (November 1974), pp. 943–958.

——— and Stephen P. Smith: "Redesigning Urban Transit Systems: A Transit-Center-Based Approach," *Transportation Research Record,* no. 798 (1981), pp. 56–65.

———, Chris Deffebach, and King Cushman: "The Timed-Transfer/Transit Center Concept as Applied in Tacoma/Pierce County, Washington," *Transportation Quarterly,* vol. 38, no. 3 (July 1984), pp. 393–402.

Schneider, Morton: "Travel Time Minimization—Transit," *C.A.T.S. Research News* (Chicago Area Transportation Study), vol. 4, no. 2 (June 2, 1961), pp. 10–16.

Sosslau, Arthur B., Amin B. Hassam, Maurice M. Carter, and George V. Wickstrom: *Quick-Response Urban Travel Estimation Techniques and Transferable Parameters: User's Guide,* National Cooperative Highway Research Program Report 187 (Washington: Transportation Research Board, 1978).

Tass, Leslie: *Modern Rapid Transit* (New York: Carlton Press, 1971).

Thelen, Keith M., Arun Chatterjee, and Frederick J. Wegmann: "Evaluation of Alternative Transit Routing Configurations in a Hypothetical Low-Density Area," *Transportation Research Record,* no. 761 (1980), pp. 53–56.

Thompson, Gregory Lee: "Planning Considerations for Alternative Transit Route Structures," *Journal of the American Institute of Planners,* vol. 43, no. 2 (April 1977), pp. 158–168.

Toronto Transit Commission: *TTC Service Standards Program: An Overview* (Toronto, Canada: Toronto Transit Commission, 1984).

Transportation Research Board: *Bus Route and Schedule Planning Guidelines,* National Cooperative Highway Research Program, Synthesis of Highway Practice No. 69 (Washington: Transportation Research Board, 1980).

Tyndall, Gene R., John Cameron, and Chip Taggart: *Strategic Planning and Management Guidelines for Transportation Agencies,* National Cooperative Highway Research Program Report 331 (Washington: Transportation Research Board, 1990).

Van Nes, Rob, Rudi Hamerslag, and Ben H. Immers: "Design of Public Transport Networks," *Transportation Research Record,* no. 1202 (1988), pp. 74–83.

Vaughan, Rodney: "The Performance of Rectangular, Radial, and Polar Bus Networks," *Traffic Engineering and Control,* vol. 26, no. 12 (December 1985), pp. 587–590.

Vuchic, Vukan R.: *Interstation Spacings for Line-Haul Passenger Transportation* (Berkeley: Institute of Transportation and Traffic Engineering, University of California, 1966).

Woodhull, Joel: "Urban Public Transportation: Specification of Service Parameters for a Two-Mode Cooperative Hierarchy," Ph.D. dissertation, Rensselaer Polytechnic Institute, Troy, New York, 1970.

9

OPERATIONS AND MANAGEMENT

This chapter discusses certain aspects of operations that are important in planning facilities and services. It does not cover the full range of activities of transit managers, many of which involve short-run operating decisions. Planners should, of course, know something about transit operations. In small systems, the same person may be responsible for both long-range and operational planning.

THE OPERATING CYCLE

From the time a vehicle leaves one stop until it leaves the following stop, the vehicle goes through an operating cycle that has five separate phases. Each of these will be discussed below. It is important to understand this cycle to estimate the time a vehicle takes between stops. By adding the times for all the intervals between stops, the planner can estimate the time to complete a route. This tells the average speed, which influences how many vehicles are needed. It is also important in determining the spacing of stops.

Acceleration

Acceleration is the rate of change of speed. It is measured in either miles per hour per second or feet per second per second (sometimes abbreviated feet/second^2). When speed is constant, the acceleration rate is zero. When speed increases at a constant rate, the acceleration rate is constant.

When a vehicle starts, if full power is applied, the acceleration rate is at its maximum. The rate falls continuously until it reaches zero at the limiting or balancing speed, which is the maximum speed of the vehicle. At this point, the forces of propulsion equal (or balance) the forces of resistance. The propulsive forces come from the motor. The two main forces of resistance are friction and aerodynamic drag, which both become stronger as the speed of a vehicle increases.

Many factors influence the acceleration curve of a vehicle in a real situation, including the grade and curvature of the guideway, temperature, air pressure, and wind speed (see Figure 9-1). It is not feasible to develop a model that accurately represents all these factors. However, a reasonable approximation can be obtained from a simple equation proposed by Haase and Holden [1964] involving only two parameters (the initial acceleration rate and limiting speed)

$$V = L(1 - e^{-(A/L)T})$$ (9-1)

where V =   velocity attained, miles per hour
        L =   limiting speed, miles per hour

FIGURE 9-1
Typical acceleration patterns for heavy rail, light rail, and bus vehicles. These were estimated by using the equation proposed by Haase and Holden (see text). For heavy rail, it was assumed that the maximum speed is 80 miles per hour and the initial acceleration rate is 3.0 miles per hour per second. For light rail, the values assumed are 55 miles per hour and 3.0 miles per hour per second. For bus, the values were 55 miles per hour and 2.4 miles per hour per second.

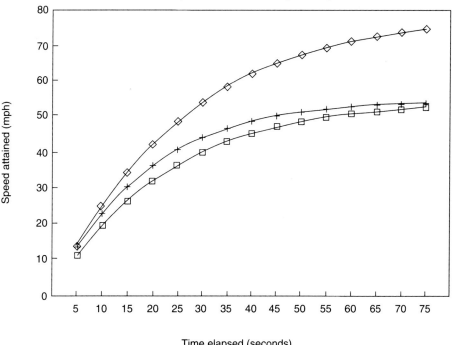

A = initial acceleration rate, miles per hour per second
T = time elapsed from the start, seconds
e = base of natural logarithms

For example, appropriate values for a heavy rail vehicle would be $L = 75$ and $A = 3$. The resulting equation is

$$V = 75\,(1 - e^{-0.04T}) \tag{9-2}$$

A vehicle that accelerates slowly takes a long time to reach top speed. If two stops are so close together that a vehicle cannot attain top speed before braking for the next stop, then there is a misfit between the vehicle and the spacing. Vehicles with high acceleration rates are needed on routes where stops are closely spaced. Vehicles with low acceleration rates should be used only on routes where stops are far apart.

The acceleration potential of railcars is seldom used. The PCC streetcar was capable of high acceleration (so high that it could knock down standing passengers). An acceleration rate of 3.0 miles per hour per second is considered the limit for passenger safety and comfort in transit vehicles. It is a different matter when all passengers are in padded seats facing forward. High-performance sports cars are capable of initial acceleration rates in excess of 10 miles per hour per second.

Railcars can accelerate faster than buses, even though a rubber tire on pavement has a higher coefficient of friction than a steel wheel on a steel rail. There are two reasons for this. (1) Buses use diesel engines, which have inherently poor acceleration. (2) Electric motors can be overloaded for brief periods, as during start-up. The initial acceleration rate of a diesel bus is only about 2.4 miles per hour per second.

The French make railcars with rubber tires that run on a concrete guideway. The railcars were introduced in Paris and are used in those cities (such as Montreal and Mexico City) where the French built subways. As one might suspect, rubber-tire trains have better acceleration than trains with steel wheels. However, the only time when this high acceleration ability is useful is when trains start while facing up a steep grade. (The other advantage of rubber-tire trains is that they are quieter.)

Cruising

After completing acceleration, a vehicle runs at a constant speed, a phase usually called *cruising*. Transit vehicles seldom run at their maximum possible speed. Trains normally cruise at less than top speed to save electricity. As with motor vehicles, it requires a disproportionate amount of energy to reach the last few miles per hour of potential speed.

In older subways like the ones in New York City, trains typically cruise at 40 to 45 miles per hour. Newer subways have cruising speeds of 60 to 70 miles per hour. Buses on exclusive lanes cruise at 45 to 55 miles per hour. Buses on city streets, of course, move with the traffic flow. They may reach higher speeds in peak periods than in off-peak periods, since average traffic speeds are often higher in peak periods. Many traffic control measures (e.g., signal timing, parking restrictions) are designed to raise peak-period speeds. There are fewer trucks in the traffic stream during the peak period because most deliveries are scheduled to avoid these times.

Coasting

When the motor is disengaged and a vehicle runs on its momentum, it is called *coasting*. Buses have little opportunity to coast, but trains have a lot. Coasting saves power and is encouraged by transit management. The desired pattern is to alternate between applying power and coasting—in other words, to keep turning the power on and off. In former times, motor operators became skilled at this, a device recorded it, and they were paid bonuses. This is not so important today because labor accounts for much more of operating cost than electricity does. However, automatic train control systems used in some places try to minimize power consumption by following this ideal pattern.

Deceleration (Braking)

The time pattern of the deceleration rate is approximately linear. There are two separate forces at work that tend to balance out: (1) Braking becomes more effective as a vehicle slows. (2) Aerodynamic drag decreases at the same time, exerting less force to stop the vehicle. It is reasonable to assume that vehicles decelerate at a constant rate. As with acceleration, considerations of passenger comfort and safety limit this rate to 3.0 miles per hour per second in normal situations. In an emergency, much higher deceleration rates can be achieved.

Station Dwell

The time during which a vehicle stands at a stop to unload and load passengers is called *station dwell*. It depends on several factors, the most obvious being the number of passengers getting on or off. Also important are the number and the width of the vehicle doors. A standard bus has two doors; passengers are supposed to board at the front door and leave by the rear door. Most heavy railcars have three doors on each side; some have four.

The platform level also plays a part. Boarding and exiting are faster with a high-level platform that is flush with the floors of the cars. This is the standard design for heavy rail systems. When passengers must negotiate two or three steps, the process is naturally slower.

Another factor is the fare collection system. If bus drivers must make change and figure out zone fares and special fares, that slows the boarding process. The move to exact fares has made some improvement. In heavy rail systems, passengers pay to pass through a turnstile and enter the platform; they do not pay when boarding a train.

According to *Highway Capacity Manual* [Transportation Research Board 1985], the dwell time at bus stops generally ranges from 15 to 60 seconds during peak periods. The average time for a passenger to board is 2 to 3 seconds when a token is deposited in a farebox, but 6 to 8 seconds when there are multiple zone fares and change is made. In analyzing rail systems, it is common to assume a dwell time of 20 seconds per stop, although this should be increased with high volumes of passengers getting off and on.

SCHEDULING

Scheduling is one of the major concerns of transit management. It directly affects operating costs, and schedules can vary widely in their efficiency. Scheduling also represents an interface with the riding public. A good schedule is likely to be taken for granted, while a bad schedule can either provoke complaints or silently cause ridership to dwindle.

There are three separate parts to scheduling. The first is to prepare a timetable listing all vehicle trips to be made on each route over the day. This requires a decision on the headway (the interval between trips). The timetable specifies when each trip starts and ends; usually the table also sets the times when vehicles are to pass certain checkpoints along a route.

There must be a layover time at the end of each trip before the vehicle starts another trip. This gives the operator(s) a short break, and it provides a time cushion in case a vehicle is late, so that delays are not passed on from one trip to the next.

Another decision required concerns when to start and stop service for the day. Some large cities provide *owl service* throughout the night. The New York City and Chicago subways run all night, but in most cities subways shut down from about 1 a.m. to 6 a.m. A few cities operate some bus routes all night, usually at 1-hour intervals, but it is not common.

Most schedules vary the frequency of service during the day: Headways are shorter during morning and afternoon peak periods, longer during midday and evening hours. Hence more operators are needed during the peak periods, and it would be advantageous to put some of them on split shifts (two working periods separated by an unpaid break). However, the labor contract may require extra payments to workers on split shifts.

Many bus systems schedule extra trips during peak periods that travel not the full length of a route, but only the most heavily used portion (normally that closest to the city center). This is called a *short turn* or a *tripper*. The object is to use vehicles and operators more efficiently by closely matching supply and demand. Trippers may be assigned to part-time operators (if permitted by the labor contract) or to regular operators as overtime. Furth [1987] and Ceder [1989] developed methods for designing short-turn schedules.

Ideally headways are uniform over long periods of time. This makes the schedules easier to remember, and it can also be shown that unequal headways increase the average waiting time for passengers. Examples of irregular schedules can be found, but they suggest neglect by management. Of course, there may need to be a gradual transition between peak and off-peak headways.

As explained in the previous chapter, an optimal headway can be calculated that balances the waiting time of passengers against operating costs. In practice, transit agencies do not try to optimize headway. Most agencies use demand-based scheduling for peak periods. This means that they schedule just enough service so that, at the maximum load point on a line, the number of passengers equals a percentage of the number of seats (such as 125 percent). During the off-peak period, policy-based scheduling is used regardless of the number of passengers. This means the scheduler follows an arbitrary rule, such as 1 bus every 15 minutes. Such rules, of course, represent policy decisions made by transit management.

The second part of scheduling is to assign vehicles to make the trips on the timetable. A series of trips performed by one vehicle is called a *block*. It starts with a *pull-out* from the garage and ends with a *pull-in*. The scheduler tries to design blocks to minimize the number of vehicles used, as this affects costs. Sometimes bus routes are paired to permit *interlining*, in which one bus alternates between two routes that terminate at a common point.

In rail systems, the length of trains may be changed during the day. After the morning peak period, some cars are removed from trains and stored until late afternoon. There may be a third track in some places that is used for this purpose.

The third and most difficult step in scheduling is to assign crews to the vehicles (a crew may be a single person, as for a bus). Since blocks often last longer than a crew's workday, many blocks are divided into pieces (a *piece* is a portion of a block handled by a single crew). The division must occur at relief points—stops where one crew can replace another.

Then the pieces must be assembled into runs (a *run* is the daily work schedule of an individual crew). The process is often called *run cutting*, and the resulting list of assignments is sometimes called a *roster*. A run can contain one, two, or three pieces. Most workers prefer a *straight run* that has a single piece lasting the entire workday. However, many operators will get a *split run* that contains two pieces separated by a long break. Sometimes there are short pieces left over; the term *tripper* is also used for such a brief work assignment.

Run cutting requires paying close attention to the labor contract, which contains work rules that have been negotiated (see Chapter 4 for a discussion of labor unions). Some rules may prohibit certain types of runs, while others require the transit authority to make extra payments (e.g., for split runs). The optimal roster would minimize these extra costs. There may also be informal rules that are not legally binding but that labor or management would prefer. For example, in a study of the transit system in Adelaide, Australia, Bennett and Potts [1968] tried to maximize consecutive days off because workers indicated this was important to them.

New schedules are prepared three or four times a year. There are some seasonal adjustments, and service on particular routes may be increased or decreased in response to changing ridership levels. After a new roster is posted, operators select runs according to seniority. Usually there are separate schedules for weekdays, Saturdays and Sundays, and occasionally for holidays.

In the past, schedules were prepared by hand by using rules of thumb. It took much skill and a great deal of time to prepare an efficient schedule. Good schedule makers, who usually required many years of experience to master their art, were considered among the most important personnel in a transit system. Once satisfactory schedules were obtained, they were sometimes kept the same for many years. Unfortunately, in some cases demand patterns changed and schedules were not adjusted, causing a mismatch between supply and demand.

In 1969, UMTA gave a grant to the San Diego Transit Corporation to develop an automated scheduling system [Hinds 1979]. The MITRE Corporation was hired, and it prepared a computer package called RUCUS, which stood for *run cutting and scheduling.* It had four components; three were called *trips, blocks,* and *runs* and corresponded to the three steps described above. The fourth was called *data management,* and it handled the flow of information from inputs through outputs.

A preliminary version of RUCUS was released to transit agencies in 1973. UMTA funded demonstration projects in Baltimore, Boston, Los Angeles, and Minneapolis, and a number of other systems experimented with RUCUS. It was first used to produce a run cut that was used on the street in Syracuse in March 1975. However, most systems found that RUCUS was not flexible enough to meet their needs, and they made numerous modifications. The runs portion proved to be generally useful, but other parts of the program were seldom used.

The original RUCUS has been superseded by other computer scheduling packages [Rousseau 1985]. RUCUS II was developed under an UMTA grant and first released in 1982. The HASTUS system is marketed by GIRO, Inc., a Canadian consulting firm, which worked with the University of Montreal. SAGE Management Consultants, also from Canada, has another package called the *Mini-Scheduler.* The BUSMAN package developed by an English firm in conjunction with the University of Leeds is widely used in Britain.

The new packages are more flexible and allow individual agencies to customize the programming for their own needs (e.g., to incorporate unique provisions of their labor contracts). Some programs are interactive so that a human scheduler can try out incremental changes and get immediate feedback. There is consensus that a human brain and a computer must work in tandem to get the best results. Today virtually all large and medium-size transit agencies in the United States and Canada use computerized scheduling, but many small systems still rely on manual scheduling.

The advantages of computerized scheduling are not limited to replacing the human effort of schedule makers. The programs often make it possible to reduce the number of vehicles and operators needed by designing more efficient schedules. Savings in operating costs of up to 5 percent have been reported. While this seems a small amount, it means several million dollars a year for a large system. Another advantage is that the programs can be used during labor negotiations to estimate the impact of proposed changes in work rules.

Schedules are normally published in smaller systems, but this may not occur in large cities. It is argued that service is so frequent that people ignore the schedule because the wait is always short (however, this also permits the transit authority to change the schedule without anyone knowing). When headways are long, passengers read the schedule and try to arrive at a stop a few minutes before the vehicle. The rule of thumb is that the dividing line comes at an interval of 20 minutes. However, some studies have indicated that it may be much less [O'Flaherty and Mangan 1970, Seddon and Day 1974].

Overcrowding during peak periods is taken for granted in large cities. As noted, peak-period service is scheduled so that some passengers will have to stand. Often in New York City, travelers cannot board the first subway train or first bus that arrives. However, overcrowding is even worse in many foreign countries. Much publicity has been given to the "pushers" on the Tokyo subway who pack the cars as fully as possible. According to a paper by Seshagiri et al. [1969], in Bombay, India, the "third bus rule" is followed in scheduling: If a passenger joins the queue as the first bus is leaving, she or he should miss the second bus and get on the third one. If the passenger makes the second bus, service is too frequent; if he or she has to wait for the fourth bus, service is not frequent enough.

ADHERING TO SCHEDULE

Transit service is unlike most businesses in that there is a high expectation of performance as scheduled. It is a serious matter if scheduled trips are canceled. You cannot tell people, "We are short-handed today; come back tomorrow." An operator who is sick must be replaced; a bus that breaks down or has an accident must be replaced. Of course, transit agencies cannot always do this, but they do fulfill a high percentage of their schedules.

Transit agencies use a personnel *extra board*, which is a list of operators on standby. The operators are called to duty in several situations: (1) when a scheduled operator is absent or on vacation; (2) when an operator is late for a run, which is called a *miss-out*; (3) when an operator takes sick and leaves early; and (4) when a vehicle breaks down and a replacement vehicle must be sent out. Sometimes people on the extra board are assigned to trippers (short pieces of work late in the day) or holiday service.

Assignment to the extra board is not considered desirable; it usually goes to workers with the least seniority. It is regarded as a way to break in new employees. However, those on the extra board are often guaranteed some minimum pay, even for a day in which they do not actually have to work. A transit agency can reduce costs by keeping the extra board short (typically it is 5 to 10 percent of the scheduled workforce). However, if the extra board is exhausted on a particular day, then a problem arises: Either some scheduled trips are canceled, or some operators are asked to work overtime. Determining the optimal size of the extra board is one of several workforce planning problems that have been studied [Koutsopoulos and Wilson 1987].

It is also important to passengers for vehicles to follow their schedules faithfully. Attitude surveys of transit users consistently show that users place high priority on the reliability of arriving at a destination on time. Further, it can be proved mathematically that passenger waiting time is minimized if vehicles arrive at stops at equal intervals. As noted before, a good schedule uses equal intervals.

One of the major operational problems of a transit system lies in making the vehicles adhere to their schedules. In particular, there is a great deal of randomness in the arrivals of buses at stops. This is partly a function of driving behavior: Drivers have individual characteristics that create differences in their average speeds. In addition, random delays occur because of traffic or the behavior of passengers.

There is a marked tendency for buses to bunch in pairs, and it is hard to overcome

[Chapman and Michel 1978]. It happens like this: If random delays cause a bus to fall behind schedule, the bus will encounter unusually large numbers of people waiting at stops. Their boarding will cause the bus to get further and further behind. The next bus will find unusually low numbers of people waiting and will get ahead of schedule. Soon one bus is right behind the other. A similar problem occurs in buildings with banks of elevators.

Transit managers try to control this randomness and make vehicles keep to schedule. To do this, managers must know what routes are unreliable and when. Complaints from passengers form one source, but in addition, bus systems often have checkers who collect data on route performance. One method is the *point check*, in which a checker is stationed at a stop and compares actual arrivals of buses with scheduled arrivals. Another is the *ride check*, in which the checker rides the bus and records the times at major schedule points. A ride check can also produce data on riders getting on and off at stops. However, the point check is more common because it requires fewer personnel.

The main way to correct the problem is to keep buses from getting ahead of schedule by making them wait (it is not easy to speed up buses that are behind schedule). In some systems, a supervisor at a stop has the authority to hold a bus that is ahead of schedule. However, this causes delays for passengers already on the bus.

Operations researchers have made studies of this problem. While it seems like a specific, limited problem, the mathematics gets very complicated. Some analysts have suggested that adhering to schedule is not the optimal policy. You should also consider delays to passengers on board the vehicle. If there are enough passengers, you should not hold the vehicle, even if it is ahead of schedule (presumably a computer could calculate this in seconds).

The problem is not so severe with grade-separated rail systems because there is little difficulty with traffic. However, there are still sources of randomness that can cause trains to be early or late. Some systems have traffic signals intended to keep trains from getting ahead of schedule. When a train waits at a station for no apparent reason, the operator may be waiting for a green light. This is one reason for interest in automatic train control. A computer should follow a consistent pattern and eliminate irregularity in driving behavior.

SPECIAL SERVICE PATTERNS

In conventional rail transit service, every train stops at every station. New York City and Philadelphia have both local and express service. Local trains stop at all stations, while express trains stop only at major stations and bypass the others. This system requires four tracks and hence is more expensive to construct. It has not been used on any rail systems built in the last 50 years.

However, there are two special types of service pattern that can improve performance at little cost without requiring extra tracks. While these have mostly been used on rail lines, they could be applied to bus routes.

Zone System

In the zone system, each train stops only at stations within a specified zone (see Figure 9-2). Black [1962] did one of the earliest studies of this pattern, proposing a two-zone

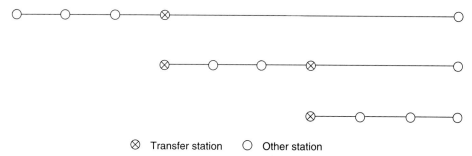

⊗ Transfer station   ○ Other station

FIGURE 9-2
The zone system. In the example shown, a rail line is divided into three zones. At top, one set of trains makes all stops within the outer zone but travels nonstop through the other zones. Another set of trains makes all stops within the middle zone (center), and another serves the inner zone (bottom). The zones overlap at transfer stations.

system for a line extending northwest from the Chicago Loop. One set of trains would stop at every station in the outer zone, but run nonstop through the inner zone to the CBD terminal. The other set of trains would stop at every station in the inner zone, but would not go into the outer zone. There would be overlap to permit transfers: The inner station of the outer zone and the outer station of the inner zone would be the same.

The system has three main advantages: (1) Passengers in the outer zone get a faster trip to the CBD because trains speed through the inner zone without stopping. (2) Trains in the inner zone do not travel as many miles, which reduces operating costs. (3) Trains for both zones have a faster turnaround, which means that less equipment is needed. In practice, the last factor seems to yield the most cost savings for the transit agency.

There are two principal disadvantages: (1) There is increased headway at every station except the one where all trains stop, so travelers may incur greater waiting time. (2) Any passengers traveling between the two zones must transfer at the one station in common. In addition, an extra track may be required if trains are close together; in practice, this has not been needed.

Later the New York Central Railroad implemented a multiple-zone system in 1965–1966 as a demonstration project [Eisele 1968]. On the Harlem division, e.g., four zones were created, each containing two or three adjacent stations. Each train stopped only at stations within its assigned zone.

Although more trains operated, there was a reduction in the number of train cars needed. This enabled the railroad to take some older equipment out of service. A zone fare system was introduced at the same time, in place of charging a different fare for every station, and all tickets were collected at Grand Central Station, instead of on the trains. This reduced the number of ticket collectors needed, which also saved money. The schedule was also simplified, making it easier for passengers to remember when trains departed.

The system was considered successful and was made permanent [Eisele 1978]. It was later adopted by the Penn Central and Long Island railroads in New York City and by the Burlington Northern and Illinois Central Gulf railroads in Chicago. The Southern Pacific Railroad used it on the line between San Francisco and San Jose.

The system works well if most passengers are going to or from the CBD terminal. This pattern is typical for commuter rail lines. But if many people travel between outer stations and will have to transfer, the resulting time losses will more than offset the savings for those passengers who benefit. Hence the scheme is not considered suitable for heavy rail systems that primarily operate within the central city.

Skip-Stop

Another pattern is the *skip-stop system* (see Figure 9-3). Alternate stations on a line are designated as A or B, and at intervals a station is designated as AB (these are for transfers). Trains are also designated: The A trains stop at A and AB stations; the B trains stop at B and AB stations. This system, used on some lines in Philadelphia and Chicago, was analyzed by Vuchic [1973].

The skip-stop system can handle diverse travel patterns and is suitable for inner-city subway-elevated lines. It is not necessary that most travelers go to the end of the line. The system does not require extra tracks unless headways are very short.

The advantages of the skip-stop system are similar to those of the zone system: Train speeds are increased, which benefits the bulk of passengers and may permit reduction in equipment needed. The major disadvantages are that headways at the A and B stops are doubled (A and B trains alternate) and travel between A and B stops requires transfers at AB stops. Hence careful planning is needed: A and B stations should have low use, and busy stations should be designated AB.

Vuchic analyzed the benefits and costs of skip-stop service on the Market-Frankford line in Philadelphia, which is 13 miles long and has 28 stations. There are 6 pairs of A and B stations (that is, 12 stations are involved), and he found this was indeed the optimal number.

FARE COLLECTION

Over the years, different fare collection systems have evolved for different transit modes. In U.S. bus operations, the driver was responsible for collecting fares and making change (European systems often had a conductor who handled fares). Passengers dropped coins into a fare box that was designed so the driver could see that the amount

FIGURE 9-3
The skip-stop system. Stations are designated as A, B, or AB. A trains stop at A and AB stations but skip B stations. B trains stop at B and AB stations but skip A stations. Transfers can be made at AB stations.

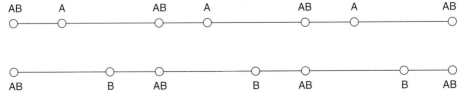

was correct. The driver then pressed a lever, and the money dropped into a compartment. From time to time, the driver emptied the compartment to get change.

Most U.S. bus systems now use the exact-fare system in which money dropped in the fare box falls into a locked vault that the driver cannot open. At the end of the day, the vault is taken to a counting room where it is unlocked. The primary reason for this arrangement is to deter robberies of bus drivers. It also speeds up the boarding process. The major disadvantage is inconvenience for passengers who do not have the exact fare available. The driver is not permitted to make change, but other passengers may do so.

In older subway-elevated systems, stations were designed with barriers to separate people who have paid from those who have not. Passengers deposit coins or tokens in turnstiles in order to be admitted to the paid area. Formerly some turnstiles accepted quarters, but now that fares usually exceed $1, tokens are used. Each station has a booth with a clerk who sells tokens, makes change, and admits people with passes. This is a labor-intensive system and adds a substantial amount to operating costs. However, the clerk is also available to give information and offers some deterrent to crime.

All new heavy rail systems use some form of automatic fare collection. In some, a passenger purchases a ticket from a vending machine and inserts it in a turnstile. More common is the fare card system, in which a passenger deposits money (up to $20) in a vending machine and receives a card with a magnetically coded strip. The person inserts the fare card in a turnstile, which opens and returns the card. At the destination station, the passenger again inserts the card in a turnstile, which computes the fare, subtracts the fare from the balance, and returns the card (unless the balance is zero).

The primary motivation for adopting the fare card system was to save labor costs (the stations can be unattended). Another advantage is that fares can be graduated by distance and time of day. However, the system requires several kinds of electronic machines, which are expensive and require considerable maintenance. When a turnstile malfunctions during rush hour, it can cause long queues to form. The machines originally used on the Washington, D.C., Metro had a high rate of failure, but eventually the bugs were worked out.

The system requires some familiarity and often confuses newcomers. Particularly nettlesome is the *add-fare* machine located in every station. It works this way: If the fare card does not have enough money left to pay for the trip, the card will be rejected by the exit turnstile. This is embarrassing if others are waiting to pass through. The traveler must then find the add-fare machine and insert more money to increase the balance on the card.

New light rail lines use self-service fare collection, also called the *no-barrier system* because there are no turnstiles. It is not really an honor system (although it is often called that) because there is enforcement. Passengers purchase tickets at vending machines at the stations or street corner stops (see Figure 9-4). Upon boarding, a passenger inserts the ticket in another machine on the vehicle that stamps the date and time. Inspectors roam the trains and make random checks of passengers. If someone has no ticket, the inspector can write a citation like one given for a traffic violation.

This system works well and requires less labor because there are no clerks in stations. It has been widely used in Europe since the 1960s [MITRE Corporation 1979]. It speeds up train operation because motormen do not collect fares and all doors of the

FIGURE 9-4
A ticket-vending machine at a light rail stop in San Diego. With self-service fare collection, passengers purchase tickets before boarding. Inspectors roam the trains and randomly check whether passengers have tickets. All new light rail systems in the United States use this system. (Photo by author.)

vehicles can be used. U.S. transit managers were reluctant to introduce it because they believed there would be more cheating than in Europe. Such fears now appear to have been unfounded.

The U.S. pioneer of this system was the Tijuana Trolley in San Diego [Carter and Powell 1982]. During the first 6 months of operation, the inspection rate was 41 percent of all riders, and the evasion rate was only 0.25 percent. The fine for not having a valid ticket was $20 for the first offense and $50 for the second offense. The inspectors (who had to be bilingual) spent more time giving information than writing citations. The system was deemed successful and has been used on all U.S. light rail systems that have opened since.

Most transit systems offer transfers for travelers who use more than one route. Often the transfers are free; in some places, there is a small charge. The date and time are indicated on the transfer, typically by tearing off strips of paper. The transfer is valid only for a specific period of time (perhaps 2 hours), so that it cannot be used on another day.

Several kinds of discounted fares are common. Many systems offer multiple-ride or monthly passes that cost less per ride. Federal law requires that systems receiving operating assistance charge elderly and disabled persons no more than half the peak-period fare during off-peak hours. Some cities charge less: In Boston, the elderly and disabled persons pay only $0.10 at any time of day. In many places, students are eligible for reduced fares. Sometimes the school system reimburses the transit agency for this.

Generally fare collection has not been a progressive aspect of U.S. transit operations, which have lagged behind Europe in making innovations. The future should bring increasing use of automatic fare collection and honor systems. There is always some loss of money when large numbers of employees handle cash; many transit managers would like to eliminate this process and go to a cashless system. Some day, passengers may pay fares with credit cards.

MARKETING

For years, transit companies largely ignored marketing. Managers were oriented toward providing a product in an efficient way; they assumed that customers would purchase the product if the quality and price were right. Some transit operators engaged in advertising, public relations, and promotions, but they devoted very little of their budgets to such activities. Some systems occasionally offered services for special events such as a ball game or convention. During horse racing season, e.g., the New York City Transit Authority runs special trains to the tracks.

A book by Schneider [1965] first directed attention to the lack of marketing in transit. Since then, many transit agencies have made serious efforts to improve marketing, and more works on the subject have appeared (see Figure 9-5). Large transit agencies employ marketing directors; in small systems this function may be combined with planning or other work. There has been a good deal of consumer research, often conducted by consultants, and much has been learned about the characteristics of transit patrons.

There is wide recognition today that public transportation is a service that needs to be sold to the public. The shift from the private to the public sector has made profits irrelevant and put emphasis on increasing ridership levels as a measure of success. Hence efforts are devoted to determining what travelers need and want and developing services to satisfy them.

Sophisticated marketing emphasizes segmentation of the market. This means analyzing the clientele and dividing it into segments that have different characteristics and behavior. Then services can be targeted to attract the individual segments, which will increase revenues, if successful. For example, two obvious segments of the transit market in large cities are (1) commuters who prefer transit to driving their cars in congested

FIGURE 9-5
A billboard promoting transit use in New York City. This was part of an advertising campaign by the Metropolitan Transportation Authority. The billboard emphasizes the traffic congestion and air pollution caused by motor vehicles. (Courtesy of the artist, Roger Shimomura.)

traffic and paying high parking fees and (2) people without cars available who rely on transit at all times of day. Other segments might include the elderly, disabled persons, students, and shoppers.

Many transit systems sell passes that offer discounts from standard fares. Most common are an all-day pass (intended for tourists), a multiple-ride pass, and a monthly pass that allows unlimited riding. However, evidence indicates that most passes are sold to regular commuters, who thus pay less than they used to, and few new riders are generated. Other objections are that passes cause revenues to drop, induce people to take extra rides for free, and are conducive to cheating. On the other hand, passes give the transit agency cash in advance of providing service, which is an advantage.

The Greater Bridgeport Transit District in Connecticut introduced an innovation in a *fare cutter card*, which allows unlimited riding at a reduced fare [Oram 1983]. The normal base fare was $0.60; with a card, it was cut to $0.25. With this approach, there are no free rides, and the district continues to gain revenue every time a card is used. The card is usually sold for $15 per month (less during promotions).

Most transit operators recognize the importance of providing information on their services to the public, yet some are negligent on this score. The most basic aid is a map of the routes; in a few cities you cannot find such a map, and in other cities you must purchase it (see Figure 9-6). At the other extreme, the London and Paris subways have electrified maps in many stations where you push a button for your destination stop and the route will light up.

Another important aid is a timetable showing the scheduled arrivals at a stop. Commuter railroads always provide timetables because headways tend to be large and irregular. Most subway-elevated systems in the United States do not publish timetables; it is argued that service is so frequent that timetables are unnecessary. It is now common to provide timetables for bus routes, except in large cities where headways are only a few minutes.

It is desirable to provide a clear indication of where bus stops are located on street corners; in some cities this also is neglected. The best method is a sign that gives the route number, a schematic map of the route, and a timetable. It is helpful if the transit authority uses a standard logo that is easily identifiable and can be seen from a distance. Vehicles should have signs that clearly give their routes and destinations. In Boston, each rail line is identified by a color, and the cars are painted the same color.

FIGURE 9-6
A passenger examining a map of BART routes. This display was located outside the Fremont station in the East Bay. It is important for transit agencies to provide such practical information for travelers. (Photo by author.)

Many transit agencies have a telephone number that patrons can call to obtain assistance in using the system. These numbers are heavily used. Some systems have booths or offices where people can get information and buy passes. One duty of fare collectors in rail stations is to give assistance to travelers. Often systems that use automatic fare collection still post personnel in stations for this purpose.

Although there has been much progress in marketing transit services, there is still room for improvement. Little attention has been paid to evaluating the various means used to attract riders. Marketing is often conducted independently of service planning and pricing. Following a review of current marketing practice, Walb and Booth [1985, p. 14] concluded that "the role of marketing must be expanded from advertising and promotion to include market research and evaluation, and the marketing function must be integrated with activities of other agency operating departments."

ACCIDENTS

Accident costs do not form a major item on the books of transit systems. Payments of claims for injuries and damages typically account for about 2 percent of operating costs. Buses average about 25,000 miles between collision accidents. This is a high rate compared to automobiles, but the rate per passenger-mile is low. Heavy rail systems average about 1 accident per 2.5 million vehicle-miles. A substantial reduction in the accident toll could be achieved by switching travelers from automobiles to transit.

Unfortunately, when transit accidents do occur, they may be serious because the vehicles carry so many passengers. Following are some of the significant transit accidents in U.S. history:

November 2, 1918   In the worst transit accident ever in the United States, all five cars of a subway train derailed at Malbone Street station in Brooklyn. There were 97 deaths on the spot; 5 others later died of injuries. The mishap occurred during a strike, and the motorman was a 23-year-old dispatcher who was filling in. He was charged with manslaughter but was acquitted. The fact that the bodies of the subway cars were made of wood contributed to the toll.

The notoriety of Malbone Street was too much to endure; the name was subsequently changed to Empire Boulevard.

August 24, 1928   An accident on the Seventh Avenue subway in New York City left 16 dead and 100 injured. The last two cars of a ten-car train jumped a faulty switch after leaving Times Square station and crashed into concrete pillars between the tracks. A maintenance worker was charged with homicide.

February 17, 1950   On this date 32 persons died, and 100 were injured in a head-on collision of two Long Island Railroad commuter trains at Rockville Center, New York. This occurred on a temporary one-track section laid down because of construction of an overpass. An eastbound train ran through a stop signal and struck a westbound train that had just left the Rockville Center station. The motorman of the eastbound train was charged with criminal negligence and manslaughter.

May 25, 1950   A streetcar collided with a gasoline truck in Chicago, and flaming gasoline engulfed the streetcar and set fire to nearby buildings and automobiles. Thirty-two persons died and 30 were hospitalized. Five buildings were destroyed, and three others were damaged. The streetcar was supposed to take a detour because of a flooded underpass; apparently the motorman had forgotten this (he died in the accident). Witnesses said the car was going too fast when it hit an open switch and veered into the path of the truck. The conductor and some passengers escaped by climbing through a rear window.

November 22, 1950   On Thanksgiving eve, 79 persons were killed and 318 injured when one Long Island Railroad commuter train plowed into the rear of another in the Richmond Hill district of Queens. The train ahead had stalled because its brakes would not release. The engineer of the following train, who died, was held responsible for going through a signal. An antiquated signaling system was a contributing factor.

February 6, 1951   An 11-car Pennsylvania Railroad commuter train derailed in Woodbridge, New Jersey, and 8 cars tipped over. The death toll was 84, and more than 400 passengers were injured. There was construction at the site, and the train was passing through a temporary track section (at 50 miles per hour, the engineer admitted).

September 15, 1958   Forty-five persons died when a Jersey Central commuter train plunged through an open lift bridge into the waters of Newark Bay. The train had two engines and five passenger cars; the engines and two cars ended up underwater, and a third car was left dangling from the bridge. Small boats rushed to the scene and rescued passengers who escaped by breaking windows. One victim was George "Snuffy" Stirnweiss, who had played second base for the New York Yankees and led the American League in batting in 1945.

The bridge had opened to let a sand dredge pass through. The train went through two caution signals and a red signal and tripped an automatic derailing device. It bounced along the wooden ties, but could not stop in time. A recording device showed the train was going at an abnormal speed. Both the engineer and fireman died. An autopsy of the engineer showed he had heart disease, and he may have suffered a heart attack.

February 4, 1977   In a freak accident in the Chicago Loop, one train ran into the rear of another that was stopped at a station. Although the crash occurred at a low speed, the train behind left the tracks and fell to the street below. The casualties were 11 dead and 189 injured [Young 1977].

January 13, 1982   A crash on the Washington, D.C., Metro left 3 dead and 25 injured. It was the first fatal accident in the Metro's history. It got little notice because it happened 27 minutes after a jet taking off from National Airport crashed into a Potomac River bridge, killing 74 persons.

A blizzard contributed to both tragedies. The government decided to send workers home early, even though the Metro was operating light midday service and advised against the move. Hence all the trains were overloaded. One train broke down at a station and was evacuated, forcing other trains to use a single track. Before operations could be restored to normal, another train jumped a switch. When that train was backed up, it derailed and the end car struck a concrete divider between the tracks. It was estimated the car carried 250 persons. A panel of experts blamed the accident on human error.

May 21, 1988   Yes, San Francisco cable cars sometimes run wild on the steep hills. On this date a cable car lost control on Hyde Street and crashed into a truck that was waiting at a red light. There were no deaths, but 31 persons were injured.

March 7, 1990   In Philadelphia, the last three cars of a six-car subway train derailed and crashed into steel pillars during the morning rush hour. Three persons died and 46 were hospitalized. Apparently a mechanical problem was at fault.

August 28, 1991   A New York City subway train derailed on the Lexington Avenue line, resulting in 5 deaths and 200 injured persons. A board of inquiry concluded that the primary cause was excessive speed while the train was going through a switch. The motorman admitted drinking alcohol before work; a grand jury indicted him for homicide. Following this mishap, the transit authority began random drug and alcohol testing of employees in safety-sensitive positions. Late in 1992 the motorman came to trial; the jury rejected the murder charge but convicted him of manslaughter.

There was a disaster in the King's Cross subway station in London in November 1987 when a smoldering fire suddenly erupted into an inferno, killing 30 persons. During the preceding hour, several passengers had reported smoke in the station. It was believed that electrical overheating was responsible.

Signaling is a vital feature of rail systems. The main object is to prevent a train from running into the one ahead, but there are also situations in which trains going in both directions must share the same track. This is usually a temporary arrangement, and it is noteworthy that several of the accidents cited above occurred in places where construction was going on.

Block signaling is almost universally used in subway-elevated systems. A *block* is a section of track that is to be used by only one train at a time. When a block is occupied, an electric impulse controls signals up the line: There is a red signal on the following block, and there are yellow signals farther on. Older systems had wayside signals; new ones have signals in the cab. If a train runs a red signal, a device in the roadbed activates a switch on the lead car that automatically brakes the train to a stop.

The idea of block signaling is to keep a safe interval between trains. This interval is a constraint on the capacity of a track. In U.S. practice, 90 seconds is considered the minimum safe interval, which means a limit of 40 trains per hour.

Some of the new rail installations utilize computers to control spacing between trains. It was intended that BART rely entirely on a central computer, and block signals were not provided, but it took several years to get the system to work correctly. The Vancouver Skytrain is fully automatic, and there are no operators on the trains. The U.S.

systems with automatic train control use a motorman who can override the computer in case of emergency.

There are other sources of accidents in rail systems besides collisions and derailments. One is overcrowding in stations. Sometimes people are pushed into the tracks or injured by closing train doors. A grisly accident occurred in the New York City subway in 1964 when a man got his arm caught in a door and was carried to his death while dozens of people on the platform watched helplessly. This led to a new operating rule: A conductor must put her or his head out of a window and look up and down the platform before pushing the button that allows the train to start.

A surprisingly large number of people leave station platforms and go into the tracks, where they are hit by trains or electrocuted. The police classify most of these incidents simply as "fell or jumped into tracks." They believe most are suicides, but a few may be homicides.

Another danger is the collapse of a motorman because of a heart attack or other illness. To counteract this, most subway trains have a *dead man's feature*. The motorman must constantly push down on the operating lever; if pressure is released, the train automatically comes to a stop. This device played a key part in the plot of a thrilling novel by John Godey [1973] about the hijacking of a New York City subway train.

Heavy rail lines tend to have the best safety systems. Some of the older light rail lines do not have automatic devices to stop trains. In fact, trains often follow each other closely; this is allowed because trains have only one or two cars and do not travel very fast. Commuter railroads have generally lagged behind in adopting safety devices that are not used in intercity railroading. This is one reason why many of the bad accidents have occurred on these lines.

CRIME

The most important crime problem in transit systems consists of robberies and assaults on passengers, both in vehicles and while they wait at stops. Transit crime often gets great publicity, so there have been strenuous efforts to combat it. Large transit systems may have their own police forces. The New York City Transit Authority employs more than 3500 officers, making it one of the largest police forces in the country.

Subway crime attracts the greatest media attention in New York City. Besides muggings and purse snatching, there are several murders and rapes every year. Street gangs are thought to roam the system, looking for victims; they intimidate people even if they do not commit crimes. It is common belief that other passengers will not help a person in trouble, and indeed, there have been incidents that confirmed this perception.

The most spectacular episode occurred on December 22, 1984, when a white man named Bernhard Goetz was approached by four black teenagers. Goetz pulled a gun and shot all four of them. He was later arrested and eventually convicted of carrying a gun without a permit. Meanwhile, he became a media hero, and the case caused great controversy. It was widely assumed that crime on the subways was out of control and drastic solutions were needed.

During this period a group of teenagers named the Guardian Angels was patrolling the subways for the avowed purpose of protecting honest citizens. The group was formed by a charismatic leader named Curtis Silwa. The implication was that the police could not do the job and that common people should band together to "take back the subways." There was understandably some friction between the police and the Guardian Angels, whom some considered to be vigilantes.

A criminal justice student named Kenney [1987] conducted an experiment to gauge the impact of the Guardian Angels' patrols on the occurrence of crime and on passengers' perceptions of the threat. During one month, patrols were intensified in one area; during the following month, the patrols were suspended. The experiment came to naught: There were so few crimes reported that the researcher could not find any statistically significant differences.

Kenney [1987, p. 58] concluded, "it would appear that the perceptions of crime on the New York subways are exaggerated beyond its actual occurrence. With an estimated nighttime victimization rate in the project area of only 6 passengers for every 100,000 subway rides, our popular images of a dangerous, crime-ridden system are hard to justify factually. . . . The important point is that the subways are really quite safe." *The New York Times* reported statistics showing that the average subway rider will be victimized once in 200 years.

Kenney also found in interviewing subway riders that almost half were "very" or "somewhat" worried about crime. The vast majority supported the Guardian Angels' efforts and felt safer because of them. Almost 25 percent reported that they usually carried something for self-defense when they rode the subways. The most popular item was a knife, which 13 percent said they carried. Almost 3 percent reported they carried a firearm.

In a study of transit crime in Los Angeles, Pearlstein and Wachs [1982] found that crime rates on the bus system were highest in the parts of the city where overall crime rates were highest. The CBD had the highest rates of all. The majority of crimes were committed against passengers, but still an individual bus driver was 10 times more likely to be a victim. Both the New York City and Los Angeles studies found that the majority of transit crimes occur during daylight hours, when the ridership level is also higher. However, the risk to the average passenger is much greater at night.

Subsequently Levine and Wachs [1986] conducted a telephone survey of a random sample of households in west central Los Angeles. They concluded that police statistics greatly undercount the number of crimes actually related to transit use. A majority of the crimes occurred not on a bus, but while the victim was waiting at a bus stop or was walking to or from a stop. Further, a high percentage of crimes were not reported to police. They found that a sizable proportion of the crimes occurred at a limited number of locations, where environmental factors contributed to the problem.

Fear of crime is clearly a deterrent to transit riding; surveys show that crime is often mentioned as a reason for not using transit. Perhaps public perception of the danger is exaggerated, but perceptions still affect behavior. Fear is greatest after dark, when bus stops and subway stations may be deserted. People feel safer on buses than on trains because there is a uniformed driver in the vehicle. If you get on the subway at night, you may be alone in the car, and you can't tell who will get on at the next stop.

The main approach to this problem is to have police patrol subway stations and ride on trains and buses. For years it has been the practice in New York City to have a uniformed officer ride every subway train during evening and night hours. In addition, the transit authority has teams of undercover agents that roam the system and watch in particular for teenage gangs. This strategy is effective, but it is labor-intensive and costly.

Subway stations are often crime sites and have sometimes acquired a reputation as very dangerous places at night, when there are few people around. Again, the usual solution is to assign police to the stations. Stronger lighting increases feelings of security and perhaps deters crime. Most new rail systems have television cameras that scan the stations.

Robberies of bus drivers once constituted a major problem. The main solution is the exact-fare system, which is now used throughout the United States and has been effective. Money drops into a metal vault that can be unlocked only at the garage. Many systems have also installed two-way radio communications with bus drivers. Sometimes there is a silent alarm that a driver can activate.

Vandalism is also a serious problem for transit authorities, although it affects passengers little. Formerly the interiors of transit vehicles sustained a great deal of damage, such as slashing of seat cushions. Now most vehicles are designed with vandal-proof materials such as plastic and fiberglass. This has mitigated the problem.

SUBWAY GRAFFITI

Graffiti on subway cars (and, to a lesser extent, in stations) was long a major problem in New York City and Philadelphia, but it never occurred much in other U.S. cities. See Figure 9-7. Each graffito is an individual creation; the most common form is a *tag* representing the nom de plume of the artist. The graffiti are inscribed with spray paint cans and felt-tipped pens, usually at night, when cars are stored in outdoor yards or on spare tracks underground called *layups*. New York has more than 6000 subway cars, and it is not feasible to guard them all.

An interesting exploration of this phenomenon is given in a book by Castleman [1982], who came to know many of the New York "writers" (as they call themselves). Apparently the practice was started in the late 1960s by a teenage boy who wrote *Taki 183* on walls, public monuments, and subway stations all over Manhattan. (He lived on 183d Street; it became popular to include one's street number in a tag.) On July 21, 1971, *The New York Times* published an interview with Taki 183, who was portrayed as an engaging youngster with a curious hobby. This publicity made a strong impression on young boys and graffiti soon became rampant.

At first, reputations were based on quantity: The "king of the line" was the one whose tag was the most prevalent on a particular subway line. Later quality became important, and those who did the most artistic work were called *style masters*. The size of the inscriptions also grew over time. Writers began doing "top-to-bottoms" and "end-to-ends." In late 1973, Flint 707 painted the first whole car. This became the specialty of the best writers, who designed murals that covered the entire side of a car.

The culmination came on July 4, 1976, when three boys named Caine, Mad 103, and Flame One covered a whole train in bicentennial decorations. The transit authority did not feel patriotic about the "Freedom Train"; it was removed from service the next day

FIGURE 9-7
Graffiti covering a New York City subway train. For years, graffiti seemed to present an insoluble problem in New York City (see text). It has now been virtually eliminated, but at considerable cost. (Photo by author.)

and painted over. Another whole train was done in December 1977 by the Fabulous Five, known as the most skilled writing group in the city. It was called the "Christmas Train" and featured reindeer, Santa Claus, a snowman, and the words *Merry Christmas to New York*.

Some of the graffiti have been recognized for artistic value. In 1972, a sociology major at Columbia University named Hugo Martinez organized a group called United Graffiti Artists, which staged several public exhibitions. They had a show of graffiti painted on canvases at an art gallery in September 1973, and their works sold for up to $3000. A second group, called Nation of Graffiti Artists, was formed in 1974 and also put on exhibitions. Several of the writers have gone to art school, and a few now make their living as professional artists.

A majority of graffiti artists are poor blacks, although all economic levels and ethnic backgrounds are represented. Most artists are between the ages of 11 and 16. Males predominate, but there are some females. Three girls became famous by "hitting" the lavatory and shower room of the all-male DeWitt Clinton High School in the Bronx. The writers consider the graffiti a form of self-expression and do not believe they are doing anything wrong. However, they steal the paint, and police say a substantial percentage of them graduate to more serious crimes.

The transit authority police have fought graffiti for years, but with no lasting effect.

A special graffiti squad of ten plainclothes officers operated from 1975 to 1979 and compiled files on more than 1500 writers. They made thousands of arrests. However, the courts have never seen graffiti as a serious crime and refused to commit the youths to institutions. The usual punishment was to spend a day scrubbing graffiti off cars. The writers actually liked this, since it created clean cars that they could hit later on.

Thus graffiti represent both an art and a crime. It is debatable which aspect is more important. Nathan Glazer [1979], a prominent sociologist, revealed fascination with the craze, but concluded that it should be curbed. He argued that graffiti are offensive to most people and contribute to the insecurity of subway riders. Because the problem cannot be controlled, it reenforces the impression that the subway is unsafe.

The writers have an entirely different attitude: They believe they are beautifying the city and think graffiti should be encouraged, not suppressed. They point out, quite accurately, that removing graffiti does not make the subways safer, faster, cheaper, or more reliable. Several times writers have gone to the transit authority and asked permission to paint cars with designs they have submitted for approval. The writers have always been refused.

After years of frustration, the transit authority (TA) has apparently succeeded in eliminating graffiti in the last few years. The TA has been purchasing new subway cars with stainless-steel exteriors that are supposed to be graffiti-proof. Strong chemicals have been developed to clean the older cars. Under a new policy, when graffiti are observed, the car is immediately removed from service and cleaned by special squads of workers who are on standby. All this, of course, is very expensive.

However, the graffiti craze seems to be spreading to other places. It struck the London Underground in the 1980s, although there had never been a graffiti problem there before. Up to 1983, no money was budgeted for graffiti removal; in 1987 it cost $1.4 million. Graffiti artists have also become active in Los Angeles, led by a boy with the tag of Chaka, named after a character in a former television series for children. The transit district is reportedly paying $10 million a year for graffiti removal.

QUESTIONS

1 What are the three major parts of the process of scheduling transit service? Why do the work rules negotiated by labor unions have so much influence on scheduling?

2 Why is it important for transit vehicles to keep to schedule? Why do transit systems hold back vehicles that get ahead of schedule? Why do the largest transit systems not bother to publish timetables?

3 Three special service patterns are used in some U.S. transit systems: separate express and local service, the zone system, and the skip-stop system. Explain the differences between them. In what situations is each one appropriate? What are the advantages and disadvantages of each?

4 U.S. transit officials have been reluctant to use the honor system for fare payment, although it has been successful in other countries. Do you think people in the United States are more prone to cheat? What are the advantages of self-service fare collection?

5 Do you think advertising actually causes any travelers to use public transportation? Would appeals to environmental consciousness work? What can transit systems do to improve their image and attract riders?

6 There are two points of view about subway graffiti: Some hold that it is a nuisance and a petty crime; others believe that it is a form of artistic expression. Which do you agree with? Why shouldn't a transit authority let young people decorate a subway train if the artists submit their designs for approval?

REFERENCES

Bennett, Brian T., and Renfrey B. Potts: "Rotating Roster for a Transit System," *Transportation Science,* vol. 2, no. 1 (February 1968), pp. 14–34.

Black, Alan: "A Method for Determining the Optimal Division of Express and Local Rail Transit Service," *Highway Research Board Bulletin,* no. 347 (1962), pp. 106–120.

Carter, Maurice M., and Langley C. Powell: "Self-Service Barrier-Free Fare Collection: An Early Look at San Diego's Experience," in *Light Rail Transit: Planning, Design, and Implementation,* Special Report 195 (Washington: Transportation Research Board, 1982), pp. 149–152.

Castleman, Craig: *Getting Up: Subway Graffiti in New York* (Cambridge, MA: MIT Press, 1982).

Ceder, Avishai: "Optimal Design of Transit Short-Turn Trips," *Transportation Research Record,* no. 1221 (1989), pp. 8–22.

Chapman, R. A., and J. F. Michel: "Modelling the Tendency of Buses to Form Pairs," *Transportation Science,* vol. 12, no. 2 (May 1978), pp. 165–175.

Eisele, Donald O.: "Application of Zone Theory to a Suburban Rail Transit Network," *Traffic Quarterly,* vol. 22, no. 1 (January 1968), pp. 49–67.

————: "Zone Theory of Suburban Rail Transit Operations: Revisited," *Traffic Quarterly,* vol. 32, no. 1 (January 1978), pp. 5–22.

Furth, Peter G.: "Short Turning on Transit Routes," *Transportation Research Record,* no. 1108 (1987), pp. 42–52.

Glazer, Nathan: "On Subway Graffiti in New York," *The Public Interest,* no. 54 (Winter 1979), pp. 3–11.

Godey, John: *The Taking of Pelham One Two Three* (New York: G. P. Putnam's Sons, 1973).

Haase, R. H., and W. H. T. Holden: *Performance of Land Transportation Vehicles,* Memorandum RM-3966-RD (Santa Monica, CA: Rand Corporation, 1964).

Hinds, David H.: "RUCUS: A Comprehensive Status Report and Assessment," *Transit Journal,* vol. 5, no. 1 (Winter 1979), pp. 17–34.

Kenney, Dennis Jay: *Crime, Fear, and the New York City Subways: The Role of Citizen Action* (New York: Praeger Publishers, 1987).

Koutsopoulos, Harilaos N., and Nigel H. M. Wilson: "Operator Workforce Planning in the Transit Industry," *Transportation Research,* vol. 21A, no. 2 (March 1987), pp. 127–138.

Levine, Ned, and Martin Wachs: "Bus Crime in Los Angeles," *Transportation Research,* vol. 20A, no. 4 (July 1986), pp. 273–293.

MITRE Corporation, Metrek Division: *Self-Service Fare Collection* (McLean, VA: MITRE Corporation, August 1979).

O'Flaherty, C. A., and D. O. Mangan: "Bus Passenger Waiting Times in Central Areas," *Traffic Engineering and Control,* vol. 11, no. 9 (January 1970), pp. 419–421.

Oram, Richard L.: "Making Transit Passes Viable in the 1980s," *Transportation Quarterly,* vol. 37, no. 2 (April 1983), pp. 289–296.

Pearlstein, Adele, and Martin Wachs: "Crime in Public Transit Systems: An Environmental Design Perspective," *Transportation,* vol. 11, no. 3 (September 1982), pp. 277–297.

Rousseau, Jean-Marc: *Computer Scheduling of Public Transport 2* (Amsterdam: North-Holland, 1985).

Schneider, Lewis M.: *Marketing Urban Mass Transit* (Cambridge, MA: Harvard University Press, 1965).

Seddon, P. A., and M. P. Day: "Bus Passenger Waiting Times in Greater Manchester," *Traffic Engineering and Control,* vol. 15, no. 9 (January 1974), pp. 442–445.

Seshagiri, N., R. Narasimhan, S. Mehndiratta, and B. K. Chanda: "Computer Generated Time-Tables and Bus Schedules for a Large Bus Transport Network," *Transportation Science,* vol. 3, no. 1 (February 1969), pp. 69–85.

Transportation Research Board: *Highway Capacity Manual,* Special Report 209 (Washington: Transportation Research Board, 1985).

Vuchic, Vukan R.: "Skip-Stop Operation as a Method for Transit Speed Increase," *Traffic Quarterly,* vol. 27, no. 2 (April 1973), pp. 307–327.

Walb, Carol, and Rosemary Booth: "Transit Marketing: The State of the Art," *Transportation Research Record,* no. 1039 (1985), pp. 9–16.

Young, David: "Anatomy of a Train Crash," *Mass Transit,* vol. 4, no. 6 (June 1977), pp. 12–16.

10

TRANSIT AND URBAN DEVELOPMENT

This is a controversial subject of special interest to those concerned with urban form, land-use development, and city planning. Advocates of transit improvements often make strong claims about the favorable land-use impacts of their proposals. They may say, e.g., that transit will revitalize the central business district (CBD), slow down suburban sprawl, or create a more efficient land-use pattern. Others dispute these assertions and argue that transit will make little or no difference. Facts and opinions become intertwined so that it is difficult to ascertain the truth.

Everyone recognizes there is a symbiotic relationship between transit and a particular form of urban development; the two support each other and need each other. Transit functions most efficiently in cities that have high population densities and are compact and highly centralized. Such cities are relatively dependent on transit and have ridership levels much greater than those of dispersed, low-density cities.

It is agreed that in the historical past, notably the 19th century, transit had a strong influence on urban form. Many historical studies have demonstrated this conclusively. However, it is disputed whether a transit facility built today can have much impact on future urban development. Transit now has a strong competitor in the automobile, whereas before 1920, the main competition was walking.

In some recent cases, development has sprung up around new transit lines and stations. These provide evidence that transit can still have some impact, but critics argue that the cases are few and far between. Further, it is uncertain whether this is a net benefit to the city caused by transit or only relocation of development that would have occurred anyway, but in a different location.

Even if it had been proved that transit could recreate the dense, compact 19th-century city, it is debatable whether this would be desirable. Some writers have favored this course, but others have dismissed it as nostalgia. This is the question of what kind of land-use pattern we want: What are our land-use goals? It is argued that popular preferences and public policy endorse the suburban lifestyle that has led to the sprawling metropolises common today.

These points will be discussed in more detail.

THE SYMBIOTIC RELATIONSHIP

The relationship between transit use and a variety of urban characteristics has been the subject of many statistical studies, such as those by Smith [1959], Schnore [1962], Schmandt and Stephens [1963], Kain and Beesley [1965], Guest and Cluett [1976], and Pushkarev and Zupan [1977]. Several variables indicating the size or structure of a metropolitan area have consistently been found to be associated with transit use. One variable is total population: Larger cities rely more on transit than smaller ones. A second is population density: Higher density favors transit use. Another variable is the age of the city: Transit is more important in older cities than in those that developed in the automobile era. Total employment in the central business district has also been shown to be positively associated with transit use [Hendrickson 1986]; this is a measure of whether a city has a strong center, which should favor transit use.

A few other variables are strongly related to transit use. One of these is automobile ownership, and another is transit service. As one would expect, transit use has been found to be associated with miles of service per capita [Carstens and Csanyi 1968], route miles [Kasoff 1970], frequency of service [Constantino 1975], and ratios of vehicle-miles per route-mile and vehicle-miles per square mile [Weisman 1981]. Of course, identifying the cause and effect is debatable: It is too facile to claim that more service produces more ridership. Perhaps cities increase (or decrease) service in response to higher (or lower) demand that results from other factors.

In one study, Black [1989] performed statistical analysis on a sample of 120 standard metropolitan statistical areas (SMSAs), using data from the 1980 Census and section 15 reports from transit agencies. He found high correlations between the percentage of persons who used transit to go to work in 1980 and the variables listed in Table 10-1. Several of these variables represent the structure of the metropolitan area, several reflect the supply of transit service, and one is a measure of automobile ownership. These variables were highly intercorrelated; they are different facets of the same pattern. What happened historically is this:

Early in the 19th century, U.S. cities were small, compact, and dense, and walking was the major mode of travel. When transit arrived in the middle of the century, the cities grew out along the transit routes. Some of these cities grew large by 1900 and are still among the largest cities in the country today (New York, Chicago, Philadelphia, St. Louis, and Boston were the five largest cities in population in the 1900 Census).

These older cities are much denser than the newer cities that didn't experience major growth until the 20th century. Automobile ownership has always been lower in these cities; high density discourages automobile use because of congestion and parking problems. At the same time, transit service is better in these cities because high density makes transit more efficient and economical. These cities have had comparatively good

TABLE 10-1
CORRELATION OF SELECTED VARIABLES WITH PERCENTAGE OF WORK TRIPS MADE BY
PUBLIC TRANSPORTATION, FOR A SAMPLE OF METROPOLITAN AREAS, 1980

Variable	Correlation coefficient
Transit operating expenses per capita	0.909
Number of transit vehicles	0.905
Number of persons employed in the CBD	0.897
Population of central city in 1920	0.872
Population density (persons per square mile)	0.841
Percentage of households with no automobile	0.831
Population of metropolitan area	0.778
Transit vehicle-miles per capita	0.765

Source: Alan Black, "Analysis of Trends in Transit Work Trips," *Journal of American Planning Association,*
vol. 55, no. 1 (Winter 1989), p. 40.

transit for a long time, and many people consider it essential. All these things combine
to cause higher transit use in cities that are old, large, and dense.

Size alone is not enough; some large cities have relatively low transit use. These are
cities that experienced their major growth after 1900, including Houston, Dallas, San
Antonio, Phoenix, San Diego, and San Jose (none of these was among the 50 largest
cities in 1900). Los Angeles, currently the second-largest U.S. city, ranked 36th in 1900.

Most of the transit-oriented cities are in the frost belt, although there are exceptions
(notably San Francisco, which was the ninth-largest city in 1900 and remains one of the
densest). Most of the automobile-oriented cities are in the sun belt; they are growing
faster than transit-oriented cities because of population migration. This does not help
transit.

Census data for the 1970s showed that transit use increased in many sun belt cities,
especially in the west, while it was stable or declined in most frost belt cities, although
there were some exceptions [Fulton 1983]. Nevertheless, the sun belt cities are not
likely to attain the levels of transit riding that used to be common in older eastern cities.

Except for automobile ownership, social and economic characteristics of city
dwellers do not explain much of the differences in transit riding among cities. Black
[1989] obtained the following correlations with transit use:

1 *Median family income:* 0.250. This modest correlation was positive, whereas one
would expect it to be negative. This probably occurred because median income tends to
be higher in large cities than small ones and in the north than in the south.

2 *Percentage of employment in manufacturing:* – 0.095. Smith [1959] found a fairly
strong positive association in his study with data from the 1950s. But in the past three
decades, most new manufacturing jobs have been located in the suburbs, where transit
service is often poor or absent.

3 *Percentage of females in the labor force:* 0.077. This low correlation was surprising because it is known that women ride transit more than men do.

4 *Race or minority status.* Black found a correlation of 0.154 with the percentage of

African-Americans in the population and a correlation of 0.053 with the percentage of Hispanics in the population. This was again surprising because minorities are more likely to use transit [Pucher and Williams 1992].

The geographic structure of a city seems to be more important than who lives in the city or what they do for a living. However, socioeconomic variables are important in explaining differences in transit use among parts of a single metropolitan area (see Hadden [1964] for a study of Milwaukee). For example, transit riders are more likely to come from low-income areas than high-income areas.

THE PAST IMPACT OF TRANSIT

There is no doubt that transit had a great impact on urban growth patterns in the 19th century. Before transit arrived, walking was the dominant mode of travel, and the geographic spread of cities was largely limited to walking distance [Schaeffer and Sclar 1975]. Horses were common, but average people could not afford them; horses were used mostly by businesses and rich people.

The successive transit improvements discussed in Chapter 2 allowed the city to grow out farther and farther. Development followed transit routes. The suburban movement that most people assume started after World War II actually started after the Civil War. It did not originate with the automobile or federal home mortgages. It was based on transit and was well advanced before automobile ownership became common in the 1920s. An empirical study of the 1880–1920 period concluded, "Expanded street railway service seems to have provided the same impetus for lower density development that automobile ownership provided in the later time periods" [Harrison 1976, p. 121].

Another mistaken belief is that the automobile was the cause of strip commercial streets. Originally it was streetcar lines that generated this pattern of development: Businesses wanted to locate near streetcar stops, which were closely spaced. Later, of course, these streets filled with motor vehicles, and the streetcar tracks were usually removed.

In the larger cities, suburban railroads created a finger pattern of development. Chicago provides an excellent example: Towns grew up along half a dozen railroad lines, while the spaces between the lines remained in farms. For a series of historical maps illustrating this, see the *Final Report* of the Chicago Area Transportation Study [1960, pp. 17–18].

Many historical studies have documented the effects of transit on urban development in the 19th century. The most thorough is Sam Bass Warner's book on Boston, *Streetcar Suburbs* [1962]. This was based on exhaustive research on streetcar line extensions and building permits in three suburban towns between 1870 and 1900. The towns—Roxbury, West Roxbury, and Dorchester—grew from a total population of 60,000 in 1870 to 227,000 in 1900. During this period, horsecar lines were extended into the area and then electrified (see Figure 10-1).

Warner divided the streetcar lines into three types of service:

1 *Pioneering lines.* These extended into sparsely developed areas and had infrequent service. They were largely patronized by the wealthy still living on farms or estates.

FIGURE 10-1
Apartment buildings on Commonwealth Avenue in Boston. Boston grew outward along streetcar lines like this one in the late 19th century. Today high residential densities help make Boston one of the most transit-oriented cities in the country. (Photo by author.)

2 *Good linear service* (a car about every 10 minutes). This brought intensive development of housing for the upper and central middle classes, but it was limited to a depth of several hundred yards from the lines (i.e., walking distance).

3 *Crosstown service.* This led to filling in the gaps between the radial lines, usually with lower-middle-class housing. These people changed jobs frequently and needed the flexibility provided by crosstown lines so they could go all over the city.

There was a close relationship between the rate of new residential construction and the amount of street railway service. Warner [1962, p. 49] demonstrated that the better the service on a line, the higher the rate of building:

> The Boston to Roxbury segment of the line gave good service, cars every eight minutes; the Roxbury to Jamaica Plain segment was a pioneering one: it had cars only every half hour. There was a marked difference in the rates of building next to the two segments, building along the Roxbury to Boston segment being far the most active.

Martin Wachs' article [1984] on Los Angeles in the 1920s presents a similar picture. People moving to the area preferred single-family homes on large lots because most came from the midwest (there were few European immigrants), had a rural background, and had enough money to afford these homes. Construction of a large network of street-car and interurban electric lines enabled fulfillment of this desire.

Thus, Wachs wrote, the Los Angeles area already had a dispersed settlement pattern, based on transit, before the automobile came into common use. But southern Californians eagerly welcomed automobiles, and from an early point Los Angeles had the highest automobile ownership rates of any U.S. city. In the mid-1920s, Los Angeles voters were given a choice. They approved a major street plan and rejected a rapid transit plan. All this happened years before the first freeway was built. (See Bottles [1987] for a detailed account.)

Both Warner and Wachs mentioned that streetcar companies often speculated in real estate. They would buy a large tract of farmland, extend a streetcar route to it, subdivide it, and try to sell off the lots. Many times the companies were successful and made more money from real estate than from transit fares. But some of these projects failed, which contributed to the financial crisis of the transit industry just after World War I.

Transit strengthened the CBD and made cities monocentric. The most important transit routes were radial lines that met at the city center. This was documented in Homer Hoyt's classic study [1933] of 100 years of land values in Chicago from 1833 to 1933. He found values in the Loop increased more rapidly than elsewhere after the first elevated line opened in 1892. People who had gone shopping in the neighborhoods started going downtown. The CBD became the dominant center of the city, not only for business, but also for government, entertainment, and cultural activities.

Other inventions complemented transit by enabling construction of skyscrapers. One was the elevator, without which tall buildings would have been impractical. Elisha Otis perfected a safety device that made elevators acceptable in 1853; he installed his first one in a New York City store in 1857. Another key invention was steel-frame construction. The first building entirely supported by a steel frame was the Home Life Insurance Building in Chicago, completed in 1885, which stood 535 feet tall. The Woolworth Building in New York City, completed in 1913, was 792 feet tall. It retained the title of tallest building in the world until the Chrysler Building (1046 feet) in New York City was completed in 1929.

The impact of transit facilities was most evident where a natural barrier was crossed by a bridge or tunnel. Opening of the Hudson Tubes (a rail tunnel under the Hudson River, now part of the PATH system) in 1908 stimulated the growth of northern New Jersey. In San Francisco, a 2.2-mile streetcar tunnel under the Twin Peaks was opened in 1918 and spurred development of the area to the west, which had been mostly farmland.

The evidence is clear that early transit improvements promoted development of the city center and made skyscrapers practical. They attracted more intensive land use along transit routes and around stations. At the same time, the transit improvements caused cities to grow horizontally, enabling middle-class families to live at lower densities.

THE IMPACT OF TRANSIT TODAY

Since transit now has major competition from the automobile, new transit lines are less likely to affect urban form than a century ago. As Knight noted, "Today's transit improvements do not provide the kind of drastic improvement in overall accessibility which was typically associated with earlier transit improvements" [1980, p. 5]. Some people argue that new transit routes have almost no impact on land use. Others claim that in the right conditions, transit can play a major role in shaping development.

The evidence is mixed. Here are some recent cases:

Toronto

After Toronto opened its first subway under Yonge Street in 1954, there was a building boom along the corridor (see Figure 10-2). This was described in an article by Warren Heenan [1968], who claimed the subway "ignited a $10 billion development explosion along the route." The city's total property valuation increased by $15 billion in 10 years, and he attributed two-thirds of this to the subway. Assessments in districts contiguous to the subway went up by 45 percent in the downtown area and 107 percent along the remainder of the route. Assessments for the rest of the city increased by an average of 25 percent.

FIGURE 10-2
Development along Yonge Street in Toronto. The city's first subway runs under this street, and high-rise buildings have been developed around the locations of stations. Land-use planning controls enhanced the impact of the rail line on development. (*Source:* American Public Transit Association.)

Heenan must be considered a biased observer as he is a developer who said he made lots of money from the subway (he argued that transit should be free because the increase in real estate values is enough to justify it). Others have studied Toronto and found the subway had less impact [Meyer and Gomez-Ibanez 1981, p. 117]. However, any visitor to Toronto would find Heenan's claims to be convincing. It is obvious from looking at the skyline where the subway lines are. Rows of skyscrapers line the routes, while the rest of the city has predominantly low buildings.

An important factor was that zoning was closely coordinated with the rail lines. The planners allowed maximum densities for commercial and apartment buildings within 1500 feet of stations, with progressively lower limits at greater distances. This doubled or tripled land values for sites close to stations. This kind of coordination has not been common for new transit facilities in the United States.

San Francisco

The BART impact study was discussed in Chapter 5. Planners of the system hoped it would greatly alter the Bay Area's growth pattern, but this did not happen. With regard to land-use and urban development impacts, Dyett et al. [1979, p. 140] concluded, "To date, the effects have been small relative to expectations, but not inconsequential. Both behavior patterns and development decisions have been affected, and the benefits of BART are reflected in small property price and rent increases near stations."

There was a building boom in downtown San Francisco, especially on Market Street (under which run both BART and a light rail line) (see Figure 10-3). This was facilitated by two redevelopment projects that cleared the unattractive area south of Market, the $35 million Market Street Beautification Project, and changes in zoning. Of course, the San Francisco metropolitan area has been one of the fastest growing in the country in the last 25 years. Many national corporations have selected it for regional headquarters. Probably most of this development would have occurred anyway, but some of it would not have been in the San Francisco CBD.

BART had much less effect on downtown Oakland and Berkeley, the secondary centers served by the system. Possibly development that would have occurred in these centers was diverted to San Francisco. Also, there has been minimal development around suburban stations. Dennis Dingemans [1978] did a case study of Contra Costa County, which received vastly improved accessibility from BART. Here are his findings:

1 Citizens and politicians in the suburbs opposed dense development (especially high-rise buildings). They were afraid BART would spoil the suburban environment they liked. As of 1978, there was only one high-rise building adjacent to a station, a 10-story building at Walnut Creek.

2 City councils in the suburbs approved large development projects (including two regional malls) that were located far from BART stations.

3 There was a boom in town house construction during the time when BART opened, but most of this did not occur near stations. The average distance from the nearest station was 4.5 miles. Only 23 percent were built within 2 miles of a station.

4 Most BART stations were surrounded by large parking lots, intended to attract park-and-ride commuters. However, these lots prevented construction of buildings

FIGURE 10-3
Skyscrapers lining Market Street in downtown San Francisco. Both a
BART line and a light rail line run under this street. While there are
doubts about BART's impact in other places, there is no question that
it played a role in San Francisco's downtown building boom. (Photo
by author.)

within easy walking distance of the stations. Because of high parking demand, many of
the lots have been expanded.

5 Only 10 percent of BART passengers walked to the stations. The vast majority (73
percent) used a car to reach them. The rest used buses.

Philadelphia

There were also impact studies of the Lindenwold line, a 14-mile rail line which opened
in 1969 between downtown Philadelphia and the New Jersey suburbs. According to

David Boyce [1980, p. 413], "The overall impact of the Line on development and location decisions in the South Jersey area was modest, but significant." There were no major developments related to the line, but garden apartment projects were built within a few miles of stations and medium-rise office buildings went up near several stations. Land prices of single-family residential property in the corridor rose. There appeared to be no effect on retail development, which is attracted more to shopping centers and busy highways. Boyce said that impacts may not happen immediately upon opening a line; it may take 5 to 10 years for them to materialize.

The line's impact on office development was investigated by Gannon and Dear [1975]. They concluded that the line was a growth stimulus in both downtown Philadelphia and the suburbs, although the amount of office construction in the corridor was fairly small and was concentrated around stations (within a 5-minute walk). Vacancy rates were much lower near stations; highway-oriented office space was not selling well. A majority of the firms that located at outlying stations had moved out from Camden, which is a declining older city in the shadow of Philadelphia.

Other Cases

Several major projects built in New York City in recent decades have capitalized on transit accessibility. These include the 59-story Pan Am Building (built over Grand Central Station), the new Madison Square Garden (built over Pennsylvania Station), and the 110-story World Trade Center (built over the Hudson Terminal, fed by several subway lines).

Three of the five tallest buildings in the world are located in the center of Chicago (including the very tallest, the Sears Tower). It is unlikely that these buildings would have been constructed if Chicago did not have an excellent rail transit system.

The Washington, D.C., Metro has attracted considerable nonresidential development to station areas [Baker 1983]. From 1979 to 1982, $2 billion out of $3.7 billion of public and private nonresidential construction in the metropolitan area occurred within $7/10$ mile of stations. The major types of development were mixed-use projects, office buildings, and hotels. The effects were greatest in downtown Washington, D.C., and the inner, older suburbs such as Rosslyn and Bethesda. There was minimal development near outlying suburban stations. Little new residential construction occurred in these station areas, perhaps because the zoning limits building heights.

A rigorous statistical analysis by Green and James [1993] confirmed that Washington's rail system has had significant development impacts, especially in regard to service and government employment. Rail corridors have developed more than other places, and within the rail corridors, station areas have grown much more than other areas.

The MARTA system in Atlanta has stimulated development at several stations. The IBM Tower, currently the tallest building in the city at 50 stories, is adjacent to the Arts Center station, which is about 2 miles from downtown. Farther out, a 27-story office building called ReSurgens Plaza was erected over the Lenox station. The developer leased air rights from 40 feet aboveground upward plus toeholds for the columns that support the building. The developer pays an annual rent of $120,000, with increases tied to the consumer price index.

There is debate whether light rail has the same impact as heavy rail. Light rail normally requires less capital investment; as a rule it provides a lower quality of service and doesn't carry as many passengers. Robert Cervero [1984] surveyed a dozen light rail projects in North America and evaluated the potential for land-use impacts, which varied considerably. He concluded that the strongest potential was in downtown areas where the lines were integrated into pedestrian malls (as in Buffalo, Calgary, Portland, and San Jose).

A paper by Arrington [1989] tabulated $693 million of new development adjacent to stations on the Portland light rail line since the decision was made to build it in 1979. This included $364 million in downtown Portland, $266 million at the nearby Lloyd Center, and $63 million at outlying stations. The author suggested that light rail may have a greater impact than heavy rail because light rail operates on the surface and makes adjacent businesses visible to thousands of passengers.

Necessary Conditions

Knight and Trygg [1977] studied the land-use impacts of four new rail systems (Toronto, Montreal, San Francisco, and Washington, D.C.). They concluded that four conditions are necessary for a new rail line to make an impact on land-use development:

1 Local government policies encourage development at the stations. Examples include rezoning for higher density, density bonuses for buildings with direct access to the stations, tax abatements, and public investment in the projects. Another recent approach is to reduce parking requirements for development near stations.

2 There is pressure for development in the region. This is manifested by population growth, employment growth, and a boom in office building. If a city is stagnant or declining, transit will probably have little impact.

3 Developable land near the stations—vacant sites or sites with old buildings that can be torn down at low cost—is available. Division of the land into small parcels with different owners deters development because it is often difficult for developers to assemble large sites.

4 The physical characteristics of the area are desirable. It should be a physically attractive area with a reputation as a good neighborhood. Slums or industrial areas are unlikely to attract development. It has been noted that the San Diego LRT line had little impact because most of it runs through an industrial belt and unwanted scrubland.

The permanence of a new transit facility makes a difference in how developers react to it. Since real estate investment requires many years to pay off, developers are interested in longevity: They want to be sure that the transit service will be there a long time. It is argued that, for this reason, new rail lines have greater impact than improvements in bus service do. A Toronto transit official commented, "our developers tell us we can't get them to develop an area with private capital along a bus route that could be taken out tomorrow. They want to see the tracks" [Young 1980, p. 24].

An exclusive busway may be different, since it can involve major investment and is unlikely to be abandoned. Houston is building the largest system of high-occupancy vehicle (HOV) lanes in the country. Already lanes are operating on four radial expressways. A study of the North Transitway (on Interstate 45N) concluded that "the land use impacts of the HOV treatments have been relatively insignificant. The study site showed only three possible instances of . . . land use impacts" [Mullins et al. 1989]. Interviews indicated that presence of the transitway may affect people's choices of where to live and work, but developers paid no attention to it.

The specific locations of routes and stations are important. A representative of the Urban Land Institute commented, "A variation of 100 or 200 feet in the transit right-of-way can make or break a major development proposal" [Jensen 1978, p. 8]. A case in point is the location of a rail line in the median strip of a freeway, which forces transit riders to walk long distances from nearby buildings. This is likely to discourage intensive development around the stations. Furthermore, the stations are often located at freeway interchanges, where highway-oriented businesses such as gas stations occupy the closest sites. Despite this, many recent rail lines have been located in freeways because the land is available at little or no cost. This practice may be penny-wise but pound-foolish.

Joint Development

Joint development has been defined as "real estate development that is closely linked to public transportation services and station facilities and relies to a considerable extent on the market and locational advantages provided by the transit facility" [Urban Land Institute 1979, p. 1]. It requires close cooperation between public and private parties in designing a station, and often the public agency gets a continuing income. An example is the ReSurgens Plaza in Atlanta, cited earlier (see Figure 10-4).

In 1978 the Carter administration began an Urban Initiatives Program to encourage joint development and earmarked $200 million in UMTA funds to aid real estate projects related to transit facilities. The Reagan administration discontinued this program, but under it a number of joint development projects were started in 1979–1980 and eventually completed.

Keefer [1985] studied nine joint development projects in cities ranging in size from Philadelphia to Davenport, Iowa. He found that the projects provided considerable leverage for private investment and were very cost-effective. Besides earning direct income for transit authorities from leases, they generated additional transit riders and fare box revenues. The cities benefited from increases in employment and property taxes. However, he found that many transit authority governing boards were reluctant to engage in joint development because they thought it was inappropriate for public agencies to make deals with private developers.

Allen [1986] described four cities that have had success with joint development: Toronto, Montreal, Washington, and Miami. Partly because of the severe winters, the Canadian cities have extensive underground walkway systems that connect subway stations with numerous buildings. Opportunities are greatest when new rail lines are built, but there have been isolated cases of joint development at stations of older systems in Boston, Chicago, New York City, and Philadelphia. Allen mentioned three cases in which joint development has not occurred: Cleveland, the Lindenwold line, and BART. Cleveland's heavy rail line was located in an old railroad right-of-way that did not serve

FIGURE 10-4
The ReSurgens Plaza office tower built over a rail station in Atlanta.
This is an excellent example of joint development. The developer
leased air rights from the transit authority, and there is a station in the
basement of the building. (Photo by author.)

any important commercial locations. In the other two cases, the policy was to emphasize park-and-ride so that stations are surrounded by parking lots.

An Urban Land Institute report [1979], containing case studies of some of the cities
cited above, stressed the complexity of making joint development work. Developers
must be involved early in the planning process; they are interested in the exact location
and design of stations. Public policy must be favorable, and zoning must be appropriate.
Developers are eager to share risk; they find it more attractive if the public entity has an
equity interest in a project. The report concludes that "the major, but often overlooked,
elements in the achievement of transit-related development are the detailed planning

and dedicated implementation efforts by the public and private sectors to encourage and accomplish joint development at individual station locations" [1979, p. 181].

Cervero et al. [1992] conducted a nationwide survey and identified 114 completed joint development projects. However, 108 of them occurred in just five cities: New York, Washington, Philadelphia, Atlanta, and Boston. Only in Washington had joint development been made a central policy consideration. Thirty-nine percent of the projects involved cost sharing between the transit agency and a private firm, 22 percent involved revenue sharing, and 34 percent involved some combination. Many of the projects were arranged when old rail stations were renovated (especially in New York).

The fact that developers are interested in joint development is proof that transit facilities can influence land use. These people are not swayed by the presumptions of planners or the critiques of scholars; developers want to make profits. However, their interest is in the immediate vicinity of stations, so the impacts are very localized. There is no evidence that transit can cause a substantial change in overall urban form.

THE IMPACT OF HIGHWAYS

Some people claim that new highways have a weaker impact than transit. The argument is that streets are ubiquitous; you can go anywhere you want by car. A new freeway causes only a slight improvement in accessibility. Short distances are less important when you are driving. It doesn't matter if you are located $1/2$ mile from a freeway interchange, because it takes only a few minutes and little effort to cover the distance. However, there is ample evidence that highways can have a strong impact on development.

There have been hundreds of studies of the impacts of new highways [Federal Highway Administration 1972]. The first generation of such studies usually dealt with the effect of building a bypass around an isolated town or small city. After construction of the interstate highway system began, the studies mostly concerned the results of building expressways in metropolitan areas.

The first major beltway in the United States was Route 128 around Boston, of which the major link was completed in 1951. During the 1950s it attracted a large number of factories and stimulated residential building in adjacent towns [Bone and Wohl 1959]. Some of the businesses moved out from central Boston; others were brand-new. Route 128 (eventually widened to eight lanes) is still a favored location for new development. Beltways in other cities have produced similar results [Payne-Maxie and Blayney-Dyett 1980].

Crossing a natural barrier with a highway has an effect similar to doing so with a transit facility. One striking case was the opening of the Tappan Zee Bridge across the Hudson River in 1955, which sparked development of Rockland County, New York [Herr 1962]. Previously the driving time to Manhattan was too high to make it attractive to commuters. Rockland County's population boomed from 89,276 in 1950 to 229,903 in 1970 (or 157.5 percent in 20 years).

Another case is the Verrazano Narrows Bridge between Brooklyn and Staten Island, which opened in 1964 and started a building boom on Staten Island. Until then it was mostly farmland, although it is part of New York City. The population of Staten Island increased from 221,991 in 1960 to 352,121 in 1980 (or 58.6 percent in 20 years).

There is usually much development around urban freeway interchanges, especially highway-oriented businesses such as motels, restaurants, and gas stations. Shopping centers, however, are often located up to a mile from an interchange. This shows short distances are not critical; there is less monopoly in the land market. Frontage on a freeway is mostly valued for advertising. This is not important for shopping malls because they are major attractors in themselves and do not depend on passing traffic.

Studies have shown that residential property values often increase in the area served by a new freeway, but the effect is quite diffuse [Federal Highway Administration 1972]. Property close to the freeway may suffer losses or experience slow sales because of the noise, dirt, and air pollution. The best location is several blocks away where you get the accessibility without suffering the nuisance.

LAND-USE THEORY AND SIMULATION

The effect of transportation on the spatial structure of cities and the distribution of land uses has been a recurrent theme in geography and land economics [Hanson 1986]. Classical works in location theory gave an important role to transportation (of course, other things besides transportation costs vary geographically, such as wage and tax rates). This is also true of the theories of urban form developed in recent decades [Wingo 1961, Alonso 1964, Muth 1969, Mills 1972]. The gist of the theories goes as follows:

The transportation system has a major effect on the internal structure of cities. Some sites have physical characteristics that make them more or less desirable (e.g., high altitude with a view or poor soils that make construction expensive). But the value of urban land is primarily determined by its location, which is a function of the transportation system. This gives some sites advantages over others. This is represented by the concept of *accessibility*. Accessibility is higher when the costs to reach a site are lower, and vice versa. The costs are borne by various parties, depending on the activity on the site: the occupier, shippers, employees, or customers.

In a smoothly functioning competitive land market, each site will go to the highest bidder. This is what real estate people call the *highest and best use*. The party that can make the most advantage from the site will bid the most and acquire it. For the production sector of the economy, this means the party that can make the most profit from the site, which largely depends on the site's accessibility.

The most accessible sites have the largest profit potential for the right kinds of activities and command the highest prices. Higher-priced land usually requires taller buildings to spread out the land cost. Hence high-rise office and apartment buildings are mostly found on very accessible sites. Retail establishments are an exception: They can earn so much income per unit of floor space that they do not need tall buildings. Generally retail firms can outbid other kinds of business for the best sites.

Superior transportation facilities create peaks and ridges of accessibility. Land prices are higher, and buildings are taller. Stores are also attracted to these locations. Areas between the routes have less accessibility and lower land values and develop at lower densities.

In the transit era, there were large differences in accessibility within a city. Subway and elevated lines provided better service than streetcars and buses, and all forms of transit were better than walking. Development intensified around the transit lines (especially in the CBD, where most rail lines converged). This changed when the automobile became the dominant travel mode. While freeways improve accessibility, the effects spread widely because the street system is ubiquitous and it is easy to drive a mile or two from a freeway exit. Accessibility became more uniform and less focused on major transportation routes. The peaks and ridges diminished. The same thing happened to land values and density: They became more evenly distributed.

Around 1960, planners became interested in translating this body of theory into practical tools that could be used to forecast future land-use development [Voorhees 1959]. Much of this research was done as an adjunct of transportation studies, since by this time transportation planners and engineers had realized that the land-use pattern has a strong influence on travel demand [Mitchell and Rapkin 1954]. Aided by rapid advances in computing, planners and scholars created mathematical models, mostly during the 1960s, to forecast future land use [Harris 1965, Lowry 1968]. These are usually called *land-use models*. Most of them used some description of the transportation system as a key input.

In theory, land-use models should enable planners to estimate the land-use impacts of major transportation improvements. This would help to answer some of the questions that are still debated. But the models have not been very useful for this purpose [Boyce et al. 1970]. Most are quite gross in scale and do not attempt predictions for small areas such as individual blocks. Since impacts of transit facilities are thought to be very localized, this capability is important. Usually the models make predictions for *traffic zones* which are fairly large (as much as 1 square mile).

Furthermore, the models are not very reliable, and nowadays few planners put much faith in the models' predictions. A period of high expectations was succeeded by one of disillusionment [Lee 1973]. There has been relatively little research aimed at developing improved land-use models since the 1970s. Transportation planners still use several of the older land-use models because it is necessary to make a land-use forecast as an input to the transportation modeling process.

MEASURING THE BENEFITS OF TRANSIT

Many transit proposals are partly justified by the claim that they will increase property values and tax revenues. It is difficult to prove there is a net benefit to the city, even after the fact. Property values might have risen anyway, so it is necessary to compare the transit-affected area with a control area. Even if there is more development in the transit area, it is questionable whether there is an actual increase in total property values in the city or merely a redistribution (what economists call a *pecuniary effect*).

Knight and Trygg [1977] found no evidence that cities with new rail transit systems were more competitive than other cities. While Toronto had a boom after its subway opened, they attributed this to external factors. Other Canadian cities that were automobile-oriented grew just as rapidly as Toronto. According to Knight [1980, p. 10], "Recent experience provides no evidence that any rapid transit improvements have led to net new urban economic or population growth. . . . This suggests that land use impacts are shifts from one part of the city to another."

Another consideration is that cities are competing with each other for new development (particularly for firms that are seeking new locations). It is understandable that city X wants to get the lion's share of this, but it is not necessarily in the national interest to favor city X over other cities. Should the federal government give a transit grant to city X so that it can take development away from city Y? Knight [1980] suggested that it might be logical for the government to steer transit investment toward economically depressed cities, but this has certainly not been a consistent policy. Large federal grants to build new rail systems have gone to such booming cities as Atlanta, Miami, and Los Angeles.

Economists say there is a net benefit from transit only if there is an increase in efficiency, so that fewer resources are used to produce the total community output. No one knows whether this happens. Possibly it does: Clustering of activities around a transit station may produce *agglomeration economies*. For example, people may make trips on foot instead of driving (for lunch or shopping). It is likely that multiple-use projects (which may be attracted to rail stations) reduce vehicular travel.

Many planners argue that a centralized city with a strong CBD is more efficient than a dispersed city. This seems plausible, but it has never been proved. It *is* clear that in a centralized, high-density city, the total mechanized travel will be less: People will make shorter trips, and some trips will be on foot. Further, there will be more transit travel because these conditions make transit service more efficient and economical. Both of these factors will cause less automobile travel, which will reduce air pollution and energy use. This is one reason why gasoline consumption per capita is lower in foreign cities than in U.S. cities [Newman and Kenworthy 1989].

The concept of *value capture* has been popular among transit planners. The idea is for a transit system to capture some of the increased land values that it creates by condemning land around station sites and later selling it. This would take some of the windfall that private landowners do not pay for and hence do not deserve.

An important point is that the value capture must be partial; if it is total, there will be no incentive for developers and nothing will happen. There must be sharing of the benefits of the transit improvement.

Many states have legal restrictions against excess condemnation (taking more land than needed for public use). Public bodies are not supposed to condemn land in order to make a profit. Hence the value-capture idea has been replaced by the joint development approach, which was discussed earlier.

THE ISSUE OF DESIRABLE URBAN FORM

Some transit supporters believe the development pattern should be manipulated to enhance the transit system and boost ridership. This could be done by increasing density in general, but especially in transit corridors and the immediate vicinity of stations. This position implies doubt about whether transit by itself is enough of a force to shape development; it suggests some help is needed. The findings of Knight and Trygg [1977] seem to confirm this.

This also implies that making the transit system succeed is a dominant goal of city planning. Most planners would reject this idea. They regard transportation as a means to an end, not an end in itself. Transportation provides an essential service to land use (like sewer and water), but it is not the *raison d'être* of a city. Therefore, planners should decide on a land-use plan first and then plan the transportation system to serve it. This sequence is followed in the orthodox transportation planning process.

However, the symbiotic relationship discussed earlier indicates that it would be unwise to plan land use without considering transportation implications. Travel takes a significant portion of personal time and money budgets, and the transportation system has many impacts on the urban environment. A compromise position seems best: Land use and transportation should be treated as a package. This was done in some of the more sophisticated transportation studies [Boyce et al. 1970].

There remains the question of whether to seek a high-density, transit-oriented city or a low-density, automobile-oriented city. Some urban observers believe that high density is not necessarily desirable and should not be encouraged. They argue that the majority of people in the United States have cast their votes for low-density suburbs. We should not try to recreate the 19th-century city; no one wants this except a few benighted planners.

Alan Altshuler [1979, chap. 10] made a strong case for not trying to shape development to favor transit. Public opinion surveys, as well as market behavior, indicate that the vast majority of people in the United States prefer low densities. People are migrating in huge numbers to the suburbs and to sprawling cities of the sun belt [pp. 377–379]. "Virtually all current urban growth is occurring in low-density regions that seem irretrievably committed to auto dominance" [p. 384].

Altshuler noted that there is no national policy to promote higher urban densities. In fact, many federal programs (such as the highway and home mortgage programs) have encouraged lower densities. At the local level, "no clearcut public consensus has yet emerged in any metropolitan area in support of high-density development as a preferred outcome of land use and transportation policy decisions" [p. 376]. It appears that politicians have correctly interpreted the public mood and not espoused a high-density policy.

Altshuler reviewed the charges that "low-density urban development entails excessive energy, environmental, economic, and social costs" [p. 393] and the rebuttals by the people who favor a real estate market that tries to satisfy consumer preferences. He concluded that many of the criticisms are inaccurate or exaggerated. There are some disadvantages and costs to low density, but most people seem willing to bear these to get the lifestyle they want. Hence, in his opinion, there is little justification for government intervention to create higher densities.

However, there has been recent interest in designing *transit-friendly land use* around rail stations. This apparently originated with San Francisco architect Peter Calthorpe, who proposed creating *pedestrian pockets* around stops on Sacramento's light rail system [Bernick 1990]. The concept envisions high-density housing, with a complement of commercial facilities, within walking distance of a station. The street system would be designed to discourage driving, and a network of pedestrian ways would make walking safe and convenient. The object is not just to enhance transit revenues, but also to create a more livable community that is not dependent on automobiles.

The concept was incorporated in a new comprehensive plan prepared for Sacramento County. Further, Calthorpe convinced a developer to apply the scheme in the Laguna West community being built 13 miles south of downtown Sacramento. A recent book by Calthorpe [1993] presents his guidelines for community design, along with summaries of other projects. These include plans for several transit station areas in New York City and California.

There are others who disagree with Altshuler's position and believe that we should strive to create transit-oriented cities. Most environmental activists strongly support mass transit and oppose urban sprawl. This is a fundamental policy decision that depends on values and cannot be settled by logical analysis. However, as Altshuler noted, there is rarely any explicit discussion of the issue in the political arena. Instead, there is tacit agreement to let market forces and consumer preferences determine urban form.

QUESTIONS

1 Transit proposals are often defended on the grounds that they will stimulate a more desirable land-use pattern. Describe how transportation facilities influenced urban form and land development in the past. Can transit improvements made today have similar effects?

2 Summarize the conditions necessary for new transit lines to have an impact on land-use development. How large an area is likely to be affected?

3 In view of the problem of suburban gridlock discussed in Chapter 4, why do local residents often oppose concentration of development around suburban transit stations?

4 The archetypical dream in the United States is to own a single-family house on a large lot in the suburbs. Under what conditions might people be willing to live at higher densities?

5 Would you rather live in a high-density, transit-oriented city or a low-density, automobile-oriented city. Why?

6 Suppose you were responsible for planning the land-use pattern in a hypothetical city. How would you design the city so as to maximize the use of mass transit? Could any of your ideas be applied to real cities?

REFERENCES

Allen, John G.: "Public-Private Joint Development at Rapid Transit Stations," *Transportation Quarterly,* vol. 40, no. 3 (July 1986), pp. 317–331.

Alonso, William: *Location and Land Use* (Cambridge, MA: Harvard University Press, 1964).

Altshuler, Alan: *The Urban Transportation System: Politics and Policy Innovation* (Cambridge, MA: MIT Press, 1979).

Arrington, G. B., Jr.: "Light Rail and Land Use: A Portland Success Story," Paper presented at Transportation Research Board meeting, Washington, D.C., January 1989.

Baker, Carole: "Tracking Washington's Metro," *American Demographics,* vol. 5, no. 11 (November 1983), pp. 30–35, 46.

Bernick, Michael: *The Promise of California's Rail Transit Lines in the Siting of New Housing* (Berkeley: Institute of Urban and Regional Development, University of California, 1990).

Black, Alan: "Analysis of Trends in Transit Work Trips," *Journal of the American Planning Association,* vol. 55, no. 1 (Winter 1989), pp. 38–43.

Bone, A. J., and Martin Wohl: "Massachusetts Route 128 Impact Study," *Highway Research Board Bulletin,* no. 227 (1959), pp. 21–49.

Bottles, Scott L.: *Los Angeles and the Automobile: The Making of the Modern City* (Berkeley: University of California Press, 1987).

Boyce, David E.: "Impact of Federal Rail Transit Investment Programs on Urban Spatial Structure," in Norman J. Glickman, ed., *The Urban Impacts of Federal Policies* (Baltimore, MD: Johns Hopkins University Press, 1980), pp. 398–425.

———, Norman D. Day, and Chris McDonald: *Metropolitan Plan Making: An Analysis of Experience with the Preparation and Evaluation of Alternative Land Use and Transportation Plans* (Philadelphia: Regional Science Research Institute, 1970).

Calthorpe, Peter: *The Next American Metropolis: Ecology, Community, and the American Dream* (New York: Princeton Architectural Press, 1993).

Carstens, R. L., and L. H. Csanyi: "A Model for Estimating Transit Usage in Cities in Iowa," *Highway Research Record,* no. 213 (1968), pp. 42–49.

Cervero, Robert: "Light Rail Transit and Urban Development," *Journal of the American Planning Association,* vol. 50, no. 2 (Spring 1984), pp. 133–147.

———, Peter Hall, and John Landis: *Transit Joint Development in the United States* (Berkeley: Institute of Urban and Regional Development, University of California, 1992).

Chicago Area Transportation Study: *Final Report,* vol. 2: *Data Projections* (Chicago: Chicago Area Transportation Study, 1960).

Constantino, D. P.: "Attributes of Transit Demand," *Traffic Quarterly,* vol. 29, no. 2 (April 1975), pp. 243–257.

Dingemans, Dennis J.: "Rapid Transit and Suburban Residential Land Use," *Traffic Quarterly,* vol. 32, no. 2 (April 1978), pp. 289–306.

Dyett, Michael, David Dornbusch, Michael Fajans, Caj Falcke, Victoria Gussman, and James Merchant: *Land Use and Urban Development Impacts of BART: Final Report* (San Francisco: John Blayney Associates/David M. Dornbusch & Co., 1979).

Federal Highway Administration: *Economic and Social Effects of Highways* (Washington: Department of Transportation, 1972).

Fulton, Philip N.: "Public Transportation: Solving the Commuting Problem?" *Transportation Research Record,* no. 928 (1983), pp. 1–9.

Gannon, Colin A., and Michael J. Dear: "Rapid Transit and Office Development," *Traffic Quarterly,* vol. 29, no. 2 (April 1975), pp. 223–242.

Green, Rodney D., and David M. Jones: *Rail Transit Station Area Development: Small Area Modeling in Washington, D.C.* (Armonk, NY: M. E. Sharpe, 1993).

Guest, Avery M., and Christopher Cluett: "Analysis of Mass Transit Ridership Using 1970 Census Data," *Traffic Quarterly,* vol. 30, no. 1 (January 1976), pp. 143–161.

Hadden, Jeffrey K.: "The Use of Public Transportation in Milwaukee, Wisconsin," *Traffic Quarterly,* vol. 18, no. 2 (April 1964), pp. 219–232.

Hanson, Susan, ed.: *The Geography of Urban Transportation* (New York: Guilford Press, 1986).

Harris, Britton, ed.: "Urban Development Models: New Tools for Planning," special issue of the *Journal of the American Institute of Planners,* vol. 31, no. 2 (May 1965).

Harrison, David, Jr.: *Transportation Technology and Urban Land Use Patterns* (Cambridge, MA: Department of City and Regional Planning, Harvard University, 1976).

Heenan, G. Warren. "The Economic Effect of Rapid Transit on Real Estate Development," *Appraisal Journal,* vol. 36, no. 2 (April 1968), pp. 212–224.

Hendrickson, Chris: "A Note on Trends in Transit Commuting in the United States Relating to Employment in the Central Business District," *Transportation Research,* vol. 20A, no. 1 (January 1986), pp. 33–37.

Herr, Philip B.: "The Timing of Highway Impact," *Traffic Quarterly,* vol. 26, no. 2 (April 1962), pp. 279–288.

Hoyt, Homer: *One Hundred Years of Land Values in Chicago* (Chicago: University of Chicago Press, 1933).

Jensen, Harold S.: "Public Transportation and Land Use: A Developer's Perspective," in *Transportation and Land Development,* Special Report 183 (Washington: Transportation Research Board, 1978), pp. 7–11.

Kain, J. F., and M. E. Beesley: "Forecasting Car Ownership and Use," *Urban Studies,* vol. 2, no. 2 (November 1965), pp. 163–185.

Kasoff, Mark J.: "The Quality of Service and Transit Use," *Traffic Quarterly,* vol. 24, no. 1 (January 1970), pp. 107–119.

Keefer, Louis E.: "Joint Development at Transit Stations in the United States," *Transportation,* vol. 12, no. 4 (May 1985), pp. 333–342.

Knight, Robert L.: "The Impact of Rail Transit on Land Use: Evidence and a Change of Perspective," *Transportation,* vol. 9, no. 1 (March 1980), pp. 3–16.

———— and Lisa L. Trygg: "Evidence of Land Use Impacts of Rapid Transit Systems," *Transportation,* vol. 6, no. 3 (September 1977), pp. 231–247.

Lee, Douglass B., Jr.: "Requiem for Large-Scale Models," *Journal of the American Institute of Planners,* vol. 39, no. 3 (May 1973), pp. 163–178.

Lowry, Ira S.: "Seven Models of Urban Development: A Structural Comparison," in *Urban Development Models,* Special Report 97 (Washington: Highway Research Board, 1968).

Meyer, John R., and Jose A. Gomez-Ibanez: *Autos, Transit, and Cities* (Cambridge, MA: Harvard University Press, 1981).

Mills, Edwin S.: *Studies in the Structure of the Urban Economy* (Baltimore, MD: Johns Hopkins Press, 1972).

Mitchell, Robert B., and Chester Rapkin: *Urban Traffic: A Function of Land Use* (New York: Columbia University Press, 1954).

Mullins, James A., Earl J. Washington, and Robert W. Stokes: "Land Use Impacts of the Houston Transitway System," Paper presented at Transportation Research Board meeting, Washington, D.C., January 1989.

Muth, Richard F.: *Cities and Housing: The Spatial Pattern of Urban Residential Land Use* (Chicago: University of Chicago Press, 1969).

Newman, Peter W. G., and Jeffrey R. Kenworthy: "Gasoline Consumption and Cities: A Comparison of U.S. Cities with a Global Survey," *Journal of the American Planning Association,* vol. 55, no. 1 (Winter 1989), pp. 24–37.

Payne-Maxie and Blayney-Dyett: *The Land Use and Urban Development Impacts of Beltways* (Washington: Department of Transportation and Department of Housing and Urban Development, June 1980).

Pucher, John, and Fred Williams: "Socioeconomic Characteristics of Urban Travelers: Evidence from the 1990–91 NPTS," *Traffic Quarterly,* vol. 46, no. 4 (October 1992), pp. 561–581.

Pushkarev, Boris S., and Jeffrey M. Zupan: *Public Transportation and Land Use Policy* (Bloomington: University of Indiana Press, 1977).

Schaeffer, K. H., and Elliot Sclar: *Access for All: Transportation and Urban Growth* (Harmondsworth, England: Penguin Books, 1975).

Schmandt, Henry J., and G. Ross Stephens: "Public Transportation and the Worker," *Traffic Quarterly,* vol. 17, no. 4 (October 1963), pp. 573–583.

Schnore, Leo F.: "The Use of Public Transportation in Urban Areas," *Traffic Quarterly,* vol. 16, no. 4 (October 1962), pp. 488–498.

Smith, Joel: *Some Social Aspects of Mass Transit in Selected American Cities* (East Lansing: Institute for Community Development and Services, Michigan State University, 1959).

Urban Land Institute: *Joint Development: Making the Real Estate-Transit Connection* (Washington: Urban Land Institute, 1979).

Voorhees, Alan M, ed.: "Land Use and Traffic Models: A Progress Report," special issue of the *Journal of the American Institute of Planners,* vol. 25, no. 2 (May 1959).

Wachs, Martin: "Autos, Transit, and the Sprawl of Los Angeles: The 1920's," *Journal of the American Planning Association,* vol. 50, no. 3 (Summer 1984), pp. 297–310.

Warner, Sam B., Jr.: *Streetcar Suburbs: The Process of Growth in Boston, 1870–1900* (Cambridge, MA: Harvard University Press, 1962).

Weisman, Mark: "Variables Influencing Transit Use," *Traffic Quarterly,* vol. 35, no. 3 (July 1981), pp. 371–383.

Wingo, Lowdon, Jr.: *Transportation and Urban Land* (Washington: Resources for the Future, 1961).

Young, David: "Toronto: Taking the Lead Again," *Mass Transit,* vol. 7, no. 11 (November 1980), pp. 6–11, 24, 50.

11

ENERGY AND
ENVIRONMENTAL IMPACTS

Energy and the environment have become major concerns of the public and policy makers in the last 25 years. Transportation plays a major role in both areas, and many problems are attributed to U.S. reliance on the automobile for personal travel. Mass transit is often proposed as one solution to these problems. Hence it is appropriate to first examine the problems generally and then look more closely at transit's potential for alleviating them.

ENERGY

Transportation—including urban and cross-country movement of persons and freight—accounted for 28 percent of total energy use in the United States in 1990 [Davis and Strang 1993]. Highway modes consumed 72.4 percent of the energy in the transportation sector, of which 39.1 percent was for automobiles and 32.5 percent for trucks (see Table 11-1). Air and water modes took more than half of the remainder. Urban transit required only 0.5 percent—0.3 percent for bus and 0.2 percent for rail.

The transportation sector depends heavily on oil, while other sectors of the economy rely more on other fuels. In 1991, 96 percent of the energy used in transportation came from petroleum products (including kerosene and diesel fuel). Consequently, transportation took 65.1 percent of the U.S. petroleum consumption (up from 51.2 percent in 1973).

Although the United States is the second-largest oil producer in the world (Russia is first), domestic production has fallen short of meeting domestic demand for many years. Hence the country imports a large amount of oil, and this is a major factor in the foreign trade deficit. Petroleum imports peaked at 8.8 million barrels per day in 1977

TABLE 11-1
TRANSPORTATION ENERGY USE BY MODE, 1990

Mode	Trillion Btu	Percent
Highway		
Automobiles	9,066.3	39.1
Motorcycles	23.9	0.1
Buses	162.8	0.7
Trucks	7,543.6	32.5
	16,796.6	72.4
Off-highway		
Construction	209.9	0.9
Farming	455.3	2.0
	665.2	2.9
Nonhighway		
Air	2,059.3	8.9
Water	1,486.9	6.4
Pipeline	927.6	4.0
Rail	507.0	2.2
	4,980.8	21.5
Military operations	757.7	3.3
Total	23,200.3	100.0

Source: Davis and Strang 1993, table 2.9.

and then declined considerably during a period of high prices (see Figure 11.1). However, the United States never came close to achieving energy independence, which President Nixon declared a national goal and President Carter called "the moral equivalent of war." Several of the measures that Carter instituted (such as the synthetic fuels program) were later abandoned.

The level of imports varies greatly in response to the world price of crude oil. The price of a barrel of crude fell from $29 in 1983 to $14 in 1986. At times there was considered to be a glut of oil. One result was that domestic production fell and U.S. imports increased. When the price is low, there is less incentive to explore for new oil fields or extract oil as fast as possible. The number of active drilling rigs in the United States fell from 2233 in 1983 to 705 in 1986 [Mintz et al. 1987].

In 1991 the United States consumed 16.6 million barrels of oil per day, of which 7.6 million barrels (or 46 percent) were imported. Domestic production has declined from 9.6 million barrels per day in 1970 to 7.4 million barrels per day in 1991. Without Alaska, the figure would be much lower. There has not been a major oil discovery in U.S. territory since 1970.

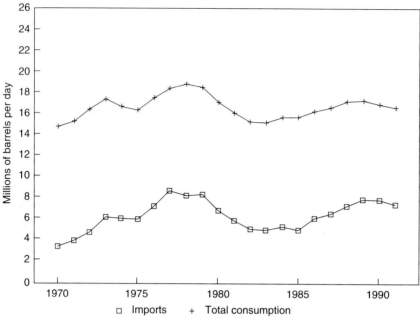

FIGURE 11-1

Total consumption and imports of petroleum in the United States, 1970 to 1991 (millions of barrels per day). While the effects of the oil shortages in 1974 and 1979 are visible, the trends have largely followed fluctuations in world oil prices. Meanwhile, domestic production (not shown) has declined fairly consistently. (*Source:* Davis and Strang 1993, table 2.2.)

Energy Policy

Our dependence on imported oil is important strategically because of insecurity about the continuing flow of foreign supplies. More than half of the world's proven crude oil reserves are in the Middle East, where it is accessible and cheap to produce. When the Organization of Petroleum Exporting Countries (OPEC) imposed an embargo on oil shipments to the United States and western Europe in October 1973, a severe gasoline shortage followed. The price of oil escalated rapidly, which badly hurt the U.S. economy. A second gas shortage occurred during the Iranian crisis in 1979.

Subsequently the United States has shifted to more dependable countries for oil imports, such as Mexico, Canada, Venezuela, Indonesia, and Nigeria. Mexico and Canada do not belong to OPEC; the other three countries do, but are not in the Middle East. However, in 1990, 33 percent of U.S. imported oil still came from Arab countries.

The Middle East has continued to be vital to U.S. allies, such as Japan, France, Germany, and Italy (Great Britain is an exception; its North Sea wells make it self-sufficient in oil). That is why the United States has been a major presence in the Persian Gulf. U.S. naval forces were sent there during the war between Iran and Iraq to keep the sea-lanes open. Clearly oil was a major consideration in the Persian Gulf War, no matter what politicians said about restoring freedom to the Kuwaiti people.

Since petroleum is a nonrenewable resource, many people wonder why there is sometimes reported to be a surplus, causing the price to fall. Why don't countries keep the price high in order to induce conservation?

The primary reason is that there is a spot market for oil on which the price changes daily and is very sensitive to short-range conditions. If there is a temporary surplus, prices fall on the spot market, and there is also an effect on the futures market. Prices do not reflect what may happen 1 year from now, and certainly not 10 years from now. There is no allowance for depletion in the current price.

According to economic theory, scarcity of a resource will eventually raise its price. This will spur greater exploration for the resource, a search for substitutes, and technological efforts to improve efficiency. In the long run, it is argued, the economy will adapt. However, in the short run a crisis can occur when no price will attract a larger supply. It takes time to remedy a shortage; discoveries and inventions do not occur overnight.

One way to cope with a temporary surplus would be to store oil until the price rose at a later date. This does happen to some extent, but it has a limited effect because annual oil production greatly exceeds storage capacity. When storage capacity is used up, oil producers must do something. One option is to reduce production; another is to cut the price to boost demand.

The oil industry has a vast system of transportation, refining, and marketing. If some of the capacity of this system goes unused, money is lost. For example, it costs money to have empty tankers sitting in ports. Hence it pays the oil companies to reduce prices to stimulate demand and keep the system operating efficiently.

Another factor is that many foreign governments get much of their income from oil (this is not true of the U.S. government, but it is true for some state governments). Either the government runs the oil business itself (as in Mexico), or it receives royalties from private firms. If production is cut, the government's income falls, which can cause an economic crisis.

Approaches

One approach to the oil problem is to increase the supply. This policy was favored by the Reagan and Bush administrations. As noted, domestic oil production declined in the 1980s because of low prices, with severe economic impacts on major oil-producing states such as Texas, Alaska, Louisiana, and Oklahoma. Among the solutions proposed were to boost exploration for offshore wells and open the Arctic National Wildlife Refuge to drilling.

Another approach is to allocate most oil for transportation and switch other sectors of the economy to more plentiful energy sources. Coal, natural gas, and nuclear power can be used for heating, manufacturing, and generating electricity. The United States has enough coal to last 300 years at current rates of consumption. However, much of our coal has high sulfur content and causes air pollution. Some western states have large reserves of low-sulfur coal, but it has to be strip-mined, which ruins the landscape and requires huge quantities of water. There are abundant supplies of natural gas in North America, but investment in pipelines is needed. The problems with nuclear power were demonstrated by the disasters at Three Mile Island and Chernobyl. Further, recent projects have suffered from tremendous cost overruns and vigorous public opposition. Hence the electric industry no longer seems interested in building nuclear plants.

Environmentalists advocate using renewable sources as much as possible. Hydroelectric power is currently the most important of these, but only 10 percent of the energy consumed by electric utilities in 1991 came from this source. It is clean, but proposals to build dams are often bitterly opposed because of impacts on fish and wildlife or threats to areas of natural beauty or recreational value. In fact, many potential sites are protected by legislation such as the Wild and Scenic Rivers Act. The best sites for hydroelectric power in the United States have already been utilized; it is estimated that 37 percent of ultimate capacity has been developed. Hence there will be no major expansion of this source.

Other renewable sources include wind, solar energy, geothermal wells, and the tides. These are quantitatively insignificant at present, and much technological development is needed to make them economical. It is unlikely that there will be much growth of these sources in the near future, but in the long run they could become important.

Another approach is to reduce the demand for oil, which mostly implies conservation. There has already been a considerable amount of conservation since the 1970s, some of it caused by regulation, but most stimulated by rising energy prices. Following are some measures that could reduce oil consumption in the transportation sector:

Improve the Fuel Efficiency of Vehicles   Congress imposed mandatory mileage standards in 1975, with a goal of 27.5 miles per gallon for 1985-model cars (see Figure 11-2). The carmakers easily met the standards at first, but Ford and General Motors did not meet the 1985 target (Chrysler did). The government temporarily rolled back the standard to 26.0 miles per gallon; the standard returned to 27.5 in 1990. Meanwhile, foreign manufacturers had little difficulty meeting the standards.

This approach has been successful. The average fuel efficiency of domestic passenger cars rose from 14.7 miles per gallon for the 1975 model year to 26.2 for the 1985 model year [Greene 1987]. In the latter year, European automobiles averaged 27.6 miles per gallon, and Japanese cars, 32.3. Total gasoline consumption in the United States declined in some years; from 1982 to 1990, it increased at an average annual rate of only 1.4 percent.

The technology to design cars that get very high mileage already exists. For years some subcompact cars have achieved more than 50 miles per gallon on the highway. There is a problem with consumer preferences: The automakers sell a variety of models ranging from subcompacts to full-size sedans. Whenever the price of gasoline drops, people buy larger cars. Allegedly the automakers gain more profit from larger vehicles and have no desire to promote the use of small cars.

There has also been increased demand for trucks and vans, which get lower mileage than automobiles. Sales of pickup trucks, vans, and special-purpose vehicles rose from 2.9 million units in 1978 to 4.2 million units in 1985 [Hu 1986]. In 1985, these vehicles averaged 20.4 miles per gallon.

Use Alternative Fuels for Motor Vehicles   The Bush administration emphasized this approach, and it still receives strong support. Methanol and ethanol are promoted as

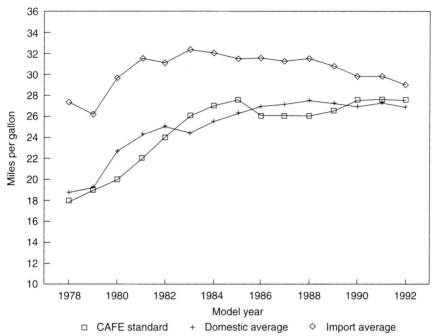

FIGURE 11-2
CAFE standards and performance, 1978 to 1992. The graph shows the corporate average fuel
economy (CAFE) standard set by the U.S. government and the estimated performance of all
domestic and all imported automobiles for each year. The government reduced the standard to
26.0 miles per gallon in 1986 under pressure from U.S. automobile manufacturers. The standard
is now 27.5 miles per gallon. *(Source:* Davis and Strang 1993, table 3.36.)

substitutes for gasoline, in part because they would contribute less to the greenhouse
effect. Other alternative fuels include electricity, compressed natural gas, propane gas,
and various blends. All the possibilities have costs as well as benefits; there is no
perfect fuel.

Methanol is the alternative fuel that has been publicized the most. Often called *wood
alcohol,* it can also be made from coal, natural gas, or solid waste. It is the fuel used in
Indianapolis 500 race cars, primarily for safety reasons. It contains only about 60 percent as much energy per gallon as gasoline, meaning that either gas tanks would have to
be larger or refueling more frequent. A major drawback is that it emits a large amount of
formaldehyde, which is an eye irritant and contributes to smog. The fuel also damages
paint, steel, and rubber.

Ethanol (which can be made from corn, grain, sugar cane, or garbage) also contains
less energy per gallon and costs about twice as much as gas. It is favored by agricultural
interests. Brazil, where sugar cane is abundant, initiated a sweeping ethanol program in
1975 to improve its foreign trade balance. By 1987, ethanol fuels constituted 27 percent
of the liquid fuels used in ground transportation [Trindade and de Carvalho 1989]. This
makes Brazil the largest user of alternative fuels in the world.

In the United States, ethanol seems more promising as an additive than as a straight fuel. Gasohol, containing 90 percent gasoline and 10 percent ethanol, has been sold by service stations since the late 1970s. Several farm states gave a tax break to encourage sales. Some environmentalists oppose ethanol because more energy is consumed in making it than is contained in the final product [Fowler 1984].

Ethanol has become a political issue in Congress, with the farm lobby favoring it and the petroleum lobby opposing it. The EPA announced a regulation that would guarantee ethanol a certain market share in areas with the worst air pollution. In August 1994, the Senate defeated a proposal to block this regulation by a 51-50 vote, with Vice President Albert Gore, Jr., casting the deciding vote.

Much publicity has been given to electric vehicles, but they still have major limitations. With current technology, batteries are very heavy (up to 1000 pounds) and must be recharged frequently, a process taking many hours. An electric automobile might be suitable as a second car for short trips within the city, but it is not attractive for general family use.

In 1984 several electric utility companies formed the Electric Vehicle Development Corporation to promote commercial use of electric vehicles [Mader and Bevilacqua 1989]. Later the automobile companies joined, apparently more for self-defense than leadership. Emphasis has been on marketing electric-powered vans that can make many short trips during the day and be recharged overnight. A British electric van called the *Griffon* was introduced in this country.

Early electric automobiles had low power, but at the 1990 Los Angeles Auto Show, General Motors exhibited a two-seat sports car called the *Impact* in an attempt to shatter that image (see Figure 11-3). The Impact can accelerate from 0 to 60 miles per hour in 8.5 seconds and has a top speed of 80 miles per hour. It has a range of 70 to 90 miles and can be recharged at home with standard 110-volt current. Late in 1993 GM announced that 50 Impacts would be manufactured, and 1000 motorists in 12 cities would be selected to test drive them for 2 to 4 weeks.

Some experts believe that compressed natural gas should be the preferred alternative fuel [Sperling and DeLuchi 1989]. The governments of New Zealand and Canada implemented moderately successful programs to encourage its use [Sathaye et al. 1989]. The main disadvantage is that it must be compressed at high pressure, both at filling stations and in the vehicles. This adds a considerable amount to the price of a car. Frequent refueling is necessary.

Propane gas has the advantages that it is already marketed widely for other uses (such as home heating) and is competitive in price. Canada began a propane vehicle program in 1981, and by 1987 there were 140,000 propane-fueled vehicles in the country [Sauve 1989]. For many years, the Chicago Transit Authority has used propane-fueled buses manufactured by Flxible.

Major obstacles to increasing the use of alternative fuels are the costs of converting vehicles and of developing a distribution and marketing system. Economic incentives are necessary, and most successful programs to date have involved substantial government subsidies or tax breaks. Expansion is most likely to occur in vehicle fleets because they are centrally fueled and maintained. This includes taxis, rental cars, delivery trucks and vans, and transit buses. There have been promising demonstrations with buses running on methanol and compressed natural gas.

FIGURE 11-3
The General Motors Impact. This electric car was first shown publicly in 1990. A small number of cars were undergoing consumer testing in 1994. General Motors has not said when the car will be available to the general public. (*Courtesy of General Motors.*)

Restore the 55 Mile per Hour Speed Limit　This speed limit was enacted early in 1974 as a conservation measure because cars use more gas at high speeds. It cut gasoline consumption by 1 percent in 1974, but the number of deaths from accidents fell by 17 percent. Hence the speed limit became more a safety issue than an energy issue. But a lower limit would save gas: According to the Federal Highway Administration, driving at a constant speed of 65 instead of 55 miles per hour caused average fuel economy losses of 12.4 percent in one study and 17.8 percent in a second study [Davis and Strang 1993].

Western states vigorously opposed the 55 mile per hour limit, and in 1987 Congress gave the states the option of raising the limit to 65 miles per hour on rural expressways. Forty states did so, but many eastern states still have a limit of 55 miles per hour.

Improve the Flow of Traffic　Stop-and-go driving is especially wasteful of gas; reducing congestion would reduce fuel consumption. While there is a great deal of variation from one model to another, most cars obtain their maximum mileage when they run at a constant speed in the range of 35 to 45 miles per hour. However, most studies indicate that traffic engineering measures would produce only modest savings and might even be counterproductive. Experience shows that in many cases increasing highway capacity causes people to travel more.

Shift Travel to More Energy-Efficient Modes   Mass transit is an obvious candidate and is often advocated by those concerned with energy. The question of how much energy transit actually saves will be discussed later.

It would help to shift travel to nonmotorized modes such as bicycles and walking. There has been tremendous growth in cycling in recent years, and it has undoubtedly had some impact. Many communities have installed bikeways and taken other steps to facilitate the use of bicycles. Walking, however, has decreased because our land-use patterns are more spread out and distances between activities are greater. According to the Census, the share of U.S. workers who walked to work dropped from 7.4 percent in 1970 to 3.9 percent in 1990.

Increase Ride Sharing   The average automobile carries only 1.5 persons, so there is much room for improvement. Some travel demand management programs adopted in California have greatly increased carpooling. Car pools are not very popular, though, in the absence of strong incentives. Probably little will change as long as gas prices stay low and people attach a high value to convenience. However, there could be a large change in an energy crisis, since carpooling is a quick, simple, and cheap response to an emergency.

Reduce Automobile Travel by More Efficient Land-Use Patterns   One way to reduce travel is to cluster development around transit stations. Another is to mix different kinds of land uses, as is done in a *planned unit development,* so that people can walk between them. In general, higher densities lead to less travel and greater use of transit. This is one reason why residents of foreign cities consume less gasoline per capita than U.S. urbanites [Newman and Kenworthy 1989]. But the immediate impact of a land-use approach would be small because it would take many years to overcome the inertia of existing development patterns. It also implies a marked change in U.S. lifestyle preferences, which *could* occur if the incentives are right.

One approach that could have a major impact would be to reduce journey-to-work distances. This could be accomplished by having the government assign workers to homes close to their jobs. At present, such regulation seems politically unacceptable in the United States; U.S. lawyers believe there is an implied constitutional right of "freedom to travel." However, Communist countries had similar controls for years, and even in Western Europe people have to obtain residence permits.

Increase the Price of Gasoline   When prices soared in the 1970s, gas consumption did decline. But since market prices fluctuate greatly, they cannot be relied on. The only way to guarantee higher prices is to impose higher fuel taxes. This in fact has happened: The federal gas tax was raised by $0.05 per gallon in 1983, another $0.05 in 1990, and $0.043 in 1993. Many states have also increased their gas taxes in recent years.

The demand for gasoline is inelastic, which means that taxes would have to be very high to cause a marked decline in consumption (it also means that such taxes would raise large amounts of revenue). It would take taxes of $0.50 to $1 per gallon to have a sizable impact on purchases. European countries have gas taxes in this range, which is one reason why they have always made fuel-efficient cars. It is unlikely that U.S. politicians would be willing to impose such high taxes short of a national emergency.

The demand for gas is more elastic in the long run than in the short run (this is a general rule in economics, but it is especially true of gasoline). When the price zooms (as in the 1970s), the immediate response of people is to travel less, mainly by forgoing discretionary trips such as vacations. But if the price remains high for several years, people react by buying more fuel-efficient vehicles and living closer to their jobs. Eventually producers adapt by marketing the cars and homes that people have come to want.

Ration Gasoline   This would be a last resort, but it might happen in a crisis. Gas was rationed during World War II, when each household was allowed 10 gallons per week (with exceptions for persons in special occupations, such as doctors). During the Iranian crisis, the Carter administration set up the administrative apparatus for rationing as a standby measure and even had coupons printed. Later the Reagan administration dismantled this program.

There is debate over whether rationing coupons should be transferable or not. With transferable coupons, it would be legal for people to buy and sell coupons (this is sometimes called a *white market*). For example, transit users could sell their coupons and use the money to pay their fares. People who wanted to take a long vacation trip could buy extra coupons. Free-market proponents favor this approach because it preserves consumer choice. If the coupons were not legally transferable (as was the case in World War II), a black market might develop and it might require much effort to enforce the restriction.

The first group of policies discussed—improving fuel efficiency, using alternative fuels, lowering the speed limit, and improving traffic flow—all implicitly accept the dominance of the automobile for personal travel and would not cause any modal shifts. In fact, they might generate more vehicle-miles traveled. The other policies should reduce automobile use, directly or indirectly.

Comparison of Modes

Conventional wisdom holds that mass transit saves energy. This turns out to be too simplistic an assumption because the situation is complicated. It is also a controversial subject. Different analysts have compared energy consumption of urban transportation modes and reached different conclusions.

The controversy began when Charles Lave, professor at the University of California at Irvine, made a detailed analysis of BART. He calculated that BART produces savings of about 13 percent in current energy use because some of the riders switched from cars. But it required a huge amount of energy to build the system because modern construction is very energy-intensive. Lave concluded that "the energy invested in BART is so enormous and the yearly operating energy savings are so small that it will take 535 years even to repay the initial investment, much less to save any energy" [1977, p. 17].

Furthermore, this computation was based on the assumption that cars would continue to get 14 miles per gallon, which was the national average at the time. If fuel effi-

Hydrocarbons, also called *volatile organic compounds,* are ingredients of fuel that are not completely burned. Emissions have been greatly reduced by catalytic converters. The transportation sector was once the largest source of hydrocarbon emissions, but its contribution decreased to 30 percent in 1991. Hydrocarbons are involved in formation of photochemical smog, and it is suspected that they cause cancer.

Nitrogen oxides are produced when air is heated to high temperatures. Emissions from automobiles have proved to be difficult to control. The devices that reduce emissions of carbon monoxide and hydrocarbons, by burning gasoline at higher temperatures, simultaneously increase emissions of nitrogen oxides. Their effects on human health are not well understood, but they contribute to photochemical smog and give it a brown color. Nitrogen oxides also play a major role in acid rain. The transportation sector was responsible for 39 percent of nitrogen oxide emissions.

Particulates are particles of solid or liquid matter ranging in size from cinders down to microscopic bits. Gasoline engines produce few of them, but diesel engines create a lot, which is obvious in the black smoke emitted from exhaust pipes. Size is a major factor in the efficiency of diesel engines, so diesel is preferred for trucks and buses. At one time diesel fuel was cheaper than gasoline, and the popularity of diesel automobiles increased to a level of 6 percent of new-car sales in 1981. Then the price of diesel fuel rose, and sales plunged [Kurani and Sperling 1988]. Particulates occur in smog, where they absorb other chemicals and eventually reach the ground. They are believed to cause lung cancer. The Environmental Protection Agency (EPA) has regulated particulate emissions from diesel vehicles since 1982, but has no standard for gasoline-powered vehicles. The transportation sector produced 21 percent of particulates in 1991; most came from heating, power plants, and factories.

Sulfur dioxide is the most dangerous air pollutant and a major component of classical smog. It irritates the respiratory system and can be fatal to persons with bronchitis or emphysema. It has been implicated in the worst air pollution incidents, such as the smog that killed 17 people in a weekend in Donora, Pennsylvania, in 1948 and the one that was blamed for 4000 excess deaths in London in 1952. The transportation sector produced only 5 percent of sulfur oxides in the air; most came from burning coal and oil in furnaces and power plants. That is the reason for interest in low-sulfur coal and oil.

Lead has been added to gas since the 1920s because it reduces engine knocking (premature combustion of the compressed fuel mixture). It was ignored in the early 1970s because lead normally occurs in the air in very small amounts, and it was not thought to pose a health threat. Its principal notoriety was that it damaged the catalytic converters that U.S. carmakers used to cut other pollutants. That is why the government mandated that unleaded gas be widely available by 1974 [Sperling and Dill 1988].

Later, scientific findings indicated that even small amounts of lead in the body can have serious effects (especially brain damage). Leaded gasoline was found to be the major source of lead in the air. Therefore, in 1985 the federal government ordered a 90 percent reduction in the lead content of leaded gas and declared that eventually it should be totally eliminated. This measure has been effective, and the transportation sector's contribution of this pollutant fell to only 33 percent in 1991.

Ozone is a secondary pollutant that results from a chemical reaction between hydrocarbons and nitrogen oxides in the presence of sunlight. It is regulated because it is a major component of photochemical smog. Ozone reduces the ability to perform physical exercise, and in sufficient concentration, it is toxic. (Note that while ozone is injurious when it is breathed, it is desirable in the upper atmosphere because it blocks harmful rays from the sun. That is why there is concern about holes in the ozone layer over the poles.)

Los Angeles County's Air Pollution Control District identified the automobile as the principal source of its smog in 1953. At the county's urging, the California legislature passed a law in 1960 requiring new cars to have crankcase controls to reduce emissions from engine blow-by. The federal government made this device mandatory on all cars sold in the United States starting in 1963. California enacted the first law regulating new-car emissions in 1966 and has often had tougher standards than those of the federal government.

Although the first federal air pollution control law was passed in 1955, the Clean Air Act of 1970 is really the cornerstone of air quality regulation. It authorized the Environmental Protection Agency to set national standards for vehicle emissions. The goal was to reduce emissions of carbon monoxide, hydrocarbons, and nitrogen oxides by 90 percent by the 1975 model year. The deadline was postponed several times at the urging of the automobile industry. Detroit decided to meet the standards by adding catalytic converters, rather than redesigning engines (some foreign manufacturers chose the latter course). The targets for carbon monoxide and hydrocarbons were eventually reached, but not the one for nitrogen oxides.

The 1970 act also required the EPA to establish National Ambient Air Quality Standards (for which measurements are made at random sites rather than at emissions sources). The states were required to submit plans to achieve the standards by 1975. The EPA disapproved of some of the plans and caused a storm of controversy. In 1973 it rejected the California Air Resources Board's plan for Los Angeles and substituted one of its own. This called for reducing automobile traffic in Los Angeles by 82 percent within 4 years! The EPA also stipulated a 68 percent reduction in traffic in nine counties of northern New Jersey. Some observers concluded that the EPA took these actions primarily for shock value.

Many metropolitan areas failed to meet the standards by 1975, and the deadline was postponed three times—until 1977, then 1982, and finally 1987. At that point 107 cities were still classified as nonattainment areas for either carbon monoxide or ozone. The EPA has the statutory authority to impose sanctions, which include withholding federal aid for highway and sewer construction. In 1987 it proposed to levy penalties on areas that did not meet standards and did not have an approved plan for doing so, but Congress imposed a moratorium on enforcement.

The plans developed by nonattainment areas often included traffic control plans with drastic measures to reduce automobile travel, such as rationing gasoline, banning cars from the downtown area, taxing parking spaces, and mandatory carpooling. Increasing transit use has inevitably been part of these plans. This might involve building new facilities, increasing service, or abolishing the transit fare. Thus, the program can be seen as another boost for transit.

However, the proposals to effect modal shift have not been taken very seriously. While early plans stressed traffic control, later plans returned emphasis to the regulation of vehicles. Because emission control devices deteriorate as cars get older, some areas have adopted inspection and maintenance programs to ensure that the devices remain effective (New Jersey initiated such a program in 1974). Some cities proposed to retrofit older vehicles with better devices.

The Clean Air Act was amended in 1977, but then no changes were made for 13 years as Congress debated revisions throughout the 1980s without reaching agreement. The Reagan administration showed no interest and would not admit that acid rain was a problem. Leading one side of the debate was Representative Henry A. Waxman of California, Chair of the House Subcommittee on Health and the Environment, who favored strict controls. Opposing him was Representative John D. Dingell of Michigan, Chair of the House Energy Committee, who defended the interests of the automobile industry.

President Bush broke the impasse by proposing his own set of amendments in 1989, after which Waxman and Dingell reached a compromise. The House and Senate negotiated for a year and finally passed a bill, which Bush signed in November 1990. Besides smog, the Clean Air Act Amendments of 1990 deal with acid rain, toxic air emissions, and depletion of the ozone layer. As with most compromises, critics on both sides attacked this one as inadequate.

The law classified ozone nonattainment areas into five categories with different deadlines: marginal, moderate, serious, severe, and extreme. Marginal areas were given 3 years to meet standards; moderate areas, 6 years; and serious areas, 9 years. There are eight severe areas, which were given 15 to 17 years: Baltimore, Chicago, Houston, Milwaukee, New York City, Philadelphia, San Diego, and Ventura County, California. Los Angeles is the only extreme area; its deadline is 20 years.

The law imposed tighter tailpipe standards on automobiles and trucks for carbon monoxide, hydrocarbons, and nitrogen oxides, to be phased in beginning with the 1994 model year. It prohibited lead from motor vehicle fuel after January 1, 1996. It required cleaner (or "reformulated") gasoline to be introduced in the nine cities in the serious and extreme ozone nonattainment categories, starting in 1995. It established a clean-fuel pilot program in California, requiring stricter emission limits for 150,000 vehicles in the 1996 model year and 300,000 by the 1999 model year.

The transit industry was concerned about the law because it regulates particulate emissions from diesel buses. Lobbyists argued for a chance to show that technological improvements could yield cleaner diesel engines. They were successful, and the EPA compromised by allowing a more lenient standard for the 1994 model year. A stricter standard will take effect with the 1996 model year. However, the EPA may eventually require buses to switch to cleaner fuels.

There has been much discussion about "unfunded mandates" by the federal government: imposing regulations without providing money to carry them out. This will not be true in this case. The ISTEA legislation passed in 1991 established a congestion mitigation and air quality improvement program and authorized funding of $6 billion over 5 years. Most of this money will go to states that contain nonattainment areas for ozone and carbon monoxide. ISTEA also requires coordination between transportation and air quality plans.

The Clean Air Act authorizes penalties for noncompliance, such as withholding of federal transportation funds. It remains to be seen whether these sanctions will ever be applied. In the past, federal regulation of ambient air quality has been a paper tiger. Planning agencies prepared plans but had no power to pass laws or impose taxes. Deadlines were ignored, and many areas did little to implement their plans. The EPA works with the states and has no authority over local governments. The federal government has been unwilling to push enforcement with politically unpopular measures. Sanctions have sometimes been threatened, but rarely carried out.

Emission controls have been successful in substantially reducing amounts of carbon monoxide, hydrocarbons, particulates, and sulfur oxides in the air. Use of unleaded gas has greatly lowered the levels of lead. Little progress has been made in curbing nitrogen dioxide, but the standard has generally been met. Ozone is considered the most widespread air quality problem. It was estimated that in 1991, 69.7 million people lived in counties that exceeded the standard [U.S. Environmental Protection Agency 1992].

Air quality has improved in many cities and is no longer a high-priority concern. However, a number of rapidly growing cities (mostly in the west) still have serious problems. Here are a couple of examples:

Denver has the worst carbon monoxide problem in the country, according to an EPA survey released in 1987. The popularity of wood stoves among people living in the Rocky Mountains contributes to the problem, but automobiles account for 75 percent of the pollutant. Since 1984, Denver has mounted an annual campaign in which commuters are asked to carpool or take the bus 1 day a week during the winter, when the problem is most severe. The program is voluntary, but reportedly it has cut pollution by a few percentage points.

Los Angeles remains the leading city in smog, although the air is cleaner than it used to be. An Associated Press story in 1988 stated that Los Angeles typically exceeds the federal ozone standard 145 times a year, while no other city has more than 35 violations a year. It was also the only city that failed the nitrogen oxide standard. Hence Los Angeles has been the locus of the most ambitious efforts to combat the problem.

In 1988 the South Coast Air Quality Management District issued Regulation XV, which instituted *transportation demand management*. It is based on *average vehicle ridership* (*AVR*), defined as the ratio of the number of workers arriving at a site between 6:00 a.m. and 10:00 a.m. to the number of vehicles arriving at the site. Regulation XV set targets of 1.75 for the downtown, 1.5 for most of the Los Angeles basin, and 1.3 for remote, low-density areas (the AVR for the region was about 1.15 in 1988). Among means for increasing the AVR are shifting to transit, ride sharing, walking, cycling, and changing work hours. Employers of 100 or more workers were required to submit plans for improving the AVR. Employers have not been penalized for failing to meet their targets, but many have been fined for failing to submit plans. Results for the first year indicated a slight but significant increase in the AVR, which came almost entirely from more carpooling [Giuliano et al. 1993].

Meanwhile, the district was embroiled in a lawsuit over not having a satisfactory plan to meet federal air quality standards. This was resolved in 1989 when the district adopted an air quality management plan that seeks to reach all federal standards by 2010. The plan has three tiers: Tier 1, to be implemented in 5 years, aims to attract automobile drivers to car pools, transit, and bicycles. Tier 2 stresses cleaner fuels for motor vehicles, especially methanol. Tier 3 puts hope in new technology such as fuel cells.

According to Baye [1993], the plan contains very optimistic projections for reducing emissions through growth management, mode shifts, and alternate work hours. Even if the projections turn out to be valid, she contended, these measures would contribute relatively little to improving air quality. "The automobile emissions problem is much more amenable to technological solutions (although the road to implementation may be far from smooth) than to remedies that rely on transportation planning and policies based on radical changes in travel behavior" [p. 73].

Along this line, the state of California has issued regulations requiring that in 1998, 2 percent of all new vehicles sold in the state have zero emissions. By 2003, 10 percent of new vehicles must have zero emissions. This has been a stimulus for automobile manufacturers and electric utilities to invest in the development of electric-powered vehicles.

Usually the highest concentrations of vehicle-caused pollutants occur in the central business district. Since most mass transit systems emphasize service to the CBD, they have the potential to alleviate the worst problems. However, a study of Chicago concluded that transit strategies would have only a modest effect on air pollution [Zerbe and Croke 1975]. This was partly because Chicago already had an extensive and heavily used transit system; the outcome might be different in other cities. The authors conceded that eliminating transit would have a disastrous effect on air quality.

A study of metropolitan New York estimated that increasing transit service would reduce emissions of carbon monoxide and hydrocarbons slightly, while letting the transit fare rise would increase emissions [Haikalis and Jordan 1984]. The most effective measures were disincentives to automobile use: increasing bridge and tunnel tolls, imposing a $1.50 charge on automobiles crossing the city line, raising the fuel tax, and placing a tax on parking. The revenues generated by these charges could be used to improve transit service.

Although transit has a role in reducing air pollution, it does not appear to be a major one. Increasing the supply of transit does not by itself attract enough automobile drivers to make a noticeable difference. Disincentives to automobile use appear to be more effective; of course, they imply increased use of transit as well as more ride sharing, cycling, and walking. Experience indicates that direct controls on vehicles emissions have produced the greatest results. Since the automobile will certainly continue to be the dominant mode of urban travel in the United States, this still seems like the best approach.

Noise

Noise from transportation facilities regularly affects several million persons in the United States. In fact, transportation may be the largest source of noise problems in the country. Repeated exposure to very loud noise causes hearing loss, but otherwise the health effects are uncertain. Noise does not cause deaths, and there is limited evidence that it causes or contributes to physical illnesses. Noise clearly causes psychological stress and can interfere with activities requiring oral communication. Real estate values are reduced in residential areas that suffer persistent noise problems.

Congress indicated its concern by enacting the Noise Control Act of 1972 and the

Quiet Communities Act of 1978. The Environmental Protection Agency established a noise abatement program in 1972 and later issued regulations governing trucks and motorcycles. However, the Reagan administration decided to terminate this program to reduce the budget, and Congress concurred. The program was phased out in 1982. One justification was that the benefits of noise abatement are highly localized, and therefore state and local governments should take the responsibility.

Aircraft noise is the biggest problem and plays a large role in airport planning. Complaints about the noise of highway traffic are also widespread. The major response in the United States has been to erect sound barriers alongside freeways that absorb noise and channel it upward. Several hundred million dollars has been spent in building such walls.

Noise is the most serious environmental impact of rail transit lines and has often prompted objection to them. In New York City, sound levels exceeding 100 decibels have been measured in trains, in subway stations, and on the street below elevated tracks [Huss and McShane 1973]. Levels of 93 to 98 decibels have been measured in Philadelphia. This compares with a level of 70 decibels from freeway traffic at a distance of 50 feet. For a thorough discussion of train noise, see Nelson [1987].

The biggest problems occur in older subway-elevated systems because they were designed without any thought given to acoustics. This was also true of the design of rail transit cars. This situation has changed in recent years. Now noise abatement is a major consideration in designing new rail lines and vehicles. The Toronto subway is considered one of the quietest in the world that uses steel wheels on steel rails; sound levels average 85 decibels. The Montreal subway, which uses rubber-tire trains, has levels of 60 to 80 decibels.

There are three places where rail noise affects humans: alongside the right-of-way (this is called *wayside noise*), in stations, and inside the vehicles. Wayside noise brings the most complaints; this is one reason why neighborhoods sometimes object to proposed rail lines.

The effects differ depending on whether the track is on an elevated structure, at grade, or in a tunnel. Older elevated lines were built on thin steel structures that readily vibrate and create very loud noise when trains pass. In some places (such as the Chicago Loop), there are buildings within a few feet of elevated tracks. Modern systems are built on concrete structures that absorb much of the vibration and hence are much quieter.

Noise from elevated and at-grade lines is mostly transmitted through the air. The situation is different with subway tunnels. Here noise and vibration are transmitted through the ground to nearby buildings. Humans inside may feel the vibration, and often they hear a low rumble. The vibration can affect delicate instruments and can even cause minor structural damage.

The major sources of noise from train operations are (1) the interaction of wheel and rail, (2) propulsion equipment, and (3) auxiliary equipment such as heating and air conditioning. Any of the three can dominate in certain conditions. At low speeds, e.g., auxiliary equipment creates the most noise. At high speeds, wheel-rail noise dominates. It is always true that the overall noise level increases with train speed.

Wheel-rail noise is greatly affected by the condition of the wheels and rails. This is another reason why older systems are noisier. Over time, wheels may develop flat spots and other irregularities, while the running surface of rails also becomes uneven. Remedies include truing the wheels (returning them to perfect circles) and grinding the rails. The Toronto Transit Commission has a monitoring program in which wayside sensors detect unusual vibrations as a train passes and set off an alarm. Then the car with the faulty wheel is removed from service for maintenance.

Formerly rails were installed in discrete sections that met at joints. If two sections become slightly out of line at a joint, that is another noise source. Modern systems are constructed with continuous welded rail, which eliminates that problem. Some transit authorities are gradually replacing jointed rail with welded rail, especially in sensitive areas such as stations.

Other approaches to noise abatement include (1) using resilient wheels or damped wheels, (2) using resilient fasteners between the rail and ties that support it, (3) installing sound-absorbing materials in car interiors and stations, and (4) erecting sound barriers alongside elevated tracks. All these measures reduce noise somewhat. When used in combination, they can produce an acoustical environment that is acceptable to most people.

Buses are fairly noisy vehicles, although usually they are less offensive than heavy trucks and motorcycles. Buses have received little attention in noise abatement, probably because they make up a small fraction of the traffic stream. However, a bus route on an otherwise quiet residential street can occasion complaints. The EPA issued regulations regarding noise emissions from newly manufactured buses in 1977, but the regulations were withdrawn in 1982. There is currently no federal regulation in this area. However, transit authorities ordering new buses are likely to include noise levels in their specifications.

Aesthetics

Rail transit lines built at ground level usually have little visual impact on the urban landscape, and of course, lines built underground have none at all. But elevated lines have been a major cause of concern ever since they were first built over a century ago. Although the vertical steel supports were thin, the structure carrying the track and the stations were often bulky and cast wide shadows on the ground. The design was strictly functional and, in the view of many, ugly. Often the lines were built over streets, which created a distinctly unpleasant environment at sidewalk level. It was common for real estate values to fall when such a line was built.

During the hiatus in building new urban rail systems that occurred in the 1950s and 1960s, construction techniques changed. Since then, steel columns have rarely been used; modern elevated lines are built on reenforced-concrete structures. These are simpler and less bulky; often there is a single row of vertical supports instead of two rows. Aesthetic judgment is subjective, but many people consider the newer elevated structures to be a positive addition to the visual environment. To illustrate the difference, Figure 11-5 shows a station on the Third Avenue elevated in New York City (which was torn down in the 1950s). Figure 11-6 shows a section of the Washington Metro at Na-

FIGURE 11-5
The Third Avenue elevated in New York City. This line was torn down in the 1950s, following which there was a real estate boom along much of Third Avenue. Early elevated structures like this were considered objectionable and often depressed property values. (Photo by author.)

tional Airport. Another attractive structure is the Detroit people mover, which was shown in Figure 7-4.

Although many older subway stations were quite plain, there was a conscious effort to make some of them attractive. When New York City's first subway opened in 1904, it was considered quite elegant. The stations were lined with white tile, and each one had a distinctive emblem made of mosaic that was repeated every few feet. For example, the emblem at the Astor Place station is a beaver, because the street was named after John Jacob Astor, who became rich in the fur trade. Unfortunately, most of these stations have become so dirty over the years that few people notice the decorations.

Another example is the Moscow subway, which is famous for its elaborate decorations, including chandeliers, statues, and murals. Most of this was done in the neoclassical style favored by Stalin. Figure 11-7 shows one of the station buildings. Later subways in Russia have been designed in the modern style.

It is now customary to employ architects to design stations. In the Montreal subway, each station was assigned to a different architectural firm, so there is considerable variety. In the BART system, groups of stations were given to different firms. Officials planning the Washington, D.C., Metro decided to use a uniform design throughout the

FIGURE 11-6
The Washington, D.C., Metro at National Airport station. Modern elevated structures are usually graceful and elegant; many people think they are aesthetically pleasing. Further, the concrete posts transmit vibrations far less than the older steel poles did. (Photo by author.)

system. Each subway station has a barrel vault lined with identical concrete panels that have a depression in the center. Incidentally, these panels contain sound-absorbing material.

Many subway stations are virtually invisible at street level, but some do have buildings that form a noticeable part of the built environment. While most of these are simple and functional, a few have received special treatment and even won architectural awards. An example is the Ruggles station on Boston's new Orange Line (see Figure 11-8).

One objection to light rail lines is that they require overhead wires. Early in the century, when electric streetcars were common, their wires were often lost in a maze of electric and telephone lines strung over streets. This situation was generally tolerated, except in a few cities (such as New York City and Washington, D.C.) that required the streetcars to use underground wires (resulting in a system very similar to the cable cars). Overhead wiring was considered much more objectionable in Europe, which retarded the spread of streetcars there.

Here again modern construction technology helps. The poles from which light rail wires are strung are generally slimmer and less obtrusive than those in older streetcar

FIGURE 11-7
A subway station in Moscow. The Moscow subway is famous for its neoclassical design and flamboyant decorations. This was the taste of Joseph Stalin when the subway was built in the 1930s. Probably few people share this taste today. (Photo by author.)

systems. Sometimes existing poles (as for street lights) are used. But it is certainly a value judgment whether any overhead wiring should be permitted.

THE ENVIRONMENTAL REVIEW PROCESS

The National Environmental Policy Act (NEPA) that took effect in 1970 requires federal agencies to submit an Environmental Impact Statement (EIS) for all "proposals for legislation and other major federal actions significantly affecting the quality of the human environment." This covers not only direct actions by federal agencies, but also actions of state and local governments and private parties which involve federal subsidies, grants, or loans. Most highway and transit projects are included. In fact, about half of all EISs involve transportation projects, mostly highways.

The sponsoring federal agency is responsible for submitting the EIS, but the EIS is usually prepared by the state or local agency applying for federal aid. Often consultants actually perform the work. Essentially, the initiator of a project arranges for the analysis, which is not conducive to objective evaluation. An agency may forgo preparing an EIS if it determines that the action would have no significant effect on the environment.

FIGURE 11-8
The Ruggles station on Boston's Orange Line. This building won architectural awards. The Orange Line, which opened in 1987, was built to replace the aging Washington Street elevated line, which was then torn down. (Photo by author.)

This is called a *negative declaration.* It must be published and can be challenged, which may happen if environmental watchdogs are alert.

An EIS is submitted to the Council on Environmental Quality, which is part of the Executive Office of the President. The council actually has no power to prohibit an action. The object of the procedure is disclosure; it is meant to inform other government agencies and the public of any environmental risks involved in a proposal. A draft EIS is referred to federal, state, and local agencies that may be affected, and public hearings may be held.

In many cases, other federal agencies have the authority to cancel, delay, or alter projects. For example, under section 404 of the Clean Water Act of 1972, anyone intending to dump dredge or fill material into wetlands must obtain a permit from the Army Corps of Engineers. The EPA has regulatory authority in several areas, including air and water quality. Often opponents of a project go to court and challenge the validity of an EIS. While the courts will not abort a project because it is environmentally damaging, they require strict adherence to the prescribed procedure. The courts have rejected many EISs for not following the rules.

One reason for rejection is inadequate analysis of alternatives. NEPA requires that an EIS include a study of alternatives to the proposed action, and this is not limited to alternatives under the jurisdiction of the sponsoring agency. For example, a transit measure under FTA jurisdiction might be an alternative to a highway proposed by the Federal Highway Administration. In general, the EIS procedure has given a boost to transit.

Transit proponents may think their projects have no adverse environmental impacts, and therefore no EIS is necessary. They believe that building a transit line instead of a highway will be better for the environment. This may be a valid generalization, but some transit projects do have adverse impacts, and an EIS is legally required. Recall that the Santa Monica Freeway diamond-lanes project was terminated because of failure to comply. The Department of Transportation has published a manual on how to prepare an EIS for transit projects [Alan M. Voorhees & Associates 1979].

Transit projects are not always popular. Any proposal to build an elevated guideway in a residential area is likely to arouse opposition. Sometimes opponents have enough influence to get plans changed. For example:

1 Voters in Berkeley, California, passed a $20 million bond issue in 1966 so that the entire BART line within the city limits (3.5 miles long) would be put underground.

2 The Buffalo light rail line was originally proposed to be elevated. There was heated protest from the neighborhoods affected and a hospital adjacent to the route, so the plan was changed. The line was built underground everywhere except in the CBD, at a considerable increase in cost.

3 In Miami, there was opposition to the proposed location of a storage yard and repair shop for the heavy rail line [Muse et al. 1979]. Consequently, the facilities were relocated, which necessitated building a 4-mile spur track. This also increases operating costs, as trains must deadhead over this spur.

The scope of an EIS is much broader than the obvious environmental factors. It must also cover economic and social impacts as well as impacts on parks, recreation areas, and historical and archeological sites.

Economic impacts include changes in land use and property values, effect on business activity and employment, and costs of relocating families and businesses. In a study of an elevated rail line in Atlanta, Nelson [1992] found that proximity to a station lowered home values in high-income neighborhoods, but raised home values in lower-income neighborhoods. There were both positive effects (increased accessibility) and negative effects (noise and other nuisances). The positive effects meant more to people with lower incomes.

Social impacts are more difficult to characterize [Stein 1977]. Displacement of families and businesses is again relevant, but in addition, effects on neighborhood cohesion and racial integration may be considered. If a rail line built at ground level divided an established neighborhood, that would be an adverse social impact. On the other hand, if the rail service improved accessibility to shopping, medical, and recreational opportunities, that would be a beneficial social impact.

There are laws governing impacts on parks and historic sites. Section 4(f) of the 1966 Transportation Act prohibits taking any park, recreational area, wildlife refuge, or historic site for a transportation project unless there is "no feasible and prudent alternative." Previously it was common for state highway departments to route new roads through parks because the land was in public ownership and hence free. Section 106 of the Historic Preservation Act of 1966 also protects buildings, sites, and districts listed in the National Register of Historic Places.

States also have environmental laws, and more than half of them have an EIS system similar to that of the federal government. There are also a few local governments that require an EIS. Some state and local regulations are stricter than those of the U.S. government, and some cover privately financed projects such as residential subdivisions.

The EIS system is controversial. Some environmentalists think it is too weak, while those who want to build complain about paperwork and delays. The Supreme Court has ruled that NEPA deals strictly with procedure, not content. Nevertheless, following the procedure correctly often brings negative publicity and political backlash. Many proposals have been killed or modified as a result. Clearly the system has reduced many potentially harmful impacts, although it has not given environmentalists all the victories they wanted.

One loophole in the system is that Congress can exempt individual projects from compliance. It did so in the case of the Alaskan pipeline and for an interstate highway in San Antonio.

The EIS was a major decision-making tool during the 1970s, when environmental consciousness was high. The Reagan administration downplayed the EIS process and put renewed emphasis on benefit/cost analysis (where evaluation is based on dollars). This is anathema to many environmentalists because it involves, among other things, estimating a dollar value for human life. No doubt there will be continuing shifts in emphasis according to the prevailing political ideology.

QUESTIONS

1 Is the huge consumption of petroleum products in the United States a serious problem that requires government action, or will market forces take care of the situation? Is dependence on foreign supplies a reason for concern?
2 What would be the most effective ways of reducing consumption of gasoline and diesel fuel (taking account of cost and political acceptance)?
3 List the alternate fuels currently being considered. Which one seems most promising?
4 From the standpoint of using energy efficiently, what are the best modes of urban travel? Does the evidence provide a good argument against building more rail transit lines?
5 Is there a smog problem in the area where you live? If so, what is being done about it? Is it getting worse?
6 There are two broad approaches to addressing the energy and environmental problems caused by U.S. dependence on motor vehicles: making the vehicles cleaner and more efficient and switching to alternate fuels, and getting people to shift to other transport modes. Which do you favor?

REFERENCES

Alan M. Voorhees & Associates: *Guidelines for Assessing the Environmental Impact of Public Mass Transportation Projects* (Washington: Department of Transportation, 1979).

Baye, Chang-Hee Christine: "Air Quality and Travel Behavior: Untying the Knot," *Journal of the American Planning Association,* vol. 59, no. 1 (Winter 1993), pp. 65–74.

Boyle, Daniel K.: "Rail Rapid Transit and Energy: A Reexamination of Current Conventional Wisdom," *Transportation Research Record,* no. 988 (1984), pp. 11–18.

Chomitz, Kenneth: "Survey and Analysis of Energy Intensity Estimates for Urban Transportation Modes," *Transportation Research Record,* no. 726 (1979), pp. 8–14.

Davis, Stacy C., and Sonja G. Strang: *Transportation Energy Data Book: Edition 13* (Oak Ridge, TN: Oak Ridge National Laboratory, 1993).

Fowler, John M.: *Energy and the Environment,* 2d ed. (New York: McGraw-Hill, 1984).

Giuliano, Genevieve, Keith Hwang, and Martin Wachs: "Employee Trip Reduction in Southern California: First Year Results," *Transportation Research,* vol. 27A, no. 2 (March 1993), pp. 125–137.

Greene, David L.: "Advances in Automobile Technology and the Market for Fuel Efficiency, 1978–1985," *Transportation Research Record,* no. 1155 (1987), pp. 18–27.

Haikalis, George, and J. David Jordan: "Stringent Transportation Measures to Reduce Vehicular Emissions in the New York City Metropolitan Area," *Transportation Research Record,* no. 963 (1984), pp. 45–52.

Hu, Patricia S.: *Motor Vehicle MPG and Market Shares Report: Model Year 1985* (Oak Ridge, TN: Oak Ridge National Laboratory, February 1986).

Huss, Martin F., and William R. McShane: "Noise in Transit Systems," *Traffic Quarterly,* vol. 27, no. 2 (April 1973), pp. 239–253.

Kurani, Kenneth S., and Daniel Sperling: "Rise and Fall of Diesel Cars: A Consumer Choice Analysis," *Transportation Research Record,* no. 1175 (1988), pp. 23–32.

Lave, Charles A.: "Rail Rapid Transit and Energy: The Adverse Effects," *Transportation Research Record,* no. 648 (1977), pp. 14–30.

Mader, Gerald H., and Oreste M. Bevilacqua: "Electric Vehicle Commercialization," in Daniel Sperling, ed., *Alternative Transportation Fuels: An Environmental and Energy Solution* (New York: Quorum Books, 1989), pp. 235–245.

Meyer, John R., and Jose A. Gomez-Ibanez: *Autos, Transit, and Cities* (Cambridge, MA: Harvard University Press, 1984.)

Mintz, Marianne Millar, Margaret Singh, Anant Vyas, and Larry Johnson: "Transportation Energy Outlook under Conditions of Persistently Low Petroleum Prices," *Transportation Research Record,* no. 1155 (1987), pp. 56–68.

Muse, Edward C., Sean T. Stewart, Billy J. Sexton, Stephen R. Beard, and Abbe Marner: "Environmental Planning and Design for Rapid Transit Facilities," *Transportation Research Record,* no. 716 (1979), pp. 1–8.

Nelson, Arthur C.: "Effects of Elevated Heavy-Rail Transit Stations on House Prices with Respect to Neighborhood Income," *Transportation Research Record,* no. 1359 (1992), pp. 127–132.

Nelson, P. M., ed.: *Transportation Noise Reference Book* (London: Butterworths, 1987).

Newman, Peter W. G., and Jeffrey R. Kenworthy: "Gasoline Consumption and Cities: A Comparison of U.S. Cities with a Global Survey," *Journal of the American Planning Association,* vol. 55, no. 1 (Winter 1989), pp. 24–37.

Sathaye, Jayant, Barbara Atkinson, and Stephen Meyers: "Promoting Alternative Transportation Fuels: The Role of Government in New Zealand, Brazil, and Canada," in Daniel Sperling, ed., *Alternative Transportation Fuels: An Environmental and Energy Solution* (New York: Quorum Books, 1989), pp. 187–204.

Sauve, Robert: "Compressed Natural Gas and Propane in the Canadian Transportation Energy Market," in Daniel Sperling, ed., *Alternative Transportation Fuels: An Environmental and Energy Solution* (New York: Quorum Books, 1989), pp. 145–162.

Shapiro, Phillip S., and Richard H. Pratt: "Energy-Saving Potential of Transit," *Transportation Research Record,* no. 648 (1977), pp. 7–14.

Sperling, Daniel, and Jennifer Dill: "Unleaded Gasoline in the United States: A Successful Model of System Innovation," *Transportation Research Record,* no. 1175 (1988), pp. 45–52.

——— and Mark A. DeLuchi: "Is Methanol the Transportation Fuel of the Future?" in Daniel Sperling, ed., *Alternative Transportation Fuels: An Environmental and Energy Solution* (New York: Quorum Books, 1989), pp. 273–292.

Stein, Martin: "Social-Impact Assessment Techniques and Their Application to Transportation Decisions," *Traffic Quarterly,* vol. 31, no. 2 (April 1977), pp. 297–316.

Trindade, Sergio C., and Arnaldo Vieira de Carvalho, Jr.: "Transportation Fuels Policy Issues and Options: The Case of Ethanol Fuels in Brazil," in Daniel Sperling, ed., *Alternative Transportation Fuels: An Environmental and Energy Solution* (New York: Quorum Books, 1989), pp. 163–185.

U.S. Congressional Budget Office: *Urban Transportation and Energy: The Potential Savings of Different Modes* (Washington: Government Printing Office, December 1977).

U.S. Environmental Protection Agency: *National Air Quality and Emissions Trends Report, 1991* (Washington: Environmental Protection Agency, October 1992).

Zerbe, Richard O., and Kevin Croke: *Urban Transportation for the Environment* (Cambridge, MA: Ballinger Publishing Company, 1975).

12

THE PEOPLE WHO RIDE TRANSIT

We shift attention from transit vehicles and facilities to the people who ride transit. This is important to transportation planners for several reasons. First, planners need to forecast transit ridership, which plays a key role in evaluating any transit proposal. Estimated passenger volumes on proposed transit lines carry great weight in decisions. Second, planners want to know the attitudes of travelers and how to attract more of them to transit. This is important in designing transit systems and marketing them. Third, there is often interest in the distribution of transit service and use among special groups of people, such as the so-called transportation-disadvantaged. Equity is a major consideration in many policy debates.

The first part of this chapter looks at transit travel as a statistical phenomenon by itself. The second part looks at the attributes of the people who travel by transit. Next comes a discussion of the attitudes of travelers and how these affect their travel choices. The final part is a brief summary of modal-split modeling. Although this is not a text on transportation planning methods, transit planners should know something about modal split.

CHARACTERISTICS OF TRANSIT TRAVEL

The most comprehensive picture of urban travel patterns comes from origin-destination studies conducted in most U.S. cities in the 1950s and 1960s. Several types of surveys were used, the most important being the home interview, in which interviewers visited a sample of households in an urban area and recorded all trips made by all household members on a single day. The results were factored up to get measurements of total travel in the area on a typical weekday.

These studies were labor-intensive and expensive. Sampling rates varied between 1 and 10 percent, which could produce a large number of interviews. For example, in each of the studies of Chicago (1956) and New York City (1963 to 1964), approximately 50,000 households were interviewed. Further, processing of the data usually took 2 years or more. Because of these drawbacks, few large-scale home-interview surveys have been conducted since 1970.

In recent years, planning agencies have tended to make smaller surveys, using less exhaustive and expensive methods. In the 1970s, most surveys focused on a particular mode (such as transit) or a particular population group (such as the elderly and disabled). In the 1980s, most dealt with a single project or corridor [Hartgen 1992]. The methodology includes roadside and onboard interviews. When households are sampled, it is usually done by telephone interviews or having the respondents mail in travel logs.

Some metropolitan planning organizations have conducted areawide travel surveys in recent years, or are planning to do so in the near future [Purvis 1990]. In 1988, the Chicago Area Transportation Study began a 5-year household travel survey. In 1990, household surveys were made in the San Francisco Bay area and the Minneapolis–St. Paul area. In all three cases, the sampled households were asked to complete travel diaries and mail them back.

Transportation planners also rely on other sources for up-to-date information on travel behavior. One of these is the Decennial Census, which questions a sample of all households in the nation (15 to 20 percent) about work trips. However, the Census collects no data on trips for other purposes. Another source is the Nationwide Personal Transportation Survey, which was conducted in 1969, 1977, 1983, and 1990–1991. It yields useful information on national trends, but does not collect data on the origins and destinations of trips.

Unfortunately, the most complete data on urban travel are quite old, but they are still worth examining for the details they reveal. Many of the findings are believed to remain valid, although of course there have been some changes (e.g., the total number of transit trips has fallen in many cities, and there has been a great increase in suburb-to-suburb travel). The following sections describe some of the special features of transit travel, which has some marked differences from automobile travel.

Purpose of the Trip

In most cities, the purpose of a majority of transit trips is to go to or from work. Of the eight or so categories into which transportation planners classify trip purpose, transit is used more than the average only for trips to work and school. This concentration of work trips on transit explains much of what follows.

Transit is used less than the average for the other major trip purposes: shopping, personal business, and social/recreation. Destinations of shopping trips are dispersed, and the trips often involve carrying packages home, which can be inconvenient on transit. Many social/recreation trips include more than one family member, which makes using a car attractive.

Table 12-1 shows the percentage of trips for each purpose made by transit, as reported in studies of New York City (made in 1963–1964), Chicago (1956), and Pitts-

TABLE 12-1
TRANSIT USE FOR EACH TRIP PURPOSE IN SELECTED TRANSPORTATION STUDIES

	Percentage of trips by transit		
Purpose	New York City	Chicago	Pittsburgh
Home	35.7	26.2	23.7
Work	38.0	32.7	23.2
Shop	13.3	18.8	14.8
School	74.1	61.1	61.3
Social/recreation	14.3	13.5	7.0
Eat a meal	—	7.1	6.3
Personal business	18.3	20.8	8.8
Serve passenger	0	0	—
Ride	0.4	0	—
All purposes	32.5	24.3	21.7

burgh (1958). In New York City, transit's share rose to 45.0 percent for trips made directly from home to work.

Time of Day

Transit is used more in the peak periods, when most work trips occur. The automobile is heavily favored during the midday and evening hours. There are two reasons why transit is more competitive in the peak period. First, highways become congested, and travel by automobile is much slower than in the off-peak period. Second, transit service is scheduled more frequently in the peak period, which means that headways and waiting times are reduced. Transit becomes more convenient, and door-to-door speed may even increase.

The New York City survey showed that 61.5 percent of all transit trips originated between 7 a.m. and 10 a.m. or between 4 p.m. and 7 p.m. This was true of only 43.4 percent of highway trips. Table 12-2 shows the variation in modal split for different periods of the day (trips were grouped by time of origin).

There are differences among the transit modes. Suburban railroad is the most peaked in its time patterns; then comes the subway-elevated. Bus trips are the most evenly spread over the day. In the New York City study, 77.8 percent of railroad trips originated during the 6 peak hours, 67.0 percent of subway-elevated trips, and 56.4 percent of bus trips.

Since World War II, transit riding has fallen more in the off-peak period than in the peak period. Transit has done best at holding onto its share of work trips, as trips for other purposes, which are more likely to occur in the off-peak period, have shifted to automobile.

This peaked pattern causes many problems for transit. Extra vehicles must be purchased to handle peak demand, although they are not needed at other times. Extra em-

TABLE 12-2
MODAL SPLIT OF TRIPS BY TIME OF DAY
(Tri-State Transportation Study of the New York City Metropolitan Region, 1963)

Mode	12 a.m.–7 a.m.	7 a.m.–10 a.m.	10 a.m.–4 p.m.	4 p.m.–7 p.m.	7 p.m.–12 p.m.	24 hours
Automobile driver	46.8	37.2	49.7	43.0	51.2	45.0
Automobile passenger	14.6	13.6	17.9	18.2	31.9	18.9
All highway	*64.3*	*52.8*	*70.1*	*63.2*	*85.9*	*66.3*
Railroad	2.3	2.6	0.4	2.6	0.6	1.6
Subway-elevated	18.7	20.5	9.4	19.5	6.7	14.8
Commercial bus	13.7	15.7	12.9	13.5	6.5	12.8
School bus	0.4	7.8	6.9	0.6	0.1	4.1
All transit	*35.7*	*47.2*	*29.9*	*36.8*	*14.1*	*33.7*
Total	*100.0*	*100.0*	*100.0*	*100.0*	*100.0*	*100.0*

Based on unlinked trips.

ployees must be hired for the peak. Contracts with the unions place restrictions on part-time workers and split shifts; hence many workers have little productive work to do for several hours a day.

Time of Week

Transit patronage is much lower on Saturdays and Sundays than on weekdays because relatively few people work on weekends. Most transit systems have less frequent service on Saturdays and Sundays. Many small cities have discontinued all weekend service because demand was so small. This has not always been the case: When the 6-day workweek was common, Saturday had as many riders as Monday through Friday. Sunday has always had the lowest ridership. Early in the century, many transit firms operated amusement parks to attract recreational trips on Sundays.

The pattern is not necessarily the same for automobile travel. In areas with concentrations of stores, Saturday is often the busiest day for traffic. On highways leading to resort areas, the heaviest volumes may occur on Sundays.

There is minor variation among the five weekdays. According to analysis of the Pittsburgh survey [Sullivan 1963a], travel by all modes was lowest on Tuesday (7 percent below the 5-day average) and highest on Friday (12 percent above the average). Work and school trips were quite consistent from day to day, while Friday had a surge of shopping and social/recreation trips. For transit trips, Tuesday was again the lowest day (6 percent below average), but Monday was the highest (3.5 percent above average).

Time of Year

Transit use is highest in the winter and lowest in the summer. Most people take vacations in the summer, and hence fewer people go to work. Another reason is that in many cities, a sizable proportion of transit trips are to school, and this number declines in the summer. While social/recreation trips increase in the summer, transit is lightly used for this trip purpose.

Weather also plays a part. Usually people with a choice like to drive in good weather, but some prefer not to when there is a storm. Rail transit is quite reliable in bad weather, including snow. Subways are largely immune to the weather, although older systems sometimes have flooding in the tunnels.

Location and Direction

Transit is most heavily used for trips to and from the central business district (CBD). The reasons are clear: There is a large concentration of jobs in a small, crowded area where parking is difficult and often expensive. Highways leading to the CBD are usually the most congested in the area during rush hours. Many people who have cars choose to use transit to reach the CBD.

This travel pattern is reenforced by the fact that most transit routes are radials and that the CBD gets the best transit service. Heavy and light rail lines are almost always radials. They provide the best transit service, while people who travel in other directions choose between automobile and lower-quality bus service. In cities without rail, the bus routes tend to be radials. Those who travel in other directions have little opportunity to use transit.

The dominance of the CBD can be striking, as shown in Table 12-3. In New York City, transit was used for 81.6 percent of all trips to the CBD (defined as all Manhattan below 60th Street), and the figure rose to 91.4 percent during the peak period. The fig-

TABLE 12-3
CHARACTERISTICS OF MASS TRANSIT TRAVEL FROM SELECTED TRANSPORTATION STUDIES

City	Year of survey	Study-area population	Percentage of trips by mass transit			
			All trips	Trips to work	Trips to CBD	Peak-hour CBD trips
New York	1963	16,301,611	32.5	38.2	81.6	91.4
Chicago	1956	5,169,663	24.3	32.7	70.9	87.2
Philadelphia	1960	4,006,951	16.0	22.2	45.4	57.9
Detroit	1953	2,968,875	16.8	20.9	47.5	54.7
Milwaukee	1963	1,674,300	9.0	13.4	34.5	43.6
Pittsburgh	1958	1,472,099	21.7	23.2	50.9	63.3
Buffalo	1962	1,218,335	7.6	11.0	33.1	36.4
Kansas City	1957	960,568	8.6	12.4	30.9	35.8
New Orleans	1960	855,500	26.5	27.3	42.8	44.0
Atlanta	1961	700,104	9.6	16.2	30.0	30.8
Hartford	1960	548,365	12.7	19.4	51.0	51.6
Honolulu	1960	500,394	10.4	11.3	22.0	26.6

Source: Urban Planning Division, Bureau of Public Roads, U.S. Department of Transportation, *Urban Transportation Planning Data* (August 1969).

ures for Chicago are only slightly lower. In all cities, transit was used much more for travel to the CBD than to elsewhere.

This is further illustrated with journey-to-work data from the 1980 Census. Table 12-4 gives a selection of large cities from the four regions of the United States. In every city, transit was used for trips to the CBD far more than to other destinations. In many cities, CBD trips accounted for at least one-third of all transit trips (48 percent in the case of Pittsburgh).

Regardless of whether transit trips go to the CBD, they are predominantly radial in direction. Many trips that do not go to the CBD go in the direction of the CBD. Reverse commuting (trips away from the center in the morning and toward the center in the afternoon) is quite small. There is a great directional imbalance in transit travel during peak periods. The pattern is more balanced during the midday.

Boyce [1967] conducted statistical tests on the distribution of trips reported in the Chicago survey to determine whether compass direction had any influence. He found that direction had no appreciable effect on automobile trips, but volumes of transit trips toward the CBD were significantly greater than would be expected in a random distribution. One reason, he suggested, was that the rail transit system was radially oriented.

TABLE 12-4
USE OF TRANSIT FOR TRIPS TO THE CBD AND ELSEWHERE FOR JOURNEY TO WORK, FOR SELECTED SMSAs, 1980

SMSA	Percentage of transit for trips to:		CBD trips as percentage of all trips	
	CBD	Elsewhere	Transit	All modes
Northeast				
Boston	58.44	12.34	24.21	6.32
Buffalo	30.37	4.39	35.96	7.51
Philadelphia	60.11	9.45	37.86	8.74
Pittsburgh	52.60	6.66	48.45	10.64
Midwest				
Chicago	74.13	12.43	36.35	8.74
Cleveland	43.43	6.45	44.81	10.75
Detroit	25.88	2.58	31.76	4.44
St. Louis	26.69	4.01	31.83	6.55
South				
Atlanta	31.41	5.42	30.90	7.16
Baltimore	36.96	8.41	20.40	5.51
New Orleans	28.64	7.68	38.17	14.21
San Antonio	14.25	3.58	26.79	8.42
West				
Denver	28.14	4.14	36.16	7.70
Los Angeles	23.84	6.16	13.74	3.95
San Francisco	52.38	11.12	39.59	12.21
Seattle	46.92	6.82	33.08	6.70

Source: 1980 Census.

Trip Length, Speed, and Time

Among the transit modes, railroad has the longest average trip length because it connects the suburbs with the CBD and stations are far apart. Subway has the next-longest trip length, which is greater that the average automobile trip. Bus trips are the shortest. Table 12-5 shows that this pattern was consistent from city to city. (Distances given in the table were approximations, measured by straight line from origin to destination.)

Overall, work trips have a longer average length than trips for other purposes. This helps to make transit trips longer. Furthermore, trips to the CBD are longer on average than trips to other parts of a metropolitan area. This also lengthens transit trips, especially those by railroad and subway.

Data on average door-to-door speed (airline miles from origin to destination divided by time from origin to destination) for different modes were given in Table 5-5. Recall that suburban railroad is the fastest of all modes, since trains often attain speeds up to 80 miles per hour and make relatively few stops. Commuting by train is usually competitive with driving on an expressway. Subway is second fastest among transit modes, but somewhat slower than automobile driver trips. Bus is the slowest of all modes.

Combining figures for trip length and speed yields the average time for a trip (including walking and waiting). Table 12-6 gives data for three cities. Railroad trips are

TABLE 12-5
AVERAGE TRIP LENGTH* BY MODE FROM SELECTED TRANSPORTATION STUDIES

Mode	New York City	Chicago	Philadelphia
Railroad	19.80	13.26	10.2
Subway-elevated	5.79	7.18	5.9
Bus or streetcar	2.41	3.63	3.0
Automobile driver	3.98	3.92	3.4
Automobile passenger	3.46	3.54	3.4
All modes	*4.12*	*4.16*	*3.6*

*Distances are measured in airline miles from origin to destination.

TABLE 12-6
AVERAGE MINUTES PER TRIP* BY MODE FROM SELECTED TRANSPORTATION STUDIES

Mode	New York City	Chicago	Philadelphia
Railroad	52	56	46
Subway-elevated	37	48	48
Bus or streetcar	34	35	33
Automobile driver	22	22	18
Automobile passenger	22	21	18
All modes	*27*	*26*	*22*

*Time is measured from origin to destination (includes walking and waiting).

the longest, with subway next and bus or streetcar third. All transit modes take more time than automobile trips. This is because many automobile trips cover short distances, and speeds are relatively good. Bus trips tend to be shorter in distance, but slow speed makes them longer in time.

CHARACTERISTICS OF TRANSIT RIDERS

Transit riders differ from the average traveler in several respects. These differences will be summarized by citing data from several sources. One is a paper by Pucher and Williams [1992] summarizing findings of the 1990–1991 Nationwide Personal Transportation Survey (NPTS) conducted for the Department of Transportation. The data are only for trips of 75 miles or less in urban areas with populations of 50,000 or more. Another source, the 1980 Census, includes only journey-to-work trips.

Income

Transit use is inversely related to income; the poor are more likely to be transit riders. The NPTS showed that 27 percent of all transit riders came from households with incomes below $15,000, while only 12 percent of automobile users had incomes this low. However, the poor still made most of their trips by automobile. In the under-$15,000 bracket, 63 percent of the trips were by automobile and 7 percent by other privately operated vehicle.

There is an exception to this pattern: Suburban railroad riders tend to have high incomes. The survey showed that 41 percent of railroad passengers came from households with incomes of $50,000 or more. Fares for this mode are the highest of all transit. New York is the only city with suburban railroads that carry a large number of working-class people.

Automobile Ownership

It should be no surprise to find that transit riders are less likely to own a car. For example, in the New York City survey, households without a car made 81.9 percent of their trips by transit. Households with one car made 28.6 percent of their trips by transit; those with two cars, 14.1 percent.

This pattern also holds nationwide, although the percentages using transit are lower. According to O'Hare and Morris [1985], the 1980 Census showed that in the 25 largest urbanized areas, workers in households with no automobile made 58.5 percent of their work trips by public transportation. Among households with one automobile, the share dropped to 15.9 percent.

There are two exceptions to the pattern. One is the case mentioned of suburban railroad passengers, who normally own cars and drive to the station. The other is an instructive anomaly: Wealthy people living in exclusive inner-city enclaves usually own cars, but still use transit a great deal because it is convenient. Such areas include the

East Side of Manhattan, Chicago's Gold Coast, Beacon Hill in Boston, and Nob Hill in San Francisco.

Automobile ownership is highly correlated with income, but the two variables have independent effects. Among people in the same income bracket, those without a car are more likely to use transit. Among households with the same number of automobiles, transit use declines with increasing income.

Race and Ethnicity

Minorities are more likely to use transit. The NPTS showed that 52.6 percent of all transit riders were African-American or Hispanic, although these groups accounted for only 21 percent of all households. However, African-Americans and Hispanics still made more than two-thirds of their trips by private vehicle.

There is an interesting difference in national averages between African-Americans and Hispanics. According to the NPTS, African-Americans made 35.7 percent of transit trips, and Hispanics made 16.9 percent. African-Americans were more likely to ride the bus (40.2 percent of all riders) than the subway (23.4 percent of riders). Hispanics were more apt to ride the subway (15.6 percent of riders) than the bus (14.7 percent). This is undoubtedly because Hispanics are concentrated in those cities with subway-elevated systems (particularly New York City), while African-Americans are more dispersed around the country in cities that have only buses.

Table 12-7, from the 1980 Census, also shows that minorities are more likely to ride transit than the overall population. The only exceptions to the pattern are among Asian-Americans in cities where they are few in number. Table 12-8 shows that in many cities, over half of all transit riders going to work are minorities. (There is some double counting, for some people report they are both black and Hispanic. The number is believed to be small.)

Residential segregation can cause marked differences between transit routes. On Chicago's South Side, there is a railroad line along the Lakefront and an elevated line farther west. Most passengers on the railroad are Caucasian because they come from the suburbs. Most passengers on the elevated are African-Americans because the neighborhoods where they live are served by the elevated with frequent stops.

Gender

The NPTS showed that 55.1 percent of transit riders were female. Women accounted for 57.2 percent of bus riders, 52.2 percent of subway riders, and only 46.5 percent of commuter rail passengers (the last being the highest-quality travel mode). Women represented 56.7 percent of automobile users, but only 34.2 percent of those using other vehicles (mostly vans and pickup trucks).

Women represent a relatively smaller percentage of transit users during the peak period and a larger share during the off-peak period. Probably this is because of traditional gender roles: Women are more likely to be homemakers who do shopping and errands during the day. (The travel problems of women are discussed in the next chapter.) The

TABLE 12-7
PERCENTAGE OF PERSONS USING PUBLIC TRANSPORTATION FOR THE JOURNEY TO
WORK, IN SELECTED SMSAs, 1980

SMSA	All persons	African-Americans	Hispanics	Asian-Americans
Northeast				
Boston	15.61	38.33	27.21	16.16
Buffalo	6.56	22.06	12.66	9.36
Philadelphia	14.03	32.66	18.86	17.35
Pittsburgh	11.50	31.16	18.33	13.33
Midwest				
Chicago	17.98	32.75	22.69	23.49
Cleveland	10.55	22.72	14.70	14.26
Detroit	3.73	14.06	5.74	2.93
St. Louis	5.72	19.28	8.08	7.28
South				
Atlanta	7.57	22.85	10.87	7.95
Baltimore	10.26	28.29	10.29	6.82
New Orleans	10.89	24.34	12.87	7.71
San Antonio	4.56	8.98	7.45	4.84
West				
Denver	6.14	14.75	8.53	7.61
Los Angeles	6.97	12.64	12.23	8.03
San Francisco	16.41	24.61	18.16	27.96
Seattle	9.57	21.53	14.05	17.36

Source: 1980 Census.

number of female heads of household is increasing, but they tend to have low incomes
and many cannot afford a car.

Age

At one time, the elderly were more likely to use transit than other people, but apparently
this has changed in recent years. The NPTS showed that persons over 65 years old made
6.2 percent of all trips, but only 5.5 percent of transit trips. Total trip making by all
modes drops off after age 55, partly because many older persons are retired. The elderly
rely heavily on taxis; they accounted for 16.2 percent of taxi trips.

Still, the vast majority of transit trips are made by persons in the peak earning years
(21 to 55 years old). And the elderly, like others, rely predominantly on the automobile:
The survey showed that people over 65 years old made 80 percent of their trips by au-

TABLE 12-8
MINORITIES AS PERCENTAGE OF PERSONS USING TRANSIT FOR THE JOURNEY TO
WORK, IN SELECTED SMSAs, 1980

SMSA	African-Americans	Hispanics	Asian-Americans	Sum
Northeast				
Boston	11.46	2.97	2.15	16.57
Buffalo	21.89	1.76	0.64	24.29
Philadelphia	33.66	2.23	1.27	37.16
Pittsburgh	16.08	0.70	0.51	17.29
Midwest				
Chicago	26.48	8.74	3.08	38.30
Cleveland	32.23	1.52	1.07	34.82
Detroit	56.00	2.02	0.69	58.71
St. Louis	44.27	1.22	0.73	46.22
South				
Atlanta	61.66	1.54	0.63	63.83
Baltimore	57.97	0.89	0.69	59.55
New Orleans	58.53	4.97	0.71	64.21
San Antonio	13.33	62.25	0.89	76.47
West				
Denver	10.21	11.86	1.69	23.76
Los Angeles	18.92	41.90	7.58	68.40
San Francisco	14.00	10.56	18.01	42.57
Seattle	6.85	2.63	7.59	17.07

Source: 1980 Census.

tomobile. Undoubtedly older persons are more likely to be passengers and less likely to
be drivers.

Occupation

Although transit has a blue-collar image, the fact is that white-collar workers use transit
more than blue-collar workers do. Clerical and sales workers form the largest occupational category among transit riders. This is partly because their jobs tend to be concentrated in the central city.

Blue-collar workers (those classified as supervisors and operatives) use automobiles
more. One reason is that many factories are now located in the suburbs where transit
service is poor or absent. Furthermore, manufacturing workers usually belong to unions
and receive wages sufficient to afford car ownership.

As you would expect from their high incomes, suburban railroad riders often come from the professional and managerial class. This group also rides subways a lot, but buses very little.

ATTITUDES OF TRAVELERS

Sociologists define an *attitude* as a predisposition to respond to an object in a particular way. Attitudes are not directly observable; they must be inferred from overt actions or research such as interviews, questionnaires, or experiments. Responses to a survey may be unreliable; people may hide their attitudes (perhaps subconsciously) or give biased answers (e.g., they may want to please the interviewer or seem socially responsible). Attitudes affect behavior, but not in a simple or direct way. The context is a mediating influence. Hence studies of attitudes do not make behavior perfectly predictable; it is still uncertain how people will actually behave.

In recent decades, many attitude surveys have been conducted regarding transportation and related planning issues. Examples include the studies reported by Hille and Martin [1967], Golob et al. [1972], and Haynes et al. [1977]. The results of these surveys should be treated with some skepticism. It is common for a large proportion of people to say they will use a transit service that is proposed, but this is an unreliable predictor of actual patronage. Couture and Dooley [1981] conducted surveys before and after bus service was inaugurated in Danville, Illinois; the number of persons who said they would ride the bus was three times the number who actually did.

Conventional wisdom in transportation planning holds that time and cost are the major determinants of mode and route choice. There is a trade-off between time and cost. Most people will pay something to travel faster, and some people will pay a great deal. These are the beliefs on which travel forecasting models are based.

The consensus of findings from attitude surveys about transit travel, as summarized by Wachs [1976], is as follows:

1 Time is indeed important, but it is not evaluated in a simple way. Total elapsed time from origin to destination is not so dominant a factor as assumed by most transportation planners.

2 Reliability is very important to many travelers (especially commuters). They want to be certain they will reach their destinations on time. Often they leave earlier (thus lengthening the time for the journey) to be sure of arriving on time. This means it is important for transit vehicles to adhere to schedule; delays and breakdowns should be minimized.

3 Out-of-vehicle time is subjectively weighted more heavily than in-vehicle time. Out-of-vehicle time includes walking, waiting, and transferring. Most studies show that walking time is two or three times as burdensome as time riding in a vehicle. Waiting time receives similar weights. This gives a great advantage to the automobile, since out-of-vehicle time is usually small (just walking to or from where the car is parked), and no transfers are required.

4 Out-of-pocket costs are important, but hidden costs are not. Usually the whole cost of transit is an out-of-pocket cost: the fare. The out-of-pocket costs for automobiles are tolls and parking charges, which most motorists do not pay. However, high parking cost is a major deterrent to automobile use. Most costs of driving are hidden, and most motorists have little idea of the full costs (including depreciation, insurance, and maintenance). In one study, 65 percent of motorists purchasing gas near the border between two states did not know which state had the lower fuel tax [Cook and Rush 1966].

5 Two aspects of comfort and amenity are important: getting a seat on the vehicle and air conditioning when the weather is hot or humid. Other amenity factors matter little. While some transit agencies spend a lot of money making vehicles luxurious, this is not likely to increase patronage.

6 Security from accidents and crime is normally taken for granted; transit users don't think about it. However, it becomes important if put in question, as by publicity about an accident or a series of assaults. BART developed a bad image after the 1979 fire in the tunnel under the bay and a rash of minor accidents and breakdowns that occurred about the same time. Many Bay Area residents claimed they didn't ride BART because it was unsafe, although this may have been a rationalization.

7 Attitudes toward transit are similar among all socioeconomic classes, except that rich people put more weight on saving time and poor people give more weight to saving money. Elderly people also give priority to saving money. People of high socioeconomic class will use transit if service is perceived to be of high quality. For example, 82 percent of those riding buses on the Shirley Busway in Virginia had a car available for the trip.

Attitude surveys are to a degree superficial and do not identify the underlying psychological motives of people. Tehan and Wachs [1972] discussed basic human psychological needs and how they affect choice of travel mode. Psychologists group the needs in two categories: (1) ego-defensive needs, which include security, conformity, rejection, and space; and (2) personal growth needs, including affiliation, esteem of others, self-identity, and autonomy.

The automobile satisfies these needs quite well, but transit does not. For example, getting in a car enables you to reject strangers and provides security because you are inside a private metal shell. The automobile industry has spent many millions of dollars on market research and plays upon these motives in its advertising. Most car buyers want something beyond fulfillment of basic travel needs; the automobile has much symbolic value. In contrast, most transit systems spend little on marketing, and transit evokes a bad image with most people (although new rail systems may be regarded in a favorable light).

Tehan and Wachs suggested several ways in which the design of transit vehicles could be modified to better fulfill these human needs (e.g., by changing seating arrangements). Their analysis of personal rapid transit (PRT) indicated that it might address these psychological factors better than conventional transit does. Small vehicles offer the opportunity for security and privacy similar to that provided by a personal automobile. Pushing a button to select a stop gives a feeling of autonomy (i.e., control of the vehicle).

Planners usually assume that travel is a necessary evil that people try to minimize. They realize there are pleasure trips, but they associate these with weekend drives in the country and summer vacations. Planners believe that within an urban area, pleasure trips are trivial in number and can be ignored.

However, there is evidence that some people get pleasure from commuting to work. The act of driving gives them satisfaction. The trip may provide a brief period of relaxation between the tension or boredom of work and other kinds of pressure at home. People who commute on trains usually spend the time reading or sometimes playing cards.

Anthropologists at Cornell University hypothesized that some people subconsciously regard driving as a form of personal expression [Roberts et al. 1966]. It is a challenge: It takes some skill; there are hazards and obstacles. These people test themselves every day while driving; if they do well, they get satisfaction.

The scholars gave a questionnaire to 130 people in Ithaca, New York, who regularly drove to work. They found that one-third of the respondents scored high on a scale measuring psychological attachment to driving. The respondents said they enjoyed driving; it gave them feelings of freedom and power. They liked to go fast and exceeded the speed limit when conditions permitted. They felt pride in their driving skill. These people were mostly middle-class and also scored high on a need-for-achievement scale.

The researchers concluded that such people would voluntarily seek a home in the suburbs and a long commuting trip. They would be unlikely to use mass transit even if it objectively appeared to have advantages.

The deficiencies of transit from the viewpoint of passengers were illuminated in an article by two sociologists [Davis and Levine 1967]. For most people, a transit trip is purely instrumental and not pleasurable. There is nothing to do, so the trip is boring, and various minor irritations can occur, such as sitting next to a talkative person. Hence, the authors claimed, most passengers are "exit-oriented": They make mental preparations to leave as soon as they board a vehicle. A notable exception, in the opinion of Davis and Levine, is the St. Charles streetcar line in New Orleans:

> It follows a slow, roundabout, but visually beautiful course between the far uptown area and lower Canal Street. Other transit lines are far more direct and rapid. The streetcar sways and jerks. Its steps are high and its acceleration rate low. But the windows open wide on the open air; and the wooden seats, the unshaded lights, the standing motorman with a hand-operated rheostat, and the constant ringing in of fares all have a nostalgia and charm about them that makes the regular patron a perpetual tourist. Among a considerable number of New Orleanians the motto is "Streetcars Desired." They simply find the ride pleasant [1967, p. 90].

MODAL-SPLIT MODELS

Transportation planners use a series of mathematical models to estimate demand for planned transportation routes (highways or transit). The process, called *travel demand forecasting,* was summarized in Chapter 8. The intent is usually to predict what will happen in the future if proposed improvements are made (especially to estimate the number of users). In most cases it requires a computer to carry out this system, as millions of calculations are involved.

After a transit system is coded into network form and stored in computer memory, the estimating process starts by specifying the number of trip origins and destinations in each zone (this is called *trip generation*). Then a *trip distribution* model calculates the number of trips between every pair of zones (called *zonal interchanges*), based on the total travel frictions from zone to zone. *Modal split* estimates how many trips will go by automobile and how many by transit. Finally, a *traffic* (or *network*) *assignment* model routes the interchanges over the network and sums up the flow on every link. In this system, modal-split models are of particular interest to transit planners (these models are also the most politically sensitive part of the process).

Two Types of Models

No single modal-split model is standard in transportation planning; many different models have been developed in various transportation studies. For a summary of nine early models, see Fertal et al. [1966]. The models are classified into two types that differ in where they come in the sequence:

Trip-end models go after the trip generation step and before the trip distribution step (see Figure 12-1). These models use variables describing characteristics of travelers or their place of residence. Common variables in the first group are automobile ownership, income, household size, age, and occupation. Examples of variables in the second group are population density and distance from the CBD. Sometimes trips are classified by purpose (usually into work and nonwork) and by whether at least one end is in the CBD.

Trip interchange models go after the trip distribution step and before the assignment step (see Figure 12-2). These models allocate trips according to the attractiveness of transit versus automobile for each zone-to-zone interchange (based on travel friction). It is not assumed that all trips choose the mode with least friction; usually the percentage that will use transit is estimated from a diversion curve based on either the ratio or difference in travel frictions (see Wynn [1969] for one example). These models may ignore socioeconomic characteristics of travelers such as income and automobile ownership.

Travel friction is measured in time and cost, which are combined by using a monetary value of time. Sometimes only total door-to-door travel time is used; sometimes this is divided into in-vehicle and out-of-vehicle time, with the latter given more weight. Cost consists only of out-of-pocket costs paid while traveling (transit fares, tolls, and parking charges). As noted before, it appears that only the marginal costs of making a trip affect the decision-making process. Some researchers have attempted to quantify attitudinal variables such as comfort and convenience, but this is not common practice.

Following is an example of a diversion curve for trip interchanges used by the author in a study of New York City:

$$Y = 39.65e^{-0.029X} \qquad (12\text{-}1)$$

where Y = percentage of trips by automobile (driver and passenger) and X = transit time minus automobile time (minutes). This was calibrated with data on trips between

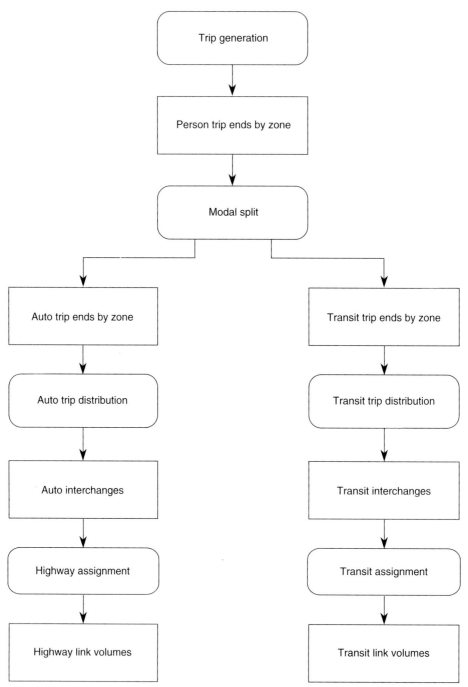

FIGURE 12-1
Forecasting sequence with trip-end modal-split model.

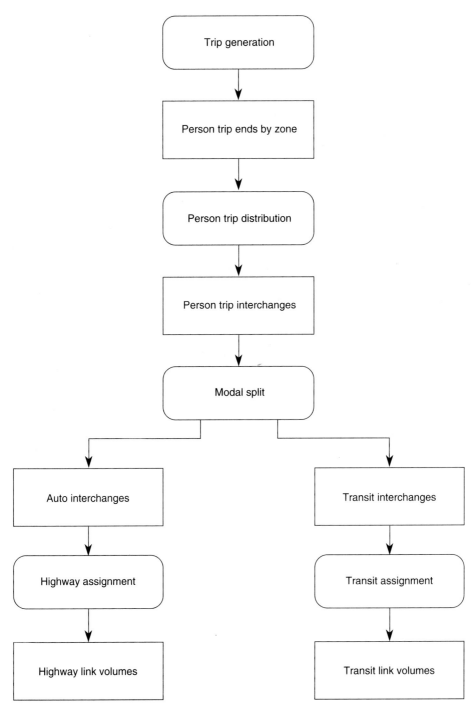

FIGURE 12-2
Forecasting sequence with trip interchange modal-split model.

Westchester County and the Manhattan central business district. Costs were converted to travel time at a rate of $0.04 per minute. The automobile costs included parking, which was expensive. Hence transit had an advantage over automobiles for most trips. The equation was used to estimate how many automobile trips would be diverted to transit if certain improvements to the transit network were made. For example, a 5-minute reduction in transit travel time would, according to the model, cause 5.4 percent of travelers to shift from automobile to transit.

Transportation planners have long debated which type of modal-split model is superior [Weiner 1969]. Trip-end models are criticized because they do not account for the transportation service available to the trip makers (i.e., how highways and transit compare for the trips the travelers want to make). Transit proponents claim this is biased against transit because the models are insensitive to improvements in transit service. The number of trips allotted to transit does not change if you build a new transit line or lower headways on an existing line. Naturally they want to show that many travelers will switch from automobile to transit as a result of such changes.

Defenders of trip-end models argue that socioeconomic characteristics and location largely determine modal choice, and that quality of service has little influence. Households without an automobile are likely to use transit even if highway travel times are less. These planners also point out that the majority of passengers on new rail lines have switched from buses rather than automobiles. However, one flaw with trip-end models is that they can assign travelers to transit in an area where there is no transit service.

Trip-end models were developed first; they continue to be used in some studies because they are simpler. However, most transportation planners now prefer trip interchange models. The notion that the demand for transit is totally inelastic with regard to quality of service seems patently unrealistic. Trip interchange models can incorporate socioeconomic characteristics to some degree by dividing travelers into groups according to automobile ownership, income, etc., before the modal split is calculated.

It might be best to use both types of models and estimate transit riding in two parts. A trip-end model could be used to estimate the number of travelers who do not have access to an automobile, and they could be assigned to the transit network. Then those travelers who have a choice between automobiles and transit would be estimated and allocated to modes by a trip interchange model. Each traveler would select automobile or transit depending on the service offered for the particular trip. Such a procedure was carried out in a study of Miami [Ferreri and Cherwony 1971].

Disaggregate Models

Older modal-split models used the traffic zones as units of analysis and aggregated responses from household surveys into zonal averages, which became the input data in modeling. This approach later was criticized on several counts. It was argued that aggregation masks variation within the population and can lead to estimating errors. For example, travel made by residents of a zone with an average of one car per household would probably be quite different if (1) every household had one car or (2) 50 percent of the households had no cars and 50 percent had two cars. Another problem was that interzonal travel frictions were also averages. It was also claimed that the models were not "policy-sensitive" and could not estimate responses to such measures as tax increases, carpooling incentives, or restraints on automobile use.

Hence travel analysts developed disaggregate models that represent the behavior of individual households or persons. Warner [1962] pioneered by creating a model of binary travel choice by individuals. Domencich and McFadden [1975] produced another seminal work in which they modeled work and shopping trips in Pittsburgh. The approach became popular in the 1970s and is now the most common methodology used in modal-split research.

These are often called *behavioral models* because they are based on explicit theories of individual human behavior, which come from the fields of economics and psychology. The models try to embody causal relationships, rather than merely statistical regularities. Theoretically this should make them more accurate for prediction, and they can be used to estimate responses to transportation alternatives not presently available (e.g., a downtown people mover). While choice of mode has received the most study, the models have also been applied to frequency of travel and choice of destination and route (sometimes simultaneously). Thus the models may incorporate all the steps of the conventional travel forecasting process.

A typical model, derived from the economic theory of consumer choice, estimates the probability of a traveler's making a particular choice based on the ratio of the utilities that could be obtained from the alternatives available. *Utility* is an abstract concept, defined as the satisfaction or subjective reward that a consumer gets. Utility is not directly observable, but it can be inferred from overt behavior and estimated statistically. The logit model is the most popular mathematical form, while the probit model and discriminant analysis have also been used. All these forms are readily adapted to multiple regression analysis, which can be used to estimate utility as a function of numerous variables. The same model may include as variables the socioeconomic characteristics of the trip maker, aspects of the trip (e.g., purpose, time of day), and measures of the transportation system (e.g., speed, headway, prices). This is one advantage of disaggregate models.

Another advantage is that the models can be calibrated with a relatively small data set [Tye et al. 1982]. Originally it was hoped that parameter values would be fairly uniform nationwide so that a standard model could be used anywhere. It is now believed that the models can be transferred from one city to another, but should be recalibrated with a small local survey, perhaps involving a few hundred interviews [Atherton and Ben-Akiva 1976]. The need for massive home-interview surveys appears to be obviated.

Flexibility is a further advantage. There is no standard disaggregate model, although the multinomial logit equation is the most popular form. The model can be adapted to the data available or to issues of interest (e.g., prices, staggered work hours, or impacts on special groups such as the elderly).

Eventually the results of disaggregated modeling must be aggregated to traffic zones for use in later parts of the forecasting process. This must be done with care because the relationships are nonlinear. Usually travelers are grouped into "market segments" that are relatively homogeneous in behavior. If data permit estimation of how each market segment is distributed among the zones, then there is no conceptual difficulty. But sometimes the available data do not provide enough detail; Koppelman [1976] offered some guidelines on how to deal with this situation.

It would be unfair to say that the older, aggregate models of modal split ignored behavioral considerations. They were based on ideas about what makes people behave in certain ways, but the ideas came from common sense rather than accepted social science theory. The emphasis was on empirical analysis, on finding regularities in the voluminous data that came from large origin-destination studies. Some people still prefer that approach, since in planning, it is the total volumes of travelers that matter, not the actions of discrete individuals. The difference between aggregate and disaggregate modeling is similar to that between macroeconomics and microeconomics.

Although behavioral modeling dominates research on modal choice, the models have not been widely used in planning. Among the reasons given by Hartgen [1981] are resistance to change, skepticism about the capabilities of disaggregate models, and the complexity of calibrating and using them. There has developed a gap between theory and practice in the analysis of modal split.

Captive versus Choice Riders

Louis Keefer, director of the Pittsburgh Area Transportation Study around 1960, introduced the distinction between *captive* and *choice* transit riders. Captive riders cannot drive or have no car available, either because the family doesn't own one or because the car is being used by another family member. Choice riders have a car available for the trips they want to make but choose transit because it is more attractive (presumably in time, cost, or convenience).

Keefer [1962] tabulated data from the origin-destination survey of Pittsburgh conducted in 1958 and found that only 14.8 percent of transit riders were choice riders (see Table 12-9). The percentage rose to 26.4 percent for trips to or from the downtown area (where congestion and parking discouraged automobile use). In fact, almost 60 percent of choice transit trips were oriented to the CBD. Choice trips were predominantly for work; they tended to be longer and faster than captive trips (an average door-to-door speed of 6.8 miles per hour compared with 5.3 miles per hour).

Keefer's findings were supported by later studies made in other cities. The ratio of captive to choice transit riders ranged from 3:1 to 9:1. The percentage of captive riders tends to be higher in small cities; there are more choice riders in large cities. Clearly this is because traffic congestion and parking are worse in large cities.

Of course, there are also captive automobile users. In parts of the suburbs, transit service does not exist; if there is no service, there can be no transit riding. There are also places where transit service is so poor that only a masochist would use it. Also, some people cannot commute by transit because they need a car during the day.

One of Keefer's planners did a study of captive and choice automobile trips in Pittsburgh, using the same data source [Sullivan 1963b]. He assumed everyone had transit service available because 95 percent of the homes in the area were within $\frac{1}{4}$ mile of a bus route. He defined a captive automobile driver as someone who used the car during the day or made a stop on the way to or from work. Persons who drove directly from home to work and then from work to home were considered choice drivers. He exam-

TABLE 12-9
CLASSIFICATION OF PITTSBURGH TRANSIT TRIPS
(Data from 1958 Home-Interview Survey)

Category of transit rider	Transit trips	Percentage
Non-car-owning households	141,354	29.8
Nondrivers in car-owning households	142,132	30.0
Drivers with no car available at time of trip	120,321	25.4
Total captive trips	403,807	85.2
Total choice trips	69,943	14.8
Total transit trips	473,750	100.0

Source: Keefer 1962, p. 26.

ined only work trips to the CBD. The results were that 70 percent drove by choice and 30 percent of the automobile drivers were captive.

Clearly these numbers are not transferable to other cities. In places with less extensive transit systems than Pittsburgh has, there would be a much higher proportion of captive automobile drivers. Furthermore, the availability of transit service is not an all-or-nothing attribute. A person who would have to make a long bus trip involving two or three transfers could reasonably be considered captive to an automobile. Time of day is also important: Transit service may be good during the peak periods but poor in midday and evening hours.

The implication of this research is that most people avoid riding transit if they can. As automobile ownership grows over the years, the captive group can be expected to decrease, and transit ridership will fall. However, there is a logical flaw to the analysis that partially biases the findings. People who prefer transit may choose not to buy a car or not to buy a second car. They will then be classified as captive transit riders, which is wrong because they have voluntarily chosen transit.

There is a policy aspect to this dichotomy. Attracting drivers out of their cars is often a major goal of transit proposals (e.g., in order to reduce road congestion and air pollution). By definition, these efforts are directed at choice travelers. This could mean neglect of captive transit riders because the resources available to improve transit are limited. As Wachs noted, "If transit authorities commit enormous resources to the improvement of regionwide commuter service, there will be less money to spend on the needs of the mobility limited. If heavy investments, on the other hand, are made in extending local bus service to unserved areas or in improving service on inner-city routes, fewer dollars will be available to spend on premium service for rush-hour commuters" [1976, p. 97].

This chapter has given an overall view of the types of people who ride transit, the reasons why, and the travel patterns that result. The next chapter will focus on special groups within the population whose travel behavior and needs are of particular interest for social or political reasons.

QUESTIONS

1 Why are city dwellers more likely to use mass transit for trips to work or school than for other purposes?

2 There are some wealthy persons who own automobiles but still use mass transit for some of their trips. In what situations does this occur?

3 What are the factors that are associated with the tendency of urban travelers to use mass transit rather than private automobiles? Make a list of the variables you would analyze in a study of modal split.

4 If people calculated the full cost of owning and using an automobile over a year, would they be more likely to ride transit instead?

5 Why do some people tell interviewers that they would use a proposed transit service, but then fail to do so after the service is started?

6 Would you place the emphasis in transit policy on providing better service to captive riders or increasing the number of choice riders? Describe the measures that seem best for achieving each objective. Are there things that would be good for both groups?

REFERENCES

Atherton, Terry J., and Moshe E. Ben-Akiva: "Transferability and Updating of Disaggregate Travel Demand Models," *Transportation Research Record,* no. 610 (1976), pp. 12–18.

Boyce, David E.: "Effect of Trip Direction on Interzonal Trip Volumes: Test of a Basic Assumption of Trip Distribution Models," *Highway Research Record,* no. 165 (1967), pp. 76–88.

Cook, Kenneth E., and Patrick A. Rush: "Consumer Awareness of Motor Fuel Tax Rates and Prices," *Highway Research Record,* no. 138 (1966), pp. 22–31.

Couture, Michael R., and Thomas Dooley: "Analyzing Traveler Attitudes to Resolve Intended and Actual Use of a New Transit Service," *Transportation Research Record,* no. 794 (1981), pp. 27–33.

Davis, Morris, and Sol Levine: "Toward a Sociology of Public Transit," *Social Problems,* vol. 15, no. 1 (Summer 1967), pp. 84–91.

Domencich, Thomas A., and Daniel McFadden: *Urban Travel Demand: A Behavioral Analysis* (New York: American Elsevier Publishing Company, 1975).

Ferguson, Erik, Catherine Ross, and Michael Meyer: "PC Software for Urban Transportation Planning," *Journal of American Planning Association,* vol. 58, no. 2 (Spring 1992), pp. 238–243.

Ferreri, Michael G., and Walter Cherwony: "Choice and Captive Modal-Split Models," *Highway Research Record,* no. 369 (1971), pp. 80–90.

Fertal, Martin J., Edward Weiner, Arthur J. Balek, and Ali F. Sevin: *Modal Split: Documentation of Nine Methods for Estimating Transit Usage* (Washington: Government Printing Office, 1966).

Golob, Thomas F., Eugene T. Canty, Richard L. Gustafson, and Joseph E. Vitt: "An Analysis of Consumer Preferences for a Public Transportation System," *Transportation Research,* vol. 6, no. 1 (March 1972), pp. 81–102.

Hartgen, David: "Behavioural Models in Transport: Perspectives, Problems and Prospects," in David Banister and Peter Hall, eds., *Transport and Public Policy Planning* (London: Mansell Publishing, 1981), pp. 331–341.

———: "Coming in the 1990s: The Agency-Friendly Travel Survey," *Transportation,* vol. 19, no. 2 (May 1992), pp. 79–95.

Haynes, J. J., J. N. Fox, and B. T. Williams: "Public Attitudes toward Transit Features and Systems," *Transportation Research Record,* no. 649 (1977), pp. 42–48.

Hille, Stanley J., and Theodore K. Martin: "Consumer Preference in Transportation," *Highway Research Record,* no. 197 (1967), pp. 44–56.

Keefer, Louis E.: "Characteristics of Captive and Choice Transit Trips in the Pittsburgh Metropolitan Area," *Highway Research Board Bulletin,* no. 347 (1962), pp. 24–33.

Koppelman, Frank S.: "Guidelines for Aggregate Travel Prediction Using Disaggregate Choice Models," *Transportation Research Record,* no. 610 (1976), pp. 19–24.

O'Hare, William, and Milton Morris: *Demographic Change and Recent Worktrip Travel Trends* (Washington: Joint Center for Political Studies, 1985).

Pucher, John, and Fred Williams: "Socioeconomic Characteristics of Urban Travelers: Evidence from the 1990–91 NPTS," *Transportation Quarterly,* vol. 46, no. 4 (October 1992), pp. 561–581.

Purvis, Charles L.: "Survey of Surveys II," *Transportation Research Record,* no. 1271 (1990), pp. 23–32.

Roberts, John, Wayne E. Thompson, and Brian Sutton Smith: "Expressive Self-Testing in Driving," *Human Organization,* vol. 25, no. 1 (Spring 1966), pp. 54–63.

Sullivan, Sheldon W.: "Variations in Personal Travel Habits by Day of Week," *Highway Research Record,* no. 41 (1963a), pp. 39–44.

———: "Choice and Captive Auto Driver Trips," *Traffic Engineering,* vol. 33, no. 12 (September 1963b), pp. 11–13.

Tehan, Claire, and Martin Wachs: *The Role of Psychological Needs in Mass Transit* (Los Angeles: School of Architecture and Urban Planning, University of California, 1972).

Tye, W. B., L. Sherman, M. Kinnucan, D. Nelson, and T. Tardiff: *Application of Disaggregate Travel Demand Models,* National Cooperative Highway Research Program Report 253 (Washington: Transportation Research Board, 1982).

Wachs, Martin: "Consumer Attitudes toward Transit Service: An Interpretive Review," *Journal of American Institute of Planners,* vol. 42, no. 1 (January 1976), pp. 96–104.

Warner, Stanley L.: *Stochastic Choice of Mode in Urban Travel: A Study in Binary Choice* (Evanston, IL: Northwestern University Press, 1962).

Weiner, Edward: "Modal Split Revisited," *Traffic Quarterly,* vol. 23, no. 1 (January 1969), pp. 5–28.

Wynn, F. Houston: "Shortcut Modal Split Formula," *Highway Research Record,* no. 283 (1969), pp. 48–56.

13

SPECIAL GROUPS OF USERS

THE TRANSPORTATION-DISADVANTAGED

The term *transportation-disadvantaged* refers to people whose ability to travel (or mobility) is restricted by not having adequate access to either an automobile or transit service. In our automobile-dominated society, lack of access to an automobile is the basic problem. Transit is a backup for those without automobiles. But if transit service is poor or unavailable, these people are constrained in what they can do outside their homes.

The transportation-disadvantaged have been identified by making studies that compare the trip-making behavior of a special group with that of the general population. The groups that have received the most attention are the poor, minorities, elderly, disabled, children, and women. The studies usually show that the group makes fewer trips per day, makes shorter trips, and travels at a slower average door-to-door speed. These are considered indicators that the group's ability to travel is constrained.

Transportation planners have decades of experience in measuring observed travel behavior, which represents manifest demand. The concept of *latent demand* was invented to signify potential travel that is suppressed because of barriers to mobility [Hoel et al. 1968]. There are many kinds of barriers; they may be physical (e.g., lack of transit service), economic (inability to pay fares), or social (racial discrimination). Some barriers exist within the individual, such as physical or mental handicaps, ignorance, or illiteracy.

If the barriers were removed, more travel would be generated. However, it is not necessarily true that each special group would travel just as much as the overall population. Some people do not need or want to travel as much as the average citizen. For example, people who are retired don't go to work. Some people live in environments that

306

require less travel. High density and mixed land use make it possible to make trips on foot that elsewhere would be made by motorized means.

Conventional wisdom assumes that people who travel more are better off. This reflects the materialistic attitude that people who have more things and do more things have a higher standard of living. However, one can argue that travel is not directly productive but is an unavoidable cost that should be minimized (except for recreational travel, which is minor within urban areas). Further, travel contributes to several societal problems such as congestion, air pollution, and energy consumption. Hence more travel is less efficient, and less travel is desirable.

This is a philosophical aside; the underlying concern is with equity. People with less mobility have fewer opportunities to obtain the rewards of life. For example, they have fewer choices of jobs and places to shop. It is harder for them to reach medical services and public facilities such as schools and libraries. They have fewer choices of where to go for leisure activities.

Although the number of vehicles in the United States has risen steadily over the years, the number of households without any vehicle available does not seem to be decreasing. Rising vehicle ownership has mostly occurred through increases in households with multiple vehicles. This is readily apparent when one drives through new suburban developments: One-car garages have given way to two-car garages, and many expensive homes now come with three-car garages. Table 13-1 shows that between 1980 and 1990 the number of households in the United States with no vehicle available increased by 2.0 percent, while households with vehicles increased by much larger percentages. The largest percentage increase was for households with two vehicles.

No matter how wealthy the country becomes, there will always be some people who do not drive. This includes the poor who cannot afford it, the young, the old, the disabled, and those who simply dislike driving. Part of the problem is that some of these people live in areas where conventional transit service does not reach them. It would be easier to serve them if they were concentrated around transit routes, but this would restrict their choice of location. Hence some type of paratransit may be the best approach.

People who do not have a motor vehicle are not necessarily confined to their homes;

TABLE 13-1

U.S. HOUSEHOLDS CLASSIFIED BY VEHICLES AVAILABLE, 1980 AND 1990

(In Thousands)

Number of vehicles	1980		1990		Change	Percentage change
	Number	Percent	Number	Percent		
0	10,390	12.9	10,602	11.5	212	2.0
1	28,565	35.6	31,039	33.8	2,474	8.7
2	27,347	34.0	34,361	37.4	7,014	25.6
3 or more	14,088	17.5	15,945	17.3	1,857	13.2
Total households	80,390	100.0	91,947	100.0	11,557	14.4

Source: U.S. Census.

they have several travel options. Some walk, but many live in low-density areas where distances to desired destinations are long. Some ride transit, but many do not have this option because they live far from transit routes or in towns or rural areas where there is no transit at all. A surprising number of people without cars use taxis, even among the poor [Lee et al. 1972]. However, the most common mode of travel is getting a ride in a car with someone else—a family member, friend, or neighbor.

The following sections discuss several groups that are considered to be transportation-disadvantaged.

THE POOR

On August 11, 1965, a California Highway Patrol officer arrested a young African-American male for drunken driving in south central Los Angeles. The man became unruly, and before he was subdued, a crowd had gathered. The episode mushroomed into one of the largest civil disturbances in U.S. history, known as the Watts riot. It lasted for 6 days and did not end until 13,900 members of the National Guard were called in to patrol the area. The final toll was 34 dead, 1032 injured, and $40 million in property damage.

The governor of California appointed a commission headed by John A. McCone, a distinguished statesman, to investigate the riot and identify its underlying causes. Among their findings was that

> . . . the inadequate and costly public transportation currently existing throughout the Los Angeles area seriously restricts the residents of the disadvantaged areas such as south central Los Angeles. This lack of adequate transportation handicaps them in seeking and holding jobs, attending schools, shopping, and in fulfilling other needs. It has had a major influence in creating a sense of isolation, with its resultant frustrations, among the residents of south central Los Angeles, particularly the Watts area. [Governor's Commission on the Los Angeles Riots 1965, p. 65]

Ironically, Watts was originally the name of a railroad station where two Pacific Electric Railroad lines crossed and transfers could be made. The last train ran in 1961.

This focused the attention of transportation planners on the travel needs of the poor, which differ from those of the middle class. This concern fit in with the civil rights movement and the War on Poverty. Planners realized that the poor and minorities have a major travel problem: They mostly live in the central city because their housing choices are restricted. But most new blue-collar jobs—for which they are logical candidates—are located in the suburbs. Hence reverse commuting is required, and conventional transit does not serve this kind of movement well. Transit is good at bringing commuters to the CBD because after they get off, they can walk to their jobs. But relatively few suburban jobs are within walking distance of transit stops.

Starting in 1966, the federal government funded demonstration projects addressed to this problem in Boston, Los Angeles, New York City, St. Louis, and several other cities [Hilton 1974]. Typically they provided bus service between ghetto areas (mostly in the inner city) and industrial areas (usually in the suburbs) where planners had identified job openings. The results were disappointing. Most routes attracted few riders for several reasons:

1 Many of the jobs were unattractive, paying minimum wage for menial work and offering no chance for advancement. Some people preferred to remain unemployed than to become janitors or do other "dirty work." For a young person in the ghetto, there are easier ways of making money than working in a fast-food restaurant.

2 Transportation was not the major obstacle for many unemployed. Some had few skills and little education. Others could not hold a steady job because they were alcoholics or drug addicts or had psychological problems. In some cases, there was discrimination so that minorities could not get jobs regardless of how qualified they were.

3 When the programs were successful in helping people get jobs, often they used their new income to buy a car and stopped riding the bus.

This policy thrust lasted about 5 years. Most of the services were dropped after the federal government stopped paying for them (usually a period of 2 years). The services often ran larger deficits than other bus routes. Only a few generated enough riders that local authorities continued them. One successful route was the Century Boulevard bus line in Los Angeles that linked Watts with the Los Angeles International Airport, a General Motors plant in South Gate, and several other concentrations of jobs. It served more than 3000 passengers a day and was made permanent, even though it lost money [Hilton 1974].

These projects were initiated with the primary objective of helping the unemployed to get and hold jobs. "Upon the termination of demonstration subsidies, however, the most important criterion considered for the justification of continuing the project routes was the financial success of the operation. Financial success was based on the economics of route operation and did not include the benefits derived by the various population segments who rode the buses" [Falcocchio and Cantilli 1974, p. 46].

No one expected transit service to eliminate unemployment, but it could alleviate the problem. Falcocchio and Cantilli made a detailed analysis of the central Brooklyn Model Cities area and estimated that 11.5 percent of unemployment among unskilled workers (omitting those classified as the hard-core unemployed) was attributable to inadequate transportation to job sites. They tested hypothetical transit improvements and found that none would be self-supporting financially. However, the transit improvements would be economically beneficial because of the earnings of workers who otherwise would contribute nothing to economic output. This is a widely accepted justification for subsidies.

The demonstration projects represented an effort to use transportation to solve some larger problems of society. It failed because the problems are broader and deeper. It is convenient to blame such problems on transportation and to make transportation responsible for solving them. Providing new transit services that will be used mostly by minorities is an easy way for politicians to address the problem of discrimination. The cost is relatively small, and it requires no behavioral change by those who are not minorities.

Nonetheless, the attention given to travel problems of the poor had a lasting effect.

Providing mobility for *all* the population has become a permanent policy objective in transportation planning. Fast and efficient movement is no longer the overriding goal, as it once was.

This is especially true in small cities, where it would be physically possible to handle all travel by automobiles with tolerable levels of congestion. But some people don't have automobiles and would be denied transportation. This is the primary justification for preserving transit in small cities. Transit riders in small cities are more likely to be poor, while in large cities they come from a wider range of income levels.

This is illustrated in Table 13-2, which shows the mean earnings of commuters, as reported in the 1980 Census, for a selection of large and small cities in the midwest. In Chicago, the most transit-oriented of the cities, there is no appreciable difference in income between transit riders and all workers. In the other large cities, the incomes of transit riders are relatively high compared to those of all commuters. In the small cities, transit riders lag well behind the overall commuting population.

Historically, the poor have been ignored in most decisions about transportation improvements. As noted, some projects were aimed specifically at the poor, but they were few and far between. The usual objective has been to get travelers to switch from automobiles to transit. If successful, this would reduce congestion, accidents, air pollution, energy consumption, and so on. But measures to induce drivers to switch may not help the poor.

The difference between captive and choice transit riders was explained in the last chapter. A large percentage of captive riders are poor. But most transit improvements of recent years have sought to increase the number of choice riders. Captive riders have

TABLE 13-2
MEAN EARNINGS ($) OF COMMUTERS IN SELECTED SMSAs IN THE MIDWEST, 1979

	Males			Females		
SMSA	All modes	Transit	Transit/all modes ratio	All modes	Transit	Transit/all modes ratio
Large cities						
Chicago	20,054	20,056	1.000	9,663	9,982	1.033
Cleveland	19,445	16,092	0.828	8,748	8,315	0.951
Detroit	21,793	13,780	0.632	9,679	8,351	0.863
Kansas City	18,463	11,477	0.622	8,655	7,531	0.870
Minneapolis	18,985	15,210	0.801	8,472	8,043	0.949
St. Louis	18,313	13,056	0.713	8,314	7,439	0.895
Small cities						
Appleton, WI	16,992	9,758	0.574	7,112	4,956	0.697
Davenport, IA	19,132	9,948	0.520	8,397	5,989	0.713
Evansville, IN	17,282	8,004	0.463	7,733	5,089	0.658
Flint, MI	20,351	8,861	0.435	9,803	5,795	0.591
Rockford, IL	18,557	9,750	0.525	7,844	6,247	0.796
Youngstown, OH	18,288	7,714	0.422	8,060	4,863	0.603

Source: 1980 Census of Population, vol. 1, *Characteristics of the Population*, chapter D, *Detailed Population Characteristics* (Washington: Government Printing Office, 1983), table 232.

been ignored, perhaps because of the very fact that they are captive. Following are some examples:

1 Wohl [1976] pointed out that high-speed rail lines from the suburbs to the CBD usually serve few poor people. The clientele largely consists of professional and managerial employees who have above-average incomes. The BART system has been especially criticized on this score, but other heavy rail projects also seem to have been designed primarily for suburbanites.

2 Rail lines to airports mostly serve middle- and upper-income people. The poor don't fly much. In recent years, Cleveland, Washington, D.C., and Chicago have built new heavy rail lines to their airports. A BART line will be extended to the San Francisco International Airport.

3 Bus lanes (or high-occupancy vehicle lanes) on expressways serve suburban commuters. This is also true of express bus services that use expressways. Most have high fares and pick up their passengers in well-to-do neighborhoods.

4 Services aimed at tourists don't help the poor much. The Tijuana Trolley in San Diego is an example: A sizable percentage of the passengers travel to Tijuana on the Mexican border. A major argument for a proposed light rail line in Kansas City is that it will connect a number of scattered hotels and boost convention business. The poor don't attend conventions much.

5 Downtown people movers help some clerical and service workers who have jobs downtown, but the people movers are primarily intended to benefit downtown businesses. It was for this reason that Dennis Kucinich, when mayor of Cleveland, declined a federal grant to build such a facility.

What can be done to help the poor with their travel needs? One idea is to help them to get automobiles. Automobile ownership is surprisingly high among the poor, but most of their vehicles are old, and operating costs are high. According to Myers [1970], for the typical annual cost of using a jalopy, one could purchase a small, inexpensive new automobile. If two or more commuters shared the car, it would probably be cheaper than relying on public transportation.

A major obstacle is that poor people do not have the assets or credit to finance a new-car purchase. Myers proposed that some organization buy cars and rent them to the poor at rates that would make the program financially viable. He labeled this plan as "new Volks for poor folks" because at the time the Volkswagen was the most popular cheap car. He did not think the federal government would undertake such a program; apparently he had in mind a private, nonprofit organization.

This is a reasonable proposal; one advantage is that it would facilitate reverse commuting to suburban jobs. However, no organization came forward to implement the plan, and it received no political support. It would be better to do things that are practical in the current political and economic climate.

It helps that the poor are usually concentrated in certain parts of the city (particularly if they are minorities). Economic segregation is pervasive in U.S. cities. This means you can target specific neighborhoods for better transit service and be sure that most of the beneficiaries will be poor.

Usually buses provide the main transit service in these areas. Often the best way to help the poor is to improve bus service in the inner city. This means shorter headways, longer hours of service, and perhaps some additional routes. More attention to scheduling could make transfers easier. Changing bus routes might be helpful. Ornati [1969] found that most bus routes in New York City followed former streetcar lines and led to older commercial centers. Service to industrial areas with thousands of blue-collar jobs was often poor, requiring transfers and double fares.

Such a systematic improvement of conventional bus service in the central city is rarely undertaken. In part, this is because decision makers often neglect the poor, but another reason is that these changes are mundane and unglamorous. A new rail line is exciting; better bus service is a bore.

The poor do not necessarily consider the bus to be a desirable mode of travel. In a study of Buffalo, New York, Paaswell and Recker [1978] found that members of carless households regularly rode the bus to work, but it tended to be the "mode of last resort" for nonwork trips. People preferred to use a car (as driver or passenger) when possible; otherwise they made most trips on foot. Most people were able to borrow a car or get a ride at least occasionally.

New rail lines can serve the poor if there are stops in the right places. This can be a political issue. In Washington, D.C., a proposed Metro line would have served the low-income Columbia Heights area, but it was deleted from the final plan despite protest [Murin 1971]. In New York City, the route of the proposed Second Avenue Subway was altered to put a stop in the Lower East Side, a poor district [Ornati 1969]. However, this project was halted and apparently will not be completed.

Paratransit services may help the poor. They are cheaper than taxis, which the poor are forced to use a great deal. Door-to-door speeds are low, so people who can afford faster transportation are not likely to use the services. Many users are elderly who are not pressed for time. Other users are parents and children in one-car households where the other parent has taken the car.

In discussions of national transportation policy, serving the poor is usually given as a major justification for spending money on transit. But in developing proposals at the local level, the poor are sometimes forgotten. It is important for transportation planners to analyze each transit proposal in terms of who pays and who gets the benefits. Information about what people would use the service should be developed; often this is not done. Many recent projects have mostly benefited people who have plenty of money.

THE ELDERLY AND DISABLED

The mobility problems of the elderly and disabled people have received a great deal of attention in the last 20 years. The group was once called the *elderly and handicapped* (or E&H), but it is now considered "politically correct" to refer to the latter as *disabled*. This is a diverse group, and simple solutions to their problems do not work well. It may be unfortunate that elderly and disabled people are often lumped together; although there is overlap, there are also differences. We discuss the two groups separately before we review programs to serve them, which are often combined.

The Elderly

The elderly are usually defined as persons at least 65 years old. The 1990 Census showed there were 31.2 million such persons in the United States, or 12.6 percent of the population. Because medical advances have increased longevity, this segment is growing and will represent an ever-larger share of the population in the future. Senior citizens have a considerable amount of political clout and lobby effectively in Washington, D.C. Many are active politically (in part because they are retired and have the time), and the elderly vote at a higher rate than any other age group.

There is a common perception that most elderly have low incomes, live in high-density areas of the central city, and rely on public transportation. Actually the elderly are very heterogeneous. Wachs [1979] made an exhaustive analysis of the elderly in Los Angeles County and identified seven lifestyles corresponding to different residence locations. One group fit the popular image, but it contained only about one-quarter of the elderly.

Of course, some elderly people are wealthy. A large share of the millionaires in the country are over age 65; they can afford chauffeur-driven limousines if they want them. Wachs labeled one group as *financially secure*; they lived in middle- and upper-income neighborhoods. In addition, many of the elderly live in homes that they own "free and clear," having paid off their mortgages. While their cash incomes might be low and might qualify them for poverty status, in fact their circumstances are reasonably comfortable.

While many of the elderly do live in the central city (especially the minorities), older people have participated in the shift to the suburbs in recent decades. Wachs found some had lived in the suburbs for many years, but others have moved there fairly recently. It is probable that an increasing proportion of the elderly will choose suburban homes in the future.

Many of the elderly own and drive cars, although the percentage is lower than that among the middle-aged. Most elderly persons do not have any handicap that prevents them from driving. It can be difficult to persuade them to stop driving, even when their ability becomes impaired (in the opinion of others). It is natural that people want to retain their independence for as long as possible.

Inevitably a higher percentage of the elderly will drive in the future. The current elderly grew up in the 1920s and 1930s when automobile ownership was much lower, and many persons never learned to drive (especially women). Many grew up in central cities and have been accustomed to using transit all their lives. Those who are currently middle-aged are more likely to have learned to drive, to have grown up in the suburbs, and not to have used transit.

Thus, increasing the supply of transit service for the elderly may be the wrong approach; it might make more sense to facilitate their use of automobiles. Wachs suggested that a small, low-powered motor vehicle be designed especially for the elderly to use in making short trips near their homes. A major problem is that it would not mix well with ordinary vehicles and should have a separate right-of-way (possibly bicycle paths). No company has come forward to market such a vehicle, but in some retirement communities with networks of off-street paths, electric golf carts are popular.

This scheme would not serve all the elderly, as some do have handicaps. Even those who are able-bodied in their 60s and 70s will eventually succumb to the aging process (the group of people 85 years or older is growing faster than any other segment of the population). Many elderly get rides from family or friends, but obviously this cannot be guaranteed. It is likely that increasingly those elderly with mobility problems will be widely scattered in low-density areas where conventional transit service is weak. Hence there will be a growing demand for specialized paratransit services.

The Disabled

While the number of elderly is known fairly accurately, the number of disabled persons is uncertain. Estimates range from 5 to 14 percent of the population. An estimate that 13.4 million persons have some type of disability that interferes with their use of public transportation is widely accepted [Katzman 1986]. However, this number may be too high.

The 1980 Census included a question that asked respondents whether they had a physical, mental, or other health condition that prevented them from using public transit. The question evoked considerable controversy and was not repeated in the 1990 Census. Tabulations showed that for the whole United States, 14.9 percent of persons aged 65 or older reported a transit disability, while 1.8 percent of those aged 16 to 64 reported one. This amounted to 3.6 million elderly persons and 2.6 million aged 16 to 64.

Part of the measurement problem lies in defining what constitutes a handicap. There was once concern that alcoholics and drug addicts would be classified as handicapped, and federal law was amended to specifically exclude them. Moreover, because surveys rely on self-reporting, they are only partially helpful: Some people readily identify themselves as handicapped, but other persons confined to wheelchairs refuse to call themselves handicapped.

There is a definition in section 16(c) of the Urban Mass Transportation Act which states that a transportation-handicapped person is "any individual who, by reason of illness, injury, age, congenital malfunction, or other permanent or temporary incapacity or disability, is unable without special facilities or special planning or design to utilize mass transportation facilities as effectively as persons who are not so affected." Note that being handicapped is not necessarily a permanent status: Someone who breaks a leg becomes handicapped for a time.

In practice, *transportation-handicapped persons* are defined as those who cannot perform one or more of the following functions: (1) negotiate a flight of stairs, an escalator, or a ramp; (2) board or alight from a transit vehicle; (3) stand in a moving transit vehicle; (4) read informational signs; (5) hear verbal announcements; (6) walk more than 200 feet; or (7) use public transportation without the aid of another person.

Many people with some degree of disability are able to perform these particular functions. Some have no difficulty in either driving or using transit. Those in wheelchairs often drive cars with hand controls. For many who are disabled, it is easier to drive a car than to take a bus.

The disabled form a heterogeneous group with a large variety of difficulties. It is a challenge to a transit system to assist people with many different needs. Publicity has focused on wheelchair lifts, but only a small fraction of the disabled use wheelchairs (see Figure 13-1). Some can walk but are unable to climb the steps of a bus. Others cannot reach the cord to signal for a bus to stop. Some are blind, and some are deaf.

It is uncertain whether the number of disabled persons will increase or decrease in the future. Improvements in medical care and prosthetic devices will tend to lower the number of people who are prevented from performing normal activities. On the other hand, the elderly population will increase, and older persons are more likely to incur disabilities.

Involvement of Social Service Agencies

There is a huge number of social service agencies, public and private, that provide special transportation services for their clients, many of whom are elderly and/or disabled. Providers include churches, schools, universities, senior citizen centers, welfare departments, and many others. Most of the operations are small, and there is no accurate count of them. In a large metropolitan area, there may be more than a hundred.

While the supply of service is large, it cannot be considered a system because typically there is no coordination. Different agencies may offer overlapping services for the same clients in the same area, causing duplication and waste. Sometimes organizations deliberately compete with each other, as bureaucracies are wont to do. Further, many social service agencies have specific and narrow eligibility requirements: One may serve the elderly; another, the disabled; still another, the poor. Some potential users may not fit the right categories or may have trouble finding the proper provider.

One remedy to these problems is the *brokerage* concept, in which a clearinghouse coordinates providers and handles requests for service. When a request is received, the brokerage ascertains the needs and eligibility of the client and tries to find a suitable provider. UMTA funded a dozen brokerages as demonstrations; the first was in Knoxville, Tennessee [Schreffler 1985]. Large cities with brokerages include Houston and Pittsburgh [Rosenbloom and Warren 1981].

There is also lack of coordination at the federal level. Rosenbloom commented, "U.S. policy aimed at increasing the mobility of the elderly and handicapped is fraught with inconsistencies and complications. Most national program efforts have begun in some confusion; many have degenerated into open conflict" [1982, p. 335].

Most of the local organizations receive federal grants which may be used to provide transportation to clients. Rosenbloom [1982] gave a long list of programs administered by the Department of Health and Human Services, the Department of Housing and Urban Development, the Department of Labor, and the Veterans Administration. Some of the services are quite specific. For example, under the Social Security Act, Medicaid recipients can be transported to doctors' offices and medical facilities. Under the Older Americans Act of 1965, persons aged 60 or older can be taken to sites for congregate meals. Other services are more general and take any elderly or handicapped person anywhere in a city. Some services are available to others, such as children or the poor.

The local agencies supply service in several ways. In small agencies, it is common for staff members or volunteers to use their own cars to carry clients. Some agencies simply reimburse clients for travel expenses, letting them find the means of travel.

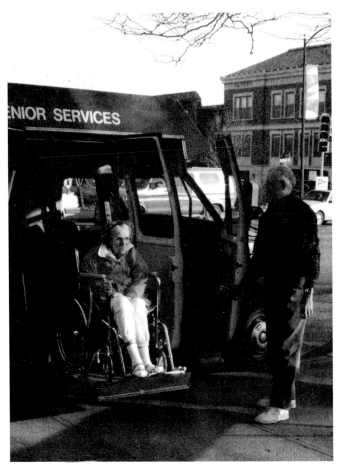

FIGURE 13-1
Using a wheelchair lift. A passenger in a wheelchair is lifted aboard a
paratransit vehicle. The driver operates the lift controls. (Photo by
author.)

Increasingly, agencies offer organized services with vans or buses purchased with federal funds. Occasionally they contract with the local transit agency to provide paratransit service. Another arrangement is for the social service agency to contract with a private transportation provider such as a taxi company.

All this is beyond the jurisdiction of the Department of Transportation, but DOT is
also concerned with transporting the elderly and disabled. Section 16 of the Urban Mass
Transportation Act deals with the planning and design of transit facilities to meet the
special needs of the elderly and handicapped and authorizes grants to purchase vehicles
to carry them. Section 18 provides grants for rural public transportation, which is available to the general public but mainly used by the elderly and handicapped. The law requires that systems receiving federal operating assistance charge no more than half-fare
to the elderly and handicapped during nonpeak hours. DOT has long been embroiled in

controversy over making transit service accessible to the disabled; this issue is discussed later.

Involvement of Transit Agencies

Local transit authorities have the legal responsibility to ensure that elderly and disabled persons have adequate transportation. There are three common approaches to fulfilling this mandate [Middendorf et al. 1983]:

Accessible Fixed-Route Bus Systems Some transit systems seek to serve the elderly and handicapped with their regular fixed routes by making their vehicles accessible to the disabled. Most often this means providing wheelchair lifts, but there are other changes that try to remove barriers presented by the design of vehicles. For example, large, illuminated signs help those who are visually impaired; nonslip floors help those who have trouble walking. This approach is good when the transit system is extensive and service is frequent. However, in many cities, transit service is limited, route coverage is sparse, and schedules are poor, with long headways and no evening or weekend service.

Transit agencies also provide financial assistance in the form of reduced fares for elderly and disabled passengers. As noted, the elderly and handicapped can be charged no more than half-fare during off-peak periods. Many transit systems charge lower fares at all times or sell cut-rate passes to eligible riders. However, this addresses only the income situation and not other needs.

Advocacy groups for the disabled favor this approach because it integrates their members with the general population. It has become the law of the land: Under the 1990 Americans with Disabilities Act (ADA), new buses purchased by transit agencies must be accessible to the disabled, including those in wheelchairs. However, there will always be some disabled persons who cannot use buses.

Specialized Transportation Services Many transit agencies provide specialized services for the elderly and disabled separate from their regular routes. This is typically demand-responsive, door-to-door service utilizing vans or small buses. Often passengers must make advance reservations. Some transit agencies supply the vehicles and personnel themselves, but many contract with private firms for the service. According to a national survey conducted in 1985, a majority of special services for the elderly and handicapped were operated by private firms [Teal 1988].

Many transit officials favor this approach, believing it to be less expensive than making full-size buses accessible. However, it does require a considerable subsidy, because the fare covers only a fraction of the cost. Such services have proved to be popular, and one problem is that demand for service may outrun supply, so that potential riders have to be put on a waiting list. More transit systems will offer these services in the future because the ADA requires that they offer complementary paratransit service to persons unable to use regular buses in the area served by the fixed bus routes.

User-Side Subsidies for Taxi Service In some places, the transit agency subsidizes qualified individuals to use taxis (which of course are operated by private companies).

This is also done by local governments in small communities that have no bus service. This is called a *user-side subsidy*. A typical arrangement is for the public body to sell vouchers that can be used to pay part of the taxi fare. The government then reimburses the taxi company for the difference.

This system has the advantage of providing door-to-door service anywhere in the community at any time. It is considered efficient, since the government pays only for service actually consumed. If demand is low, the cost will be low. The cost per trip is substantially less than when the elderly and handicapped are carried in specialized services. The approach is favored by free-market advocates, who believe that it approximates a competitive market. This is true only if there is more than one taxi company, and many cities have only one. However, it is argued that the system encourages competition in the taxi business. Spear [1982] summarized findings from several demonstrations and case studies.

There have been some problems with this method. Some taxi firms give these passengers a low priority, serving them only when the firms are not busy. Hence the companies need to be monitored. Taxi drivers can be insensitive; they should receive special training in dealing with the disabled. While many taxi firms have joined these programs, some have declined for various reasons, such as claiming they did not want to be bothered with the paperwork.

Comparing the three approaches is difficult because they tend to serve different segments of the elderly and handicapped population. Studies show that equipping buses with wheelchair lifts is generally not very cost-effective because there are few users. The best performance has been recorded in Seattle, where there are more users than in other cities and the cost per lift boarding was only $16 in 1980. Providing specialized services is cheaper, and subsidizing taxi rides is the cheapest alternative, although the ranges of reported costs overlap. Middendorf et al. concluded that "it is not possible to recommend a single transportation solution that is clearly the most cost-effective for all handicapped people in all situations. The cost-effectiveness of any alternative can vary widely, depending on local conditions and many other factors" [1983, p. 90].

The Mentally Retarded

It is estimated that there are 6.7 million mentally retarded persons in the United States [Starks 1986]. About 87 percent are classified as mildly retarded (with IQ scores ranging from 55 to 70) and have the potential to travel by scheduled public transportation if they have proper training. At present, many utilize special paratransit services, the costs of which are rapidly rising. Because independent living has been widely encouraged, many of the retarded travel regularly to jobs, schooling, and recreational activities. Their demand for travel is greater than that of most disabled persons and is more likely to occur in peak periods.

About 250,000 mentally retarded persons live in institutions. Although there is no alternative for the severely or profoundly retarded, about three-quarters of those now institutionalized could live in the community if they were able to travel alone. This would have several benefits: It would reduce social service costs, enable the retarded to take jobs, give them fuller lives, and enhance their self-esteem.

According to Starks [1981, p. 21], "current federal policy overlooks the transportation needs of the educable mentally retarded in this country, who constitute a large portion of the travel handicapped." The Urban Mass Transportation Act nowhere mentions the mentally retarded, but section 504 of the Rehabilitation Act of 1973 states that "mental impairments which substantially limit one or more such person's major life activities" constitute a qualifying disability. Thus there is no legal question that transportation programs to serve the disabled should cover the retarded.

This group is unique because the nature of the handicap means that they are unlikely to organize themselves for political action. Militant activists have arisen among the wheelchair-bound, but this will not happen with the retarded. Typically they are shy and have trouble asserting themselves. This probably explains why policy makers have neglected them.

Measures that address other handicaps, such as the use of wheelchair lifts, are mostly irrelevant to the retarded. The design of buses is of little importance to them, except for those individuals who also have physical handicaps. Clear markings of routes and destinations are helpful, but flashing signs can be disorienting. What the mentally retarded mostly need is training in how to ride buses. Some social service agencies have developed travel training programs for the retarded. These programs are based upon earlier programs for the blind, since learning pedestrian skills is an important aspect.

Educable mentally retarded persons can learn the routine involved in making the same trip day after day. They learn where to wait for a bus, how to recognize the right bus to get on, how to pay the fare, and where to get off. However, candidates should be screened because some have emotional problems. To ride a bus, they need enough emotional stability so they will not panic if something unexpected happens (such as an accident or breakdown that requires switching to another bus). They must be assertive enough to ask for help if they need it, and some find this difficult. Bus drivers should be trained to recognize mentally retarded passengers and assist them as needed.

In a demonstration project staged in Sacramento, 95 out of 97 clients completed a 25-hour course with one-on-one training by an instructor [Starks et al. 1984]. Three months later, 85 clients were still riding the buses regularly. However, the transit authority then changed its routes, and some of the individuals had to be retrained.

DOT does not provide any funds for mobility training and has generally ignored the mentally retarded in its efforts to serve the transportation-handicapped. There is presently no incentive for local transit authorities to take responsibility, and few have done so. Of course, they do not have the background to conduct travel training themselves, but they could contract with the social agencies that do have the appropriate experience.

THE ACCESSIBILITY ISSUE

Section 16, added to the Mass Transportation Act in 1970, established the policy "that elderly and handicapped persons have the same right as other persons to utilize mass transportation facilities and services, that special efforts shall be made in the planning and design of mass transportation facilities and services so that the availability to elderly and handicapped persons of mass transportation which they can effectively utilize will be assured." It authorized grants and loans for capital investment in services for the elderly and handicapped. Section 16(b)(1) covers public agencies, while section

16(b)(2) is the only part of federal law that allows transit grants directly to private organizations (which must be nonprofit). Section 16 is called the *Biaggi amendment* because it was introduced by Congressman Mario Biaggi of New York, who in 1988 was convicted of taking payoffs in the Wedtech scandal.

The first case that became a public issue was the Washington, D.C., Metro, which as originally designed had no provision for wheelchairs. Organizations of the disabled complained, and in 1972 a congressional committee held a stormy hearing during which it was charged that the transit authority had "simply flouted the law" [Fielding 1982, p. 276]. The upshot was that Congress added a $65 million appropriation to the 1973 Highway Act so that all Metro stations would have elevators or ramps (see Figure 13-2).

Another key law is section 504 of the Rehabilitation Act of 1973, which bans discrimination against handicapped persons. This applies to all programs receiving federal aid, not just those in transportation. It was administered by the Department of Health, Education, and Welfare (HEW), which took the position that the act conferred certain civil rights on the disabled.

DOT at first sought to fulfill its obligations by forcing the redesign of buses. In 1972

FIGURE 13-2
Elevator at a transit station. An elevator for the disabled is located on the platform of the National Airport station on the Washington, D.C., Metro. The original design for the Metro had no provision for wheelchair users, and this became a controversial issue. (Photo by author.)

it awarded grants totaling $28 million to the three U.S. bus manufacturers to design a new model called *Transbus*. It would have wider doors, better lighting, a lower floor, kneeling capability (meaning the buses could be lowered to make it easier to climb the steps), and a wheelchair lift. However, the companies encountered technical problems in meeting Transbus specifications and proceeded with their own "advanced design" models. In January 1975, UMTA announced that Transbus would be introduced nationwide, but in July 1976, it decided that Transbus would not be required.

Another shift came after the Carter administration took office. Secretary of Transportation Brock Adams decreed in May 1977 that after September 30, 1979, all new buses purchased with federal aid must be of the Transbus design. The bus manufacturers resisted because they thought there was too much financial risk involved. Los Angeles, Miami, and Philadelphia formed a consortium to place an order for 530 buses. At the bid opening on May 2, 1979, not a single bid was received. That spelled the end of Transbus, and DOT rescinded its order.

Meanwhile, DOT had issued regulations in 1976 based upon the idea of "special efforts" mentioned in section 16. Each transit system was allowed to design its own solution to the problem of serving the elderly and handicapped, but it was supposed to do something. In response, many cities started special services for the elderly and handicapped, some of which were very successful. Usually they were dial-a-ride services provided by minibuses or vans equipped with wheelchair lifts. Some cities contracted with taxi companies to provide the service.

However, the response was uneven. Many cities did little or nothing, and there was no real enforcement by UMTA. In some places, disabled persons brought suit to force the initiation of services. Many transit systems did not have extra money available to start special services, which were expensive (the cost per passenger often exceeded $10). Sometimes demand exceeded supply, and applicants were put on a waiting list. Often advance reservations were required, and hours of operation were limited.

This approach was also opposed by some of the disabled, who called it "separate but equal" treatment and compared it to racially segregated schools. They lobbied for accessibility to all regular transit vehicles. This approach is known as *mainstreaming*. The two main arguments for it are that it would compel "normal" people to interact with the disabled and help them overcome prejudice and that it would keep the disabled from feeling isolated from society.

The main objection to mainstreaming was cost. A wheelchair lift on a bus cost $10,000 to $13,000 (more if it is a retrofit) and increased the operating cost an average of $2000 per year [Middendorf et al. 1983]. Making a rail station accessible to wheelchairs could run into millions of dollars. It was also argued that disabled persons cause delays that defeat the aim of providing speedy and convenient service for as many passengers as possible.

Katzman [1986] wrote a thorough account of the controversy. On one side were those who believed that *effective mobility* for the disabled was the goal, and that it should be accomplished by the most cost-effective means. This group included the transit industry and many local officials. On the other side were those who believed that the civil rights of the handicapped were abridged if these people could not use the same vehicles and services as the general population. This group included organizations of the disabled (such as the Paralyzed Veterans of America) and HEW. DOT was caught in the middle and over the years shifted its position back and forth.

Because of the Vietnam war, the disabled had some young and aggressive leaders [Fielding 1982]. They gained support in Congress (a few members of Congress were disabled, including Senator Daniel Inouye of Hawaii and Senator Robert Dole of Kansas, and some had relatives or friends with disabilities). Brock Adams was also convinced, and in May 1979, DOT canceled the 1976 regulations and issued new ones. It put emphasis on access to people in wheelchairs, although only a small percentage of the disabled use wheelchairs (7 percent, by one estimate).

The new rules required that (1) all new buses have wheelchair lifts and kneeling capability, (2) at least one car on every rapid transit train be equipped to tie down wheelchairs, (3) all stations on new subway-elevated systems be accessible to wheelchairs (by either elevators or ramps), and (4) all *key stations* on older rail systems be retrofitted for wheelchairs. Key stations were those with high passenger volumes or transfer points or terminals; it was estimated that 40 percent of stations would be affected.

In November 1979 the Congressional Budget Office published a report on the impact of section 504 on the transit industry [U.S. Congressional Budget Office 1979]. The study estimated that making all transit vehicles accessible to wheelchairs would serve only 7 percent of the wheelchair population, at a cost of $38 per trip. The total cost to the country over 30 years was put at $6.8 billion. The alternative of providing separate demand-responsive service for the handicapped would serve 26 percent of the wheelchair population, at a cost of $7.26 per trip. The total cost would be $4.4 billion.

This did not impress those who thought section 504 conferred civil rights on the disabled: ". . . they saw funding constraints as irrelevant; rights are absolute and cannot be compromised by fiscal considerations" [Katzman 1986, p. 100].

The transit industry opposed the new rules; the American Public Transit Association (APTA) and eleven member transit systems sued to block implementation. In February 1980, the U.S. District Court in Washington ruled against the plaintiffs, but they appealed. In May 1981 the Court of Appeals reversed that decision and threw out the 1979 regulations, saying that section 504 did not give DOT sufficient authority. The court invited DOT to submit alternative justification, but by then the Reagan administration had taken office with a promise to minimize federal regulation. DOT rescinded the 1979 rules and went back to the 1976 rules and the "special efforts" approach.

In 1983 DOT issued new rules that let each transit system choose from three options: (1) It could make at least 50 percent of the buses used in the peak period accessible to wheelchairs, (2) it could offer separate paratransit service for the elderly and handicapped, or (3) it could develop some mix of the first two options. Existing subway stations did not have to be retrofitted. Further, total expenditures on the elderly and handicapped could be capped at 7.1 percent of the recipient's UMTA assistance, or 3 percent of its operating budget. Critics saw this as a loophole that would allow transit authorities to get away with doing very little for the elderly and handicapped. For example, expenditures by social service agencies could be counted toward the caps. Conceivably a transit authority could satisfy the rules without doing anything. These rules became final in 1986.

It was first expected that most cities would choose to provide special services for the elderly and handicapped. However, some large cities opted to make half of their bus fleets accessible to wheelchairs. In Seattle, for example, 75 percent of the 1000-bus fleet was equipped with wheelchair lifts. According to a 1990 survey by APTA, 18 percent of transit systems offered only accessible fixed-route service, 44 percent provided only paratransit service, and 38 percent used a combination [Bellucci 1990].

Activists among the disabled continued to press their cause through the 1980s. Since existing law was vague and DOT regulations had changed course several times, activists sought legislation that would state requirements in specific terms and limit the scope of administrative interpretation. Congress was receptive, and the Bush administration supported their efforts.

In 1990 Congress passed the Americans with Disabilities Act (ADA) with overwhelming majorities. The law stipulated the following: (1) All new buses and rail vehicles ordered after August 26, 1990, must be accessible to disabled persons, including those in wheelchairs. (2) Existing rail systems must have one accessible car per train by July 26, 1995. (3) All new bus and rail stations must be accessible. (4) Existing key stations in rail systems must be made accessible by July 26, 1993, unless an extension is granted. (5) Transit authorities must offer comparable paratransit services to disabled persons who cannot use fixed-route services.

The last provision has caused the most concern. It means that it is not sufficient to make fixed-route services accessible. Under regulations issued by DOT in 1991, any fixed-route transit system must provide paratransit service to origins and destinations within corridors $3/4$-mile wide on each side of a bus route. For rail systems, the service area consists of circles with a $3/4$-mile radius around each station. The service must operate the same hours and days as the fixed-route service.

Individuals are eligible if they are unable to board, ride, or disembark from the fixed-route vehicle, or if they are unable to get to the boarding location or from the disembarking location to their destination. There can be no restrictions based on trip purpose (e.g., priority cannot be given to work trips). Service cannot be denied because of capacity constraints, and there can be no waiting lists. Service must be provided if requested any time the previous day. Fares cannot exceed twice the fare for a similar fixed-route trip.

Transit agencies were required to submit plans to meet the paratransit requirement by January 26, 1992, and to begin implementing them immediately. Full implementation must be achieved by January 1997. However, the law has a loophole by which DOT can grant waivers if the rule would impose an undue financial burden. For further details about ADA, see Simon [1993].

It is uncertain at this point how great the financial impact will be on the transit industry. Some officials of small bus systems have claimed that the requirements will force them to go out of business. DOT projected that the cost of meeting all ADA targets would range between $850 million and $1.3 billion per year. The largest part of this cost would be for complementary paratransit, estimated to range from $590 million to $940 million annually.

WOMEN

Since the 1970s, there has been concern about the travel problems of women. In 1978, the Department of Transportation sponsored a Conference on Women's Travel Issues that focused attention on this topic [Rosenbloom 1978]. This concern no doubt reflects the growth of feminism to some extent, but more important, it recognizes that social and economic trends have overturned traditional notions about family structure and travel behavior.

Perhaps women who are homemakers do not need to travel as much as others, but a shrinking proportion of women have this as their primary role. More and more women work outside the home: Participation of working-age women in the labor force increased from 34 percent in 1950 to 57 percent in 1990, and it is expected to go higher. There has been a large increase in families with two wage earners. Another persistent trend is the growth of female-headed households.

According to Fox [1983], empirical studies have shown that women have the characteristics of a transportation-disadvantaged group: (1) They make fewer trips per day than men. (2) Their trips are shorter in length than those of men, especially work trips (an average distance of 11 miles for men versus 7 miles for women). (3) Women use transit more than men (almost twice as much for work trips). (4) Women take less time per trip, another indication that their trips are shorter.

Data from the 1980 Census suggest a continuation of culturally based gender roles: The man drives, and the woman rides. Table 13-3 shows the percentage of females

TABLE 13-3
PERCENTAGE OF FEMALES AMONG PERSONS USING DIFFERENT MODES FOR THE JOURNEY TO WORK, IN SELECTED SMSAs, 1980

SMSA	All modes	Drive alone	Car pool	Transit
Northeast				
Boston	45.35	39.72	50.35	56.41
Buffalo	42.03	37.00	49.05	63.00
Philadelphia	42.15	37.39	45.78	54.96
Pittsburgh	40.30	34.23	43.65	59.25
Midwest				
Chicago	42.98	37.25	49.07	52.85
Cleveland	42.47	37.45	49.53	59.40
Detroit	41.65	39.35	45.96	58.27
St. Louis	43.37	40.28	47.54	60.37
South				
Atlanta	44.09	41.61	47.38	59.92
Baltimore	42.75	39.03	45.72	58.02
New Orleans	40.93	36.80	43.55	60.82
San Antonio	40.78	38.59	46.84	58.64
West				
Denver	42.90	40.72	45.75	55.01
Los Angeles	42.72	40.14	47.39	57.77
San Francisco	43.73	40.89	46.42	52.62
Seattle	41.91	39.08	43.50	56.18

Source: 1980 Census.

among those using the major travel modes to get to work. Women were least likely to drive alone, more likely to carpool, and most likely to ride transit. A majority of transit riders were female in all the cities listed, although women consistently represented only 40 to 45 percent of all commuters.

Following are some explanations offered for these facts:

1 If a family has only one car, the man has first call on it and takes it to reach his job. The woman must rely on transit or walking. In part this may be because the man usually earns a higher income, but it also reflects traditional gender roles. Although the percentage of women who have driver's licenses has been increasing, it is still lower than that of men. When a man and a woman travel together, more often the man drives.

2 When both spouses work, the typical sequence of choices is this: (*a*) The man takes a job. (*b*) They find a residence convenient for the man's journey to work. (*c*) The woman looks for a job. Unless they have two cars, this limits the woman's job opportunities to places accessible by transit or walking. Even if the woman has a car, she may feel it necessary to stay close to home. Having a smaller choice of jobs contributes to the fact that women have lower incomes.

3 Even if the woman works outside the home, she still performs most of the duties of a homemaker. Summarizing the results of a survey in Toronto, Michelson reported, "The fulfillment of multiple responsibilities on the part of employed women was largely done without significant adjustment and help from other family members. Husbands of women with full-time jobs participated in more household activities than other males in the sample, but in no way approached equality in household division of labor" [1983, p. x].

In particular, the woman usually carries the major responsibility for the children. A sizable proportion of women's trips are made to take young children to day care or older children to school and other activities. The woman is chauffeur much more than the man. Rosenbloom [1987] uncovered a striking fact in a study of working women in Austin, Texas: If a child is sick and one parent must stay home, the mother is four times as likely as the father to be the one who misses work.

In effect, the working wife has two jobs. She cleans the house, does the laundry, cooks the meals. Shopping is also a traditional responsibility of women, and surveys show that women do spend much more time in shopping trips. The outcome is that women have less time than men for discretionary travel. The difference is very marked on weekends, when women are more likely to do shopping and errands; men are more apt to take social and recreational trips.

Aggravating the situation is the popularity of the suburbs, where low densities make walking arduous, transit service is usually poor, and zoning practices isolate most residences from other types of land use. Many young people live in the central city until they have children; they then move to the suburbs where the environment is supposedly better for raising children. Many working women would be better off if they lived in the central city.

Obviously these problems reflect the fact that women have lower status in U.S. society. A revolution in gender roles does not seem imminent; in the meantime, here are some measures suggested by Fox [1983] to improve the mobility of women:

Flexible Working Hours This would permit women to reduce or reorganize the hours they must spend at their jobs so they could use midday hours for shopping, child care, or recreation. Working a 4-day week would also help.

Longer Hours for Businesses and Public Facilities If these places were open evenings and weekends, women would have more opportunity to benefit. This has been the trend among shopping centers and supermarkets, but many other places such as banks and post offices still have limited hours.

Land-Use Changes Many women live in homogeneous residential areas where retail and public facilities can be reached only by automobile. There could be more mixing of activities so homes would not be so isolated. Some zoning ordinances permit *planned unit developments,* where office and retail uses are integrated with housing. Another problem is that many suburban jobs are in office and industrial parks that are segregated from other activities. If homes and workplaces were intermixed, it could reduce the journey to work.

Better Transit Service This might involve shorter headways, longer hours of service, and more routes in the suburbs. Paratransit might assist women living in low-density suburban areas. While transit does not offer as high accessibility as the automobile, many women will continue to need it.

Strong interest continues in meeting the travel needs of women and the other special groups discussed above. Although the level of militancy about these issues has declined somewhat in recent years, there is a widespread realization that these are pervasive problems that should be addressed in transportation planning.

QUESTIONS

1 Have recent transit improvements been of more benefit to the poor or the rich? Why is an improvement in bus service more likely to benefit the poor than the building of new rail lines?
2 One of the travel problems of many poor people is that they live in the inner city, while most new blue-collar jobs are now located in the suburbs. What can be done to remedy this?
3 What do you think of the idea of providing every poor family in the country with a small, inexpensive automobile?
4 Increasingly older people in the United States live in the suburbs and drive cars. Is there a need for any kind of public transportation to serve them?
5 There has long been a dispute over two approaches to providing transit service to the disabled: making all transit services accessible to this group, or offering special (and separate) services for them. Which approach do you think is better?
6 Do you think the travel needs of women deserve special attention? Is the U.S. transportation system biased against women? Will this change in the future?

REFERENCES

Bellucci, Angela: "Accessibility at a Price," *Mass Transit,* vol. 17, no. 3 (March 1990), pp. 24–26.

Falcocchio, John C., and Edmund J. Cantilli: *Transportation and the Disadvantaged: The Poor, the Young, the Elderly, the Handicapped* (Lexington, MA: D.C. Heath, 1974).

Fielding, Gordon J.: "Transportation for the Handicapped: The Politics of Full Accessibility," *Transportation Quarterly,* vol. 36, no. 2 (April 1982), pp. 269–282.

Fox, Marion B.: "Working Women and Travel: The Access of Women to Work and Community Facilities," *Journal of the American Planning Association,* vol. 49, no. 2 (Spring 1983), pp. 156–170.

Governor's Commission on the Los Angeles Riots: *Violence in the City—An End or a Beginning?* (Los Angeles: Governor's Commission on the Los Angeles Riots, 1965).

Hilton, George W.: *Federal Transit Subsidies: The Urban Mass Transportation Assistance Program* (Washington: American Enterprise Institute for Public Policy Research, 1974).

Hoel, Lester A., Eugene D. Perle, Karel J. Kansky, Alfred A. Kuehn, Ervin S. Roszner, and Hugh P. Nesbitt: *Latent Demand for Urban Transportation* (Pittsburgh: Transportation Research Institute, Carnegie-Mellon University, 1968).

Katzman, Robert A.: *Institutional Disability: The Saga of Transportation Policy for the Disabled* (Washington: The Brookings Institution, 1986).

Lee, Bumjung, John C. Falcocchio, and Edmund J. Cantilli: "Taxicab Usage in New York City Poverty Areas," *Highway Research Record,* no. 403 (1972), pp. 1–5.

Michelson, William: *The Impact of Changing Women's Roles on Transportation Needs and Usage* (Irvine: Institute of Transportation Studies and Program in Social Ecology, University of California, Irvine, 1983).

Middendorf, D. P., K. W. Heathington, F. J. Wegmann, M. W. Redford, A. Chatterjee, and T. L. Bell: *Cost-Effectiveness of Transportation Services for Handicapped Persons: Research Report,* National Cooperative Highway Research Program Report 261 (Washington: Transportation Research Board, 1983).

Murin, William J.: *Mass Transit Policy Planning* (Lexington, MA: D.C. Heath, 1971).

Myers, Sumner: "Personal Transportation for the Poor," *Traffic Quarterly,* vol. 24, no. 2 (April 1970), pp. 191–206.

Ornati, Oscar A., James W. Whittaker, and Richard Solomon: *Transportation Needs of the Poor: A Case Study of New York City* (New York: Praeger, 1969).

Paaswell, Robert E., and Wilfred W. Recker: *Problems of the Carless* (New York: Praeger, 1978).

Rosenbloom, Sandra, ed.: *Women's Travel Issues: Research Needs and Priorities* (Washington: Department of Transportation, 1978).

————: "Federal Policies to Increase the Mobility of the Elderly and the Handicapped," *Journal of American Planning Association,* vol. 48, no. 3 (Summer 1982), pp. 335–350.

————: "The Impact of Growing Children on Their Parents' Travel Behavior: A Comparative Analysis," *Transportation Research Record,* no. 1135 (1987), pp. 17–25.

———— and David Warren: "Comparison of Two Brokerages: Lessons to Be Learned from Houston and Pittsburgh," *Transportation Research Record,* no. 830 (1981), pp. 7–15.

Schreffler, Eric N.: "Transportation Brokerage: Key Findings from Crosscutting Analysis," *Transportation Research Record,* no. 1018 (1985), pp. 47–54.

Simon, Rosalyn M.: "Americans with Disabilities Act of 1990: Mandate for Full Accessibility," *TR News,* no. 168 (September-October 1993), pp. 17–23.

Spear, Bruce D.: "User-Side Subsidies: Delivering Special-Needs Transportation through Private Providers," *Transportation Research Record,* no. 850 (1982), pp. 13–18.

Starks, Jane K.: "Mobility Training for the Retarded: An Issue of Public Transit Accessibility," *Transportation Research Record,* no. 830 (1981), pp. 21–25.

————: "Overview of the Transportation Demand of Mentally Retarded Persons," *Transportation Research Record,* no. 1098 (1986), pp. 1–8.

————, Catie Simpson, and Heather Menninger: "Mobility Training Program: Methods and Costs of Teaching Mentally Retarded Persons to Ride Public Mass Transit in Sacramento," *Transportation Research Record,* no. 973 (1984), pp. 52–59.

Teal, Roger F.: "Public Transit Service Contracting: A Status Report," *Transportation Quarterly,* vol. 42, no. 2 (April 1988), pp. 207–222.

U.S. Congressional Budget Office: *Urban Transportation for Handicapped Persons: Alternative Federal Approaches* (Washington: U.S. Congressional Budget Office, 1979).

Wachs, Martin: *Transportation for the Elderly: Changing Lifestyles, Changing Needs* (Berkeley: University of California Press, 1979).

Wohl, Martin: "Equity Considerations of Urban Transportation Planning," in Andrew Hamer, ed., *Out of Cars/Into Transit: The Urban Transportation Planning Crisis* (Atlanta: School of Business Administration, Georgia State University, 1976), pp. 83–91.

14

ESTIMATING SYSTEM COSTS

Twenty years ago it was common to downplay the role of money and give costs low priority in decision making. Environmental values were regarded as priceless, and millions of dollars might be spent to save the habitat of an endangered creature. Attitudes have changed in recent years, and decision makers are now very dollar-conscious. It is unlikely that anyone will dispute the claim that costs are important.

The bottom line in evaluating any transit proposal is the comparison of total returns with total costs. Estimating costs is a critical step in the process. Underestimating costs is common and can lead to serious trouble in the future. There is a bias because the agency making a transit proposal usually prepares the cost estimates. It is tempting to underestimate costs since this will make the project more attractive politically.

Evaluation of a public project involves both an economic decision and a financial decision, which are different. An economic decision seeks efficient use of resources; the goal is to maximize the net social gain. The key question is: Is it worthwhile to society to do this? Benefit/cost analysis and cost-effectiveness analysis are popular methods for determining this.

A financial decision concerns actual cash flows and involves the comparison of revenues and expenditures. They key question is: Will it pay for itself? If not, money must come from other sources, or the project will be forgone.

Usually a private firm cares about only the financial decision, although sometimes intangible factors play a role. Both kinds of decisions are important in the public sector. A project may be economically beneficial but not self-supporting. Then money must be found elsewhere, often from taxes on the general public.

A classic case of conflict between the two kinds of decisions was described by M. E. Beesley [1973]. In 1962 he and C. D. Foster presented a benefit/cost analysis of the Victoria Line, a proposed addition to the London Underground. It showed that the project was economically justified. A critical factor was that 52 percent of the benefits would accrue to travelers who would *not* use the line, including motorists who would benefit from reduced street congestion because other motorists would switch to transit.

The researchers assumed that fares would remain the same and estimated that the project would increase the system's operating deficit. Because of this, the London Transport Executive proposed to raise fares throughout the system. Beesley and Foster made another study, assuming the higher fares, which showed that ridership would decrease to the point where the Victoria Line would no longer be a socially desirable investment. However, the line was built and opened in 1969.

The following sections discuss major categories of costs.

CONSTRUCTION COSTS

This is the most variable cost category because it depends greatly on the particular sites chosen. Average costs vary from city to city because of differences in wage and price levels, but there is even more variation within a single city, for it can cost far more to build in one location than in another.

According to Cambridge Systematics, Inc. [1992], recent costs for four heavy rail lines ranged from $64 million per mile in Miami to $132 million per mile in Washington, D.C. (in 1988 dollars). Underground construction is much more expensive; the Miami project had none. For five light rail projects, the costs ranged from $10.3 million per mile in Sacramento to $36.6 million per mile in Los Angeles (in 1990 dollars). The Sacramento figure is probably lowest because more than half of the route had a single track.

Two exclusive busways were built in Pittsburgh. The South Busway cost $6.8 million per mile; the East Busway, $13.7 million per mile. Costs of six high-occupancy vehicle (HOV) lane projects ranged from $2.8 million per mile in Houston to $5.1 million per mile in Los Angeles.

Components

The major components of construction cost are as follows:

Land Acquisition   Costs can vary greatly within a single city. Some right-of-way is free, such as streets, alleys, and parks, because it is already in the public domain. Tunnels and elevated structures often use such right-of-way and require no land acquisition. A route that cuts diagonally through a block usually requires the taking of private property.

In several cases, surplus railroad tracks have been purchased for very little (as in San Diego). Land in a freeway right-of-way is relatively cheap because most of the cost is charged to the highway lanes. Typically a freeway requires the taking of a strip that is a whole city block wide, and the transit facility does not require additional land.

Guideway for the Vehicles   The elements of this are as follows:

1 Site preparation. This includes the clearing of land, excavation, and relocation of utilities. Shallow tunnels usually interfere with underground utility lines and involve extra costs, while deep tunnels go below utilities.

2 Structures such as tunnel walls, bridges, and viaducts.

3 Roadbed and track (for rail) or pavement (for bus).

4 Signals and control system (for rail).

5 Power transmission (for rail).

6 Ventilation in tunnels. This is a major problem for buses because of the exhaust from diesel engines. Hence bus tunnels are uncommon and usually very short. Seattle built a bus tunnel over a mile long, but the buses switch to electric power when they enter it. Subways for rail vehicles are self-ventilating to some extent because of the pistonlike action of trains, but mechanical ventilation may be necessary.

7 Drainage to remove water. This is very important in tunnels, which may be constructed below the water table.

Stations   The cost of stations depends on the length and height of platforms. The platform length sets a maximum length on trains (eight-car trains cannot be used if the platforms are long enough for only six cars). Hence this is a key decision made in planning a rail system. The method of fare collection also affects the design and cost of stations. Heavy rail systems usually have barriers to separate those who have paid their fares from those who have not. Light rail lines use self-service fare collection and have no barriers.

Storage Yards and Maintenance Facilities   There must be a place to store vehicles at night and shops to service the vehicles. An addition to an existing system may not call for such facilities, but a new system will. It is best to locate these facilities at the terminal of a line to minimize deadheading, but it is not always possible.

Parking Facilities at Stations   Most rail lines (as well as some express bus routes) depend on park-and-ride travelers for a large portion of their patronage. Parking could be left to private enterprise, but it is usual for a transit authority to construct such facilities as part of a new line.

Construction cost depends greatly on the vertical alignment of the guideway. In general, building at ground level is cheapest, an elevated structure is more expensive, and a tunnel is the most expensive. The cost of tunneling depends on the engineering method used. Usually the cheapest approach is to cut and cover: A trench is excavated, the tunnel structure is built, and then the tunnel is covered over. However, this causes considerable disruption during the construction period if the tunnel is located under a street.

Boring through rock avoids this problem and has become cheaper with technological advances, but usually it still costs more than the cut-and-cover method. Underwater tunnels are expensive and require innovative engineering. The BART tunnel under San Francisco Bay was made of prefabricated concrete sections that were floated into place and sunk to the bottom.

Cost Overruns

Cost overruns have persistently troubled transit projects and generated unfavorable publicity. For example, the $792 million bond issue that voters approved for BART turned out to be inadequate; federal and state governments had to come up with additional funds.

According to Merewitz [1973], an economics professor at the University of California, Berkeley, the ability to estimate costs accurately depends on experience with similar types of construction. He assembled data on a large number of public works projects and found that the record for rapid transit was better than for other major projects of an ad hoc nature (such as airports). Table 14-1 summarizes his findings. The best records were for highways and water resources projects; in both cases the same type of facility is built over and over. BART's cost overrun (45 percent as of 1971) was slightly below the average for rapid transit projects.

Merewitz identified the following causes of overruns:

1 General inflation greater than expected (project estimates include an allowance for inflation, but it may not be enough).

2 Unanticipated price increases for specific inputs, such as electricity or the wages of skilled workers. Certain prices may rise much more quickly than standard price indices, which are averages.

3 Delays. When capital is tied up, interest must be paid, whether or not the capital is productive. BART was delayed several years by a lawsuit.

4 Changes in design, which result in some work being wasted or more expensive things being added.

5 Poor management or poor estimation of costs.

As discussed in Chapter 5, Pickrell [1989] analyzed ten rail transit projects and found that the capital outlay had been underestimated in every case. He believed that the system for distributing federal capital grants poses incentives to make cost estimates unrealistically low: Lower cost makes proposals seem more cost-effective, and the fed-

TABLE 14-1
SUMMARY OF COST ESTIMATION EXPERIENCE

Type of project	Number of projects	Ratio of actual to estimated cost
Highway	49	1.26
Water resources	49	1.38
Rapid transit	17	1.54
Building	59	1.63
Ad hoc	15	2.14
Grand mean	189	1.59

Source: Leonard Merewitz, "How Do Urban Rapid Transit Projects Compare in Cost Estimating Experience?" *Proceedings of the International Conference on Transportation Research,* Bruges, Belgium, June 1973. (Chicago: Transportation Research Forum, 1974.)

eral government pays a large share of overruns. In some cases, local residents must vote on proposals, and lower cost makes the proposals more attractive politically.

Menendez [1993] made a thorough analysis of the problem, including case studies of the light rail projects in Buffalo and San Jose and a proposed suburban rail service in Boston. He found that there is some room for improvement in the technical process of cost estimating and that there should be greater use of sensitivity analysis and computer-based information systems. But the main problem is political: A proposed project (such as a rail line) garners support from politicians, interest groups, and the public, and only then are technical studies undertaken. There is considerable pressure to make sure that the technical work justifies the project to which people are already committed. Cost estimates tend to be biased to meet the criteria of funding agencies at the federal and state levels. After approval, there are often cost-raising design changes to meet objections that were not considered in the early planning.

VEHICLE COSTS

Heavy Rail

Rail transit cars are custom-made to fit local specifications, so there is considerable variation in the costs. New York City often pays higher prices because it demands stronger and heavier materials than other cities and because it gets special features to combat vandalism and graffiti. In the past decade, the price of a heavy railcar has usually exceeded $1 million. Table 14-2 lists recent purchases, including the price per car and the manufacturer.

BART raised prices to a new level when it ordered its C car in 1982. The C car can be used as either a lead car or a midtrain car, unlike the specialized A and B cars that

TABLE 14-2
RECENT PURCHASES OF HEAVY RAILCARS

Date	Number	Price per car, $	Purchaser	Manufacturer
September 1982	50	1,136,000	Atlanta	Hitachi/C. Itoh
October 1982	150	1,522,000	San Francisco	Alsthom Atlantique
November 1982	225	1,180,000	New York City (MTA)	Westinghouse-Amrail
April 1984	58	980,000	Boston	UTDC
November 1984	95	1,000,000	New York City (PATH)	Nissho Iwai & Kawasaki
1987	200	1,150,000	New York City (MTA)	Kawasaki
May 1989	100	1,220,000	Washington	Breda
February 1990	257	848,000	Chicago	Morrison Knudsen
December 1990	86	1,540,000	Boston	Bombardier
March 1992	80	1,770,000	San Francisco	Morrison Knudsen
June 1994	42	2,017,000	Los Angeles	Breda

FIGURE 14-1
BART railcars. The C car (on the left) was the first transit railcar to cost more than $1.5 million apiece. The original BART fleet consisted of the A car (on the right), which contained operating controls, and the B car, which did not. The C car can be used either as the lead car or in the middle of a train. (*Source:* American Public Transit Association.)

BART had previously (see Figure 14-1). The contract for 150 cars, costing $1,522,000 each, went to a subsidiary of Alsthom Atlantique of France. The cars were assembled in California to meet the Buy America requirements.

UMTA began a railcar cost containment program in 1988. Administrator Alfred A. DelliBovi noted that the average cost of a railcar had quadrupled since 1972 and cited the BART C cars as an example of runaway costs. Technical study grants were given to several transit agencies to develop specifications and bidding procedures that would result in lower-priced cars. A study in Atlanta pinpointed potential cost savings of $69,260 per car, which would be a small percentage of the total cost.

Light Rail

One motive for developing the Standard Light Rail Vehicle in the early 1970s was to lower costs through mass production. In 1972, Boeing-Vertol submitted low bids of $293,422 per car to Boston and $316,616 per car to San Francisco [Silien and Mora 1975]. These figures were way below the low bid of $473,000 per unit that San Francisco had received in 1971 (and rejected). However, it eventually cost Boeing-Vertol about $550,000 to manufacture each car. The company lost a great deal of money on the orders and subsequently withdrew from the business.

The Standard Light Rail Vehicle is no longer made, and hopes for relatively inexpensive cars have faded. Many recent orders for light rail transit (LRT) vehicles have exceeded $2 million per unit. Generally the cost of a light railcar is greater than that of a heavy railcar, partly because most light railcars are articulated and have greater seating capacity.

Table 14-3 lists recent orders for light railcars. All the manufacturers are foreign: Siemens, and Duewag are German; ABB Traction is Swedish; Breda is Italian; the other firms are Japanese.

Bus

A transit bus is a more standardized product than a railcar, but there is still variation in local specifications. You cannot actually purchase a bus "off the shelf." There was more uniformity when General Motors dominated the U.S. market; now there is competition among several firms, which offer some different features. Most buses are 40 feet long, but some cities order smaller ones that are 35 feet long.

Recently the base price for a 40-foot bus has run from $150,000 to $175,000. Optional equipment—such as automatic transmission, power steering, air conditioning, and wheelchair lifts—adds many thousands of dollars. Table 14-4 itemizes some recent purchases of conventional buses.

There has been a trend toward larger buses, mostly for use in peak periods. This increases the productivity of drivers, and the savings in operating costs can justify the higher initial cost. Double-decker buses are still the rule in Great Britain, but few have been used in the United States. More common are articulated buses, which bend in the middle to go around corners. They have long been used in Europe, and several U.S.

TABLE 14-3
RECENT PURCHASES OF LIGHT RAILCARS

Date	Number	Price per car, $	Purchaser	Manufacturer
March 1986	50	1,200,000	Boston	Kinki Sharyo and C. Itoh
April 1987	54	1,170,000	Los Angeles	Sumitomo and Nippon Sharyo
September 1987	20	1,050,000	San Diego	Siemens
Late 1988	31	1,465,000	St. Louis	Siemens
June 1989	35	1,743,000	Baltimore	ABB Traction
July 1991	75	1,627,000	San Diego	Duewag
January 1992	35	2,345,000	San Francisco	Breda
January 1992	8	1,600,000	Denver	Siemens Duewag
October 1992	15	2,900,000	Los Angeles	Sumitomo
December 1992	40	2,625,000	Dallas	Kinki Sharyo
May 1993	37	2,340,500	Portland	Siemens Duewag
August 1993	72	2,708,000	Los Angeles	Siemens Duewag

TABLE 14-4
RECENT PURCHASES OF BUSES

Date	Number	Price per bus, $	Purchaser	Manufacturer
April 1987	94	156,400	Honolulu	Saab-Scania
June 1988	491	174,284	Chicago	Transport Mfg. Corp.
October 1988	150	180,000	Los Angeles	Flxible Corp.
November 1988	200	175,000	Boston	Transport Mfg. Corp.
May 1989	77	148,182	Cleveland	Transport Mfg. Corp.
January 1990	103	162,500	Los Angeles	Transport Mfg. Corp.
January 1990	120	201,726	Pittsburgh	Bus Industries of America
February 1990	79	189,639	El Paso	Transport Mfg. Corp.
February 1990	174	193,000	Washington	Flxible Corp.
April 1990	300	193,000	Houston	Ikarus
July 1991	162	228,000	Dallas	Motor Coach Industries
April 1994	250	217,600	Boston	Transport Mfg. Corp.

cities purchased them in the 1980s. These buses contain 70 to 75 seats, whereas a standard bus has 45 to 55 seats. The cost currently ranges from $200,000 to $300,000 per vehicle.

The most expensive buses ever built were purchased by Seattle for use in its downtown bus tunnel, which opened in 1990. An order for 236 buses, at $576,300 each, was placed with Breda Costruzioni Ferroviarie of Italy in 1986. The buses have both diesel and electric motors; they use the latter when running in the tunnel, to eliminate exhaust.

Estimating Vehicle Needs

In preparing a transit proposal, it is necessary to estimate the number of vehicles required. This consists of the number needed in the peak period plus an allowance for spares (usually 15 to 20 percent), because some vehicles are always out of service for repairs or routine maintenance.

The peak-period need for each route depends on headway and the time it takes each vehicle to make a round trip. Usually headways are shorter during the peak period, and the round trip takes longer because of congestion (this is even true on rail lines because it takes longer to load and unload passengers).

The number of vehicles needed on a route can be calculated by the ratio of round-trip time to headway. For example, suppose that during the peak period, the round trip time on a bus route is 60 minutes and the headway is 10 minutes. Then $60/10 = 6$ buses are needed. Repeat this calculation for each route, and sum the results to find the total number of buses needed.

During the off-peak period, the round-trip time might be 45 minutes, and the headway, 15 minutes. Then only $45/15 = 3$ buses are needed. This illustrates why the peak period determines fleet size and the off-peak period is irrelevant.

OPERATING COSTS

Section 15 Requirements

Transit systems used to follow different accounting formats, and it was difficult to compile uniform data. That problem was solved by section 15 of the Urban Mass Transportation Act, which imposed a uniform accounting system on all agencies that receive federal operating aid. It was added to the act in 1974, but did not take effect until the 1978–1979 fiscal year. FTA compiles the annual reports from across the country and publishes a summary, which is a valuable source of data for research. It includes performance indicators so that transit managers can determine how their operations compare with others.

The system uses a matrix approach for reporting expenses. Operators fill in tables in which each cost is classified on two dimensions: expense object class and function. The expense object classes include salaries and wages, fringe benefits, services, fuels and lubricants, tires and tubes, other materials and supplies, utilities, and casualty and liability costs. The four functions are vehicle operations, vehicle maintenance, nonvehicle maintenance, and general administration. Agencies that operate more than one mode file separate reports for each mode.

Besides costs, operators must submit data on revenues, classified by source, and operating characteristics such as accidents and energy consumption. Operators also report service supplied (measured in vehicle-miles and vehicle-hours) and service consumed (measured in passenger trips and passenger-miles traveled). Some transit systems have electronic systems that routinely record these data, but most do not. To comply with the requirements, they conduct an annual sample survey and make estimates of passenger trips and miles traveled.

Recent Trends in Costs

Transit operating costs have increased greatly in the past 30 years and sometimes appear to be out of control. Since fare revenues have risen at a much slower rate, there have been recurrent financial crises, and a few systems have suspended service temporarily. This is not a new situation for transit; costs also rose sharply after World War I, causing a spate of bankruptcies. Today most systems are publicly owned and will not go out of business, but they seem to require ever-growing amounts of subsidy.

According to a study by Pickrell [1983], from 1960 to 1980 the operating expense per seat-mile in bus service went up 58 percent in constant dollars (that is, 58 percent more than general inflation). Rising unit costs for labor were responsible for more than three-quarters of the increase; higher fuel costs accounted for most of the remainder. The average annual compensation per transit employee (in constant 1980 dollars) rose from $14,560 in 1960 to $25,930 in 1980, an increase of 78 percent.

Furthermore, Pickrell found that labor productivity increased by only 10 percent during this period, from 564,400 annual seat-miles per employee in 1960 to 620,800 in

1980. Most of the gain resulted from the trend to larger buses with more seats. Productivity actually declined from 1970 to 1980.

Ortner and Wachs [1979] made case studies of four large transit systems and found that both system efficiency (vehicle-miles of service per dollar) and effectiveness (passengers per dollar) consistently declined in the 1960s and 1970s. Direct labor costs rose considerably, but expenditures on pensions and fringe benefits increased more than any other type of cost. Power and fuel costs went up, but they accounted for less than 5 percent of total costs.

Labor accounts for an overwhelming majority of operating costs. Table 14-5 summarizes operating expenses for all U.S. transit services in 1992; it shows that salaries and wages represented 46.7 percent of the total, and fringe benefits, 26.5 percent. Wage rates vary greatly from city to city. Generally they are higher in large cities, partly because the cost of living is higher and partly because the unions are stronger. A strike threat is taken more seriously in a city where many people depend on transit. There are unions in all large cities, but some small cities do not have them.

Labor unions have had a major impact, as discussed in Chapter 4. The New York City transit strike in 1966 resulted in large wage increases and initiated a period of rapidly rising labor costs. Since pattern bargaining is the rule in the industry, wage hikes tend to spread from city to city. It is claimed that section 13(c), the labor protection clause, gives the unions a strong weapon to use in obtaining higher wages and greater benefits.

Another reason for declining performance is that many transit systems have increased the vehicle-miles of service by extending bus routes into suburban areas. Typically the new routes attract light passenger loads, causing low productivity that drags down the systemwide averages. Further, public transit officials are often unwilling to

TABLE 14-5
TRANSIT OPERATING EXPENSE FOR 1992
(All Transit Services in the United States)

Type of cost	Amount ($ thousands)	Percent
Salaries and wages	7,777,600	46.72
Fringe benefits	4,404,700	26.46
Services	934,800	5.62
Fuels and lubricants	453,900	2.73
Materials and supplies	1,109,300	6.66
Utilities	615,200	3.70
Casualty and liability costs	556,200	3.34
Purchased transportation	1,473,900	8.85
Other	(679,900)	−4.08
Total	16,645,700	100.00

Source: Transit Fact Book, 1993 edition (Washington: American Public Transit Association, 1993), table 15.

reduce or eliminate service on routes with low ridership. While cost-conscious private managers readily cut out money-losing operations, public agencies are subject to political pressure or have social objectives to meet as well as economic ones.

It is believed that subsidies contribute to higher costs by distorting the decisions of transit officials. Costs have indeed escalated rapidly since federal operating subsidies were enacted in 1974. It is argued that there is little incentive for management to be efficient when deficits are covered by subsidies. Purportedly transit authority boards yield easily to union demands for large increases in wages and benefits. Federal subsidies are allocated by formulas that do not include any measures of performance or efficiency.

This rationale was given in the Reagan administration's (unsuccessful) attempt to end federal operating subsidies. However, the U.S. government is not the major source of subsidies. According to Pucher [1982], the federal government provided only 30 percent of transit subsidies in 1980. State governments provided 23 percent, and 47 percent came from local sources. Many metropolitan areas have adopted taxes earmarked for transit (especially sales taxes). Sometimes a new tax has created a windfall for the transit authority, which suddenly gets more money than it knows what to do with.

Pucher performed multiple regression analysis on data from 86 bus systems across the country. He found a very strong relationship between cost per bus-hour and federal operating subsidy, and a weaker but still significant relationship between cost per bus-hour and the state operating subsidy. He also found that the existence of dedicated state or local funding was associated with higher costs.

This situation has given ammunition to people who want to end subsidies for transit. Pucher did not propose to stop subsidies, but rather to rationalize them by basing grants on measures of productivity and efficiency.

There is debate among scholars on whether there are economies of scale in bus operations [Berechman and Giuliano 1985]. Early studies mostly showed that there are constant returns to scale, but more recent work has indicated that increasing returns exist in many cases (meaning that the unit cost goes down as output goes up). Berechman and Giuliano concluded that the results depend on the theoretical base, the analytical model used, and the selection of data.

It is believed that there are increasing returns to scale in rail systems for two reasons: (1) Whenever there is large capital investment in fixed facilities, unit costs will decrease as the facilities are used more. (2) Train length can be varied in response to demand. Since a train crew is the same regardless of train length, longer trains are more economical.

Peak versus Off-Peak Periods

Split shifts greatly increase labor costs. The marginal operating cost per passenger is higher in the peak period because extra workers are hired to handle the demand. Often these workers receive premiums for split shifts or guaranteed minimum pay. Economists believe differential pricing by time of day is desirable, as will be discussed in the next chapter.

Another approach to the problem is to use *part-time operators* (PTOs) in the peak periods. The unions strongly resisted this, and traditionally labor contracts prohibited it. In 1971, the Seattle Metro became the first large transit agency to win the right to use part-timers. This began a trend that accelerated in the 1980s. In many cases, management gave concessions in the form of better wages and benefits in exchange for permission to use PTOs. This of course offset the potential cost savings.

The Massachusetts Bay Transportation Authority (MBTA), which serves Boston, started hiring part-timers in 1982 after the state legislature passed a law permitting it to do so regardless of previous agreements with the unions. According to Attanucci et al. [1984], this produced cost savings of $5.6 million per year. There were some problems, though: Accident rates were higher among the part-time operators, as were absenteeism and turnover.

Wells et al. [1985] made a nationwide survey for UMTA in 1984 and found that 77 percent of the transit agencies in the sample were permitted to use part-time operators. The authors concluded that "the use of PTOs is widely regarded as a means of reducing the cost of providing peak-period transit service" [p. 48]. However, Chomitz et al. [1985] found in five case studies that overall system cost savings were generally less than 10 percent. They also learned that part-timers consistently have lower absentee rates than full-time workers (perhaps because often part-timers do not receive sick pay). The evidence on accident rates was inconclusive.

Estimating Operating Costs

Most transit planners use simple mathematical models to estimate operating costs. Most of the models were developed for bus systems because they are more common than rail systems. Data are assembled for individual routes or, in larger systems, divisions consisting of groups of routes. The models are used to assess the impact of making incremental changes in service, such as adding or dropping routes. The models may also be used in budget forecasting and long-range planning.

There are several types of operating cost models for bus systems, as described by Cherwony et al. [1982]. The most popular takes the following form:

$$OC = A(VM) + B(VH) + C(PV) \qquad (14\text{-}1)$$

where OC = operating cost
    VM = vehicle-miles of service
    VH = vehicle-hours of service
    PV = peak-hour vehicles in service

Often values of the parameters (A, B, and C) are estimated by the unit cost approach. Major categories of costs from the agency's accounts are assigned to the variables that seem logical, and unit costs are calculated. For example, fuel, tires, parts, and maintenance of vehicles are based on vehicle-miles. Wages of operators and supervisors (plus fringe benefits) are based on vehicle-hours. Administrative and overhead costs are considered a function of system size and are based on vehicles used in the peak hour, a standard measure of size used by the FTA.

Similar models are used with more or fewer variables. Two other variables that may appear are route-miles and the number of passengers carried. The simplest model uses only one variable, which will usually be vehicle-hours (considered most important because of the scope of labor costs).

An alternative to the judgmental approach is to use multiple regression analysis, which has been done by several researchers. The variables hypothesized are usually the same as in the unit cost approach. Of course, the estimating equation calculated includes only the significant variables that emerge from the analysis.

Similar models are used to estimate the operating costs of rail systems. Following is the model recommended by Roess et al. [1977]:

$$OC = A(CM) + B(CH) + C(PV) + D(RP) \qquad (14\text{-}2)$$

where OC = operating cost
    CM = car-miles
    CH = car-hours
    PV = peak-period railcars in operation
    RP = revenue passengers

More sophisticated models have been designed in recent years to give more accurate estimates and analyze other problems (such as the impact of price increases or changes in work rules). Herzenberg [1983] and Jones [1982] developed models to estimate bus drivers' wages that took account of scheduling practice and labor contract provisions. Some models separate fixed and variable costs. Comprehensive models—such as those by Cervero [1982] or Stopher et al. [1987]—may be programmed to run on a microcomputer.

Because of concern about the higher costs of peak-period service, as discussed in the previous section, there is interest in getting an accurate allocation of operating costs between the peak period and the rest of the day. Several models were specifically designed to do this, such as those by Cherwony and Mundle [1978], Levinson [1978], and Reilly [1977].

To estimate the costs of a proposed route, values of the variables must be predicted. To do this precisely requires compiling a timetable for the route. This is routinely done for incremental changes, and computer scheduling programs like RUCUS make it easy. However, it cannot be totally accurate because the wage bill will depend on the particular persons assigned to the route (e.g., a worker with greater seniority will get higher pay).

In long-range planning, it is not usual to prepare full timetables. Approximations are used to make rough estimates. For example, the number of daily peak-period trips can be estimated by assuming the length of the period and dividing by the average headway. Multiplying this by the round-trip distance gives the number of vehicle-miles. Applying the average speed gives the number of vehicle-hours. The process is repeated for the off-peak period (probably headway and average speed would be different). If more detail is desired, separate estimates can be made for evenings, Saturdays, and Sundays.

A challenging situation arises where a new transit mode is to be introduced (such as a rail line or an exclusive busway). This is not a marginal change, and there are no existing local data. Values can be borrowed from comparable cities, but the values should be adjusted for differences in wage rates. Of course, express buses cruising at high speeds have different operating costs than ordinary buses running on city streets.

USER COSTS

User costs are borne by the passengers, rather than the operator. Hence user costs do not appear in a section 15 report or the accounts of a transit agency. But these costs are important in making an economic decision and must be included in a benefit/cost analysis.

Fares are not counted as costs in an economic analysis, although they are counted in a financial analysis. Fares are regarded as transfer payments, like taxes, that reflect political decisions on raising money rather than the consumption of resources. Another way to look at it is this: A benefit/cost analysis takes the viewpoint of society as a whole, including all consumers and producers. While the fares are costs to transit passengers, the fares are revenue to the transit agency, and the two sums balance out to zero.

Travel Time

Passengers' travel time is the major user cost included in an economic analysis. It is routinely calculated by the computer models that carry out travel demand forecasting. The components are as follows:

Travel to and from Transit Stops   This may be by automobile or walking. There have been many studies of pedestrian behavior, and it is established that the average walking speed is 3 miles per hour [Fruin 1971].

Waiting Time   The usual practice is to estimate the average waiting time of passengers at one-half the headway between buses or trains. This is actually true only under two assumptions. The first assumption is that the vehicles arrive at equal intervals; otherwise the average waiting time is larger. Since uniform arrivals are seldom achieved, the assumption leads to an underestimate, but it is probably not serious in most cases.

The second assumption is that passengers arrive randomly at a transit stop according to a uniform distribution. If arrivals are bunched just before the vehicle comes, the average waiting time is less. This implies that people know the schedule. The usual assumption is that arrivals are uniform up to a headway of 20 minutes (equivalent to an average wait of 10 minutes). With longer headways, people learn the schedule and time their arrivals.

In-Vehicle Time   This depends on the average speed of the vehicle, which in turn depends on (1) the cruising speed of the vehicle, (2) the spacing of stations, (3) acceleration and deceleration rates, and (4) station dwell time. The particulars of the operating cycle for a transit vehicle were discussed in Chapter 9. As noted, station spacing is usually more important than the maximum speed that a vehicle can attain.

Transfer Time This applies only when a traveler transfers between routes. This consists of (1) the walking time (if any) between where the person gets off and where she or he gets on (this can be substantial in large subway stations) and (2) the waiting time of one-half the headway on the second route. This assumes there is no coordination between schedules on the two routes; under the timed-transfer system, waiting time should be less.

Money Valuation of Travel Time

To combine travel time with dollar outlays in a benefit/cost analysis, time must be converted to money. This requires estimating the monetary value of an hour of travel time, since time is not a commodity explicitly traded in a market. This is an example of what economists call a *shadow price* or *imputed price*. There is a large body of literature, both theoretical and empirical, on estimating the dollar value of travel time. While some people object to the practice, no one doubts that saving time is a primary justification for most transportation improvements.

There are several approaches to estimating the value of travel time. One, called the *income*, or *productivity*, *method*, bases the value of 1 hour of travel time on the hourly wage rate. Sometimes the minimum wage is used, sometimes the average wage for manufacturing workers. The rationale is that an hour of travel time saved could be used to work another hour, and so should be valued at the wage for that hour.

This method was dissected in a classic article by Moses and Williamson [1964]. Their theoretical analysis showed that the approach is correct only if a worker is able to choose the number of hours worked and is paid by the hour. Of course, this is not the typical situation. Most people have a fixed workweek, such as 40 hours, and salaried employees are not paid more for working extra hours. Another objection to the approach is that it applies only to people who work for cash income, which excludes a large portion of the population (such as homemakers, children, and retired persons).

Another approach, which is now preferred, is the *willingness-to-pay method*. It involves empirical studies to determine what people actually pay to save travel time. It is an example of what economists call *revealed preference* methodology: Consumers reveal their values by their behavior, although they are not conscious of them and could not tell them in response to direct questions.

In such a study, some travelers must have a choice between an option that is faster and more expensive and one that is cheaper and slower. These are called *traders*; such people face a trade-off between time and money. A sample of travelers is interviewed, data are collected, and a calculation is made of how much money is paid to save a minute of travel time. Several statistical techniques have been used; they were summarized by Watson [1974, chapter 7].

Many studies have been made over the past 60 years. Hensher [1976] compiled a review of the empirical literature. Some studies have used urban locales; others have dealt with intercity travel. Many have involved route choice; the most popular type is a comparison of toll roads versus free roads. There are numerous places in the United States in which an automobile trip can be made on either a turnpike or a free highway (e.g., between Dallas and Fort Worth or between Kansas City and Topeka).

Other studies have examined mode choice, usually by comparing automobiles and transit. Since time and cost are major variables affecting the choice of mode, studies of modal split and of the value of time are closely linked. In one famous study, Beesley [1973, chapter 6] analyzed choices among transit options in London, where British Railway trains are generally faster and have higher fares than the Underground. However, only 27.5 percent of the respondents were traders; most had a dominant alternative that was both faster and cheaper.

What is the value of travel time? Because there was much variation in practice, the government sponsored an extensive research effort by Stanford Research Institute during the 1960s. This included surveys at eight locations with toll road–free road choices scattered from Maine to Texas. The researchers recommended a value of $2.82 per hour for commuting trips of at least 5 miles in length and 10 minutes in time [Thomas 1968]. Other results were summarized by Bruzelius [1979, p. 153]. One would expect the value of travel time to rise over time because of inflation. However, many planners have been conservative and preferred to use a value that is on the low side (a higher value might lead to overinvestment).

It is of interest to compare findings of these studies with wage rates (which would be used in the alternative approach). The results have varied widely, showing that people value time at anywhere from one-fifth to two-thirds of their hourly wage [Watson 1974, p. 153]. Beesley calculated that lower-income commuters paid one-third of their wage rate to save travel time, while those with higher incomes paid up to one-half.

Quarmby [1967] estimated that out-of-vehicle time (for walking, waiting, and transfers) is subjectively valued at 2.5 to 3 times as much as in-vehicle time. Later studies have confirmed that out-of-vehicle time is weighted more heavily, but again the results have varied considerably. Some studies show that walking time and waiting time are valued differently (walking requires more effort, but waiting is boring).

It is common to apply a uniform value of travel time (i.e., an average value) to the total time savings produced by a transportation project. There have been objections to this. Thomas and Thompson [1970] argued that the value of time for commuters is a function of their incomes and the amount of time saved. With regard to income, it makes sense that the rich will pay more to save time than the poor will. The authors analyzed the data collected by Stanford Research Institute and estimated that those persons with an income over $20,000 per year will pay 4 to 5 times as much as those with an income below $4000 per year.

However, if the high values placed by the rich were taken into account, it might lead to building facilities that they want more than the poor do (such as high-speed rail lines to the suburbs). Hence some people have asserted that using a constant value is more desirable from the standpoint of equity. For this reason, the British Department of Transport has a policy of using a single value of time [Bruzelius 1979, pp. 179–180].

Thomas and Thompson also claimed that there is a nonlinear relationship between the amount of time saved and its total value to a traveler. They calculated that savings up to 10 minutes have a low value per minute, while savings from 10 to 20 minutes have a much higher value per minute. It does seem plausible that very small time savings have no perceived value. This is an important point because the sum of hours saved by a project often consists of a small average savings of a few minutes for many thousands of people. Using a constant value of time may overestimate benefits in such a situation.

A final issue is whether travel time is really a cost for all travelers. Customarily it is assumed that travel is not intrinsically productive or rewarding and that people want to minimize travel time. An obvious exception is sightseeing or travel for pleasure, which planners generally brush aside as insignificant within urban areas. More relevant, many people like to drive, and some enjoy riding transit and watching other passengers or looking out the window. Suburban railroad passengers frequently read or play cards. As noted in Chapter 12, some people find the journey to work enjoyable or interesting. In these cases, people would probably not pay money to save travel time.

These arguments are usually ignored in transportation planning practice. It is theoretically possible to classify the beneficiaries of a project by income level and amount of time saved, but it would complicate an estimating process that is already long and elaborate.

Other User Costs

Several other types of user costs are considered less important and are often ignored in analyses. These include the intangible factors discussed in Chapter 12 such as comfort, convenience, reliability, and security. No one doubts that these factors do influence people's travel behavior to some extent. A few studies have incorporated comfort [Nicolaidis 1975] and convenience [Spear 1976], but these variables are usually omitted because they are hard to measure.

Empirical studies usually turn up a minority of travelers who prefer an alternative that seems inferior on all counts. For example, Beesley found in his study that 6.3 percent of respondents chose an option that was both slower and more expensive. On the surface, this appears to be irrational behavior. Clearly he omitted some variables that do affect choices. Possibly it was comfort that was important. In New York City, where both local and express trains stop at many subway stations, some riders take the slower local trains because seats are available, while the express trains are crowded.

Accident costs are not estimated separately in most transit studies. It is usually assumed that accident costs are covered in operating costs (transit agencies include insurance or a reserve for payment of claims in their budgets). This contrasts with the practice in highway studies, where considerable effort may be expended to estimate accident costs. This reflects the fact that accidents are far more common on the highways.

Some transit lines attract many park-and-ride travelers. While their travel time in reaching a station is counted, the costs of operating the automobiles and parking are sometimes omitted. They should, of course, be included.

QUESTIONS

1 Describe the factors that cause cost overruns in public works projects such as the building of rail transit systems. Why do proponents of a project tend to underestimate costs? Can this tendency be corrected?

2 Sketch a proposed new transit route in your city. Decide on the frequency of service, and then estimate the time to complete a trip. Finally, calculate the number of vehicles that would be required for the route.

3 The operating costs of mass transit systems in the United States have risen greatly in recent years. What factors are responsible for these increases? What could be done to moderate the increases in the future?

4 What are the advantages and disadvantages of using part-time operators in transit service? Why have labor unions opposed this practice?

5 What are the important variables to include in a model to estimate transit operating costs? How does the average speed of vehicles affect the operating cost?

6 Do you agree that saving travel time is worth money? What would you be willing to pay to save 5 minutes on each trip? Why do different persons put different values on saving time?

REFERENCES

Attanucci, John, Nigel H. M. Wilson, and David Vozzolo: "An Assessment of the Use of Part-Time Operators at the Massachusetts Bay Transportation Authority," *Transportation Research Record,* no. 961 (1984), pp. 21–28.

Beesley, M. E.: *Urban Transport: Studies in Economic Policy* (London: Butterworth & Co., 1973).

Berechman, Joseph, and Genevieve Giuliano: "Economies of Scale in Bus Transit: A Review of Concepts and Evidence," *Transportation,* vol. 12, no. 4 (May 1985), pp. 313–332.

Bruzelius, Nils: *The Value of Travel Time: Theory and Measurement* (London: Croom Helm, 1979).

Cambridge Systematics, Inc.: *Characteristics of Urban Transportation Systems,* rev. ed. (Washington: Federal Transit Administration, September 1992).

Cervero, Robert: "Multistage Approach for Estimating Transit Costs," *Transportation Research Record,* no. 877 (1982), pp. 67–75.

Cherwony, Walter, and Subhash R. Mundle: "Peak-Base Cost Allocation Models," *Transportation Research Record,* no. 663 (1978), pp. 52–56.

———, Subhash R. Mundle, Benjamin D. Porter, and Gregory R. Gleichman: "Review of Bus Costing Procedures," *Transportation Research Record,* no. 854 (1982), pp. 54–60.

Chomitz, Kenneth, Genevieve Giuliano, and Charles Lave: "Part-Time Public Transit Operators: Experiences and Prospects," *Transportation Research Record,* no. 1013 (1985), pp. 32–38.

Fruin, John J.: *Pedestrian Planning and Design* (New York: Metropolitan Association of Urban Designers and Environmental Planners, 1971).

Hensher, David A.: "Review of Studies Leading to Existing Values of Travel Time," *Transportation Research Record,* no. 587 (1976), pp. 30–41.

Herzenberg, Ann: "Method for Estimating the Cost of Drivers' Wages for Bus Services," *Transportation Research Record,* no. 947 (1983), pp. 7–14.

Jones, Janet: "Tri-Met Bus Operator Costing Methodology," *Transportation Research Record,* no. 862 (1982), pp. 47–57.

Levinson, Herbert S.: "Peak–Off Peak Revenue and Cost Allocation Model," *Transportation Research Record,* no. 662 (1978), pp. 29–33.

Menendez, Aurelio: *Estimating Capital and Operating Costs in Urban Transportation Planning* (Westport, CT: Praeger Publishers, 1993).

Merewitz, Leonard: "Cost Overruns in Public Works," in William Niskanen et al., eds., *Benefit Cost and Policy Analysis 1972* (Chicago: Aldine Publishers, 1973), pp. 277–295.

Moses, Leon N., and Harold F. Williamson, Jr.: "Value of Time, Choice of Mode, and the Subsidy Issue in Urban Transportation," *Journal of Political Economy,* vol. 71, no. 3 (June 1964), pp. 247–264.

Nicolaidis, Greogy C.: "Quantification of the Comfort Variable," *Transportation Research,* vol. 9, no. 1 (February 1975), pp. 55–66.

Ortner, James, and Martin Wachs: "The Cost-Revenue Squeeze in American Public Transit," *Journal of the American Planning Association,* vol. 45, no. 1 (January 1979), pp. 10–21.

Pickrell, Don H.: "Sources of Rising Operating Deficits in Urban Bus Transit," *Transportation Research Record,* no. 915 (1983), pp. 18–24.

————: *Urban Rail Transit Projects: Forecast versus Actual Ridership and Costs* (Cambridge, MA: Transportation Systems Center, U.S. Department of Transportation, October 1989).

Pucher, John: "Effects of Subsidies on Transit Costs," *Transportation Quarterly,* vol. 36, no. 4 (October 1982), pp. 549–562.

Quarmby, David A.: "Choice of Travel Mode for the Journey to Work: Some Findings," *Journal of Transport Economics and Policy,* vol. 1, no. 3 (September 1967), pp. 273–314.

Reilly, John M.: "Transit Costs during Peak and Off-Peak Hours," *Transportation Research Record,* no. 625 (1977), pp. 22–26.

Roess, Roger P., Martin F. Huss, and Claire S. Kwicklis: "Operating and Maintenance Costs for Rail Rapid Transit," *Transportation Engineering Journal,* vol. TE3 (May 1977), pp. 421–439.

Silien, Joseph S., and Jeffrey G. Mora: "North American Light Rail Vehicles," *Light Rail Transit,* Special Report 161 (Washington: Transportation Research Board, 1975), pp. 93–98.

Spear, Bruce D.: "Generalized Attribute Variable for Models of Mode Choice Behavior," *Transportation Research Record,* no. 592 (1976), pp. 6–11.

Stopher, Peter R., Len Brandrup, Byron Lee, and Stephen T. Parry: "Development of a Bus Operating Cost Allocation Model Compatible with UMTA Urban Transportation Planning System Models," *Transportation Research Record,* no. 1108 (1987), pp. 31–42.

Thomas, Thomas C.: "Value of Time for Commuting Motorists," *Highway Research Record,* no. 245 (1968), pp. 17–35.

———— and Gordon I. Thompson: "The Value of Time for Commuting Motorists as a Function of Their Income Level and Amount of Time Saved," *Highway Research Record,* no. 314 (1970), pp. 1–19.

Watson, Peter L.: *The Value of Time: Behavioral Models of Modal Choice* (Lexington, MA: D.C. Heath, 1974).

Wells, Martin J., Brian McCollom, and Thomas Dooley: "Review of the Use of Part-Time Transit Operators and Methods for Assigning Part-Time Work," *Transportation Research Record,* no. 1013 (1985), pp. 39–48.

15

PRICING AND FINANCING

The previous chapter covered the costs of building and operating transit systems. This one deals with the other side of the ledger: Where does the money come from to pay the costs? A decreasing portion comes from the price charged for the service—the fare. In 1992, passenger revenues paid for only 37 percent of operating expenses for all transit systems in the United States, and total operating revenues covered only 42 percent. Table 15-1 shows that the operating deficit has been increasing steadily over the years. But many believe that better pricing strategies could improve transit's revenue yield.

Since virtually all U.S. public transit systems operate at a deficit, they are obviously obtaining funds from other sources to balance their books and stay in operation. These funds come from federal, state, and local governments (and ultimately from taxpayers). Money provided to cover a deficit is usually called a *subsidy,* so this topic will also be discussed here. Since the word *subsidy* has a negative connotation with many people, it is common to use instead terms such as *grant* or *operating assistance.*

There are also the costs of capital investment, of building tracks, busways, and stations, and of purchasing transit vehicles. Normally a private firm uses part of the net operating revenue to pay off investment costs (including interest charges and depreciation). Public transit agencies cannot do this because their net operating revenue is negative. Since the 1960s, it has been largely accepted in the United States that transit capital costs are financed from other sources (i.e., subsidized). The extent to which operating losses should be subsidized is a more controversial issue.

ELASTICITY OF DEMAND

One of transit's basic problems is weak demand. The reason is clear: The automobile is a close substitute that most people prefer. Although automobile travel costs more, most

TABLE 15-1
TREND OF OPERATING REVENUE AND EXPENSES FOR ALL TRANSIT SYSTEMS IN THE U.S.
($ millions)

Year	Operating revenue	Operating expense	Operating deficit	Revenue as percentage of expense
1975	2,043.0	3,537.3	(1,494.3)	57.76
1976	2,236.1	3,857.4	(1,621.3)	57.97
1977	2,353.6	4,121.0	(1,767.4)	57.11
1978	2,449.9	4,539.1	(2,089.2)	53.97
1979	2,647.8	5,231.7	(2,583.9)	50.61
1980	2,805.1	6,246.5	(3,441.4)	44.91
1981	3,045.2	7,024.3	(3,979.1)	43.35
1982	3,457.0	7,552.9	(4,095.9)	45.77
1983	3,504.1	7,956.0	(4,451.9)	44.04
1984	5,228.2	11,574.0	(6,345.8)	45.17
1985	5,276.5	12,380.9	(7,104.4)	42.62
1986	5,850.4	12,951.7	(7,101.3)	45.17
1987	5,890.7	13,472.1	(7,581.4)	43.73
1988	6,065.3	14,287.3	(8,222.0)	42.45
1989	6,256.6	14,972.3	(8,715.7)	41.79
1990	6,785.8	15,742.1	(8,956.3)	43.11
1991	6,804.0	16,541.4	(9,737.4)	41.13
1992	6,985.6	16,645.7	(9,660.1)	41.97

Note: Series not continuous between 1983 and 1984. Prior to 1984, data exclude commuter railroad, automated guideway, ferry boat, demand responsive, and most rural and smaller systems.
Source: Transit Fact Book, 1993 edition (Washington: American Public Transit Association, 1993), tables 16 and 20.

consumers consider it to be worth the money. Much of the demand that does exist for transit comes from people who cannot afford automobiles.

Economists summarize such preferences in a demand function, which may be presented as an equation, a table of values, or a curve on a graph. It shows the quantity of a product that will be purchased at any given price. Normally a demand curve slopes downward, meaning that the quantity purchased rises as the price falls, and vice versa. For transit, we measure quantity in the number of trips or rides, and price in the fare.

An important characteristic of a demand curve is its *elasticity,* which means *sensitivity* or *responsiveness.* Of particular concern is the *price elasticity,* or sensitivity to price changes. How much will transit ridership go up if the fare is reduced, or down if the fare is raised? *Price elasticity* is defined as the percentage change in the quantity purchased (the number of rides) divided by the percentage change in price (the fare). Stated another way, price elasticity is the percentage change in rides resulting from a 1 percent change in the fare.

The elasticity at a single point on the demand curve is called the *point elasticity*. This can be calculated only if the equation for the demand curve is known. Sometimes analysts estimate the equation statistically, but in most cases there are not enough data to do so. Hence another measure called the *arc elasticity* is used more often. This measures the elasticity between two points on the demand curve (i.e., an arc of the curve). Frequently data are known for two points: before and after a price change. There are different ways to define arc elasticity, depending on whether percentage changes are based on the before or after situation. The most common approach is to average the before and after conditions, resulting in the following formula:

$$\left(\frac{q_2 - q_1}{p_2 - p_1}\right)\left(\frac{p_1 + p_2}{q_1 + q_2}\right) \tag{15-1}$$

Here p_1 and p_2 are the prices before and after the change, while q_1 and q_2 are the quantities before and after.

Values of elasticity are negative if the demand curve slopes downward (which is the normal case and holds for transit). The value can vary between zero and minus infinity. When elasticity is zero, the demand curve is a vertical line, meaning the same quantity will be sold regardless of price. When elasticity is infinite, the demand curve is a horizontal line. A producer can sell as much as desired up to a certain price, but nothing above that price.

These extremes exist only in theory. Of practical interest are values of elasticity in the vicinity of -1. Demand is said to be *elastic* when the ratio is more negative than -1 and *inelastic* when the ratio is between 0 and -1. These terms have important implications:

1 When demand is elastic, a price cut will increase total expenditures (the product of price and quantity), while a price hike will decrease them. Of course, expenditures by consumers are equal to revenues for producers.

2 When elasticity is exactly -1, a change in price will leave the total expenditures the same. This borderline situation is called *unit elasticity*.

3 When demand is inelastic, a drop in price will decrease the total expenditures, and a rise in price will increase them.

This implies two simple rules for a firm to maximize profit: (1) If demand is elastic, lower the price. (2) If demand is inelastic, raise the price. These rules should be modified to account for the cost of increasing or decreasing output. The first rule is valid only if the (lower) price is still greater than the marginal cost of increasing output. The second rule should always hold: A higher price should lead to lower output and reduce cost, which will further improve the profit picture.

Many empirical studies of the elasticity of demand for transit have been made over several decades, and all have shown the demand to be inelastic. The transit industry often uses an elasticity of -0.33 as a rule of thumb, after the recommendation of the engineering firm of Simpson and Curtin. Curtin [1968] based this finding on 77 cases of bus fare changes (mostly increases) made across the United States between 1952 and 1963. This implies that ridership will drop by one-third of a fare increase. For example, if the fare is raised 30 percent, ridership will fall by 10 percent.

In 1972, the bus fare in Atlanta was dropped from \$0.40 to \$0.15, a decrease of 62.5 percent, after voters approved a 1 percent sales tax to finance building the MARTA rail system. The fare cut was offered as a way to offset the regressive nature of a sales tax. Ridership immediately increased by 18.5 percent, which is close to what the Simpson and Curtin formula would suggest [Bates 1974]. After 8 months, ridership was up by 30.2 percent, partially due to increases in service.

Bus passengers seem to have higher elasticity than rail passengers. When the New York City transit fare was raised from \$0.15 to \$0.20 cents in 1966, subway ridership declined by only 2.4 percent, while bus ridership fell by 10 percent [Lassow 1968]. The explanation is that rail trips are more likely to have a work purpose, while bus trips are more likely to be discretionary.

Using time-series data, Pushkarev and Zupan [1977] estimated that the fare elasticity of New York City subway riding over a 25-year period was -0.147. The elasticity for bus trips was greater (-0.305). They explained that a high percentage of subway trips go to or from Manhattan, where there are few good alternatives. Bus trips occur more often in the other boroughs, where travel by automobile is more competitive. They compared their findings with results of other studies, which were similar. Mayworm [1982] summarized more recent research. Boyle [1985] investigated the question of whether transit riders were becoming less sensitive to fare increases over time, but found no evidence to support the hypothesis.

This means that the companies that once owned transit systems behaved in a rational manner by raising fares. Today transit authorities still face a strong temptation to raise fares: Ridership will decline only a little, and revenues will go up. Possibly service can be cut, which will reduce operating costs. Conceivably fares could be raised, and service lowered, to the point where the authority makes a profit. The reason for not doing this is to achieve the social benefits of transit, which are judged worthy of subsidy.

Fare elasticity can be measured accurately only if all other conditions that affect ridership remain constant (the famous *ceteris paribus* assumption of economists). It is not unusual for a transit system with financial problems to reduce service at the same time as it raises the fare. Then it is difficult to distinguish the separate effects of the two changes. Demand also depends on the prices of substitutes (this is called *cross-elasticity*). Thus, a higher price of gasoline can offset an increase in the transit fare. Indeed, this happened during the gasoline shortage in 1979, when many transit fares were raised without any subsequent decline in ridership [Boyle 1985].

While it is simpler to use one average value of fare elasticity, this can lead to erroneous forecasts. "Ridership response will be different in different cities, for different transit services and levels of service, for different periods of the day, for different trip lengths, and perhaps for different fare levels. All of this suggests that a single fare elasticity value is of little use to most transit companies if accurate ridership and revenue forecasts are required" [Mayworm 1982, p. 31]. In particular, demand is relatively inelastic for commuting trips, compared with nonwork trips made outside the peak period. Pushkarev and Zupan [1977] found that elasticities tend to be higher in smaller cities, where congestion is less and automobile travel easier than in large cities.

The total price that a transit rider pays includes not only the fare but also travel time and subjective factors such as discomfort and anxiety. Time elasticity can be estimated, but the other factors are difficult to measure. Empirical studies have shown that elasticity with regard to travel time is greater than that for the fare. Thus travelers place a higher value on time than on money. One implication is that they would be willing to pay a higher fare for better service, and there might be no loss in ridership.

Elasticity relates to the idea of captive and choice riders, discussed in Chapter 12. In fact, captive riders can be defined as those who have inelastic demand; they will continue to ride transit despite substantial fare hikes. Choice riders, who have an automobile available, have more elasticity; even a small fare hike may send some back to their cars. Walking is an alternative for very short trips, which have a higher fare elasticity than longer trips.

PRICING

The Economists' Rule

The economic rule for price setting is that the price should equal the marginal cost (the cost of producing the last or marginal unit). Price should be set at the level at which the demand curve intersects the marginal cost curve. This means that the cost of the marginal unit is just equal to what some purchaser is willing to pay. This yields the most efficient allocation of resources and maximizes social welfare.

In a normal situation (see Figure 15-1), the demand curve intersects the marginal cost curve at an output where the average cost is increasing, so that the marginal cost is higher that the average cost. Assuming a uniform price (which is the custom in most markets), the price is the same as the average revenue. If the price is set equal to the marginal cost, then the average revenue will exceed the average cost, total revenue will exceed total cost, and the firm will make a profit.

However, a situation can arise (see Figure 15-2) in which the demand curve crosses the marginal cost curve at an output where the average cost is decreasing, and the marginal cost is lower than the average cost. Then if the price is set equal to the marginal cost, the average revenue will be less than the average cost, total revenue will be less than total cost, and the firm will suffer a loss.

This case is called a *decreasing cost industry,* and unfortunately it applies to transit. Fixed costs are large, especially for rail systems, and variable costs are relatively small. The marginal cost is low because transit systems usually operate at less than capacity; they could carry more riders with little increase in costs. Therefore, if the price is set equal to the marginal cost, transit operators will lose money.

One possible remedy is *average cost pricing,* which many utilities use. The price is set equal to the average cost instead of the marginal cost. Then the average revenue equals the average cost, total revenue equals total cost, and the firm breaks even. But compared with marginal cost pricing, the output is lower and the price higher. Some consumers would be willing to pay more than the marginal cost to expand output.

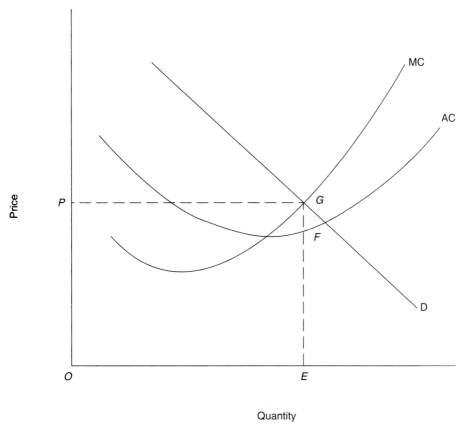

Quantity

FIGURE 15-1
Pricing in a normal market. Price and quantity are determined by the intersection of the demand curve (D) and the marginal cost curve (MC) at point *G*. At quantity *OE*, the average cost curve (AC) is below the marginal cost curve. Average revenue is *EG* and average cost is *EF*, so there is a profit of *FG* on each unit sold.

Hence average cost pricing does not maximize social welfare and is economically inefficient. It is used only when there is no practical alternative.

Another solution is *price discrimination,* in which different prices are charged to different buyers. It is necessary to segregate consumers into identifiable groups that differ in their willingness to pay for a product (usually stemming from income differences). Then a higher price is charged to those who will pay more, a lower price to others. This can lift a firm's revenues and possibly turn a money-losing situation into a profitable one.

It is possible to use price discrimination in transit markets. It is approximated in some cities where well-off commuters pay high fares for suburban railroad service, while middle- and low-income commuters pay lower fares to use subways or buses. However, the railroad service is usually of better quality, so the product is not uniform. It has been proposed to charge lower fares for the same service to the poor, who would

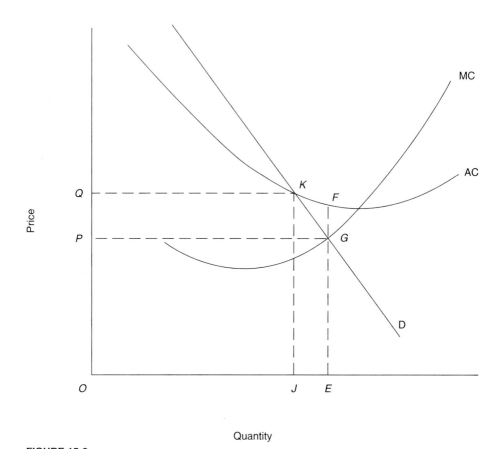

FIGURE 15-2
Pricing with a decreasing cost industry. The demand curve and marginal cost curve intersect at point *G*, which is the economically efficient solution. However, at quantity *OE*, the average cost of *EF* is greater than the average revenue of *EG*, and there is a loss of *FG* on each unit sold. An alternative is average cost pricing, based on point *K*, where the demand curve and average cost curve intersect. This is a break-even solution, but it is inefficient because consumers represented by the distance *JE* are willing to pay more than the marginal cost of supplying them.

be certified and carry identification cards. This would be an example of price discrimination.

In practice, transit authorities pay little heed to the rules of economics. Fares are sometimes set to achieve a target adopted as a policy decision by the board of directors. One common target is a revenue/cost ratio. For example, policy makers may decide that fares should cover 40 percent of operating costs. Another is a subsidy-per-passenger target. For example, the goal may be to hold the subsidy to $0.50 per passenger.

Such rules, while arbitrary, offer some guidance to transit management. In many cases, it is alleged, political decisions on fares are expedient and irrational. According

to Kirby, "the repeated introduction of new sources of subsidy funds has averted one financial crisis after another, with each new funding source providing a breathing space
during which unrealistically low (but politically popular) fares could be maintained"
[1982, p. 327].

Fare Structure

The majority of U.S. transit systems charge a flat fare—the same for all riders on all
routes at all times. This appeals to management because of its simplicity; it is incontro-
vertibly argued that passengers understand it well. The popularity of the exact-fare system, in which bus drivers do not make change, has led to an increase in the use of flat
fares.

Customarily transit agencies charge lower fares for special groups, but they are still
flat fares. Federal law requires transit agencies receiving federal operating assistance to
charge the elderly and disabled no more than half-fare in the off-peak period. In many
cities, students get reduced fares. Some systems give discounts to frequent riders in the
form of multiride or monthly passes. This is mostly a marketing tool.

Two alternatives to flat fares are widely advocated as steps toward more rational
pricing that could improve the financial situation of transit systems and increase equity.
They are compatible; both could be used simultaneously. They are discussed in the following sections.

Distance-Based Fares

It seems logical that people who travel longer distances should pay higher fares because
it costs more to carry them. The marginal cost pricing rule calls for this. With a flat fare,
short-distance travelers subsidize long-distance travelers, which is both uneconomical
and unfair. Further, people making short trips may walk instead of taking transit because the fare seems so high for going less than a mile. There is nothing wrong with
walking, but it lowers the income of the transit operator.

This has equity implications. The poor tend to live in the central city and the rich, in
the suburbs. On the average, poor people make shorter trips than rich people. Thus, a
flat fare results in the poor subsidizing the rich.

Graduated fares relate price to distance traveled. These fares were long used on suburban railroads and foreign rail systems such as the London Underground, where there
was a different fare for each station-to-station pair. This was a labor-intensive system;
tickets were issued and had to be checked by conductors or gatekeepers. London no
longer uses this system.

Currently the popular way to base fares on distance traveled is to have *zone fares,* in
which the charge goes up whenever a passenger enters a new zone. Many bus systems
formerly used zone fares, but it has become less common. New heavy rail systems such
as BART and the Washington, D.C., Metro have electronic fare collection machines
that calculate zone fares. Older subway-elevated systems in the United States still use
flat fares.

Peak-Period Pricing

Demand for some products is distributed unevenly through time. There can be large variations by season, day of the week, or time of day. When demand is much higher in peak periods, producers must have the capacity to supply extra output that is not needed at other times. Hence the marginal cost is higher for peak-period users than for others. Under the marginal cost pricing rule, peak-period users should pay a higher price than off-peak users. This will cause a more efficient use of resources. It may induce some users to shift from the peak period to the off-peak period, which may reduce costs.

This situation obviously applies to transit: The greater demand during the two peak periods each day creates extra costs for equipment and labor. On the average, twice as many vehicles are used in the peak period as in midday. Union contracts make the extra cost of labor especially heavy.

The idea of charging higher fares in the rush hour was long ago suggested by economist William S. Vickrey [1955], who served on a commission appointed by the mayor of New York City to find ways to eliminate the transit deficit. New York City never followed his recommendation, and for many years, few did, although many economists advocated the practice. Recently there has been experimentation with time-of-day pricing, but it remains the exception rather than the rule. It is done with automatic fare collection in new rail systems.

An article by Cervero [1985] summarized recent experience with charging higher fares in the peak period. As of 1983, he found 23 cities that used some form of time-of-day pricing. There were two approaches: to impose a surcharge on the base fare during the peak period or to offer a discount from the base fare during the off-peak period. The resulting pattern is the same, but the impact on revenues was different. Systems that used a surcharge had better revenue/expense ratios than those that used a discount.

The schemes worked well but had little impact on patronage. Typical changes in ridership were around 10 percent, partly because the fare differentials were small. In a few cases, transit operators were able to reduce peak-period service, which saved some cost. Public acceptance of the schemes was mostly good. There were disputes with passengers around the time when the fare was changed. This was solved by making the change when a bus started a new run, so everyone getting on a bus paid the same fare. There were complaints that the peak period was too long and did not give people an opportunity to adjust their time of travel.

Despite a large body of literature citing the advantages of differential pricing, few transit authorities use it. Markowitz [1986] made a nationwide survey of transit professionals to find out why. He learned that almost all respondents knew of the arguments for time-of-day pricing and supported the concept. Political barriers were not insurmountable; most boards of directors were appointed rather than elected and were not preoccupied with winning votes.

Practical aspects concerned the transit officials the most. First, they did not feel confident that they could predict the effects of fare changes well enough to justify these changes to their directors and the public. Second, fare collection equipment would have to be replaced with more advanced devices. Third, the public prefers the simplicity of flat fares and would be confused by differential fares. All these obstacles seem capable of being overcome.

On the average, Markowitz found, the transit agencies surveyed made fare changes every other year. In 34 percent of the cases, the change was made in response to a financial crisis; in another 34 percent of cases, as part of the annual budgetary process. Only 11 percent of cases made scheduled changes following a plan.

Congestion Pricing

There is an analogous situation with regard to highway use: There are peak periods of demand, during which marginal costs are higher than otherwise, and peak-period users do not pay the full marginal cost. This affects transit because underpricing of highways decreases transit use. Raising highway prices might cause dramatic boosts in transit riding.

The price that each driver pays consists of the vehicle operating cost plus travel time. When traffic flows freely, users impose no marginal costs on each other. Under the marginal cost pricing rule, there should be no charge for using the highway (as is generally the case).

The situation changes when a highway becomes congested. Each additional driver who enters the highway does pay a higher price in travel time (because speed is slower), but also causes delays for other users. Thus the marginal user does not pay the full marginal social cost. The price for using the highway is too low, causing overuse.

The proposed remedy is to tax vehicles during periods of congestion on highways. Economists such as Vickrey [1963] have proposed this for many years. The obstacle to implementation seemed to be figuring out an efficient and inexpensive way to administer a pricing system. Visions of long backups at tollbooths came readily to mind.

In 1975, Singapore became the first city in the world to implement congestion pricing [Watson and Holland 1978]. It adopted an *area licensing* scheme with a cordon designated around the central business district. Any car entering during the morning peak period had to display a permit on the windshield, which cost the equivalent of $26 per month. There were 22 entry points, where police watched cars and recorded the plate numbers of violators. Buses, commercial vehicles, and automobiles with four or more persons were exempt.

The system reduced morning traffic by 40 percent. Administration went smoothly. Police issued about 100 tickets per week to cars that entered the restricted area illegally. At first, congestion occurred before and after the designated period of 7:30 a.m. to 9:30 a.m.; the ending time was extended to 10:15 a.m. Transit ridership went up, and buses completed their trips faster with downtown streets clear. The scheme also produced considerable revenue for the government. It is still in effect, and the price has been raised several times over the years.

The Singapore example has received much favorable publicity, but one scholar is critical. Wilson made a calculation of travelers' utility and concluded that "some commuters are clearly worse off . . . and the available evidence indicates that society as a whole may be worse off" [1988, p. 208]. He claimed that bus passengers incurred greater travel times because increased ridership slowed the buses.

During 1983 to 1985, Hong Kong staged a pilot project with electronic road pricing [Hau 1990]. Each of 2600 vehicles was fitted with an *electronic license plate* (ELP), a small cassette carrying magnetically coded data. A detector buried in the pavement in-terrogated the ELP as a vehicle passed over and transmitted the information to a com-puter. Accounts were kept, and a monthly bill was sent to each vehicle owner. A video camera taped vehicles without an ELP, and the owners were sent tickets. This demon-stration removed doubts about technical performance, since the accuracy was well over 99 percent. However, a proposal to implement the system on a larger scale met strong public and political opposition and was shelved.

Several other cities besides Singapore have implemented area licensing programs, including Bergen and Oslo in Norway and Milan in Italy [Orski 1991].

There have been few efforts to implement the idea in the United States [Higgins 1986]. However, it has attracted considerable attention in the last few years. The na-tional transportation policy issued in 1990 gave favorable mention to congestion pric-ing. The ISTEA legislation passed in 1991 provided $25 million per year to fund five pilot projects. However, when the Federal Highway Administration solicited proposals, it received only one that it considered acceptable. This involved raising peak-period tolls on the San Francisco–Oakland Bay Bridge.

It is uncertain whether congestion pricing will ever be accepted in the United States. The technology is available, as electronic toll collection has been used in Atlanta, Dal-las, and New Orleans. Many people in the United States are hostile to new taxes and in-sist on the right to drive anywhere at any time without restraint. Another objection is that the scheme is inequitable and would tax low-income drivers off the road. It remains to be seen whether the technical capability will be matched by political approval.

Another approach is to levy a parking tax in congested areas such as the central busi-ness district. San Francisco imposed a 25 percent tax on off-street, nonresidential park-ing spaces from 1970 to 1972 [Kulash 1974]. The purpose was to raise revenue, not to discourage driving, and the tax did generate $5.5 million per year. The effect on traffic was negligible, and the number of parked cars declined very little. However, parking fa-cility operators suffered large decreases in profits and lobbied against the tax, which was lowered to 10 percent in 1972.

FREE TRANSIT

There has long been some sentiment that transit service should be free; there should be no fares. Local governments provide many free services, such as schools, libraries, parks, snow removal, police and fire protection. Why not add transit to this list? The federal government sponsored a study of the concept that resulted in a book titled *Free Transit* [Domencich and Kraft 1970]. UMTA later funded several demonstration proj-ects to test the idea.

O'Connell [1973] proposed a plan that would combine congestion pricing with free transit. The scheme is to charge everyone who drives to work a fee, which he estimated should be $1.75 per day. The money would go into a transit trust fund and pay all costs of the transit system, which would be free. The objective is to have half of commuters drive and half ride transit. This would end congestion on streets, so that those who choose to pay for driving would be getting something for their money. The approach is superficially appealing, but no one came forward to put it into practice (he looked to businesses for support, rather than government).

Arguments in Favor

A zero fare is the price that will maximize transit ridership (although a few writers have suggested negative fares). The more people who switch from cars to transit, the larger will be the community benefits, such as reductions in air pollution, energy consumption, accidents, and traffic congestion.

The policy should also ameliorate the redistribution of income to the poor, who use transit a lot. It would ensure that no one is ever denied transit service because of a lack of money.

A practical benefit would be the elimination of the cost of fare collection. Most bus operations use the exact-fare system, so there would be little effect on the drivers. Passengers would load the vehicles more quickly (both doors could be used), which would bring a slight improvement in bus travel times. The incentive to rob drivers would be eliminated.

In rail operations, the cost of fare collection is larger. In older systems such as the one in New York City, there is a fare collector or change maker at every station. This position could be dropped, but there would probably have to be someone in every station to give information to travelers and provide security. It is uncertain whether there could be reductions in personnel (which would be opposed by the unions in any event). Domencich and Kraft estimated that dropping fare collection in Boston would reduce operating costs by 5 percent; they felt this was the upper bound for systems elsewhere.

Newer rail systems have machines that dispense tickets and make change. Hence no savings in labor costs would occur. However, the machines could be removed; they are expensive and require maintenance. In all cases, the costs of transporting and counting money, accounting, etc., would be obviated.

Arguments Against

Skeptics point out that since the demand for transit is quite inelastic, ridership will not increase much. They believe that only a small number of drivers will switch to transit, and hence the purported benefits of less traffic will be negligible. Domencich and Kraft reached this conclusion after using an econometric model to estimate the result of eliminating the transit fare in Boston. They believed that reducing travel times on transit would be more effective than lowering fares if one wants to attract more passengers.

On the other hand, inelastic demand doesn't mean there is *no* response to a lower fare; it just means the response is relatively small. If ridership goes up very much, then additional service will have to be supplied to avoid overcrowding. More vehicles will be needed, and operating costs will go up. The subsidy to the transit system will have to be increased; it will be larger than just the loss of current passenger revenues.

Indeed, this happened when Atlanta cut its bus fare from $0.40 to $0.15 in 1972. This caused a much larger increase in passengers than expected, and the transit authority was not prepared to handle it. Overcrowding persisted for months until the authority could get more buses [Bates 1974].

Domencich and Kraft estimated that eliminating fares in Boston would increase ridership by 28 percent, assuming no additional capacity is supplied. But there would be overcrowding; to keep loading standards the same, more service would have to be added, increasing the system's operating costs by 12 percent. The better service would attract still more passengers, bringing the total increase to 32 percent.

It is also argued that free transit is an inefficient way to redistribute income to the poor. All passengers will benefit, including those who have high or middle incomes (which is a substantial number in transit-oriented cities such as New York and Chicago). It would be more effective to give passes to people who qualify as low-income. Further, many economists believe the best way to alter the income distribution is to give cash to the poor, rather than services that they may or may not want.

It is also claimed that eliminating fares would create management problems. Fare receipts indicate the value of service to passengers; a rational consumer pays a price only if the utility of the commodity is worth at least that price. Without these market signals, it would be more difficult for transit managers to evaluate different routes, levels of service, etc., and to allocate resources appropriately.

The absence of fares might remove incentives for transit managers to be efficient. Cost control might be ignored because no one could compare costs and revenues. Although most systems lose money, managers are expected to keep costs down, and they may be penalized if deficits exceed expectations.

Experiments

UMTA sponsored systemwide demonstrations of free transit in Trenton, New Jersey, and Denver, Colorado, starting in 1978. This was done only in off-peak hours and on weekends. According to Studenmund et al. [1979], off-peak ridership rose by 45 percent in Trenton and 74 to 155 percent in Denver (depending on the estimation method used). System revenues fell by 25 percent in Trenton and 37 percent in Denver. Operating costs went up slightly (less than 1 percent in Denver) because some buses had to be added to handle the additional riders.

But the experiments turned up an unexpected problem: Many teenagers rode the buses, especially in the evening and often for joy riding. Incidents of vandalism, rowdiness, and harassment of other passengers increased in both cities. This apparently caused a decrease in the number of elderly riders. There was unfavorable publicity, and some people demanded that the experiments end. They seemed to create a bad public image for transit.

The program affected quality of service in other ways. The availability of seats declined, and some buses were crowded. Reliability suffered, because buses were more likely to fall behind schedule. Both crowding and lateness prompted many complaints from passengers who were used to better service.

Almost all the bus drivers disliked the system. "One of the most severe impacts of free fares appears to be a drop in driver morale. Increased ridership has added to the responsibilities of drivers and affected their run times. In addition, drivers appear to be receiving the brunt of negative patron comments about the program and are having to deal with increased harassment and vandalism by youths" [Studenmund et al. 1979, p. 20].

Both demonstrations continued for a year. After they ended, off-peak ridership dropped sharply, but remained slightly higher than before they began. The impact on highway traffic was insignificant: "Approximately 9 percent of the free-fare trips in Trenton and 15 percent of the Denver trips would have been made by car. At the outside, free fare reduced weekly car VMT [vehicle-miles of travel] in Denver by less than 0.5 of 1 percent and in Trenton by slightly more than 0.1 of 1 percent. These changes are so small as to be unobservable within total VMT" [Doxsey and Spear 1981, p. 48].

One situation in which free transit is common is within the central business district of large cities. Seattle introduced a free-fare zone in a 108-block downtown area in 1973, Portland did likewise the following year, and since then other cities have followed suit. In cities with a downtown transit mall (e.g., Buffalo and Denver), fares are not charged on this section. Usually the prime motive is to promote downtown business, and merchants exert political pressure for the system. It may also reduce street congestion and air pollution by enticing some drivers to park outside the CBD.

SUBSIDIES

Definition

Most dictionaries define a subsidy as government financial assistance given to a private individual or firm. That definition is too narrow; the term is used in broader senses. Here is an attempt at a better definition:

A *subsidy* is a payment that does not require an exchange of goods or services of equal market value in return, and it is used to accomplish a specific objective or has a specific effect.

A subsidy is not a market transaction, where value given equals value received. It is an example of what economists call a *transfer payment.* A subsidy is also not a gift, where use of the money is at the discretion of the recipient. It is not free money; there are strings attached.

Often a public body awards a subsidy to achieve a specific purpose. State and local governments may give money to a transit agency threatened with bankruptcy. Programs of continuing operating assistance to transit agencies are meant to keep them in business without recurring financial crises. Reduced fares for pupils reflect the view that education is good for society, and the transit agency should not bear an undue burden for it.

There are also *hidden subsidies* where the transfer was never intended or anticipated (it is usually identified by researchers after the fact). Nobody planned for off-peak transit riders to subsidize peak-period riders; it just happened because of aversion to changing fares in the middle of the day.

Another common term is *cross-subsidy.* In this situation, one group pays for more than the benefits it gets, and another group receives more benefits than it pays for. The first group subsidizes the second. With a flat fare, e.g., short-distance transit riders subsidize long-distance riders.

Not all subsidies are in the public sector. In earlier years, many electric utility companies used part of the profits from power sales to cover the deficits of their transit subsidiaries. Today thousands of firms provide free parking for their employees, which is a subsidy because the beneficiaries do not pay the costs. This is a controversial topic because federal tax policy on fringe benefits has long had an antitransit bias. Under the Comprehensive National Energy Act of 1992, an employer can give an employee $60 per month for transit use (including vanpooling) free of tax, but anything above $60 is taxed as income. Free parking is not taxed unless the value exceeds $155 per month. Prior to this law, there was a $21-per-month cap on transit benefits, and free parking was totally a tax-free benefit.

A subsidy need not involve a cash payment; it may take the form of goods or services provided free. For example, the U.S. Postal Service delivers free the mail of blind persons and organizations that serve the blind. This is a classic case of subsidy: Congress wrote this into law to help the blind.

Traditionally, subsidies were considered to be money that the public sector gave to the private sector. This is the basis for the emotional reaction that has made *subsidy* a pejorative term for many people. Use has broadened in recent years, and payments from one government unit to another are now called subsidies. There should be no blanket condemnation of subsidies; they can be desirable or undesirable, depending on one's point of view.

Many public services (such as police and fire protection) collect no revenues. Technically they are subsidized, but few taxpayers object. Government always involves taking money from some persons and delivering services to others, because it is not practicable to put all operations on a fee-for-service basis. One role of elected representatives is to decide who should be taxed and who should be subsidized. Subsidies are inevitable.

Justification

Economists (and others) have offered some justifications for subsidies, among which the following are often cited:

The Decreasing-Cost Industry   This is the case discussed previously in which setting the price equal to the marginal cost causes a loss because the marginal cost is less than the average cost. The difference can be made up by subsidy if it is deemed to be in the public interest. As noted, transit falls in the group of relevant industries.

Positive Externalities   When the economic behavior of some parties creates benefits that spill over to others who do not pay, these are called *positive externalities*. When some people switch from automobile to transit, this reduces air pollution, noise, and congestion, which benefits other people who are not transit users. These other people cannot be made to pay directly for their benefits, but they can pay indirectly through taxes.

Research and Development   Sometimes private firms are unable or unwilling to search for innovations because the costs and risks are large. The government may pay the costs of research and absorb the risks, at least until the promise of success seems high. This is really a type of positive externality: Society benefits from technological advances, but firms that spend money seeking them have a good chance of failing and suffering losses. This was the rationale for several UMTA initiatives, such as designing the Standard Light Rail Vehicle and building the Morgantown PRT.

Redistribution of Income to Certain Groups   This is a major argument for subsidizing transit; it transfers real income in the form of transit service rather than cash. Since the subsidies go to transit providers, the effectiveness of the redistribution depends on the extent to which the target groups use transit. Critics have argued that in some large cities, many middle- and upper-income persons use transit.

Hence some experts favor *user-side subsidies,* which go to members of the target groups instead of to service providers. Persons certified as eligible receive vouchers or coupons that can be used to pay some of or all the cost of the transportation [Kirby and McGillivray 1976]. Free-market advocates prefer this approach because presumably it encourages competition among providers. It has been tried in a number of places, but has not become widespread. It is mostly used to enable elderly and disabled persons to ride taxis at low cost.

Compensation for Other Subsidies   Transit proponents argue that highways are subsidized, so transit should be subsidized to create a "level playing field." This would make a fairer price comparison for travelers, who would supposedly choose transit more. Wachs [1981] agreed that automobile use is subsidized; he noted that 93 percent of workers get free parking, and U.S. fuel taxes are much lower than in other countries. However, he concluded that neither highways nor transit should be subsidized to the current extent because the underpricing of both modes encourages more travel and leads to inefficient, dispersed land-use patterns.

Several economists have made theoretical derivations of optimal transit fares, but their recommendations are usually not very practical. It is basically a political decision as to what amount of subsidy is warranted. At present, FTA pays 50 percent of operating deficits (up to a limit set by formula) and up to 80 percent of capital costs. A majority of the states give additional subsidies for local transit. They vary widely; there is no standard pattern. Highly urban states such as New York and New Jersey subsidize transit heavily; largely rural states may have no subsidies.

The consensus is that the price should equal the marginal social cost (including externalities). When the price that travelers pay does not equal the marginal social cost, a correction would increase social welfare. If the price is too low, a tax should be imposed (this is the rationale for congestion pricing). If the price is too high, a subsidy should be used to lower it. If a hidden subsidy causes underpricing, it should be removed (as with free parking).

Are Highways Subsidized?

It is worth examining the question of whether highways are actually subsidized because it is a claim often made by transit advocates. Following are the facts, which reveal a complicated situation.

The Census Bureau annually reports data on finances for all levels of government in the United States. Table 15-2 shows that revenues from highway sources (including fuel taxes, license fees, and tolls) totaled $54.5 billion in the 1990–1991 fiscal year. Table 15-3 shows that direct public expenditures for highways totaled 65.6 billion. This suggests that overall, highways received a subsidy of more than $11 billion.

However, this does not tell the whole story. The revenues do not include (1) property taxes paid on motor vehicles, (2) sales taxes for vehicle purchases and fuel, and (3) special assessments on property owners for street construction. The expenditures do not include the costs of police service, much of which is devoted to traffic control, enforcement, and accidents.

Federal fuel taxes go into the Highway Trust Fund, which has accumulated a surplus of many billion dollars in recent years. This has been done in order to reduce the federal deficit, and of course it is a practice strongly opposed by highway interests. Thus, the U.S. government has been taxing motorists faster than it spends on them (and part of the fund goes for transit). However, the opposite is true for state and local governments.

It is well established that there are several cross-subsidies within the overall picture. Urban areas subsidize rural areas. Rural highways cost a great deal to build and maintain because there are long distances to cover and hence many miles of rural roads. But

TABLE 15-2
GOVERNMENT REVENUES FROM HIGHWAY SOURCES, 1990–1991 FISCAL YEAR
($ millions)

Source	Federal	State	Local	Total
Motor fuel tax	16,917	20,639	677	38,233
Motor vehicle licenses	0	10,131	784	10,915
Operators' licenses	0	865	0	865
Highway charges	0	2,826	1,687	4,513
Totals	16,917	34,461	3,148	54,526

Source: U.S. Bureau of the Census, *Government Finances, 1990–1991,* Series GF–91-5 (Washington: Government Printing Office, 1993), table 6.

TABLE 15-3
DIRECT GOVERNMENT EXPENDITURES FOR HIGHWAYS, 1990–1991 FISCAL YEAR
($ millions)

Activity	Federal	State	Local	Total
Current operation	384	12,087	16,441	28,912
Capital outlay	143	26,824	9,585	36,552
Other	138	0	0	138
Totals	665	38,911	26,026	65,602

Source: U.S. Bureau of the Census, *Government Finances: 1990–1991,* Series GF–91-5 (Washington: Government Printing Office, 1993), table 8.

most of these roads have light traffic and produce little in fuel taxes. This situation occurs partly because, for historical reasons, many state legislatures are dominated by rural members.

It is also clear that in urban areas, off-peak-period users subsidize peak-period users. This is the same pattern as for transit, but the peaking is not so severe; automobile travel is spread more evenly throughout the day.

Expressway users are subsidized by drivers on other streets. The taxes paid by vehicles on expressways do not cover their costs. People driving on residential streets pay a large sum in gas taxes, but the cost of building the streets usually falls on developers (and is passed on to property owners).

Note that the users of toll facilities (bridges, tunnels, and turnpikes) are taxed twice. They pay tolls as well as gas taxes; hence they subsidize motorists who use free routes.

Some claims of subsidy arise from the fact that states may allocate revenues in a manner that corresponds poorly with the sources of the revenues. For example, gas taxes paid by central-city residents may be only partially returned to the city (in the form of state grants for construction and maintenance of state highways). Thus the central city may be subsidizing the suburbs and rural areas. This situation varies from state to state.

This discussion has dealt with only the financial picture. From a broader point of view, it is often argued that highways are subsidized because their users do not pay for such external costs as air pollution, energy waste, and noise. The costs of highway accidents also represent a substantial bill that is not included in the statistics given above.

SOURCES OF FUNDS FOR TRANSIT

The money to subsidize transit comes from a variety of government revenue sources. Much of the federal support comes from general revenues, which derive from various taxes (individual and corporate income taxes are the biggest sources). Of the gas tax, $0.015 per gallon goes into a transit trust fund; this generates about $2 billion per year. Thus, motorists pay a considerable portion of transit subsidies.

But the bulk of transit subsidies come from state and local governments. The sources of funds for these include the following:

General Revenues   Some transit systems are operated as departments of municipal governments, as in Honolulu and San Francisco (for the Muni only). In Pittsburgh, Allegheny County makes up the transit system's operating deficit. Three states (Connecticut, Maryland, and Rhode Island) own and operate local transit systems. Several other states (such as Illinois, New Jersey, and Pennsylvania) make capital and operating assistance grants to local transit systems that are funded from general revenues. In these cases, the funds come from the same mix of revenue sources as other public services.

Sometimes state and local governments provide grants as an emergency measure when a transit authority faces a financial crisis. There are also hidden subsidies for police and students. The New York City transit police are paid by the police department, not the transit authority. Illinois has a program in which pupils pay half-fare and the state reimburses the transit system for the difference. Several states subsidize reduced fares for the elderly and disabled.

Sales Taxes   This is now the most popular way to cover transit losses. Pucher [1981] found that in 1978, 41 percent of nonfederal support for transit came from sales taxes. Major cities with a sales tax for transit include Atlanta, Chicago, Cleveland, Denver, Houston, Kansas City, Los Angeles, New Orleans, St. Louis, San Antonio, San Diego, San Francisco, and Seattle. California and Indiana have state sales taxes earmarked for transit.

Economists consider the sales tax to be regressive, although this depends on whether essentials such as food, clothing, and drugs are taxed. But people seem to prefer it to other taxes, probably because it is paid in dribbles and is "invisible."

Property Taxes   Pucher found that 28 percent of nonfederal support came from this source. The Twin Cities in Minnesota is one major metropolitan area that supports its transit system with property taxes. Property owners in the San Francisco Bay area pay taxes to retire the bonds that financed construction of BART. This also happens in other cities that have sold bonds for transit projects.

Boston has one of the longest histories of subsidizing its transit system with public funds; this has been going on since 1918 [Cudahy 1973]. The Massachusetts Bay Transportation Authority (MBTA) was created in 1964 with power to assess annual charges on Boston and 78 surrounding cities and towns. Each municipality receives an annual bill; a surcharge is added to the local property taxes to pay the bill. This is controversial because a few of the towns do not contain any MBTA routes.

Income and Payroll Taxes   Oregon permits transit districts to levy a payroll tax, and this is done in Portland and Eugene. Cincinnati and Louisville have municipal income taxes which finance transit subsidies.

Bridge and Tunnel Tolls   This source is important in three cities. In New York City, surpluses of the Triborough Bridge and Tunnel Authority help cover transit authority deficits. The Port Authority runs the PATH subway system between New Jersey and Manhattan and uses bridge and tunnel tolls to meet the operating deficit. In Philadelphia, Delaware River Port Authority bridge tolls financed construction of the Lindenwold rail line and help pay operating costs. In San Francisco, tolls on the Bay Bridge paid for construction of the BART tunnel under the bay. Tolls on the Golden Gate Bridge pay for bus and ferry service to Marin County.

Fuel Taxes   Baltimore, Chicago, and Detroit have local gas taxes which help support transit. A few states (including California and Michigan) have a gas tax earmarked for transit and distribute revenues to local governments by formula. This is how San Diego built the Tijuana Trolley without federal aid.

Miscellaneous Sources   Washington state permits transit districts to levy a tax on electric utility bills. Massachusetts allocated part of its cigarette tax to transit in 1965, but ended this arrangement 10 years later. Birmingham, Alabama, adopted a tax on beer in 1983 after a financial crisis closed down its bus system. Pennsylvania and Arizona dedicate part of the receipts from the state lottery. New Jersey spends part of receipts from the Atlantic City casinos on transportation for the elderly and disabled.

As discussed in Chapter 2, at one time many transit systems were owned by utility companies. They used profits on sales of electricity to cover losses on transit. This mostly ended when the electric trusts sold their transit operations in the 1930s. However, the New Orleans transit system was still owned by the local utility until quite recently. For years, New Orleans had one of the lowest fares in the country, and per capita ridership was unusually high [Ristroph 1959].

Several states (such as Maryland, New Jersey, and Virginia) have established combined transportation trust funds that are used for both highways and transit. Receipts come from a mix of sources, including sales taxes, fuel taxes, vehicle registration fees, and bridge and tunnel tolls.

Cervero [1983] conducted a national survey of state and local transit officials about tax sources and found a strong preference for automobile-related taxes such as fuel taxes and vehicle registration fees. This reflected a belief that "public transportation should be financed from revenues generated within the transportation sector, and moreover that motorists have some obligation to pay transit's bills. . . . The use of highway-related funds to support public transit has long been advocated as a way to induce motorists to switch to the transit mode" [p. 28].

However, there is an inherent contradiction in using automobile-based taxes to support transit. If this approach were successful in inducing thousands of motorists to shift to transit, then the revenue source would diminish. At the extreme, if everyone opted for transit, there would be no money to pay for it.

Next in popularity among the transit officials was the sales tax, while the property tax and income tax ranked low. Another survey found that local politicians preferred the sales tax. It is clear that many citizens find the sales tax acceptable, as most of the existing sales taxes dedicated to transit were approved at public elections. The property tax seems to be the most objectionable, partly because it comes in large bills once or twice a year.

EARMARKED TAXES AND TRUST FUNDS

Some taxes are earmarked or dedicated for expenditure on one specific use. Often they go into a trust fund, and if receipts exceed expenditures in any year, the surplus is saved for future years. Earmarked taxes are distinct from general revenues, which can be spent on any legitimate purpose as decided in the annual budget. Trust funds are outside the normal budgeting process.

Public administrators generally oppose trust funds because the funds reduce flexibility in budgeting. The administrators believe that raising money and spending money should be handled separately. The various expenditure needs of a government should be compared with each other on merit, and not influenced by how much money happens to be available in particular funds. This position seems reasonable, but not everyone agrees that the sources of money should be ignored in deciding how to spend it.

Economists are more sympathetic with trust funds; they believe that the funds can be justified by the *benefit principle* of taxation. This holds that those who receive the benefits of a public service should pay the costs through fees or taxes. Highway trust funds are considered fairly good in this respect because truckers and motorists pay most of the taxes and get most of the benefits. However, it is questionable whether the benefit principle applies to many earmarked taxes.

In truth, creation of a trust fund to receive earmarked taxes is often a highly political act. Supporters of a particular program want to commit a tax source and guarantee permanent funding for that program. Thus they largely escape the kind of legislative scrutiny that is applied to an annual budget. Transit supporters are not immune to this temptation.

The best-known trust fund is the federal Highway Trust Fund, created in 1956 to pay for the interstate highway system. Its receipts come from federal fuel taxes. This means of financing was chosen because it was estimated that tolls would not raise enough money (the states had preempted the most financially attractive routes for their own toll roads, built in the 1940s and 1950s). For years, this fund could be spent only for construction of new highways. Since it was "busted" in 1973, part has been used for transit capital improvements, but not for operating subsidies.

Most states have their own highway trust funds. Years ago, state gas taxes were often diverted to nonhighway purposes. (New Jersey was famous for this; it enabled the state to avoid both an income tax and a sales tax for many years.) This became a major issue in the 1930s, and highway supporters were able to get gas taxes dedicated in most states. A 1934 federal law penalized states that increased the diversion of their gas taxes to nonhighway use.

Now there are many taxes earmarked for transit. As noted, part of the federal gas tax goes into a transit account in the Highway Trust Fund. Many of the state and local taxes mentioned above are earmarked for transit. This is especially true of local sales taxes.

Obviously transit people welcome this trend since it is in their self-interest. However, there are valid objections. For one, the sales tax is regressive; it would be better to use the personal income tax. It is also questionable whether the benefit principle applies. It can be argued that motorists benefit from promoting transit use, but not everyone agrees motorists should be taxed for this.

In reality, political expediency has been a major factor. In the typical scenario, legislators became tired of facing the financial crises of the transit system year after year and seeing transit take a larger and larger share of annual budgets. They wanted to get transit out of the way. They proposed a new tax to save the transit system. This was important enough to voters that they usually (but not always) approved the tax.

Earmarked taxes are not completely reliable. Sales tax receipts depend on the volume of retail sales and go down during a recession. For many years, fuel tax receipts climbed steadily in what seemed a predictable trend. That changed with the energy crisis in the 1970s. As the public switched to more fuel-efficient vehicles, tax receipts dipped and many state highway departments encountered financial difficulties. The problem was eventually remedied by raising the tax rates.

While there is room for debate, earmarked taxes do not seem desirable to this writer. It would be better if we never had highway trust funds. It would be preferable to raise money for transit in some other way. Income taxes are probably the best because they are the most progressive.

EQUITY IN TRANSIT FINANCE

There has been much interest among scholars in determining whether the system of transit finance redistributes income to disadvantaged groups. Several studies have estimated the consumption of transit service and compared it with the distribution of payments (fares and taxes), either for different population groups or for geographical areas. The object is to find out who benefits and who pays.

Dajani et al. [1975] analyzed selected districts in Atlanta and calculated that families in all areas would receive net benefits from the MARTA rail system. They found that the level of net benefits was strongly related to distance from the nearest station, but there was no significant relationship with income. This study was made before the system opened and was based on projected ridership.

Hoachlander studied BART and concluded that "Relative to their incomes and their proportions in the BART district, the wealthy ride BART, and the poor pay for it" [1976, p. 35]. BART riders were underrepresented among households with low income, African-Americans, Hispanics, children, and the elderly. Local subsidies for BART come from sales and property taxes, which are regressive (the poor pay a higher percentage of their incomes than the rich do). This was perhaps an inevitable result of designing the network largely to bring suburban commuters to downtown San Francisco and Oakland.

Hodge [1988] analyzed the bus system in metropolitan Seattle and estimated that peripheral areas received a higher subsidy per passenger than the central city did. However, the peripheral areas also paid more in taxes and had a higher ratio of total payments to total costs. This occurred because these areas had high proportions of nonusers who paid taxes but received no direct benefits.

The most comprehensive study was made by Pucher, who concluded that "those types of transit most frequently used by the poor are the least subsidized, and those most used by the affluent are the most heavily subsidized" [1981, p. 389]. Bus riders get the least subsidy, subway riders get more, and commuter rail passengers get the most. However, the poor use transit more and are more likely to gain from the subsidies. Overall, Pucher found, the distribution of subsidies by income class was roughly proportional to the distribution of the population. In other words, the subsidies had a neutral effect on income distribution; they did not redistribute income.

The other side of the picture is: Who pays for the transit subsidies? This depends on what types of taxes finance the subsidies and the incidence of those taxes. Pucher found that overall, tax financing of the subsidies was progressive—largely because 53 percent of transit aid came from the federal government and federal taxes are progressive.

When benefits and payments were combined, transit aid was progressive. Benefits exceeded tax payments for the poor; middle-income people came out about even; and the rich paid more in taxes than they got in benefits.

This was mainly because the federal government played a large role in the year for which the analysis was done (1978). Since then, the federal government has reduced transit aid and shifted the burden to state and local governments. This means that transit aid is becoming less progressive because state and local taxation is regressive (it relies more on sales and property taxes than income taxes).

QUESTIONS

1 In theory, a transit agency could set its fare at a level at which it would break even financially (average cost pricing). If a transit agency did this, what would be the results? Why is this possibility rarely considered?

2 Evaluate the current practices for pricing mass transit in the United States. What changes would you recommend in the ways in which passengers are charged for their rides?

3 Is congestion pricing of highways a good idea? Is it likely to be implemented in the United States? Would it benefit the rich more than the poor?

4 Some transportation experts believe that transit service should be free. They argue that transit is an essential public service—like schools, libraries, and police and fire protection—and the benefits to the community justify this. Do you agree with this position? What problems might it cause?

5 The Reagan administration tried (but failed) to eliminate federal subsidies for transit operating costs. Do you think these subsidies should be ended? What would the effects be?

6 What are the most popular revenue sources used to finance transit operations? Which ones seem to be most acceptable to taxpayers? What changes would you make in the way money is raised to pay for transit?

REFERENCES

Bates, John W.: "Effect of Fare Reduction on Transit Ridership in the Atlanta Region: Summary of Transit Passenger Data," *Transportation Research Record,* no. 499 (1974), pp. 1–11.

Boyle, Daniel K.: "Are Transit Riders Becoming Less Sensitive to Fare Increases?" *Transportation Research Record,* no. 1039 (1985), pp. 43–45.

Cervero, Robert: "Views on Transit Tax Financing in the U.S.," *Transportation,* vol. 12, no. 1 (August 1983), pp. 21–43.

———: "Experiences with Time-of-Day Transit Pricing in the United States," *Transportation Research Record,* no. 1039 (1985), pp. 21–30.

Cudahy, Brian J.: "Financing Transit: The Boston Experience," *Highway Research Record,* no. 476 (1973), pp. 4–7.

Curtin, John F.: "Effect of Fares on Transit Riding," *Highway Research Record,* no. 213 (1968), pp. 8–20.

Dajani, Jarir, M. Michael Egan, and Marjorie B. McElroy: "The Redistributive Impact of the Atlanta Mass Transit System," *Southern Economic Journal,* vol. 42, no. 1 (July 1975), pp. 49–60.

Domencich, Thomas A., and Gerald Kraft: *Free Transit* (Lexington, MA: D.C. Heath, 1970).

Doxsey, Lawrence D., and Bruce D. Spear: "Free-Fare Transit: Some Empirical Findings," *Transportation Research Record,* no. 799 (1981), pp. 47–49.

Hau, Timothy D.: "Electronic Road Pricing: Developments in Hong Kong 1983–1989," *Journal of Transport Economics and Policy,* vol. 24, no. 2 (May 1990), pp. 203–214.

Higgins, Thomas J.: "Road-Pricing Attempts in the United States," *Transportation Research,* vol. 20A, no. 2 (March 1986), pp. 145–150.

Hoachlander, E. Gareth: *Bay Area Rapid Transit: Who Pays and Who Benefits?* (Berkeley: Institute of Urban and Regional Development, University of California, July 1976).

Hodge, David C.: "Fiscal Equity in Urban Mass Transit Systems: A Geographical Analysis," *Annals of the Association of American Geographers,* vol. 78, no. 2 (1988), pp. 288–306.

Kirby, Ronald F.: "Pricing Strategies for Public Transportation," *Journal of the American Planning Association,* vol. 48, no. 3 (Summer 1982), pp. 327–334.

——— and Robert G. McGillivray: "Alternative Subsidy Techniques for Urban Public Transportation," *Transportation Research Record,* no. 589 (1976), pp. 25–29.

Kulash, Damian: "Parking Taxes as Roadway Prices: A Case Study of the San Francisco Experience," *Transportation Research Record,* no. 494 (1974), pp. 25–34.

Lassow, William: "Effect of the Fare Increase of July 1966 on the Number of Passengers Carried on the New York City Transit System," *Highway Research Record,* no. 213 (1968), pp. 1–7.

Markowitz, Joel E.: "Prospects for Differential Transit Pricing in the United States," *Transportation Research Record,* no. 1078 (1986), pp. 39–48.

Mayworm, Patrick D.: "Transit Fare Elasticity: Role in Fare Policy and Planning," *Transportation Research Record,* no. 862 (1982), pp. 29–35.

O'Connell, W. H.: *Ride Free, Drive Free: The Transit Trust Fund and the Robin Hood Principle* (New York: John Day Company, 1973).

Orski, C. Kenneth: "Congestion Pricing: Its Promise and Its Limitations," *Transportation Planning,* vol. 18, no. 2 (Summer 1991), pp. 15–20.

Pucher, John: "Equity in Transit Finance: Distribution of Transit Subsidy Benefits and Costs among Income Classes," *Journal of the American Planning Association,* vol. 47, no. 4 (October 1981), pp. 387–407.

Pushkarev, Boris S., and Jeffrey M. Zupan: *Public Transportation and Land Use Policy* (Bloomington: Indiana University Press, 1977).

Ristroph, Paul L.: "New Orleans' Seven-Cent Bus Fare," *Traffic Quarterly,* vol. 13, no. 3 (July 1959), pp. 402–407.

Studenmund, A. H., Sherrill Swan, and David Connor: "Interim Analysis of Free-Fare Transit Experiments," *Transportation Research Record,* no. 719 (1979), pp. 13–21.

Vickrey, William S.: "A Proposal for Revising New York's Subway Fare Structure," *Operations Research,* vol. 3, no. 1 (February 1955), pp. 38–68.

———: "Pricing in Urban and Suburban Transport," *American Economic Review,* vol. 53, no. 2 (May 1963), pp. 452–465.

Wachs, Martin: "Pricing Urban Transportation: A Critique of Current Policy," *Journal of the American Planning Association,* vol. 47, no. 3 (July 1981), pp. 243–251.

Watson, Peter L., and Edward P. Holland: "Congestion Pricing: The Example of Singapore," in *Urban Transportation Economics,* Special Report 181 (Washington: Transportation Research Board, 1978), pp. 27–30.

Wilson, Paul W.: "Welfare Effects of Congestion Pricing in Singapore," *Transportation,* vol. 15, no. 3 (1988), pp. 191–210.

16

POLICIES FOR THE FUTURE

It seems inevitable that the automobile will remain the primary mode of personal transportation in the United States for several decades to come. Perhaps in the distant future, petroleum resources will near exhaustion; then alternate fuels may come into widespread use. The preference for individual transportation is very strong, although it can be partially satisfied by bicycles and walking.

There is little possibility of a return to 19th-century conditions in which public transportation was dominant. The pertinent issue is whether mass transit will survive. In the author's opinion, the answer is yes. Large cities such as New York and Chicago are not going to disappear, and the central business district remains an important focal point for certain activities. Such cities could not function if all travel were by private vehicles. In addition, there will always be part of the population who cannot afford automobiles or who are unable to use them.

This chapter begins with a summary of future trends that will affect transit. This is followed by a recapitulation of major policy issues that have remained prominent for many years and will continue to do so. Next are brief discussions of two approaches that offer promise; one is reforming the automobile, and the other involves major changes in land-use patterns. The chapter concludes with the author's views on policies that are feasible in the current economic and political climate and that could enhance the effectiveness of mass transit.

FUTURE TRENDS

Let us consider at this point the directions in which urban transportation is likely to go in the coming years. This involves speculation, but it is probable that many current trends will persist for some time, while some emerging changes are already visible.

From the viewpoint of mass transit, some of the trends will be harmful, others will be helpful, and still others will have little effect one way or another. (For a fuller discussion of the trends, see Transportation Research Board [1988].)

Bad for Transit

Recent population shifts in the United States have caused decreases in transit use, and these movements seem certain to continue. One is the persistent growth of the suburbs. As jobs have moved out from the central city, the dominant commuting pattern is now from suburb to suburb [Pisarski 1987]. Fixed-route transit cannot serve this pattern economically and efficiently. Although automobile travel is easy in many areas, in the suburbs of the largest metropolitan areas, highway congestion has become a problem attracting considerable attention [Cervero 1986]. The main approach is travel demand management, with emphasis on increased ride sharing. However, there is likely to be an increased supply of demand-responsive transit in suburban areas.

Another major trend is the migration to the southern and western states known collectively as the sun belt. California, Texas, and Florida are attracting the most migrants. This trend seems sure to persist, as people in the United States opt for warmer climates and geographic areas with more amenities. This trend also tends to decrease transit use. Most sun belt cities have low population densities that are difficult for transit to serve. Meanwhile, most large cities in the frost belt are growing slowly or are even losing population (see Table 16-1 for a comparison of regions). Basically, people are moving from transit-oriented cities to automobile-oriented cities.

Growth of the fleet of private vehicles should continue, but at a lower rate than in the past, as the market approaches saturation. This will largely occur through families owning multiple vehicles, as the number of one-car households declines. This will provide more mobility for spouses and teenaged children, but it will also affect transit ridership. There is also an increase in the popularity of specialized vehicles such as vans, pickup trucks, and recreational vehicles. This means some families will have more vehicles than persons, as different vehicles are used for different purposes.

The costs of providing transit service have risen rapidly in recent years, and there is no sign of their abating. This includes the cost of building new transit lines, of purchasing vehicles, and of operating services. Efforts at cost containment have met with only modest success. One factor is the growth in federal regulation, exemplified by the Buy America clause and the 1990 Americans with Disabilities Act. Another factor is the power of labor unions, which will remain strong in large cities. Privatization may produce some cost savings, but it is likely to occur on a modest scale.

Although there is strong interest in reducing the federal deficit, it will be many years before the federal government has a balanced budget. Since tax increases are difficult to obtain, there will be increasing pressure to cut expenditures. Hence large increases in federal transit subsidies are unlikely. Reductions in defense expenditures may bring a "peace dividend," but there will be numerous claimants on the money competing with the transit lobby. On the other hand, the spending authorized by ISTEA, together with the flexibility in allocating funds between highways and transit, should bring some increased capital investment in new transit facilities.

TABLE 16-1
FASTEST-GROWING METROPOLITAN AREAS* IN EACH REGION, 1980 TO 1990

| Metropolitan area | Population | | | Percentage increase |
	1980	1990	Increase	
Northeast				
Hartford	1,013,508	1,085,837	72,329	7.1
Providence	1,083,139	1,141,510	58,371	5.4
Boston	3,971,792	4,171,643	199,851	5.0
Philadelphia	5,680,509	5,899,345	218,836	3.9
Midwest				
Minneapolis–St. Paul	2,137,133	2,464,124	326,991	15.3
Columbus	1,243,827	1,377,419	133,592	10.7
Kansas City	1,433,464	1,566,280	132,816	9.3
Indianapolis	1,166,575	1,249,822	83,247	7.1
South				
Orlando	699,904	1,072,748	372,844	53.3
Dallas–Fort Worth	2,930,568	3,885,415	954,847	32.6
Atlanta	2,138,136	2,833,511	695,375	32.5
Tampa–St. Petersburg	1,613,600	2,067,959	454,359	28.2
West				
Phoenix	1,509,175	2,122,101	612,926	40.6
Sacramento	1,099,814	1,481,102	381,288	34.7
San Diego	1,861,846	2,498,015	636,169	34.2
Los Angeles	11,497,549	14,531,529	3,033,980	26.4

*Only areas with a 1990 population of 1 million or more.
Source: 1990 Census.

Good for Transit

There is renewed emphasis on air quality problems, shown by enactment of the Clean Air Act Amendments of 1990. This law imposes specific deadlines for nonattainment areas to meet ambient air standards. Earlier laws have succeeded in reducing the level of emissions per vehicle, but in fast-growing metropolitan areas, this effect has been swamped by growth in the number of vehicles. Los Angeles remains the "smog capital" of the country, while some other sun belt cities (such as Denver) have seen their air quality markedly deteriorate.

In most urban areas, motor vehicles form the major contributor to air pollution. Hence there will be increasing pressure to get people to switch to alternate means of travel, such as ride sharing, transit, bicycles, and walking. Regulation XV in southern California is an example. However, the success of this approach will depend on how strictly the laws are enforced. In the past, penalties available under law have seldom been imposed.

There is continuing concern about energy consumption, the depletion of oil reserves, and U.S. dependence on imported oil. This is reflected in the energy bill that Congress passed and President Bush signed in 1992. Raising the corporate average fuel economy (CAFE) standard is a political issue, since this might adversely affect the automobile industry. Again, switching travelers to alternate modes such as transit is an approach favored by many.

A major energy crisis is one scenario that might drastically alter consumption patterns. A study of the future of the automobile industry concluded that technological developments (such as conversion to alternate fuels) should adequately address such a situation [Altshuler et al. 1984]. However, technological changes tend to raise prices, and higher prices deter the acquisition and use of automobiles. It takes a long time to implement new technology on a wide scale, during which many travelers would shift to transit.

There seems to be greater public acceptance of high-density living, which makes transit more feasible. During the 1950s and 1960s, most new housing took the form of single-family suburban homes, and the larger the lot, the better. In the last two decades, there has been more construction of garden apartments in the suburbs. The town house has also become a popular form of suburban development (with densities as high as 20 units per acre). There is still a preference for large lots, but rapidly escalating prices of new homes have forced many people to compromise.

Large suburban developments called *megacenters* have arisen in many large metropolitan areas. They contain thousands of jobs in relatively small areas. This offers some potential for fixed-route transit if services are designed innovatively (e.g., the transit center and timed-transfer concepts).

The central business district is still a major concentration of white-collar employment in most cities. Besides offices, this location has been favored for hotels, public buildings, and some retail projects such as Quincy Market in Boston and Harborplace in Baltimore. Even in older central cities where there is relatively little investment, the CBD has been a strong point in the real estate market. Almost every large or medium-size city has had a downtown building boom at some time in the past two decades. Thus traditional transit services focusing on the CBD will continue to attract patrons.

It would be incorrect to say that ride sharing is becoming more popular, since 1990 Census data show a large increase in solo commuting and a decrease in carpooling. However, ride sharing may become more acceptable to people fed up with suburban gridlock. There is political approval, as traffic reduction ordinances have been adopted in some communities (although mostly in California). Employers have also shown support in the voluntary formation of transportation management associations. Probably increased ride sharing will be the major approach to solving congestion problems in suburban areas.

There will be more flexibility in urban transportation funding, especially at the federal level. Some politicians and academics have long favored a federal block grant for transportation, which could be allocated among various modes at state or local discretion. ISTEA takes a step in this direction, but does not go all the way. A true block grant will probably come in the future. This will mean more funding for transit in highly urbanized states such as New York and Massachusetts, where many people rely on transit and it is a popular cause. Rural states will spend most of their money on highways, and bus systems in small cities may suffer.

There seems to be more willingness by urban residents to accept higher taxes to support local transit systems. Federal financial aid to transit declined during the Reagan years, but state and local governments increased their support. The most popular form is a local sales tax earmarked for transit, which usually requires approval at a public election. Voters have passed many such proposals, although some have been defeated. Economists consider sales taxes to be regressive; it would be preferable to finance transit with income taxes. However, there is no sign of a trend to use income taxes for this purpose. There is great popular resistance to taxes that are paid in large sums on infrequent occasions. The sales tax is an "invisible" tax that is paid in small amounts frequently.

Technological advances will have some impact on transit, but there is not likely to be any kind of revolution. Automated rail systems will probably be built in several U.S. cities. The technology has been proved in Vancouver and the Docklands light rail line in London. Some people claim that people in the United States will not accept trains driven by computers, but there has been little objection to automated people movers used in several airports and CBDs. It is worth noting that at one time, there were thousands of elevator operators in the United States; now there are almost none. Other new technology will not have major impacts. In the author's opinion, intelligent vehicle-highway systems will not be widely implemented, although some features may prove to be practical and useful.

Local governments will continue to own and operate most transit services, but there will be increasing opportunities for private enterprise. Monopolistic transit authorities will have their power diminished, and there will be more competition among providers. This will increase efficiency and flexibility in some cases, because private firms are more responsive to market forces. Some cost reductions are likely, but these stem mostly from paying lower wage rates than public agencies. This cost advantage may disappear in time.

Neutral for Transit

There has been much discussion about the substitution of communications for travel, and several scholars specialize in this subject. There has been rapid dissemination of such electronic devices as personal computers, facsimile machines, and cellular phones. For many years, white-collar employment has been increasing, while blue-collar jobs have declined. Some economists believe the so-called quarternary sector, involving the processing of information, will become the dominant part of the economy.

The possibilities were identified in a review article by Salomon [1986]. The most important involves large numbers of white-collar workers performing their duties at home, obviating the journey to work. Many people already work at home, but they tend to be self-employed business people or those engaged in research or creative work (such as writers, artists, and scholars). Perhaps clerical workers could work at home, retrieving information from files over telephone lines and transmitting documents by fax. An alternative is to have people report to neighborhood work centers dispersed throughout a metropolitan area, instead of traveling to a central office in the CBD. Such arrangements are called *telecommuting*.

Census data show a substantial increase in the number of persons who worked at home between 1980 and 1990 (see Table 16-2). This reversed a decline that had gone on for two decades. Since these are totals for the entire United States, the decline was attributed to a decrease in the number of persons engaged in farming.

Telecommunications might replace travel for other purposes. People might do their shopping and banking via home computers. Teleconferencing already occurs; people in different locations hold meetings via telephone or television. There have also been applications in the field of education. Some universities transmit lectures to satellite classrooms by television. In some places one can receive instruction at home on cable television.

There are several reasons for a firm to congregate workers at one site. In the past, the major reason was that the workers operated machines or handled materials. However, employment in manufacturing has declined for many years as a result of automation and higher productivity. The machines many workers use today are computers, which could just as well be located at home. Central files—a reason to bring workers to office buildings—are now usually kept in computer memory, which can be accessed at home.

The main argument against telecommuting is the value of face-to-face contact. This is clearly important for activities such as selling, negotiating, listening to complaints, and evaluating the immediate reactions of others. However, many routine jobs do not require these functions. Chance encounters can be productive in making new contacts and stimulating ideas. Socializing with colleagues is an attractive feature of the workday for many; it boosts worker morale. Then there is the question of supervision: Who can be sure that people working at home are making the effort that is expected of them?

These points are well taken. They suggest that the work-at-home trend will be gradual, and that traditional factories, stores, and offices will not disappear any time soon. A key factor is that telecommuting seems to offer limited benefit for employers. It is the workers who would benefit by eliminating the journey to work, which is not paid time.

TABLE 16-2
PERSONS WHO WORKED AT HOME IN THE UNITED STATES

Year	Total workers	Worked at home	
		Number	Percent
1960	61,873,929	4,662,750	7.54
1970	76,852,389	2,685,144	3.49
1980	96,617,296	2,179,863	2.26
1990	115,070,274	3,406,025	2.96

Source: U.S. Census.

Thus, many firms have little incentive to change. However, some companies might be able to reduce their office space or parking facilities. Also, some firms may be forced by regulation to adopt this approach (which is an acceptable means of meeting trip reduction targets).

Mokhtarian [1991] summarized recent evidence on telecommuting in the United States: It is clearly on the rise. She cited a 1991 survey that showed that 5.5 million persons telecommute from home; this was 2.5 times the number in 1988. However, only 16 percent of these telecommuted 35 hours or more per week. Studies show that noncommute trips do not increase—they actually decrease. There is strong interest in telecommuting among transportation planners and policy makers. Several states have taken initiatives to promote it, and the concept was endorsed by President Bush.

The unanswered question is: To what extent will telecommunications replace travel? Working at home will be popular with many, and employers may find it valuable in attracting and retaining workers. Clearly the major impact would be on automobile travel, since this is the dominant urban travel mode. Ride sharing might become less convenient, and transit use might fall somewhat.

A related development is the use of staggered work hours, flextime, and the 4-day workweek. The first two would shift some travel to off-peak times, which would be helpful for both highways and transit. The 4-day workweek presumably would eliminate 20 percent of commuting trips; this would affect both roads and transit. It is uncertain how widespread these practices will become. They are popular with some people because greater flexibility essentially means greater freedom. The idea of a 3-day weekend is very attractive to many.

A societal trend that is ineluctable is the aging of the population. The number of elderly persons will grow steadily in coming decades. This will probably have little effect on transit. In the past, the elderly were above-average users of transit, but in recent years more of this group have been living in the suburbs and driving cars. There may be some increased demand for paratransit services for those senior citizens who can no longer drive.

Although the bicycle and pedestrian modes receive little attention from transportation planners today, these modes may get more emphasis in the future. They have obvious benefits, such as requiring no mechanical energy and being good for personal health. Both modes are slow, which makes it possible to observe the immediate environment; some people consider this an amenity. The popularity of bicycles has been increasing for years, especially in college towns like Davis, California. Bike lanes and separate roadways for cyclists may become more common. There will probably be greater use of automobile-free zones, particularly in downtown areas and college campuses.

MAJOR POLICY ISSUES

Many controversies involving urban transportation have been discussed in this book. Following is a summary of the five major policy issues that have dominated the field for many years and are likely to remain in the forefront for a long time.

Highways versus Transit

This remains a top issue after all these years. It is partially a liberal versus conservative issue: Liberals tend to favor transit, while conservatives favor highways. But local interests transcend these labels. Senator Alfonse D'Amato of New York, a conservative Republican, has been one of the strongest supporters of federal aid for transit (he comes from Long Island, and transit is important to many of his constituents).

Transit advocates have done well in Congress in the last three decades. They got their own federal agency (now called the Federal Transit Administration) in 1968. They "busted" the Highway Trust Fund in 1973 and won federal operating subsidies in 1974. A transit trust fund was established in 1982, with dedicated receipts from the federal fuel tax.

The highway interests made a comeback when Reagan was President, and there was a revival of highway building around the country. The federal gas tax was raised in 1982 and 1990, with a majority of the money going to highway construction. The federal government cut funding for transit, while funding for highways increased substantially. With the passage of ISTEA in 1991, expenditures on both highways and transit are likely to rise.

There is a vast literature on this subject. Many of the works embody an attack on the automobile/highway system. Mumford [1964], Mowbray [1969], and Leavitt [1970] criticized the interstate highway program. Keats [1958] ridiculed the design of automobiles. Nader [1965] focused public attention on the safety defects of motor vehicles. Schneider [1971] decried the impact of the automobile on urban life. Rothschild [1973] and Yates [1983] chronicled the decline of the U.S. automobile industry.

A counterattack to this genre was a book written by Bruce-Briggs [1977] that defended the automobile. Here is the gist of his argument:

People in the United States live in a mass production society whose benefits have filtered down to the entire population to a remarkable degree. While some people live in poverty, they comprise a minority. The average family can afford many of the same material goods as the rich—in particular, owning a car and living in a single-family home in the suburbs.

Upper-class enjoyment of such benefits was spoiled when they became available to the masses. Highways became crowded with ever more vehicles. The suburbs were once attractive; when they grew into urban sprawl, they became ugly. The upper class resents spreading of these advantages; they want other people to stay in the central city and ride transit.

The intellectuals who mold public opinion mostly come from the upper and upper-middle classes. They may not be personally wealthy, but they crystallize and disseminate the views of the upper class. This group is often called the *Eastern establishment*; Bruce-Briggs called them the *new class*. This elite has led the attack on the automobile and on suburbs. Since they control the media, they have succeeded in influencing many people.

Bruce-Briggs cited members of the new class who have criticized the automobile, including Mumford, Keats, and Senator Daniel Patrick Moynihan, who wrote some anti-automobile articles when he was a professor at Harvard. Bruce-Briggs noted that

Nader is a graduate of Princeton and Harvard Law School. Rothschild is a member of one of the richest families in the world.

According to Bruce-Briggs, the "silent majority" of people in the United States are better off than ever before. They want to keep their automobiles and suburban homes. Since this is supposed to be a democratic country, we should let them do so. We should build more highways and stop creating obstacles to automobile ownership. While this book must be considered extremist, Bruce-Briggs does make some telling points.

Choice of Transit Technology

The debate between rail and bus proponents remains heated; apparently this issue will never die. Light rail transit (LRT), seen by some as a compromise, is currently very popular. From 1981 through 1993, eight U.S. cities opened new LRT systems. As of this writing, additional lines are under construction in Dallas, Denver, and Los Angeles. Several other cities are planning light rail lines, and some of these will probably be built.

Prospects for new heavy rail systems seem less bright because they are so expensive to build. The Los Angeles subway opened in 1993, and it is going to be extended. Several other cities, such as Houston and Honolulu, have seriously considered building new rail transit lines, but the persistent federal deficit may prevent these schemes from being realized.

Meanwhile, busways and high-occupancy vehicle (HOV) lanes have been constructed in a score of U.S. cities. They seem to work well, and most are relatively inexpensive. Seattle pioneered in building a tunnel for buses under its CBD, but this was a very costly project. The spending authorized by ISTEA may bring a new round of large-capital projects, involving both rail and bus.

Responsibility for Transit

The dominant issue of the 1980s was the privatization policy initiated by the Reagan administration. Most local transit officials opposed it because they are running monopolies and do not want competition. Since they are often unresponsive to changing patterns of demand and timid about innovations, there is justification for opening up opportunities for private firms.

However, there will not be any major shift of transit back to the private sector. There are many small private operations, some well established, others new. There are some affluent markets for transit, but not many. The bulk of transit serves the poor, and it is unlikely that anyone can make a profit providing transit to the poor. The major involvement of private firms will be seen in contracting with public agencies to supply supplemental services (such as demand-responsive service for the disabled).

The other aspect is the role of state and local governments. The Reagan administration succeeded in transferring some of the responsibility for transit to them, and this trend should continue. ISTEA gives more discretion to state and local officials in allocating federal aid between highways and transit. To many, this seems a wise approach:

The federal government has more ability to raise money, while the lower levels of government are closer to the people and understand local needs better. However, some transit proponents are skeptical. If state and local governments have more choice, some will spend more for highways and less for transit. Only in highly urban states, such as New Jersey and Maryland, will transit get a large share.

Financing

Operating costs continue to rise, as well as the deficits of transit agencies. Transit people are anxious to keep fares down in order to keep ridership up. They want to avoid getting into a spiral of higher fares, lower ridership, higher fares, etc., such as happened in the 1950s and 1960s.

Federal aid declined during the 1980s. This was offset by increased revenues from state and local governments, which are assuming more of the financial burden. The sales tax is a popular option because it seems to be politically acceptable. Voters in many metropolitan areas have approved sales taxes earmarked for transit. There is also a trend toward taxing motorists to help pay for transit. Congestion pricing of highways has been widely discussed; it could produce large revenues, some of which might go to transit. However, this approach may encounter strong political opposition.

Some experts believe there should be unrestricted federal block grants for transportation. This would eliminate separate funding for highways and transit, and separate funding for capital investment and operating costs. Local officials could decide how to spend the money. As noted, ISTEA does grant greater flexibility, so there is movement in this direction.

Equity

Concern for the transportation-disadvantaged received less attention in the 1980s, but it has returned as a major issue. In 1990 Congress enacted the Americans with Disabilities Act, which is rewriting the rules on service to the disabled. The elderly also continue to be a strong lobbying force. Helping the poor is one motive behind the desire of many planners and politicians to keep fares in check.

Equity can be a major issue at the local level, as in Cleveland [Krumholz and Cogger 1985]. Transit proposals may be examined closely to determine what groups will benefit the most. Ever since analysis of BART showed that it mostly benefited people with above-average incomes, rail lines to the suburbs have been opposed on these grounds. Clearly low fares and improved bus service in the inner city would serve the poor better.

There is no sign that poverty will be eliminated in the United States. In fact, the number of persons below the poverty line has been increasing in recent years. There will always be some people without access to an automobile, because of income, age, disability, or other barriers. There will be a continuing need to provide transit service for these people, who have been left behind in the evolution of our automobile-dominated society.

REFORMING THE AUTOMOBILE

Background

When Brock Adams became Secretary of Transportation in 1977, there was a rethinking of urban transportation policy. It was decided that supporting transit was not a successful approach because (1) transit ridership had grown relatively little, (2) transit required ever-increasing subsidies, and (3) automobile use continued to multiply. Instead, Adams took a policy approach that was popularly called *reinventing the automobile*.

Adams announced this policy in a speech to the Detroit Economic Club in 1978. He suggested the automobile industry and federal government cooperate in an effort to mass-produce an optimum automobile by 1990. The emphasis was on energy conservation, with a goal of 50 miles per gallon as the fleet average. The car should also meet all emissions and safety standards.

Soon the Department of Transportation was deluged with proposals from hundreds of inventors with ideas about how to improve the automobile. A task force was set up to screen these. In February 1979, 700 delegates from the automobile industry attended a technical conference in Boston. In May, President Carter met the heads of the automobile companies at the White House.

This initiative faded after Adams unexpectedly left office. President Carter reshuffled his cabinet in the summer of 1979; Adams was one of those not asked to stay. He was replaced by Neil Goldschmidt, mayor of Portland, Oregon, who was considered a transit advocate.

The Reagan administration showed no interest in this approach, and it was forgotten for a time. But it seems relevant again with the federal endorsement of programs to find alternate fuels for automobiles and to develop intelligent vehicle-highway systems. Is it a good idea? Following is an evaluation of the pros and cons of reinventing the automobile with regard to major aspects of the urban transportation problem.

Evaluation

It is technologically feasible to design a car that gets 100 miles per gallon, which would promote energy conservation. It would be light and small, since weight is a major factor in fuel consumption. There has been a trend toward better-mileage cars; some now on the market get more than 50 miles per gallon. There is much experimentation with alternate fuels, which could reduce U.S. dependence on petroleum imports. However, it is uncertain whether these fuels will be economical.

Air pollution could be reduced. Better mileage is generally compatible with lower emissions because the less gas you burn, the less the emissions. Early emission control devices did reduce automobile mileage noticeably, but this problem has been largely solved. Control devices do add some weight to the vehicle.

Safety seems to be the biggest concern about the concept. The automobile companies argue that smaller, lighter vehicles do not hold up as well in accidents. Many studies indicate that small foreign cars do not protect their occupants as well as U.S. cars in a crash (the Volkswagen Beetle had an especially bad record). Collisions between small cars and big cars are tough on the small cars. If all cars were small, it would not be such a problem.

However, engineers can increase safety through better design, and they might be able to offset the disadvantages. Other measures such as airbags, stronger bumpers, safer highways, and reduction of drunk driving would all help to lower the accident toll.

With the technological improvements, the new cars would undoubtedly be more expensive. Hence the approach would not raise the mobility of the transportation-disadvantaged, since many of the poor would be unable to afford them. Some people will never be able to drive in any case. Transit services would have to remain to serve these people.

The idea is compatible with preferences in the United States for personal mobility and the suburban lifestyle. Except for the automobile manufacturers, there should be little political or popular resistance. Consumers would retain freedom of choice, and restraints on behavior would be minimal.

A major drawback is that better mileage means lower travel cost per mile. This would encourage more travel, and the number of vehicle-miles driven would increase (exactly how much depends on the elasticity of demand). Hence energy savings would be less than you might expect. There could be some reduction in traffic congestion because short cars use less road space than long cars [McClenahan and Simkowitz 1969]. There would be no impact on land use; the present dispersed, low-density settlement pattern would continue. Further, fuel tax receipts would decrease, and there would be less money available for transportation improvements, unless the tax rates were increased.

In summary, it appears that an optimum automobile could have major benefits in energy conservation and reduction of air pollution. It might have an adverse impact on vehicular safety. It would have little effect on other aspects of the transportation problem. It appears it could not replace transit, but it might be a desirable supplement to a good transit program.

LAND-USE POLICY

There is a strong interrelationship between transportation and land use. This was emphasized by Newman and Kenworthy [1989], who ascribed the large differences between countries in gasoline consumption to differences in physical planning. The urban transportation problem partly stems from the settlement pattern that has become common in the United States. Two possible land-use policies, of a long-range nature, would help to solve the problem (these are similar to the scenarios described by Robinson [1985]).

Disperse the Population

One is to disperse the population from the large metropolitan areas where most people live to small and medium-size cities. This would reduce travel distances and improve accessibility. Densities would be lower, and congestion would be reduced. People might make more trips, but the trips would be shorter. It is best if the cities are isolated or well separated. Ideally they should be self-contained so that people will not commute to other cities.

This is already happening to a degree; many large, older metropolises have lost population. The problem is how to keep the smaller cities from growing too large. Some places that were long considered to be nice small cities are becoming fairly large metropolitan areas with all the concomitant problems. For example, in 1990 the Austin metropolitan area had a population of 782,000; Tucson had 667,000; and Charleston, South Carolina, had 507,000.

Transit has little part in this approach. Basically, it concedes urban travel to the automobile. The idea is to spread out the automobile travel to mitigate the problems that it causes (some, such as congestion and air pollution, result from high density on the land surface).

Concentrate the Population

The opposite approach is also reasonable: Concentrate the population in large cities, at high densities, with the land-use and transportation systems closely coordinated. High population density has several advantages: (1) It promotes greater transit use because better transit service can be provided in a high-density setting. (2) It reduces automobile ownership because of the cost and inconvenience of owning a car. (3) It encourages walking because many activities are located within a short distance. (4) If the city is compact, trips will be shorter. It is urban sprawl that creates the need for long automobile trips.

Development should be planned in corridors along rapid transit lines (rail or busways). There should be clusters of activity at transit stations (office and retail at some, high-rise housing at others). Single-family homes should be located between the corridors. High employment density in the CBD is desirable because transit can serve it efficiently. This is similar to the "reurbanization" approach favored by Newman and Kenworthy [1989].

To conclude, either approach would make a big difference, but both approaches are politically difficult because they involve major government intervention, especially in land use. Real estate interests have great power on the local level and strongly oppose regulation. There is no land-use legislation at the national level, and there is very little at the state level.

HOW TO SOLVE THE URBAN TRANSPORTATION PROBLEM

With the interstate highway system finally nearing completion, much thought has been given in recent years to the future direction of national transportation policy. This has resulted in documents prepared by the American Association of State Highway and Transportation Officials [1985], the National Council on Public Works Improvement [Kirby and Reno 1987], and the American Public Transit Association's Transit 2000 Task Force [1989]. The federal government itself has issued a policy statement [U.S.

Department of Transportation 1990]. Wachs [1992] also wrote a concise summary of ten proposals to save transit. The author has drawn on this material in formulating the following recommendations.

Process and Institutions

A multimodal approach to urban transportation is clearly desirable. Although the federal government and most state governments now have departments of transportation, they are usually organized along modal lines, and activities of the different modal agencies may be uncoordinated or even competitive. The relevant committees in Congress and state legislatures also tend to be divided by mode. Supporters of each mode jealously guard their turf.

This is also a problem at the local level. Most transit authorities are interested in conventional rail and bus service only; they have little or no involvement with paratransit. Metropolitan planning organizations deal with federal aid programs for highways and transit. As a rule, these organizations have no jurisdiction over taxis, school buses, ride sharing, or bicycle and pedestrian facilities. Each metropolitan area should have a comprehensive transportation agency that covers everything from walking to heavy rail.

Kirby and Reno [1987] believe that policy making should be separated from the delivery of services. In each metropolitan area, a public body would be responsible for planning, adopting policies, and oversight. Contracts to provide service would be awarded competitively, with both public and private organizations eligible. This would end the monopolies that many transit authorities have in their metropolitan areas and would increase opportunities for the private sector.

Reforms are needed in the federal funding process. First, categorical grants should be abolished, and local officials should be able to use federal aid for either operating costs or capital investment, as they wish. Second, discretionary grants should be abolished, and all federal aid should be distributed on a formula basis, which would diminish political influence. Third, establish block grants for transportation which local authorities could allocate among modes as they think best. The federal government should require high quality in planning, design, and management, but should not dictate what the money is spent for.

There are many institutional barriers and constraints that interfere with the delivery of transportation services. The federal government has gotten the most criticism for excessive regulation; the labor protection clause and the Buy America clause are two oft-cited examples. Some states have regulations that hinder the formation of vanpools. At the local level, many communities still have ordinances that prohibit shared riding of taxis (hence jitneys). Many of these restrictions have outlived their usefulness and should be modified or repealed.

The Automobile

Many experts believe that automobiles and highways are heavily subsidized in the United States. Pucher [1988] argued that public policies favoring automobile use are responsible for the sizable differences in modal split between cities in North America and in Western Europe. The standard of living is similar in all countries, but taxes are quite different. Policies and taxes can be changed, if the political process so determines.

Regardless of whether one agrees about the extent of subsidization, it is clear that making it more expensive to drive an automobile in the city would take cars off the road. This would boost transit use and mitigate automobile-related problems such as accidents and air pollution. There are several ways to accomplish this:

1 Raise fuel taxes, which are lower than those in almost every other country. Ross Perot proposed to add $0.50 per gallon to the federal tax.

2 Raise annual vehicle registration fees. It is debatable whether fees should be based on weight or engine size (which would encourage better-mileage cars) or on value (which would be more beneficial to the poor).

3 Implement congestion pricing or an area licensing scheme, as in Singapore. This has the virtue of being a targeted approach that would aim at the most congested spots (motorists on uncrowded rural roads would pay nothing). An easy step in this direction would be for existing toll facilities to charge higher fees in the peak period than at other times of day. At the least, commuter discounts could be eliminated.

4 Eliminate the subsidies that parking often gets. Free parking at work could be made a 100 percent taxable fringe benefit. It is also conceivable to impose a tax on parking spaces in certain locations. At the least, paid parking should be priced to attract short-term users and discourage all-day parkers (contrary to existing practice).

Unfortunately, all these proposals would be unpopular with motorists, and they would protest mightily. It is questionable whether political leaders would be willing to adopt these proposals, since motorists obviously form a majority of voters. It is particularly difficult to take away privileges (such as free parking) that people are accustomed to. Only in times of crisis (such as war or a fuel shortage) do most people in the United States voluntarily make personal sacrifices.

Altshuler noted, "The least acceptable innovations are those that entail substantial costs or interference with widespread patterns of behavior, imposed in such a manner that the blame is likely to fall squarely upon the public officials who adopt the innovation" [1979, p. 414]. He cited gas tax increases and parking surcharges as examples. However, he also stated, "The bounds of feasibility are constantly evolving. Constraints that seem new and outrageous today may seem commonplace a few years hence" [p. 415].

It would also help to put more constraints on where automobiles can be driven. There should be more automobile-free zones and transit/pedestrian malls in activity centers such as the CBD and university campuses. Innovative designs like the Dutch *woonerf* scheme permit limited access by automobiles traveling at low speeds while discouraging heavy traffic. Design with the pedestrian in mind; don't force people to use their cars to cross the street.

Transit

There is no single best approach to improving transit systems. What is needed is a mix of improvements that offers a range of opportunities to travelers. Improving service is more effective, if one wishes to attract riders, than lowering fares or taking cosmetic measures like bus shelters and elegant graphics. That means faster service, more frequent service, and better route coverage.

There should be thorough analysis of each problem and an unbiased study of alternative solutions, including those that do not involve capital investment. Often there occurs what John Kain called the "premature imposition of constraints" [1972]. An early decision is made to take a certain action (such as building a rail line), and most of the planning is intended to justify the decision. Many politicians have pet projects; they feel certain things boost a city's image. No matter how good national transportation policy is, many key decisions are made at the local level. These decisions could be better made.

The author believes that bus improvements should be undertaken much more than they are. Better bus service in the inner city is probably the best way to serve the poor and minorities. Express buses from the suburbs, busways, and high-occupancy vehicle (HOV) lanes have been successful where they have been tried. Increasing bus service is relatively inexpensive, compared to building rail lines. There is consensus among experts that bus is a very energy-efficient mode.

However, there may be several places in which building new light rail lines would be cost-effective. In the most favorable situation, there is heavy demand in a corridor, and existing right-of-way is available. Putting lines in the middle of streets in the CBD seems to work well and saves a lot of money. It is doubtful that light rail will have much impact in low-density, automobile-oriented metropolitan areas in the sun belt.

There is probably no need to start any more heavy rail systems in U.S. cities, but some extensions of existing systems might be warranted. Older systems in Boston, Chicago, New York City, and Philadelphia need a great deal of money for rehabilitation and modernization. These cities are very dependent on their subway-elevated systems, as becomes painfully clear in a transit strike.

There should be a great expansion of paratransit. Demand-responsive services—utilizing taxis, vans, and small buses—will be the best way to provide public transportation in low-density suburbs and small towns. This can serve as a safety net for the minority of people who don't have a car available in situations where most people do. This will also be a major way of serving the elderly and disabled.

Carpooling and vanpooling are still not very popular, but they will definitely become more important. Many private parties are now promoting ride sharing in heavily congested areas such as southern California. Local governments will become more active in promoting and requiring ride sharing in the future. There are ways to make it more attractive, such as providing matching services and installing HOV lanes.

In the area of innovative technology, people movers seem to be the most successful concept. They have proved to be valuable in activity centers such as airports and amusement parks. Whether people movers are worthwhile in the CBD is questionable because they cost more to build in this location. Some rail systems should be fully automated, and several other technological advances should bring incremental improvements in transit service.

More rational pricing of transit services should be widely adopted. This includes charging higher fares in the peak period and basing fares on distance traveled. Self-service fare collection is a desirable innovation that should be extended. It reduces operating costs and is compatible with graduated fares.

There are some permanent markets for transit, even though the automobile will remain the primary mode of urban transportation. Meyer and Gomez-Ibanez identified three: (1) "long-distance worktrips to the centers of the two dozen or so largest and most congested metropolitan areas," (2) "paratransit for the physically handicapped, the elderly, and others who cannot easily use automobiles or conventional public transit," and (3) "serving short-haul worktrips and shoppingtrips to and from the inner-city neighborhoods and central business districts of older, more compact cities" [1981, pp. 280–281].

The transportation problem is not simple, and it has no simple solution. A broad-based attack is needed. In the metaphor of Anthony Downs, it takes "one hundred small cuts" for a woodsman to cut down a huge tree with an axe [1992, p. 34]. There will be no technological breakthrough that makes urban travel costless and painless. As long as most people choose to live in cities and keep the lifestyles they now prefer, travel will cause some difficulties.

CONCLUSION

Overall, the transit industry today is in a fairly stable situation. Federal programs are well established; the Reagan administration's attempt to slash them failed because many in Congress support transit. State governments have taken a larger role (financially and otherwise), and many local leaders have accepted transit as an essential public service. Ridership has been increasing gradually, although it accounts for a decreasing share of urban travel. There has been growth in transit use in sun belt cities, but it has been partially offset by declines in frost belt cities.

Is a strong revival of transit—a large growth in ridership—possible in the future? This is only likely to happen following a prolonged energy crisis, perhaps stemming from depletion of oil reserves. More likely there will be incremental changes in the next few decades. The election of environmentally conscious politicians could well lead to partial implementation of the recommendations given here.

Urban transit has a permanent role in U.S. society, in providing an alternative to congested roads in large cities, and in serving the transportation-disadvantaged everywhere. Transit will survive and will get better. Hopefully this book will assist transit planners in designing and operating improved transit services in the future.

QUESTIONS

1 Will fixed-route transit survive in the United States? Will the buses and trains we know today eventually disappear? Since most people in the United States prefer to live in low-density areas, will demand-responsive service become the major form of transit in the 21st century?

2 To what extent will telecommunications replace travel? Will most people work at home someday, or is this science fiction?

3 Do you agree with Bruce-Briggs that the intellectual elite is responsible for most of the criticism of the U.S. automobile-dominated culture? Should policy makers cater to the wishes of

the middle class and expand the highway system? Will intelligent vehicle-highway systems make this strategy a realistic possibility?

4 Should the federal government put renewed emphasis on "reinventing the automobile"? In terms of investing money, would you give this a higher priority than building more transit systems?

5 Do you think many people in the United States will move to small towns in the future? How much would this help to solve the urban transportation problem? Should the federal government have a policy of encouraging people to leave the large metropolitan areas?

6 To what extent will new technology change the form of public transportation in the 21st century? What technological advances are most likely to come into common use?

REFERENCES

Altshuler, Alan: *The Urban Transportation System: Politics and Policy Innovation* (Cambridge, MA: MIT Press, 1979).

————, Martin Anderson, Daniel Jones, Daniel Roos, and James Womack: *The Future of the Automobile: The Report of MIT's International Automobile Program* (Cambridge, MA: MIT Press, 1984).

American Association of State Highway and Transportation Officials: *A Study on Future Directions of Public Transportation in the United States* (Washington: American Association of State Highway and Transportation Officials, February 1985).

American Public Transit Association, Transit 2000 Task Force: *Managing Mobility: A New Generation of National Policies for the 21st Century* (Washington: American Public Transit Association, November 1989).

Bruce-Briggs, B.: *The War Against the Automobile* (New York: E. P. Dutton, 1977).

Cervero, Robert: *Suburban Gridlock* (New Brunswick, NJ: Center for Urban Policy Research, Rutgers University, 1986).

Downs, Anthony: *Stuck in Traffic: Coping with Peak-Hour Traffic Congestion* (Washington: The Brookings Institution, 1992).

Kain, John F.: "How to Improve Urban Transportation at Practically No Cost," *Public Policy*, vol. 20, no. 3 (Summer 1972), pp. 335–358.

Keats, John: *The Insolent Chariots* (Philadelphia: Lippincott, 1958).

Kirby, Ronald F., and Arlee T. Reno: *The Nation's Public Works: Report on Mass Transit* (Washington: National Council on Public Works Improvement, May 1987).

Krumholz, Norman, and Janice Cogger: "Urban Transportation Equity in Cleveland," in Barry Checkoway and Carl V. Patton, eds., *The Metropolitan Midwest* (Urbana: University of Illinois Press, 1985), pp. 211–228.

Leavitt, Helen: *Superhighway—Superhoax* (Garden City, NY: Doubleday, 1970).

McClenahan, John W., and Howard J. Simkowitz: "The Effect of Short Cars on Flow and Speed in Downtown Traffic: A Simulation Model and Some Results," *Transportation Science*, vol. 3, no. 2 (May 1969), pp. 126–139.

Meyer, John R., and Jose A. Gomez-Ibanez: *Autos, Transit, and Cities* (Cambridge, MA: Harvard University Press, 1981).

Mokhtarian, Patricia L.: "Telecommuting and Travel: State of the Practice, State of the Art," *Transportation*, vol. 18, no. 4 (1991), pp. 319–342.

Mowbray, A. Q.: *Road to Ruin* (Philadelphia: Lippincott, 1969).

Mumford, Lewis: *The Highway and the City* (New York: New American Library, 1964).

Nader, Ralph: *Unsafe at Any Speed* (New York: Grossman, 1965).

Newman, Peter W. G., and Jeffrey R. Kenworthy: "Gasoline Consumption and Cities: A Comparison of U.S. Cities with a Global Survey," *Journal of American Planning Association*, vol. 55, no. 1 (Winter 1989), pp. 24–37.

Pisarski, Alan E.: *Commuting in America: A National Report on Commuting Patterns and Trends* (Westport, CT: Eno Foundation for Transportation, 1987).

Pucher, John: "Urban Travel Behavior as the Outcome of Public Policy: The Example of Modal Split in Western Europe and North America," *Journal of American Planning Association*, vol. 54, no. 4 (Autumn 1988), pp. 509–520.

Robinson, Ira M.: "Energy and Urban Form: Relationships between Energy Conservation, Transportation and Spatial Structures," in John Byrne and Daniel Rich, eds., *Energy and Cities* (New Brunswick, NJ: Transaction Books, 1985), pp. 7–50.

Rothschild, Emma: *Paradise Lost: The Decline of the Auto-Industrial Age* (New York: Random House, 1973).

Salomon, Ilan: "Telecommunications and Travel Relationships: A Review," *Transportation Research*, vol. 20A, no. 3 (May 1986), pp. 223–238.

Schneider, Kenneth R.: *Autokind vs. Mankind: An Analysis of Tyranny; A Proposal for Rebellion; A Plan for Reconstruction* (New York: W. W. Norton & Company, 1971).

Transportation Research Board: *A Look Ahead: Year 2020*, Special Report 220 (Washington: Transportation Research Board, 1988).

U.S. Department of Transportation: *Moving America: New Directions, New Opportunities* (Washington: Department of Transportation, February 1990).

Wachs, Martin: *Can Transit Be Saved? Of Course It Can!* (Los Angeles: Graduate School of Architecture and Urban Planning, University of California, Los Angeles, June 1992).

Yates, Brock: *The Decline and Fall of the American Automobile Industry* (New York: Empire Books, 1983).

LANDMARKS IN
THE HISTORY OF
URBAN MASS TRANSIT

1662   Blaise Pascal inaugurated low-priced coach service on five routes in Paris. He died the same year, and service ceased after 2 years.

1819   The era of urban transit arrived with a stagecoach line in Paris. A new vehicle called the *omnibus* was introduced in 1825.

1827   The first urban transit service in the United States began—a stagecoach line running on Broadway in New York City.

1829   Regularly scheduled omnibus service was initiated in London. In 1832 it was made legal to pick up and discharge passengers along the route.

1832   The first horse-drawn street railway in the world opened in New York City.

1838   The first suburban railroad line in the world began service in London. The first U.S. commuter trains ran from Worcester to Boston in 1843.

1855   The first horsecar line in Europe began operation in Paris.

1863   The world's first subway began operation in London. Trains were pulled by steam locomotives, and it was called the *sewer railway.*

1868   The first elevated railway in the world opened in New York City. Cable traction proved unsuccessful, and it was converted to steam locomotives.

1870   A pneumatically operated subway was opened in New York City. Only 300 feet long, it ceased operation after 3 years. The tunnel is still there.

1872   The Great Epizootic killed thousands of horses in east coast cities and caused a crisis for operators of horse-drawn railways. They began looking for other means of propulsion.

Cincinnati got its first inclined railway. These were later built in Los Angeles, Pittsburgh, and Duluth and on the New Jersey Palisades.

An elevated railway (the S-Bahn) opened for service in Berlin.

1873   Andrew Hallidie successfully demonstrated the cable car in San Francisco. Regular service started a month later.

1880   Construction of a railway tunnel under the Hudson River was halted when a cave-in killed 20 workers. Work was resumed in 1902, and the Hudson Tubes (now used by PATH trains) were finally opened in 1908.

1881   The world's first electric trolley service was opened in a suburb of Berlin. Werner von Siemens was the inventor.

1882   Cable cars started running in Chicago in January, proving that climate was no barrier to the technology. Eventually lines operated in 30 U.S. cities. Chicago had the second-largest system, after San Francisco.

1883   The first interurban electric railway in the world began service at Giant's Causeway in Northern Ireland. This line lasted until 1949.

1888   Frank J. Sprague opened a 12-mile electric streetcar system in Richmond. Its success stimulated wide development of electric trolley systems.

1890   The first electrically powered subway in the world was opened in London. It was very successful, and by 1906 an extensive network was in place.

1892   The South Side elevated line was opened in Chicago. At first trains were pulled by steam locomotives; electric trains began running in 1895.

1896   In May, Budapest became the second city in the world with underground transit (actually a tram line). In December, Glasgow became the third with a 6.6-mile loop powered by cables.

1897   Boston became the first city in the United States with a subway when a streetcar line under Tremont Street began operation. The tunnel is still in use.

The Chicago Loop was completed. By this time all elevated trains were using electricity. They had the *multiple-unit* system invented by Sprague, in which every car has its own motor.

1899   The first motor buses in the world went into service in London.

1900   The first Metro line in Paris was opened for service.

1901   The first monorail line in the world, 8 miles long, began operation in Wuppertal, Germany. It is still in use.

1902   Berlin's first subway (the U-Bahn) was opened.

1904   New York City's first subway line was opened; it ran under Fourth Avenue and Broadway from the Brooklyn Bridge to 145th Street. This was the first line with four tracks, for local and express service.

1905   The first motor bus line in the United States went into service, with double-deckers running on Fifth Avenue in New York City.

1907   Rapid transit came to Philadelphia with a combination subway and elevated line along Market Street.

1910   The first trackless trolley line in the United States was opened in Hollywood, California. It was preceded by others in Europe.

1912   A party of officials traveled from Boston to New York City by streetcar, using a dozen lines and going via Worcester, Springfield, Hartford, New Haven, and Bridgeport. The total fare would have been $2.40.

1913   The first subway line in Latin America was opened in Buenos Aires.

1914   Jitney service appeared in Los Angeles, posing a great threat to the streetcar business. Jitneys were soon outlawed in most U.S. cities.

1917   In the worst transit accident in U.S. history, 97 persons were killed in a subway crash at Malbone Street in Brooklyn, New York.

1919   Madrid's Metro was opened. It long led the world in passengers per route-mile, due to the split workday, with four peak periods.

1923   This was the peak year for streetcar patronage in the United States—13.6 billion passengers.

1926   A 3-mile tunnel for streetcars was opened in Sydney, Australia.

1927   The Ginza line in Tokyo was opened—the first subway in Asia.

1935   The first line of the Moscow subway was opened. The Moscow system now carries more passengers than any other in the world.

1936   The first PCC streetcars began service in New York City. They were developed in an effort to standardize equipment in the transit industry.

1937   Paris became the first large city in the world to abandon streetcars. It was followed by Manchester (1949), London (1952), Edinburgh (1956), Sydney (1961), Glasgow (1962), and Bombay (1964).

1943   Chicago's first subway began operating under State Street.

1946   This was the peak year for transit riding in the United States—23.4 billion passengers. Patronage on subway-elevated systems also peaked in 1946; on buses, in 1948; and on trackless trolleys, in 1949.

1949   The Long Island Railroad went bankrupt, initiating an era of decline for commuter railroads. It was the largest commuter carrier in the United States, but it carried little freight. It was bought by New York State.

1952   The last PCC streetcars made in the United States arrived in San Francisco.

1954   The Yonge Street line was opened in Toronto—Canada's first subway.

1955   Cleveland's one rapid transit line was put into service. This was the first postwar subway construction in the United States.

Service was discontinued on the Third Avenue elevated line in New York City, and the structure was removed the following year. There followed a major real estate boom along Third Avenue.

1956   Rubber-tire trains began operation on one line of the Paris subway in the first demonstration of this design. It is used in the Montreal and Mexico City subways, both built with French assistance.

The last streetcar line in New York City was abandoned. Detroit and Dallas did likewise the same year. Kansas City took this step in 1957, Chicago in 1958, Washington, D.C., in 1962, and Los Angeles in 1963.

1958   A rapid transit line was opened in the median strip of the Congress Expressway in Chicago—the first use of this concept. Similar lines were opened in two other Chicago expressways in 1969 and 1970.

The Highland Branch of the Boston & Albany Railroad was electrified and added to the Boston transit network as the Riverside Line.

1962   An Alweg monorail line, 1.2 miles long, was built in Seattle for the World's Fair. It is still in operation.

1964   The Skokie Swift went into service as a 5-mile extension of Chicago's rapid transit system. It had been part of a railroad line.

An Alweg monorail line opened between downtown Tokyo and Haneda Airport.

1966   The New York City transit strike caused a partial shutdown of the city for 12 days, with high absenteeism. The settlement stimulated a nationwide trend to higher transit wages and subsequent fare hikes.

Montreal's Metro was opened in anticipation of the World's Fair held the following summer.

1968   Cleveland extended its rapid transit line to Hopkins Airport, becoming the first U.S. city with rail service to its airport.

1969   The first exclusive busway in the world was opened on the Shirley Highway in Virginia, leading to the Washington CBD.

The Lindenwold rapid transit line was opened between the New Jersey suburbs and downtown Philadelphia.

Mexico City's Metro initiated service.

The first new subway in central London in 60 years was opened—the Victoria Line, connecting several existing lines. It is 10.5 miles long and cost $170 million. It was the first rail system in the world with automatic fare collection. At the opening ceremony, Queen Elizabeth II had to borrow the fare, as the Queen never carries cash.

1970   One lane of a New Jersey expressway leading to the Lincoln Tunnel was set aside for buses during the morning rush hour. It carries over 500 buses per hour—probably the highest bus volume in the world.

1972   The first section of the Bay Area Rapid Transit system was opened. Because of computer problems, trains did not run in the tunnel under San Francisco Bay until 1974. The final cost for BART was $1.6 billion.

1973   Boston and San Francisco placed the first orders for new streetcars made in this country since 1952. Boston put the new Standard Light Rail Vehicle, built by Boeing Vertol, into service in 1976.

1974   The Dallas–Fort Worth Airport opened, including the AIRTRANS system of driverless vehicles connecting terminals, parking lots, and a hotel. It has 13 miles of guideway and 14 stations.

1975   A major demonstration of dial-a-ride service in Haddonfield, New Jersey, ended after a 3-year trial. Federal funding ended, and the state of New Jersey declined to take over. Peak ridership was 1300 persons per day.

The major demonstration of personal rapid transit (PRT) began in Morgantown, West Virginia. The 2.2-mile line connected the downtown with the University of West Virginia. The line was later extended; there are now five stations.

1976   The first segment of Washington's Metro opened for service. Later extensions brought the system to 89 miles with 74 stations by the end of 1993.

A Los Angeles judge halted the Santa Monica diamond-lanes project after 21 weeks because no Environmental Impact Statement had been filed. It took two lanes from regular traffic and reserved them for buses and car pools. It was unpopular, and no effort was made to revive it.

1977   A bizarre slow-motion collision of two trains on Chicago's Loop left 11 persons dead and 189 injured when four cars left the tracks. It was the worst transit accident in Chicago's history.

1978   The first light rail system in North America went into service in Edmonton, Canada. The line has now been extended to 6.5 miles.

1979   The first segment of Atlanta's MARTA subway opened. The system was eventually expanded to 32 miles and 29 stations.

A 9.6-mile contraflow lane for buses and vanpools—the longest in the United States— went into operation on Interstate 45 in Houston.

1980   The Tyne and Wear Metro opened in Newcastle, England, as Great Britain's first light rail system. The network now comprises 34.5 route-miles.

1981   A 7.8-mile light rail transit (LRT) line opened in Calgary, Canada. A second line opened in 1985, and a third in 1987 in time for the Winter Olympics.

San Diego opened the first light rail line in the United States. The Tijuana Trolley runs 16 miles from the CBD to the Mexican border. A second line was completed in 1989; the system now has 31.9 route-miles.

1983   Baltimore opened a subway 8 miles long and costing $797 million.

1984   Service began on the 11-mile South Line of Miami's heavy rail transit system. A 1.9-mile people mover system was opened in 1986.

Chicago opened an 8-mile heavy rail extension to O'Hare Airport, located in the median strip of the Kennedy Expressway. It cost $196 million.

1986   The Vancouver SkyTrain opened in anticipation of a World's Fair. It was the first fully automated rail line in North America. The final cost exceeded $1 billion Canadian.

MAX service began in Portland, Oregon. The 15-mile light rail line, which runs along the Banfield Expressway, cost $240 million.

Buffalo completed a 6.4-mile light rail line. The cost was high ($550 million) because most of the route is underground.

1987 Sacramento opened the first line of its 18.3-mile light rail system in March, the second line in September. It cost $176 million.

General Motors, long the dominant U.S. bus manufacturer, agreed to sell its transit bus division to the Transportation Manufacturing Group of Greyhound Corporation.

The new Orange Line of Boston's heavy rail system opened, replacing elevated tracks built in 1901. The 4.7-mile facility cost $743 million.

Cairo opened the first subway in Africa in October. It connects two suburban railroad lines and permits through-running.

1988 Santa Clara County began LRT service to downtown San Jose in June. The 20-mile Guadalupe Line, completed in April 1991, cost $500 million.

Detroit's downtown people mover opened in July. A dozen vehicles move in one direction around a 2.9-mile loop with 13 stations.

1990 Los Angeles opened the Blue Line in July, marking the return of rail transit after 30 years. The 22-mile light rail line connects downtown Los Angeles and Long Beach. It cost $877 million.

In September, Seattle opened a 1.3-mile bus tunnel under the CBD. It cost $450 million. Specially designed buses switch to electricity when they enter the tunnel.

1992 Baltimore opened the first link of its central light rail line in May.

1993 The Los Angeles subway, called the Red Line, began service in January. It is 4.4 miles long and cost $1.4 billion. Construction of an extension is already underway.

Part of St. Louis' light rail line, Metrolink, was opened in July. It will stretch 18 miles from Illinois through downtown to Lambert Airport.

1994 Denver opened a light rail line, 5.3 miles long, in October. Construction of an 8.7-mile extension has been approved.

PUBLIC ELECTIONS ON
MASS TRANSIT PROPOSALS

November 1958 A $16,900,000 bond issue proposed by the Alameda-Contra Costa Transit District in California was defeated. It received over 50 percent of the votes, but two-thirds was required. The district was formed in 1957 to take over the decaying Key System, which was privately owned and largely financed by General Motors.

October 1959 After the state legislature amended the law to require only a simple majority vote, a new $16,500,000 bond proposal by the Alameda-Contra Costa Transit District was passed, receiving just over 50 percent of the votes. This enabled the district to buy 850 buses and expand its service.

November 1959 New Jersey voters turned down a proposal to permit use of surplus earnings from the New Jersey Turnpike to subsidize railroad commutation. The margin was over 200,000 votes.

November 1962 A $792 million bond issue to finance the San Francisco Bay Area Rapid Transit system was approved by 61.2 percent of voters in three counties (60 percent was required). The bonds are being retired with property taxes. The eventual cost of the system rose to $1.6 billion.

November 1964 Philadelphia voters approved a $77 million bond issue to finance extensions to two subway lines.

Voters of five counties of metropolitan Atlanta passed an amendment to the state constitution to permit creation of a public authority engaged in mass transportation.

June 1965 Voters in four counties around Atlanta passed a referendum to create a met-

	ropolitan authority to build and operate a rapid transit system. One county voted against the proposal and was omitted from the system.
June 1966	Chicago voters passed a $22,886,000 bond issue to build rail transit lines in the median strips of two expressways.
October 1966	By a 4-to-1 margin, Berkeley, California, voters approved a $20,500,000 bond issue to put a BART line underground within the city limits.
November 1966	A $96,500,000 bond issue to buy new equipment for the San Francisco Municipal Railway failed to receive the two-thirds approval that was required.
November 1967	New York State voters approved a $2.5 billion transportation bond issue, including $1 billion for transit improvements, mostly in New York City. The vote in favor was 59 percent.
February 1968	A $385 million bond issue to build a rapid transit system in Seattle received a favorable vote of 50.3 percent, but failed because 60 percent was needed under state law.
November 1968	A $2.515 billion mass transit bond proposal for Los Angeles County, including an 89-mile rail system, was favored by only 44.7 percent of the voters (60 percent was needed to pass). Bonds were to be retired by an increase in the sales tax.
	Voters in Atlanta and two suburban counties rejected a $993 million bond issue to build a rapid transit system. It would have required an increase in the property tax.
	New Jersey voters approved a $200 million bond issue for transit improvements.
	One county of Maryland and two counties of Virginia passed bond issues totaling $208 million to finance their portions of the Washington Metro system.
June 1969	Voters of San Mateo County, California, defeated the West Bay Rapid Transit Authority's plan for a new system of bus routes.
September 1969	Voters in Santa Clara County, California, rejected a plan for a countywide bus system, plus purchase of right-of-way for eventual connection to BART. This was proposed by a special transit district, which was later dissolved.
May 1970	A $440 million bond issue for the Seattle rapid transit system did worse at the polls the second time, receiving a favorable vote of only 46.6 percent.
November 1970	Only 45.9 percent of California voters favored a proposition to divert state fuel taxes to transit and antismog devices after a hot campaign with heavy advertising by oil companies.
November 1971	By a margin of 0.2 percent, voters approved the $1.4 billion plan of the Metropolitan Atlanta Rapid Transit Authority, including 56 miles of rail lines. The system was partly financed by a 1 percent sales tax. The proposal included a reduction in the bus fare from $0.40 to $0.15, which took effect in March 1972.

Another $2.5 billion transportation bond issue for New York State was soundly defeated. It included a $1.25 billion for transit, but was attacked as being lopsided in favor of highways. Part of the money would have gone for a rail line in Buffalo.

September 1972   Voters in the Seattle region approved a countywide bus system costing $96 million. This provided for new buses, 25 park-and-ride lots, and exclusive bus lanes. It was financed partly with a 0.3 percent sales tax.

November 1972   Voters of Dade County, Florida, approved $132.5 million in bonds to finance the initial 54 miles of a rail system.

April 1973   Voters in Ann Arbor, Michigan, approved a plan to convert all bus service to dial-a-ride. The favorable vote was 61 percent, even though it was forecast that 80 to 85 percent of operating costs would have to be subsidized. The money comes from property taxes and the state gas tax.

September 1973   Denver voters approved a $425 million bond issue to finance the local share of a $1.5 billion people mover system—a 98-mile network of remote-controlled 12-passenger vehicles. The vote in favor was 57 percent. The system was never built.

October 1973   Voters in Harris County, Texas, defeated a proposal to create a Houston Area Rapid Transit Authority. Only 16 percent of registered voters turned out; 73.4 percent were opposed.

November 1973   New York State voters again rejected a huge transportation bond issue, with only 43.3 percent in favor. This one was for $3.5 billion—$2.1 billion for transit and $1.4 billion for highways. While opponents painted the proposal as pro-highway, it was largely defeated by votes from upstate, highway-oriented counties. One object of the proposal was to hold the New York City subway fare at $0.35.

March 1974   Creation of a Regional Transit Authority for the six counties of the Chicago metropolitan area was approved by a margin of 13,000 votes out of 1,400,000 cast. The new agency took over the Chicago Transit Authority and has the power to levy taxes.

June 1974   On the second try, California voters approved an amendment to the state constitution permitting use of gas taxes for mass transit. The vote in favor was 60.3 percent.

November 1974   Voters in the Los Angeles area defeated a proposal to levy a 1 percent sales tax for transit. This would have provided the local share for a $4.3 billion transit improvement plan, including 145 miles of rail transit and 1500 new buses.

Michigan voters rejected a $1.1 billion public transportation bond issue, with 57 percent against. The measure included $540 million for the Detroit area, which would have covered the local share for 75 miles of rail transit and 179 miles of bus/carpool lanes. Voters also turned down a constitutional amendment to limit the diversion of gas taxes to transit.

New York State voters approved a $250 million railroad bond issue by a margin of almost 2 to 1. The package included $102 million to improve commuter rail service to New York City. A similar proposal for $100 million was defeated in New Jersey, with 51.1 percent of the voters opposed.

November 1977   Voters in the San Antonio area approved creation of a metropolitan transit authority, to be supported with a 0.5 percent sales tax. The authority took over the city's bus system and began expanding the bus fleet and route network.

March 1978   After a heated campaign, voters in Dade County, Florida, barely defeated a referendum to repeal the bond issue that had been passed in 1972. A Miami lawyer formed a group called *STOP* (Stop Transit Over People) and got enough signatures on a petition to call the election. However, 50.5 percent of the vote went against him, and plans for the rail line proceeded.

August 1978   Voters in Harris County, Texas, approved creation of a transit authority with power to levy a 1¢ sales tax. The authority encompasses Houston and 16 suburban communities that had no transit service at the time. The overall vote was 57 percent in favor, but several suburbs voted not to join. The authority took over the HouTran bus system in January 1979.

June 1979   Voters in Columbus, Ohio, rejected a 0.5 percent sales tax to support the Central Ohio Transit Authority by just 5000 votes. Because a deficit was projected, authority officials said they would cut back service and raise fares.

August 1980   A proposal to create the Lone Star Transportation Authority was soundly defeated by voters in Dallas, Fort Worth, and 62 suburbs. The measure would have raised the sales tax by 1¢. A system of *transitways* (with technology to be determined later) was proposed.

November 1980   Los Angeles County voters adopted Proposition A, which guaranteed local funding for transit by adding $1/2$¢ to the sales tax. The vote was 54.2 percent in favor. Part of the revenues went for construction of two rail lines. The election was challenged in court, but in May 1982 the state supreme court ruled that a majority vote was sufficient.

Denver voters rejected a sales tax to finance a proposed light rail transit system, with 53 percent opposed.

Plans for a downtown people mover in St. Paul were ended when 71 percent of voters passed a referendum that prohibited the city from spending public funds to build the system.

November 1981   Voters in Youngstown, Ohio, declined to raise the property tax to maintain bus service (52 percent voted against). Subsequently the 85 buses were taken off the streets for a month. The proposal was resubmitted to voters in February 1982, and this time 62.9 percent approved.

August 1982   Voters in Nashville defeated a referendum that would have imposed a tax of 1¢ per gallon on gasoline to help fund transit service. In response, the transit authority reduced service by 10 percent and personnel by 14 percent.

June 1983   Houston voters rejected a $2.35 billion bond issue for construction of an

18.5-mile rail line. The vote was 62.4 percent opposed. Three months later voters approved $900 million in bonds to build 57 miles of new toll roads.

August 1983

Dallas voters passed a referendum to raise the sales tax by 1¢ to finance transit improvements without federal assistance. The money would double the bus fleet and build a huge light rail system (160 miles by the year 2010) that would cost $8.7 billion. The vote was 58 percent in favor.

November 1983

Voters in Arlington County, Virginia, approved a $13 million bond issue to continue extension of the Washington Metro into the county. The vote was 76 percent in favor.

January 1985

Voters in Austin, Texas, approved creating the Capital Metropolitan Transportation Authority by a 59 percent majority. The authority was granted a 1¢ sales tax to carry out a plan for a fivefold increase in bus service.

May 1986

A property tax increase requested by the Toledo Area Regional Transit Authority was defeated by voters. Much of the funding was intended to improve service to the elderly and disabled.

December 1987

El Paso voters approved a $1/2$¢ sales tax to fund public transit. The measure failed twice before; this time it passed by a margin of 69 votes.

A majority of 53 percent of San Diego voters approved Proposition A, which raised the sales tax by $1/2$¢ to fund transportation improvements. One-third of the revenues go to transit (mostly to extend the light rail system).

January 1988

Houston residents passed a nonbinding referendum for a $2.6 billion expansion program for the regional transit authority. The plan included a 20-mile rail loop to connect radial bus lines. The measure did not involve a tax increase and was favored by 60 percent of voters.

June 1988

Dallas-area voters rejected a long-term financing proposal by Dallas Area Rapid Transit to build a 93-mile light rail system by the year 2010. The vote was 58 percent opposed.

March 1989

Phoenix voters defeated the $8.5 billion ValTrans system, including 103 miles of automated rail lines. Only 39.1 percent voted in favor.

June 1990

By a 52 percent majority, California voters passed Proposition 111, which doubled the state's gas tax and would raise $18.5 billion over 10 years for highway and transit projects. The measure was opposed by the building industry because local governments must initiate traffic reduction programs to qualify for funds. Voters also approved two related proposals for rail transit construction.

November 1990

Voters in Los Angeles County agreed to raise the sales tax by $1/2$¢, with the anticipated annual revenue of $400 million going for transit and anticongestion improvements. Voters in nearby Orange County adopted a $1/2$¢ sales tax that will finance commuter rail projects, after rejecting similar measures in 1984 and 1989. However, proposed sales taxes to fund mass transit were defeated in three other California counties and in Dade County, Florida.

A $125 million bond issue to expand the light rail system in Portland, Oregon, was approved at the polls. However, voters in suburban Gwinnett County, Georgia, rejected a proposal to extend the MARTA system into the county.

November 1992   California voters defeated Proposition 156, which would have authorized $1 billion in bonds for rail transit, including projects in San Diego, Los Angeles, Sacramento, San Jose, and San Francisco. The vote was 51.5 percent opposed.

In Salt Lake City, 56 percent of voters turned down a measure to impose a $1/4$¢ sales tax to fund a light rail line.

November 1993   Residents of St. Clair County, Illinois, approved a $1/2$¢ sales tax to fund an extension of the St. Louis Metrolink rail system.

August 1994   Voters approved a $1/4$¢ sales tax dedicated to funding the Bi-State Development Agency in St. Louis. The agency operates Metrolink and the bus system in the St. Louis metropolitan area.

INDEX